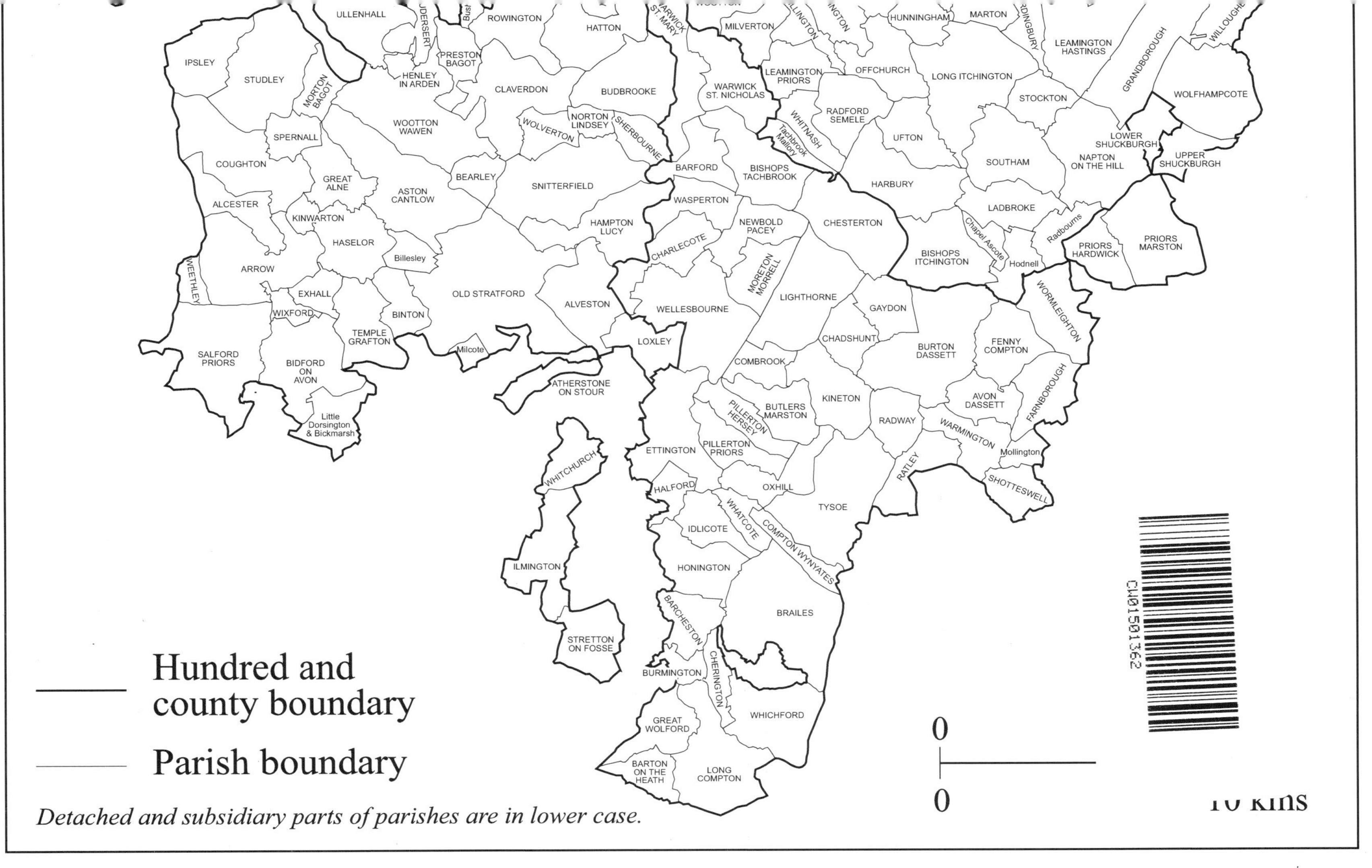

ULLENHALL
ROWINGTON
HATTON
MILVERTON
HUNNINGHAM
MARTON
LEAMINGTON HASTINGS
GRANDBOROUGH
IPSLEY
STUDLEY
MORTON BAGOT
PRESTON BAGOT
HENLEY IN ARDEN
CLAVERDON
BUDBROOKE
WARWICK ST. NICHOLAS
LEAMINGTON PRIORS
OFFCHURCH
LONG ITCHINGTON
WOLFHAMPCOTE
STOCKTON
RADFORD SEMELE
WOOTTON WAWEN
SPERNALL
NORTON LINDSEY
WOLVERTON
SHERBOURNE
WHITNASH
Tachbrook Mallory
UFTON
LOWER SHUCKBURGH
UPPER SHUCKBURGH
NAPTON ON THE HILL
SOUTHAM
COUGHTON
GREAT ALNE
ASTON CANTLOW
BEARLEY
SNITTERFIELD
BARFORD
BISHOPS TACHBROOK
HARBURY
ALCESTER
KINWARTON
WASPERTON
LADBROKE
HASELOR
HAMPTON LUCY
NEWBOLD PACEY
CHESTERTON
Chapel Ascote
Radbourns
PRIORS HARDWICK
PRIORS MARSTON
ARROW
Billesley
CHARLECOTE
MORETON MORRELL
BISHOPS ITCHINGTON
Hodnell
WEETHLEY
EXHALL
OLD STRATFORD
ALVESTON
LIGHTHORNE
GAYDON
WORMLEIGHTON
WIXFORD
BINTON
WELLESBOURNE
TEMPLE GRAFTON
Milcote
LOXLEY
CHADSHUNT
BURTON DASSETT
FENNY COMPTON
SALFORD PRIORS
BIDFORD ON AVON
COMBROOK
ATHERSTONE ON STOUR
KINETON
AVON DASSETT
FARNBOROUGH
Little Dorsington & Bickmarsh
BUTLERS MARSTON
PILLERTON HERSEY
RADWAY
WARMINGTON
ETTINGTON
PILLERTON PRIORS
Mollington
WHITCHURCH
RATLEY
SHOTTESWELL
HALFORD
OXHILL
TYSOE
IDLICOTE
WHATCOTE
COMPTON WYNYATES
ILMINGTON
HONINGTON
BARCHESTON
BRAILES
STRETTON ON FOSSE
BURMINGTON
CHERINGTON
WHICHFORD
GREAT WOLFORD
BARTON ON THE HEATH
LONG COMPTON
0
0
10 kms
Hundred and county boundary
Parish boundary
Detached and subsidiary parts of parishes are in lower case.

THE DUGDALE SOCIETY
ROBERT BEARMAN, B.A., PH.D., F.R.HIST.S., *General Editor*

BRITISH RECORD SOCIETY
CATHERINE FERGUSON, M.A., PH.D., *General Editor, Hearth Tax Series*

CENTRE FOR HEARTH TAX RESEARCH
ROEHAMPTON UNIVERSITY LONDON
ANDREW WAREHAM, PH.D., F.R.HIST.S., *Director*

WARWICKSHIRE HEARTH TAX

[INDEX … ME VII

I

The Dugdale Society

Registered Charity No. 1051033

THE DUGDALE SOCIETY, named after Warwickshire's distinguished antiquary, Sir William Dugdale (1605–86), was founded in 1920 with the objects of publishing original documents relating to the history of the County of Warwick, fostering interest in historical records and their preservation and generally encouraging the study of local history and its sources.

The Society publishes as frequently as its resources and circumstances permit and to date forty-two volumes in the Main Record Series have appeared, as well as forty-four Occasional Papers.

Membership of the Society is open to any person, library or corporate body interested in promoting the interests of the Society. Members receive a free copy of all publications issued. An Annual Meeting takes place in the autumn, at which a paper is presented, and a summer social event is usually held.

Applications for membership are welcome. They should be sent to the Secretary of the Dugdale Society, c/o The Shakespeare Centre, Stratford-upon-Avon, Warwickshire CV37 6QW (email: dugdale-society@hotmail.co.uk)

The British Record Society

Registered Charity No. 248874

THE BRITISH RECORD SOCIETY was founded in 1889 to compile, edit and publish calendars and transcripts of historical records in public or private custody throughout Great Britain. For many years it has concentrated on producing indexes to English probate records to facilitate the study of English history and genealogy and took over publishing the Index Library founded in 1888. In addition, since 1995, it has been collaborating with the British Academy Hearth Tax Project at Roehampton University to publish transcripts and analyses of Hearth Tax returns, concentrating on those counties where no transcript has yet been printed.

The Society's work is dependent upon subscription income and voluntary labour and, while it aims to publish a new volume annually, that is dependent upon resources and availability of volunteers. During the period 1992 to 2009 not every year saw a new publication, but 20 volumes were produced which subscribers received free of charge.

Applications for membership are welcome from any person, library or corporate body. They should be sent to Hon Secretary, P.L. Dickinson, College of Arms, Queen Victoria Street, London EC4V 4BT (email: richmondherald@dial.pipex.com)

WARWICKSHIRE HEARTH TAX RETURNS: MICHAELMAS 1670 with Coventry Lady Day 1666

Edited by
TOM ARKELL

with
NAT ALCOCK

Published by the Dugdale Society
c/o the Secretary
Shakespeare Centre
Stratford-upon-Avon
CV37 6QW

ISBN 978–0–85220–091–9

and the British Record Society
c/o Patric Dickinson
The College of Arms
Queen Victoria Street
London EC4V 4BT

ISBN 978–0–901505–55–2

Printed in Great Britain by 4Word Ltd, Bristol

Contents

List of Illustrations

List of Maps

List of Tables

Picture Credits

Permission to reproduce the following illustrations is gratefully acknowledged:

Figures 2–4; 7–14, 17: © N.W. Alcock
Figure 15: Birmingham Archives and Heritage Service
Figure 18: © James Kerr [www.jameskerr.co.uk]
Figure 19: © Trevor Lucas, courtesy of Images of England
Figures 23–25: The National Archives
Figures 5, 6, 20–2: Warwickshire County Record Office

Figure 1 was originated by Cathy Millwood

Maps 1–3 were prepared by the staff of the Department of Geography, Earth and Environmental Sciences, University of Birmingham, under the direction of Canon Terry Slater

Maps 4–18 and the endpapers were prepared by Mike Shand of the Department of Geographical and Earth Sciences, University of Glasgow, with the support of the British Academy Hearth Tax Project

Historic Units of Currency and Land Area

The historic units in use in the seventeenth century were:

£1 = 20 shillings(s)	1 acre(ac) (0.405 hectare) = 4 rods (r)
1s = 12 pence(d)	1 rod = 40 perches (p)

Abbreviations

BAHS	Birmingham Archives and Heritage Service
LRO	Lichfield Record Office
SCLA	Shakespeare Centre Library and Archive, Stratford upon Avon
TNA	The National Archives
WCRO	Warwickshire County Record Office

General Editor's Preface
Dugdale Society

The Dugdale Society has long cherished the hope that an edition of the Warwickshire Hearth Tax would be published as one of its volumes. However, it had always been accepted that this would be no easy task. In Warwickshire's case, the survival of uniquely extensive documentation presented potential editors with enormous difficulties, as the pioneer efforts of Philip Styles had already amply demonstrated. No quick results were expected, then, when in 1981 Tom Arkell offered to take up the challenge. But with remarkable doggedness, and in the face of many setbacks, he has now brought this project to fruition, inspired in more recent years by Margaret Spufford's wider ambition to publish returns for every English county, under the auspices of the British Record Society. The Dugdale Society has therefore welcomed this opportunity to publish this volume as part of the Hearth Tax Series in recognition of its value both locally and nationally, and thanks the British Record Society, and in particular the past and present general editors of the series, Margaret Spufford and Catherine Ferguson, and Andrew Wareham, Director of the Hearth Tax Project at Roehampton University, for their enthusiastic and helpful collaboration in the final stages. This volume would also not be what it is without valuable input by Nat Alcock who, from the late 1990s, has generously given much time to its evolution: to him, as well as Tom Arkell, the Society is deeply indebted.

Robert Bearman
General Editor
Dugdale Society

General Editor's Preface
British Record Society, Hearth Tax Series

This is the seventh volume in the British Record Society Hearth Tax Series, produced in association with the British Academy Hearth Tax Project at Roehampton University, and we are delighted in this instance that the Dugdale Society, who had long intended to publish a volume devoted to the Warwickshire Hearth Tax, has taken the lead in bringing this to fruition in the form of a joint publication. This is a significant volume, as not only does Warwickshire have an impressive set of hearth tax returns, but it is also the first Midlands county in the British Record Society Hearth Tax Series. The publication of this volume, together with the analysis by Tom Arkell and Nat Alcock, adds considerably to the body of scholarship of seventeenth-century social and economic history and helps contribute towards a better understanding of many issues in that period, including the complexities of wealth and poverty across the country.

The aim of the Hearth Tax Series is to provide a national survey of population, households and their relationship with social and economic status in Restoration England and Wales. To this end, the Roehampton University Centre for Hearth Tax Research was established in 1995 under the direction of Professor Margaret Spufford, and in 2004 it was adopted as a British Academy Research Project. The Hearth Tax Project uses volunteers and palaeographical consultants to transcribe hearth tax documents, and consultants skilled in GIS and statistics to present the data. The partnership between the British Academy, the British Record Society and Roehampton University continues to flourish. Hearth tax volumes have now been published for returns on Cambridgeshire (2000), Kent (2000), County Durham (2006), West Riding of Yorkshire (2007), Westmorland (2009) and now Warwickshire, as well as the Norfolk exemption certificates volume (2001). In the next few years volumes will follow on several counties, including Essex, London and Middlesex, thereby widening the geographical and topographical coverage of the series.

The initial stated aim of the Project was to publish the best unpublished return for the county in question. Since then, however, the Hearth Tax Project, encouraged by the British Academy, has extended its scope. The Cambridgeshire and Durham volumes included additional material and the Westmorland volume printed four documents (1670 Michaelmas return and three surveys for 1674-5). Multiple lists, where one list does not provide comprehensive coverage, are going to be our future goal. The edition for London and Middlesex will draw upon both the 1663 and 1666 returns in order to provide comprehensive coverage of the whole of the City of London. At the same time the use of other sources, such as exemption certificates and probate inventories, will continue as an area of interest to the Hearth Tax Project, thereby adding to understanding of distributions of wealth and poverty, the development of vernacular architecture and related themes.

In all these respects the Warwickshire volume is a most welcome addition and we should like to thank Tom Arkell and Nat Alcock for their scholarly contribution, Robert Bearman and the Dugdale Society's editorial team for their major role in the production of this volume, and the transcribers, consultants and members of the Hearth Tax Project who have also played an important part in its evolution including Elizabeth Parkinson, John Price, Margaret Spufford, Mike Shand, Sue Stearn, Susan Rose and Trevor Dean. Finally, without the support of the Project's funders, it would not be possible to bring hearth tax volumes into the public domain. In addition to the British Academy generous assistance is provided by the Aurelius Trust and the Marc Fitch Fund.

Catherine Ferguson
General Editor
British Record Society
Hearth Tax Series

Andrew Wareham
Director
British Academy
Hearth Tax Project

Feast Day of Saint Bernard, 2009

Preface

In the steps of Philip Styles

'On a huge hill,
Cragg'd, and steep, Truth stands, and hee that will
Reach her, about must, and about must goe.'
John Donne, *Satyre III*

Anyone who explores seriously the abundant surviving material from the Warwickshire hearth tax will discover sooner or later that they are following in the pioneering footsteps of Philip Styles.[1] He was a lecturer in local history at the University of Birmingham when he first proposed in May 1936 to transcribe and publish the county's complete assessment list for Lady Day 1664.[2] Two months later the Records Committee of the County Council accepted his proposal on the understanding that his transcript would be ready for publication in 1938 and subsequently paid him £23 15s. 0d. for it at the agreed rate of one shilling per 72 words.[3] This list, like most of the other Warwickshire hearth tax returns, was preserved at Warwick, but within a year C.A.F. Meekings, the catalyst for hearth tax studies nationwide, had introduced Styles to many additional Warwickshire hearth tax documents in the Public Record Office, now The National Archives. He thus learned that Warwickshire had more surviving hearth tax documents from the period 1662 to 1674 than any other county. As an impeccable scholar, Styles abandoned his initial plan to publish just one single list and instead decided to study all eight Warwickshire returns first, including the two in the Public Record Office, which were photostatted and bound for him. In the summer of 1939 he presented the Records Committee with two alternative proposals for eventual publication in four or two volumes, but since Styles was committed by then to producing the Barlichway hundred volume of the Victoria County History of Warwickshire, his hearth tax studies were placed on hold until 1945.

And so it was only as the Second World War drew to a close that Styles returned to the hearth tax with renewed enthusiasm and built up a large bank of data in a card index system.[4] Early in 1945 he agreed to produce three volumes between 1947 and 1949. The first two were to contain a comparative analysis of all the county's hearth

1 See Styles, *Studies*, pp. ix-xvii for two brief appreciations of Philip Styles (1905–1976) as a person and an historian by H.A. Cronne and E.A.O. Whiteman.

2 WCRO, CR1520/Box70/RE66/IV/9/1 contains the correspondence between Styles and the clerk to the County Council on which this paragraph is based. Styles gave 1663 as the date for this assessment, which was the year when it was drawn up, but in this volume assessments are dated consistently according to the last collections for which they were used.

3 WCRO, CR1741/13/4 & 8 contain Styles's transcripts of Knightlow, Barlichway and Kineton hundreds.

4 WCRO, CR1741/13/26–131 contain Styles's card index for the householders in Barlichway together with his folders of notes and transcripts for 105 parishes in Barlichway and Kineton hundreds.

tax data and the third an extensive editorial introduction and index. The clerk of the council's letters disclose the very different climate in which academics then operated. In January 1945 he reported that the Records Committee had agreed to let Styles work on the hearth tax rolls at home and also asked 'perhaps you would be good enough to indicate what you consider would be satisfactory to you by way of remuneration?' A fortnight later they agreed on 'one shilling per folio of 72 words manuscript' plus his expenses incurred while consulting other documents. In 1946 the clerk wanted the county archivist to go over to Birmingham to see Styles to finalise questions about the content and layout of the text with its related biographical notes 'at whatever date would be most convenient to you'.[1]

Evidently all was not going according to plan because the task which Styles had set himself was much more challenging than he had realised. In the end it defeated his powers of organisation, but not his erudition. In 1952 he finally revealed to Meekings his method of analysing the data for all the households recorded in every return, based upon the assessment for Lady Day 1664, but Meekings was not impressed. He considered the tables were too elaborate, too confusing and lacking in rationale and advised Styles instead to divide his work into two basic texts that covered the periods 1662–66 and 1669–74 separately.[2] But Styles rejected this sound advice and made only one further alteration to his approach, using the first assessment for 1662–3 as the basis for his analyses in place of the second one for 1664. In theory this was more logical, but in practice it was a mistake because this initial list did not include the exempt and so made his presentation of the data even more confused. In the event just one volume of his projected series was published in 1957, which contained his promised general introduction and an analysis of two divisions from Hemlingford hundred done by Margaret Walker according to Styles's plan, but not the biographical notes that he had intended originally to include.[3] Nearly everyone who has attempted to use it since has been frustrated by the complexities of its layout so that it has done little to sustain his reputation as the outstanding scholar on the Warwickshire hearth tax that he undoubtedly was.

Although Styles lived for nearly twenty more years, he suffered from creeping and then devastating ill health and published little more on the hearth tax. After his death in 1976 his copious notes were lodged in the Warwickshire County Record Office as a silent witness to the extent and quality of his unfinished work.[4] Two years later a collection of his articles and papers was published as a memorial to him, but without anything on the hearth tax, even though Anne Whiteman in her foreword claimed that his work on it was 'in some ways his most substantial achievement' and 'a model of its kind'.[5] His magisterial introduction on the administration of the Warwickshire

1 WCRO, CR1741/13/6: letters from Edgar Stephens to Philip Styles dated 15 & 25 January 1945 and 12 July 1946.

2 WCRO, CR1741/13/6: letter from C.A.F. Meekings to Philip Styles dated 15 July 1952.

3 Styles, 'Hearth tax'.

4 WCRO, CR1741.

5 Styles, *Studies*, p. xvi.

hearth tax is therefore the sole published proof of this claim. It is a piece of outstanding scholarship which I have plundered appropriately, together with some of his notes.

But this volume too has developed a history of its own. It started with a rather indeterminate proposal in 1981 from me to the Dugdale Society for a comparative study of all these elusive hearth tax returns. At first I set out to record on computer, more cryptically than Styles had done, all the available data for each householder by alphabetical order within each parish, but not based on any particular return. When this proved to be unsatisfactory, I abandoned it four years later.[1] Next I planned to confine my comparative study to the last four assessment lists, based upon the one for 1670, but this was halted within a few years by illness and a subsequent move to west Cornwall. After a long fallow period it was finally revived in 1997 when Margaret Spufford suggested a collaboration with the British Record Society, as an integral part of their Hearth Tax Series, which Joan Lane endorsed enthusiastically on behalf of the Dugdale Society. I decided that the volume would now concentrate on Warwickshire's hearth tax return for 1670 because it was the first in a unique sequence of four returns which, when combined with a similar cache of contemporary exemption certificates, can provide diligent historians with an amazing insight into Warwickshire's households between 1670 and 1674. The 1670 return is also the most thorough and the nearest in time to Coventry's best surviving hearth tax list from 1666. Margaret Spufford also approached Nat Alcock who happily agreed to collaborate in seeing the project through to completion. He had already studied the 1674 hearth tax return in some detail together with aspects of the county's domestic architecture and brought his computing skills to the project.

In 2004 the British Academy Hearth Tax Project provided the Dugdale Society with a copy of the transcripts of the relevant returns, which I vetted against the originals several times during the following year. Since then they have been supplemented with transcripts of 41 exemption certificates and as illuminating an introduction as the space available would permit, backed up with appropriate statistical analyses, especially the four main Tables 8, 9, 28 and 29, which cover all the parishes. Nat Alcock's specific contribution to these endeavours has been the section on houses in the introduction, some initial work on the Coventry transcript and sole responsibility for collaborating with Mike Shand of the Hearth Tax Project in the production of the detailed maps that the Hearth Tax Project require. In addition, he has compiled two of the indexes and taken part in countless stimulating discussions. While every effort has been made to check and recheck every aspect of the text, no volume of this complexity can ever be entirely error free, and I accept full responsibility for those that remain.

Tom Arkell, St Just-in-Penwith

[1] This was undertaken for Kineton hundred and part of Hemlingford and subsequent analyses of the data were used in Arkell, 'Warwickshire'.

Acknowledgements

We owe an enormous debt of cumulative gratitude to the many people who have provided help, support and advice in the preparation of this book. They include Margaret Spufford, Steve Hindle, Elizabeth Parkinson; the changing staff at the Warwick County Record Office, especially Mark Booth who alone has remained in post throughout the last three decades, Jonathan Mackman, Peter Seaman and Helen Watt at The National Archives, Andrew George at the Lichfield Record Office, Gwyn de Jong, Duncan Harrington, Susan Rose and Mike Shand from the British Academy Hearth Tax Project, Terry Slater of Birmingham University with his cartographers, and from Warwickshire, Christine Hodgetts, Cathy Millwood, Janet Saunders and Joy Woodall.

Throughout the lengthy gestation period of this book, we have greatly appreciated the wise counsel, hard work and persuasive diplomacy of our general editor, Robert Bearman.

Tom Arkell
Nat Alcock

Introduction: Part 1

by Tom Arkell

1. Restoration Warwickshire

The economy[1]

Although Warwickshire lay at the centre or heart of England, it lacked both economic and administrative coherence. By the mid-seventeenth century the simple traditional division of the county into the pastoral forest region of the Arden, north of the River Avon, and the arable open-field Felden to the south no longer obtained. However, its legacy still survived of small scattered settlements in the Arden and mainly larger nucleated ones in the Felden, although with very complex village plans compared to County Durham.[2] In fact, two centuries of cumulative economic development had divided the county into some seven regions, 'which often had more in common with the economies of neighbouring counties than they had with other parts of Warwickshire'.[3] The Felden was broadly divided between the heavier clay soils in the east, where large scale sheep farming had generated some enclosure, and the more fertile soils towards the west, where wheat and barley flourished in a mixed farming context that also predominated in the county's lower Avon valley, which had experienced much piecemeal enclosure. On the poorer soils of Dunsmore Heath and the area north of Rugby in east Warwickshire, sheep farming and cattle grazing were the norm. By then the Forest of Arden, which had also covered much of east Worcestershire, had been virtually destroyed by the heavy demand for timber and charcoal of the growing iron industry round Birmingham, while its agriculture had been transformed from mainly pastoral to dairying, mixed with cereal growing, to meet the increasing demand for food from its rapidly growing population.[4]

The Black Country covered parts of Staffordshire and Worcestershire as well as north-west Warwickshire. It was one of the most prosperous iron smelting areas of the country and relied on Birmingham as its centre for both marketing and extended credit.[5] Its main trades included nail-making and cutlery, which were run under the putting-out system and controlled increasingly by entrepreneurs. The county's other main industrial area lay on or near the coalfield, which stretched southwards from Tamworth to Coventry, where the potential market for coal was huge, but so were the problems that bedevilled the working of the mines, from drainage and steep seams to the limitations of overland carting. Thus the Warwickshire coalfield

1 This section draws heavily on the excellent opening chapter in Hughes, *Warwickshire*, pp. 1–20.
2 Roberts, 'Village', pp. 126–32.
3 Hughes, *Warwickshire*, p. 1. These sub-regions are discussed in some detail in section 5 below and delineated in Map 3.
4 Skipp, *Crisis*, pp. 42–3, 50–1; Thirsk, 'Midlands', pp. 180–4.
5 Rowlands, 'Society', p. 52.

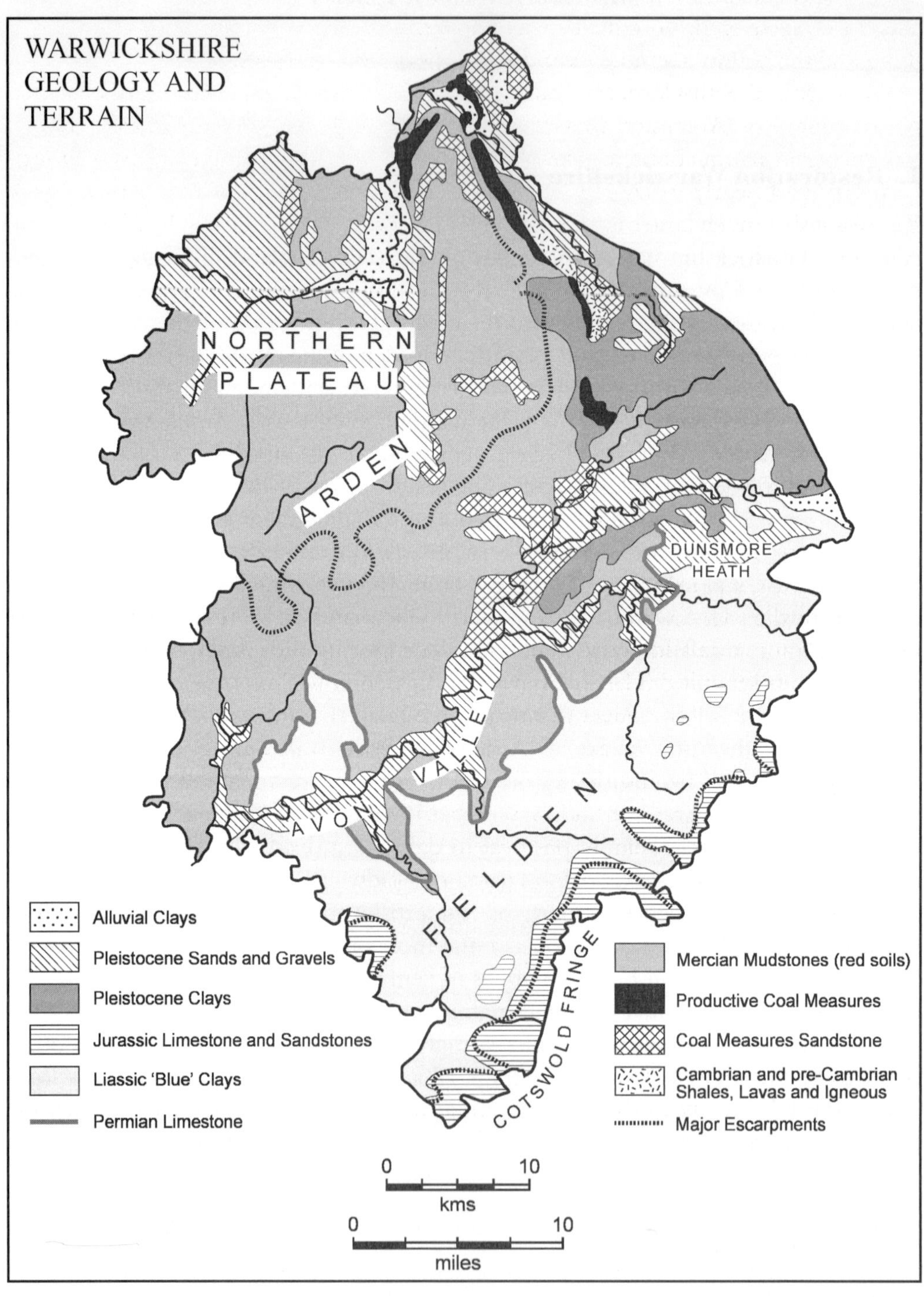
WARWICKSHIRE
GEOLOGY AND
TERRAIN
NORTHERN
PLATEAU
ARDEN
DUNSMORE
HEATH
AVON
VALLEY
FELDEN
COTSWOLD FRINGE
Alluvial Clays
Pleistocene Sands and Gravels
Pleistocene Clays
Jurassic Limestone and Sandstones
Liassic 'Blue' Clays
Permian Limestone
Mercian Mudstones (red soils)
Productive Coal Measures
Coal Measures Sandstone
Cambrian and pre-Cambrian
Shales, Lavas and Igneous
Major Escarpments
0
10
kms
0
10
miles

Map 1 Warwickshire geology and terrain.

tantalized speculative entrepreneurs and landowners with promises of riches, which they rarely delivered: no colliery was apparently active for more than one year in three and the county's annual output did not exceed 30,000 tons.[1]

Warwickshire-with-Coventry had no single town comparable to Leicester, Northampton or Worcester 'that was sufficiently large, conveniently placed, and all embracing in its functions to provide a focus for the whole county'.[2] Even though Coventry had nearly twice as many people as Birmingham, the next largest town, and was also a much larger manufacturing and commercial centre, it had been in relative decline since the early sixteenth century with an obstinately stagnant cloth trade. However, Coventry still nurtured a wide range of trades in leather, food, drink and building among others, benefited from lying on the main road from London to Chester and even had its own mint until the end of the seventeenth century.[3] It also ran thriving markets for the exchange of grain, wool, cattle and coal that penetrated into parts of Northamptonshire and Oxfordshire. But socially and administratively the city of Coventry remained aloof from the rest of Warwickshire, a proud separate county in its own right with its own Quarter Sessions. Warwick borough was the county town where Warwickshire's Quarter Sessions and assizes were held and where the gentry from the centre and south of the county congregated regularly, unlike those living to the north of Coventry for whom Warwick was too remote. It was also an important centre for trade in corn and horses, retailing and a range of services and overall about half its active adults were engaged in trade and manufacture, such as mercery and tanning. The sole navigable waterway in this landlocked county was the lower reaches of the River Avon below Stratford upon Avon, its fourth largest town, which thus became a river port uniquely linked to Bristol. It prospered with a growing trade in heavy and bulky goods in addition to its well-established market in corn and dairy products, such as cheese, that were interchanged between the Felden and the Arden. Stratford also had flourishing glove-making and malting trades and a thriving horse fair that attracted sellers mostly from the north and east and buyers from the south and west.[4] In addition, it enjoyed a certain independence through its status as a borough.

Local government

For administrative purposes Warwickshire was split into four hundreds, with each then subdivided into four autonomous divisions under their own high constables, who reported directly to the county's high sheriff and were responsible for all the petty constables in their area.[5] Warwickshire's 16 divisions therefore operated like the

1 Grant, 'Coalfield', pp. 327–32.

2 Hughes, *Warwickshire*, p. 17.

3 *VCH*, viii, pp. 164–7.

4 Edwards, 'Horse trade', pp. 95–6.

5 TNA, E179/194/343: 'The account of Henry Ferrers esq high sheriff of the county of Warwick for the hearth money due to his Majesty at Lady Day 1664' which lists the constables and their constableries for each division. See also *Quarter Sessions*, vii, pp. lvi–lviii, for more about the high constables and the relationship between the divisions and hundreds in Warwickshire.

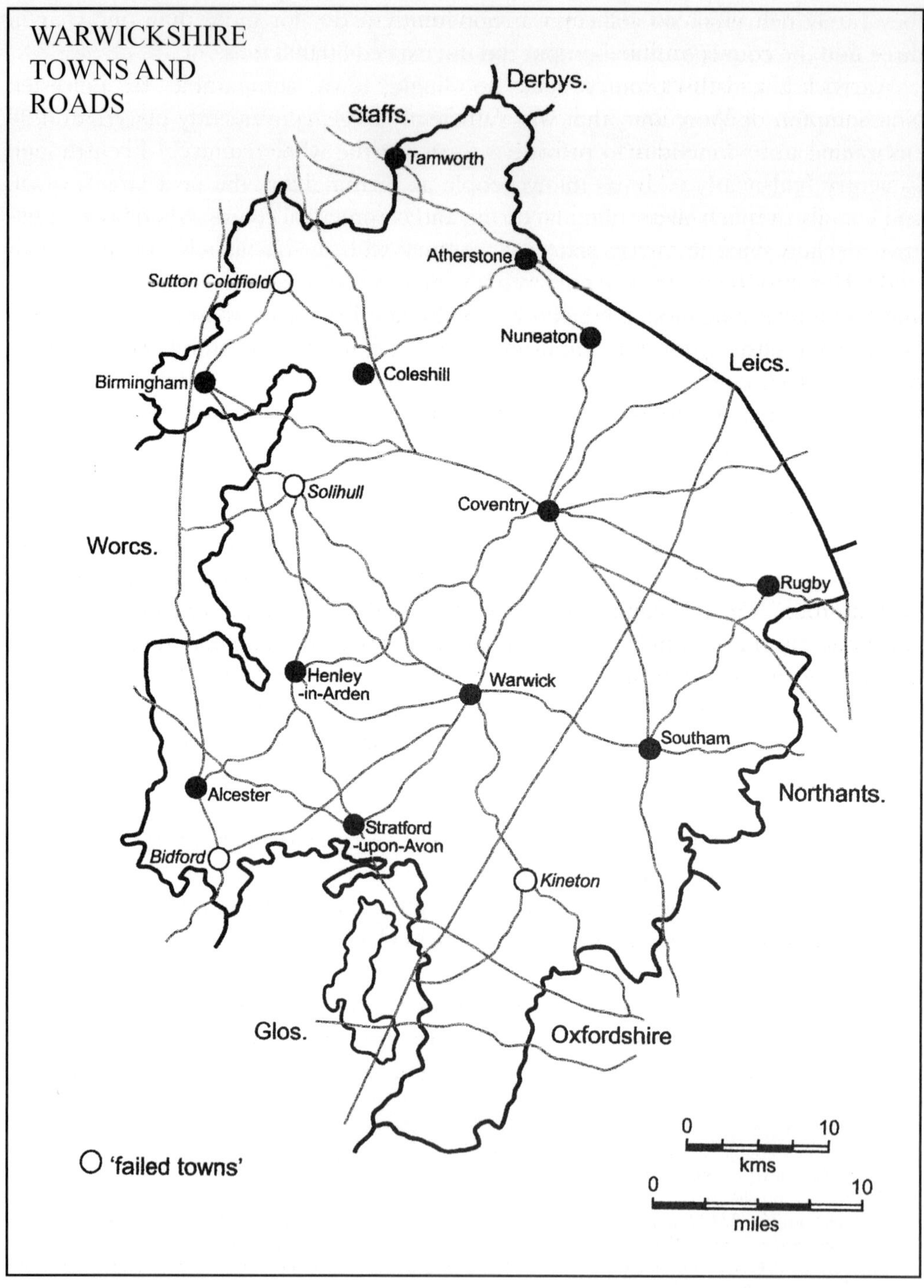

Map 2 Towns and roads of early modern Warwickshire. Roads from Robert Morden, *Map of Warwickshire*, 1695 and John Ogilby, *Britannia*, 1675.

smaller hundreds of Devon and East Anglia, for example, while the role of its so-called hundreds was limited to minor legal functions and collective organising.[1] Petty constables were responsible for the maintenance of law and order, including the supervision of alehouses and the accuracy of weights and measures, for aspects of the application of the poor laws and the collection of some national taxes and the county rate. The latter was used mainly for the upkeep of the county's principal bridges and some roads, its gaol and house of correction as well as for payments to maimed soldiers and other travellers.[2] In 1662 the constables were also empowered to raise money to pay for their own expenses and were charged with collecting the hearth tax.

By the mid-seventeenth century, however, major complications affected the powers and appointment of these petty constables. In fact the whole system of local government was in flux, as the crumbling manorial system gave way to one based on the parish, and responsibility for civil administration was transferred from the manor to the parish vestry.[3] Where the courts leet still operated, each appointed its own constable with powers strictly limited to the extent of the manor but, where they were no longer held, parish vestries often filled the void by nominating the constables for appointment by the justices. This caused considerable confusion over the areas for which they were responsible when the parish and manorial or constablery boundaries did not coincide, especially when they shared the same name, such as Burton Dassett or Maxstoke.[4] Further complications were caused by the appointment of assistant constables or thirdboroughs as subordinates to the petty constables in some areas, just as they had been previously in sub-manors. Thus, the thirdborough of Moxhull in Wishaw parish reported to the constable of Curdworth parish and the parishes of Barcheston and Stretton under Fosse each had their own thirdborough, who was subordinate to the constable of Honington parish, while Kingsbury parish covered parts of five different constableries.[5] According to Styles, Claverdon was an unusually large constablery that stemmed from the common overlordship of the medieval earls of Warwick over several manors and sub-manors in the parishes of Claverdon, Beaudesert, Preston Bagot and several scattered hamlets in Wootton Wawen parish.[6] Furthermore, most of the hamlet of Langley in Claverdon parish constituted a separate manor, while the southern part of Preston Bagot parish belonged to the manor of Wootton Wawen. The constable of Claverdon was elected by its court leet with a jurisdiction confined to the manors of Claverdon and Langley, while Beaudesert, Preston Bagot and Aspley in Wootton Wawen had their own thirdboroughs, who

1 *Quarter Sessions*, vi, pp. xxi–iv; *Quarter Sessions*, vii, pp. liv–viii.

2 *Quarter Sessions*, v, pp. xxxi–lxviii.

3 Hindle, *State*, pp. 207–15.

4 WCRO, CR1741/13/20 (unpublished typescript by P. Styles on 'The Constabulary of Claverdon'), pp. 1–4; *Quarter Sessions*, iv, p. xxxv. The traditional spelling of the word 'constablery' has been used consistently throughout this volume to stress the fact that it refers to the jurisdiction of a single petty constable and not to the modern meaning of a group of policemen and women.

5 Walker, *Hemlingford*, pp. 68–9; *Quarter Sessions*, ii, pp.142–3; *Quarter Sessions*, i, p. 9.

6 WCRO, CR1741/13/20 (Styles, 'The Constabulary of Claverdon'), pp. 1–4.

were chosen at different vestry meetings, but were subordinate to the Claverdon constable until the 1730s.

Warwickshire was further fragmented by its ecclesiastical organisation, which was split into six deaneries under two archdeacons' courts in two dioceses with headquarters outside the county. Worcester's two deaneries covered most of Kineton hundred and all of Barlichway in the south and west, while the four in Lichfield and Coventry diocese accounted for Hemlingford and Knightlow hundreds in the north and east, together with the rest of Kineton and the county of Coventry.[1] During the 120 years between the dissolution of the monasteries and the Restoration of Charles II various statutes transformed each parish from an area that was simply served by a minister and his churchwardens into a civil parish or unit of secular administration as well.[2] One of the main elements in this process was the granting of powers from 1598 to raise compulsory levies for the relief of the poor, which took almost a century to become fully operational, strengthened in 1662 by the Act of Settlement.[3] But Warwickshire still wrestled with various unresolved parochial anomalies. These included the status of defunct parishes, which were victims of population decline and enclosure and had become extra-parochial areas loosely attached to neighbouring parishes. At the same time, former monastic and Templar properties, such as Pinley and Ernesford Grange, were also extra-parochial and clung for as long as possible to their independence.[4] In addition, the larger parishes were subdivided into townships or their equivalents for civil purposes, others had detached portions or subordinate chapelries, of which some were semi-independent, such as Castle Bromwich and Deritend in Aston parish, while ten chapelries were truly independent, with their own chapel, minister, registers and finances.[5] Particular confusion arose over the boundary between Lower Shuckburgh chapelry and the parish of Upper Shuckburgh. Both were described as 'parishes' in 1637 when the Quarter Sessions could not determine which ratepayers and paupers claiming relief belonged to which area; and this enduring uncertainty is reflected in the hearth tax when most who were listed under Upper Shuckburgh in the 1660s appeared under Lower Shuckburgh in the 1670s.[6]

The increased financial demands placed upon each parish's limited resources were of even greater concern, however, and created considerable tension with persistent demands for the burden to be shared more widely and more fairly.[7] Traditionally, most local taxes had been raised according to the size of a landowner's holding in the

1 For the composition of these deaneries see Whiteman, *Compton*, pp. 183–7, 449–53, which also notes the existence of various dependent chapelries.

2 Hindle, *State*, pp. 206–7, 215–7.

3 Styles, 'Settlement', pp. 175–90.

4 *Quarter Sessions*, iv, pp. 35, 79, 286; *Quarter Sessions*, vii, pp. 70, 91; *VCH*, iii, pp. 150–1.

5 Table 28 below (pp. 450–62) records the extra-parochial places and the parishes to which they were attached, together with the detached portions of other parishes and the fully independent chapelries. Although Castle Bromwich had its own registers for baptisms and marriages from 1619, all its burials were undertaken at Aston until 1810, and its parishioners were also required to attend Easter communion there in the seventeenth century. Deritend did not have its own chaplain until 1677 nor its own registers before 1700 (*VCH*, vii, p. 364).

6 *Quarter Sessions*, i, p. 261; *Quarter Sessions*, ii, p. 2.

7 Hindle, *Parish*, pp. 243–53.

parish's common fields, measured by the yardland, but a uniform valuation for all farmland did not measure wealth equitably because pasture and most enclosed land were more valuable than arable and the omission of personal estates compounded it further.[1] In order to impose a bigger share of this burden on the better-off, new methods of assessment based upon the yearly value of the land or pound rent were devised, discussed, approved as 'most consonant to law and reason' at the county's Quarter Sessions in the 1630s, and subsequently implemented in many parishes, especially between 1646 and 1653.[2] After the Restoration some parishes, mostly in south Warwickshire, reverted to assessment by the yardland, including Brinklow, Fenny Compton, Leamington Priors and Oxhill, but an attempt by some inhabitants in Rugby to return to this old practice in 1662 was thwarted seven years later.[3]

Thus the whole rating process became a battleground fought over between competing interests, both in and outside the parish vestry, which sometimes spilled over into the proceedings of the Quarter Sessions. In 1626, for example, the inhabitants of Studley were ordered to settle their levies openly in their parish church and not secretly in private houses, and in 1672 it was ruled that ten days notice of a comparable meeting in Long Itchington should be given to its main absentee landowner, Richard Newdigate of Arbury.[4] Other disputes concerned the proportions to be borne by the different parts of larger parishes[5] and the contributions of particular individuals, including the ministers of Meriden, Radway, Rugby and Whichford.[6] Two prominent dissidents were Lord Leigh of Stoneleigh, a former sheriff, who was ordered several times in 1647–8 to pay his share of all levies for the demesne lands according to their true value, and Richard Newdigate, who held out for a year against paying his share of the Long Itchington levies by pound rent.[7] Other recalcitrant landowners emerged between 1664 and 1674 in Bearley, Dunchurch, Frankton, Pillerton Priors, Polesworth and Withybrook.[8] Evidence that sometimes the value of people's personal estates was assessed appears mostly in Birmingham and east Warwickshire: for example, in Harborough Magna, Monks Kirby, Newbold on Avon, Polesworth and Rugby parishes.[9] But when absentee landlords were double-taxed on possessions that they held elsewhere, this was clearly unjust.[10] Countywide, therefore, there was no uniformity in establishing liability for, or exemption from, these local taxes, which had implications for how the hearth tax was assessed and so for a thorough understanding of its surviving hearth tax documents.

1 Hindle, *Parish*, pp. 365–78; *Quarter Sessions*, ii, p. 38.
2 *Quarter Sessions*, ii, p. 23; *Quarter Sessions*, iv, p. xxix; Hughes, *Warwickshire*, pp. 281–2; Hindle, *Welfare*, p. 19.
3 *Quarter Sessions*, iv, pp. 129, 171, 176–7, 206; *Quarter Sessions*, v, pp. 41–2, 104–5, 221–2.
4 *Quarter Sessions*, i, p. 38; *Quarter Sessions*, v, p. 186.
5 *Quarter Sessions*, ii, p. 189; *Quarter Sessions*, iv, pp. 25, 117, 289, concern Mancetter, Nuneaton and Stratford.
6 *Quarter Sessions*, iii, pp. 197, 251, 295; *Quarter Sessions*, iv, pp. 28, 282.
7 *Quarter Sessions*, ii, pp. 168, 170, 186–7, 213; *Quarter Sessions*, v, p. 206.
8 *Quarter Sessions*, iv, p. 290; *Quarter Sessions*, v, pp. 126, 135, 151, 188, 208, 224.
9 *Quarter Sessions*, i, p. 135; *Quarter Sessions*, iii, p. 102; *Quarter Sessions*, v, pp. 122, 199.
10 *Quarter Sessions*, iii, p. 129.

Understanding the hearth tax

2. The administration of the hearth tax in Warwickshire

After Charles II was restored to the throne in May 1660 the survival of his new regime depended above all on its financial security. Parliament had agreed that he needed an annual income of £1.2 million to govern the country, but it was soon clear that the revenue which he had been given fell short by some £300,000 a year so that additional taxes were needed to close the gap and keep the government solvent.[1] In the event, the only acceptable proposal to emerge was one for a house tax, graduated according to the number of its hearths. This was probably the brainchild of Sir William Petty, although Sir Edmund Sawyer took charge of implementing it in 1662.[2] Unjustified optimism, based upon ignorance of the number and size of houses in the country, led people to assume that this new hearth tax would cover the shortfall fully, but in the event its yield never came close to the required £300,000.[3]

Sawyer's original proposal was rather nebulous when presented to the House of Commons on 1 March 1662. It planned to tax each hearth or fireplace in every house one shilling (or 5 per cent of one pound) every six months, to be paid at Michaelmas (29 September) and Lady Day (25 March) by either the owner or the occupier. The petty constables were made responsible for collecting the money, under the supervision of the high constables of each hundred or division and of the sheriffs of each county. When Members of Parliament started to examine this bill it became apparent that the liability for paying the tax needed to be clarified and so they placed the onus on the occupier and not the owner, thus making the household the basic unit of taxation and not the house.[4] One consequence of this decision was the obvious inability of some occupiers to pay the new tax and so Members hastily cobbled together in less than two weeks three different exemption clauses that were worded confusingly, partly overlapped and so created an administrative muddle.[5] Another consequence was the uncertain status of empty dwellings, but this was not resolved until later. Thus the bill that the House of Commons approved on 12 March was radically different and more complex than the initial proposal. Most unusually the hearth tax was granted to the crown in perpetuity and not for the king's lifetime. However, it soon became apparent after the first collection at Michaelmas 1662 that, despite the best endeavours to improve the tax, it was still badly flawed.

1 Seaward, *Cavalier*, pp. 103–7.

2 Chandaman, *Revenue*, pp. 77–80; Styles, 'Hearth tax', pp. xii-xiii.

3 Parkinson, *Establishment*, pp. 5–8; Seaward, *Cavalier*, p. 111.

4 13 & 14 Car. II, c. 10 (1662), ss. 1, 2 & 20. Sections 15 to 21 were all amendments added to the Act and included the statement in no. 20 that the tax 'shall be charged only on the occupier for the time being'. This contrasts with 'the owner or occupier' being made responsible in section 2 for supplying a true account of the number of hearths in each house.

5 13 & 14 Car. II, c. 10, ss. 16, 17 & 19.

The Sheriffs' administration, 1662–64

Sawyer thought he could make the hearth tax palatable to the landed gentry by using the machinery of local government to assess and collect it, but in the event it became a hostage to fortune.[1] The petty constables had to identify every taxpayer in their jurisdiction, agree with each the number of hearths for which they were liable and later note any reductions that occurred to the number of hearths in each dwelling. After writing up a list of their names, they had to provide a copy to their high constable for transmission to the county's Quarter Sessions, where the justices were meant to inspect them before the clerk of the peace made an enrolled assessment for the whole county and a duplicate for the Exchequer in Westminster.[2] A very tight nine-week timetable was also prescribed for the money that was collected to reach the Exchequer by the beginning of December and June each year. The petty constables were given just six days to collect the tax, issue receipts and, if possible, levy the duty by distraint from those who had refused to pay, and then a fortnight to hand over the money, along with a list of the taxpayers and any defaulters, to their high constables. The latter then had a further 10 days in which to transmit these to the sheriffs, who were given 30 more days in which to make their return to the Exchequer. There the clerks had to check the sums received against the relevant assessment lists and so identify all the non-payers.[3] In return for their pains the petty constables received two old pennies in the pound (that is less than one per cent) of the money that they handled, while the high constables and clerks of the peace had one penny each and the sheriffs three pence. In cities such as Coventry, where the constables reported directly to the sheriffs, the administration was greatly simplified: the sheriffs took direct responsibility for collecting the tax and the money was required to reach the capital within six weeks, with no poundage paid to any constable.[4]

This was the system that operated for the first three collections until Michaelmas 1663. By then the government was so appalled at receiving only £115,000 a year, or little more than a third of the expected yield, that they tried to restructure the whole administration of the tax. But they were thwarted by Parliament and so compromised with a hastily drafted Revising Act in July 1663, which concentrated on improving the method of assessment. The main innovations of this Act required the petty constables to enter the homes of the chargeable in the company of two local 'substantial inhabitants' to check the accuracy of their returns and to return a complete list of the names and number of hearths of the non-chargeable householders as well as of the chargeable.[5] In the event this was applied only to the 1664 Lady Day collection, which was the last to be administered by the sheriffs, but it was the first of several complex changes that were introduced so quickly in the 1660s that

1 Chandaman, *Revenue*, pp. 81–5; Styles, 'Hearth tax', p. xxiv.
2 13 & 14 Car. II, c. 10, ss. 3–5.
3 13 & 14 Car. II, c. 10, ss. 8–10.
4 13 & 14 Car. II, c. 10, s. 11.
5 15 Car. II, c. 13 (1663).

they generated more confusion and opposition to the hearth tax than improvements to its collection.[1]

The surviving hearth tax documents for Warwickshire, which was administered separately from Coventry, show why this initial attempt to devolve the management of the tax to the sheriffs failed. For a start, since a new sheriff was appointed every November, there was no continuity or accumulated experience as three different men were responsible for the first four collections: Thomas Boughton of Bilton (Michaelmas 1662), Walter Chetwynd of Grendon (Lady Day and Michaelmas 1663) and Henry Ferrers of Baddesley Clinton (Lady Day 1664). The notion that they would return to the Exchequer all the money that was due to be collected within nine weeks was quite unrealistic. In fact five months elapsed before Boughton paid in his first instalment of about one third of what he owed and another two months before his next tranche, while his final third dribbled into the Exchequer over a year later in four instalments which still left him some £50 in arrears.[2] Chetwynd managed to return his money to the Exchequer more quickly in seven instalments between October 1663 and August 1664, but the total sum remitted was much smaller because his arrears for both collections came to nearly £450.[3] Ferrers returned the bulk of his collection within 15 months, but the government remained displeased because, although it was the product of the new assessment ordered by the 1663 Act, this return listed about 5 per cent fewer chargeable householders than in 1662 and 10 per cent fewer chargeable hearths.[4] In 1666 Francis Dormer managed to recover about half the outstanding arrears of the three sheriffs, but as late as 1676 one high constable was still being pursued for some £30 that he owed.[5] The sudden death of the sheriff's deputy-receiver in 1664 and the subsequent loss of his papers had contributed to some of this delay.[6] The sheriffs in Coventry, where two were elected every year, were even more dilatory: their first payment to the Exchequer for the 1662 collection was not made until March 1665, but then their accounts for all four collections were cleared within another year.[7]

Ferrers's account for the 'Hearth money' due at Lady Day 1664 was a copy of the returns made by his high constables under the 1663 Revising Act and shows just how much he depended on the cooperation of both levels of constable.[8] The high constable of the Snitterfield division, for example, as well as the two petty constables for Kenilworth, had neither made any return nor paid in any money, while the high constable for the Tamworth division had paid in his receipts, but without any breakdown, as had nearly one petty constable in six. Most petty constables, however, listed

1 Chandaman, *Revenue*, pp. 82–3, 89–90; Seaward, *Cavalier*, pp. 113–8; Meekings, *Dorset*, pp. viii–ix.
2 Styles, 'Hearth tax', pp. xxi–xxiii.
3 Styles, 'Hearth tax', pp. xxvii–xxix.
4 WCRO, QS11/1–5; Styles, 'Hearth tax', pp. xxxv–xxxvi.
5 Styles, 'Hearth tax', pp. xxiii, xxix–xxx, xxxvi.
6 Styles, 'Hearth tax', p. xviii.
7 Styles, 'Hearth tax', p. xl.
8 TNA, E179/194/343/1. This account was presented for audit at Leicester in October 1665.

their exempt and about a quarter also included particulars of their empty houses, hearths taken up and/or those from whom no distress or distraint could be had. There was, in short, a wide spectrum between conscientiousness and incompetence among the constables, over whom the sheriffs lacked leverage.[1] They were also hampered by the fact that the constables' periods of office, like their own, normally began in November.[2]

The surviving documents also reveal widespread and enduring confusion over the exemption process. The first set of instructions issued for the constables in 1662 was deceptively simple, drawing solely from part of the first exemption clause with 'none to be charged by this Act that is exempted from the usual taxes, payments and contributions towards the church and poor'.[3] This not only ignored the second exemption clause but failed to restrict the first to those who were excused from paying their local levies 'by reason of their poverty or the smallness of their estate' rather than because their landlord paid them or because their occupant undertook such unpaid local offices as churchwarden or petty constable.[4] By law exemption was also granted to the occupiers of properties that had a rental value of one pound a year or less 'upon the full improved rent' with possessions of not more than £10 capital value, so long as they also had an annual certificate signed by their minister, one or more churchwardens or overseers of the poor, and attested by two local justices.[5] Warwickshire's earliest surviving exemption certificates were nearly all for individual householders until the requirement of the 1663 Act to name all the exempt led to the creation of group certificates of non-liability from Lady Day 1664 onwards.[6] Finally, the third exemption clause excused all the almshouses (except for those with endowments worth more than £100 *per annum*) along with private ovens in chargeable houses, blowing houses, stamps, furnaces and kilns.[7] The legal nuances of this clause caused few problems for the Warwickshire sheriffs but in due course bitter disputes arose over its application to smiths' forges and even bakers' ovens.

The first Receivers' administration, 1664–66

By the spring of 1664 the sheriffs had failed so obviously to manage the hearth tax that the House of Commons could not hold out any longer against the king's demand to replace them with dedicated tax-collectors operating directly under his control.[8] The second Revising Act, which came into force on 24 June, replaced the sheriffs with receivers who were responsible for every aspect of the hearth tax administration

1 Styles, 'Hearth tax', p. xxxiv.
2 Chandaman, *Revenue*, p. 82.
3 TNA, E179/360.
4 13 & 14 Car. II, c. 10, s. 16; Arkell, 'Regional', pp. 148–9.
5 13 & 14 Car. II, c. 10, s. 17.
6 TNA, E179/194/343/1 contains the earliest evidence for their existence in Warwickshire.
7 13 & 14 Car. II, c. 10, s. 19.
8 Chandaman, *Revenue*, pp. 84–5; Seaward, *Cavalier*, p. 119; Parkinson, *Establishment*, pp. 40–51. Relatively little material has survived to illuminate the receivers' administration in comparison with the sheriffs, but Elizabeth Parkinson's account is by far the best from the scraps which are available.

in their area.[1] They chose their own deputies and subordinate collectors or 'chimney men' who, when accompanied by a petty constable, were empowered to enter each house once a year to check the number of its hearths and to levy the duty by distraint from those who refused to pay after an interval of one hour. Some collectors therefore undertook both the assessment and collection at the same time.[2] Under the new Act no dwelling with more than two hearths could be exempted nor any property that had been previously assessed as chargeable nor one that was subsequently subdivided if this reduced its value below the exemption level.[3] Otherwise the law concerning exemption certificates remained unaltered, although further confusion was caused by some badly worded instructions.[4]

The receiver for Warwickshire, which was now administered with Coventry, was Francis Dormer.[5] He was appointed in July 1664 by the newly created Exchequer Commission, which issued a very detailed set of printed instructions, drafted by Sawyer, to all receivers. Among other things, these told them not to make a new assessment but to amend and update a copy of the most recent one for Lady Day 1664 and to insert all omissions, both chargeable and non-chargeable, at the end of each place to which they belonged.[6] But since the Exchequer could not provide them with these copies in time for the Michaelmas collection, it substituted the one from 1662 instead. Thus Dormer and his chimney men struggled, like others, to revise an out-of-date list with no non-chargeable entries, making it impossible for them to follow Sawyer's detailed instructions. In the end this new list was used for the three collections from Michaelmas 1664 to Michaelmas 1665 before it was enrolled.[7] Overall it recorded more chargeable households and hearths than the most recent one compiled under Ferrers, but fewer than Boughton's original list of 1662.[8] Very little is known about the collectors who worked under Dormer, although he appears to have appointed at least five for Warwickshire and Coventry. The minor variations in the format of the returns for each hundred suggest that they had some degree of independence as do the different sequences of the names in each place, with many following the 1662 order, some the one for Lady Day 1664 and others neither, implying that sometimes the collectors made fresh surveys. The much closer connection between assessment and collection that obtained under the receivers led in some places to alterations being made to the returns after each collection. This happened at Stratford and Coventry, though not in Warwick nor in many other parishes or constableries. This may reflect how much

1 16 Car. II, c. 3 (1664); Meekings, *Dorset,* pp. xi–xv.
2 Styles, 'Hearth tax', pp. xxxvii–xxxviii, xliv.
3 16 Car. II, c. 3, s. 6; Parkinson, 'Understanding', p. 11.
4 Arkell, 'Instructions', pp. 49–50.
5 Styles, 'Hearth tax', p. xli.
6 Arkell, 'Instructions', pp. 44–6, 51–2, 56–61.
7 Styles, 'Hearth tax', pp. xlii–xlviii.
8 TNA, E179/259/10.

the collectors still depended on the petty constables to complete their task, even though they were no longer responsible directly for drawing up the lists of the chargeable and non-chargeable. In addition, the fact that under the receivers the poundage for the petty constables remained unaltered at two (old) pennies implies that Sawyer realised that they still had a crucial role to play in the smooth working of the hearth tax.

The poundage awarded to the receivers was one shilling or 5 per cent, which may sound generous but, because it had to reward their sub-collectors as well as themselves, it eventually left many receivers with a relatively small profit. According to Styles, this method of payment created financial difficulties for many receivers who took even longer than the sheriffs to clear their accounts.[1] In due course Dormer handed over £3,500 in six instalments, with the first in February 1665 and the next five between January 1666 and August 1667, but his account was not cleared finally until he had settled several small outstanding sums in 1670.[2] Like the other receivers, Dormer had worked under the threat of dismissal if he did not deliver his half-yearly instalments within three months of each collection, but this had little impact. The receivers were also charged with collecting the arrears from the sheriffs' time, but Dormer did not start to pursue them until July 1666 when his administration had ceased to operate. The outbreak of the Second Dutch War left the government so short of money in 1665 that it mortgaged the future yield from that year's two hearth tax collections as surety for loans of £200,000 from the City of London, knowing that it would take some time before they could be repaid.[3] The outbreak of plague in London, the east Midlands and elsewhere during the second half of 1665 undermined further the collection of the hearth tax so that the new regime of semi-professional tax collectors proved no more efficient than its predecessor.[4] With no sign of an end to the Dutch War, the government was becoming ever more desperate for money. It therefore decided not to try to improve the receivers' administration but to replace it in 1666 with a totally different approach that promised to yield both a regular income and an immediate advance.[5]

The first Farmers' administration, 1666–69

This new departure involved privatising or farming out the administration of the hearth tax for an agreed annual rent to a consortium of wealthy businessmen. On 30 March 1666, just as the receivers were preparing to collect the hearth tax that had become due five days earlier, three leading London merchants took over full responsibility for all aspects of raising the tax from the Michaelmas 1666 collection

[1] Styles, 'Hearth tax', p. xxxix.
[2] Styles, 'Hearth tax', pp. xlix–li.
[3] Chandaman, *Revenue*, pp. 91–2; Meekings, 'Loans'.
[4] Parkinson, *Establishment*, p. 49.
[5] Seaward, *Cavalier*, pp. 125–7.

onwards.[1] Even though it took the farmers several months to settle their sub-farmers' areas and then appoint them and their subordinates, the sudden change of regime prompted most receivers to stop work and hand over the collection for Lady Day 1666 to the sub-farmers.[2] Undertaking this collection was a more long drawn-out and messy process than anticipated because in most counties new assessment lists had to be made before the money could be collected. By then this was long overdue and such retrospective payments were very unpopular.

John Best, a London financier, became the sub-farmer for Warwickshire with Coventry sometime in the spring of 1666. Unfortunately nothing is known about his staff, although Styles concluded that the confused sequence and inaccurate wording of some place names in the assessment list probably indicate that 'most of his sub-collectors were not Warwickshire men'.[3] Because this list did not divide the householders' names between the chargeable and non-chargeable, but concentrated instead on separating those who had paid from those who had not, it is not possible to determine the precise number of chargeable hearths and households at this collection. According to Styles, however, both were greater than in all the previous returns, although, since some 20 per cent or so remained in arrears, much less money was collected.[4] It is not recorded when Best handed over this money to the farmers but it was probably between July 1668, when he presented his assessment for audit, and April 1670, when the farmers claimed to have handed over all the money for Lady Day 1666; however, the Exchequer did not clear Best's own account until September 1671.[5]

Long before then the farming of the hearth tax had unravelled so badly that the farmers had surrendered their lease at the earliest opportunity after the Lady Day 1669 collection. There were several reasons for this disastrous failure, not least Charles II's inability to get Parliament to approve the farming of the tax and to tighten up the law on exemption certificates.[6] When the Commons met in September 1666, just after the Great Fire of London, many Members were so annoyed by the government's mishandling of the war against the Dutch and their constant demands for funds to pay for it that they introduced two abortive bills to abolish the hearth tax and then to regulate many of its alleged abuses. Their hostility reflected the widespread distress and mounting opposition in the country to a tax that was now being collected by private individuals for their own profit, while local officials were only involved in the granting of exemption certificates which the king now

1 Styles, 'Hearth tax', pp. li–lxvi.
2 Parkinson, *Establishment*, pp. 51–2.
3 TNA, E179/259/9; Styles, 'Hearth tax', pp. lviii–lix.
4 Styles, 'Hearth tax', p. lix. Styles counted as exempt those who were described as 'certified' or receiving alms and as chargeable those noted as 'poor' or 'pauper' and whose tax was unpaid.
5 Styles, 'Hearth tax', pp. lxv–lxvi.
6 Marshall, 'Levying', p. 633; *CSPD 1666–7*, p. 359. The king consequently resorted on 19 December 1666 to a proclamation which ordered rigorous proceedings against all those who concealed their hearths or made false returns.

clearly wished to curtail.[1] Opposition to the farmers took numerous forms, including riots, violence and the threat of violence to the hated chimney men, outright refusal to pay, false claims that houses were empty or chimneys blocked up, the granting of 'undue' certificates to the technically liable by some justices and the insistence that smiths' forges were not chargeable.[2] In such a climate it became impossible for the sub-collectors to gather all the money that was due and the leading farmers were arrested temporarily when they failed to repay the loan that was overdue to the City of London. Exemption from paying the hearth tax was then granted for seven years to those who rebuilt their houses that were destroyed in the Fire of London, but without adequate compensation to the farmers. These were the last straws that drove the farmers to apply in November 1668 to surrender their lease, but wrangling with the Treasury over such details continued until 1682 when the farmers' accounts were finally cleared.[3]

The second Receivers' administration, 1670–74

Despite receiving clear advanced warning, the government dithered for a whole year over how the hearth tax should be administered after the Lady Day 1669 collection. They really wanted to farm it again, but no one would tender for it after the experiences of the first farmers. The government therefore settled in March 1670 on an improved form of direct collection for the five years to Lady Day 1674 under the second receivers. This time they were vetted more carefully for their administrative competence than their predecessors had been and were also directed centrally from a newly-created Hearthmoney Office in London by two agents, Richard Sherwyn and William Webb. These agents operated under the general supervision of the Treasury lords and kept a very close watch on the local administration of the tax and the processing of its accounts. They imposed greater efficiency through a comprehensive manual of instructions, derived from those of Sawyer and the farmers, printed exemption certificates and increased poundages for the receivers that varied according to the administrative difficulties of their areas.[4] This new arrangement was so successful that the agents were soon put in charge of several other direct taxes.[5] However, these second receivers had to overcome a major hurdle from the outset because Michaelmas 1670 was almost upon them by the time that they had drawn up their first assessment lists and they had to collect the two previous half years retrospectively at the same time as the current one. Restarting the hearth tax collection in such circumstances was a formidable task, even with the support and direction of the hearthmoney agents.[6]

1 Chandaman, *Revenue*, pp. 92–5; Seaward, *Cavalier*, pp. 129–30.
2 Braddick, *Taxation*, pp. 252–66.
3 Styles, 'Hearth tax', pp. liv–lvi.
4 Chandaman, *Revenue*, pp. 95–7; Styles, 'Hearth tax', pp. lxvi–lxvii.
5 Ward, 'Taxes', pp. 204–5.
6 Styles, 'Hearth tax', p. lxxiii.

John Newsham (1633–97) became the receiver for Warwickshire and Coventry in May 1670, when his elder brother Charles Newsham of Chadshunt and brother-in-law William Loggin of Butlers Marston were his sureties.[1] He thus belonged to a well-connected south Warwickshire gentry family that enabled him as a younger son to carve out a profitable career in financial administration. He had already served as a deputy receiver for the hearth tax under Dormer and, from 1666 onwards, as receiver for the royal aid, the poll tax and other direct taxes for Warwickshire and Coventry and so was a natural choice for the hearth tax receivership. He soon proved to be a very good one. By 1671 John Newsham had moved into a seven- or eight-hearth house in Butlers Marston, close to his brother-in-law and on the other side of Kineton from his brother's 13-hearth abode in Chadshunt.

So much hearth tax material has survived for Warwickshire from the early 1670s that it can provide us with a good picture of how Newsham tackled his task. For the triple collection at Michaelmas 1670, he divided responsibility for Warwickshire rather unevenly between four collectors, with Warberton Hull taking charge of the eight divisions in Barlichway and Knightlow hundreds, William Wainman of the four in Kineton hundred, Richard Samon of the Solihull division and Henry Hargrave of the other three in Hemlingford hundred. In 1671 Hargrave took over the whole of Hemlingford while Samon replaced Wainman in Kineton. Further changes in personnel occurred when William Phipps took responsibility for Kineton hundred in 1673–4 and Robert Johnson junior for Barlichway and Knightlow, while Hargrave retained Hemlingford. These collectors have been identified from their signatures on the relevant lists (see Figures 20–22) but most of their subordinates remain anonymous. One exception was Phipps, who was a deputy to Samon in Kineton hundred before he replaced him, and another was the 18-year-old Thomas Woolmer of Stratford, who acted as one of Newsham's own assistants in 1674.[2] The administrative burden involved in collecting the hearth tax was immense, with a continuous need to check, amend and copy out lists and accounts, to provide receipts every half year to every paying householder, to guard very carefully every shilling that had been collected and to chase up all arrears. It is impossible, however, to know how many people were engaged in carrying out all these tasks under the Newsham regime.[3]

All the available evidence indicates that Newsham was one of the more diligent and efficient county receivers, although it is doubtful if he encouraged his collectors in the summer of 1670 to use Best's survey of 1666 for their first assessment lists.[4] During the next three years Newsham refined his format so that the processes of assessment, payment and audit could be undertaken with just one list. When the

1 Styles, 'Hearth tax', pp. lxvii–lxix.
2 Styles, 'Hearth tax', pp. lxx–lxxiii.
3 Parkinson, *Establishment*, pp. 73–82; Arkell, 'Regional', p. 154.
4 Styles, 'Hearth tax', pp. lxxiii–lxv. Styles's assertion that the sequence of names in 1670 follows those of 1666 is quite misleading. In fact this was the exception and not the norm.

previous sequence of names was preserved, it was thus much easier to spot changes to, and omissions from, the chargeable. This improved administrative efficiency led to a small increase in the liable hearths detected by Newsham's collectors and a doubling of the recorded exempt but its impact was greatest on the collection of the money. The tax was gathered more and more promptly until all the money from the final collections for the last two assessments in 1673 and 1674 reached the Exchequer within twelve and then nine months, while the arrears that Newsham's team failed to collect fell to as low as 2 or 3 per cent.[1] With similar improvements in the effectiveness of the collection elsewhere, the net annual yield from the second receivers' collection rose overall to £145,000 *per annum*, or almost half of the figure originally anticipated. Chandaman thought that 'a sense of relief at the replacement of the farmers' was partly responsible for this together with the strict control and direction applied by the hearthmoney agents to well-motivated receivers.[2]

However, there was one problem that remained unresolved in 1674. From the time of the farmers onwards the government had tried without success to curtail eligibility for exemption from the hearth tax to the second exemption clause alone, without any change in the law. This was the only clause that made the exemption certificates both legal and compulsory and without them the government would be powerless to control or monitor those who were excused from paying the hearth tax.[3] On the other hand, this attempt to restrict exemption to the occupants of houses that were worth at most 20 shillings a year, threatened to deprive Warwickshire's officials of their power to apply exemption flexibly according to each household's circumstances, while in London and the south-east, where rental values were much higher, the threat was even worse.[4] This initiative therefore met strong resistance and, until 1674 at least, the first exemption clause, excusing most who did not pay their local levies, continued to be applied widely in Warwickshire and elsewhere. At the same time it also helped to block the application of that part of the second Revising Act of 1664 which prohibited dwellings that had once been chargeable from ever gaining exemption.

The last fifteen years, 1674–89

Despite the relative success of this return to direct collection, the government did not, as might have been expected, persevere with it after 1674. Instead the new Lord Treasurer, Danby, strongly favoured privatising the collection of taxes because it gave him a clearer idea of his likely future revenue and also provided him with some money in advance. This was urgently needed in the spring of 1674 to cope with a chronic shortage of government funds and to pay off many of the armed forces at the

1 Styles, 'Hearth tax', pp. lxxxv–lxxxvi.
2 Chandaman, *Revenue*, pp. 97–9.
3 Arkell, 'Exemption', pp. 18–21.
4 Guillery, *London*, p. 44; Gerhold, *Putney*, pp. 53–4; Arkell, 'Poverty', pp. 35–6.

conclusion of the Third Dutch War.[1] Danby therefore negotiated a second farm for five years under closer scrutiny by the Treasury than before, but with no intermediate sub-farmers. In the winter of 1674–5 a very thorough fresh survey of all householders was undertaken, which may have increased the eventual number of assessed liable hearths by up to 10 per cent nationwide, but not the net yield to the Exchequer.[2] This revival of the farm generated more attacks against the hearth tax in the House of Commons, but the king managed to head them off, allowing Danby to arrange a fresh farm for another five years from 1679 with another group of financiers, who agreed to return a 'perfect survey' of hearths to the Exchequer in 1680.[3] When it became clear that they were collecting some £50,000 a year more than the £157,000 that they paid annually to the Exchequer, the government decided to return to direct collection for the next five-year period from 1684 to ensure that it benefited from this increase.[4]

By then the excise was no longer being farmed but managed by a body of salaried commissioners. It was therefore decided to make them responsible for the hearth tax also, with two extra commissioners well-experienced in hearth tax matters and a well-staffed Hearthmoney Office to direct operations.[5] Detailed new instructions were prepared to guide their local officers, most of whom had worked previously for the farmers and were now supervised even more closely than before.[6] Their new survey towards the end of 1684 again appears to have increased the number of chargeable hearths nationally by some 2 to 3 per cent, perhaps stimulated by renewed financial inducements to uncover new hearths and eliminate dubious exemptions. As a result the net yield to the Exchequer in the late 1680s rose dramatically to £216,000 a year, or double the lowest total of 25 years earlier, while the gross receipts of around £240,000 a year crept towards the original projection. This increase stemmed from the greater efficiency with which the whole business was conducted, the rapid recovery and expansion of London and its suburbs, and the ending of widespread evasion and under-enumeration both there and in the remoter parts of Wales and the north.[7] In addition, as Gregory King noted, a new and stricter interpretation of the application of exemption made most landlords responsible by stealth for their formerly non-chargeable rented properties, without any change in the law.[8] However,

1 Styles, 'Hearth tax', p. xc; Chandaman, *Revenue*, p. 98.

2 Chandaman, *Revenue*, p. 100; Ramsden, *Westmorland*, pp. ii–iv; Arkell, 'Regional', p. 156. One of the few surviving assessment lists from this period comes from Westmorland for 1674–5. A comparison with that county's earlier list for 1670 shows that 6 per cent more households with two hearths were recorded in 1674–5 and another 5 per cent with three or more hearths.

3 Marshall, 'Levying', pp. 641–6.

4 Chandaman, *Revenue*, pp. 101–4.

5 Chandaman, *Revenue*, p. 105; Styles, 'Hearth tax', p. xci.

6 Arkell, 'Instructions', pp. 47–8.

7 Chandaman, *Revenue*, pp. 105–9; Styles, 'Hearth tax', p. xciv, n. 1.

8 TNA, T64/302 (G. King, 'The tax upon windows, Miscellany Papers'), p. 2. In a marginal note, King calculated that the number of exempt hearths fell from 380,000 to 60,000 'when the landlords were forced to pay for their tenants'.

Lady Day 1689 was the last occasion when the hearth tax was collected in England and Wales: a month later William and Mary agreed to abolish it.[1] According to Chandaman, this came ironically 'at a time when, with its administrative problems largely solved, the tax had at last succeeded in realizing something like its full potential'.[2]

Unfortunately nothing is known about the administration of the hearth tax in Warwickshire under the second farmers and little more during the two subsequent regimes. During the third farm, from 1679 to 1684, Warwickshire was administered along with Northamptonshire, Oxfordshire and four other counties to the south, according to Styles, although it shared a receiver with Worcestershire for the first three collections at least.[3] Under the commissioners Warwickshire and Northamptonshire were again grouped together, but with four different counties to the north that included Staffordshire, but not Shropshire as claimed by Styles.[4] The few scraps of hearth tax documents surviving from this last decade suggest that the new survey made for the third farmers in 1679–80 recorded more names in Coventry than in 1666, but not more chargeable hearths.[5] The available evidence also suggests that the collectors were rather slack in keeping an up-to-date record of all the changes that occurred to the householders. They also ignored the high constables' divisions and listed the parishes, hamlets and other places somewhat illogically within the hundreds.[6] Other documents from the early 1680s relate to the continuing battle in the Birmingham area between the collectors and the smiths over their refusal to pay for their forges.[7] Some rather dubious figures from this period imply that the revenue collected for the hearth tax was increasing in Warwickshire as elsewhere, but they cannot be confirmed. Perhaps the county was paying for around 3,000 or even 4,000 more hearths in 1689 than in 1674, but this is by no means certain.[8]

3. Warwickshire's surviving hearth tax documents

More hearth tax documents have survived for Warwickshire, though not for Coventry, than for any other county in England and Wales. They are preserved in both the

1 1 Gul. & Mar., c. 10 (1689).
2 Chandaman, *Revenue*, p. 109.
3 Styles, 'Hearth tax', p. xciii; Meekings, Porter & Roy, *Worcester*, p. 12.
4 Meekings, *Accounts*, p. 142.
5 Styles, 'Hearth tax', p. xciv.
6 Styles, 'Hearth tax', pp. xcv–xcvi; Styles, *Studies*, pp. 111–15. When Gregory King extracted the names of those with five hearths or more from the hearth tax books in the Hearth Office in London in 1682 for the heralds' visitation to the Midlands, they included some who had died in 1676 and others who did not move into their homes until 1679, while the Coventry return for 1679 recorded William Dugdale as an esquire, even though he had been knighted in 1677. Styles thought that King had consulted several assessments from 1676 onwards but it seems much more likely that the Hearth Office had shown him their new survey for 1679, which was not fully up to date.
7 Styles, 'Hearth tax', pp. xcvi–xcvii.
8 Styles, 'Hearth tax', pp. xciii–xciv. The claim by Styles that the total number of hearths in 1684 was over 6,000 more than in 1674 seems greatly exaggerated and is unlikely to have been more than 3,500.

Warwick County Record Office and The National Archives and are summarised in Table 1. The dates in square brackets apply to the last collection of each return and are used consistently to identify them in the text and tables that follow. Those documents that are transcribed in whole or in part in this volume are indicated in bold type.

The returns

The first two surviving Warwickshire lists are the Quarter Sessions copies for the sheriffs' administration. Both are straightforward assessments of those who ought to pay, with the second for Lady Day 1664 recording most of the non-chargeable and a few chargeable householders who had blocked up or demolished some hearths. The third is an Exchequer duplicate that was written up after the first receiver's first three collections. It recorded some but not all of the changes that occurred between Michaelmas 1664 and Michaelmas 1665 and, contrary to the first revising act, listed the exempt quite separately from the chargeable.[1] The return for Lady Day 1666 is another Exchequer duplicate for the first receiver's last collection. It was carried out retrospectively by the farmers, who were more concerned to identify those who had and had not paid than those who were officially not chargeable. All four of the second receiver's returns are the county's Quarter Sessions copies. The first is predominantly another assessment made in time for the last of his first three collections due at Michaelmas 1670, while the one for 1671 records the sums of money raised from its two collections. The last two for 1672–4 summarise in four columns the total number of hearths that were liable for a whole or half a year together with empty dwellings and those that were exempt. The surviving fragments of the Exchequer duplicates replicate closely the county copies.

Because the petty constables were responsible during the sheriffs' administration for identifying the taxpayers and collecting their money under the supervision of the high constables, their returns for the first two assessments were based upon their constableries within each high constable's division. This is evident from the high constables' returns for the Lady Day 1664 collection to the sheriff, Henry Ferrers, and a similar pattern was repeated under the first receivers as the petty constables continued to help them draw up their assessments.[2] Precise knowledge of the constablery boundaries are as elusive today as they were for contemporary strangers, such as John Best when he took over the Warwickshire farm in 1666. Therefore, since the petty constables do not appear to have contributed to this assessment, Best's return used the parish more often as its basic unit of assessment, although with numerous exceptions, without indicating the high constables' divisions. Newsham's collectors also followed a mainly parochial approach, but within the high constables' divisions. Such differences between the various areas assessed in the earlier and later returns, combined with our ignorance of many constablery boundaries, often undermine

1 Styles, 'Hearth tax', pp. xlv-xlvii.
2 TNA, E179/194/343/1.

attempts to plot them on a map or to compare one return with another. The best way of making these comparisons is to use the contemporary parochial boundaries wherever possible. This is how the data in Table 8 below (pp. 48–54) has been assembled, showing clearly the differing number of households in each extant return and demonstrating both the very extensive coverage of these surviving Warwickshire returns and their variable quality.

Table 1 The surviving hearth tax documents for Warwickshire and Coventry

Collections	*[last year]*	*References*	*Coverage*
Assessment lists/returns			
1662M-63M	[1663]	QS11/1–4	county apart from Birmingham & part of Atherstone divisions
1664L	[1664]	QS11/5	county
1664M-65M	[1665]	E179/259/10	county & Coventry
1666L	[1666]	E179/259/9	county & **Coventry**
1669M-70M	[1670]	QS11/7–23	**county**
1671L & M	[1671]	QS11/24–8, 31–3	seven Hemlingford & Kineton divisions, omitting Birmingham
		E179/194/325; E179/338; E179/368/2/1–2	county, all divisions: fragments of badly damaged roll
1672L-73L	[1673]	QS11/29–30, 34–45	county
1673M-74L	[1674]	QS11/46–59	county
		E179/259/12/1–2	parts of Hemlingford & Kineton: fragments of damaged roll
1679M-80		E179/259/11/1	part of Coventry city
		E179/259/11/2	part of Coleshill & Fillongley parishes
1682M-84		QS11/6, 60–3; E179/375/1	Birmingham division: smiths' hearths & new houses
Exemption certificates			
1662–64		E179/329/2–9	Coventry
1664L		E179/194/343/1	county: Sheriff's Account including copies of many certificates
1662–64, 1670–74		E179/347	**county** & Coventry (unsorted)
1671–72		E179/194/334	**county** & Coventry (sorted)
Accounts, arrears etc for 1662–66			
Most of the relevant documents are contained in the following E179 pieces: 194/327; 194/329/1; 194/331/1–2; 194/343/2, 4, 5, 7, 8; 259/6; 265/28; 319/7; 355; 356; 374/4–5.			
Declared accounts for 1670–74			
E360/168.			

Documents with references E179 and E360 are at TNA; those with QS at WCRO.
Items described as 'county' exclude Coventry.
Bold type identifies documents transcribed in this volume in whole or in part.
L = Lady Day; M = Michaelmas.

A full set of eight enumerations has survived for the whole of Brailes and most of Kineton, Priors Marston and Tanworth divisions in Kineton hundred along with all of Tamworth, most of Solihull and about half of Atherstone divisions in Hemlingford hundred. Complete sets also survive for twelve small parishes or places in the other two hundreds, of which the largest are Hunningham (with 29 households in 1670), Norton Lindsey (27) and Ashow (23). For most other places in Warwickshire seven hearth tax lists have survived, apart from Birmingham division which has only six. At the other end of the spectrum come Stretton Baskerville (6 households in 1670), with just three extant lists, Fulbrook (4) with four and Combe Fields (14) with five. The return for Lady Day 1666 had the worst coverage with nine such omissions overall, including Haselor (58 households in 1670), Baxterley (32) and Bentley (31). On the other hand, Table 8 shows that Newsham's lists from the 1670s covered everywhere.

Establishing definitive entry or household totals for each return is an elusive task. While some entries, for example, indicate that they relate to two or more dwellings, so do others that are not so flagged. These include houses or tenements with a single owner and several occupiers, dwellings that were shared between two close relatives or elderly widows, and large mansions where the hearth total covered other dwellings on the estate. Empty houses were recorded even less consistently, with many being omitted entirely or not recorded as such, especially in the earlier returns, while the status of those entries with just a landlord's name are even more opaque. Gregory King estimated that some 2–2½ per cent of the houses were normally empty and an analysis of all the eight returns for Kineton hundred supports this. There 2.7 per cent of the entries were reported as empty in 1673, compared with just 1.2 per cent in 1670 and a mere 0.1 per cent in 1664.[1] Another problem concerns the recording of almshouses, which may either have been omitted or listed as single multi-hearth properties or as several separate dwellings with one or two hearths each. Although not very numerous, wherever possible, they are treated as separate households in Table 8.

The exemption certificates

The first exemption certificates were little more than handwritten slips of paper that excused individual householders. Most of those that have survived for Coventry and Warwickshire come from the first two years of the hearth tax and their varied wording reflects the initial confusion over exactly who were exempt. Thus one individual 'doth pay to his landlady but ten shillings a year for his house so that we conceive he is not to pay the hearth money', while two others were 'unpayable both by rent and estates' and 'not within the compass of the Act for chimney money nor able to pay'.[2]

1 Arkell, 'King', p. 36; Arkell, 'Warwickshire', p. 184.

2 Styles, 'Hearth tax', pp. xix–xx. TNA, E179/347 is an uncatalogued collection of exemption certificates for Warwickshire and Coventry mainly from 1670–4, but with a few from the early 1660s. Those quoted here are for Chesterton, Deritend and Coleshill.

The first evidence of collective certificates for groups of people from the same place appears in the copies made for the sheriff's account for Lady Day 1664.[1] There the exempt are named for nearly half the county in eight divisions, mostly in Hemlingford and Kineton hundreds. Exemption certificates were administered in divisions, just like the collectors' returns. Those that survive for 1670–74 from Warwickshire relate to all four hearth tax returns, apart from those for the Hemlingford divisions of Atherstone, Birmingham and Tamworth in 1670. When studied together, they provide a unique opportunity to unravel the different ways in which the non-chargeable were identified and recorded. The varying totals for these exemption certificates and hearth tax returns are compared in Table 29 (pp. 463–72), which reveals for most places numerous inconsistencies in the numbers recorded as exempt.

In theory these certificates should have been used to vet those who qualified for exemption before they were recorded in the returns but in practice this became the exception rather than the norm. Because the receivers had to provide the Exchequer with bundles of current exemption certificates along with their returns, John Newsham and his collectors became more concerned with meeting this target than with following the correct sequence. According to Styles, who studied all of Newsham's 767 surviving certificates, Hull, who was the collector for Barlichway and Knightlow hundreds, copied out most of the certificates from the assessments in 1671 and 1673, ready for the minister and local officers to sign, and in a few instances even wrote the signatories' names himself.[2] In Hemlingford, on the other hand, Hargrave took more trouble over ensuring that the certificates were completed properly than that the returns included all the exempt. Thus the intention that the certificates should be used as independent checks on the accuracy of the assessments was frequently short-circuited and the commitment that local justices would carefully inspect them was undermined when they signed batches of certificates from several divisions at one sitting. Furthermore, because the certificates were valid for only 12 months, new ones were required every year (from one Lady Day to the next). This meant that most were not produced in time for those returns with a last collection at Michaelmas. Thus only 38 certificates for 1670–1 were dated before Michaelmas 1670 and just 15 from 1671–2 before Michaelmas 1671. All this changed when the final collection for the next return was delayed until Lady Day 1673, when a mere 16 exemption certificates for 1672–3 were late. But the old pattern returned for Newsham's last return at Lady Day 1674 when only 30 current certificates had been produced, mostly from Hemlingford hundred.

Normally each parish should have had its own separate exemption certificate but in Warwickshire there were many complex exceptions. Shared certificates, for instance, were frequently applied to the smaller parishes and chapelries and were also

[1] TNA, E179/194/343/1. The eight divisions are Atherstone, Bidford, Kineton, Priors Marston, Solihull, Southam, Tamworth and Tanworth.

[2] Styles, 'Hearth tax', pp. lxxvi–lxxxii.

common in 1671–2 in the Knightlow divisions of Southam, Kenilworth and Rugby. Sometimes, when just one parish is named, it can be very misleading: Weethley, for example, followed Kinwarton incognito in 1674. Some were also grouped illogically, such as Hatton, which was twinned with Haseley and Honiley parishes in 1673, while the two other parts of Hatton parish, Beausale and Shrewley, were covered elsewhere. Although these certificates were intended to relate to parishes and not constableries, Longdon End and part of Widney End, in Knowle constablery and Solihull parish, were included consistently in the certificates for Knowle chapelry and not Solihull. Kingswood Brook in Lapworth parish, on the other hand, was a detached part of Wellesbourne constablery and was recorded in both certificates in 1671, but was not identified separately as such in the Lapworth list. On a few occasions two certificates were made for the same place in the same year. In addition, Newsham tried in 1670–1 to remove some people from the lists for seven parishes in Kineton and Priors Marston divisions whom he claimed were incorrectly certified as exempt, but subsequently gave up the effort.[1] Other anomalies are also indicated in Table 29. Most unusually the first three certificates for Rugby all failed to name the inhabitants of 40 poor cottages whom they exempted, while those for another 12 parishes in 1672–3 contained more anonymous exempt.

Inconsistencies

Data taken from Tables 8 and 29 for a sample of 11 larger parishes are presented in Table 2 to show by how much the number of households and exempt recorded in these documents could vary from one place to another. In Monks Kirby and Wolfhampcote, for example, the difference between the highest and lowest household totals in all the returns, apart from the first which excluded the exempt, was only 10 per cent, while Priors Marston had two very different but consistent levels, with household totals in the 1660s between 71 and 79 and 102 to 105 in the 1670s. By contrast, the largest totals in Alcester and Polesworth were more than double those of their smallest returns and nearly four times as great in Barford. Since neither the highest nor lowest totals for all these parishes date from the same year, any so-called 'best' return with the most households for the whole county cannot be the 'best' for all its parishes.

Although one might expect the number of exempt in each hearth tax return to coincide with those in a contemporary exemption certificate, it has already been explained why this was often not the case. Thus while the totals for both are very close in such parishes as Alcester, Barford and Priors Marston, only in 1674 do they match in Polesworth and Solihull. Overall, the exempt were recorded less efficiently in 1674 in half of these sample parishes, most obviously in Salford Priors, while in Barford they were omitted completely. In Brailes, on the other hand, the exempt seem to have been under-recorded in 1670. Other suspect non-chargeable totals appear in some

[1] See, for example, the transcript of the 1670 exemption certificate for Avon Dassett below, p. 419.

returns for six of these parishes, where many were numbered but not named. This affects Polesworth in particular and partly explains the erratic totals that were recorded for its exempt. Sometimes lower household totals can be linked directly with the recording of fewer exempt, as at Solihull in 1673 and Monks Kirby in 1674. But in Chilvers Coton, for example, the number of recorded households fell from 183 in 1671 to 176 in 1674, while its non-chargeable increased by eight and their proportion from 48 to 55 per cent.

Table 2 Hearth tax data for 11 selected parishes
(a) Household totals 1664–74

Parish (division)	**Ratio*	*1664*	*1665*	*1666*	*1670*	*1671*	*1673*	*1674*
Monks Kirby (MK)	1.1	243	*232*	**263**	**263**	–	255	239
Wolfhampcote (Sou)	1.1	85	86	88	85	–	**92**	*84*
Wellesbourne (Tan)	1.4	76	78	*58*	80	80	**83**	82
Priors Marston (PM)	1.5	*71*	79	72	102	104	103	**105**
Solihull (Sol)	1.6	**324**	283	309	309	304	*204*	301
Brailes (Bra)	1.6	166	183	*121*	188	186	185	**199**
Chilvers Coton (Ath)	1.6	**188**	150	*116*	**188**	183	177	176
Salford Priors (Bid)	1.6	132	130	101	133	–	**135**	*86*
Polesworth (Tam)	2.1	*101*	199	**213**	195	174	175	187
Alcester (Alc)	2.2	*140*	**312**	166	270	–	275	267
Barford (Tan)	3.8	52	*20*	68	**75**	71	73	44

* = ratio of highest to lowest total

(b) Exempt totals 1670–74

Parish	*HT70*	*EC70–1*	*HT71*	*EC71–2*	*HT73*	*EC72–3*	*HT74*	*EC73–4*
Monks Kirby	**88**	86	–	79	86	85	*71*	71
Wolfhampcote	17	–	–	16	**21**	21	*15*	15
Wellesbourne	32	33	33	34	**39**	35	*29*	31
Priors Marston	34	34	**38**	37	34	*33*	34	34
Solihull	133	**144**	126	130	(23)*26*	128	127	128
Brailes	*70*	79	82	**86**	82	81	(85)**86**	85
Chilvers Coton	(39)93	–	*88*	**106**	(55)90	95	96	99
Salford Priors	64	63	–	58	**65**	63	(14)16	*14*
Polesworth	(52)96	–	(32)77	100	(68)*76*	**102**	92	92
Alcester	125	–	–	124	**133**	133(113)*121*		121
Barford	29	29	28	28	**31**	30	*0*	–

HT = hearth tax return; EC = exemption certificate; (brackets) indicate number of exempt who were not named, but are included within the succeeding total.
The highest totals are recorded in **bold** and the lowest in *italics*.

Source: Tables 8 and 29.

4. Warwickshire's hearth tax returns for 1670

The transcript of the Warwickshire hearth tax return for 1670, which forms the core of this volume, is the county or Quarter Sessions copy. It has been made from 17 separate documents written in six different hands, with one booklet for each high constable's division and an extra one for Warwick borough. (Because the Coventry return for 1670 is missing it has been replaced by the relevant part of the one for 1666.) When these assessments were made in the summer of 1670 the hearth tax had not been collected for over 12 months so that they covered simultaneously the three collections from Michaelmas 1669 to Michaelmas 1670. They were compiled by the county's receiver and his four collectors with the assistance of the petty constables and others. All their returns shared a common framework in which the householders' names were followed by two columns that recorded the hearths of the non-chargeable on the left and those of the chargeable on the right, thus reversing their order in the 1666 return. The booklets, however, show numerous differences. These include discrepancies arising from the abbreviations used, how they recorded the non-chargeable and how closely they followed the previous enumeration of 1666. They also reveal a marked contrast between the 12 divisions which simply listed what was due for collection and the other five that amended their returns after the tax was collected.[1] These and other details relating to their compilation are summarised in Tables 3 and 4.

The collectors

Warberton Hull, who was the collector for all eight divisions in Barlichway and Knightlow hundreds, produced the simplest and most consistent returns in his own hand, with the non-chargeable entries being interspersed among the chargeable and indicated regularly with a 'C' for certified. In addition, the fact that most parishes and constableries in all but two of these divisions (the exceptions were for Bidford and Henley) were recorded separately as having been 'viewed' or surveyed by Hull and a named constable proves that the petty constables were deeply involved in this assessment process. The other nine returns from Hemlingford and Kineton hundreds were copied out by five different people, which accounts for numerous discrepancies between them (see Figures 20–22). Thus the non-chargeable in the second half of the Priors Marston division were separated from the chargeable and described as discharged by legal certificate. Brailes, on the other hand, was the sole division in these two hundreds that endorsed its exempt with a 'C' for certified. It was also one of four where the collector only confirmed once that he had viewed the whole return without mentioning the petty constables. The other three divisions were Atherstone, Birmingham and Tamworth in Hemlingford hundred, which were 'viewed and collected' and copied out by their collector, Henry Hargrave. He

1 Styles, 'Hearth tax', p. lxiii.

grouped their non-chargeable households together at the end of each place and recorded some merely as totals made up of unnamed persons, whom he described somewhat dubiously as living in town houses or on the waste or common and receiving collection.

The major difference between Hargrave's three divisions and the others, however, was that his returns did not just apply to those who were assessed in 1670, but were amended to cover the assessments for 1671. Their sub-totals for the chargeable hearths therefore relate to those who were assessed in 1671 and not 1670. But when they refer to some of the chargeable householders who had not paid, this applies to the 1670 collection, and not 1671, which was covered in a later return. This explains why Hargrave's returns for 1670 include a scattering of such comments as: 'empty', 'refuseth to pay', 'unpaid', 'in prison', 'paid ½ year', '1 s[hilling]', 'formerly cert' and 'now holds land', or entered, payable or tenanted at Lady Day, midsummer or Michaelmas 1671. The way in which the forges or smiths' hearths were treated in Hargrave's divisions was also quite different from all the others. Most were omitted at first and only entered later in a different hand so that they are additional to the given

Table 3 The compilation of the 1670 hearth tax returns

Hundred & division	*Collector*	*Scribe*	*ass 70*	*Coverage coll 70*	*ass 71*
Barlichway					
Alcester	Hull	Hull	x		
Bidford	Hull	Hull	x		
Henley	Hull	Hull	x		
Stratford	Hull	Hull	x		
Hemlingford					
Atherstone	Hargrave	Hargrave	x	x	x
Birmingham	Hargrave	Hargrave	x	x	x
Solihull	Samon	unknown & Samon*	x	x	
Tamworth	Hargrave	Hargrave	x	x	x
Kineton					
Brailes	Wainman	Samon*	x	x	
Kineton	Wainman	Newsham	x		
Priors Marston	Wainman	Newsham	x		
Tanworth	Wainman	Wainman	x		
Warwick borough	Wainman	Wainman	x		
Knightlow					
Kenilworth	Hull	Hull	x		
Monks Kirby	Hull	Hull	x		
Rugby	Hull	Hull	x		
Southam	Hull	Hull	x		

ass = assessment; coll = collection; * = sub-totals omitted.

totals for their dwellings and not included within them, as was the case elsewhere. The remaining Hemlingford division was Solihull, which was the only one entrusted to its collector, Richard Samon. His return was dated Michaelmas 1671, but in fact covered only the assessment and collection for 1670 and ignored all new liabilities for 1671. Compared with the neat presentation of Hargrave's returns, Solihull's was an untidy manuscript that has the appearance of a rough copy. Most of it was written by an unknown scribe before Samon completed the last four pages, made numerous corrections and added another page at the start for two small places that had been left out.

Solihull was also one of the two divisions that did not provide any sub-totals for the chargeable hearths in each parish or separately enumerated place. The other was Brailes in Kineton hundred, which also covered the collection for 1670 as well as its assessment, and so was more concerned with how much was actually collected than with estimating what this ought to have been. The return of the Brailes manuscript was delayed until 24 November 1671 after it had been written up by Richard Samon, who replaced William Wainman in 1671 as the collector for all of Kineton hundred. In 1670 Wainman copied out only two of his five returns – those for Warwick borough and Tanworth division – while the receiver, John Newsham, himself tackled the remaining two for Kineton and Priors Marston divisions, which were adjacent to where he lived. The heading for the Warwick borough return in 1670 states incorrectly that it was part of Kineton division and not Tanworth. Styles, however, has argued convincingly that Warwick was 'treated as a separate division' under the second receiver because none of the three following returns for Warwick borough mentioned either Kineton or Tanworth division.[1] One more small difference should also be noted. Newsham listed the names of the places in his two divisions at the front of these returns, and so did Hull for three divisions in Barlichway, while Newsham also inserted a list of contents into Wainman's manuscript for Tanworth. However, they have been excluded from this transcript as the other 11 divisions had no such list.

Less apparent differences between the divisions involve the way in which the various scribes used some words and abbreviations. For example, Hargrave alone referred to 'owner' rather than 'landlord', while only Wainman preferred 'void' to 'empty'. As for using abbreviated forenames, 'Tho' was the only one employed regularly by all six. Newsham also resorted to 'Will' and 'Nick' but otherwise normally wrote out all forenames in full, unlike the other five who used many more abbreviations in various other forms. Some of these were responsible for subsequent errors, as will be explained later, but an awareness of these differences does serve to explain what otherwise might appear as random variations. Thus William was shortened to 'Will' by Wainman, but to 'Willm' by Hargrave and 'W^{m}' by the rest, while Nicholas

[1] Styles, 'Hearth tax', p. lxx.

normally appears as 'Nick' or 'Nich', but as 'Nicho' when shortened by Hargrave. Only Wainman used 'wid' for widow rather than 'widd'. He was also the sole exponent of 'Rob' rather than 'Robt' for Robert, but was joined by the Solihull scribe in preferring 'Edw' to 'Edwd' for Edward, and only Samon added a 'd' to 'Rich' for Richard. The treatment of the name John was more complex because not everyone seems to have been aware of the need to distinguish it from Jonathan. Thus Hargrave appears to have applied 'Jno' to both and Hull to have alternated between 'Jo' and 'John' for no apparent reason. Exceptions to some of these practices can, however, always be found.

Comparison with 1666

According to Styles, the assessments made by Newsham's collectors were derived from Best's earlier return but a detailed comparison shows that he greatly exaggerated the extent to which their 'order of names and general lay-out' followed those of 1666.[1] In fact, the various places were only enumerated in a similar sequence in five divisions (Brailes and all four in Barlichway) and in ten there were large discrepancies between the total number of entries recorded in both lists. In five other divisions, where the places were listed in vaguely recognisable sequences, only Kenilworth and Solihull had reasonably comparable entry totals. By contrast the places in Rugby and Monks Kirby divisions were intermingled in the 1666 return, while the sequence of those in the remaining five divisions (Kineton, Southam, Tamworth, Tanworth and Warwick) were quite unrelated to how they were presented four years later. And yet only Kineton and Tanworth in this group of seven divisions had many more entries in 1670 than in 1666. The data in Table 4 show that the 10 divisions with many additional entries ranged from Atherstone and most of Birmingham, with over 30 per cent, to Bidford and Tanworth divisions with 40 per cent more, Brailes, Henley and Priors Marston with 45 per cent, and Alcester, Kineton and Stratford divisions with well over 50 per cent more.[2] Most of these additional entries stemmed from the failure of Best's assistants to record many of the non-chargeable householders, which must have created major difficulties for those collectors who had hoped to use the 1666 return as the main source for their new assessment in 1670.

The order in which the names were recorded in each place is even more significant. After allowing for the turnover of occupants in the four intervening years, the closest match between the two lists was in Knightlow's four divisions (Kenilworth, Monks Kirby, Rugby and Southam) and Warwick borough, with a few individual exceptions such as Leamington Hastings and Marton parishes and two wards in Warwick which started differently. The two other divisions with comparable entry

1 Styles, 'Hearth tax', p. lxxiii.

2 The relevant proportion for all of Birmingham division was 23 per cent, but for Aston, Birmingham, Coleshill and Edgbaston parishes it was 31 per cent and just 3 per cent for the rest.

Table 4 Total hearth tax entries in 1670 compared with 1666 by division

Hundred & division	*Total entries 1666*	*1670*	*Diff %*	*Hundred & division*	*Total entries 1666*	*1670*	*Diff %*
Barlichway				**Kineton**			
Alcester	514	789	154	Brailes	555	805	145
Bidford	381	527	138	Kineton	510	778	153
Henley	353	510	144	Priors Marston	420	608	145
Stratford	733	1157	158	Tanworth	550	772	140
				Warwick	634	617	97
Hemlingford				**Knightlow**			
Atherstone	1124	1483	132	Kenilworth	940	1003	107
Birmingham: most	1094	1432	131	Monks Kirby	1341	1376	103
Birmingham: rest	440	454	103	Rugby	1117	1143	102
Solihull	1124	1150	102	Southam: most	832	835	100
Tamworth	1040	1084	104	Southam: rest	58	144	248
				Warwickshire	**13760**	**16667**	**121**

The figures for 1666 have been amended to allow for places that were omitted.
Birmingham: most = Aston, Birmingham, Coleshill & Edgbaston parishes.
Southam: rest = Leamington Hastings & Marton parishes.

totals were much more diverse. In Solihull division only three whole parishes had very similar sequences (Hampton in Arden, Meriden and Great Packington) and Tamworth division had even fewer. In both, however, good matches do occur in parts of some parishes, with blocks of some households being reversed in, for example, Balsall and Austrey. However, the decision to group the non-chargeable at the end of most places in the Hemlingford divisions and part of Priors Marston division meant that, whereas they had formerly been interspersed, they now became separated from the chargeable households; while in a few parishes, such as Birmingham and Chilvers Coton, the previous sequences were abandoned. In the remaining seven divisions of Barlichway and Kineton hundreds, the collectors and petty constables discovered that they had to expand their woefully inadequate lists from 1666 by about 40 to 55 per cent and did so in several different ways. In those parishes, such as Stratford and Lapworth, which had previously recorded very few non-chargeable households, the main thrust in 1670 was to insert them in the appropriate places among the chargeable. In other parishes, such as Kineton and Tysoe, the 1666 enumeration was so shoddy that the chargeable had to be overhauled as well as the non-chargeable, although only Lower and Middle Tysoe (but not Upper Tysoe) were revised in 1670. Sometimes the previous return was left unaltered and the missing entries were tacked on to it at the end. This was a common practice in Brailes division and it also occurred in Snitterfield parish, where two extra groups of four chargeable households were included together with eleven certified as exempt. A coherent summary of all these various responses is not possible without a much more detailed analysis, but it should by now be apparent that, although the 1666 return provided the collectors and constables with a launching pad, most of them had to work almost as hard on the 1670 assessment as on a new survey, which indeed is what many in the end produced.

Topographical order

The most efficient way of administering the hearth tax was to record all the householders with their hearths in strict topographical order or 'as they lie most contiguous', according to the Instructions of 1684.[1] We do not know when this policy was first advocated, but Newsham's collectors did begin to use it in Warwickshire, especially in the larger towns. This is apparent in Birmingham, where different sections of the High Street and Digbeth were indicated in 1670 as being on the left or right hand side, although without any non-chargeable households, while some contiguous layouts can be traced elsewhere, with help from other sources. Thus the return for West Street in Warwick starts on the north-west side close to Lord Leycester's hospital and proceeds south-westwards through the suburbs to the hamlet of Longbridge where it crosses the road and returns towards Warwick on the south-east side.[2] Similarly, the Henley Street list in Stratford goes north-westwards up the north-east side until it reaches some 15 exempt and two other small dwellings at the end before coming back down the south-west side.[3] The first part of this street is explored in much more detail below.

In rural areas the houses were so scattered, especially in the remnants of the Arden forest, that strict topographical order could only be applied to small groups, but it is still evident that some petty constables or collectors followed a coherent route. The 145 households in Stoneleigh parish, for example, were grouped in eight different named areas and, although by contrast the 131 in Rowington appear quite amorphous, their opacity dissolves when Joy Woodall's work on the parish is studied alongside the hearth tax return for 1665, which placed the chargeable householders in seven ends, although in a different sequence from the 1670 list which starts with Turners End, followed by Rowington End, Mouseley End and then Lowson End. Finwood End and Poundley End were entered next before the constable returned to Lowson End. He then listed Pinley End and finally revisited three other ends.[4] The sequence in smaller parishes was often much more straightforward, as in Wasperton, where the names spread eastwards from the River Avon in 1670 but, with one exception, corrected in 1671, when Mr Doelittle in the vicarage and Mr Warner's six-hearth farmhouse, which was closer to the river, were reversed.[5] A similar study

1 *CTB*, vii, p. 1366.
2 Information provided by personal communication from Christine Hodgetts.
3 Data held in street-based card index system in the Shakespeare Centre Library and Archive.
4 Woodall, *Hroca*, pp. 161–5. For more details, see note to the Rowington transcript, p. 237.
5 Barratt, 'Wasperton'.

Table 5 Households in part of Henley Street, Stratford borough, 1666–74

	Householders	*1666*	*1670*	*1673*	*1674*
	[North-east side]				
1	**Mr Jo Careless** [yeoman]	3	3	2 –	2
2	**Ann Walker**	4	3		
	Ed Faulks			3	3
3	**Rich Ward**		1	1 p	1 c
4	**Mr John Bradley** [maltster]	3	3	3	3
5	**Mrs Mary Beane**	3	3	3	3
6	Edward Allen	1			
	Mary Mullinux		1		
	Will Feasy, late Barber			1	1
7	**Wm Hall** [glover]	1	1	1 p	
8	**Rich George**		1 c		
	Mic George			1 p	1 c
9	**Mr Wm Atwood** [yeoman, maltster]	3	2	2	2
10	**Mr Step Edkins** [maltster] [#Atkins]	2	2	2 #	
	Will Atkins				2
11	**Rich Kings**		1 c		
12	**Jos Cole**		1Fc		
	Tho Turner			3	2
13	**James Tranie**		2E		
	Jo Ward			2	3
14	**Joane Hornobey**		1 c		
15	**James Tranie** [glazier] [#Straine]	2E	2	2 #	2 #
16	**John Tomes** ['Maidenhead']	6	6		6
	Jo Cooper			6	
17	**Geo Heart**		1	1	1
18	**Walter Gilkes**		1 c	2 +	2
19	**Geo Heart**		1Ec		
20	**Mr Horne mayor** Thomas ['Swan']	6	6	6	6
21	[**Mr Horne**] owner	2E	2E		
	Wid Burford			1 p	
	Will Burfoote				1 c
22	**Mr Hen Harbadge** ['White Lion']	9 +	11	11	11
23	**Tho George**		1	2	2
24	**John Hornoby**		1Fc	2 p	2 c
25	**Geo Masson**		1 c		
	Widow Ferris				1E
26	**Rich Peacock**	3	3	3E	
	John Burnam [maltster]				3
27	**John Smith**	4	4	4	4

	Householders	*1666*	*1670*	*1673*	*1674*
	[*North-west end*]				
28	Thomas Collet	2			
	Kath Barton		2 c	2 p	2 c
29	**Rich Sitch**		1 c	1 p	
30	**Tho Cleaver**	1	1	1	1
31	**John Hunt** [#Hart]		1 c	1 p	1 c#
32	**John Bentley**		1 c	1 p	1 c
33	**Wm Harding**		1 c	1 p	1 c
34	**Robt Ward**		1 c	1 p	1 c
35	**John Cooper**		1	1 p	1 c
36	**Tho Holmes**		1 c	1 p	1 c
37	**Rich Joyles** [#Gilkes]		1 c	1 p#	1 c

The names in bold are taken from the entries in the 1670 hearth tax return.
The left hand column gives the sequence of each separate dwelling recorded there.
Where a different householder occupied that property in 1666 or 1673–4 they are included under the same number on a separate line and indented.
The numbers in the last four columns give the total hearths recorded for each dwelling in each return.
Additional information from the other returns is added after the 1670 householders' names.
Square brackets indicate an editorial comment or addition from another source.

E = empty; F = forge (excluded from the hearth total); c = certified; p = poor or pauper; # = different name; + = new building reported; – = reduction of hearths reported.

reveals that a topographical approach was abandoned in Warmington parish when the small hamlet of Arlescote, which was enumerated separately in 1665, was mingled with the other householders in 1670. In addition, late insertions were always prone to being misplaced, whilst in some subdivided parishes the boundaries of their ends or townships were not always well enough known for all householders to be allocated to the same place each time, as occurred in Fillongley and Chilvers Coton. Thus, although proof of a topographical approach can sometimes be confirmed, its extent cannot be established without more research.

On those rare occasions when several returns have survived in topographical order for the same place, it is possible to study both continuity and turnover among the occupants and to detect more of the collectors' problems and mistakes. This is demonstrated in Table 5 with four returns from 1666 to 1674 for the north-east side of Henley Street in Stratford. There every household that was recorded in 1670 has been given a separate number with their householder's name printed in bold which, when compared with the 1666 return, shows how the chimney men in 1670 followed the same route taken by their predecessors. In 1666 they had omitted the non-chargeable dwellings, but now they listed them with the chargeable ones in the order that they encountered them, as did their successors in 1674. In between, the return from 1671 is missing and the one for 1673 separated the exempt from the chargeable, while still retaining the same sequence for each group. A century earlier, Shakespeare was born on this side of the street and his birthplace now occupies the site of No.16 where John Tomes kept his inn. The Birthplace publications building now stands where Joseph Coles had his house and forge in No. 12. Several other non-chargeable households, like his, were interspersed with the chargeable, but the bulk lived in a group at the end of the street, half of whom are listed here.

The juxtaposition of these returns also exposes many more minor inconsistencies than one might anticipate. New building is recorded as the cause of the extra hearths for Gilkes (18) and Harbadge (22), but not for Turner (12) and Ward (13), whose increased totals may have included their neighbours' small houses that were no longer mentioned. Then again, an entry for Careless (1) noted the reduction of one hearth, but not those for Walker (2) or Atwood (9), who may thus have evaded paying for one hearth each. Similarly, Ward (3) and Cooper (35), who were chargeable in 1670, were exempt in 1673 and 1674. In contrast with the continuity of occupancy revealed for Mrs Beane (5) and many others, the 1673 entry for Feasy (6) implies that Barber lived there in 1671 and that the occupants of this dwelling changed three times in six years. However, since Stephen Edkins (10) was recorded as Atkins in 1673, it seems safe to assume that his property stayed within the family when Will Atkins followed him in 1674. Elsewhere Peacock's house (26) stood empty in 1673 before Burnam moved in. The return of John Tomes (16) in 1674 suggests that Cooper was a temporary, and perhaps an unsatisfactory, tenant of his inn.

Reliability

Similar comparisons for other locations between the 1670 and 1666 returns, and with other sources, confirm that Warwickshire's hearth tax list for 1670 was in fact far from perfect. They also challenge the assumption that the neat subdivision found in most hearth tax returns between the non-chargeable and chargeable, with their differing hearth totals, reflects clear-cut and enduring social distinctions between their households. On the contrary, such exercises suggest that Plato's well-known analogy of the cave provides a better insight into the reality, as an observer contemplates the flickering images that an unseen fire throws onto a wall, which change as the fire flares up or dies down. Together the surviving hearth tax returns and exemption certificates reveal many differences in their total numbers of chargeable, non-chargeable and empty dwellings as well as many variations in the number of hearths allotted to individual households, in the number of forges and ovens that they identified and in the forms of their householders' names. All must be examined in some detail before one can judge the relative reliability of the 1670 return. It will then become apparent that, apart from the turnover in occupancy, most of the differences between these lists reflect the varying levels of competence of those who drew them up rather than actual changes on the ground.

(i) Household totals

A comparison between the data for 1666 and 1670 in Table 4 shows that the later return recorded some 21 per cent more households overall. But when the focus is altered to parish level some flaws emerge in the later return. Places that had a larger total in 1666 included Warwick borough with 17 more entries, Polesworth (18), Berkswell (9) and Ladbroke (9). After all the other returns that are set out in Table 8 are examined, 38 parishes in all appear with at least five more entries in some year other than 1670. These were most notably Birmingham with 94 more households, Mancetter (47), Alcester (42) and Aston, Bickenhill, Bidford and Sutton Coldfield parishes with an additional 32 to 35. However, this picture is altered when the contemporary exemption certificates are considered because many excused more householders than were recorded in the 1670 return, and so identified many omitted from it. In order to ensure that these cover only those who were definite omissions, all detectable duplicated entries were discounted and an arbitrary margin of error established which ignores all differences of less than five between the two sources. By this means a total of 386 missing households were found in the exemption certificates, with five or more extra exempt in 22 parishes, of which 17 were in Atherstone, Birmingham and Solihull divisions. Most of these errant householders belonged to the parishes of Birmingham (88), Mancetter (41), Berkswell (28) and Aston, Bickenhill, Bidford, Nuneaton and Sutton Coldfield with between 20 and 24 each. They are indicated in brackets in Tables 8 and 28 and are absorbed into the relevant parish totals and all subsequent calculations. This approach reduces the gap between the totals for 1670 and another return to just six in both Birmingham and Mancetter and to between 9 and 13 in Aston, Bickenhill, Bidford and Sutton Coldfield and so leaves Alcester as the sole parish with more than 30 entries recorded at some time other than 1670.

(ii) Hearth numbers

Disparities between the number of hearths recorded in individual households in 1666 and 1670 are not uncommon. The claims that some hearths had been 'pulled up' (Warwick, High Street), 'taken up' (Shotteswell) and 'decayed' (Nuneaton) in 1666 appear to have been false because these 'non-existent' hearths were all charged four years later without a challenge and without evidence of any rebuilding. Variations in the number of hearths recorded for the same property provide further evidence of evasion and are most apparent among the larger houses. Thus the moated hall at Baddesley Clinton, which was the home of Henry Ferrers, the high sheriff in 1664, was assessed for 15 hearths in 1670 and 1671 but for 20 in 1666, 1673 and 1674, while the return for Aston Hall, where the very active justice Sir Robert Holt lived, was trimmed from 42 to 41 hearths in 1670 and John Ridgley's house in Curdworth also 'lost' three of its 13 hearths. Proof of further slackness in the 1670 assessment is found in Birmingham division, where two other households in Curdworth were reduced from five to three hearths in 1670 and another from two to one, together with two more such instances in Minworth, three in Water Orton, six in Coleshill and five in Sutton Coldfield.

A detailed study of six other divisions reveals that such evasion was widespread, since about one household in twenty escaped being assessed for at least one hearth in 1670 or 1666, but without any consistent pattern between the two returns. In Solihull division, 65 households had a different hearth total in 1670 from 1666, of whom nine had fewer, to only one with more. In the three divisions of Brailes, Tanworth and Warwick, the ratio among 84 households was three with fewer hearths in 1670 to two with more. In Newsham's 'home' divisions of Kineton and Priors Marston the ratio among 53 entries slightly favoured those with more. Thus both assessments were flawed, but it is easier to detect those households that had more hearths in 1670 than in 1666. Altogether those with increased totals accounted for 3 per cent of all the entries in 1666 in Brailes, Kineton and Priors Marston divisions compared with 1.6 per cent in Tanworth, 1.3 per cent in Warwick and just 0.5 per cent in Solihull division. By contrast, the tax evaders in 1670 can only show up among those who had at least two hearths in 1666. They reveal significant proportions of households with fewer recorded hearths in 1670, ranging from about 4 per cent in Warwick, 5 per cent in Kineton division, 6 per cent in Priors Marston and Tanworth, 8 per cent in Brailes division to as high as 15 per cent in Solihull division. Since half the households in Warwick contained two or more hearths and one third elsewhere, and some householders almost certainly escaped paying for some hearths on both occasions, the proportion of these evaders in all dwellings in 1670 was at least 2 per cent in four divisions, 3 per cent in Brailes and 5 per cent in Solihull divisions. Because the returns for the latter two were the last to be completed, some sharp-witted householders may have seized the chance to reduce their tax burden illegally as the collectors struggled to complete their new survey. Meanwhile the more officious or competent collectors elsewhere were increasing the number of hearths of those who paid.

(iii) Forges and ovens

Smiths' forges and bakers' ovens were also under-recorded in this 1670 assessment. Indeed the total of 299 forges that were enumerated then probably accounted for only half of those that actually existed. A close comparison with the 1666 assessment raises the number by two thirds to 505, with 440 forges being noted in 1666 and another 65 omitted then, but not in 1670. Of these 206 additional forges, 98 or nearly half were in the three parishes of Birmingham, Aston and Sutton Coldfield and another 52 in Atherstone and Solihull divisions. On the other hand, no extra forges identified from the1666 return were in Alcester, Bidford, Priors Marston or Rugby divisions and very few in several others. Although there were far fewer public or bakers' ovens than forges, the total of 72 ovens in 1670 can be raised to 109, by combing through the 1666 return. This does not boost the oven totals in eight divisions, including Tanworth, where only a few flax ovens were recorded, or

Birmingham, Tamworth and Priors Marston divisions, which appear in 1670 without any bakers' ovens at all. However, the 1666 return uncovered 13 more ovens in Birmingham division, 5 in Monks Kirby and 4 each in Kenilworth, Solihull and Tamworth divisions. But we will never know how many more went undetected, apart from five in Nuneaton. There nine bakers' ovens were recorded as being in arrears in 1664, before they fell to four in 1666 and 1670 and none in 1671, when it was claimed implausibly that new occupants had demolished the last four.

The explanation why more forges and ovens were listed in 1666 than in 1670 stems from the third exemption clause that was tacked on to the original Hearth Tax Act in 1662.[1] Its rather confused wording – that the act 'shall not extend to charge any blowing house and stamp furnace or kiln or any private oven within any of the houses hereby charged' – failed to make it crystal clear that smiths' forges and bakers' ovens were not excused. It was not until the farmers began to administer the hearth tax in 1666 that they tried to track down and tax all the forges and ovens to raise every possible extra shilling. This aroused so much opposition, especially over the forges, that the House of Commons tried and failed to exempt them officially in 1667–8.[2] In Warwickshire Sir Robert Holt encouraged this resistance to paying for the forges and was supported strongly by the specialist metal workers in the Birmingham area, but not by the local blacksmiths and wheelwrights elsewhere. Thus, under the second receivers, there was less incentive to identify the forges of those who paid up willingly or those in the areas where this resistance was implacable and widespread. The specialist metal workers held out until December 1683 (four years after Sir Robert's death) when a survey of smiths' hearths listed 178 in Birmingham parish, 15 in Edgbaston and 78 in most of Aston parish, giving a total of 271 forges compared with the 145 recorded in the same area in 1666 and just 76 in 1670. One cannot tell how many were new forges built between 1670 and 1683, but, on the assumption that most had escaped the hearth tax during this time, close to 600 forges existed in Warwickshire in 1670 or twice as many as the collectors recorded then.[3]

(iv) Family and personal names

A cursory inspection of the 1666 and 1670 returns soon reveals many discrepancies between the names in these two lists, such as 'Wm Simonds of the Lodge' in Kingsbury turning into 'Willm Simonlog' in 1670 and 'Wm' into 'Em' in Solihull, while 'Wm Wallis' became 'Harris' in Polesworth, 'Widow Robins' 'Pobbins' in Willoughby, 'Widow Pierce' 'Deire' in Long Itchington and so on. But spotting such differences is a relatively easy exercise compared with determining which version was

1 13 & 14 Car. II, c. 10, s. 19.

2 Marshall, 'Levying', p. 641.

3 Styles, 'Hearth tax', pp. xcvi–ii; WCRO, QS11/6, 61–3; Meekings, Porter & Roy, *Worcester*, p. 12. Some of these figures do not accord with those in Styles, who also implied that these surveys were for 'new hearths and forges' whereas in fact they were of 'firehearths and stoves in new erected houses and also of smiths' hearths', which had to be assessed officially first before they could be taxed legally.

correct or whether an idiosyncratic version of one name had become a different one. Although this task can be eased by consulting the three later returns for 1671–4, it can never be conclusive because once a wrong name was established it might be copied out again, as even happened to someone as prominent as Michael Armstead, the minister of Caldecote and Weddington who became 'Nicholas' in the last three hearth tax lists.[1] Many such inaccuracies occurred when the final returns were compiled from rough or partial lists by men who were frequently in a hurry to meet tight deadlines and so were prone to making errors, as anyone who has ever tried to transcribe precisely a hearth tax list or similar document under duress may appreciate. Even so, it is still difficult to comprehend how some mistakes crept in. A few may have arisen when the scribe misheard a name that someone else read out to him, such as Veale for Beale in Bridge End, Warwick, or Elias Lenthall for Lewis Lenton in Chilvers Coton, while haste can only account for the conversion of Thomas Southam [*of*] Loxley in Sheep Street, Stratford, into Thomas Loxley. There are also some intriguing sequences, including two in Lapworth where Duncalfe became Duncastle and then Doncaster, and Weekes was transformed first into Wickes before reverting to Weekes and ending as Wilkes. In Charlecote, Cornehill was converted into Thornhill and then Cornewell, both closer to and further away from its original version. In order to measure and so establish the prevalence of such phenomena, a large sample of 3,275 named entries in 1670 from north, central and south Warwickshire was compared with the next three returns. This analysis is presented in Table 6 and suggests that the overall proportion of unsound names was about 7 per cent, with a margin of error of perhaps one per cent to allow for some uncertainty. However, this does not mean that about one name in 14 was wrong because it seems safe to assume that one version of each name was probably sound, even if we cannot tell which it was. Thus if one can assume that little more than half of those identified as suspect in any one list were wrong, then about 4 per cent of the householders in 1670 were named incorrectly, with the ratio of erroneous surnames to faulty forenames being about two to one.

Because there is no principle that can distinguish with certainty variants of one surname from those that are definitely different, Table 7 demonstrates the range of the problem and how some of the borderline cases behind Table 6 have been treated here. The doubling of single letters is always ignored, while surnames that differ by just one vowel, such as Bludden/Bladen or Mason/Musson are normally assumed to be the same unless they create a recognised alternative name such as Bull/Ball. On the other hand, those that start with different consonants (Wall/Hall or Masson/Nasson) are invariably treated as different names, but not if they began with a different vowel (Archard/Orchard). Longer names can obviously absorb more diversity, especially when it occurs towards the end, as with Frenchman/Frensham or Wagstaffe/Wagster, but not when it occurs in the first syllable where a name's

[1] Walker, *Hemlingford*, pp. 224–6.

Table 6 Percentages of named entries in 1670 with different names in 1671–4

Area	*1670 named entries*	*1671–4 different names* all	s'n	f'n	*Percentage with different names* all	s'n	f'n	*Half percent.* all
		n	n	n	%	%	%	%
Tanworth division	785	56	38	18	7.1	4.8	2.3	3.6
Atherstone division	1350	95	62	33	7.0	4.6	2.4	3.5
Stratford parish	523	36	25	11	6.9	4.8	2.1	3.5
Warwick borough	617	34	22	12	5.5	3.6	1.9	2.8
Total	**3275**	**221**	**147**	**74**	**6.7**	**4.4**	**2.3**	**3.4**

s'n = surnames; f'n = forenames; percent = percentage.

Table 7 Interpretations of some surname variations in the hearth tax returns of 1670–4

Clearly different	*Close but different*	*Variant of same name*
Bracebridge: Baresby *Nuneaton*	Ashbey: Ashley *Packwood*	Archard: Orchard *Ch.Coton*
Chadman: Cadmore *Fillongley*	Bainton: Bampton *N.Whitacre*	Bludden: Bladen *Atherstone*
Clarke: Church *Tanworth*	Barton: Baston *Tanworth*	Frenchman: Frensham *Stratford*
Far: Starr *Packwood*	Beale: Veale *Warwick*	Gibbins: Gibson *Stratford*
Farmer: Freeman *N.Whitacre*	Bredon: Burden *Newbold Pacey*	Hickcox: Hitchcock *Stratford*
Gibson: Gisborne *Lea Marston*	Bull: Ball *Atherstone*	Legg: Lego *Shustoke*
Griggs: Biggs *Mancetter*	Hyman: Hinman *Chilvers Coton*	Mason: Musson *Atherstone*
Long: Large *Nuneaton*	Masson: Mace *Stratford*	Miller: Milner *Maxstoke*
Lukeman: Hickman *Lapworth*	Masson: Nasson *Stratford*	Roadway: Radway *Lapworth*
More: Roe *Warwick*	Miller: Millard *Stratford*	Tarpe: Tapp *Nuneaton*
Pimly: Phinies *Atherstone*	Monsall: Mowsall *Atherstone*	Topp: Tapp *Nuneaton*
Twicrofft: Taseroft *Lapworth*	Parsley: Pashley *Warwick*	Wagstaffe: Wagster *Ch.Coton*
	Tolton: Tarleton *Fillongley*	
	Tomlins: Tomkins *B.Tachbrook*	
	Tyso: Tysall *Maxstoke*	
	Wall: Hall *Wellesbourne*	
	Walton: Watson *Stratford*	
	Whitell: Writtell *Over Whitacre*	

The first name is the version recorded in 1670 and the second the variant for the same householder in one or more of the returns for 1671–4, followed by their parish or town.

complexion may be altered by just one crucial letter, such as Barton/Baston or Hyman/Hinman. Paradoxically perhaps, Tarpe and Topp are both acceptable as variants of the name Tapp, but not as alternatives to each other, while those names that are established as regular variants to each other include Hickcox/Hitchcock and Miller/Milner, but not Miller/Millard.[1] And yet, this intractable problem can never be freed entirely from intuitive judgement and so uncertainty.

Since the range of available forenames was so much more limited, it may come as a surprise to discover that there was about one corrupt forename for every two corrupt surnames. This stems from the fact that most Christian names appeared in an abbreviated form, which is what the scribes had to decipher. Thus William was rarely written out in full but shortened to 'Wm' or 'Will', for example, and in the latter form might be mistaken for 'Widd' or widow. This was a very common error, but still very difficult to disentangle unless a sequence of 'Will/widd/Will' can be detected, as occurred in Atherstone, Wellesbourne and elsewhere. On the other hand, a very obvious corruption of 'Will' appears in the 1671 return for Chilvers Coton, where William Avery was succeeded by 'Widd Avery late Wid' after he was buried five days before Michaelmas 1671. The two other most common mistakes were confusing Edmund with Edward or rather 'Edmd' with 'Edwd' and Mary with Margaret, especially when shortened to 'Marg^{t}'. Other occasional confusions involved Kath(erine) with Nath(aniel) and Mich(ael) with Nich(olas) or Rich(ard). Interchanges between Job, Jos(eph), Josh(ua) and 'Jo' or 'Jno' for John are also not unusual nor are Joan(e) for Jane or Eli(nor) for Eliz(abeth). (Perhaps even more surprisingly, the exemption certificate for Avon Dassett, that Newsham attempted to correct, printed below on p. 419, records the same person as Elisha and then Elizabeth Smith.) Unwary scribes were sometimes caught out by abbreviations of the more rarely used forenames, with Silv(anus) being converted into Sylvester, for example, Ben(jamin) into Bernard, both Laurence and Lazarus into Leonard, Anth(ony) into Arth(ur), Reginald into Roger, Valentine into Walter and even Marm(aduke) into Marg(aret). Even more unusually, in Nether Whitacre, Geo(rge) was once turned into Tho(mas) and 'Willm' into 'Tho', which reflects the confusion between their forenames and surname of Tompson.

After such a litany, one may be surprised to learn that not many more than one forename in 100 was recorded incorrectly. But, when combined with the surname errors discussed above, an overall unreliability count of 4 per 100 or so must still warn those engaged in family history or nominal linkage to proceed carefully. Table 6 shows that in Warwick borough half of the proportion of those with different names was 2.8 per cent. This is significantly lower than the 3.5 per cent or so in the other three sampled areas, where the figures are remarkably similar, even though Hargrave wrote out all the four returns for Atherstone division himself and might have been

[1] *Dictionary of Surnames*, pp. 254, 368–9.

expected to have been more accurate. It therefore seems that under Newsham most returns were not copied from the previous one but from recent rough or working lists, while the greater consistency found in Warwick may have resulted from better-educated constables compiling the returns or perhaps just those with a better local knowledge.

(v) Chilvers Coton

More insight into these returns can be gleaned by exploring a unique collection of documents for the large parish of Chilvers Coton near Nuneaton from a decade later. At its core is a very detailed manorial survey, which Sir Richard Newdigate initiated in 1681 and pushed through to completion in December 1684.[1] At Michaelmas 1670, when he was aged 26, he paid for 32 hearths at Arbury Hall, which his father had settled on him at his wedding five years earlier together with an annual income from land in Chilvers Coton, Astley and Long Itchington of over £1,500.[2] Eight years later he inherited his father's baronetcy and more property in Middlesex, Warwickshire and elsewhere in the Midlands. Eventually, after his widowed mother died, his income rose to nearly £4,000 a year, making him 'one of the wealthiest non-noble landowners in Warwickshire and not far behind his relatives the barons Leigh of Stoneleigh'.[3] Newdigate was an impulsive man, who became more concerned with improving his Arbury estate than with the wider world and more adept at losing rather than making money, especially in coalmining enterprises. His manorial survey or 'great work' contains exceptional detail on the ownership of land and tenants' holdings in the parish, a census-type listing of nearly all its inhabitants, the entitlement of many to seats in the church, a large scale map with thumb-nail sketches of three quarters of its houses, and much more besides.[4] Together they illuminate much of what lay behind the hearth tax lists and are used several times for this purpose in this introduction.[5]

Although both the 'census' of 1684 and the hearth tax return of 1674 recorded a total of 176 households in Chilvers Coton, this was not the full picture. In the 1670 return there was a higher total of 188, including four that were recorded as empty. From the relevant sections of the survey that described all the dwellings in the parish in 1684, 202 in all can be identified, although 10 of these appear to have been too decayed to be habitable.[6] But of the other additional 16 houses, we cannot tell how many were either occupied or empty. Since six of them were described unequivocally in the survey as being empty, there were 10 more dwellings that were either empty or

1 Gooder, *Arbury*, pp. 26–8, 30–4, 48–55, 78–89; Larminie, *Wealth*, pp. 101, 139–40.
2 Larminie, *Wealth*, pp. 56–61.
3 Larminie, *Wealth*, pp. 62.
4 WCRO, CR136/V12, V13, V101, V109, V122, M14. For a most perceptive study of the unique range of, and background to, the Chilvers Coton survey see Hindle, 'Great survey', pp. 164–86.
5 Gooder, *Arbury*, p. 85; Spufford, *Poverty*, p. 13.
6 WCRO, CR136/V12 (pp. 64–73), M14, V101 (pp. 25–8).

occupied by households omitted from the 'census'; or more probably a combination of both.[1] Overall, this survey does suggest that some 10 or 12 habitable houses were unoccupied in 1684, compared with the four that were recorded specifically as such in 1670. Thus, Chilvers Coton had more empty and ruinous houses than were indicated by the hearth tax and a more fluid occupancy as well. The survey recorded one farmer as holding 'what was formerly four houses … but now reduced to one farm' while another had 'a middling farm twas two houses'.[2] Another house was specifically described as being in two parts for a father and his son and in several instances close relatives were shown living next to each other in divided houses. A note added to the survey eight years later reported that another house had been 'removed and made a reckning house of in coalpit field'. The listing of sites where other tenements once stood before 1684 may indicate similar removals or fates like the 'house where JB did live pulled down'.[3] Yet other entries remind us just how flimsy and vulnerable many of these timber-framed houses were, with more than one burnt down and not rebuilt, and several others 'very much out of repair and ready to fall down'.[4] A bitter-sweet outcome awaited one of these, owned by Sir Richard Newdigate. After he had spent £6 on its renovation, the cottage was described as 'now in the year '85 in good repair', so the landlord then raised its rent of 20 shillings a year by another six shillings, making it chargeable for the hearth tax.[5]

Further exploration of the manorial survey reveals that only 17 out of the 192 dwellings in Chilvers Coton (or one in 10) were occupied by their owners in 1684, while seven more were rented by the owner of another house in the parish. In addition to the five 'town' or parish houses, 47 different people owned houses in Chilvers Coton, of whom 28 had just one property and 16 between two and four. The remaining three were Mr Parker, who was a resident with six houses, Mr Wood, who was an absentee with 20, and Sir Richard Newdigate who owned 90 houses, including Arbury Hall. This breakdown does not match precisely the situation in 1670, when Sir Richard had somewhat fewer properties, but it does demonstrate why the collection of the hearth tax was such an administrative nightmare. If Parliament had decided to tax the house owners in 1662, and not the occupiers, the hearth tax would have been no more complicated to administer than the local levies for the poor. Then the constables in Chilvers Coton would have dealt with about 50 tax payers, or a quarter of those whom they had to list, and no one would have had to wrestle with annual exemption certificates or identify the properties that were worth 20 shillings a year or less. In 1691 47 landowners in Chilvers Coton paid a total of £27 14s. 5d. for the poor rate at 6½d. in the pound, including 34 who contributed less than 2 shillings

1 WCRO, CR136/V101, pp. 27–8.
2 WCRO, CR136/V101, pp. 27, 101.
3 WCRO, CR136/V122, p. 44.
4 WCRO, CR136/V122, p. 34.
5 WCRO, CR136/V101, pp. 25–8.

each, while Sir Richard paid £16 7s. 2d. or 60 per cent of the total.[1] By contrast, the hearth tax was much more complex to administer and raised less money. Only 190 of the 283 hearths listed in Chilvers Coton parish were liable for the hearth tax in 1670, which made £19 the maximum yield for one year and enabled the main landowners to escape very lightly, with Newdigate paying just £1 12s. 0d. or less than 10 per cent of the total.

Conclusion

Hunting for errors, omissions and inconsistencies within these hearth tax lists is a lengthy and tedious business, made possible only by the survival of so many returns and exemption certificates for Warwickshire. Those that have been uncovered here are only the minima as any errors that were repeated in all these lists cannot have been detected.[2] Even when dressed in the seductive guise of an immaculate fair copy, sufficient flaws have been exposed in these hearth tax returns to undermine expectations of precision when they are analysed and to warn of the need to treat them with scholarly caution. And yet, the better acquainted one becomes with the relative failings of the Newsham lists, the more robust they seem to have been overall. Collectively they provide a unique basis for the study of crucial aspects of Warwickshire's society, which will be demonstrated in the rest of this introduction, starting with its towns and rural sub-regions.

1 WCRO, CR136/C1203.

2 Although Middleton Hall, for example, was assessed consistently with 26 hearths between 1664 and 1674, it was recorded with 29 in 1663 and 29 or 30 in the late 1670s (see Walker, *Hemlingford*, p. 60).

Parish analyses: Tables 8 and 9

Table 8 Total hearth tax entries for all parishes, 1663–74

(a) Warwickshire 1663–74

	Total entries by year							
Parish etc	*1663*	*1664*	*1665*	*1666*	*1670(inc)*	*1671*	*1673*	*1674*
Barlichway Hundred								
Alcester Division								
Alcester	127	140	**312**	166	**270**	–	**275**	267
Arrow	23	63	62	40	**60**	–	61	63
Coughton	66	106	109	73	**94**	–	97	92
Great Alne	31	49	51	40	**53**	–	52	41
Ipsley	36	55	53	34	**55**	–	54	30
Kinwarton	8	17	16	12	**14**	15	13	12
Morton Bagot	23	38	36	22	**40**	–	36	38
Spernall	13	15	15	14	**16**	16	15	15
Studley	57	112	119	64	**121**	–	116	118
Tardebigg (pt)	46	55	52	42	**56**(5)	–	51	39
Weethley chap	12	16	15	9	**15**	15	15	11
Bidford Division								
Aston Cantlow	65	95	94	55	**105**	–	105	108
Bidford on Avon	77	*75	**203**	127	**190**(20)	–	172	153
Binton	18	22	25	19	**25**	–	24	19
Exhall	10	16	16	15	**15**	–	15	15
Haselor	44	56	55	–	**58**	–	56	36
Salford Priors	77	132	130	101	**133**	–	135	86
Temple Grafton	34	*36	41	30	**45**	–	42	40
Billesley (det)	1	1	1	1	**1**	–	1	1
Welford (pt)	–	–	7	4	**5**	–	5	5
Weston on Avon (pt)	3	6	5	5	**5**	–	5	5
Wixford	16	9	22	24	**23**	–	23	23
Henley Division								
Beaudesert	16	20	25	14	**26**	–	26	24
Claverdon	65	**97**	90	*84	**87**	–	*87	*85
Henley in Arden chap	76	93	145	74	**137**	–	111	131
Preston Bagot	12	17	20	–	**15**	–	17	**21**
Rowington	76	121	128	96	**131**	–	135	135
Ullenhall chap	32	51	50	*32	**60**	–	*60	*55
Wootton Wawen	52	61	64	*53	**69**	–	*63	*63

Parish etc	*1663*	*1664*	*1665*	*1666*	*1670(inc)*	*1671*	*1673*	*1674*
				Total entries by year				
Stratford Division								
Alveston	35	34	76	58	**72**	–	**79**	70
Bearley	11	20	20	11	**17**	–	19	20
Budbrooke	44	63	65	48	**61**	–	52	53
Hampton Lucy	40	40	51	42	**54**	–	55	54
Haseley	26	36	39	25	**40**	–	42	39
Hatton	65	111	110	53	**107**	–	110	107
Honiley	12	21	21	15	**18**	19	**26**	26
Loxley	15	20	22	15	**25**	–	25	25
Norton Lindsey	15	27	22	28	**27**	27	28	27
Sherbourne	19	41	43	–	**44**	–	46	45
Snitterfield	40	58	62	48	**65**	–	67	62
Fulbrook e.p.	–	–	4	–	**4**	–	4	4
Stratford upon Avon (pt)	63	118	83	105	**135**	–	127	125
Stratford borough	199	390	385	233	**427**	–	411	395
Bushwood (det)	6	8	5	5	**18**	–	18	17
Wolverton	15	17	13	14	**16**	–	17	17
Wroxall	26	33	31	28	**31**	–	33	31
Hemlingford Hundred								
Atherstone Division								
Ansley	57	89	77	65	**89**	87	88	86
Baxterley	–	24	24	–	**32**	30	30	21
Caldecote	11	14	13	15	**14**	14	13	13
Chilvers Coton	101	188	150	116	**188**	183	177	176
Corley	–	43	34	33	**46**(8)	37	37	47
Fillongley	–	131	136	121	**136**	133	132	134
Lea Marston	–	51	40	39	**47**	47	47	45
Mancetter (pt)	33	75	69	56	**84**(4)	79	79	76
Atherstone	58	**272**	266	177	**257**(37)	211	219	218
Maxstoke	–	56	47	42	**55**	54	52	54
Merevale (most)	–	31	9	10	**28**(16)	28	12	27
Nether Whitacre	–	80	68	75	**97**(6)	87	88	89
Nuneaton (pt)	81	132	*106	77	**137**	122	126	120
Nuneaton town	139	**314**	*304	206	**302**(24)	265	272	267
Over Whitacre	–	39	31	43	**39**	38	38	42
Shustoke	–	56	41	44	**54**	49	50	47
Bentley (det)	–	27	21	–	**31**	32	32	31
Weddington	4	5	4	5	**5**	5	5	5
Birmingham Division								
Aston	–	**533**	397	*416	**521**(23)	–	506	**527**

Table 8 *contd*

Parish etc	*1663*	*1664*	*1665*	*1666*	*1670(inc)*	*1671*	*1673*	*1674*
				Total entries by year				
Birmingham	–	405	*674	*492	**780**(88)	–	687	**786**
Coleshill	–	199	*200	148	**197**(8)	–	167	187
Curdworth	–	32	33	35	**40**	–	41	43
Minworth (det)	–	32	38	45	**41**	–	44	44
Edgbaston	–	56	40	38	**60**(7)	–	58	57
Sheldon	–	**69**	55	56	**63**(12)	–	51	61
Sutton Coldfield	–	293	298	262	**304**(24)	–	309	**313**
Wishaw	–	28	33	42	**42**	–	39	39
Solihull Division								
Baddesley Clinton	9	20	19	17	**19**	18	18	*20
Barston	37	47	45	51	**52**	49	52	50
Berkswell	141	210	144	197	**216**(28)	181	186	187
Bickenhill[1]	68	**99**	89	36	**89**(22)	69	68	68
Elmdon	17	20	17	–	**20**	19	20	18
Great Packington	44	52	44	50	**49**	48	48	48
Hampton in Arden	38	53	55	61	**58**	55	55	54
Balsall (det)	129	135	133	172	**168**	166	166	164
Kinwalsey (det)	5	5	5	–	**5**	5	5	5
Nuthurst (det)	11	17	17	16	**16**	16	16	16
Knowle chap	62	*128	*126	112	**126**(17)	107	*112	103
Little Packington	20	27	26	15	**28**	28	20	*28
Meriden	66	89	95	88	**95**(8)	86	85	81
Solihull	174	*324	*283	309	**319**(10)	304	*204	301
Tamworth Division								
Austrey	63	76	76	69	**87**	78	77	79
Baddesley Ensor	24	32	25	36	**34**	33	35	38
Grendon	55	67	60	67	***66**(6)	*60	*59	56
Kingsbury (all)	88	143	152	154	***175**	*166	*168	163
Middleton	59	78	67	59	**85**	79	78	79
Newton Regis	28	37	35	36	**37**	35	36	37
Polesworth	108	101	199	**213**	**195**	174	175	187
Seckington	*10	*16	10	9	**15**	16	15	15
Shuttington	*18	*23	16	**25**	**19**	21	21	23
Tamworth (pt)	125	135	138	188	**183**	152	171	188
Tamworth borough (pt)	108	116	163	184	**194**	155	171	167

[1] Lyndon End was detached from the rest of Bickenhill, but only the 1670 return identified it separately.

Parish etc	*1663*	*1664*	*1665*	*1666*	*1670(inc)*	*1671*	*1673*	*1674*
				Total entries by year				
Kineton Hundred								
Brailes Division								
Barcheston	16	**31**	29	16	**25**	25	25	25
Barton on the Heath	20	37	33	19	**30**	**36**	36	33
Brailes	91	166	183	121	**188**	186	185	**199**
Burmington	19	25	25	17	**28**	27	28	28
Cherington	25	37	40	29	**41**	39	39	39
Great Wolford	46	83	86	67	**84**	86	86	83
Honington	41	47	39	28	**52**	53	52	53
Idlicote	16	21	21	13	**22**	24	24	23
Long Compton	74	100	105	70	**103**	***113**	109	110
Pillerton Hersey	18	29	31	23	**29**	31	31	30
Pillerton Priors	16	27	27	19	**28**	28	28	28
Stretton on Fosse	25	47	46	32	**46**	47	47	49
Whatcote	21	30	31	19	**28**	29	29	29
Whichford	82	105	94	82	**101**	101	102	99
Kineton Division								
Atherstone on Stour	13	16	*11	13	**18**	19	18	18
Butlers Marston	18	26	17	17	**35**	35	36	37
Chadshunt	14	22	25	19	**24**	24	24	23
Combrook chap	21	29	31	22	**31**	31	30	31
Compton Wynyates	–	–	3	3	**4**	5	5	5
Ettington	49	60	64	49	**67**	64	67	66
Gaydon	20	27	24	22	**37**	38	38	38
Halford	26	39	39	26	**37**	38	36	36
Ilmington	37	57	81	63	**95**	95	95	97
Kineton	66	108	117	72	**124**	111	122	119
Lighthorne	18	30	30	23	**30**	30	30	31
Compton Verney e.p.	–	1	1	1	3	3	3	3
Oxhill	36	41	37	27	**41**	42	43	43
Radway (all)	*29	*50	*52	38	**53**	54	52	45
Tysoe	82	132	139	95	**150**	148	151	152
Whitchurch	17	26	*26	20	**29**	29	29	28
Priors Marston Division								
Avon Dassett	21	34	32	23	**34**	36	35	34
Burton Dassett	*33	*72	*71	38	**76**	74	76	71
Cropredy (pt)	18	29	28	15	**19**	19	**25**	25
Farnborough	20	36	*35	22	**43**	43	43	43
Fenny Compton	42	86	87	49	**91**	92	92	87
Hodnell & Watergall e.p.	3	–	3	3	**3**	3	3	3

Table 8 *contd*

	Total entries by year							
Parish etc	*1663*	*1664*	*1665*	*1666*	*1670(inc)*	*1671*	*1673*	*1674*
Lower Shuckburgh chap	29	30	35	31	**34**	34	34	35
Priors Hardwick	30	37	34	36	**36**	37	37	**44**
Priors Marston chap	69	71	79	72	**102**	104	103	105
Ratley	15	34	36	22	**36**	36	37	37
Shotteswell	37	50	51	45	**55**	55	55	56
Warmington	42	64	62	49	**63**	62	62	62
Wormleighton	14	15	15	15	**16**	16	16	16
Tanworth Division								
Avon								
Barford	21	52	20	68	**75**	71	73	44
Bishops Tachbrook (all)	42	62	53	43	**64**	57	63	64
Charlecote	12	18	20	–	**19**	19	18	18
Chesterton	21	22	23	14	**22**	22	22	22
Moreton Morrell	19	30	29	22	**30**	29	30	30
Newbold Pacey	18	*27	*30	15	**36**	38	37	29
Wasperton	16	19	18	20	**20**	21	21	22
Wellesbourne	52	*76	*78	58	**80**	80	83	82
Arden								
Lapworth	63	82	77	59	**89**	91	91	*93
Packwood	31	55	64	34	**63**	64	61	60
Tanworth in Arden	180	241	292	217	**293**	287	292	291
Warwick Borough	458	542	434	634	**617**	627	618	**638**
Knightlow Hundred								
Kenilworth Division								
Ashow	17	23	18	22	**23**	22	21	23
Baginton	25	34	20	31	**35**	–	35	34
Bubbenhall	22	34	34	39	**35**	–	34	36
Cubbington	39	54	65	60	**67**	–	65	65
Harbury	75	105	98	114	**118**	–	114	119
Kenilworth	132	241	150	220	**244**	–	241	223
Leamington Priors	29	46	54	54	**56**	–	53	58
Leek Wootton	42	51	50	54	**58**	–	56	54
Lillington	23	35	44	41	**40**	–	40	38
Milverton	23	27	28	26	**28**	–	26	24
Offchurch	34	42	40	39	**40**	–	34	29
Radford Semele	35	50	54	54	**54**	–	52	53
Stoneleigh	94	133	149	124	**145**	–	147	137
Ufton	24	33	36	33	**32**	–	33	32
Whitnash	24	24	23	29	**28**	–	28	28

Parish etc	1663	1664	1665	1666	1670(inc)	1671	1673	1674
			Total entries by year					
Monks Kirby Division								
Allesley	87	83	89	105	**110**	–	**118**	112
Arley	29	–	35	34	**33**	–	32	32
Astley	40	51	52	46	**49**	–	49	45
Bedworth	54	255	**291**	271	**281**	–	274	251
Binley	23	30	23	29	**28**	–	29	30
Combe Fields e.p.	13	–	–	13	**14**	–	14	14
Brinklow	62	95	92	100	**99**	–	94	96
Bulkington	127	*148	146	145	**145**	–	*135	***150**
Burton Hastings	18	21	22	22	**22**	–	21	22
Stretton Baskerville e.p.	–	–	–	–	**6**	–	6	5
Cov H.T: Coundon (det)	15	25	24	24	**24**	–	*22	25
Willenhall (det)	15	16	16	17	**15**	16	15	13
Harborough Magna	31	43	43	44	**44**	–	*25	43
Monks Kirby	187	243	232	263	**263**	–	255	239
Shilton	18	*30	32	31	**32**	–	*26	*32
Walsgrave on Sowe (pt)	30	33	**43**	37	**38**	–	37	37
Wibtoft chap	15	20	19	18	**18**	–	18	18
Willey	12	29	26	29	**28**	–	28	24
Withybrook	40	**55**	53	49	**49**	–	48	48
Wolvey	53	86	56	64	**84**	–	83	**89**
Rugby Division								
Bilton	30	62	32	66	**65**	–	62	54
Bourton on Dunsmore	38	39	52	52	**53**	–	52	50
Brownsover chap	14	14	14	14	**14**	13	13	13
Church Lawford	24	34	34	37	**35**	–	35	33
Churchover	32	48	49	49	**52**	–	52	50
Clifton upon Dunsmore	50	79	80	83	**81**	–	82	82
Dunchurch	69	130	131	137	**133**	–	132	95
Frankton	15	28	36	37	**34**	–	34	31
Hillmorton	68	97	103	80	**107**	–	103	100
Kings Newnham	9	9	12	12	**11**	11	11	8
Newbold on Avon	66	109	114	111	**111**	–	109	89
Rugby	107	160	162	169	**177**	–	**182**	171
Ryton on Dunsmore	29	49	49	47	**47**	–	49	47
Stretton on Dunsmore chap	47	65	*67	71	**68**	–	66	68
Willoughby	33	53	49	49	**52**	–	51	53
Wolston (all)	70	103	99	103	**103**	–	103	103
Southam Division								
Birdingbury	19	31	*28	25	**27**	–	31	29
Bishops Itchington	47	54	59	53	**56**	–	60	57

Table 8 *contd*

Parish etc	*1663*	*1664*	*1665*	*1666*	*1670(inc)*	*1671*	*1673*	*1674*
				Total entries by year				
Grandborough	50	64	52	64	**67**	–	67	62
Hunningham	23	24	21	28	**29**	28	27	26
Ladbroke	31	45	47	**63**	**54**	–	55	50
Leamington Hastings	55	85	87	37	**94**	–	83	79
Long Itchington	75	79	73	99	**105**	–	**116**	92
Marton	21	31	*29	21	**50**	–	49	38
Napton on the Hill	107	128	141	144	**155**(8)	–	150	143
Radbournes e.p.	2	–	2	3	**3**	3	3	2
Chapel Ascote e.p. (det)	1	–	1	1	**1**	1	1	1
Southam	73	105	108	138	**140**(5)	–	138	125
Stockton	25	36	30	41	**42**	–	46	43
Upper Shuckburgh	9	18	18	18	**19**	–	18	17
Wappenbury	24	39	41	44	**42**	–	41	38
Weston under Wetherley	13	18	26	23	**23**	–	23	25
Wolfhampcote	64	85	86	88	**85**	–	**92**	84

(b) County of Coventry 1665–6

	total entries	
	1665	*1666*
Coventry city	1226	**1428**
Outlying parts		
Ansty	27	**28**
Exhall	64	**77**
Foleshill	102	**140**
H.T: Radford	14	**15**
St M: Keresley (det)	14	**22**
St M: Pinley & Whitley	6	**6**
Stivichall	36	**37**
Stoke	59	**61**
Walsgrave on Sowe (pt)	19	**65**
Wyken	21	**24**

chap = chapelry   Cov = Coventry
det = detached   H.T. = Holy Trinity
e.p. = extra parochial   St M = St Michael
pt = part
* = uncertainty over boundaries or damaged manuscript
(inc) = contemporary exemption certificate with five or more additional non-chargeable included in the total for 1670

Table 9 Percentages of households in hearth tax groups for all parishes

(a) Warwickshire 1670

Parish etc	*Division & hundred*	*Total h'holds n*	*Percentage of households in hearth tax groups* 1 %	2 %	3–4 %	5–9 %	10+ %	3+ %	NC %
Alcester	Alc:B	270	64	20	13	3	0	16	46
Allesley	MK:Kn	110	54	19	16	10	1	27	15
Alveston	Str:B	72	67	18	13	3	0	15	42
Ansley	Ath:H	89	60	28	9	2	1	12	37
Arley	MK:Kn	33	39	39	18	0	3	21	12
Arrow +	Alc:B	60	70	15	7	7	2	15	45
Ashow	Ken:Kn	23	65	22	13	0	0	13	22
Astley *	MK:Kn	49	53	29	14	2	2	18	14
Aston +	Bir:H	521	70	13	12	2	2	16	46
Aston Cantlow	Bid:B	105	70	18	10	1	1	12	34
Atherstone on Stour	Kin:Ki	18	50	17	28	6	0	33	28
Austrey	Tam:H	87	79	11	8	1	0	9	17
Avon Dassett	PM:Ki	34	56	18	15	12	0	26	24
Baddesley Clinton	Sol:H	19	74	16	5	0	5	11	42
Baddesley Ensor	Tam:H	34	56	18	18	9	0	26	47
Baginton	Ken:Kn	35	57	20	14	6	3	23	26
Barcheston +	Bra:Ki	25	60	8	16	16	0	32	36
Barford	Tan:Ki	75	79	9	7	5	0	12	39
Barston	Sol:H	52	58	31	6	6	0	12	21
Barton on the Heath *	Bra:Ki	30	43	23	17	10	7	33	43
Baxterley	Ath:H	32	75	16	6	3	0	9	28
Bearley	Str:B	17	71	12	18	0	0	18	35
Beaudesert	Hen:B	26	77	15	8	0	0	8	54
Bedworth	MK:Kn	281	93	6	1	>0	0	1	79
Berkswell *	Sol:H	216	67	16	12	5	1	18	37
Bickenhill	Sol:H	69	71	14	9	6	0	14	36
Lyndon End (det)	Sol:H	20	75	20	0	5	0	5	35
Bidford on Avon *	Bid:B	190	85	9	4	1	1	6	67
Bilton	Rug:Kn	65	85	9	3	2	2	6	55
Binley +	MK:Kn	42	60	19	14	5	2	21	26
Binton	Bid:B	25	68	8	16	8	0	24	24
Birdingbury	Sou:Kn	27	63	22	7	4	4	15	22
Birmingham	Bir:H	780	53	24	16	6	1	23	47
Bishops Itchington	Sou:Kn	56	68	18	7	5	2	14	34
Bishops Tachbrook +	Tan:Ki+Ken:Kn	64	73	9	14	2	2	17	28
Bourton on Dunsmore	Rug:Kn	53	62	26	4	8	0	11	40
Brailes +	Bra:Ki	188	69	16	12	2	1	15	37

Table 9 *contd*

Parish etc	*Division & hundred*	*Total h'holds* n	*Percentage of households in hearth tax groups* 1 %	2 %	3–4 %	5–9 %	10+ %	3+ %	NC %
Brinklow	MK:Kn	99	76	12	9	3	0	12	34
Brownsover chap	Rug:Kn	14	36	43	21	0	0	21	0
Bubbenhall	Ken:Kn	35	54	26	14	6	0	20	34
Budbrooke	Str:B	61	74	15	8	2	2	11	36
Bulkington	MK:Kn	145	63	26	9	1	1	12	19
Burmington	Bra:Ki	28	75	14	7	4	0	11	39
Burton Dassett +	PM:Ki	76	58	17	16	8	1	25	32
Burton Hastings +	MK:Kn	28	50	29	14	7	0	21	18
Butlers Marston	Kin:Ki	35	60	14	17	6	3	26	14
Caldecote	Ath:H	14	50	21	21	0	7	29	14
Chadshunt	Kin:Ki	24	79	17	0	0	4	4	13
Charlecote	Tan:Ki	19	53	26	16	0	5	21	37
Cherington	Bra:Ki	41	61	22	15	2	0	17	32
Chesterton	Tan:Ki	22	64	14	9	9	5	23	27
Chilvers Coton *	Ath:H	188	82	10	6	2	1	9	49
Church Lawford	Rug:Kn	35	86	3	6	6	0	11	34
Churchover	Rug:Kn	52	75	10	10	4	2	15	29
Claverdon +	Hen:B	87	67	18	11	3	0	15	30
Clifton upon Dunsmore +	Rug:Kn	81	65	16	15	4	0	19	33
Coleshill	Bir:H	197	67	18	8	6	1	15	29
Combrook chap	Kin:Ki	31	74	13	10	3	0	13	23
Compton Wynyates	Kin:Ki	4	75	0	0	0	25	25	25
Corley	Ath:H	46	72	17	9	2	0	11	24
Coughton +	Alc:B	94	65	14	15	4	2	21	28
Cov.HT: Coundon (det)	MK:Kn	24	71	17	8	4	0	13	17
Cov.HT: Willenhall (det)	MK:Kn	15	40	33	13	13	0	27	20
Cropredy (part)	PM:Ki+Oxf	19	47	21	21	5	5	32	26
Cubbington	Ken:Kn	67	75	6	13	6	0	19	45
Curdworth	Bir:H	40	73	13	10	3	3	15	28
Minworth (det)	Bir:H	41	71	17	12	0	0	12	34
Dunchurch +	Rug:Kn	133	66	17	11	5	2	17	49
Edgbaston	Bir:H	60	75	8	10	5	2	17	28
Elmdon	Sol:H	20	60	25	10	0	5	15	15
Ettington	Kin:Ki	67	73	9	13	3	1	18	24
Exhall	Bid:B	15	60	27	0	13	0	13	33
Farnborough	PM:Ki	43	63	19	14	2	2	19	42

Parish etc	*Division & hundred*	*Total h'holds n*	*Percentage of households in hearth tax groups* *1* %	*2* %	*3–4* %	*5–9* %	*10+* %	*3+* %	*NC* %
Fenny Compton +	PM:Ki+Sou:Kn	94	79	12	4	5	0	10	35
Fillongley *	Ath:H	136	53	24	13	10	0	24	29
Frankton	Rug:Kn	34	53	32	9	6	0	15	35
Gaydon	Kin:Ki	37	57	16	24	3	0	27	11
Grandborough +	Sou:Kn	67	54	31	10	4	0	15	27
Great Alne	Alc:B	53	74	9	11	6	0	17	30
Great Packington	Sol:H	49	82	12	4	0	2	6	24
Great Wolford +	Bra:Ki	84	71	14	10	4	1	14	36
Grendon +	Tam:H	66	65	24	6	3	2	11	23
Halford *	Kin:Ki	37	65	8	22	5	0	27	32
Hampton in Arden	Sol:H	58	72	12	10	5	0	16	36
Balsall (det)	Sol:H	168	73	14	10	4	0	13	33
Kinwalsey (det)	Sol:H	5	60	0	40	0	0	40	0
Nuthurst (det)	Sol:H	16	69	13	13	6	0	19	31
Hampton Lucy	Str:B	54	65	17	13	6	0	19	30
Harborough Magna	MK:Kn	44	68	18	11	0	2	14	43
Harbury *	Ken:Kn	118	80	12	7	2	0	8	24
Haseley	Str:B	40	78	15	5	0	3	8	48
Haselor	Bid:B	58	69	28	3	0	0	3	36
Hatton +	Str:B	107	71	19	9	1	0	10	41
Henley in Arden chap	Hen:B	137	72	18	6	4	0	9	56
Hillmorton	Rug:Kn	107	70	21	5	4	0	8	36
Honiley	Str:B	18	67	11	17	0	6	22	28
Honington	Bra:Ki	52	62	25	8	4	2	13	40
Hunningham	Sou:Kn	29	66	21	10	0	3	14	41
Idlicote	Bra:Ki	22	55	18	18	5	5	27	36
Ilmington	Kin:Ki+Glou	95	64	18	14	2	2	18	35
Ipsley *	Alc:B+Worc	55	65	16	13	2	4	18	42
Kenilworth *	Ken:Kn	244	70	12	11	6	0	17	41
Kineton	Kin:Ki	124	73	15	11	1	1	13	23
Kings Newnham	Rug:Kn	11	45	36	9	0	9	18	27
Kingsbury +	Tam:H+Ath:H	175	65	17	12	5	1	18	36
Kinwarton	Alc:B	14	64	7	14	14	0	29	43
Knowle chap	Sol:H	126	69	9	10	12	0	22	48
Ladbroke	Sou:Kn	54	67	15	13	6	0	19	37
Lapworth	Tan:Ki	89	62	19	16	3	0	19	36

Table 9 *contd*

Parish etc	Division & hundred	Total h'holds n	Percentage of households in hearth tax groups 1 %	2 %	3–4 %	5–9 %	10+ %	3+ %	NC %
Lea Marston	Ath:H	47	74	15	6	2	2	11	34
Leamington Hastings	Sou:Kn	94	67	23	7	1	1	10	48
Leamington Priors	Ken:Kn	56	77	9	11	4	0	14	45
Leek Wooton	Ken:Kn	58	79	12	3	3	2	9	24
Lighthorne +	Kin:Ki	33	52	30	9	6	3	18	18
Lillington *	Ken:Kn	40	73	28	0	0	0	0	45
Little Packington	Sol:H	28	79	11	11	0	0	11	29
Long Compton	Bra:Ki	103	62	14	20	3	1	24	32
Long Itchington	Sou:Kn	105	74	16	7	2	1	10	47
Lower Shuckburgh chap	PM:Ki	34	68	24	6	3	0	9	32
Loxley	Str:B	25	64	24	4	4	4	12	40
Mancetter +	Ath:H	341	62	13	15	8	1	24	45
Marton	Sou:Kn	50	72	14	8	6	0	14	54
Maxstoke	Ath:H	55	56	31	5	4	4	13	20
Merevale (most)	Ath:H+Leic	28	75	11	11	4	0	14	64
Meriden	Sol:H	95	64	13	13	7	3	23	40
Middleton	Tam:H	85	69	22	6	1	1	8	28
Milverton	Ken:Kn	28	71	11	11	4	4	18	21
Monks Kirby +	MK:Kn	263	61	23	13	2	1	16	33
Moreton Morrell	Tan:Ki	30	53	30	13	0	3	17	30
Morton Bagot	Alc:B	40	65	13	15	8	0	23	53
Napton on the Hill +	Sou:Kn	158	79	16	4	1	0	5	30
Chapel Ascote (det)	Sou:Kn	1	0	100	0	0	0	0	0
Nether Whitacre	Ath:H	97	70	16	10	2	1	13	23
Newbold on Avon +	Rug:Kn	111	68	16	14	2	1	16	41
Newbold Pacey	Tan:Ki	36	75	11	3	11	0	14	44
Newton Regis	Tam:H	37	62	22	16	0	0	16	14
Norton Lindsey	Str:B	27	85	7	4	4	0	7	37
Nuneaton +	Ath:H	439	69	14	13	4	1	17	49
Offchurch	Ken:Kn	40	85	10	3	0	3	5	53
Over Whitacre	Ath:H	39	62	15	18	5	0	23	26
Oxhill	Kin:Ki	41	59	22	10	10	0	20	20
Packwood	Tan:Ki	63	75	14	8	2	2	11	43
Pillerton Hersey	Bra:Ki	29	69	7	21	3	0	24	24
Pillerton Priors	Bra:Ki	28	71	14	11	4	0	14	21
Polesworth	Tam:H	195	73	13	9	3	2	13	49

Parish etc	Division & hundred	Total h'holds n	Percentage of households in hearth tax groups 1 %	2 %	3–4 %	5–9 %	10+ %	3+ %	NC %
Preston Bagot	Hen:B	15	60	13	27	0	0	27	40
Priors Hardwick *	PM:Ki	36	44	25	28	3	0	31	19
Priors Marston chap	PM:Ki	102	69	14	14	4	0	18	33
Radford Semele	Ken:Kn	54	69	20	7	2	2	11	22
Radway	Kin:Ki+PM:Ki	53	60	23	15	2	0	17	19
Ratley +	PM:Ki	36	50	19	17	8	6	31	31
Rowington	Hen:B	131	52	19	21	8	0	29	40
Rugby	Rug:Kn	177	68	9	17	5	1	23	41
Ryton on Dunsmore	Rug:Kn	47	72	17	6	4	0	11	32
Salford Priors	Bid:B	133	71	21	5	2	1	8	48
Seckington	Tam:H	15	67	13	13	0	7	20	53
Sheldon	Bir:H	63	62	14	13	10	2	24	32
Sherbourne	Str:B	44	77	14	5	5	0	9	41
Shilton	MK:Kn	32	56	31	9	3	0	13	47
Shotteswell	PM:Ki	55	71	15	13	2	0	15	31
Shustoke *	Ath:H	54	56	17	15	13	0	28	33
Bentley (det)	Ath:H	31	84	13	3	0	0	3	42
Shuttington	Tam:H	19	53	37	11	0	0	11	21
Snitterfield +	Str:B	69	61	17	19	1	1	22	36
Solihull *	Sol:H	319	71	13	10	5	1	16	45
Southam	Sou:Kn	140	61	21	11	7	0	19	41
Spernall	Alc:B	16	44	13	31	13	0	44	13
Stockton	Sou:Kn	42	71	21	5	2	0	7	52
Stoneleigh	Ken:Kn	145	66	15	11	6	1	19	28
Stratford upon Avon +	Str:B+Bid:B	562	60	15	17	7	1	26	47
Bushwood (det)	Str:B	18	78	11	11	0	0	11	72
Stretton on Dunsmore cp +	Rug:Kn	68	76	15	3	6	0	9	43
Stretton on Fosse	Bra:Ki	46	63	15	15	4	2	22	33
Studley	Alc:B	121	77	8	10	4	1	15	47
Sutton Coldfield	Bir:H	304	62	18	13	6	2	20	38
Tamworth (part) +	Tam:H+Staf	377	64	19	13	3	1	17	43
Tanworth in Arden	Tan:Ki	293	74	14	9	2	>0	12	40
Tardebigg (part)	Alc:B+Worc	56	57	23	14	4	2	20	25
Temple Grafton	Bid:B	45	76	2	11	11	0	22	42
Billesley (det)	Bid:B	1	0	0	0	0	100	100	0
Tysoe	Kin:Ki	150	67	10	20	3	0	23	19
Ufton	Ken:Kn	32	59	31	9	0	0	9	31

Table 9 *contd*

Parish etc	*Division & hundred*	*Total h'holds n*	*Percentage of households in hearth tax groups* 1 %	2 %	3–4 %	5–9 %	10+ %	3+ %	NC %
Ullenhall chap	Hen:B	60	65	20	10	5	0	15	45
Upper Shuckburgh	Sou:Kn	19	95	0	0	0	5	5	42
Walsgrave on Sowe (part)	MK:Kn+Cov	38	53	32	8	8	0	16	32
Wappenbury +	Sou:Kn	42	67	21	2	10	0	12	45
Warmington	PM:Ki	63	68	8	14	10	0	24	21
Warwick: St Mary	War:Ki	471	48	16	19	12	4	36	41
Warwick: St Nicholas	War:Ki	146	52	16	23	8	1	32	34
Wasperton	Tan:Ki	20	65	20	10	5	0	15	30
Weddington	Ath:H	5	20	20	0	40	20	60	0
Weethley chap	Alc:B	15	73	20	0	7	0	7	53
Welford (part)	Bid:B+Glou	5	60	20	0	20	0	20	20
Wellesbourne +	Tan:Ki	80	63	15	14	8	1	23	40
Weston on Avon (part)	Bid:B+Glou	5	80	0	0	20	0	20	0
Weston under Wetherley	Sou:Kn	23	48	30	17	0	4	22	30
Whatcote	Bra:Ki	28	71	21	7	0	0	7	14
Whichford +	Bra:Ki	101	50	23	23	4	0	27	29
Whitchurch	Kin:Ki	29	69	14	10	7	0	17	31
Whitnash	Ken:Kn	28	61	21	7	11	0	18	18
Wibtoft chap	MK:Kn	18	50	17	28	6	0	33	28
Willey	MK:Kn	28	68	18	11	4	0	14	39
Willoughby	Rug:Kn	52	67	17	12	2	2	15	35
Wishaw	Bir:H	42	71	19	5	2	2	10	24
Withybrook	MK:Kn	49	55	33	6	6	0	12	27
Wixford	Bid:B	23	70	17	4	4	4	13	48
Wolfhampcote +	Sou:Kn	85	61	24	13	2	0	15	20
Wolston +	Rug:Kn+MK:Kn	103	66	19	9	4	2	15	25
Wolverton	Str:B	16	69	6	19	6	0	25	6
Wolvey	MK:Kn	84	75	15	6	2	1	10	37
Wootton Wawen	Hen:B	69	75	12	10	0	3	13	32
Wormleighton	PM:Ki	16	69	13	13	0	6	19	31
Wroxall *	Str:B	31	45	42	6	3	3	13	26
Warwickshire		**17243**	**66**	**17**	**12**	**4**	**1**	**17**	**38**

(b) County of Coventry 1666

Parish etc	*County*	*Total h'holds n*	*1 %*	*2 %*	*3–4 %*	*5–9 %*	*10+ %*	*3+ %*	*Cert %*
Ansty	Cov	28	50	25	18	7	0	7	29
Coventry city +	Cov	#1428	44	24	20	10	2	32	41
Exhall	Cov	# 77	70	16	9	4	1	14	37
Foleshill	Cov	140	79	16	4	2	0	6	52
HT: Radford	Cov	# 15	57	29	14	0	0	14	7
St M: Keresley (det)	Cov	22	59	5	18	18	0	36	27
St M: Pinley & Whitley	Cov	6	33	0	0	67	0	67	0
Stivichall	Cov	37	70	22	0	5	3	8	41
Stoke	Cov	# 61	65	15	3	15	2	20	50
Walsgrave on Sowe (part)	Cov	65	75	11	11	3	0	14	62
Wyken	Cov	24	67	21	8	0	4	13	29
Coventry		**#1903**	**50**	**22**	**17**	**9**	**2**	**27**	**42**

Source: Table 28

>0 indicates a percentage above 0 and below 0.5.
# indicates that entries without hearth numbers are included in the total, but were not used to calculate any percentages.
* indicates that a histogram of this parish is included in Figure 1.
+ indicates that this parish has been subdivided in Table 27 and on Maps 4–13.

NC = not chargeable; Cert = certified exempt; chap, cp = chapelry; det = detached.
HT = Coventry: Holy Trinity parish; St M = Coventry: St Michael parish.

Divisions

Alc = Alcester	Hen = Henley	Rug = Rugby	Tam = Tamworth
Ath = Atherstone	Ken = Kenilworth	Sol = Solihull	Tan = Tanworth
Bid = Bidford	Kin = Kineton	Sou = Southam	War = Warwick borough
Bir = Birmingham	MK = Monks Kirby	Str = Stratford	
Bra = Brailes	PM = Priors Marston		

Hundreds

B = Barlichway H = Hemlingford Ki = Kineton Kn = Knightlow

Counties

Cov = Coventry	Leic = Leicestershire	Staf = Staffordshire
Glos = Gloucestershire	Oxf = Oxfordshire	Worc = Worcestershire

Combined data

For Tamworth and Walsgrave on Sowe parishes, it is possible to combine the data from the 1670 Warwickshire returns with those from Staffordshire for 1665 (TNA, E179/256/31) and Coventry for 1666. These provide the following percentages:

		h'hlds	*1*	*2*	*3–4*	*5–9*	*10+*	*3+*	*NC*
Tamworth (part)	Staf	129	74	9	12	4	1	17	40
Tamworth (all)	Tam:H+Staf	506	66	16	13	3	1	17	42
Walsgrave on Sowe (all)	MK:Kn+Cov	103	77	18	10	5	0	15	50

Interpreting the hearth tax

5. Urban and rural Warwickshire with Coventry

The best starting point for understanding Warwickshire's society in the reign of Charles II is to compare its towns with the countryside. This approach reflects Peter Borsay's perception of most towns as 'islands amidst a sea of countryside' that service its needs.[1] In this study therefore the county's exceptional hearth tax data will be used to reveal, in a much sharper focus than previously, some crucial aspects of this relationship. It starts with a methodology that has been applied to identifying regional variations throughout England and Wales and contrasting various towns.[2] For the task of spotting those parishes that were broadly similar and then grouping them together in rural sub-regions or hinterlands of the towns, a single comparator is essential. Almost certainly the best one for this purpose is the proportion of households with three or more hearths. This was the lowest total above the two-hearth cut-off point for claiming exemption from the hearth tax so that every dwelling in this category was chargeable, regardless of their occupants' circumstances. In addition, their proportions were not so vulnerable to flaws in the data as those that are based upon just one hearth or the exempt alone, although happily for Warwickshire this problem is of very little concern.

The towns

'Town' is one of those frustrating words that has changed its meaning since the seventeenth century.[3] Then it could be applied to any village of consequence with a church, such as Aston Cantlow, Chilvers Coton, Edgbaston, Fillongley and Tanworth in Arden in the hearth tax returns.[4] Now towns are assumed to be of a different order from villages, although separated by a grey area. The deciding factor for most modern historians in identifying Stuart towns is the existence of markets and this has yielded a general consensus that Restoration Warwickshire had some fifteen towns of varying size plus Coventry.[5] However four of them (Bidford, Kineton, Solihull and Sutton Coldfield) were so small, with between 76 and 88 households in the hearth tax returns (and so populations of around 350–400 people), that they cannot be regarded as 'urban', even if their markets did continue to function. They are therefore classified as failed towns in Table 10 and treated as rural communities for the rest of this discussion. Only Sutton Coldfield had more three-plus hearth households than the norm for the Warwickshire countryside but, with 29 per cent in 76 households, it was comparable to Knowle's 27 per cent in 68. The inhabitants of the 12 other towns also

1 Borsay, 'Towns', pp. 191, 205–7.
2 Arkell, 'Regional', pp. 153–5.
3 Dyer, 'Introduction', p. 4.
4 Chilvers Coton in 1664; Aston Cantlow, Edgbaston and Tanworth in Arden in 1670; Fillongley in 1674.
5 Everitt, 'Market', p. 475; Dyer, 'Towns', pp. 122–8; Borsay, 'Towns', pp. 188–91.

kept in close touch with rural life, but in environments that differed to a greater or lesser extent from the countryside.[1] Together they housed one quarter of the families in the two counties of Warwickshire and Coventry.

Imperfect returns often sabotage attempts to establish precise household totals from the hearth tax but not in Warwickshire.[2] Here the uncertainties concerning the towns are of a different order and in particular involve the areas in which they were enumerated. Thus the non-chargeable for Coleshill town had to be estimated because they were not differentiated from the other settlements in this parish. Similarly in Staffordshire's part of Tamworth the hearth tax of 1665 made no distinction between those who lived in or outside the borough.[3] Stratford upon Avon's urban area encroached beyond its 110 acres to cover part of Old Stratford between its parish church and the borough. Conversely, the populations of those towns that were assessed in areas of over 1,000 acres may be over-estimated. Warwick borough (5,600 acres) had many rural houses in Bridge End ward and parts of two others, while in Alcester (1,800 acres) some ten households were located outside the town in Kings Coughton.[4] Most of these household totals also included empty dwellings, often some 2 per cent, but as much as 5 per cent in Coventry, which will affect population estimates. More uncertainty is created by the choice of multipliers to estimate the numbers of people from household totals, which may therefore be better indicators of size on their own. For example, in over a hundred communities studied outside the London region in the later Stuart period, only some two thirds had a mean household size, within the range of plus or minus 10 per cent, of 4.3. And so when single multipliers are used to make such calculations they will inevitably introduce a similar margin of error.[5]

When the 12 towns are ranked according to their size they cluster into three distinct groups. At the bottom come the four smallest (Coleshill, Henley, Rugby and Southam) with approximately 150 households each and, assuming a mean household size of around 4.3, population totals of between about 600 to 750 people. The four medium sized towns (Alcester, Atherstone, Nuneaton and Tamworth) probably had between 250 and 300 households each and so perhaps 1,100 to 1,300 inhabitants. The four largest were more diverse and ranged from Stratford with some 2,000 people in about 450 households to Warwick with around 2,500 in 600 or so households, Birmingham probably close to 3,500 inhabitants in 800 households and Coventry with a population of approximately 6,000 in about 1,400 occupied dwellings. These last four towns together contained two thirds of the urban households in Warwickshire with Coventry; reasons for their dominance were discussed at the start of this introduction.

1 Borsay, 'Towns', pp. 196–8.
2 This problem bedevilled the West Riding of Yorkshire, for example. See Hey, 'West Riding', pp. 16–18.
3 For more detail about Tamworth see the note on Combined data to Table 9, p. 61.
4 Borsay, 'Towns', p. 196.
5 Arkell, 'Multiplying factors', pp. 53–5.

Table 10 The towns of Warwickshire with Coventry

Towns (ranked by % 3+ hearths)	*Total h'hlds*	*3+ %*	*Hearths per household 1 %*	*2 %*	*3–4 %*	*5–9 %*	*10+ %*	*NC %*	*Acres approx*
Highest									
Warwick borough	617	35	49	16	20	11	4	40	5600
Coventry city	1428	32	44	24	20	10	2	41	5500
	2045	33	45	22	20	11	3	41	
Middle									
Stratford borough	427	27	59	14	19	7	1	46	110
Tamworth borough (part)	194	26	52	23	19	6	1	39	50
Atherstone	257	25	61	14	16	7	2	47	950
Birmingham	780	23	53	24	16	6	1	47	3000
Rugby	177	23	68	9	17	5	1	41	1650
Nuneaton	302	22	65	13	16	5	1	52	n.a.
	2137	24	58	18	17	6	1	46	
Lowest									
Southam	140	19	61	21	11	7	0	41	3100
Alcester	270	16	64	20	13	3	0	46	1800
Coleshill	est.145	14	69	17	9	3	1	est.32	n.a.
Henley in Arden	137	9	72	18	6	4	0	56	350
	692	15	66	19	10	4	0.3	44	
All 'urban' towns	**4874**	**26**	**54**	**20**	**17**	**8**	**2**	**44**	
[*All rural regions*	*14269*	*15*	*68*	*16*	*10*	*4*	*1*	*37*]	
Failed towns									
Sutton Coldfield borough	est.76	29	49	22	14	12	3	est.39	n.a.
Kineton	88	14	72	15	13	1	0	26	n.a.
Solihull borough	86	13	76	12	6	7	0	65	n.a.
Bidford	76	4	87	9	3	1	0	66	n.a.
	326	15	71	14	9	5	1	49	
Subdivisions									
Coventry city									
central & south[a]	*535*	*40*	*35*	*25*	*22*	*13*	*4*	*31*	
central & east[b]	*498*	*26*	*46*	*26*	*19*	*8*	*1*	*47*	
north & west[c]	*395*	*26*	*52*	*22*	*17*	*9*	*1*	*47*	
Warwick borough									
inner[d]	*200*	*57*	*23*	*21*	*28*	*22*	*7*	*18*	
south & east[e]	*149*	*40*	*44*	*16*	*27*	*10*	*3*	*34*	
outer[f]	*268*	*16*	*71*	*13*	*11*	*4*	*1*	*59*	
Stratford borough									
north-east[g]	*68*	*65*	*13*	*22*	*38*	*25*	*1*	*4*	
rest[h]	*359*	*20*	*68*	*13*	*15*	*4*	*1*	*54*	

a = Broadgate, Cross Cheaping, Little Park St & Smithford St wards
b = Bayley Lane, Gosford St, Jordan Well & Much Park St wards
c = Bishop St & Spon St wards
d = High St, Jury St & Market Place wards
e = Castle St & Smith St wards
f = Bridge End, Saltisford & West St wards
g = Bridge St & High St wards
h = Church & Chapel St, Henley St, Sheep St & Wood St wards
Source: Table 28; *VCH*, ii, pp. 182–92.

In Table 10 these towns are not ordered according to their size but by the proportion of their households with three hearths or more. This enables a comparison of the particular hearth tax characteristics for each town to be made with the others and any marked social zoning within them to be identified. By this approach Warwick and Coventry are placed in the top group with as many as 35 and 32 per cent of their households having three or more hearths. Warwick also had the more distinct social zoning, with 57 per cent of the households in its inner wards enjoying three-plus hearths, 40 per cent round the castle and down Smith Street and just 16 per cent in its three outer wards. Coventry was more homogeneous, with 40 per cent of a group of four wards in its centre and south having three or more hearths and 26 per cent elsewhere. The spread in the next band of six towns ranged from Stratford upon Avon (with 27 per cent) to Nuneaton (22 per cent). In Stratford, 65 per cent of the households in two small wards near the bridge had three-plus hearths compared with just 20 per cent in the rest of the borough. Birmingham's 23 per cent reflects its lack of an administrative and professional cadre, but it has no apparent zonal differences because of how its hearth tax was assessed. Alcester (16 per cent) was one of the four towns in the lower group with a range of 19 to 9 per cent that differed little from the rural norms.

Other data in this table reveal that the difference of 3 per cent between Warwick and Coventry was accounted for by their households with five or more hearths, which may have reflected Warwick's status as a county town. Coventry, Tamworth and Birmingham, on the other hand, had fewer one-hearth and more two-hearth dwellings than the urban norm, while Rugby had more one-hearth and fewer two-hearth ones. Of much greater significance is the very consistent proportion of the exempt recorded for most of these towns regardless of their size. Overall this was 7 per cent higher than the rural mean. Conversely, the proportion of one-hearth households in the towns was on average some 14 per cent lower than in the countryside. Thus many more households had one chargeable hearth in the countryside (31 per cent) than in the towns (10 per cent). But before the relationship between these towns and their rural surroundings can be explored further, the rural sub-regions must be identified.

Table 11 Comparative analysis of hearths in the rural areas of selected midland counties

		Hearths per household						
	HT	*3+*	*1*	*2*	*3–4*	*5–9*	*10+*	*NC*
County	*date*	*%*	*%*	*%*	*%*	*%*	*%*	*%*
Gloucestershire	1671/2	22	60	18	16	5	1	40
Bedfordshire	1670	20	62	17	14	5	1	30
Herefordshire	1671	16	71	13	11	4	1	32
Warwickshire	**1670**	**15**	**68**	**16**	**10**	**4**	**1**	**37**
Northamptonshire	1674	15	71	15	10	4	1	40
Leicestershire	1670	12	66	21	8	3	1	33
Staffordshire	1665	12	75	14	8	3	1	31

The numbers of households in this sample range from 7,757 in Bedfordshire to 18,694 in Northamptonshire.
Source: Arkell, 'Regional', p. 159.

The countryside

Three quarters of the families in Warwickshire with Coventry lived in the countryside. Two in three of them occupied single-hearth dwellings, while one in six had two hearths, and the remaining one in six had three hearths or more. A similar pattern obtained in the rural parts of other midland counties, but with fewer three-plus households towards the north. Table 11 shows how Warwickshire and Northamptonshire, with 15 per cent each, were sandwiched between Gloucestershire (22 per cent) and Bedfordshire (20 per cent) to the south and Leicestershire and Staffordshire (both 12 per cent) to the north. Unfortunately the surviving returns from Oxfordshire and Worcestershire are too incomplete for meaningful analysis.[1] These countywide figures naturally conceal huge variations between individual parishes, constableries and townships which are mapped in great detail according to the principles of the British Academy Hearth Tax Project in Maps 4–13 below. Here, however, the prime concern is to identify in Warwickshire the distinct rural regions with at least a thousand households, along with any significant sub-divisions, before locating those larger parishes that stand out from their peers. The boundaries of these sub-regions were established without any preconceived ideas of exactly where they should come. Instead, each one was created by grouping together sufficient parishes that had broadly similar proportions of households with three-plus hearths, as are revealed in Table 9.[2] However, since these areas

[1] Arkell, 'Regional', p. 156.

[2] Many years ago, I received very valuable advice concerning the identification of Warwickshire's sub-regions from Terry Slater of Birmingham University. He persuaded me not to approach the problem of determining where their boundaries lay with preconceived ideas, but to wait for an analysis of the data to suggest where they should best be drawn.

cannot be defined precisely, the dividing lines on Map 3 should not be treated as exact either. Confining this study to Warwickshire is also far from satisfactory because the county was not a self-contained economic unit. Thus, a few parishes to the north of the coalfield should not belong with it, but with more comparable parishes across the border in Leicestershire, while three others on the northern edge of the Felden have been incorporated with Dunsmore Heath rather than Northamptonshire.

By these means seven regions in all have been identified, of which four were further subdivided. Their details are contained in Table 12, which shows that the county's rural norms were 15 per cent for the households with three or more hearths and 37 per cent for the non-chargeable. The Felden was the region with the highest proportion of the former (19 per cent) and the lowest of the latter (29 per cent). Moving clockwise round the county takes us next to the upper reaches of the Avon valley. There the feature that stands out was the 10 per cent more non-liable south of Warwick (45 per cent) than in the area to the north, although the difference between their one-hearth dwellings was only 2 per cent. The Arden forest comes closest to the countywide norms, except in its central part which had far fewer households with five to nine hearths (2 per cent) than the other two parts, while the northern one was more densely populated. The three parts of the former wooded Northern plateau to the north and east of Birmingham were more diverse. Its western sub-region, which consisted principally of Aston and Sutton Coldfield parishes on the edge of the Black Country, was the most polarised, with both more non-chargeable (41 per cent) and more three-plus hearth households (18 per cent) than usual. In the eastern part nearest to the coalfield, the proportion of three-plus hearth households (21 per cent) was the highest in Warwickshire, while its one-hearth (60 per cent) and exempt households (27 per cent) were the lowest, apart from the small central area in between. There both the three-plus households (11 per cent) and the exempt (26 per cent) were exceptionally low. The extended coalfield, which stretched northwards from Coventry to Wilnecote in Tamworth parish, had predictably the fewest households with three-plus hearths (9 per cent), the most non-chargeable (49 per cent) and the most dense population (39 per 1,000 acres). The mainly pastoral area to the east of Coventry and north of Rugby, with 17 per cent three-plus households, had 5 per cent fewer one-hearth dwellings and 4 per cent more two-hearth ones than the norm. Finally comes Dunsmore Heath and the area immediately to the south, as far as Southam. There the proportion of households with three or more hearths was very low (10 per cent) with the sole significant difference between the region's two parts being the 8 per cent more exempt living on the poor soils of the heath.

This brief survey of the salient differences among the seven rural regions and their subdivisions provides a coherent context for the otherwise bewildering diversity among all the individual parishes contained in Table 9 above. Because the proportions of the different hearth tax categories fluctuate most in the smaller parishes they

Table 12 Rural sub-regions in Warwickshire with Coventry

Sub-region	*Total h'hlds*	*Hearths per household* *3+ %*	*1 %*	*2 %*	*3–4 %*	*5–9 %*	*10+ %*	*NC %*	*H'hlds 1000 acres*
Felden	2275	19	65	16	14	4	1	29	24
Northern plateau	2286	18	65	17	12	5	1	33	26
east	*899*	*21*	*60*	*19*	*13*	*6*	*1*	*27*	*26*
west	*989*	*18*	*68*	*15*	*12*	*4*	*2*	*41*	*29*
central	*398*	*11*	*70*	*19*	*6*	*3*	*2*	*26*	*21*
East	1420	17	63	20	11	4	1	32	24
Arden	3041	16	69	15	11	4	1	38	25
south-west	*620*	*17*	*68*	*15*	*11*	*5*	*1*	*38*	*23*
north	*1048*	*16*	*70*	*14*	*10*	*6*	*1*	*39*	*30*
central	*1373*	*15*	*69*	*16*	*12*	*2*	*1*	*38*	*24*
Avon	1905	16	70	15	10	5	1	40	23
upper	*825*	*16*	*69*	*15*	*10*	*6*	*1*	*35*	*25*
lower	*1080*	*15*	*71*	*15*	*10*	*4*	*1*	*45*	*21*
Dunsmore	1705	10	71	18	7	3	1	38	26
heath	*660*	*11*	*72*	*18*	*6*	*4*	*1*	*41*	*26*
south	*1045*	*10*	*71*	*19*	*7*	*2*	*1*	*35*	*26*
Coalfield	1637	9	77	14	7	2	1	49	39
All rural regions	14269	15	68	16	10	4	1	37	26

These figures are rounded to the nearest whole number and so do not always add up to 100%.
Source: Table 28.

are not considered here. Indeed, there is a diminishing validity among those with 20 households in particular, as just one household accounts on its own for 5, 10 or even 20 per cent of their proportions. And yet huge differences still emerge between those parishes that had at least 30 households. In the Arden, for example, the proportion of households with three or more hearths ranged from Rowington (29 per cent) to Haselor (3 per cent) and on the coalfield from Baddesley Ensor (26 per cent) to Bedworth (1 per cent); but the span in the Dunsmore area was much narrower from Dunchurch (17 per cent) to Napton on the Hill (5 per cent).

Comparative analyses of the differences in the household structures of 15 representative parishes are presented as histograms in Figure 1. In this form the main hearth tax characteristics of any parish can be absorbed at a glance. The breakdowns for Solihull, Berkswell and Ipsley, for example, are similar to Warwickshire's rural norms, while the others reveal very diverse patterns, with proportions of one-hearth dwellings ranging from 85 to 43 per cent and the non-chargeable from 67 to 14 per cent. Wroxall stands out because it had an almost equal number of one- and

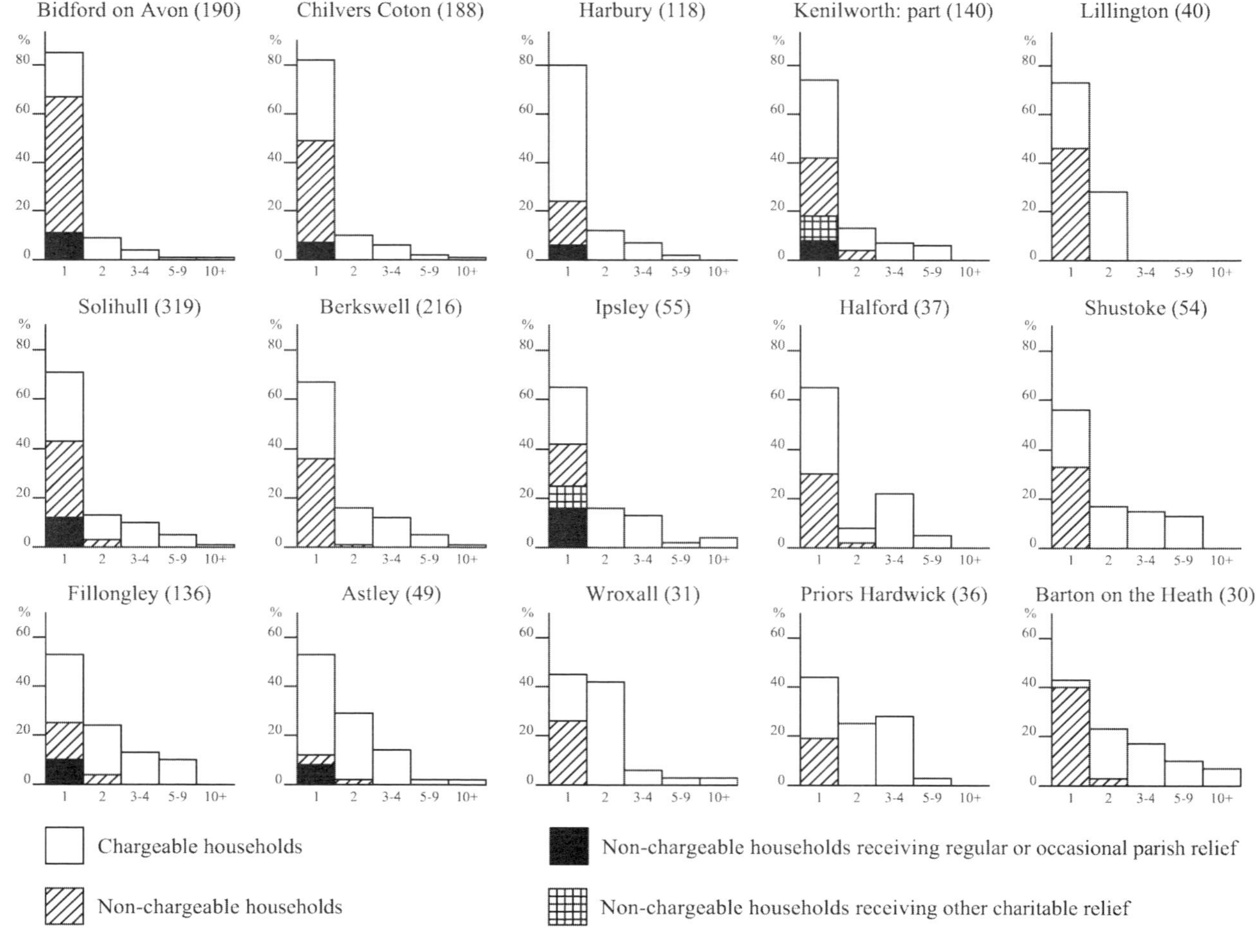

Figure 1 Households grouped by hearth numbers in 15 parishes.
Figures in brackets record the household totals in each parish. Kenilworth covers only the Augmentation part of the parish (*Source*: Tables 9, 22, 28).

two-hearth dwellings, Priors Hardwick because the number of its households with two hearths was very similar to those with three to four, while Halford had many more with three to four hearths than with two. Lillington's high proportion of two-hearth households but none with three or more contrasts sharply with Shustoke, which had three very similar groups containing two, three to four, and five to nine hearths. Although about half the households with a single hearth were often exempt, the diagrams show that this proportion was much smaller in Harbury and Astley, for example, and much greater in Bidford on Avon and Barton on the Heath. (Comparable data for all the other parishes is supplied in Table 9.) Further insight is gained from superimposing upon the non-chargeable in eight parishes data from Table 22 concerning those households that received both regular and casual poor relief. The recipients of additional charity (such as a small dole or their house rent) are also indicated in Ipsley and the Augmentation half of Kenilworth parish.[1] Even though these parishes functioned as distinct communities that were centred upon their churches and parish vestries, they should not be treated in isolation because they interacted continuously with other parishes, often for food, resources and labour, and so were not discrete social or economic units.[2]

Comparisons

As a result of these two separate studies the towns can now be placed within their rural context as plotted on Map 3 where the relative proportions of households with three or more hearths and of the exempt in ten of the towns are compared with their adjacent countryside.[3] Coventry, which was surrounded by four different regions, and Tamworth, which was partly in Staffordshire, cannot be treated in this way, but the other 10 clearly belong to one of three well-defined groups. The first contains five towns that had many more three-plus hearth households (between 12 & 20 per cent) but the same proportion of non-chargeable as the countryside around them. Warwick heads this list with respectively 19 & 0 per cent extra when contrasted with both parts of the Avon, followed by Atherstone and Nuneaton from the coalfield, Stratford in the lower Avon, and Rugby (12 per cent & 0 per cent) on Dunsmore Heath. The surplus of three-plus hearth households was smaller (8 per cent at most) in the next group of three towns, which also had more non-chargeable than their adjacent rural parishes. These are Southam to the south of Dunsmore, Birmingham (5 per cent & 6 per cent) on the west of the northern plateau and Coleshill in its centre. The final two towns had no more multi-hearth dwellings than their surrounding countryside, but many more non-chargeable ones. They are Alcester (0 per cent & 8 per cent) and Henley (-6 per cent & 18 per cent) in the Arden. These figures, it must be stressed, do not follow Table 8 in comparing the

1 The incidence of, and sources for, poor relief in Warwickshire are discussed in section 7 below.

2 Dyer, 'Villages', pp. 22–4.

3 Differences of three percentage points or less have been ignored in this analysis.

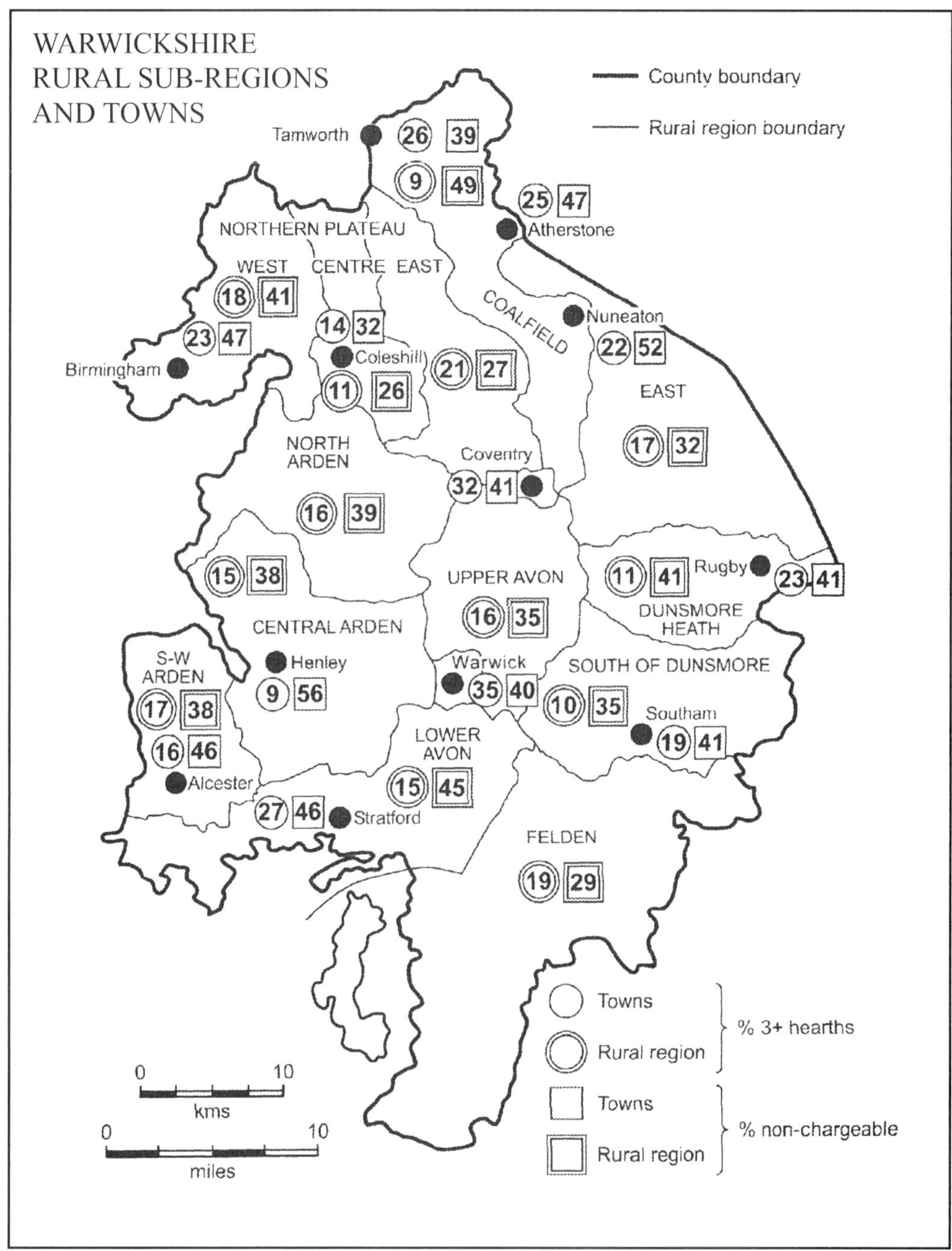

Map 3 Warwickshire hearth tax: rural sub-regions and towns.
Source: Tables 9, 10, 28.

towns directly with each other, but only with their rural hinterlands. This novel approach towards a better understanding of Warwickshire's towns is more sophisticated than an earlier study of some hundred English towns because of the high quality of their hearth tax data.[1]

Two other facets of Warwickshire's urban and rural society can also be quantified with some confidence. The population density for the whole of Warwickshire and Coventry, as measured by the average number of households per 1,000 acres, was 33, but for the countryside alone it was 26. The rural areas where the population was most dense were the coalfield (39) and the northern part of the Arden (30), while it was least dense in the lower Avon (21) and the central part of the northern plateau (21), as appears in Table 12. The mean for the towns was about 200 households per 1,000 acres. However, there is very little point in calculating separately the apparent densities for each town (as well as some parishes) because of the huge variations in the areas included within their boundaries as recorded in Table 10.

Establishing the proportions of households headed by women is another important topic worthy of attention. The norm for Warwickshire was 16.5 per cent, or about one household in six, with very little difference between the towns (18 per cent) and the countryside (16 per cent).[2] Unlike the men, women were responsible for more non-chargeable (10 per cent) than chargeable households (6 per cent). Altogether they headed 27 per cent of the non-chargeable households, but just 10 per cent of the chargeable ones. Table 13 shows that the spread of all female-headed households in the towns went from 23 per cent in Alcester, Atherstone and Coleshill to as low as 7 per cent in Warwickshire's part of Tamworth borough. The proportions of their non-chargeable households in the towns ranged from 40 per cent in Alcester and Coleshill to 15 per cent in Tamworth and of the chargeable from 17 per cent in Atherstone to none at all in Henley. In the rural regions, the overall proportion of female-headed households ranged more narrowly from 14 per cent in the Felden to 19 per cent in the coalfield, but there were much greater differences in some of the larger parishes. Women ran 32 per cent of the 44 households in Sherbourne, 29 per cent in Knowle (with 126 households) and 27 per cent in both Temple Grafton (45) and Bedworth (281). At the other extreme, only 6 per cent of the households in Whichford (101) and Shustoke (54) and 8 per cent in Bulkington (145) and Austrey (87) had female heads. Thus good quality hearth tax returns can reveal very significant differences between one area or community and another in a variety of crucial ways.

Finally, much of this section has been based upon the unspoken assumption that there was an approximate, if non-specific, connection between hearth numbers,

1 Arkell, 'Regional', pp. 162, 168–9. The earlier approach was based upon the ratios of the proportion of three-plus hearth households in each town divided by the comparable figure for the surrounding countryside. Had it been applied here, it would have created just two groups, with Southam in the top one (with ratios of 1.8 to 2.8) and the other four clustered together with ratios between 0.6 and 1.3.

2 These figures may be too low by a percentage point or so because there was always doubt about the gender of some names such as Francis.

Table 13 Percentages of households headed by females in Warwickshire with Coventry

Rural region	*All* %	*NC* %	*Ch* %	*Towns*	*All* %	*NC* %	*Ch* %
Felden	14	25	10	Tamworth	7	15	3
East	15	27	9	Birmingham	13	20	7
Northern	16	24	12	Henley	13	23	–
Dunsmore	16	28	9	Warwick	16	22	12
Avon	17	26	11	Nuneaton	17	23	10
Arden	17	28	11	Coventry	18	29	11
Coalfield	19	30	9	Southam	19	26	14
Overall	16	27	10	Rugby	20	34	10
				Stratford	20	29	12
Means				Alcester	23	40	9
Rural	16	27	10	Atherstone	23	31	17
Towns	18	27	10	Coleshill	23	40	14
All	17	27	10	*Overall*	18	27	10

house size and various socio-economic factors. This is explored in the rest of this introduction and will show that, although hearth numbers on their own are normally poor guides to the financial standing or occupation of individual householders or to the number of rooms in their houses, yet they are not entirely unconnected either. Although householders or families should not be stereotyped according to the number of their hearths alone, general conclusions about the circumstances of groups of inhabitants in particular localities that derive from local research are normally valid when sensitively drawn. But this does not endorse the mechanical application nationwide of a one-size-fits-all wealth-to-poverty spectrum onto a range of differing hearth numbers.[1]

6. Warwickshire's social and occupational structure

That there was a significant connection between the number of hearths in each house or household and the occupations or social status of their inhabitants is beyond doubt, but how close and predictable this connection was is much more problematical. When studied in combination with other contemporary documents, the hearth tax returns provide a unique opportunity to deconstruct this tantalising connection and so approach closer to the reality of social relations in Restoration Warwickshire.

1 These conclusions accord very closely with those of Nigel Goose in his perceptive and probing study of the data for Cambridge and Reading (Goose, 'Wealth', pp. 58–60).

This in turn has profound implications for our perceptions of late seventeenth-century social structure, which emerges as more complex and more subtle than traditional descriptions suggest.

Two substantial articles that Styles published half a century ago are the essential starting point for this exploration.[1] In the later one he showed how the status and occupations of those who contributed to the Free and Voluntary Gift in 1661 can be analysed and compared with the number of their hearths in 1663 and 1664 to confirm the conventional picture of a stratified society divided between gentlemen, yeomen, husbandmen and labourers, with the mean value of each group's subscriptions and the average number of their hearths per household neatly graduated.[2] But he then proceeded to demonstrate that this simple stereotype was unreliable since other documents often described people differently, while those with trades and crafts found no place in this hierarchy.[3] Since the mid-sixteenth century, English society had become more fluid and complex with broader and more economically-based class distinctions, as the hierarchical rigidities of an earlier feudal military society were eroded by the expansion of trade and manufacture together with a rising population and price inflation.[4] According to Styles, its social divisions contained 'a complex structure of intermediate grades, here distinct and there merging one into the other', based partly on differences of wealth and descent as well as on 'the estimation in which a man was held by his neighbours', which defied precise quantification.[5] This hybrid society was thus in a flux that matched the transitional state of the administrative system. Heralds and those of an antiquarian frame of mind, such as Gregory King, could still perceive enough of the old order submerged in contemporary society to want to preserve it, but they were rowing against the tide.[6]

The gentry

The identification of the gentry in the hearth tax returns is not reliably achieved by simply concentrating upon all the entries in a single list with the status of 'gent' and above. This is because the various status terms that appear in the different hearth tax lists were not recorded consistently nor were the numbers to whom they were given. Opinions also differ as to whether those described as 'Mr' should count as gentry or not. In addition, some gentry owned second homes and properties that they rented out, which cannot always be distinguished from their main residences in these returns. This explains why Styles failed to analyse coherently the various ranks of gentry in Kineton hundred when he wrestled with all its 482 householders who were recorded with some title or prefix in one or more of its eight hearth tax returns. He discovered in particular that, although the honorific term , 'gentleman', was applied

1 Styles, 'Heralds'; Styles, 'Kineton'.
2 The Free and Voluntary Gift was an emergency measure to raise money, similar to the Tudor benevolences.
3 Styles, 'Kineton', pp. 152–4.
4 Wilson, *Apprenticeship*, pp. 3–19; Styles, 'Heralds', pp. 130–1; Styles, 'Kineton', p. 158.
5 Styles, 'Kineton', pp. 167–9.
6 Wilson, *Apprenticeship*, pp. 4–6; Arkell, 'King', pp. 51–5.

extensively in the 1660s, it was replaced by 'Mr' in the 1670s.[1] The highest ranked in this sample consisted of one resident peer, 10 resident baronets and knights, and 34 esquires, of whom just 12 were consistently so recorded. The mean number of hearths for these esquires varied from 10.5 in 1666 to 13.5 in 1674. Others covered by this analysis appeared sometimes as 'gent' or 'Mr' or even with no honorific at all. They included 65 clergymen who were described as 'Mr' and 61 women who were styled as 'Mrs'. As a result, there were significant differences in the mean number of hearths per household for the 'gent' and 'Mr' groups among the different returns. Apparently the coverage of those with gentry titles was more variable in the towns than in the countryside. In Stratford borough, for example, the number of gentry entries fell from 32 in 1670 to 17 in 1674, but from just 42 to 37 in the rest of Stratford division.[2] In Warwick borough the 1660s were more volatile, with a swing from 75 in 1663 to 46 in 1665, compared with the 1670s when those recorded as gentry varied between 68 in 1673 and 54 in 1674.

This inconsistency prevented Styles from establishing any definitive averages for the different levels of gentry in Kineton hundred. Thus, when Nicholas Cooper compared the gentry in Warwickshire with those in six other counties, he only used a small sample from Styles's work from 1663 for the south of the county.[3] This sample was based on just three knights, five esquires and 103 gentlemen (but no 'Mr'), whose mean hearths per head were respectively 16.3, 10.6 and 5.7.[4] Cooper also excluded all entries for 'Mr' from the other counties, and appears to have applied a minimum cut-off point of five hearths for the greater gentry at least.[5] Since then, analyses of the returns for Kent and Durham have been added to this study by others, who have included the 'Mr' entries among their lesser gentry for good reasons and abandoned the five-hearth threshold.[6] In short, because like was not always compared with like, this simplistic approach to measuring and comparing the gentry has to be questioned. The trigger for Cooper's five-hearth minimum, which Spufford also favours, was provided by Styles's article on the heralds' visitation of Warwickshire in 1682–3.[7] This was the point below which Gregory King did not expect to find many potential gentry, who were entitled to a coat of arms. In his search for everyone in Warwickshire 'with any pretensions at all to gentility', King first reduced its 847 householders with five or more hearths to 441, by omitting all the non-£20 freeholders who were not eligible for Quarter Sessions jury service, and then adding another 66 who had less than five hearths but were mostly £20 freeholders.[8] Even then, when King sent his revised list to Sir William Dugdale, he still doubted whether 'there is not above a third part if

1 Styles, 'Kineton', pp. 158–63.
2 WCRO, QS11/12, 41, 51.
3 Cooper, *Houses*, p. 6.
4 Styles, 'Kineton', pp. 151–3.
5 Cooper, *Houses*, pp. 330 n. 9, 347.
6 Pearson, 'Kent', pp. xli–xliii; Green, 'Durham', pp. lxix–lxxi.
7 Cooper, *Houses*, p. 330 n. 10; Spufford, 'Potential', p. 206.
8 Styles, 'Heralds', pp. 112–5, 137.

so many that are really gentlemen'.[1] King thus believed that only one in five or six of those who had at least five hearths in Warwickshire were genuine gentry. Although this archaic view may have prevailed temporarily after the Restoration, it was by then no longer in tune with the times.

An alternative perception of gentility as well as of the varying proportions of those who were recorded as gentry can be explored by studying a sizeable sample from Warwickshire's unrivalled cache of hearth tax returns (Table 14). In the Hemlingford divisions of Atherstone and Tamworth, which covered the north-east of the county and included most of its coalfield, the 1670 assessment contained 171 entries for the dwellings of persons with some status label.[2] However, from their wording and a comparison with the other returns, it is evident that 24 of these houses were either unoccupied or let out to other people. Conversely, another 42 householders who were deprived of any status in 1670, appeared as 'Mr' or 'Mrs' in at least one of the other lists in the 1670s and so have been added to this group of householders with some kind of gentry status. Altogether they comprised 6.8 per cent of all householders in this part of north-east Warwickshire. Two thirds lived in the countryside (where the proportion was 6.5 per cent) and the rest in the three towns of Nuneaton (4.6 per cent), Atherstone (5.8 per cent) and Warwickshire's part of Tamworth (14.9 per cent). A similar spread obtained among the large rural parishes, from Fillongley (14.7 per cent) and Kingsbury (9.7 per cent) to Polesworth (3.6 per cent) and Chilvers Coton (2.7 per cent). This demonstrates how easily substantial differences between individual parishes may be obscured by an average figure for the proportion of gentry families in a much wider area.

The hearth numbers analysed in Table 14 also show that nearly half of these gentry had fewer than five hearths in both town and country and that as many as 15 per cent lived in dwellings with just one or two hearths. At the other end of the scale, the largest houses with 13 hearths or more were occupied exclusively by the esquires and above, while the gentry as a whole, with the most inclusive definition, occupied 83 per cent of the houses with seven to nine hearths. This proportion fell to 60 per cent among those with five or six hearths. Below them, those with some kind of status title occupied one third of the dwellings with four hearths and one sixth of those with three hearths. Finally, in the light of this variability, it must be stressed that this analysis covers only part of Warwickshire and different patterns probably obtained elsewhere.

A brief survey of a few individuals will help to clarify some of the huge differences in the circumstances of these gentry. At the lowest level, three distressed gentlefolk lived in Tamworth division.[3] Mr Thomas Briggs occupied a one-hearth non-chargeable property in Bolehall from 1666 to 1674, while Mr Jeffery Bach was excused payment for his two hearths in Church Street in Tamworth borough from 1670 to 1673, confirmed by two exemption certificates. In Polesworth Mrs Reeves's decline is

1 Styles, 'Heralds', pp. 115, 137.

2 The analysis in this paragraph derives from the data contained in Walker, *Hemlingford*.

3 Walker, *Hemlingford*, pp. 35, 56, 109, 113.

Table 14 Gentry households in Atherstone and Tamworth divisions in 1670

(a) Hearths per gentry household by status

	Number of hearths per household							
Status	*1*	*2*	*3–4*	*5–6*	*7–9*	*10–12*	*13+*	*total*
Sir, Esq & their widows	–	–	–	–	1	3	14	18
Mr (inc gent)	4	16	28	35	14	4	–	101
Additional Mr	1	3	17	11	8	2	–	42
Mrs	2	–	4	3	–	2	–	11
Clergy	–	2	11	2	2	–	–	17
Total	**7**	**21**	**60**	**51**	**25**	**11**	**14**	**189**
Three towns	–	9	17	18	9	5	2	60
Countryside	7	12	43	33	16	6	12	129
(Empty or tenanted	*10*	*5*	*7*	*2*	–	–	–	*24)*

'Additional Mr' indicates those who were not given gentry status in 1670, but were recorded in a later return as 'Mr' etc.
The empty houses and those known to have been tenanted are omitted from the main totals.

(b) Percentages of gentry in households with three or more hearths

	Number of hearths per household					
	3	*4*	*5*	*6*	*7–9*	*10+*
	%	%	%	%	%	%
Three towns	14	16	50	42	73	88
Countryside	19	41	67	68	89	100
Overall	**17**	**30**	**60**	**58**	**83**	**96**
(household total	*202*	*108*	*55*	*31*	*29*	*26)*

Source: Walker, *Hemlingford*.

the more obvious because she shared responsibility with Mr Beck for five hearths in Holt Hall before she was certified as exempt from 1670 to 1674 with a single hearth at nearby Hallend. At the other end of the spectrum we find Sir Richard Newdigate in 1684 living at Arbury Hall (32 hearths in 1670–4) with a large family and 28 servants, including his chaplain Mr Scott and housekeeper Mrs Searle.[1] At the same time the recently-widowed Mr Thomas Sprat paid £16 a year rent for six acres and a four-hearth house in Chilvers Coton where he lived with one servant and two unmarried daughters. The vicar, Mr John Perkins, lived in some comfort with his wife, four children and two servants in the Chilvers Coton vicarage, which had five hearths, four bedrooms, a hall, parlour, study, kitchen, dairy, buttery and cellar. When he died

[1] WCRO, CR136/V12, pp. 64, 69, 73.

at the age of 53 his household goods, which were valued at £62, included a clock and looking glass, a silver salt cellar, upholstered chairs, down and feather mattresses and in one bedroom curtains for both the windows and round the bed.[1] But sometimes hearth numbers may be no guide at all to a man's wealth or status. Mr William Wood, who was the second largest landowner in Chilvers Coton, rented out 20 houses, including the one occupied by Mr Sprat, and about one fifth of the land. Yet his own moated farmhouse in Sutton Coldfield parish was consistently assessed for a mere two hearths. As for the gentry who lived in four- and five-hearth houses in the towns, it is not unusual to find them in other documents engaged in trade as drapers, mercers and so on.[2] The flexibility of some family arrangements is revealed by Tib Hall in Hurley (Kingsbury), where Mr Thomas Musson and his mother were charged quite differently for its five hearths from one return to another.[3] On the other hand, Wooleston Adderley esquire, who paid for 15 hearths for his manor house in Weddington, was an absentee who lived with his friend Sir Robert Okeover in north Staffordshire.[4]

Peter Laslett, in his seminal volume, *The world we have lost*, asserted that 'the term gentleman marked the exact point at which the traditional system divided up the population into two extremely unequal sections', with some 5 per cent belonging to the ranks of all the gentry. Together they owned most of the nation's wealth, exercised virtually all the power and did not work with their hands on necessary, as opposed to leisurely, activities.[5] The attractive simplicity of this stereotype may match the static hierarchy that is apparent in single hearth tax returns, but not the reality that Styles uncovered and that has been confirmed here. And yet Laslett, in admitting that his 5 per cent was some three times greater than the proportion of families whom King recognized as gentlemen and that the other two thirds were the 'self-reputed or locally recognized gentlemen rather than those living on estates in land,' had himself begun to undermine the stereotype.[6] By the time that he revised his book for the third edition, Laslett had supervised Graham Kerby's outstanding doctoral thesis on inequality in pre-industrial Cheshire, accepted his overwhelming proof of widespread inconsistency in the application of status titles to the lesser gentry, and conceded 'that there must have been quite a considerable intermediate area of uncertain status between the élite and the mass'.[7] Kerby, however, argued that the only clear boundary between the élite and the others came after the knights and that

1 LRO, Probate Records: John Perkins 1691.

2 WCRO, CR1741/13/26.

3 Walker, *Hemlingford*, pp. 81, 85. However, most arrangements between two generations sharing the same house are probably not disclosed like this by the hearth tax returns. For example, the eminent naturalist Francis Willoughby esquire owned Middleton Hall and lived there in 1670 with his new wife and first-born son, while his widowed mother paid the hearth tax: Gribbin, *Science*, pp. 206–10.

4 Walker, *Hemlingford*, pp. 224–5.

5 Laslett, *World*, pp. 26–9.

6 Laslett, *World*, p. 43.

7 Laslett, *World*, 3rd *edn.*, p. 29.

below them the gentlemen did not constitute a social entity, but a continuum of contiguous gentries that resisted measuring and counting and merged imperceptibly with the yeomen below.[1] Because hearth numbers alone do not identify the gentry, a comparable picture has emerged from this exploration of part of the Warwickshire hearth tax. There, even the lesser esquires were not recorded consistently and all distinctions below them were overlaid from the 1670s by the ubiquitous use of 'Mr', giving in all a total of nearly 7 per cent of the families in two divisions with gentry titles. Furthermore, many on the fringe, the 'pseudo gentry', were labelled haphazardly as gentry in the different returns and even Styles, with his unrivalled knowledge of the lesser gentry and prosperous yeomen farmers in the south, could find no reason why some were regarded as gentlemen and others were not.[2]

Below the gentry

The social hierarchy beneath the gentry consisted of two virtually parallel strands. The thicker one contained the yeomen, husbandmen and labourers in descending order, although they were neither defined consistently nor separated by rigid boundaries. The other comprised the merchants, professionals, tradesmen and craftsmen who did not belong to homogeneous occupational groupings in any ordained sequence but enjoyed a social standing that could stem from their personal circumstances as much as from their occupations. This is often obscured by the fact that in formal legal documents men were required to be identified by their rank or occupation, which ignored dual occupations and conveys a false sense of a well-defined hierarchy.[3] Keith Wrightson was prompted by such confusing perceptions to explore the emerging use of more general phrases for dividing people into 'better', 'common' and occasionally 'middle' sorts.[4] He concluded that these precursors of the concept of class were still in their infancy in the later seventeenth century, when society exhibited coexisting elements of both hierarchy and class in different proportions in different places.[5]

One must therefore try to establish how applicable these views are to Warwickshire and whether the available evidence endorses Chris Husbands's conclusion that 'the hearth tax returns present a broad continuum, with the rich at the top of the scale, the poor at the bottom, and much overlap of groups in between'.[6] For this purpose the main focus will be on the variations in hearth numbers of those whose occupations can be identified in other sources, and especially from a very large, but unfinished, collection of index cards that Styles made for Kineton hundred and some Barlichway parishes. They include the hearth tax data for each householder and their

1 Kerby, *Inequality*, pp. 131, 253–4, 399, 451–6. It is interesting to note Kerby's praise for Styles as one of the few historians who had studied the use of gentry titles.
2 Styles, 'Kineton', p. 163.
3 Wrightson, 'Order', pp. 179–83.
4 Wrightson, 'Sorts', pp. 28–51.
5 Wrightson, 'Order', p. 198.
6 Husbands, 'Hearths', p. 75.

Table 15 Hearth numbers and occupations in Kineton and part of Barlichway hundreds

(a) Distribution by occupation and status of household heads

	mean	*h'hld*		*number of hearths per household*									
				Towns[a]					*Rural*				
	h'ths	*total*	*Mr*	*(1N*)1*	*(2N*)2*	*3*	*4*	*5+*	*(1N*)1*	*(2N*)2*	*3*	*4*	*5+*
Farming													
Yeoman	2.4	247		2	3	3	–	3	(3)50	89	61	33	3
Husbandman	1.6	473		10	1	3	–	–	(17)256	(2)136	53	9	5
Labourer	1.2	76		(4)5	2	–	–	–	(23)59	8	2	–	–
Shepherd/herdsman	1.2	16		(1)1	–	–	–	–	(3)12	(1)3	–	–	–
Sub-total		812		(5)18	6	6	–	3	(46)377	(3)236	116	42	8
Trades, crafts etc													
10+ households													
Innholder/-keeper	5.2	13		–	–	1	6	6					
Mercer/haberdasher[b]	4.0	28	14	(1)2	4	4	5	11	–	2	–	–	–
Medical[c]	3.3	14	3	(1)1	5	4	2	2					
Baker[h]	3.1	25	4	1	(1)6	7	4	4	1	2	–	–	–
Other dealers/retailers[d]	3.1	11	3	(1)2	1	3	4	1					
Maltster	2.2	28	3	7	(1)9	11	1	–					
Shoemaker/cordwainer	1.8	32		(6)14	(1)8	2	2	2	4	–	–	–	–
Victualler/aleseller	1.6	10		–	(2)2	–	–	–	(3)4	(2)4	–	–	–
Glover	1.5	15		(7)10	3	2	–	–					
Currier/skinner	1.5	11		(4)8	1	2	–	–					
Smith[h]	1.4	37		(2)7	5	2	1	–	(3)18	4	–	–	–
Tailor	1.4	23		(7)11	4	1	–	–	(2)5	1	1	–	–
Butcher	1.4	18		(4)7	6	–	–	–	3	2	–	–	–
Mason/tiler	1.4	16		(5)7	1	–	–	–	(1)4	3	1	–	–
Carpenter/joiner	1.2	21		(5)5	1	2	–	–	(5)13	–	–	–	–
Weaver	1.2	21		(2)5	(2)2	1	–	–	(3)12	1	–	–	–
5–9 households													
Dyer	3.0	5		–	1	2	–	–	–	–	1	1	–
Tanner	2.4	9	1	(1)1	1	3	–	1	1	2	–	–	–
Wheel/plough-wright	2.4	7		(1)1	1	–	–	1	1	2	–	1	–
Leather harness maker[e]	2.2	6		(1)2	(1)1	1	–	1	1	–	–	–	–
Carrier	2.0	7		(2)3	1	–	2	–	(1)1	–	–	–	–
Cooper	1.8	5		(1)2	–	1	–	–	1	–	1	–	–
Miller	1.7	6		1	–	1	–	–	(1)2	2	–	–	–
Clothworker etc[f]	1.0	5		(3)3	–	–	–	–	2	–	–	–	–
Sub-total		373	28	(54)100	(8)63	50	27	29	(19)73	(2)25	4	2	–
Miscellaneous[g]	2.2	31	2	(5)10	(1)3	4	7	1	(1)5	–	1	–	–
Totals		1216	30	(64)128	(9)72	60	34	33	(66)455	(5)261	121	44	8

N* = The figures in brackets record the non-chargeable whose total is also included in the column to their right.

a = Alcester, Henley in Arden, Stratford upon Avon, Warwick.

b = Mercer (14), haberdasher (5), chandler (5), draper (3), grocer (1).

c = Surgeon (6), barber (4), apothecary (3), physician (2).

d = Ironmonger (3), salter (3), fellmonger (2), bookseller (1), costermonger (1), woodmonger (1).

e = Collarmaker (3), whittawer (2), saddler (1).

f = Clothworker (3), fuller (1), furrier (1).

g = Farmer (4), gardener (2), glazier (2), roper (2), school teacher (2), bailiff, bellringer, cardboardmaker, charcoal burner, clockmaker, cook, fisherman, grazier, hayward, limner, locksmith, painter, pavier, plumber, scrivener, servant, tobacco pipemaker, turner, woodman (1 each).

h = All recorded ovens and forges are excluded from the hearth numbers.

Source: WCRO, CR1741/13/26

(b) Percentages of hearth numbers per household in composite occupational and status groups

				Hearths per household				
	mean h'ths	*h'hld total*	*(NC) %*	*1 %*	*2 %*	*3 %*	*4 %*	*5+ %*
Farming								
Yeomen	2.4	247	(1)	21	37	26	13	2
Husbandmen	1.6	473	(4)	56	29	12	2	1
Labourers etc	1.2	92	(35)	84	14	2	–	–
		812						
Trades & crafts								
Upper band	5.2–3.0	96	(4)	7	22	23	23	25
Middle band	2.4–1.7	100	(17)	42	27	20	6	5
Lower band	1.6–1.4	130	(32)	65	28	7	1	–
Bottom band	1.2–1.0	47	(43)	85	9	6	–	–
		373						
Miscellaneous	2.2	31	(23)	48	10	16	23	3

NC = Percentage of non-chargeable additional to the data in the other columns.

occupations or status when he could trace them.[1] These data are analysed in Table 15(a), which covers 327 householders in the towns of Warwick, Stratford, Alcester and Henley and 889 from the rural south and west of the county.[2] Altogether two thirds of this sample were occupied in farming and one third had a trade, craft or profession, with nearly three times as many of the latter living and working in towns than in the countryside.

The mean number of hearths per household for each occupational group provides a simple guide to their comparative hearth tax standing, but such bald figures on their own usually hide as much as they reveal. At first sight, the means for the yeomen (2.4), husbandmen (1.6) and labourers (1.2) in this sample appear to confirm the concept of a clear-cut hierarchy, but an analysis of the spread of their hearth numbers partly undermines this picture. Thus the data in table 15(b) show that 44 per cent of the husbandmen who occupied dwellings with two or more hearths had the same number or more hearths than 58 per cent of these yeomen. A smaller sample from Knowle constablery on the northern edge of the former Arden forest introduces further complexities.[3] The averages for the Knowle poll tax return of 1660 combined with its first two hearth tax assessments cover a wider spread, with 4.2 hearths for the yeomen, 1.8 for the husbandmen and 1.0 for the labourers. In addition, the occupational descriptions for many who contributed to the Free and Voluntary Gift in 1661 do not match their poll tax entries. Indeed, of the 16 yeomen who were listed in the poll tax, only five were recorded as such a year later, along with eight who were described as gentlemen, two as husbandmen and one as a gunsmith. This inconsistency partly reflects the changing perceptions of the creeping expansion of the gentry and of the erosion of yeoman status. However, since Styles discovered eight yeomen but no husbandmen in Avon Dassett and 14 husbandmen but no yeomen in Lower Shuckburgh, it is possible that the use of these ascriptions also varied from place to place.[4] In Knowle, the Free and Voluntary Gift also listed 18 more householders as husbandmen than the poll tax, including nine who had been described previously as craftsmen. Because many farms or holdings in this area were too small to support a family adequately, the husbandmen often worked part-time at a variety of crafts and so could be described as engaged in either.[5]

Those who were involved in the trades, crafts and professions are analysed in two groups here, with one having a minimum of ten male householders and the other between five and nine.[6] They have been created from Styles's cards and are presented

1 WCRO, CR1741/13/26.

2 Half of these rural householders come from just 14 parishes, led by Tanworth in Arden (95), Priors Marston (34) and Tysoe (30).

3 Downing, *Knowle*, pp. 379–93, contains a transcript of this document, which has since disappeared; Arkell, 'Poll taxes', pp. 150–2.

4 WCRO, CR1741/13/26.

5 Skipp, *Crisis*, p. 9.

6 These cut-off points are, of course, arbitrary, but those with ten or more hearths in particular do provide samples of a reasonable size for viable analysis.

in Table 15(b) according to the mean number of their hearths per household. For this purpose those with 10 or more households are divided into three large bands and one smaller one. Those in the uppermost of these bands had three or more hearths per head, with half occupying properties with four or more hearths and very few with only one. They ranged from the innkeepers (5.2), mercers and similar retailers (4.0) to medical men, bakers and a few dyers. Although one in four in this band were labelled 'Mr' at some time, they are included in this analysis because it covers everyone in each occupational category. The principal members of the middle band, with averages between those of the yeomen and husbandmen, were the maltsters (2.2) and shoemakers (1.8) with six much smaller groups comprising tanners and leather harness makers, wheelwrights and coopers, millers and carriers. The next band that fell just below the husbandmen, with means of mainly 1.6–1.4 hearths per head, was dominated by the smiths and tailors and included butchers, masons, glovers and curriers as well as victuallers. At the bottom of these groupings of craftsmen came the carpenters and weavers, with the same mean as the labourers of 1.2 hearths. Most of them lived and worked in the countryside like the smiths and victuallers. This pattern for south and west Warwickshire is broadly similar to that summarized by Michael Power for 1,300 men in 45 different occupations in London, where most of those engaged in selling and in the professions lived 'in the largest dwellings, craftsmen in much smaller homes, and semi-skilled workers in the smallest of all', with 'small' in London applying to households of three to five hearths.[1]

Unfortunately, analyses that concentrate on one mean for each group can never illuminate the whole complex picture. As Wrightson warned, 'tabulation can suggest a spurious rigour in social differentiation' because it ignores the 'very considerable degree of overlap between adjacent categories', and this is supported by a closer examination of the Warwickshire data for the various occupational groups, presented in Table 15(b).[2] Here, in the adjacent bands of those engaged in trades and crafts, only a minority differed from each other, since, when paired together, no more than two fifths to one fifth of the households in one band had a different number of hearths from the next. In addition, all four bands had very similar proportions (between 20 and 27 per cent) of households with two hearths. Among the individual occupations, the mean of 1.6 for the victuallers conceals the fact that two thirds were exempted from paying the hearth tax, unlike one third of the whole lower band. Clearly Husbands was right to conclude that 'knowledge of occupation is a poor predictor of hearth accountability in individual cases, and vice versa'.[3]

Evidence for dual occupations is usually elusive, but small gleanings can be extracted from two Warwickshire sources. In Knowle constablery, 11 householders with non-agricultural occupations – five weavers, an ironmonger, a victualler, an

1 Power, 'London', pp. 213–5.
2 Wrightson, 'Order', p. 188.
3 Husbands, 'Hearths', p. 73.

innholder, a carpenter, a tailor and a mason – were listed in the 1660 poll tax as owning small holdings or small farms worth between £1 and £11 a year, while one cooper held much more.[1] Nothing is known about how many other trades and craftsmen in Knowle cultivated rented land but the Chilvers Coton survey of 1684 does record both the freeholders' and tenants' land holdings, although in ways that prevent precise estimates of their size or acreage. From this it appears that about one third of the parish's 52 labourers and perhaps a quarter of its 72 other male householders with non-agricultural occupations rented enough land (a minimum of two or three acres) to boost their lifestyle significantly.[2] The latter group included at least one each of a collier, a mason, a nailer, a rakemaker, a tailor and a tanner, while among those with more than 12 acres or so were a miller, a silk-weaver, a skinner and a wheelwright as well as six or seven labourers. The probate inventories for one blacksmith and two carpenters, who died between 1684 and 1687, reveal how well off some craftsmen were when they also worked part-time as husbandmen.[3] These three examples also show how small the differences could be between those who had one or two hearths. At death, their movable possessions were valued at £60 to £88, with their animals, crops, cheese and farm equipment accounting for well over half these totals. However, the low valuations for their tools, with £6 for the blacksmith and just 10 shillings and £2 for the carpenters, are deceptive because they do not reveal the relative contributions from these occupations to their incomes. The younger carpenter (Richard Sutton), who died at the age of 59, lived in some comfort in a one-hearth house with five rooms, a buttery and a barn, with household goods valued at £22. Similarly, the blacksmith (Samuel Browne aged 39), who owned his own house and also had two tenants, had furniture and other household things worth £30 in the seven rooms and cellar in his house, which had a second hearth recorded in 1674. By contrast, the older carpenter (Daniel Ball aged 74), who rented a new two-hearth farmhouse with four rooms and a dairy, appears to have been less well off with household goods valued at only £6, probably a reflection of his age.

The circumstances of these three craftsmen have been described in some detail to provide some insight into the dual employment of some farming craftsmen and to show how, for those below the gentry, renting land could raise their social standing locally. The 12 jurors whom Newdigate appointed in 1681 to conduct the Chilvers Coton survey illustrate this further. These pillars of the community comprised two yeomen, six husbandmen, one of whom kept an inn, a miller, a fellmonger, a skinner and a labourer. Their apparent diversity hides their common attribute, which was a substantial holding of land. It was this, combined with their personal qualities, that made them their parish's 'chief inhabitants' below the gentry and hence perhaps the

[1] Downing, *Knowle*, pp. 379–93.
[2] WCRO, CR136/V12, V101, V109.
[3] LRO, Probate Records: Samuel Browne 1685, Daniel Ball 1686, Richard Sutton 1687.

core of an embryonic 'middle sort' that may have just begun to emerge at parochial level by then.[1]

The meaner sort

The concept of the meaner, common, vulgar or poorer sort sprang from varying attempts to differentiate the lower orders on cultural, behavioural or economic grounds from their superiors, who often perceived them as a potential threat.[2] Although these terms are too vague to be defined precisely or quantified, they do approximate more closely than is often realised to those who were excused from paying the hearth tax.

The falseness of the very widely-held belief that exemption from the hearth tax was granted simply on grounds of poverty has been explained above. It stems from a crucial misreading of the wording of the first of the two main clauses of 1662, which are summarized briefly here. By law, householders were exempted from the hearth tax either because they occupied a property that was already excused from paying the local levies to church and poor or because it was worth 20 shillings (£1) a year at most. Major complications arose from the overlap between these two clauses and from the qualifications that were added to them, which led to the first being commonly described as exempt 'by reason of poverty'. This misleading phrase was a shortened version of the explanation why some people, who did not pay their local rates or levies for such reasons as their landlords paid them, were not exempted from the hearth tax. And so the first clause spelled out that only those who were excused from paying the levies to the church and poor 'by reason of their poverty or the smallness of their estate' were exempted from the hearth tax and not because they were judged officially to be poor.

Further confusion over exactly who was excused in the early 1670s under the second receivers also arises from the government's attempt to jettison the first exemption clause in favour of the second one alone, which concentrated on the rental value of each property and made annual exemption certificates compulsory.[3]

An examination of Warwickshire's three overseers of the poor's levies and of two by the churchwardens that have survived intact show that the dividing line between the chargeable and non-chargeable came close to the one between those who did and did not pay their parochial levies by the pound rate, rather than by the yardland. In the three substantial parishes of Bishops Tachbrook, Ipsley and Nether Whitacre, with between 55 and 97 households each, the levies were based on pound rates.[4] Nevertheless, two or three non-chargeable householders in each parish paid small sums to their poor or church so that a slightly more generous threshold appears to

1 For a profound and illuminating discussion of the rural 'middle sort' within the ecclesiastical parish see French, *The middle sort*, especially pp. 17–29.

2 Wrightson, 'Sorts', pp. 33–5.

3 Arkell, 'Exemption', pp. 18–20.

4 WCRO, DR480/55 (Bishops Tachbrook Overseers' accounts); DRB27/5 (Nether Whitacre Churchwardens' accounts); CR1741/28 (Ipsley Overseers' accounts: transcript).

have been applied to exemption from the hearth tax than from the local rates. Conversely, in the smaller parish of Stockton with 42 households, where the churchwardens' levy was made by the yardland, seven who were chargeable for the hearth tax, along with all the 22 who were not, paid nothing towards the church.[1] The reason for this apparent mismatch is simple. No one with less than eight acres was charged for their parochial levy by Stockton's churchwardens who therefore seem to have used a notional pound rate to assess non-liability for the hearth tax. The 380 ratepayers recorded in Birmingham's overseers' accounts for 1664–5 also correspond reasonably closely to the 349 chargeable households in the 1665 hearth tax return, with 300 householders common to both.[2] The residual mismatch is explained partly by the omission of some 50 households from the list of the chargeable in 1665 and this comparison is further impaired by illegibility among some names of the non-chargeable. However, evidence that at least 11 ratepayers in Birmingham did not pay the hearth tax is found among those listed as chargeable, but who were described as 'poore', with no recorded hearths. Despite such minor inconsistencies, all five levies indicate a close correlation between those who were excused from paying both the hearth tax and their local rates for church or poor. Following the establishment of compulsory rates in most parishes, the distinction between those who did and did not pay them was seen increasingly as a natural division in society, unlike the 20 shilling rental threshold. As a result, a sense of group identity and consciousness of social superiority developed among the more substantial ratepayers, who increasingly came to perceive the non-ratepayers as an inferior group or 'meaner sort', even though this distinction was slightly blurred by the few who contributed small sums to the rates.[3]

An occupational analysis of the exempt should provide a better understanding of this group's composition than collective descriptions, such as the poor or landless cottagers. According to the sample in Table 16 of some 250 non-chargeable male householders from both north and south of the county, two fifths were engaged in farming as labourers or husbandmen and another two fifths worked in a range of crafts involving cloth, leather, wood or metal.[4] The main difference between the occupations of these non-chargeable and those who paid is the very small proportion of husbandmen (4 per cent) among the exempt, some of whom were probably too old or too unfit for work. The labourers, on the other hand, were divided equally between liable and non-liable, as were the glovers. About one third of those who worked in many other non-farming trades and crafts were exempt from the hearth tax, including the weavers, carpenters, tailors and, masons. The lower percentages recorded in Table 16 of those who were not chargeable among the smiths (15 per

1 WCRO, DR193 (Stockton Churchwardens' accounts).

2 BAHS, MS no. 334441 (Birmingham Overseers' account).

3 Arkell, 'King', p. 60.

4 Three fifths of the householders in this sample have been taken from Styles's work on Kineton and part of Barlichway hundreds used in Table 13 and the rest from Knowle and Chilvers Coton in Hemlingford hundred. The occupational data for Knowle comes from the 1660 poll tax, which excused and omitted all the paupers who received alms, and for Chilvers Coton from the manorial survey analysed in Arkell, 'Poverty', p. 37, table 7.

Table 16 Principal occupations of some non-chargeable male householders

Occupation	*NC n*	*all n*	*NC %*	*Occupation*	*NC n*	*all n*	*NC %*
Labourer	80	152	53	Shepherd	6	17	35
Husbandman	20	512	4	Smith	6	40	15
Weaver	15	40	38	Currier	4	11	36
Carpenter	11	30	37	Carrier	3	7	43
Shoemaker	10	39	26	Clothworker	3	5	60
Nailer	9	9	100	Sawyer	3	3	100
Tailor	9	27	33	Turner	3	5	60
Mason	8	21	38	Wheelwright	3	10	30
Butcher	7	21	33	Yeoman	3	264	1
Collier	7	9	78				
Glover	7	15	47	Others	21		
Victualler	7	10	70	Total	245		

Area covered: Kineton and part of Barlichway hundreds, as in Table 15(a), with Chilvers Coton parish and Knowle constablery.
Source: WCRO, CR1741/13/26; Arkell, 'Poverty', p. 37, Table 7.

cent) and shoemakers (26 per cent) show that most of them paid the tax, in contrast to the nailers and most colliers and victuallers who did not. Thus, except for the husbandmen and a few specific occupations, the main differences between these non-chargeable male householders and those who occupied one-hearth chargeable dwellings was one of degree and not one of kind.

Although this analysis of the exempt is more precise than conventional collective descriptions, it still suffers from an inability to take account of any secondary occupations or of the work of the women who headed a quarter of the non-chargeable households. (Women also, of course, contributed to the income of many other households which they did not head.) Nonetheless, detailed research does reveal that there were numerous overlapping sub-groups across the whole social spectrum, that simple hearth numbers alone can rarely be equated with different occupations or status, and that Warwickshire's society was far too complex to be divided into a few broad occupational or hearth tax blocks. This approach has modified considerably the conclusions of Gregory King as expressed in his well-known, but oversimplified, social Scheme for 1688. In it he not only underestimated the number of gentry and people engaged in trade and manufacture and distorted most occupational groupings, but also overestimated the size of the meaner sort who 'decreased the wealth of the kingdom'.[1]

1 These issues are discussed at length in Arkell, 'King'.

7. Wealth and poverty: the elusive issue

Wealth and poverty are very common concepts but when attempts are made to define and measure them, they can often become frustratingly elusive. For a start, poverty is not just the absence of wealth but also of income. This is well explained by Overton and colleagues, who describe wealth as 'anything that members of the household possess which can be sold for money or used to acquire other commodities: real property, durable goods, financial assets and human capital'. Thus, 'unlike income which is a flow', the concept of wealth is of a stock at one point in time and, when measured, must take into account debts and liabilities as well as the value of property and financial assets.[1] Because information about income in the seventeenth century is very scarce, historians have sought to identify the best substitute sources that indicate wealth, preferably with a broad coverage and of reasonable reliability. This is why, since the pioneering work of W.G. Hoskins, many have come to regard the number of hearths in a householder's premises as one of the best available surrogates for wealth.[2] This section therefore sets out to explore how far the numbers of fireplaces in some dwellings may indicate the wealth of their householders, by comparing them with several other relevant sources from different parts of Warwickshire. It will reveal the range of some forms of wealth among the different hearth tax bands for the chargeable, and the extent of poverty among the exempt, and also show that hearth numbers on their own are not a reliable guide to the economic standing of most householders.

Wealth

Land and buildings were the main form of tangible wealth in Restoration Warwickshire but what people owned or rented can only be traced in a few parishes and often without the knowledge of how much property they may have held elsewhere. Thus in Chilvers Coton parish, Sir Richard Newdigate owned half the land, as measured by its rental value, while Mr Wood and another absentee landlord shared another quarter: but the 1684 survey discloses nothing about their other substantial holdings, such as Newdigate's in at least four other Warwickshire parishes, and in Middlesex and several other counties.[3] The poll tax return for Knowle constablery is similarly unhelpful in this respect but it does show that the ownership of land there was distributed more evenly among its owner-occupiers; 43 per cent of the chargeable householders who were assessed for the poll tax owned some land, with the three wealthiest sharing 30 per cent of the total rental value between them.[4] The value and size of these holdings, of course, varied greatly, ranging from the top three, assessed at £123, £170 and £206 a year, to the nine at the bottom worth less than £5

1 Overton et al., *Households*, p. 138.
2 Hoskins, *Exeter*, pp. 111–12; Spufford, 'Potential', p. 205.
3 WCRO, CR136/ V12, V101, V109.
4 Downing, *Knowle*, pp. 379–93.

Table 17 Distribution of landowning in Knowle constablery from the 1660 poll tax

Chargeable hearths	*H'hld total*	*Annual value of land in pounds (£)*					
		1–4	*5–10*	*11–20*	*24–42*	*66–78*	*100–206*
1	12	5	4	2	1		
2	12	4	4	3	1		
3	7	–	1	4	2		
4	4	–	1	–	3		
5–6	8	–	1	1	2	2	2
7–8	5	–	–	–	–	4	1
10	2	–	–	–	–	1	1
	50						

Two exempt households with one hearth each and land worth £1 p.a. are also included.

Source: see p. 88, footnote 4.

a year. The correlation in Table 17 between the value of these landholdings and the number of hearths in their associated houses confirms that in Knowle constablery more hearths generally meant more land, although this pattern was uneven and far from uniform. Thus there was very little difference between those with one and two chargeable hearths, while most of those with three and four hearths had land worth between £11 and £42 a year, and only those with five or more hearths had land valued at over £50.

The pound rate measured a rather different form of wealth. Because it could be assessed on both landed and non-landed assets, Henry French has argued that there was a definite connection between these assessments and the perceived annual incomes of the chief inhabitants of most parishes.[1] However, the evidence in Warwickshire is much more equivocal because proof that the occupiers rather than the owners paid their rates is found in only a few parishes, such as Birmingham, Atherstone, Polesworth and Rugby, where personal estates were definitely included.[2] Unfortunately the analyses of those few levies which have survived are also problematic because their pound rates were calculated on unknown but clearly different bases and so cannot be compared directly. And yet, those for the three parishes in Table 18 still reveal an uneven progression of wealth with considerable overlapping, similar to the situation in Knowle. Thus there is little difference between the rating of those with two and three hearths in either Ipsley or Bishops Tachbrook, but a great difference between them and the few with three and four hearths, while in Nether Whitacre this pattern was reversed completely.[3]

1 French, *Middle sort*, pp. 89, 103–5, 111–2.

2 *Quarter Sessions*, iii, pp. 102, 208, 225; *Quarter Sessions*, v, pp. 122, 199.

3 WCRO, DR480/55 (Bishops Tachbrook Overseers' accounts); DRB27/5 (Nether Whitacre Churchwardens' accounts); CR1741/28 (Ipsley Overseers' accounts: transcript).

Table 18 Parochial levies in three Warwickshire parishes

		Rateable values in shillings & pence						
Chargeable hearths	*H'hld total*	*1d-6d*	*7d-1s*	*1s1d-1s6d*	*1s7d-2s*	*2s1d-5s*	*5s1d-10s*	*10s1d+*
Bishops Tachbrook								
1	22	8	4	3	3	4		
2	6	–	–	1	–	2	2	1
3	6	–	1	–	1	4		
4	2	–	–	–	–	–	1	1
7	1	–	–	–	–	–	1	
14	1	–	–	–	–	–	–	1
	38							
Ipsley								
1	14	6	4	4				
2	6	–	2	4				
3	8	1	1	4	2			
4	1	–	–	–	1			
5	1	–	–	–	1			
32	1	–	–	–	–	–	–	1
	31							
Nether Whitacre								
1	29	10	7	6	3	3		
2	9	3	2	1	–	3		
3	4	–	–	–	–	4		
4	3	–	–	–	1	1	1	
8	1	–	–	–	–	–	1	
22	1	–	–	–	–	–	–	1
	47							

These parishes were rated on different bases.
Three non-chargeable householders also paid rates in Bishops Tachbrook and Nether Whitacre and two in Ipsley.
Source: see p. 89, footnote 3.

The Birmingham overseers' receipts from their ratepayers for the year 1664–5 are related more closely to the hearth tax because they were based more on the value of each dwelling and less on land.[1] They also provide a more substantial sample, with 300 householders matched against the liable in the 1665 hearth tax. These overseers collected their levies weekly from each householder for the equivalent of 47 weeks to ensure that all expenses were covered. Thus everyone in Birmingham paid 3s. 11d.

[1] BAHS, MS no. 334441 (Birmingham Overseers' account).

(or nearly one fifth of a pound) for every penny for which they were rated, virtually the same as the annual charge for two hearths. The medians for the different groups in Table 19 (p. 92) rose from 1d. per week for the ratepayers with one chargeable hearth to 2d. for those with two hearths, but then remain constant at 3d. for those with three, four and five hearths before rising again to 5d. for those with six and seven hearths. However, a closer inspection of the data in Table 19 reveals that this progression is not as neat as at first appears. Among the 80 householders who were rated at 3d. or 4d. a week, some can be found in every hearth tax category from one to seven hearths. Similarly, the 205 who lived in dwellings with two to four hearths included some ratepayers in every band, paying from 1d. to 7d. or more a week. Meanwhile almost all of the much smaller group of 29 householders with five to seven hearths were rated at between 3d. and 6d. per week. Thus the medians on their own present an oversimplified picture. Here the very broad range for those with two to four hearths, for instance, provides a weak correlation in Birmingham between the value of people's homes and the number of their hearths. Exceptionally, among those listed with seven hearths in 1670, there was one widow who was reported as being 'miserably poore with nothing to be found but children and raggs'.

Probate inventories

The most widely-used source for estimating wealth in this period is probate inventories. At first sight they appear ideal for this purpose because they survive in relative profusion and normally list and value the movable possessions of all but the wealthiest and those with personal estates of little value. But they also contain traps for the unwary.[1] The appraisers who compiled these inventories were not always thorough nor competent at arithmetic nor were they consistent over the amount of detail that they recorded. They omitted all real estate, apart from chattel leases, and never indicated whether the deceased owned or rented his or her home. They listed haphazardly debts that were owed to the deceased but very rarely the money that was owed by them. In addition, the value of their goods relating to their work might vary considerably according to their occupations, as will be explained later.[2] Such inconsistencies pose a major challenge to historians over how to extract the best surrogates for wealth. Despite their well-known flaws and serious doubts over what they measured and how these movable goods should be best described, traditionally most scholars have based their calculations upon total inventory valuations (TIVs) that at first appear exact and attractively quantifiable.[3] During the last twenty years, others have developed more sophisticated approaches, with Weatherill and Wrightson, for example, concentrating on in-depth analyses of the deceased's household goods, and

1 Overton et al., *Households*, pp. 13–18; Spufford, 'Limitations', pp. 142–51.
2 Overton et al., *Households*, p. 139.
3 Arkell, 'Inventories', pp. 95–6.

Table 19 Overseers' levy in Birmingham in 1664–5

Chargeable hearths	*H'hld total*	*Rateable value per week in pence for 47 weeks*						
		1d	*1½d*	*2d*	*3d*	*4d*	*5–6d*	*7d+*
1	61	39	4	11	4	3	–	–
2	119	41	9	38	15	9	5	2
3	50	6	2	14	10	6	11	1
4	36	2	2	2	12	9	7	2
5	9	–	–	1	4	1	3	–
6	11	–	–	–	2	1	6	2
7	9	–	–	–	2	2	5	–
8+	5	–	–	–	–	–	1	4
Total	300	88	17	66	49	31	38	11

Source: see p. 90, footnote 1.

Overton extending them to include all consumption goods.[1] Overton's team also devised another category for its study of Cornwall and Kent, termed 'material wealth'. This included everything devoted to the production of goods for sale or exchange together with the consumption goods.[2] Both of these approaches are compared with the TIVs in the brief study of some Warwickshire inventories below. This shows that the values of the consumption goods correlate better than the others with their householders' hearth numbers. They also come much closer to reflecting each family's lifestyle or 'material culture' than their much more elusive wealth or income.[3]

The sample of 50 inventories, on which Table 20 is based, was only made possible by the very careful matching with the hearth tax returns that Nat Alcock undertook for his work for Table 25 below.[4] These inventories have been selected from 18 scattered rural parishes in north and east Warwickshire for the period from 1670 to 1674.[5] This balanced sample is far too small for definitive conclusions but it does illustrate many of the problems involved and the relative strengths and weaknesses of Overton's three approaches to analysing the contents of probate inventories. For example, two of the 50 include leases which account for 72 per cent of the total value (£166) of one and 15 per cent of the other (£103). Three others record the debts owed by the testator. These reduce their total values from £140 to £21, £108 to £48,

1 Weatherill, *Consumer*, pp. 25–42, 185–9, 212–4; Levine & Wrightson, *Whickham*, pp. 158–63; Overton et al., *Households*, pp. 139, 225, n. 6.

2 Overton et al., *Households*, p. 138.

3 Overton et al., *Households*, pp. 88, 150.

4 These have been selected from a total of some 680 inventories at the Lichfield Record Office that Nat Alcock identified as being suitable for this task.

5 These are the parishes followed by the number of inventories in brackets: Avon Dassett (1), Berkswell (6), Hampton in Arden (3), Harbury (2), Hillmorton (3), Kenilworth (3), Napton (3), Polesworth (3), Priors Hardwick (2), Priors Marston (1), Radford Semele (4), Rugby (2), Shustoke (3), Solihull (5), Stoneleigh (2), Sutton Coldfield (3), Withybrook (3) and Wolfhampcote (1).

and £8 to £6, to leave them with a net wealth that is 85, 55 and 25 per cent lower than their apparent probate wealth. Nineteen listed varying sums that were owed to the deceased from £1 to £175, with the latter including £38 of debts that were described as desperate. Altogether these credits accounted for more than half the personal estate of five inventories and over a quarter for another six, but we cannot tell how many more of these deceased may have been owed money that was not recorded or who may have been debtors themselves. Spufford's study of the debts that were owed by some deceased in Lincolnshire reinforces this conclusion; she asserted that their TIVs 'must be disbelieved as guides to wealth' since 'not only is the sum at the foot of the inventory no guide to the individual's net wealth, but it is no guide at all even to his financial standing within the same occupational or social group'.[1]

This explains why the Overton team regarded all comparisons between the TIVs as invalid and insisted that all debts and leases be excluded 'to ensure consistency in the measurement of wealth between individuals'.[2] Thus the aggregate of all movable goods devoted to both production and consumption became their strongly preferred comparative option, even though their value could vary considerably according to their householders' occupations.[3] As Overton explained:

> the inventory of a farmer includes much of his working capital (livestock and farm implements) and if the inventory were made in the summer, the revenue from his crops for an entire year. On the other hand, the inventory of a clothier will contain some stocks but is unlikely to include a year's worth of working capital. Thus in terms of movable goods, the farmer might appear wealthier than the clothier, whereas in terms of income flows the reverse may well be the case.[4]

Other occupations that were even more undervalued by the inventory data included tailors who 'needed only a pair of shears or scissors, a smoothing iron, cloth, needle and thread'.[5] A comparison between the farm and trade stocks of the 14 craftsmen and tradesmen included in the Warwickshire sample of 50 inventories partly demonstrates this imbalance. None of the four tailors had trade goods of any worth at all, nor did the barber, while for the butcher, carpenter and shoemaker they were valued at only one or two pounds each. Above them came three smiths with trade goods valued at about £7 per head, followed by the wheelwright's at £14, a hatter's at £21 and finally a woolcomber's at £33. Altogether their farm stocks were worth four times more than their trade goods and only the woolcomber had farm stock (£9) that was worth much less than his trade goods.

1 Spufford, 'Limitations', pp. 173–4.
2 Overton et al., *Households*, p. 138.
3 Overton et al., *Households*, p. 139.
4 Overton et al., *Households*, p. 88.
5 Overton et al., *Households*, p. 35.

This is the context that led French to reject as too unreliable the comparative valuations of each household's material wealth and to favour instead the value of their household goods alone.[1] In his words, 'this latter figure provides a uniform basis on which to compare inventories, unlike total valuation figures, which could vary dramatically according to how much of the testator's trade stock fell within appraisers' remit'.[2] He also argued that this category equates closely to the Overton definition of consumption goods because it was 'very difficult to differentiate between production for use and production for exchange in many probate inventories'.[3] The main difference concerned such items as bacon, cheese and wool, with Overton and his colleagues estimating the quantities that each household was likely to use for their own consumption and those that were for sale or exchange. The analysis of the 50–inventory sample has also tried to follow the Overton approach, but as always some valuations are more approximate than others because of the vagaries with which the goods were described, grouped and valued by the appraisers, while the deceased's clothes and ready money were normally valued together.[4] Finally, it should be stressed that there was very little connection between what a household spent on consumption and the value of their consumption or household goods. For most of them, their greatest expenditure was on food, but their inventories never reflect this.[5]

Matching inventories to hearth tax entries is never an exact science, especially when some names are corrupted, the widows lack forenames or more than one entry has the same name. Nonetheless, there is virtually no time lag here between the two sources, often a problem that mars similar exercises. In Table 20(a) the means and medians of the three different approaches to analysing the valuations within the inventories are compared for five separate hearth tax categories, from the non-chargeable with one hearth to the chargeable with five.[6] A much larger sample would be needed to produce anything approaching a firm conclusion but this probe does suggest that the best correlation is the one between the hearth numbers and the value of their occupants' consumption goods. Only the median and mean values for the consumption goods have well-spaced progressions, from £7 or £8 for the non-chargeable households to £42 or £82 for those with five hearths. But still Table 20(b) shows up the limitations of this approach because there was considerable overlapping within these apparently neat gradations for the consumption goods. All these hearth-tax groups had at least one household with goods worth between £10 and £20, while among the 15 with two hearths, two were valued at under £10 and another two at

1 French, *Middle sort*, p. 146, n. 20.

2 French, *Middle sort*, p. 158.

3 French, *Middle sort*, p. 158, n. 51.

4 See Arkell, 'Inventories', pp. 92–3, for a brief discussion of this topic. In east Devon, for example, the average value of inventoried clothing was £3 at this time, but in nine inventories, which listed wearing apparel separately in this sample, it averaged £2 a head.

5 Overton et al., *Households*, p. 87.

6 Those with more hearths have been ignored because there are relatively few inventories for them at Lichfield.

Table 20 Analysis of 50 sample Warwickshire inventories, 1670–4

(a) Mean and median values for Overton's three different movable wealth categories

Hearths	*Invs.*	*Mean values*			*Median values*		
		TIV	*MW*	*CG*	*TIV*	*MW*	*CG*
		£	£	£	£	£	£
1 NC	4	30	20	8	29	18	7
1 Ch	17	76	52	15	61	50	17
2	15	135	97	27	80	78	24
3–4	9	136	117	45	130	89	34
5	5	140	129	82	101	91	42

TIV = total inventory valuations
MW = material wealth
CG = consumption goods

(b) Value of Consumption Goods

Value £	*Invs.*	*Hearth tax categories* *1NC*	*1Ch*	*2*	*3–4*	*5*
0–9	12	3	7	2	–	–
10–9	11	1	4	4	1	1
20–9	13	–	5	6	2	–
30–9	6	–	1	–	4	1
40–9	4	–	–	1	1	2
50–99	2	–	–	2	–	–
100+	2	–	–	–	1	1
	50	4	17	15	9	5

Source: see p. 92, footnotes 4 and 5.

over £60. This should come as no surprise since people who live in similar sized houses often have different lifestyles, but Nat Alcock has also demonstrated in Table 25(b) below just how much the number of rooms (and so house size) varied between houses with the same number of hearths.

An examination of the hearth numbers and status or occupations of several selected individuals, together with their consumption or household goods, will therefore show that the latter usually provide the best evidence for their lifestyles or standards of living. The spread of the testators in the 50 inventory sample ranged from four in the higher reaches of the non-chargeable to two from the lower ranks of the gentry, who inhabited houses with five and three hearths and had consumption goods valued at £274 and £154 respectively. These stood out way above all the others. Indeed William Tylman of Rugby's wine and beer cellar and his silver goods, which were together valued at £80, were worth more than the consumption goods of all the other 48 householders.[1] However, knowledge of both the hearth numbers and status or occupations of those below the gentry is an inadequate guide in this sample to the value of their goods. For instance, even though two of the 16 described as yeomen had five hearths and two more had four, the three yeomen with the most valuable consumption goods (worth £76–£47) lived in houses with just two recorded hearths. (And indeed, when the man with £47 worth of goods died, he had the largest TIV of all in this sample.[2]) The nine who were recorded as husbandmen included two exempt but it was the occupant of a two-hearth chargeable house who had the lowest consumption goods (£7) and another with one hearth the highest (£24). Similar anomalies occur among the six widows, especially Mrs Christian Cookes, who had five hearths in Harbury and household goods that were valued at just £15, while a comparison between her will and inventory confirms that the latter did not exclude her more valuable bequests.[3]

Without a detailed study of several hundred more inventories one cannot determine how representative are the different proportions in Table 20(b) and how comparable were the household contents of broadly similar value, as Wrightson discovered in Whickham on the Durham coalfield.[4] But a very brief taster is provided by a small group of five inventories summarized in Table 21, with consumption goods worth between £14 and £17. Their beds and bedding accounted for approximately two fifths of their value, their other furniture and furnishings for about one fifth and their utensils used for cooking and preparing food and drink for another fifth. The remaining fifth was split almost equally between eating utensils and consumption materials such as cheese, bacon and flax. Only the one exempt household in this group had no feather mattress, but more surprisingly Mrs Cookes alone lacked pewter platters and dishes and was also the sole owner of iron rather than brass pots for cooking. All five had two or three chairs and a few cushions, but very different quantities of sheets and napkins. This glance into the lifestyles and relative comfort of five households with consumption goods worth about £15 gives a tantalising hint of what a much more extended study could achieve.

No analysis of these consumption goods, however thorough, nor any concentration on just one aspect of these inventories, will ever provide a rounded picture of any individual's financial standing. Wealth is such a multi-faceted concept that to comprehend it fully one must explore as many aspects as possible. In Table 21 the TIVs of the five with consumption goods worth about £15 ranged from £35 to £130, with

1 LRO, Probate Records: William Tylman 1670.

2 LRO, Probate Records: Leonard Bird 1674 (Solihull). His TIV was £539.

3 LRO, Probate Records: Christian Cookes 1673/4.

4 Levine & Wrightson, *Whickham*, pp. 231–9; Arkell, 'Inventories', pp. 89–91. For this exercise, it appears as if an analysis of the household contents rather than of the consumption goods may be more suitable. It led Wrightson to divide Whickham's inventories into three broad categories according to the value of their domestic goods, with the dividing lines set approximately at £5 and £15. In west Cornwall the more appropriate cut-off points were about £10 and £20.

Table 21 Diversity in nine sample probate inventories, 1670–4

Name	*Occup., etc*	*Hearths* *n*	*TIV* £	*Cons. goods* £	*Farm+ trade** £	*Money+ clothes* £	*Credit* £	*Debts* £
Mrs Cookes	widow	5	35	15	13	7		
G. Stoneley	husbandman	1NC	52	14	23	2	13	
T. Hickson	woolcomber	1	61	17	*42	2		
J. Mann	carpenter	1	107	17	*89	1		
I. Mason	wheelwright	3	130	16	*72	7	35	
R. Erpe	hatter	3	130	28	*74	28		
J. Weston	yeoman	5	130	42	78	10		
W. Garrett	husbandman	1	134	24	108	2		
W. Harrison	smith	1	140	26	*25	9	80	(119)

* Indicates that trade goods are included; cons = consumption.

Source: LRO, Probate Records: Christian Cookes 1673/4 (*Harbury*); Rowland Erpe 1672 (*Shustoke*); William Garrett 1670 (*Napton*); William Harrison 1673 (*Solihull*); Thomas Hickson 1674 (*Napton*); John Mann 1673 (*Stoneleigh*); Isaac Mason 1670 (*Hampton in Arden*); Gabriel Stoneley 1674 (*Radford Semele*); John Weston 1672 (*Polesworth*).

the differences in the value of their farm and trade stock (of £13 to £89) being responsible for most of this along with the credits that were owed to two of them. For those with very similar TIVs of £130 to £140, the consumption goods of two (valued at £16 and £42) were very different from the other three with £24–£28. Overton's category of material wealth is met by adding to these totals the value of their farm and trade stocks. Here, those for Harrison and Garratt (at £25 and £108) differed greatly from the rest, while Erpe had at least £25 of ready money in his house when he died. In addition, credit accounted for over half the value of Harrison's inventory, if one ignores his debts, while the TIVs for both Garratt and Mason were somewhat exaggerated because they were made in July when their crops and hay (assessed at £47 and £30 respectively) were at their most valuable. Such analyses will always take one much closer to the reality of each household's economic circumstances than any simple TIV can ever achieve.

Poverty

Before the concept of a poverty line was developed in the later nineteenth century, it is almost impossible to establish the extent and degree of poverty. References to the 'poor' in Restoration Warwickshire normally denote the 'labouring poor' or lower orders and so were less precise than we would expect now. Further confusion also stems from contemporary use of the word 'pauper', which only began to mean those who received poor relief in the later eighteenth century. In the Stuart period it was applied to those who did not pay their poor rates, for example, or whose goods were

Table 22 Adult poor relief and the hearth tax exempt in 14 parishes

Parish	*OPA* Date	*Hearth tax 1670* H'hold total	Exempt total	*Adult paupers* Regular	Occasional	Doles	*OPA exp.* total
(a)							
Farnborough	1670	43	18	5(2)	2(2)	–	£10
Astley	1670	49	7	2	4(2)	–	£11
Ipsley	1670	55	23	9(1)	2(1)	–	£21
Bishops Tachbrook	1670	64	18	3(1)	3(2)	–	£8
Harbury	1671	118	28	7(3)	2(1)	–	£20
Fillongley	1671	136	40	2	13(3)	–	£15
Kenilworth: Augmentation	1670	140	64	5(1)	10(4)	13	£54
Southam	1674/73	140	57	8(3)	–	23(6)	£25
Napton	1670	158	48	12(7)	6(4)	–	£27
Bidford on Avon	1670	190	128	c 9(1)	16(9)	–	£36
Solihull	1670	319	143	32(9)	11(6)	–	£47
		1412	574	94(28)	69(34)	36(6)	
(b)							
Walsgrave on Sowe: War	1669	38	12	5	8	12	£19
Chilvers Coton	1689	188	93	10	4	–	£44
Birmingham	1664	780	365	70	18	–	£222
		1071	510	85	30	12	

OPA = overseers of the poor's accounts; exp. = expenditure.
Figures in brackets record those who were not traced among the exempt from the hearth tax and are included in the adjacent total.
Source: see p. 99, footnote 1.

worth less than £5 for probate purposes.[1] Thus contemporary descriptions of the hearth tax exempt as 'poor' or even 'paupers' mean no more than that they were excused from paying their parish rates, or the hearth tax. In order to discover anything about actual poverty in Warwickshire at the time of the hearth tax, we need to turn to the surviving accounts of the overseers of the poor and other related documents. These will reveal the existence of four different levels among the hearth tax exempt, with two that received poor relief and two that did not.

The 14 overseers' accounts that are analysed in Table 22 are divided between 11, which can be compared directly with their hearth tax returns for 1670, and three

[1] Styles, 'Census', p. 99; private communication from Anne Tarver referring to the 1768 edition of Blackstone's *Commentaries on the laws of England*.

which cannot.[1] All covered the year from Easter to Easter, but without a common pattern over how they were compiled and what they recorded. Most provide the names of those who received collection or regular pensions together with the sum per week or month, the length of time for which it was paid and any special circumstances, such as fostering someone else's child – except in Bidford where only the annual totals for each pauper (in the modern sense) were listed. Altogether these 14 parishes had a total of nearly 2,500 householders, among whom 179 adults received weekly collection. They represented some 7 per cent of all the households or about 16 per cent of the non-chargeable. These proportions, however, should probably be reduced by a percentage point or two to allow for those pensioners who did not head a household, but lodged, for example, in other people's houses. The extent to which this might affect these calculations is demonstrated by the figures in brackets in the first part of Table 22, which show that nearly three in 10 pensioners were not traceable among the relevant exempt. No doubt some were omitted from the hearth tax or recorded under a different name, so that the exact proportion of householders who received regular relief cannot be established. Nonetheless, it is clear that they accounted for less than 5 per cent of all the households in 10 of these 14 parishes and a somewhat higher proportion only in Birmingham, Solihull, Ipsley and Farnborough. Women received 60 per cent of all these pensions, which were intended to support a very basic standard of living and so varied in value according to individual circumstances. The payments ranged from 3d. a week to 24d. (or two shillings), with two thirds concentrated between 6d. and 12d. Some parishes also appear to have been more generous than others. In Birmingham, for example, one third of the weekly pensions were worth more than 12d., while none were so large in Solihull or Napton.

Before examining those who received occasional relief, a rare but crucial misunderstanding by Styles needs to be corrected. The hearth tax lists from 1670 to 1673 contain many entries for groups of unnamed people who were claimed to be receiving weekly collection etc, which Styles assumed should be taken at face value. Most occurred in Hemlingford hundred, where they accounted for 56.3 per cent of its exemptions in 1670, and as many as 81.5 per cent in Tamworth division in 1671 and 59 per cent in Atherstone division in 1673. These figures led Styles to conclude that 'they formed a high proportion of the certified' throughout the county.[2] In order to bolster this conclusion Styles then misleadingly asserted that the hearth tax was a more reliable source than the accounts of the overseers of the poor for recording those who were given weekly collection. A generation later Beier followed Styles in

1 Overseers of the poor's accounts: WCRO, DR19/251–5 (Astley), HR71/11 (Bidford on Avon), DR408/55 (Bishops Tachbrook), CR136/B5243–4 (Chilvers Coton), DR30B/2 (Farnborough), DR404/87 (Fillongley), CR607/2 (Harbury), CR1741/28 (Ipsley: transcript), DR296/43 (Kenilworth Augmentation manor), NI/15–16 (Napton), DRB64/63 (Solihull), DR583/41 (Southam), DRO104/63 (Walsgrave on Sowe); BAHS, MS no. 334441 (Birmingham).

2 Styles, 'Hearth tax', pp. lxxvii–lxxviii, lxxxiv. Styles's misunderstanding of exemption from the hearth tax has misled other historians. His belief that possessions worth less than £10 was another criterion and not a limitation imposed on the occupants of dwellings worth £1 a year was repeated wrongly in Arkell, 'Poverty', p. 33, for example.

maintaining that those who received weekly collection formed between 56.3 and 81.5 per cent of the Hemlingford exemptions.[1]

Proof of the inaccuracy of these figures can be found in the hearth tax returns for four parishes in Table 22. In the hamlet of Marlcliff in Bidford, 11 not chargeable were named in 1670, of whom none received regular pensions and only one occasional relief. Three years later, however, all were recorded anonymously as living in cottages that received collection. The situation in Fillongley was similar. There, the return for 1673 stated that 18 'receive weekly collection and live in town houses and upon the common', followed by a list of 20 names. But only two of them appeared in the overseers' account for 1674 with regular pensions. The hearth tax returns for Chilvers Coton claim that 35 received weekly collection in 1670 and 66 in 1673, which is a huge mismatch with the, albeit much later, surviving overseers' account for 1689 when the parish had only ten adult pensioners. These samples may be insufficient to support definitive conclusions but the collectioners in the last two parishes, which were in Atherstone division, accounted for well under 15 per cent of their exempt, not the 59 per cent which Styles deduced from the hearth tax returns. Birmingham was another Hemlingford parish. In its hearth tax return for 1670 only 77 non-chargeable householders were named, but another 200 were claimed to be living 'in town houses that receive collection', while 88 more were omitted entirely, even though they are listed in a contemporary exemption certificate. This claim that 200 households received regular collection is undermined by Birmingham's only surviving overseers' account from six years earlier, which listed only 70 adult pensioners, or not more than 16 or 17 per cent of its non-chargeable householders if we allow for some who were not householders. The ratepayers of Birmingham already contributed almost twice as much towards their poor as they paid in hearth tax, but their poor law burden would have been more than five times greater than the hearth tax had they really supported 200 pensioners (or 55 per cent of their exempt). The main reason why these fictional figures appear in the hearth tax is the very tight schedule imposed upon the receivers for submitting each return, with the threat of financial penalties. This was compounded in Hemlingford hundred by Hargrave's greater commitment, compared with the other collectors, to using recent exemption certificates to identify his non-chargeable households.[2] Thus, when he had no up-to-date certificate for all or part of a parish, he seems to have covered his back by inventing swathes of nameless pensioners. Apparently this satisfied the Exchequer but set a trap later for both Styles and Beier.[3]

Evidence concerning those who were given occasional relief by their parish was recorded much more haphazardly than those on regular relief. Thus the figures in Table 22 are minima, but it does seem that in many places about a half of the

[1] Beier, 'Poverty', p. 239.
[2] Styles, 'Hearth tax', p. lxxxii.
[3] Meekings, *Accounts*, pp. 83–6.

non-chargeable householders received some charitable relief. One-off payments for adults were awarded for a variety of reasons. These included people falling ill, or the cost of their funerals, or to provide them with bread, fuel, clothing, shoes or their house rents, or occasionally to support deserted wives. In addition, small doles were often disbursed annually. We have proof of this in three parishes, but they must also have occurred elsewhere. Thus 14 shillings, collected as fines for non-attendance at church in Southam in 1673, were then distributed by the overseers as bread or money to 26 people. Three of them were pensioners and another six were not recorded in the hearth tax, but the remaining 17 were non-liable householders who were thus (in the modern sense) occasional paupers.[1] Similarly, in Walsgrave on Sowe, where five adults received pensions and eight had occasional relief in 1669, there were 12 more occasional paupers among the 23 who shared £1 8s. 0d. from the 'interest money for use of the poor'; but because most of this parish lay in the county of Coventry, we cannot discover how many were householders.[2] In the Augmentation part of Kenilworth parish, 15 of its 64 non-chargeable householders in 1670 received weekly or occasional relief or lived in the town houses that were noted in the 1673 hearth tax list. In addition, another 13 occasional paupers can be detected there among those who were listed by the churchwardens as receiving about 6d. each from the annual rent for Mr Denton's house.[3] Thus nearly half the non-chargeable householders in these three parishes received some kind of relief. Similar proportions are likely to have occurred elsewhere, especially since many doles were distributed privately or through the church and so escaped the attention of the overseers, who never noted the allocation of benefits in kind.[4] Exceptionally, in the mid 1660s the overseers in Ipsley recorded that Lady Huband supplied £10 a year to pay for the house rents of 14 named persons, nine of whom were pensioners but the other five additional paupers.[5] This raised the proportion of all paupers there to 25 per cent of all households and more than half of the exempt.

If these suppositions are sound, then the non-liable for the hearth tax were divided into two approximate halves – the pauper and non-pauper exempt – both of whom can be subdivided further into two quite unequal parts. At the top of the non-pauper exempt was a small group of householders on the cusp of being chargeable, who never made up more than a few per cent of all households. Three levies from very different parts of the county reveal that they were excused from paying the hearth tax, but not their local rates, implying that this was probably not unusual. The other non-pauper exempt included many who might well seek help from their overseers at a later stage in their lives but for the moment at least were not regarded as eligible for assistance. Most of the pauper exempt were relieved very infrequently, receiving in

1 WCRO, DR583/20 (Southam Churchwardens' accounts).
2 WCRO, DRO104/63 (Walsgrave on Sowe Overseers' accounts).
3 WCRO, DR296/6 (Kenilworth Churchwardens' accounts).
4 Hindle, *Parish*, pp. 96–9.
5 WCRO, CR1741/28 (Ipsley Overseers' accounts: transcript).

general less than one shilling a year and only very occasionally more than a pound. Below them came the collectioners with regular pensions mostly in the range of 6d. to 12d. per week. In 10 of the 14 sample parishes they occupied fewer than 5 per cent of all households, but with a somewhat higher proportion in the other four.

Attempts to determine the living standards or extent of poverty of those within each of these layers of exempt are hampered by ignorance, especially of their incomes and diet. However, many pensioners almost certainly survived on the edge of destitution. Those paupers who received occasional relief were at the mercy of differing perceptions of need by particular ministers, vestries and officials and of the varying levels of parochial charity and endowments available to them.[1] Most will therefore have resorted to a raft of strategies to 'make shift' to survive. It is impossible to tell if their living standards differed significantly from those of the non-pauper exempt who struggled to make ends meet on irregular and inadequate wages, unlike those who enjoyed more regular employment and pay. Victor Skipp was certainly right to describe the vast majority of the exempt as landless cottagers, so long as 'landless' can be interpreted as including small gardens, which could be used to raise their living standards.[2] The manorial survey of Chilvers Coton shows that the rents of most houses without any land were well below one pound a year, while those that came close to this figure could have up to an acre or so of ground attached to them.[3] The sample study of some probate inventories shows that some non-chargeable householders possessed movable goods worth well over ten pounds when they died, confirming the impression that a few exempt householders were markedly better off than most of the others. But whether this indicates a significantly higher standard of living or just greater security is far from clear. By modern standards all of these 'poorer sort' were desperately poor, but for contemporaries the distinction between those who did or did not receive poor relief was at least as significant as that between those who did or did not pay their local taxes or the hearth tax.[4]

Wealth and poverty, then, are complex, multi-faceted concepts that cannot be adequately portrayed or measured by one single factor. Most hierarchies of wealth are at their simplest and most straightforward at each end of the spectrum, when the same people are normally identified by different criteria as being either the richest or the poorest, but towards the middle it becomes increasingly confused. There the apparent differences between each household or individual are often very small and the criteria normally overlap. This accounts in part for most of the inconsistencies that have been observed between many households with from one to six chargeable hearths. It also helps to explain why the numbers of exempt from the hearth tax on their own are such superficial indicators of poverty and the poor.

1 Hindle, *Parish*, pp. 15–26.
2 Skipp, *Crisis*, p. 78.
3 Arkell, 'Poverty', pp. 33–6.
4 For example, the only adults exempted from the three poll taxes of Charles II's reign were those who received alms.

8. Summary

Single hearth tax lists invariably project a deceptive impression of certainty. This has been confirmed here by studying Warwickshire's unique sequence of hearth tax returns together with their exemption certificates and other contemporary sources.[1] They provide a major new perspective, with many fresh insights into the composition and contents of the county's return for 1670, and a novel sense of flexibility that has also exposed numerous errors, omissions and inconsistencies. Nearly 400 non-chargeable households that were omitted in 1670 have been detected as well as some 300 forges and at least 40 bakers' ovens. In addition, at least three households in every 100 seem to have escaped from paying for all their hearths and about four householders in every 100 were given wrong names.[2] Two other misleading impressions conveyed by single hearth tax lists are the existence of a finite stock of housing in each parish and a settled number of exempt householders. In fact, the number of households and of the exempt that were recorded in many parishes often fluctuated considerably between one return and another, with some being reported falsely as receiving poor relief. Empty dwellings were noted even more haphazardly, while timber-framed houses that were left unoccupied for any length of time could soon become semi-ruinous and their existence ignored, as the Chilvers Coton survey showed.

In order to carry out these comparisons with confidence, the various places that were assessed separately for the hearth tax were grouped into some 215 areas that operated in the 1670s as full scale parishes, together with about 10 detached portions.[3] This task was far from straightforward but it has ensured that all the hearth tax data presented in Tables 8, 9, 28 and 29 relate to effective contemporary parochial organisations.[4] Direct comparisons between the individual parishes reveal huge contrasts among some in the proportions of their main hearth tax groups and, among others, in the proportions of their households headed by women or by those who were recorded as gentry. Crucial though this approach is for a better understanding of each parish, it does not detect regional differences. These were established by studying the twelve towns separately from the countryside as well as each individual parish. By this means, thirteen different rural sub-regions were identified in Warwickshire and further insight gained by comparing them with their adjacent towns. This new approach to using the hearth tax returns to establish the county's

[1] The potential of the exemption certificates to supplement some omissions from the hearth tax returns has been well demonstrated by Duncan Harrington in Parkinson, *Durham*, pp. 216–65.

[2] This uncertainty arises from the fact that normally evasion and wrong names can only be detected by discovering inconsistencies between the 1670 return and its contiguous ones. But even when they matched, they may still have been wrong. This seems to have happened, for example, at Middleton Hall, where 26 hearths were recorded consistently from 1664 to 1674 compared with 29 in both 1663 and the late 1670s. See Walker, *Hemlingford*, p. 60.

[3] With the exception of the city of Coventry, where it has not been possible to match the hearth tax return to the boundary between the parishes of St Michael and Holy Trinity.

[4] Nat Alcock, who has had sole responsibility for mapping the hearth tax statistics (Maps 4–13), has followed an alternative policy by separately mapping, where feasible, the subdivisions of parishes given in the hearth tax returns, using later civil parish and other boundaries. See section 10 below.

topographical diversity relies heavily upon the quality of the available data. In Warwickshire this is especially good in the towns, unlike many other counties, where the urban assessments are usually the least reliable.

Further invaluable cumulative insights into the social structure of the later seventeenth century emerge when these exceptional hearth tax returns and exemption certificates are studied along with samples from other contemporary sources such as probate inventories, assessments for parish rates and the 1660 poll tax. These demonstrate that, although each householder's hearth numbers may indicate very approximately their occupation, social standing or economic circumstances, hearth numbers on their own can never do so with any precision. Differences of one or even two hearths between individual householders are rarely of great consequence. Instead, society in Warwickshire emerges as being less rigidly stratified than traditional notions of the hierarchy at this time assume, with many overlapping sub-groups across the social spectrum, which are sometimes gathered together loosely into 'sorts'. This is supported variously by, for example, the haphazard recording of many esquires, the imperceptible merging of the gentry into the yeomanry, and yeomen into husbandmen, the many husbandmen who can be traced with dual occupations, and the overriding importance of holding or renting different amounts of land. The discovery of at least four different levels of non-chargeable householders at the base of society undermines any concept that the exempt formed a homogeneous block of poor families.[1]

This survey of the Warwickshire hearth tax ends with two glimpses of John Newsham at work and a brief reflection on two imponderable questions. In the first, while checking some printed exemption certificates in 1670, he encounters one for Oxhill, which he knows well, signed by the rector. It contains 16 names. At first Newsham crosses out four of them and then insists that another four were also liable; indeed, three pay rents of 40 shillings a year and one was entered under the wrong name.[2] Subsequently ten were approved as exempt in Oxhill for the next assessment, but only six for the last two. *So how many households were really non-chargeable or poor in this parish in 1670?* On the second occasion Newsham visited Billesley manor in 1674 to receive the hearth money due for two collections from Sir Charles Lee. But Sir Charles was not at home so one of his servants handed over 48 shillings, which Newsham accepted knowing that the house had been assessed previously for 25 hearths. He then noted in his return that he had paid the missing two shillings himself.[3] *So did Billesley manor definitely have no more than 25 hearths?* While both incidents may remind us that elements of uncertainty lurk within the apparent precision of all hearth tax lists, they also bear witness to the huge amount of careful work and even heartache that lay behind their compilation.

[1] This study has not examined the exempt households with two hearths separately from those with one, as in Whickham, for example: Levine & Wrightson, *Whickham*, p. 162.

[2] TNA, E179/347; Styles, 'Hearth tax', p. lxxx.

[3] WCRO, QS11/54, f. 7.

Introduction: Part 2

by Nat Alcock

9. Houses and the hearth tax

The theme of this section is the relationship between the numbers of hearths listed in the hearth tax returns and the houses in which they were found. Occasionally it is possible to examine this directly, when surviving houses can be identified with their entries in the tax list, and individual examples are described in the final part of the section. Other evidence is drawn from the linking of hearths to a large sample of probate inventories from the archdeaconry of Coventry (diocese of Lichfield and Coventry), covering north and east Warwickshire.[1] The inventories that give room names are used to identify the numbers and types of rooms associated with particular numbers of hearths, and so give insights into the character of the corresponding houses. The section starts with a brief overview of the types of houses found in seventeenth century Warwickshire and of the nature of their heating.

Types of Warwickshire houses

Materials and plans

Seventeenth-century Warwickshire was dominated by timber-framing, as indeed its vernacular buildings still are; this was used from the smallest cottages up to houses as grand as Packwood House. Only in limited areas and for the grandest houses does stone play a major role. In the 1660s, brick was the coming material for substantial farms and gentry houses, though it would be a half-century or more before it became universal for smaller houses.[2]

The structural pattern for smaller timber-framed houses is straightforward: a division into bays, each normally corresponding to one room in plan, with two to four in-line bays being the most common arrangements. Larger houses have more varied plans, often with one or two crosswings (Figures 13, 14), though their layouts are too varied for easy classification. By the later seventeenth century, most houses had upper floors over some (but not necessarily all) rooms. A significant proportion of surviving Warwickshire houses dates from the mid-sixteenth century or before and sometimes uses other framing methods than the standard box-frame construction (with crucks, for example) but which do not generally differ appreciably in plan.

1 The archdeaconry included the County of Coventry, and the whole of Hemlingford and Knightlow hundreds, together with a group of parishes in the north-east part of Kineton hundred. Most of the remainder of the county (71 parishes) was in Worcester diocese, with a few parishes in Gloucester diocese.
2 Alcock, 'Innovation'.

Stone as a building material was universal only in a narrow strip along the south-eastern border of the county, from Long Compton approximately as far north as Napton on the Hill. The plans of smaller seventeenth-century stone houses are, however, very similar to those built with timber-framing.[1] Elsewhere, stone was used occasionally, where it was readily available; thus, the blue lias of Wilmcote in Aston Cantlow (near Stratford upon Avon), is found in houses in the village, sometimes in combination with timber-framing.

Chimneys and fireplaces

In principle, the type of chimney used in a Warwickshire house – whether of wattle-and-daub, stone or brick – might be expected to control the number of hearths provided but the reality seems to be that tradition rather than construction was the more important determinant. Similarly, the age of the house has little effect: this contrasts with Kent, where the surviving medieval houses (often more substantial than those in Warwickshire) seem to have had significantly fewer hearths than new-built houses of corresponding size.[2]

In medieval houses, in Warwickshire as elsewhere, the principal heating was provided by the open hearth in the hall. We have only the slightest of evidence suggesting that these ever remained in use as late as the 1670s. Most notable is the comment (Figure 25) against Sir Richard Hopkins's house in Coventry (Palace Yard in Earl Street; see p. 126) '& 1 in his hall which hee will not pay for'; this surely refers to a hearth in a still-open hall that was probably only used intermittently on formal occasions. It might have resembled the still-surviving hearth in the hall at Penshurst Place, Kent.[3] One probate inventory, that of Richard Kymbell of Avon Dassett (1677), names both the hall and the 'room where the chimney is', suggesting that the hall had only an open hearth. Uniquely, the constable of Balsall recorded one house as having 'a funnill only', and two others as having 'a funnill to an oven' (see pp. 325–6); it is difficult to imagine quite what the latter were like, but the 'funnill' itself may have been a hood over an open hearth.

In south-east England, many sixteenth-century houses incorporate smoke bays, narrow bays divided off down to eaves level (or sometimes lower) collecting the smoke of the open hearth; however, in Warwickshire this form of structure has only been recorded occasionally.[4] Hardly more common are examples of the simplest type of chimney, the timber-framed fireplace and stack. In this, the fireplace opening is defined by posts holding the lintel, and these carry a wattle-and-daub hood. They may once have been very numerous, but only a handful of Warwickshire survivors have been recognised. Figure 2 illustrates the fireplace inserted, probably in the later

1 See, for example, Wood-Jones, *Banbury*.
2 Pearson, 'Kent', p. c.
3 Wood, *Medieval House*, Plate XL.A.
4 Alcock & Moir, 'Alcester'; Alcock, 'Smoke bay'.

sixteenth century into a medieval cottage in Coventry.[1] It was almost impossible to include an upper floor fireplace in a framed stack,[2] and the limited evidence indicates that most houses had only one such stack, inserted in the former open hall of an earlier house, or serving the hall of a new-built one.

The great majority of surviving timber-framed houses have chimneys of brick, either as originally built, as inserted into open halls, or as replacements for framed stacks (Figure 3). Even though these stacks could easily incorporate first floor fireplaces, the majority of seventeenth-century householders seem to have been content with fireplaces only on the ground floor: the next step up from the hall fireplace would be a separate kitchen stack, rather than a chamber fireplace.[3] The exceptions are mainly in houses of relatively high status. Thus, a house mostly rebuilt in about 1649 by John Holyoake of Morton Bagot (Figure 4(a)) has a central stack with two hearths on each floor, all decorated in painted plaster (Figures 4(b–c)). It is listed in 1670 with four hearths.[4]

In the stone-building region in the south-east of the county, chimney stacks were universally of stone. Most of the existing buildings there are post-medieval, built with original stacks; stone stacks are also occasionally found elsewhere in the county, even in areas where timber-framing is ubiquitous (Figure 13, for example). These stone stacks give the impression that they included upper floor fireplaces more frequently than did brick stacks, but a suggestion made previously that this part of the county had more houses with eight hearths and upwards than elsewhere has not been confirmed.[5] Rather, a statistical analysis of the proportion of multi-hearth houses in the Felden as a whole and in the stone-building region (Table 23) shows that the differences are small, and if anything in the opposite direction. This is consistent,

Table 23 Comparative distribution of hearths in the Felden and in stone-building parishes.

Region	*All Felden*	*21 stone-building parishes*
Households	2275	1435
3+ hearths (%)	19.3	18.3
3–4 hearths (%)	14.1	13.6
5–9 hearths (%)	4.2	4.1
10+ hearths (%)	1.1	0.6

Source: Table 28, compiled by Tom Arkell.

1 The chimneys themselves are difficult to photograph, but an example that can be visited is to be found at Mary Arden's House, Wilmcote.

2 Barnwell, 'Houses', p. 179.

3 Back-to-back fireplaces which are common in East Anglia are rarely found in Warwickshire.

4 The stack included provision for a fifth fireplace in a rear wing, but this was never completed. In the eighteenth century, a large kitchen fireplace was added in the retained wing of the earlier house: N.W. Alcock, 'Netherstead, Morton Bagot: a history and architectural survey', unpublished report, 2006 (copy at WCRO). See also Alcock, 'Rich man', p. 143, for further information about John Holyoake.

5 Alcock, 'Warwickshire', p. 109.

of course, with the general similarity of timber-framed and stone houses in Warwickshire.

In great houses, fireplaces proliferated and could be of surpassing splendour; the pilastered and ornamented surround and overmantel in the Great Chamber at Combe Abbey (Figure 5) is typical of the early seventeenth century and Baddesley Clinton (Figure 17), for example, has several fireplaces in a similar style.

Grates and coal[1]

In the later seventeenth century, Warwickshire was in the midst of a heating revolution, the replacement of wood as a fuel by coal. This change is occasionally directly identifiable in probate inventories by the inclusion of a stock of coal but is more often indicated by the presence of one or more grates, which appear to have been used exclusively for burning coal.[2] Grates at this period did not resemble either the later kitchen ranges (Figure 2) or the grates filling small chimney apertures in the parlours and bedrooms of nineteenth-century houses. Rather, they seem to have had the form of fire-baskets, keeping the coals together and admitting the extra air needed for coal as opposed to wood burning on the ground or on andirons.[3] These grates were placed within an ordinary wide fireplace, surrounded by the usual impedimenta. Furthermore, the use of coal was by no means exclusive and a number of inventories indicate the use of both coal and wood. Thus, Robert Lea of Sutton Coldfield (1674) had in his hall 'a pair of tongs, two pairs of pot-hangers, two spits and a pair of cobirons (spit supports), a pair of irons to lay wood on, and an iron grate'. Similarly Thomas Chattock of Bickenhill (1674) had a large supply of 'coals and wood', valued at £2, to serve the three grates in his kitchen. Edward Lapworth of Coventry (1674/5) had iron grates in his kitchen and back kitchen, and a small grate in the Little Parlour, but only brass andirons in the Great Parlour.

A more systematic study of the progressive replacement of wood by coal has been obtained from two groups of inventories, namely the sample of 50 inventories used for the discussion of wealth (section 7) and 38 inventories, predominantly for the smallest houses, examined in detail as part of the survey considered later in this section. These throw valuable light on the use of coal as a domestic fuel in Warwickshire in the 1660s and 1670s, either as a supplement to, or a replacement for, wood. In these inventories, mentions of either coal or a grate reveal that at least 40 per cent and probably nearer a half of these probated households burned coal. Some coal and one or more grates were recorded in six inventories, coal alone in six more and grates on their own in another 22, with one more grate being identified in a testator's will. These figures can be contrasted with just 3 per cent found by Overton's team in Cornwall and 13 per cent in Kent (for the period 1660–89).[4]

1 This section has been written jointly with Tom Arkell.

2 Coal is comparatively rarely mentioned, perhaps because of its low value. Richard Dolphyn of Aston (1679) had a 'Colehouse', but its contents, 'coles, one old wheele and one bench' were only worth 1s.

3 Eveleigh, *Firegrates*, pp. 1–2.

4 Overton et al., *Households*, pp. 98–9.

This minimum of 35 out of 88 households may be a considerable underestimate since inventories do not prove the absence of anything, only its presence. So few individual items were recorded in five of the inventories that their appraisers would have been unlikely to list grates or coal, even if they were present. In addition, the price of coal varied enormously according to its transport costs. It was so cheap in parishes close to the pits that it may have been ignored by the appraisers more frequently than in more distant ones.[1] Undoubtedly, however, not all households, even among the most prosperous, had taken up the use of coal by the 1670s. The 1672 six-room inventory of Margery Lewis of Bentley, not very far from the coal-producing areas, has no grates and makes no mention of coal, even though it goes into the exceptional detail of including the apples and honey in the chamber. Similarly, the inventory of Robert Webb of Wolfhampcote (1672) lists 'old wood for fireing' but no coal.

The households identified as using coal ranged across the social spectrum. They include one of the four non-chargeable and one third of those who were chargeable with both one and two hearths. Among those with three or four hearths the proportion rises to three quarters but falls, surprisingly, to just one out of the five that had five hearths, making it difficult to believe that more of these did not in reality use coal. These households with coal were not just confined to the area near the coalfield but were scattered evenly across the whole of the archdeaconry of Coventry. They came from as far away as Hillmorton to the east and Avon Dassett to the south with others located in the parishes of Harbury, Kenilworth, Napton and Radford Semele. Equally, the penetration of coal was patchy, particularly for those least well-off. As an illustration, none of a group of seven inventories (three of them for exempt householders) from around Bishops Itchington in the south of the archdeaconry included grates or coal.[2] In Stoneleigh, a parish three miles south of Coventry with large woods within the parish, grates only became common at the end of the seventeenth century, being used first in parlours and chambers.[3]

The location of the identified coal-users indicates that a network based on Coventry, already well established for coal-dealing in parts of Northamptonshire and Oxfordshire, naturally covered east and south Warwickshire as well.[4] Evidence for part-time coal dealers away from the mines is understandably very elusive but it is possible that George Kimberley of Berkswell was one. He was a husbandman who had four old horses and a cart and is recorded with coal and coal bags worth £3, which may represent three tons or more.[5]

1 Trinder & Cox, *Telford*, p. 109; Trinder & Cox, *Severn Gorge*, pp. 56–7.

2 LRO, P/C/11, Peculiar of Bishops Itchington: Robert Clarke (2; 1674); John Cornish (1NC; 1672); Anne Garlick (1; 1672); Richard Penn (1C; 1672); William Poole (1; 1670); John Sabin (2; 1672); Richard Worrall (2 NC; 1670).

3 Alcock, *People at home*, pp. 99, 203.

4 Hughes, *Warwickshire*, p. 15.

5 LRO, B/C/11: George Kimberley, 1672. According to Spufford, coal sold for £1 a ton in Market Harborough but it may have been cheaper in Berkswell because it was closer to the nearest mines: Spufford, 'Chimneys', p. 29.

Forges and ovens

The hearth tax returns are inconsistent in their mention of forges and ovens, with many more recorded in 1666 than in 1670 (pp. 40–1). Virtually nothing can be said about them from standing structures. These 'public' ovens were certainly not the small domestic, usually brick-lined, ovens projecting from kitchen chimneys and heated by burning brushwood within them, which proliferated in the eighteenth and nineteenth centuries. Rather, we should interpret them as large ovens operated commercially by bakers. For forges, whether those of village smiths or the industrial hearths of Birmingham, we have no surviving Warwickshire examples that can be dated before the nineteenth century.

Rooms and hearths

This section examines 681 probate inventories that can be linked to the corresponding number of hearths in the tax returns and, in particular, the 537 of these that include the names of rooms. They provide quantitative data to compare with the individual houses that are discussed in the following section, and they represent the largest such sample yet analysed.[1] The correlation is limited to Lichfield and Coventry diocese: only here was a spreadsheet available, providing a list of the probate records sortable by place and name. Matching of the probates was carried out from 1670 to 1680 for Warwickshire and from 1666 to 1676 for Coventry.[2] Clearly, many people listed in the returns would still have been alive ten years later, but these limits were chosen to reduce the risk of spurious matches when, for example, the people concerned had moved to a different house or the parish contained more than one family of the same name. Obvious problem cases have been removed from the sample, and it is believed that any remaining misidentifications will be so few as to have little or no influence on the overall statistics.[3] Table 24 summarises the numbers of households and inventories, and the numbers matched. Tables 25(a) and (b) analyse the correlation between the numbers of hearths per household and the total

1 Overton and his co-workers (*Households*, pp. 24–5) have matched 341 Kentish and 657 Cornish inventories with the corresponding hearth tax data (including all name matches up to 1699). However, the number of the Cornish inventories that include room names appears to be only about 80 (not explicitly stated). The range of rooms listed is examined (pp. 124ff.) but not the correlation between the numbers of hearths and of rooms.

2 Warwickshire probates dated between 1 January and 1 July 1670 were examined, but have been excluded from the tabulation, since these people should have been replaced in the hearth tax lists: in reality, many of those who died in the first half of 1670 seem still to be listed in the returns. For Coventry, the 1666 return was compiled retrospectively, with the result that none of the 11 people with inventories for that year is found in the hearth tax list.

3 Some 20 apparent matches were excluded, either because of missing data or because of gross inconsistency between the inventoried wealth and the apparent number of hearths. Because of the large number of inventories, they had to be examined on microfilm of variable and often poor quality. The originals of those that could not be deciphered at all were checked, but possible filming or transcription errors may have marginally affected some of the others. It is surprising that the 681 total matches represent only 56 per cent of the probate records with inventories for the period. The failure to identify more inventories with the hearth tax returns is principally attributed to mis-spelling or alternative spelling of surnames (see pp. 44ff).

Table 24 Probate inventories linked with hearth tax returns in the Archdeaconry of Coventry

Households in the Archdeaconry of Coventry	11,424
Probate records 1670–1680* [1666–1676 for Coventry]	1,498
Probate records with inventories	1,208
Matched inventories with useable total inventory valuations	681
Matched inventories with useable room information	537

* Including only July–December 1670.

inventory valuations, and the numbers of hearths and the numbers of inventoried rooms respectively.

Inevitably, in making this correlation, the problems that affect the use of probate inventories as historical evidence need to be borne in mind.[1] Those that relate to inventory valuations have already been discussed (pp. 91ff); the direct correlation of the hearths identified in an inventory with the corresponding number in the hearth tax return is not normally possible (and has not been attempted), since the recognition of a hearth depends on its fire irons or fittings being mentioned. The listing of rooms is also not problem-free. Occasionally, the lists are clearly incomplete, as when the 'Chamber over the Shop' is listed, but not the 'Shop' itself; such obvious omissions have been corrected in counting the number of rooms. More generally, rooms would be omitted if they contained nothing belonging to the deceased, being perhaps occupied by a relative or lodger or empty.[2] It is impossible to quantify such omissions but a study of Stoneleigh identified a number of paired inventories relating to the same house, showing satisfactorily similar numbers of rooms listed.[3]

The correlation of total inventory values with numbers of hearths in Table 25(a) is important for its evidence on bias in the sample. Among householders with two to eight hearths, 7–8 per cent have wealth information (though this involves small numbers for seven and eight hearth households). For houses with nine or more hearths, the proportion drops abruptly, with only two inventories identified (0.03 per cent, compared to 1 per cent of households): thus this sample tells us almost nothing about the homes of the most substantial members of the community.[4] At the other end of the scale, only 3.4 per cent of householders paying for one hearth and 1.0 per cent of those exempted appear in the probate records, though, because of the large

1 See in particular Spufford, 'Limitations'.

2 See Orlin, 'Fictions', p. 57.

3 Alcock, *People at home*, p. 6. However, it is not surprising to find one list differing from another by one room or so.

4 To help correct this deficiency, a few individual inventories are discussed below, that have been identified in estate records or among the inventories of the Prerogative Court of Canterbury (TNA, PROB4). Systematic study of the 240 Warwickshire inventories which survive in the latter collection for the period 1670–80 would certainly correct this under-representation: they, of course, derive from both Lichfield and Worcester dioceses.

Table 25 Correlation of probate inventories and hearth tax returns in the Archdeaconry of Coventry

(a) Hearths and total inventory valuations (TIV)

Hearths	*1NC*	*1*	*2NC*	*2*	*3*	*4*	*5*	*6*	*7*	*8*	*9*	*10+*	*Total*
Households	4,185	3,489	132	1,802	807	422	211	130	62	61	17	106	11,424
Inventories	47	284	6	181	75	42	18	15	6	5	1	1*	681
Inventories as % of households	1.1	8.1	4.5	10.0	9.3	10.0	8.5	11.5	9.7	8.2	5.9	0.9	6.0
Minimum TIV (£)	3	3	5	7	10	15	19	25	56	85			
Median TIV (£)	19	48	10	92	98	105	123	105	105	195	866	695	
Max TIV (£)	109	1372	16	631	631	1359	356	373	788	654			
Average TIV (£)	28	68	10	120	150	193	149	150	229	264	866	695	
Total inventory valuation													
<£11	14	20	4	4	2	–	–	–	–	–	–	–	44
£11–30	19	73	2	23	7	4	2	2	–	–	–	–	132
£31–50	6	59	–	22	6	5	1	2	–	–	–	–	101
£51–100	6	86	–	54	24	11	2	3	3	1	–	–	190
£101–200	2	35	–	52	22	10	8	4	1	2	–	–	136
£201–300	–	5	–	15	11	7	3	1	1	1	–	–	44
£301–500	–	5	–	8	2	1	2	3	–	–	–	–	21
£501–750	–	–	–	3	1	2	–	–	–	1	–	1	8
>£750	–	1	–	–	–	2	–	–	1	–	1	–	5

(b) Hearths and room numbers listed in inventories

Hearths	*1NC*	*1*	*2NC*	*2*	*3*	*4*	*5*	*6*	*7*	*8*	*9*	*10+*	*Totals*	*%*	*Rescaled %*	*Mean hearths*
Households	4,185	3,489	132	1,802	807	422	211	130	62	61	17	106	11,424			
Inventories	27	218	4	156	65	32	14	11	4	4	1	1*	537			
2 rooms	4	10	–	–	–	–	–	–	–	–	–	–	14	2.6	6.8	1.0
3 rooms	2	32	3	6	1	–	–	–	–	–	–	–	44	8.2	8.8	1.3
4 rooms	12	46	–	20	3	–	–	–	–	–	–	–	81	15.1	25.1	1.3
5 rooms	5	58	–	33	4	–	–	–	–	–	–	–	100	18.6	18.7	1.4
6 rooms	2	33	–	29	12	1	–	–	–	–	–	–	77	14.3	11.7	1.7
7 rooms	1	18	1	30	13	3	2	3	1	–	–	–	72	13.4	9.8	2.3
8 rooms	1	19	–	16	8	10	2	2	–	–	–	–	58	10.8	8.1	2.4
9 rooms	–	2	–	10	5	3	2	–	–	–	–	–	22	4.1	2.3	2.7
10 rooms	–	–	–	7	6	2	1	2	–	–	–	–	18	3.4	1.9	3.2
11 rooms	–	–	–	4	5	4	1	–	1	2	–	–	17	3.2	1.9	3.9
12 rooms	–	–	–	–	3	2	3	1	–	–	–	–	9	1.7	1.1	4.2
13 rooms	–	–	–	–	3	3	1	1	–	–	–	–	8	1.5	0.9	4.0
14 rooms	–	–	–	1	–	2	–	1	1	–	–	–	5	0.9	0.6	4.6
15 rooms	–	–	–	–	2	1	–	–	–	–	–	1	4	0.7	1.3	5.0
16 rooms	–	–	–	–	–	–	1	–	–	–	–	–	1	0.2	0.1	5.0
17 rooms	–	–	–	–	–	1	1	–	1	2	–	–	5	0.9	0.7	6.4
20 rooms	–	–	–	–	–	–	–	1	–	–	1	–	2	0.4	0.3	7.5
Mean no. of rooms	**4.2**	**5.0**	**4.0**	**6.4**	**8.1**	**10.0**	**10.8**	**10.5**	**12.3**	**14.0**	**20.0**	**15.0**	**6.4**			
Median no. of rooms	**4**	**5**	**3**	**6**	**7**	**9**	**11**	**10**	**13**	**14**	**20**	**15**				

* 11 hearths.

NC = not chargeable.

Source: Archdeaconry of Coventry probate inventories (see p. 110).

proportion of one-hearth houses, this still provides a substantial sample (331 and 53 inventories respectively).[1] The median valuation shows a systematic increase between the exempt and the non-exempt as would be expected, while the minimum valuation in either category was only £3; thus, any bias resulting from the systematic omission of poorer estates should not be severe.

Room names (Table 25(b)) are given in a very high proportion of the matched inventories (78 per cent overall) and only for people exempt from the hearth tax does it fall significantly below this (to 59 per cent). This listing of rooms in inventories was not a legal obligation but was purely for the assessors' convenience, though it was clearly a generally accepted practice in Lichfield and Coventry diocese at this period.[2] The evidence indicates that only for the smallest houses were the appraisers less likely to bother with recording room names. But they did not systematically ignore the rooms in all small houses, nor in those of probated estates of low value: among the 44 exempt one-hearth estates, the median valuations for the 27 with room names and the 10 without are identical at £8, and both have minimum valuations of £3.

A related question is whether some homes had only one room and thus were smaller than any described by the inventories: indeed, it has sometimes been suggested that inventories which named no rooms did so because the house contained only a single room. In general this supposition is undoubtedly incorrect, as is demonstrated by the consistent 80:20 ratio between inventories that do and do not name rooms.[3] In general, the very modest valuations at the bottom end of the sample do not allow of many gradations of poverty below this, even if the sample does represent the minority whose estates entered probate and whose inventories sometimes included room names. The smallest house matched with the hearth tax return is listed as having 'His Room and a Lean-to', which in living standards might be equated to a 'room and a half'.[4] Apart from this example, the most modest houses included at least two rooms. We might suppose that a few of the Warwickshire's poorest would have had their meagre possessions in just one room, and we can be certain

1 Overton suggests that the poorest 40 per cent of society are not represented by inventories. This contrasts with the view taken here, based on the identification of the inventories associated with exempt and one-hearth households, that any such blanket cut-off is at a much lower level. Rather, the present analysis gives a direct indication of the proportion of the least wealthy section of the population represented in inventories.

2 See Alcock, *People at home*, p. 13.

3 Pairs of inventories for the same house can also sometimes be identified, one of which does and one does not name rooms: Alcock, *People at home*, pp. 211ff. From this evidence, the calculation of room size for all Kent inventories in Overton et al., *Households*, pp. 122–3, appears to be methodologically flawed, since it is based on the assumption that all inventories not naming rooms related to houses with three or fewer rooms, which is not consistent with the Warwickshire evidence. Irrespective of this problem, the calculation is of little significance since it does not take account of the relationship between estates with inventories and those without.

4 Matthew Morrell of Frankton, labourer: his probate is dated 19 May 1670, so has been excluded from the tabulations, though he is apparently listed in the 1670 assessment, with one hearth (not exempt), as in 1666. A similar description is found in a Stoneleigh inventory of 1697 (Alcock, *People at home*, pp. 121, 204): notably, this is the only two-room house described there in the 1660–1700 period. One inventory (Richard Penn of Bishops Itchington, 1672) lists just a 'Nether Room', but this name implies the presence of an upper room as well.

that such people might share a house with another family, as is occasionally indicated in the hearth tax returns, by the naming of two people against one hearth number. However, the evidence indicates that such cases were rare.

Hearths and room numbers

The correlation of hearth and room numbers is summarised in Table 25(b).[1] The mean numbers rise from 5.0 rooms for one-hearth chargeable households to 6.4 for two hearths, 9.1 for three and a relatively constant 10–11 rooms for 4–6 hearths; beyond this, we have too few identifications for meaningful calculations.[2] As we might expect, the exempt one-hearth householders lived in slightly smaller houses than those paying the tax (mean 4.2 rooms, median 4). Some similar evidence has previously been presented for Cambridge, Cambridgeshire and Richmond (Yorkshire), though all relate to smaller samples.[3] The comparison shows very significant differences, particularly in one-hearth houses, where the medians are three and two rooms respectively, compared to Warwickshire's five rooms; the Yorkshire figures confirm the low housing standards revealed by our knowledge of the region's vernacular architecture. The difference between Warwickshire and Cambridgeshire, though more modest, is less easily understood. In Cambridgeshire also, a comparison between rural houses and those in Cambridge itself showed that the city had a significantly higher proportion of rooms heated. Surprisingly, a corresponding analysis for rural Warwickshire compared to Coventry and other urban centres shows only marginal and irregular differences, although only for one- and two-hearth households are there sufficient linked inventories in 'rural' and 'urban' categories for meaningful analysis. One- and two-hearth households in the major urban settlements (Birmingham and Coventry) have means of 5.4 and 5.9 rooms respectively, compared to 4.9 and 6.3 for rural settlements, but when the smaller towns (Atherstone, Coleshill, Nuneaton, Rugby, Southam and Tamworth) are included, the urban and rural means are identical.

Table 25(b) also reveals that the averages conceal wide variations in the numbers of rooms. Thus, one-hearth chargeable dwellings have between two and nine rooms, though with a concentration at 3–6 rooms. For the one-hearth exempt householders the spread is smaller, peaking sharply at four rooms. In the houses with more hearths, the spread in the number of rooms is even greater, with three quarters of those with two and three hearths having 5–9 and 6–11 rooms respectively. Above this

1 The conventions used in counting rooms are: combinations (e.g. *Buttery and Dairy*) are counted as two rooms, as are plural names, for example *Chambers*, *Cheese Chambers* and the like. *Shops* (usually meaning workshops) are also included as this is judged to give the clearest comparison with standing buildings. Many inventories indicate (by such descriptions as 'Chamber over the shop') that the shop was within the main footprint of the house; however, their exclusion would have no effect on the median values, reducing the mean numbers of rooms by at most 0.1–0.2 in the middling categories. Farm buildings are excluded.

2 The median values are very similar to the means.

3 Cited in Arkell, 'Inventories', p. 88. These samples are based on 40, 101 and 41 matched inventories respectively.

level, the numbers of rooms varies too widely for meaningful analysis. The maximum number of rooms (20) was recorded in only two inventories. Comparison across rather than down the table reveals that all two-room houses had only one hearth, and only a handful of those with three to five rooms had three hearths. Only in houses of seven rooms and upwards do we find significant numbers with three or more hearths and an average of more than two hearths per house.

We can also make the assumption that the numbers of rooms found in the probate inventories for each hearth group represent a reasonably unbiased estimate of the numbers within the group as a whole. We can therefore use the ratio between the number of matched inventories and the total number of households to estimate the total number of houses of each size within each group: for example, the existence of 33 houses with five rooms and two hearths in the inventory sample leads to the expectation that there were about 381 such houses in the archdeaconry of Coventry as a whole (33 x 1,802 ÷ 156). Applying this to the total number of houses of all sizes in Table 25(b) provides an estimate of the numbers of rooms for all houses within the archdeaconry, not only those that appeared in probate inventories (the 'Rescaled %' column in the table).[1] The effect of this calculation is to increase the proportion of smaller houses over that indicated by the inventory sample itself. The result indicates that houses with four (rather than five) rooms were commonest, and that almost 60 per cent of Warwickshire houses had five rooms or fewer, substantially more than the uncorrected figure of 45 per cent.

Rooms in the house

In turning to the house as a whole, the present analysis concentrates on the smallest buildings, those with up to five rooms – the least likely to survive among buildings now standing – though many of the points discussed below also apply to larger houses. The principal living room in the great majority of these houses was called indifferently *Hall, Hall House, House,* or *Dwelling House* (here generally called *Hall* for convenience); the alternative, *Fire Room,* was used twice, clearly reflecting a building tradition in which houses had only a single heated room.[2] The main room for sleeping, almost invariably on the ground floor, was the *Parlour*; only a few houses had all their bedchambers on upper floors by the later seventeenth century. In this respect, a transition has been identified in the detailed analysis of Stoneleigh inventories, in which the pair of principal rooms, *Hall* and *Parlour*, was replaced by *Parlour* and *Kitchen*; at the same time, their functions were rearranged, so that cooking moved from the hall to the kitchen, and the use of the hall as a living room moved to the parlour, while the latter's role as the main sleeping room was transferred to an upstairs

1 This calculation, of course, cannot accurately reflect the 1 per cent of houses with 10 hearths or more that are inadequately represented in the sample.

2 In the inventories of Daniel Pettipher of Withybrook (1671; four rooms) and Richard Ford of Shuckburgh (1677; five rooms).

chamber.[1] However, in the present sample, covering more of Warwickshire and restricted to the 1670s, this development seems only to be in its earliest stages.

As the size of houses increased, so did the variety of rooms. *Butteries* appear occasionally among three-room houses,[2] *Dairies* or *Milk-houses* in five-room houses, sometimes accompanied by *Cheese Chambers*. Five- to six-room houses might have both a *Hall* and a *Kitchen*. The first *Study*, *Brewhouse* and *Wool House* are found in six-room houses, though a few five-room houses had a *Bolting House* or a *Meal House*, and one hall was accompanied by a *House or Kitchen* that contained a 'horse mill to make oatmeal & cuttlings';[3] this must have been a back kitchen where little if any cooking went on.

After the functions of the principal rooms, the most important factor controlling both the size and the layout of houses was the extent of upper floors. Of the 14 two-room houses, the majority (9) were single-storied, with *Hall* (or *House*) and *Parlour*; the remainder had one-room plans, with a *Low Room* and *Upper Chamber*, or *Hall House* and *Upper Room*.[4] This arrangement was to become the norm for cottages in the eighteenth and nineteenth centuries, a trend that was clearly only beginning in the 1670s.

Among the more numerous three-room houses, the commonest combination was of *Hall*, *Parlour* and *Chamber*; the latter can be assumed to have been upstairs, as is sometimes made explicit when it is called *High Chamber*, *Parlour Chamber* or *Chamber over the Parlour*.[5] The upper room was identified as for storage in two cases ('Upper room for corn'; 'Store Chamber').[6] A few houses were clearly single-storey, generally with a *Buttery* alongside the *Hall* and *Parlour*. A handful of the three-room houses had two hearths, but their rooms show no obvious differences from the remainder, and in some cases, the additional hearth must have been upstairs.

With four and five rooms in the house, the possible permutations of rooms and their layout increase greatly. Almost half the four-room houses (34/78) had the obvious arrangement of two ground floor rooms, usually *Hall* and *Parlour*, and two chambers above. With three ground floor rooms, the most usual addition was of a *Buttery*, though a few had both a *Hall* and a *Kitchen*. By no means all of the latter had two hearths, so their kitchens were presumably unheated and little different from butteries.[7] A couple of four-room houses have only ground-floor rooms listed (*Hall* and *Parlour* with either *Kitchen* and *Dairy*, or *Buttery* and *Little Parlour*).[8]

1 Alcock, *People at home*, pp. 202–3.
2 In large houses, the buttery was used to store liquids, with dry goods in the pantry. However, in these small houses, the buttery was a general store room, for food, drink and dishes particularly.
3 Isabella Richards of Nuneaton, 1672. Cutlings are husked oats or coarse oatmeal (*OED*).
4 Edward Ward of Marton, 1677; Joan Furley of Long Itchington, 1671. Both had one hearth and were exempt.
5 Richard Knatt of Hillmorton, 1670; Thomas Hartopp of Newbold on Avon, 1674; William Burgesse of Nuneaton, 1670 (all one hearth, the first exempt).
6 Anne Garlick of Gaydon, 1672; Edward Brookes of Bickenhill, 1679.
7 E.g. John Clarke of Ansley, 1670 (two hearths); Henry Holden of Erdington, 1680 (one hearth).
8 William Coleburne of Sowe, 1674 (two hearths); Clement Fisher of Solihull, 1671 (one hearth).

The principal distinction in five-room houses is also in the number of ground-floor rooms. Some half-dozen houses had just two rooms in plan, *Hall* and *Buttery* (usually) with chambers over and a *Cockloft* (attic room). The great majority (65) were of three-room plan: *Hall, Parlour,* and *Kitchen*, *Buttery* or *Dairy*, sometimes with both *Hall* and *Kitchen*. The 23 houses apparently with four ground-floor rooms show a variety of patterns, though principally combining *Hall* and *Parlour* with dairies, butteries, kitchens, and second parlours. One of these is the intriguing house mentioned above, with a 'Room where the Chimney is' distinct from the hall; it also had a *Hall Chamber, Day House* and *Meal House*.[1]

Not surprisingly, as the number of rooms increases further, so does the variety of room combinations, to the extent that no clear patterns can be identified, though generally the same individual rooms are named as in smaller houses.

Standing buildings

The identification of existing houses (and those illustrated in antiquarian drawings or photographs) with their hearth tax assessments is relatively easy for houses of gentry status or the equivalent: castles, manor houses, rectories and the like, whose owners' names may appear in Dugdale's *Antiquities of Warwickshire*, or the *Victoria County History*. Each parish has at most one or two such houses, standing out in the hearth tax lists. Research on individual houses for which good documentary evidence survives may also provide links to the assessments, though these tend also to have been occupied by the more substantial members of the community. Thus, in Stratford upon Avon, Harvard House (26 High Street) has been shown to be occupied by John Capp, blacksmith, paying for two hearths (with a forge as well); however, for Halls Croft (Old Town, Stratford) the ownership is known but it was occupied by unidentifiable tenants (and perhaps subdivided).[2]

Smaller houses generally lack the sequences of title deeds or similar evidence that make such identifications possible. Matching them with the hearth tax is generally only feasible if a near-contemporary estate map and sufficient documents exist to link the occupants named on the map to the tax lists, and if a number of houses still survive. In Warwickshire, these conditions are met in very few places.

Chilvers Coton

Not a single seventeenth-century building remains standing in and around the village of Chilvers Coton, and the only direct evidence that we have of them comes from early twentieth-century photographs showing two simple timber-framed cottages, similar to those surviving elsewhere in Warwickshire. However, the houses that were listed in the 1670 hearth tax are illustrated, if only schematically, in the map that

1 Richard Kymbell of Avon Dassett, 1677.

2 N.W. Alcock & Bob Meeson, unpublished reports for Shakespeare Birthplace Trust (copies at SCLA).

accompanies the manorial survey of 1684 (Figure 6).[1] The hearth tax return shows that four fifths of all these houses had just one hearth in the early 1670s, but the numbers of hearths for specific houses shown on the map often cannot be established: only about one quarter of the names can be matched with those in the hearth tax and some of those located had undoubtedly moved in the meantime.

The great majority of these houses are drawn uniformly, with two windows, a door and a central chimney: these must represent typical Warwickshire one-hearth houses, with two ground-floor rooms, entered either directly into one room or with a lobby entry. They correspond well to our expectation from the description of a group of houses standing away from the village centre on what must have been small encroachments on former common land. They are described in the schedule of houses associated with the map as 'Small tenements on the west side of the lane in the place called the Heath End'. What is lacking for the smaller houses is any distinction between them that would indicate that they were being drawn individually: equally, no indication is given of the outbuildings that must have existed on many of the holdings. Drawings of the larger houses are differentiated and appear to represent the individual buildings.

As specific examples, along the south street of the village (Figure 6(a)), the large house in the centre of the figure belonged to Mr John Parker, gentleman (three hearths): it is shown as L-shaped with two chimneys.[2] The faintly drawn house next to his was that of widow Mary Hughes, probably the Widow Hughes with one exempt hearth in 1671 (perhaps among the unnamed exempt in 1670), followed by Paul Hinman (1 hearth, paying), whose inventory taken in 1690 indicates a house of six rooms. The only other identifiable exempt cottage is that of Christopher Pain, at the southern end of the street. On the west (upper) side, the drawing of the large house of Henry Baker clearly indicates the presence of a central gable, flanked apparently by two cross-wings (compare the very similar appearance seen in Figure 14): unfortunately, the 1670 tenant is unknown. Next was Robert Ball (paying for one hearth) and then Samuel Browne. The latter had one hearth with a forge in 1670 and had a second 'new-built' hearth by 1674; his 1685 inventory names eight rooms (see p. 84). His tenant, George Wagster (rake-maker), lived in what appears to be a single-bay cottage standing on his croft (unnamed in 1670).[3] Next to them, Richard Sutton (one hearth) had six rooms in his 1687 inventory (p. 84). The cottage cut out of this relatively large croft, was occupied in 1684 by Samuel Suffolk, a locksmith, but the 1670 tenant is

1 WCRO, CR136/V101, including a schedule of locations, tenants and owners of the houses mapped; CR136/M14. This matching relates only to the area mapped (Chilvers Coton village), omitting the other sections of the parish, and is based on the assumption that people of the same name can be matched. More of the houses could undoubtedly be matched with their hearth numbers by using the extensive estate documentation. See also pp. 45ff.

2 It can be recognised in a watercolour of 'Cottages at Coton near Nuneaton, 1822' by Edward Rudge (Bedfordshire Record Office, X69/7, p. 33); although an administration grant was made in 1703 for John Parker's personal estate, no inventory survives.

3 Other Chilvers Coton documents show that William Hough (also named here) lived elsewhere in 1670.

unknown. All these single-hearth houses are represented in the same way (as is Samuel Browne's two-hearth house), though it is noticeable that Richard Sutton's house is longer, suggesting a three-bay dwelling. Almost all are shown with red roofs suggesting tiles, though this seems likely to be a convention, since thatch must surely have been the dominant roofing material for these cottages.

Links between the map and the hearth tax are possible for two other substantial inhabitants. The vicarage had five hearths[1] in a house that is represented very similarly to that of Henry Baker, with a central gable, though with its chimney off-centre, suggesting the presence of a cross-passage (Figure 6(b)). Again it appears to have two cross-wings, which would fit well with the rooms named in Mr John Perkins's 1691 inventory (pp. 77–8). From the drawing and the inventory together, we can suggest that the vicarage had a hall and service rooms (buttery and cellar) on each side of the central passage, with a parlour wing to the right and a service wing to the left (or perhaps in-line rooms decorated with an applied gable, as seen in the centre of Figure 14): the latter probably accommodated the kitchen and dairy, though no kitchen chimney is shown. The chambers would have been on the first floor, with the vicar's study in the room behind the central gable (which may indicate a two-storey porch).

The house of Mr (Thomas) Spratt was among a cluster of small houses in Paradise End. It had four hearths in what appears to have been a still larger house, with two central gables (Figure 6(c)). The uncoloured roof might suggest thatch, though tiles would be more likely for a gentry house. Just above it (to the west) is the house of Christopher Smith, nailer (in 1670 the home of Thomas Knight, also a nailer, paying for one hearth). Smith's 1696 inventory indicates how simple some of these houses were. It lists a living room called 'the house', furnished with a table, bench and cupboard, and also two bedsteads, a chamber containing only cheese and odd things, and his workshop, consistent with a two-bay building containing 'house' and workshop, with the chamber upstairs.[2] The tiny building in the corner of the plot is not the workshop, as might be thought, but the home of Widow Wagster, who is listed with one exempt hearth in 1670 (as Wagstaffe). Exceptionally, this sketch does suggest that the house was tiny, certainly with only a single bay and with a thatched roof.

Smaller houses in Stoneleigh parish (1–2 hearths)

The many standing buildings in Stoneleigh parish provide a glimpse of the reality of the village hierarchy behind the bald statistics of the hearth tax. It and its small neighbour, Ashow, contain some 40 surviving timber-framed houses, extending in status to the lowest level of village society, and the numbers of hearths for most of them can be established by correlation of the returns with the excellent estate records of the

1 For Mr Edward Abbott, the vicar in 1670.

2 His inventory is printed in Alcock, 'Rich man', p. 163, which includes further discussion of Chilvers Coton and Stoneleigh in relation to the hearth tax.

Stoneleigh Abbey estate.[1] The one-hearth households in Stoneleigh comprised 66 per cent of the total (168), almost identical to the county average, though only 28 per cent were exempt from the tax, considerably below the county-wide average of 38 per cent.

The standing vernacular buildings of Stoneleigh are an eclectic mixture, dating from the middle ages to the nineteenth century, with the earlier examples always timber-framed. Only one house in the village has the most characteristic form of small seventeenth-century Warwickshire houses, of two bays with a central chimney. This is 11–12 Vicarage Road (Figure 7(a)), a one-hearth house, built in about 1665 and occupied in 1670 by Edward Godard (or Goddard). Apart from originally having had an unusual end rather than a central door, it matches very closely the appearance of the houses drawn on the Chilvers Coton map.[2] Other one-hearth houses have two or three rooms in plan, though the distinction between the exempt and those who paid the tax is not obvious from their houses – and indeed their status sometimes varied from one return to the next. Those that were exempt include two medieval cruck houses (Figure 8(a–b)) that lacked any significant land holding. The first, occupied by Francis Whitmore, had only two rooms, as its upper floors had probably not yet been inserted.[3] The other with three bays had four rooms and was occupied by Humphrey Dixon.[4] Katherine Dyto, widow, lived in Fir Tree Cottage, Ashow (Figure 7(b)), probably with three rooms; this was also a medieval house, but had been reconstructed in the seventeenth century.[5] It is probably no coincidence that all these houses originated in the medieval period. What was then the norm in housing for people of many social levels had by the later seventeenth century become acceptable only for the lowest stratum in the village.[6]

An illustration of the accepted standards of housing provision at this social level is also given by the block of ten Stoneleigh almshouses that still exist. Each unit had one hearth (exempt, of course), heating the ground-floor living room, with an unheated chamber above.

Among houses paying the tax on one hearth, we find smaller farms, such as one of 30 acres with five rooms, now Bridge Cottage (Figure 9).[7] The house now known as

[1] The parish lies some three miles south of Coventry. It is examined in detail in Alcock, *People at home*. Some of this material has also been discussed in Alcock, 'Warwickshire', and in Alcock, 'Rich man'. Through the use of estate records, the correlation of houses, probate inventories and hearth numbers can be extended both before and after the 1670–80 period.

[2] Alcock, *People at home*, p. 133. The original entry at the north end was replaced by two doors on the front when the house was subdivided in the eighteenth century. In 1663, Edward Goddard had two hearths, but the return notes 'the house fallen down'; the present house can be identified with its successor with one hearth, for which he normally paid, but which was certified as exempt in 1666.

[3] He was exempt in other returns, but paid the tax in 1670.

[4] In the seventeenth century, the medieval layout with three ground-floor rooms, one of them floored, was altered by turning the floored end into a barn (removing its floor) and inserting floors over the other two rooms.

[5] This house was associated with a landholding of about 25 acres in 1612, but the land was later assigned to another tenant, perhaps in 1664 when Katherine Dyto succeeded her husband Francis. She was thereafter recorded as exempt from the tax on her one hearth.

[6] Alcock, *People at home*, p. 121. Three other non-chargeable houses, each with one hearth, are also recorded in probate inventories, though they do not still stand; they had two, three and four rooms respectively.

[7] Inventory of John Unton, 1700.

1–2 Coventry Road, Stoneleigh (Figure 10) had been occupied by a shoemaker, Roger Hudson, whose 1662 inventory lists seven rooms, counting his workshop (his successor in 1670 was John Hudson). These correspond to the three-floored bays of the main house, with an added unfloored bay for the workshop.

Fewer houses have been identified with two hearths but one well-documented example is Ivy Farm, Canley (Figure 11), the home of Thomas Gibbs in 1670, who farmed some 50 acres. The house was built earlier in the seventeenth century, with about eight rooms; presumably the first hearth served the hall/kitchen in the main range and the second the parlour in the wing.

Middling houses in Warwickshire (3–9 hearths)

One three-hearth house in Stoneleigh is well-preserved, 11–12 Coventry Road (Figure 12), a 60–acre farm with three hearths (two in the house, and one in a now demolished detached kitchen): the inventory of Thomas Hill, yeoman, lists ten rooms in 1631.[1] The village inn also had three hearths, a substantial building with some fourteen rooms listed in inventories, demolished in about 1820.[2]

For other houses in this group, we need to cast the net wider. One four-hearth house, Netherstead, Morton Bagot, has already been discussed (Figure 4; p. 107), and a five-hearth house, Lower Ingon Farm, Hampton Lucy (Figure 13), had a rather similar history. Its most prominent part, with substantial stone chimneys on each gable, is a two-bay parlour wing with hearths for both the ground and first floors, added in the early seventeenth century to an earlier range that was retained as the kitchen. The house belonged to the Cookes family (of Upper Ingon) and in 1670 was in the hands of a tenant, apparently one John Meades.[3]

An impressive example of a nine-hearth house is Manor Farm, Stoneleigh, a 73-acre farm in the seventeenth century (Figure 14). In 1670 it was empty, but thereafter was occupied by Christopher Leigh, esquire, great-uncle to Lord Leigh of Stoneleigh: perhaps in view of his intended tenancy, the house had been enlarged since 1664 (when four hearths were 'in building') by the addition of a back-to-back fireplace in the parlour wing. The house had a courtyard plan, and some of the nine hearths may have been in service buildings located in the demolished rear range. Twenty rooms are listed in Christopher Leigh's 1673 probate inventory.[4] After his death, the house declined in status, being divided between two tenants, John Holbech, gentleman (1687 will) and Francis Clayton, yeoman.[5]

1 Alcock, *People at home*, pp. 64–70. Earlier inventories list six (1551) and seven (1610) rooms, while a later one (1699) names only five main rooms and the kitchen, apparently ignoring several service rooms.

2 Alcock, *People at home*, pp. 181, 212.

3 In 1666, it was occupied by Widow Cookes: N.W. Alcock, 'Lower Ingon Farm, Hampton Lucy, Warwickshire', unpublished report, 2000 (copy at SCLA).

4 His probate administration was granted by the Prerogative Court, but the inventory only survives in the estate archives (SCLA, DR18/4/63).

5 Alcock, *People at home*, pp. 71–4.

The largest houses (10 or more hearths)

Houses with 10 or more hearths account for just 1 per cent of the entries in the Warwickshire and Coventry hearth tax returns, but their importance greatly outweighs this modest figure. The distinction adopted in previous county hearth tax volumes has been between the 'Great Houses', with 20 or more hearths, and the 'Large Houses', with upwards of 10 hearths: to allow comparisons, the same mapping is adopted here. Houses with 10 hearths or more (Map 10) were distributed relatively evenly across the countryside, with the highest proportion (1.6 per cent of total households) in the north-west of the county, and the lowest on the coalfield and in the northern part of the Arden (both 0.5 per cent), and in the 21 stone-dominated parishes in the south-east (0.6 per cent: see Table 23). Although these large houses were predominantly rural, a significant proportion were found in the towns – 25 in Coventry (2 per cent), 22 in Warwick (3.6 per cent) and four in Atherstone (1.6 per cent) (Table 10). The six in Birmingham and Stratford correspond to no more than the county-wide average, while Alcester, Southam and Henley had none at all. The 'Great Houses' in Warwickshire (Map 11) are also evenly spread, though notably absent from the south-east, apart from the isolated Shuckburgh Hall.

A number of these houses share common histories, some as converted monastic houses: abbeys at Combe (51 hearths), Stoneleigh (70) and Wroxall (22), and priories at Arbury (32) and Warwick (36). Updated castles were found at Warwick (47 hearths), Tamworth (20), Astley (18), and Maxstoke (17). Neither of these groups has survived well in their seventeenth-century form, with the great majority demolished, rebuilt or with their early structure concealed by later refurbishment, though some are recorded in engravings and early views.[1] Amongst the houses that have retained a substantial resemblance to their hearth tax appearance are Aston Hall (41 hearths), Compton Wynyates (26), Baddesley Clinton (20), Pooley Hall (19) and Little Wolford (11). All these are principally of brick or stone but some of the rural houses were undoubtedly timber-framed in 1670. A few large timber-framed houses survive, like the compact Packwood House (10 hearths): however, the burden of maintaining their fabric has since led to their almost complete disappearance, though their appearance is sometimes recorded in early drawings, such as that of Weston under Wetherley Hall, demolished in the 1730s (20 hearths; Figure 15).

Great houses (25 hearths upwards)

In classifying the largest houses for Warwickshire, it appears more appropriate to place the border between the greatest houses and those below them at about 25 hearths rather than 20, judging by the coherence of the resulting groups. The first comprises the 17 houses listed in Table 26(a), ranging from 70 down to 25 hearths. However, Combe Abbey's 51 hearths included both 'the manor house and lodge', and the same is certainly true at Stoneleigh, where the gatehouse is not identified

1 Tyack, *Country houses*, gives well-illustrated brief accounts of many of the houses discussed in this section.

Table 26 Houses with 20 or more hearths in 1666/1670 (plotted on Map 11)

(a) Great houses with 25–70 hearths

Location	*Hearths*	*Owner/occupier as listed in the hearth tax return*
Stoneleigh Abbey	70	Thomas, Lord Leigh
Combe Abbey	51	William, Earl of Craven (non-resident)
Warwick Castle	47	Robert Greville, Lord Brooke
Charlecote House	42	Richard Lucy, esquire
Aston Hall	41	Sir Robert Holt, baronet
Weston House	38	Ralph Sheldon, esquire
Coughton Court	37	Sir Francis Throckmorton, baronet
Warwick Priory	36	Sir Henry Puckering, baronet
Newnham Paddox	34	Basil Feilding, Earl of Denbigh
Arbury Hall	32	Richard Newdigate, esquire
Packington Hall	32	Sir Clement Fisher, baronet
Coleshill Hall	30	Lady Digby (widow of Kildare, Baron Digby)
Snitterfield House	28	Thomas Coventry, esquire
Compton Wynyates House	26	James Compton, Earl of Northampton (non-resident)
Middleton Hall	26	Lady Willoughby (widow of Sir Francis Willoughby, knight; owned by his son, Francis Willoughby, esquire)
Studley, Skilts[1]	26	Ralph Sheldon, esquire (non-resident)
Billesley Hall	25	Sir Charles Lee, knight

(b) Houses with 20–22 hearths

Location	*Hearths*	*Owner/occupier as listed in the hearth tax return*
Fletchamstead Hall	22	Thomas, Lord Leigh (listed with 22 hearths in 1670 and previously occupied as a single house, but known to have been divided between several tenants by 1666)
Keresley (unidentified)	22	Samuell Clearke ('in building' in 1666)
Nether Whitacre Hall	22	Lady King (widow of Sir Robert King, knight, but describing herself as Viscountess Wimbledon, from her first husband)
Wootton Wawen Hall	22	Lord Carrington
Edgbaston Hall	22	Sir John Gage, baronet
Lawford Hall	22	Sir Edward Boughton, baronet
Shuckburgh Hall	22	Robert Harvey, esquire
Wroxall Abbey	22	Sir Roger Burgoyne, baronet
Compton Verney House	21	Lady Verney (widow of Sir Grevill Verney, knight)
Castle Bromwich Hall	21	John Bridgman, esquire
Bull Inn, Coventry	21	Edward Childes

[1] Skilts was the second seat of the Sheldon family, built in about 1560 before they moved to Weston Hall, built in 1588–9 (Tyack, *Country houses*, pp. 216, 264).

Location	*Hearths*	*Owner/occupier as listed in the hearth tax return*
Ragley Hall	20	Lord Conway
Caldecote Hall	20	William Purefey, esquire
Grendon Hall	20	Sir Wooleston Dixey, baronet (husband of Frances, widow of former owner, Walter Chetwynd)
Ipsley Court	20	Lady Huband (mother of Sir John Huband, baronet, who was under age)
Baddesley Clinton	20	Henry Ferrers, esquire (listed in 1670–1 with 15 hearths, but with 20 hearths in other returns)
Tamworth Castle	20	John Ferrers, esquire
Weston under Wetherley	20	Mrs Morgan
Swan Inn, Warwick	20	Moses Holloway

separately. Thus, the hearths listed were not necessarily all within the main house. Variations in the figures between one return and another also indicate that evasion was not unknown, even at this social level.

All these houses were the centres of major estates, appropriate in size and quality to their owners' status. Their decoration could be of unsurpassed magnificence, as already illustrated by the chimney-piece at Combe Abbey. For some, probate inventories survive (principally in estate collections) that reveal more of their character than the number of hearths alone. At Stoneleigh in 1672, Lord Leigh had 102 rooms. Warwick Castle had 67 rooms listed in an inventory of 1643, where the appraisers went in stately procession round the courtyard and up each tower in turn. Aston Hall in 1654 contained 41 rooms within the house itself, headed by the imposing but little-used hall, with more functional summer and winter parlours and the usual chambers and services: a further 13 rooms were in service ranges.[1]

Substantial houses (15–22 hearths)

A group of 54 smaller, though still very substantial, houses can be identified with between 15 and 22 hearths.[2] Many of these shared the attributes of the great houses, albeit on a slightly lesser scale, but they also included two distinctive groups of urban houses. The first comprised the largest of the homes of the merchant and professional classes, such as Dr Richard Higgs of Little Park Street, Coventry (15 hearths). The second group is exemplified by the 20–hearth house of Moses Holloway in Warwick, and that of Edward Childes with 21 hearths in Coventry. Both these can be identified from other sources as major inns: remarkably, the second had the largest number of hearths of any building in Coventry. Moses Holloway's house was the

1 Stoneleigh: SCLA, DR18/4/4 (inventory of Stoneleigh Abbey); Warwick: WCRO, CR1886/6739; Aston: BAHS, MS 3889/Acc 1926–008/347952 (information from Geoffrey Tyack).

2 Those with 20–22 hearths (included on Map 11) are listed in Table 26(b). No houses had 23 or 24 hearths.

Swan in High Street, Warwick, which had 34 bays of building when it was burnt to the ground in 1694: it must have had fireplaces in most of its chambers.[1] Edward Childes was the landlord of the Bull Inn in Smithford Street, though little is known of him or the inn, which was demolished in 1793.[2] Thus, these great urban inns surpassed the great majority of gentry town houses in their size and quality.[3] They probably had courtyard plans, similar to that of the one urban gentry mansion which can be illustrated, although it was destroyed in 1940: Palace Yard in Coventry, the home of Sir Richard Hopkins (16 hearths; Figure 16).[4]

Of the rural houses, Baddesley Clinton (Figure 17), the home of Henry Ferrers, esquire, was a sixteenth-century house that had been updated internally but not externally: some 40 rooms are listed in an inventory of 1760.[5] His distant cousin, John Ferrers of Tamworth Castle (20 hearths) had 36 rooms in 1680.[6] William Purefoy 're-edified' Caldecote Hall (20 hearths) as a 'fair house of brick and stone', represented in a drawing of c. 1800.[7] The Leigh family owned a second house in Stoneleigh, Fletchamstead Hall, a 'fair manor house' with 47 rooms and 22 hearths, of a quality appropriate to the son of the family. It had been built in the 1560s by Sir Thomas Leigh, second son of the head of the family but by 1670 had ceased to be needed for its original purpose and had been divided between several tenants.[8]

One building of particular significance in this group is Maxstoke Castle, occupied by Mrs (Honor) Dilke, the widow of William Dilke, esquire, who had died in 1669, with 20 rooms listed in his inventory:[9] she paid for 17 hearths in 1670, and 19 in 1674. The quadrangular curtain wall of the castle, with gatehouse and corner towers, survives almost as built in 1345, topped by numerous original chimneys (Figure 18), although the lodging ranges that lined the wall have mostly vanished.[10] We can identify about 23 original fireplaces in the existing building, only two of which served the demolished ranges. To these, by the seventeenth century, must be added about six in the refurbished hall and kitchen area.[11] Thus, the hearth tax returns must have

1 Farr, *Great fire*, p. 137.

2 See Alcock, 'Warwickshire', p. 119.

3 Major urban inns must also exist among other Warwick houses with 10 hearths and upwards, though they have still to be identified. Mr John Lax of Coventry (15 hearths) kept the Star Inn, Earl Street (Alcock, 'Warwickshire', p. 118).

4 *VCH*, viii, p. 148; and see above, p. 106.

5 Alcock & Meeson, 'Baddesley Clinton'. The 1670 hearth tax return lists only 15 hearths here but others give a more plausible 20 hearths.

6 TNA, PROB 4/5450.

7 Tyack, *Country houses*, pp. 234–5.

8 Dugdale, *Antiquities*, p. 264; SCLA, DR18/4/1 (inventory of Stoneleigh Abbey and Fletchamstead Hall). It survived to be recorded in an eighteenth-century watercolour as a rambling timber-framed structure (Alcock, *People at home*, p. 84). The number of hearths varied from return to return, the largest being 24 in 1664; the 1671 return (p. 290), shows it subdivided between individual tenants.

9 The inventory is not very detailed and must have ignored many empty or sparsely furnished rooms. The only fire fittings mentioned are andirons etc. in the kitchen and a grate in the little kitchen.

10 Alcock, Faulkner & Jones, 'Maxstoke Castle'.

11 Four chimneys heat the upper floor rooms inserted into the medieval hall, and an adjoining area that was reconstructed in 1698 presumably also included heating before this.

ignored a substantial number of the seventeenth-century hearths, since they survive to this day.[1]

Most of the inventories cited mention great halls, though they were usually sparsely furnished. Intriguingly, at both Sir Fulwar Skipwith's Newbold Revel (1679), and in an incomplete inventory of Arbury of 1600, the principal object in the hall was a 'shovel-board'.[2] Like the hall at Palace Yard, Coventry, these rooms may well have retained their open hearths; since they were no longer the pivotal rooms in the house, they probably had little need for up-dated heating.

Lesser houses (10–14 hearths)

The figure of 137 houses with between 10 and 14 hearths provides a particular insight into the difference between town and country in seventeenth-century Warwickshire. More than a third (52) were located in towns large and small across the county, far above the statistical average; as with the larger houses, they were predominantly occupied by the urban merchant and professional elite.[3] Very little direct evidence has survived of these urban houses, as a consequence of redevelopment in Coventry and Birmingham, and the destruction caused by the 1694 fire in Warwick. A notable exception is Jury Street House in Warwick, the town house of the Archer family (13 hearths), which was drawn before its nineteenth-century reconstruction.[4] It was built of stone with decorated gables, with a courtyard plan open to the street – an ostentatious use of space in the cramped main street of the town. A probate inventory of 1673 identifies 15 rooms in the house of Mr John Rylands, rector of St Martin's, Birmingham, and another of 1677 lists 22 rooms in the home of John Brownell of Coventry, gentleman (both with 11 hearths).[5] The latter's house had been the Mermaid Inn: it had no hall but two kitchens and a series of well-furnished chambers, with fittings including glass, 'wrought or stained' with 'the severall months'.

A few of the rural houses in this group retain much of their seventeenth-century character or can be seen in early illustrations. At Little Wolford Manor, the home of Hastings Ingram (11 hearths), two wings remain of a former U-shaped building, principally of stone though with some timber-framing on its upper floor: it now has eight rooms in plan.[6] Sheldon Hall (11 hearths, Figure 19), the home of George Devereux, has a central block of brick, flanked by timber-framed wings with brick chimneys. Parts of John Stanton's house at Longbridge outside Warwick (10 hearths)

1 The most obvious areas to have been excluded are the eastern towers and the gatehouse, with a total of 10 hearths. Most of these rooms appear not to have been occupied since the seventeenth century and the fireplaces (and many chimneys) survive as they were built.

2 TNA, PROB 4/9337; WCRO, CR136/B551.

3 Such people as Thomas King, brewer and mayor of Coventry, and Humphrey Burton, the city's town clerk from 1636 to 1683, both with 11 hearths.

4 *VCH*, viii, pp. 427–8 & Plate.

5 LRO, B/C/5, 15 Apr 1673 and 31 Oct 1677. See also Alcock, 'Broadgate', pp. 20–1.

6 *VCH*, v, pp. 213–4, with plan.

also survive: it too was mostly timber-framed, with 19 rooms listed in an inventory of 1674.[1] Other houses have disappeared completely, like that of Charles Newsham of Chadshunt (13 hearths), a drawing of which shows a stone house with gables.[2] The houses of Ambrose Holbech at Mollington (now Mansion House Farm), and John Palmer at Compton Scorpion, Ilmington (10 and 11 hearths), were both built of Cotswold stone in the seventeenth century. However, the existing buildings have plans with three and four rooms respectively: though both are three storied, it is not easy to see how they could have accommodated these hearths within their existing footprints.[3] It may be that they had extensive service ranges that have disappeared – an example of the difficulties often encountered in matching the hearth tax with surviving buildings.

Conclusion

The correlation between the number of hearths and the size of house is at its clearest when averages are considered. However, individual houses with a given number of hearths, have a considerable range in the numbers of rooms identified in probate inventories. Thus, we cannot predict accurately how many rooms a dwelling listed in the hearth tax returns might have had, based on its number of hearths. The example of Maxstoke Castle also warns us that substantial parts of old-fashioned residences might be deemed to be out of use and their hearths thus ignored by the collectors, who lacked the authority to challenge the numbers of hearths returned by the rich and powerful. Furthermore, until the linking of hearths and inventories undertaken here for Lichfield and Coventry diocese is extended to inventories produced at the Prerogative Court of Canterbury, it will not be possible to examine systematically the correlation of rooms and hearths in the largest houses.

With these caveats, we may conclude that the smallest standing buildings, of two bays in plan, correspond well to our expectations based on the evidence of probate inventories that houses with one hearth, intermittently or regularly exempt from the hearth tax, predominantly had between two and four rooms. As the number of hearths increased, the buildings corresponding to them rapidly became more complex, though it is rare for the larger standing buildings to have survived unaltered in their seventeenth-century form; in particular, major houses have often suffered from partial demolition.

1 *VCH*, viii, p. 435; TNA, PROB 4/3439.

2 Tyack, *Country houses*, pp. 236–7.

3 For the Holbech house, see *VCH, Oxfordshire*, x, pp. 197–206; Wood-Jones, *Banbury*, pp. 114–15, 219; N.W. Alcock, 'Compton Scorpion Manor, Ilmington, Warwickshire, a history and architectural survey' (unpublished report, 2008, copy at WCRO).

10. Mapping the Warwickshire hearth tax

Mapping units

The confusing jumble of parishes, chapelries, extra parochial places, townships, constableries and even manors and hamlets that are recorded in the Warwickshire hearth tax returns inevitably presents a major challenge for mapping. Elsewhere in this volume, Tom Arkell has imposed order on this apparent chaos by grouping together all these various entities into the fully-operational parishes, and chapelries that were effectively parishes, in the later seventeenth century (see especially Tables 8 and 9). The places given separate entries in the returns were, by definition, administratively distinct in so far as the hearth tax collectors listed them separately, although some were no more than hamlets within the parishes. In some cases, however, these administrative sub-divisions also seem to have reflected genuine differences in topography and agricultural practice, with the inhabitants of individual settlements or townships farming their own fields within their own boundaries, which may have given rise to different patterns of economic development. The individuality of these different areas is concealed within composite averages for whole parishes, and only appears when separate statistics are calculated for each. For this reason, rather than mapping only the whole parishes as they existed in the seventeenth century, the principle that has been adopted is to map separately those entities (here called 'mapping units') for which distinct boundaries could be identified.

Crucial for this approach is the establishment of the boundaries of each mapping unit. A significant proportion of these entities later became civil parishes, so the starting point for this exercise has been the mapping of parishes and their subdivisions that was carried out by the Ordnance Survey in the 1880s, combined with the compilation by Kain and Oliver of boundaries of parishes and other areas as in 1851.[1] (Digital versions of both were provided by the Hearth Tax Project.) It is of course impossible to be certain that all of these nineteenth-century boundaries correspond to the earlier ones, but in most instances this seems to be a reasonable presumption. Most of the units mapped by the Ordnance Survey derived from traditional administrative areas used for collecting taxes etc. that were previously described as townships or an equivalent such as 'ends' in Warwickshire's Arden. However, the coverage in these maps of the places identified in the hearth tax is incomplete and other boundaries have been obtained from sources, such as enclosure awards and tithe commutation maps (sometimes with an element of approximation). Altogether, one third of the parishes in Warwickshire and Coventry (74 in all) were subdivided in the 1670 hearth tax returns and the boundaries of their components have been established in half of them.[2] In the other parishes with multiple entries in the returns, either the individual entities appear not to have had distinct boundaries or insufficient evidence exists to establish them: these are mapped by parish.

[1] Kain and Oliver, *Parishes*, pp. 12–21.

[2] Marked '+' in Table 9 and listed in Table 27 with the corresponding mapping statistics.

By these means important differences in the character of some settlements within parishes have been illustrated. Thus, in Nuneaton, the town has been separated from the rural areas of Attleborough and Stockingford. In Burton Dassett parish, the northern half of the parish contains the populous hamlets of Knightcote and Northend, sharing an open field system only enclosed in 1772. To their south, the larger area of Burton and Little Dassett had been enclosed in 1497 and was largely used for grazing land: in the seventeenth century they contained only a quarter of the number of households in Knightcote and Northend and had a significantly different hearth distribution.[1] Here, Knightcote and Northend are plotted as a single unit, as are Burton and Little Dassett. Other large parishes whose subdivisions have been mapped include Aston with 10 entities, Kingsbury with six and Monks Kirby with six mapped out of nine (the remaining three being locations within the civil parish of Monks Kirby itself). By contrast, for Stoneleigh (eight entities), numerous early maps survive, but most of the individual places did not have distinct boundaries.

Frustratingly, for some places, even though the entities within a parish were clearly independent, we lack the evidence to map them: in Aston Cantlow, for example, the hamlet of Wilmcote had its own field system,[2] as probably did Little Alne, Newnham and Shelfield, but the parish was enclosed as a single entity in 1743, and it has not proved possible to reconstruct the individual boundaries. Among the other large parishes whose subdivisions have not been mapped are Bidford on Avon (six locations named), Polesworth (seven), Solihull (eight), and Sutton Coldfield (five). A few places that can be mapped individually were conflated with others in the hearth tax returns and so have had to be combined for statistical purposes.

The Maps

The data used for mapping the Warwickshire hearth tax statistics are collected under parishes and chapelries in Table 9, while the data for the additional mapping units, into which the individual entities have been subdivided in 35 of these parishes, are recorded in Table 27. Altogether the mapping covers 180 complete parishes or chapelries, 100 subdivided entities, and ten detached portions of parishes; their locations are shown on the back end-paper map.

The statistical mapping is presented in Maps 4–13. The small-scale variability these maps reveal has already been noted in the context of the regional analysis in Section 5. It is worth reiterating this feature, since it is the most immediately obvious aspect for anyone examining the maps with an interest in individual places, and it is only at a regional level that coherent trends can be recognised. The variability is at its most extreme in the mapping of the percentage of exempt households (Map 12), where we find areas in the highest category (blue), juxtaposed with those in the lowest – or even, as for Binley (39 per cent exempt), adjoining Combe Fields with no exempt at all: the latter corresponds to the depopulated parish of Smite, later combined

[1] Alcock, *Grazier*, pp. 27ff.

[2] It also formerly had its own chapel, though it was not described as a chapelry in 1670.

ecclesiastically with Binley parish. The larger houses, with 5–9 hearths (Map 9) again show extreme variability in their density, with areas of concentration scattered over the county. The contrasts illustrated by the maps also correspond, of course, to those revealed in more detail for selected parishes by the histograms presented in Figure 1. To some extent, these differences must also relate to the social character of the individual parishes, and in particular whether they were 'open' or 'closed'; the numerous and generally more poverty-stricken inhabitants of the former would undoubtedly find employment in the neighbouring more prosperous parishes.

The fluctuations in household density (Map 4) are rather more systematic, corresponding to the urban/rural and regional differentiation established in section 5. The towns, of course, appear with very large densities, up to several hundred households per acre, and the most populous rural parishes are widely scattered, with the concentration around the north Warwickshire coalfield particularly notable (p. 67). An area of generally lower population density is apparent in the south of the county, as already highlighted. Similarly, low values are also apparent in the mapping of density of hearths (Map 5), even though the marked variations in average numbers of hearths per household are also incorporated into these figures.

Table 27 Percentages of households in hearth tax groups for additional mapping units

(a) Warwickshire 1670

		Total	*Percentage of households in hearth tax groups*						
	Division	*h'holds*	*1*	*2*	*3–4*	*5–9*	*10+*	*3+*	*NC*
Parish & subdivision	*& Hundred*	*n*	*%*	*%*	*%*	*%*	*%*	*%*	*%*
Arrow	Alc:B								
Arrow		30	70	17	7	3	3	13	37
Oversley		30	70	13	7	10	0	17	53
Aston	Bir:H								
Aston		18	61	11	17	6	6	28	28
Bordesley		81	73	17	5	5	0	10	40
Castle Bromwich		70	61	10	23	1	4	29	46
Deritend		92	74	12	13	1	0	14	60
Duddeston		13	77	8	8	8	0	15	54
Erdington		116	77	8	12	2	2	16	51
Little Bromwich		38	55	29	11	3	3	16	24
Washwood and Saltley		42	79	10	10	2	0	12	55
Water Orton		23	57	22	22	0	0	22	26
Witton		28	71	18	7	0	4	11	36
Barcheston	Bra:Ki								
Barcheston		4	50	0	0	50	0	50	0
Willington		21	62	10	19	10	0	29	43
Binley	MK:Kn								
Combe Fields		14	57	29	0	7	7	14	0
Binley		28	61	14	21	4	0	25	39

Table 27(a) *contd*

Parish & subdivision	*Division & Hundred*	*Total h'holds* n	*Percentage of households in hearth tax groups* 1 %	2 %	3–4 %	5–9 %	10+ %	3+ %	NC %
Bishops Tachbrook									
Bishops Tachbrook	Tan:Ki	58	78	7	14	2	0	16	31
Tachbrook Mallory	Ken:Kn	6	33	33	17	0	17	33	0
Brailes	Bra:Ki								
Lower Brailes		111	73	12	12	3	1	15	45
Upper Brailes & Chelmscote		53	57	26	17	0	0	17	25
Winderton		24	79	13	4	4	0	8	29
Burton Dassett	PM:Ki								
Burton and Little Dassett		15	47	20	13	13	7	33	33
Knightcote and Northend		61	61	16	16	7	0	23	31
Burton Hastings	MK:Kn								
Burton Hastings		22	36	36	18	9	0	27	18
Hydes Pasture & Stretton Baskerville		6	100	0	0	0	0	0	17
Claverdon	Hen:B								
Claverdon		61	64	18	13	5	0	18	25
Langley		26	73	19	8	0	0	8	42
Clifton on Dunsmore	Rug:Kn								
Clifton on Dunsmore		48	65	15	17	4	0	21	33
Newton and Biggin		33	67	18	12	3	0	15	33
Coughton	Alc:B								
Coughton		41	71	12	10	2	5	17	41
Sambourne		53	60	15	19	6	0	25	17
Dunchurch	Rug:Kn								
Cawston		3	67	0	0	0	33	33	33
Dunchurch		64	59	14	19	6	2	27	47
Thurlaston		66	73	20	5	3	0	8	52
Fenny Compton									
Fenny Compton	PM:Ki	91	81	11	3	4	0	8	36
Watergall with Hodnell	Sou:Kn	3	0	33	33	33	0	67	0
Grandborough	Sou:Kn								
Grandborough		53	64	28	6	2	0	8	32
Woolscott		14	14	43	29	14	0	43	7
Great Wolford	Bra:Ki								
Great Wolford		42	62	24	10	5	0	14	36
Little Wolford		42	81	5	10	2	2	14	36
Grendon+	Tam:H								
Grendon		47	64	23	6	4	2	13	19
Whittington		13	54	38	8	0	0	8	+
Hatton	Str:B								
Beausale		42	76	19	5	0	0	5	48
Hatton		30	70	20	7	3	0	10	33
Shrewley		35	66	17	17	0	0	17	40

Parish & subdivision	*Division & Hundred*	*Total h'holds n*	*Percentage of households in hearth tax groups* 1 %	2 %	3–4 %	5–9 %	10+ %	3+ %	NC %
Kingsbury									
Coton	Ath:H	8	63	13	13	13	0	25	50
Dosthill	Tam:H	11	36	27	27	9	0	36	18
Holt, Slately and Cliff	Tam:H	16	81	0	6	6	6	19	44
Hurley	Tam:H	83	71	12	14	2	0	17	41
Kingsbury	Tam:H	42	60	31	2	5	2	10	19
Whateley^{+}	Tam:H	15	53	20	20	7	0	27	53
Lighthorne	Kin:Ki								
Compton Verney		3	67	0	0	0	33	33	0
Lighthorne		30	50	33	10	7	0	17	20
Mancetter	Ath:H								
Atherstone		257	61	14	16	7	2	25	47
Hartshill		43	60	16	12	12	0	23	35
Mancetter		41	73	2	10	12	2	24	39
Monks Kirby	MK:Kn								
Cestersover		7	43	29	14	14	0	29	43
Copston Magna		27	63	33	4	0	0	4	41
Easenhall		26	58	31	8	4	0	12	27
Monks Kirby		99	59	23	17	0	1	18	36
Pailton		78	68	18	12	3	0	14	29
Stretton under Fosse		26	58	15	19	4	4	27	31
Napton on the Hill	Sou:Kn								
Napton on the Hill		155	80	15	3	1	0	5	30
Chapel Ascote		1	0	100	0	0	0	0	0
Lower & Upper Radbourne; Wills Pasture		3	33	33	33	0	0	33	33
Newbold on Avon	Rug:Kn								
Cosford		19	58	21	16	5	0	21	42
Harborough Parva		4	25	50	25	0	0	25	0
Long and Little Lawford		57	77	16	5	0	2	7	39
Newbold on Avon		31	61	10	26	3	0	29	52
Nuneaton	Ath:H								
Attleborough		66	74	21	5	0	0	5	48
Nuneaton		302	65	13	16	5	1	22	52
Stockingford		71	79	11	10	0	0	10	32
Ratley	PM:Ki								
Ratley		34	53	18	18	9	3	29	32
Upton		2	0	50	0	0	50	50	0
Snitterfield	Str:B								
Fulbrook		4	50	25	25	0	0	25	0
Snitterfield		65	62	17	18	2	2	22	38
Stratford upon Avon									
Drayton and Luddington	Bid:B	27	67	15	19	0	0	19	33
Old Stratford	Str:B	108	60	18	13	6	3	22	54
Stratford borough	Str:B	427	59	14	19	7	1	27	46

Table 27(a) *contd*

Parish & subdivision	*Division & Hundred*	*Total h'holds n*	*1 %*	*2 %*	*3–4 %*	*5–9 %*	*10+ %*	*3+ %*	*NC %*
			Percentage of households in hearth tax groups						
Stretton on Dunsmore	Rug:Kn								
Princethorpe		18	72	17	0	11	0	11	17
Stretton on Dunsmore		50	78	14	4	4	0	8	52
Tamworth (part)	Tam:H								
Amington and Stonydelph		40	73	18	8	0	3	10	35
Bolehall and Glascote		31	61	26	13	0	0	13	29
Borough (part) & Castle Liberty		194	52	23	19	6	1	26	39
Wilnecote		112	82	12	5	1	0	6	56
Wappenbury	Sou:Kn								
Eathorpe		23	78	9	4	9	0	13	48
Wappenbury		19	53	37	0	11	0	11	42
Wellesbourne	Tan:Ki								
Wellesbourne Hastings		27	52	19	26	4	0	30	26
Wellesbourne Mountford		39	64	15	10	10	0	21	44
Walton Deyville		14	79	7	0	7	7	14	57
Whichford	Bra:Ki								
Ascott and Whichford		69	45	26	25	4	0	29	30
Stourton		32	63	16	19	3	0	22	25
Wolfhampcote	Sou:Kn								
Flecknoe		56	68	23	9	0	0	9	29
Wolfhampcote & Sawbridge		29	48	24	21	7	0	28	3
Wolston									
Brandon and Bretford	MK:Kn	41	56	20	17	7	0	24	17
Wolston	Rug:Kn	62	73	19	3	2	3	8	31

+ See pp. 390 and 414 for notes on the exempt in Grendon, Whittington and Whateley.

(b) Coventry 1666: City parishes (estimated figures*)

Parish	*Total h'holds n*	*1 %*	*2 %*	*3–4 %*	*5–9 %*	*10+ %*	*3+ %*	*NC %*
		Percentage of households in hearth tax groups						
Holy Trinity (incl. Radford)	600	45	25	18	10	2	30	41
St Michael	843	45	23	20	10	2	32	39

Source: Table 28.
Key: see Table 9 (p. 61).

*The hearth tax data is listed by ward, of which Bayley Lane, Jordan Well and Gosford Street Wards overlap between the two parishes. The approximate subdivision of the ward data between the parishes has therefore been estimated from the street lengths of the wards within each parish, and from the 1674 Exemption Certificates, which give both ward and parish (Table 29(b)). Both estimates give very similar ratios, 25:75, 55:45 and 70:30 between Holy Trinity and St Michael for the three wards. Fortunately, the maps themselves are not very sensitive to the precise ratios.

Figure 2 Timber-framed fireplace at 121 Upper Spon Street, Coventry, inserted into the open hall of a mid fifteenth-century cottage. The original wattle-and-daub infill survives on one side but the remainder of the stack has been replaced in brick. A nineteenth-century range has been inserted in the fireplace.

Figure 3 A seventeenth-century cooking fireplace in a brick stack, in the kitchen/hall at Packington Old Hall, a house dated to 1679.

Figure 4 Netherstead, Morton Bagot, a house mostly rebuilt in c. 1649 for John Holyoake, gentleman, with four hearths.

(a) Exterior from south (framing exposed and restored in 2003–4). The brick section on the right conceals the framing of a sixteenth-century cross-wing retained from an earlier house.

(b) Parlour fireplace.

(c) Hall chamber fireplace.

Figure 5 Engraving of the chimney-piece in the Great Chamber at Combe Abbey, by C.J. Richardson, c. 1840 (WCRO, CR361/76, taken from Richardson, *Architectural remains*, Pl. 14).

Figure 6 Houses on the 1684 map of Chilvers Coton (WCRO, CR136/M14). North is to the right.
(a) Street running south from the village centre.

(b) The vicar's house (east of the village centre).

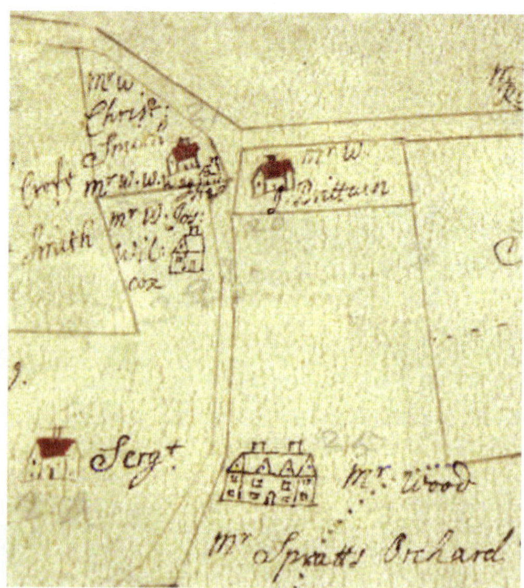

(c) Paradise End.

Figure 7 One-hearth houses in Stoneleigh and Ashow, both usually exempt.
(a) 11–12 Vicarage Road, Stoneleigh, built in about 1665.

(b) Fir Tree Cottage, Ashow, a medieval and later box-framed house with one hearth.

Figure 8 Cruck houses in Stoneleigh.
(a) 3 Birmingham Road, Stoneleigh, a two-bay medieval cruck house with one hearth (exempt in most hearth tax returns).

(b) 1 Birmingham Road, Stoneleigh, a three-bay medieval cruck house with one exempt hearth.

Figure 9 Bridge Cottage, Stoneleigh, a house with five rooms, of two main bays with a smaller one-bay extension, formerly single-storeyed (far end), paying for one hearth.

Figure 10 1–2 Coventry Road, Stoneleigh, a one-hearth, three-bay house with an additional bay at the near end (originally single-storey) that probably held the workshop of Roger Hudson, shoemaker.

Figure 11 Ivy Farm, Canley, Stoneleigh, a two-hearth house with about eight rooms, serving a 30-acre farm.

Figure 12 11–12 Coventry Road, Stoneleigh, a three-hearth house with ten rooms in 1631.

Figure 13 Lower Ingon Farm, Hampton Lucy, a five-hearth house.
(a) View from south-west (b) Parlour fireplace

(c) Kitchen fireplace

Figure 14 Manor Farm, Stoneleigh, a nine-hearth house with 20 rooms in 1673. The added parlour wing is on the right-hand side: the other two gables are purely decorative, applied to an in-line range.

Figure 15 Weston under Wetherley Hall, a house of 20 hearths, described as being taken 'from a painting by W. Hollar dated 1635 in the possession of the Throgmortons' (BAHS, Aylesford Collection, IIR61, Vol.2/722).

Figure 16 Palace Yard, Coventry, the house of Sir Richard Hopkins in 1666 (16 hearths) (destroyed in 1940): nineteenth-century engraving from Poole, *Coventry*.

Figure 17 Baddesley Clinton, the moated manor house of Henry Ferrers, with about 20 hearths and at least 40 rooms.

Figure 18 Maxstoke Castle, the gatehouse range. This was the home of Mrs Honor Dilke who paid for 17 hearths in 1670 (photo copyright: James Kerr).

Figure 19 Sheldon Hall, Sheldon, a house belonging to George Devereux with 11 hearths (photo copyright: Trevor Lucas).

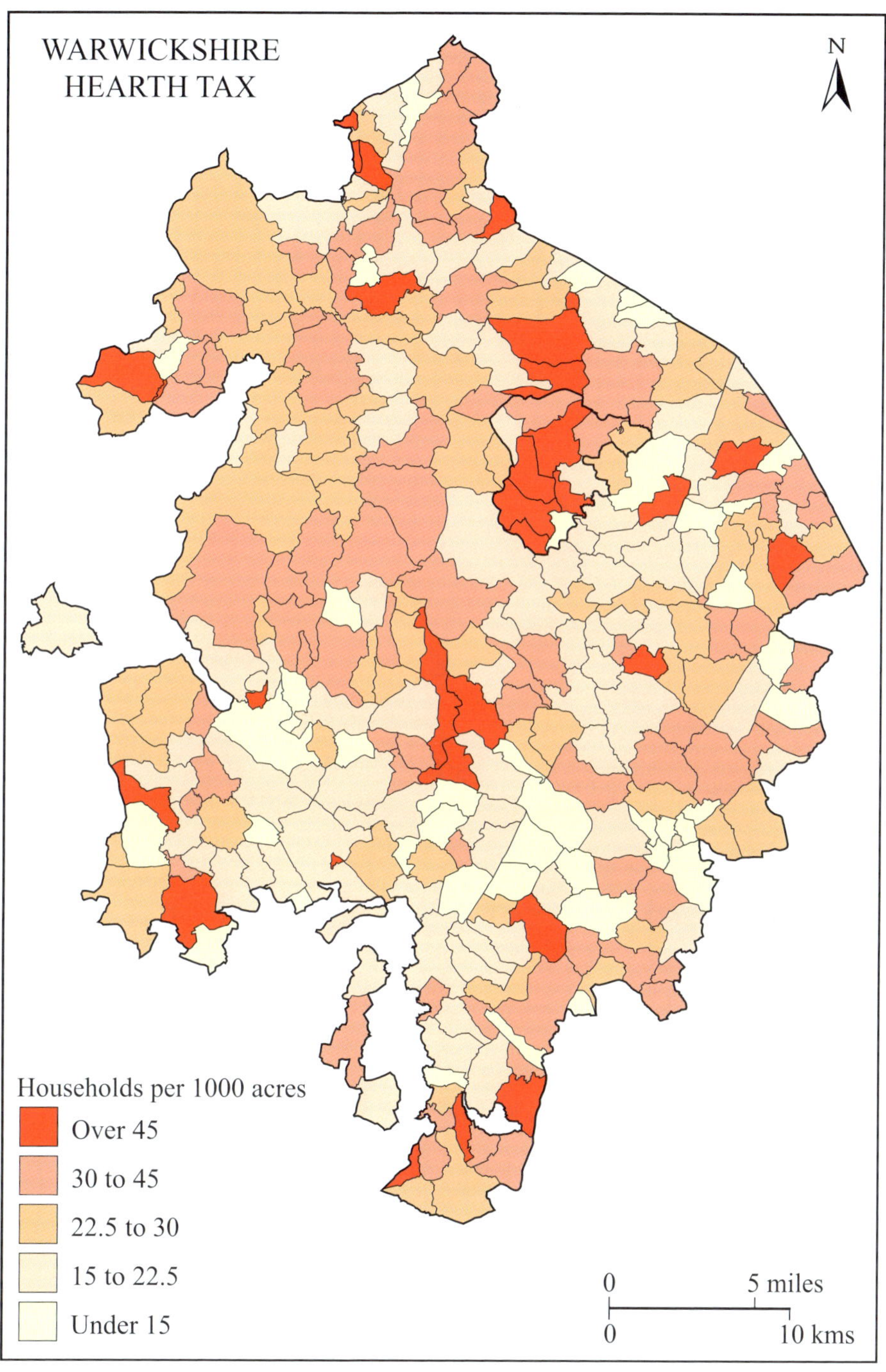

Map 4 Households per 1000 acres: Warwickshire (1670) and Coventry (1666).

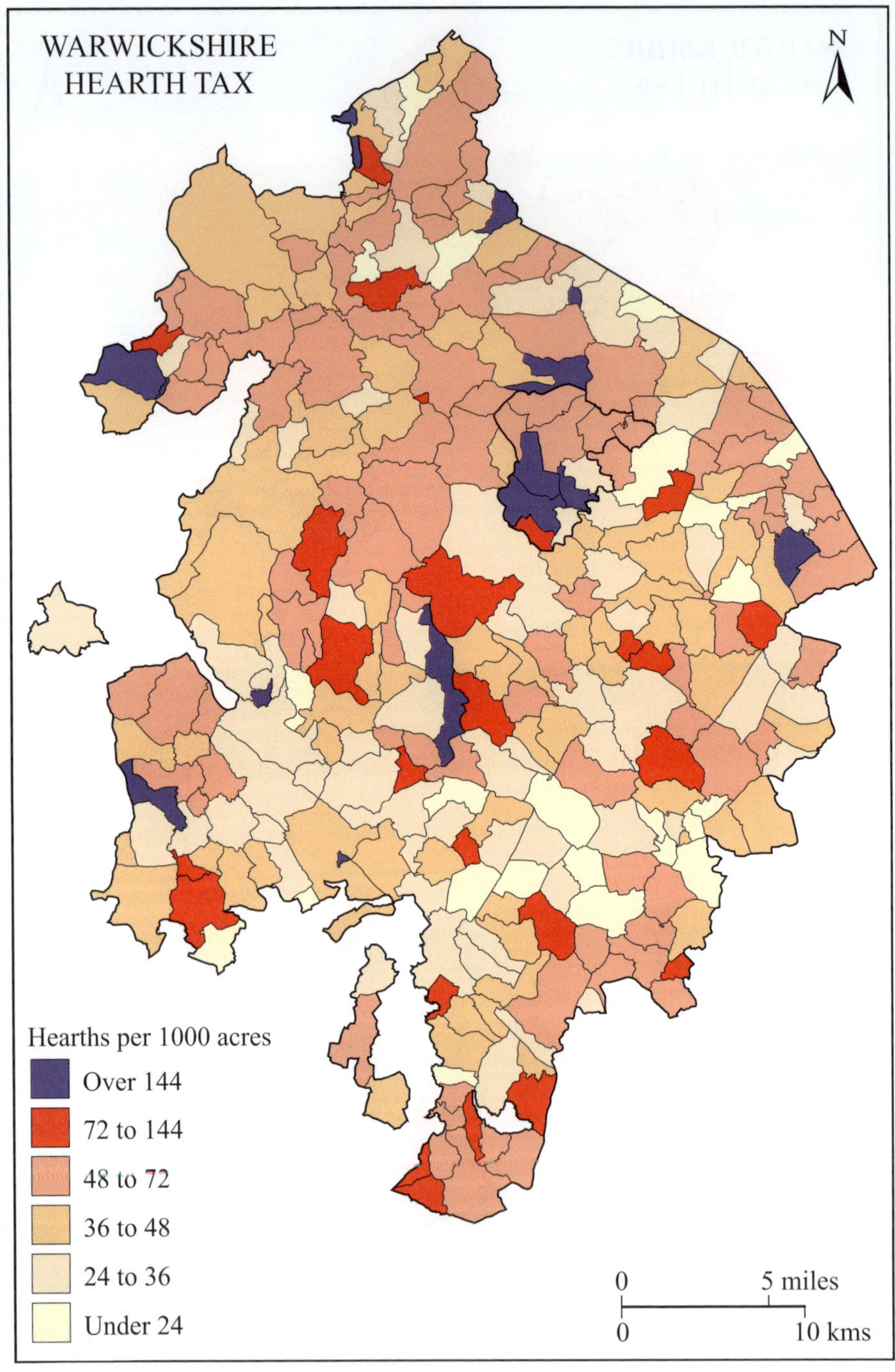

Map 5 Hearths per 1000 acres: Warwickshire (1670) and Coventry (1666).

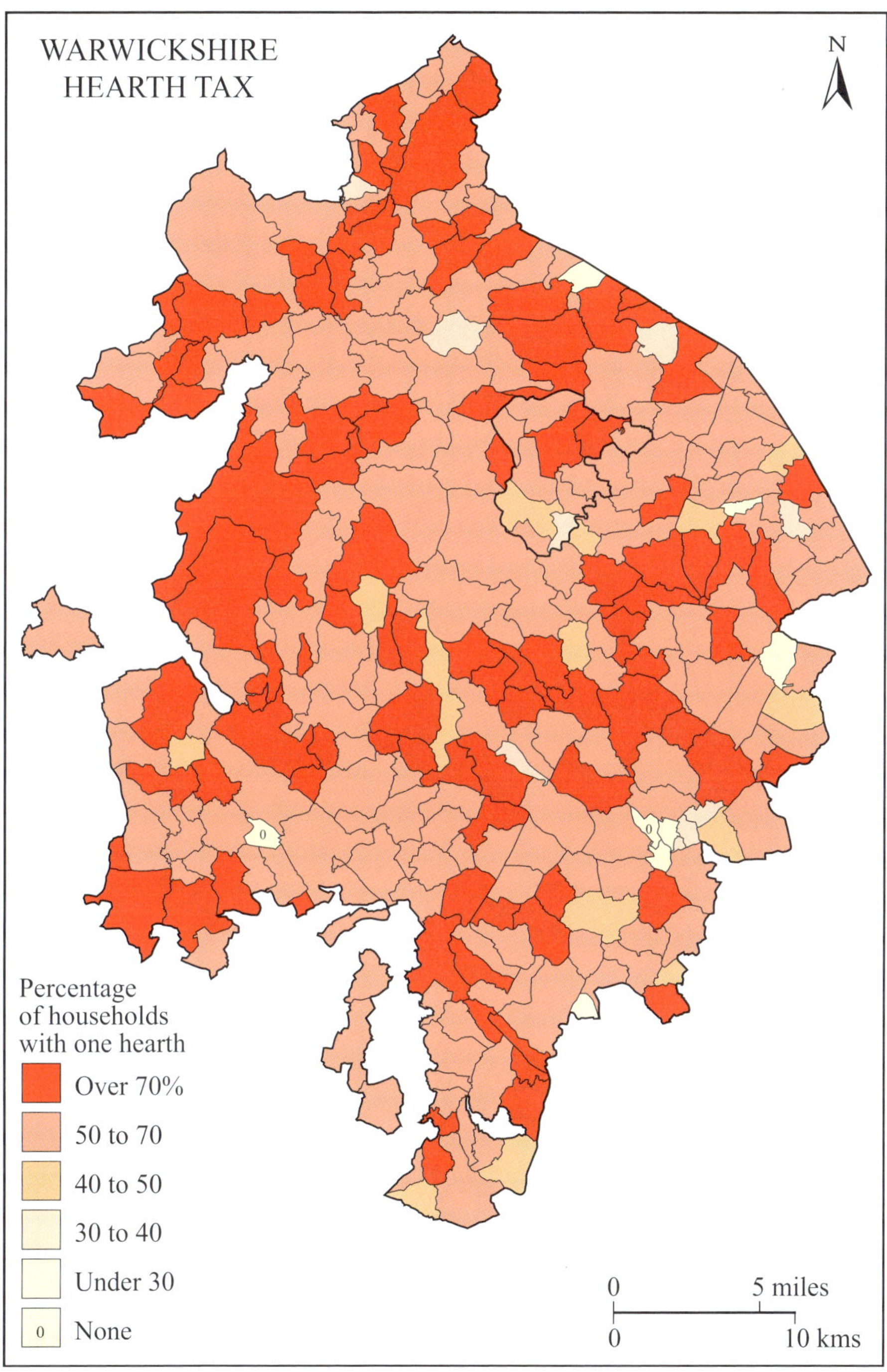

Map 6 Percentage of households with one hearth: Warwickshire (1670) and Coventry (1666).

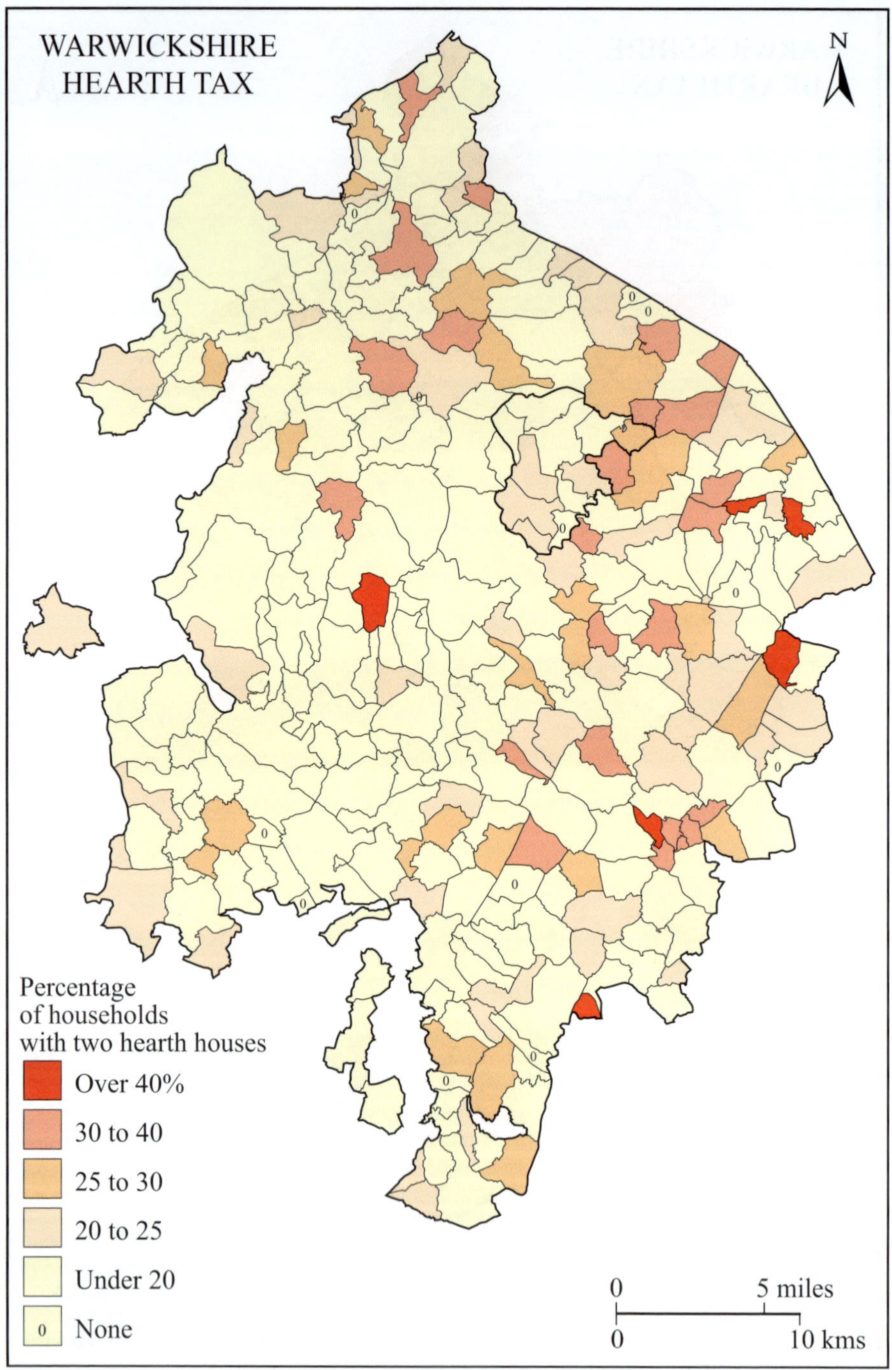

Map 7 Percentage of households with two hearths: Warwickshire (1670) and Coventry (1666).

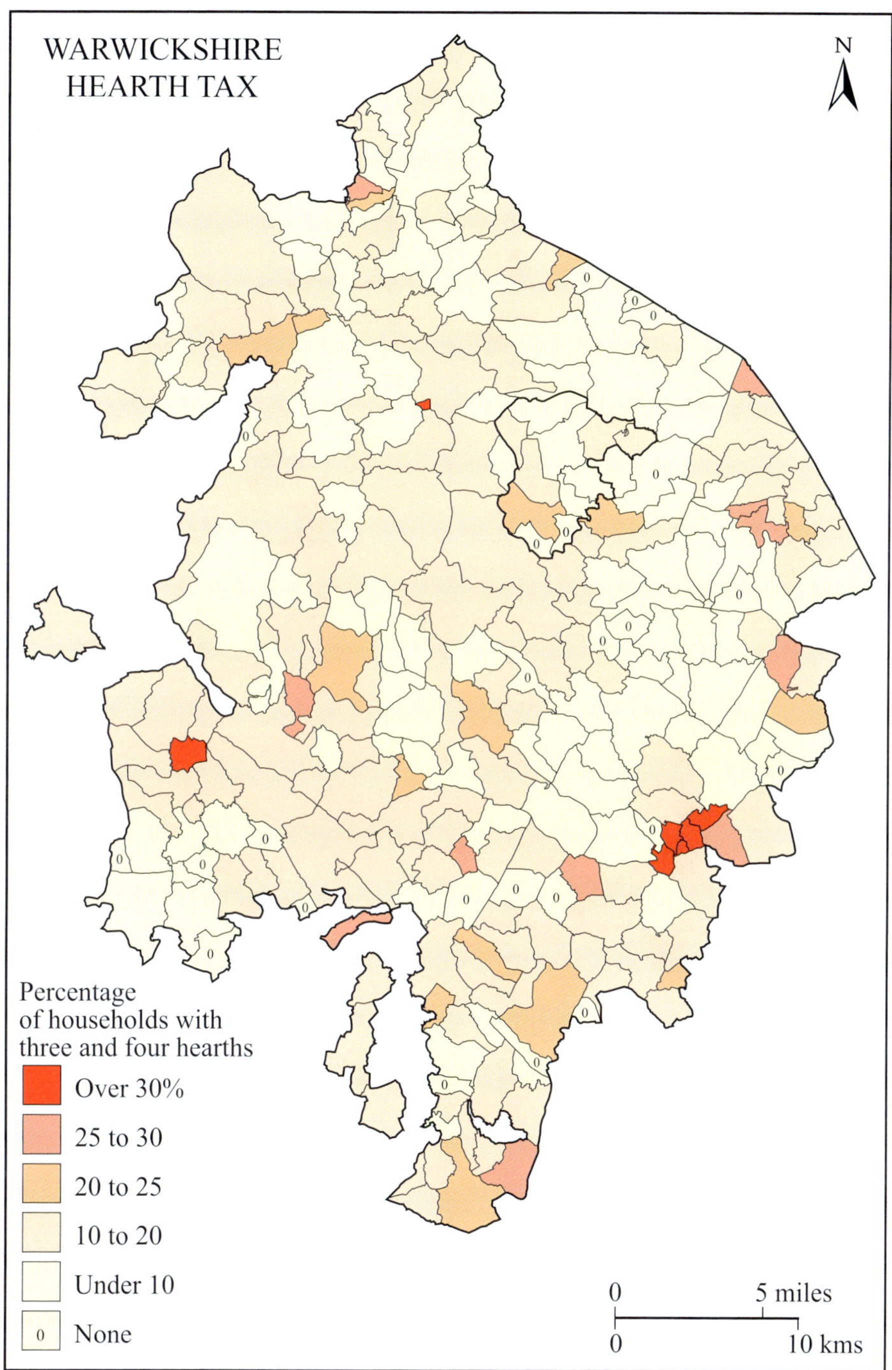

Map 8 Percentage of households with three and four hearths: Warwickshire (1670) and Coventry (1666).

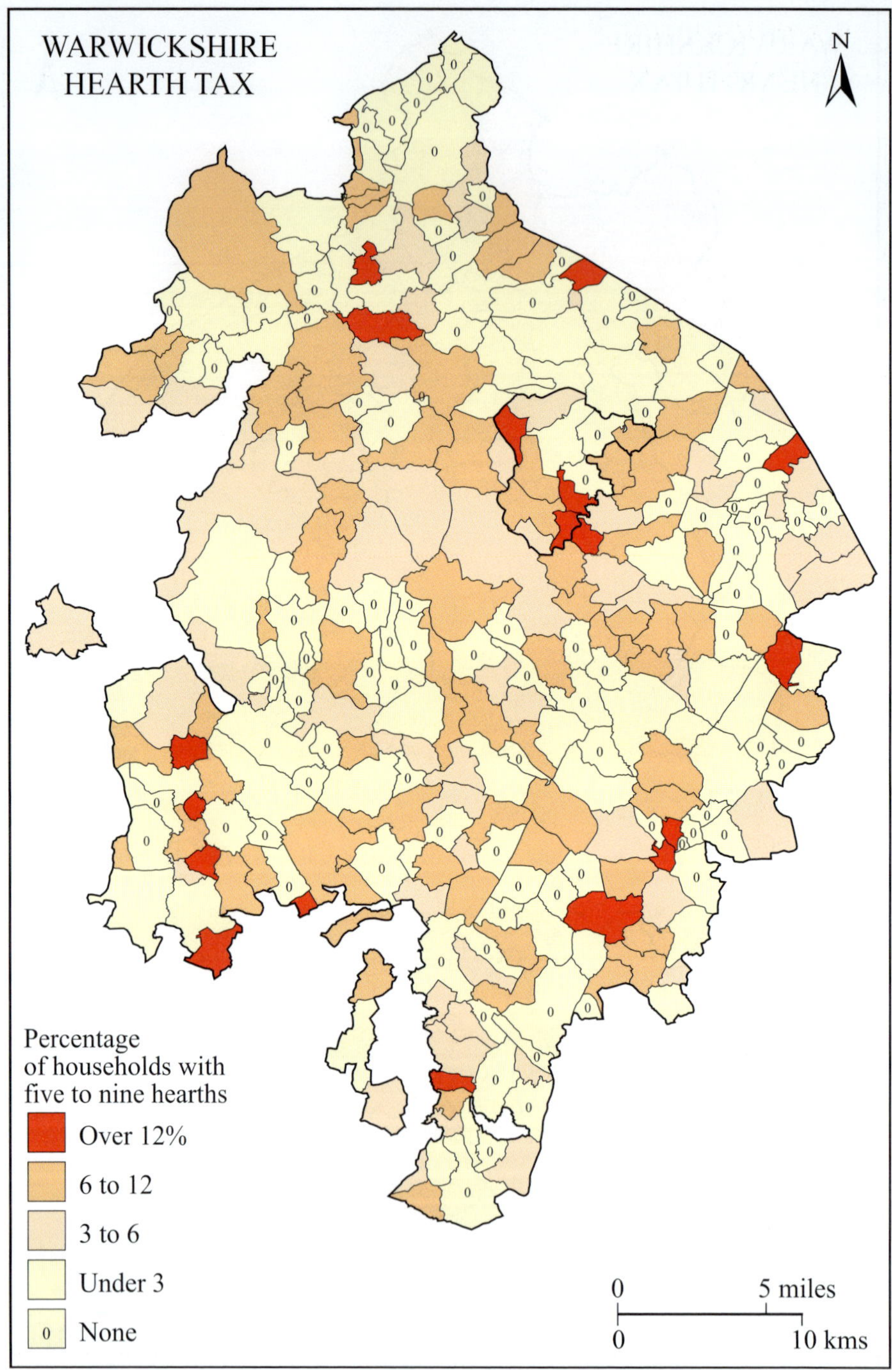

Map 9 Percentage of households with five to nine hearths: Warwickshire (1670) and Coventry (1666).

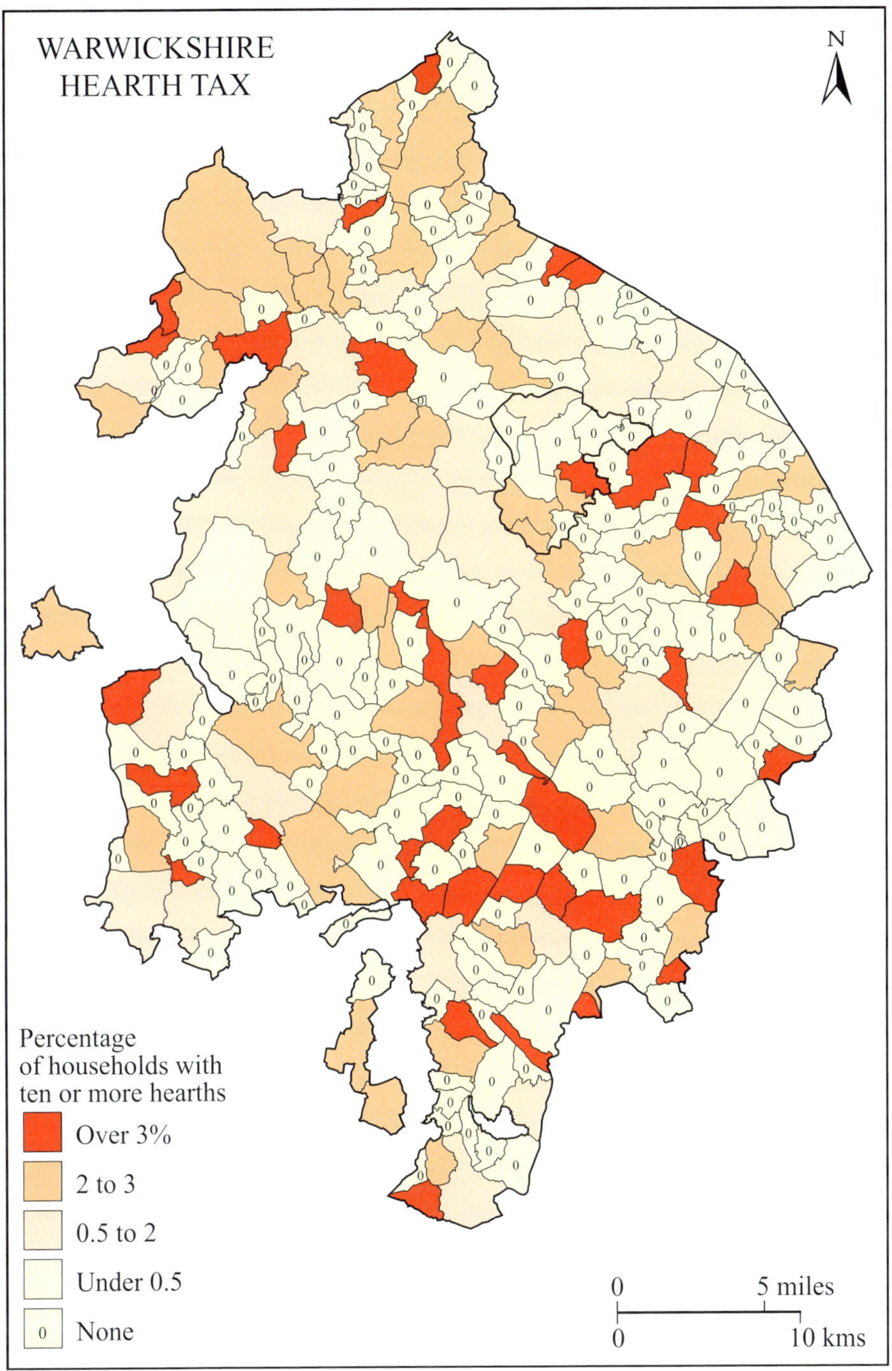

Map 10 Percentage of households with ten or more hearths: Warwickshire (1670) and Coventry (1666).

Map 11 Houses with 20 or more hearths: Warwickshire (1670) and Coventry (1666). The symbols for peers, knights and gentlemen also include houses listed under their widows. Baddesley Clinton is listed in 1670–1 with 15 hearths but with 20 hearths in other returns. Fletchamstead Hall is listed with 22 hearths and was previously occupied as a single house, but is known to have been divided between several tenants by 1666. Keresley (22 hearths) was in-building in 1666. Not all of these houses were the principal residences of their owners (see Table 26).

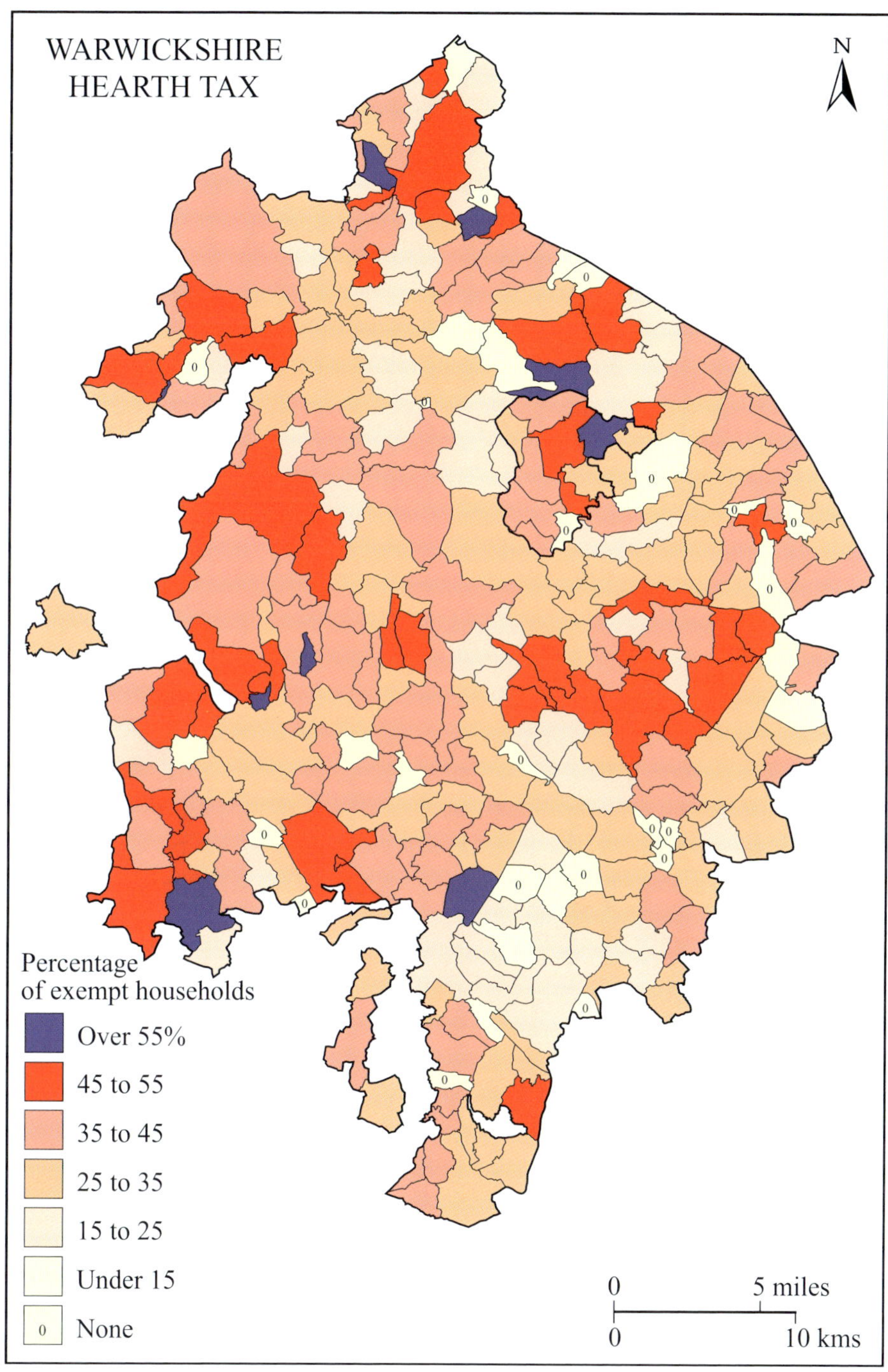

Map 12 Percentage of exempt households: Warwickshire (1670) and Coventry (1666).

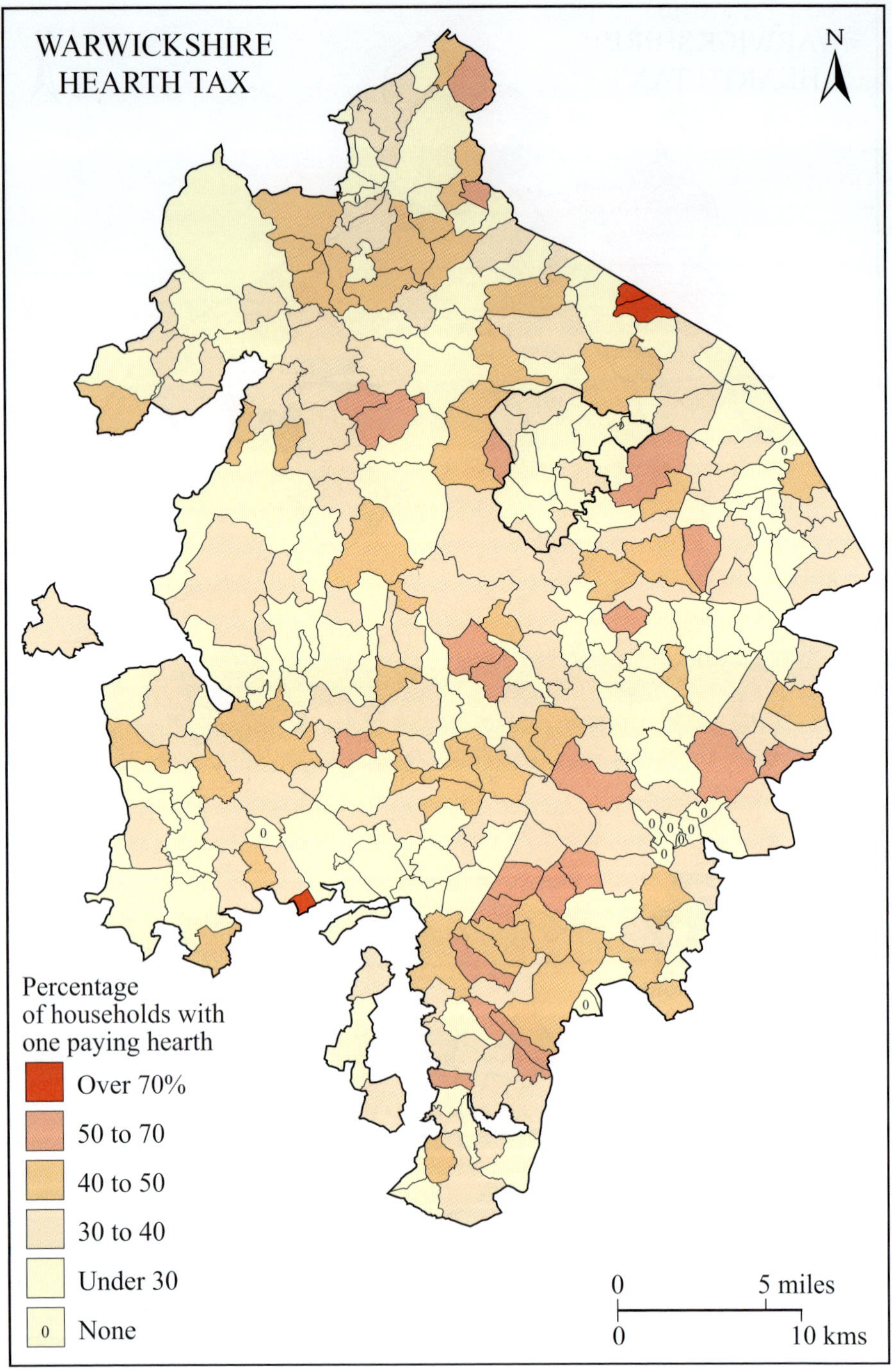

Map 13 Percentage of households with one paying hearth: Warwickshire (1670) and Coventry (1666).

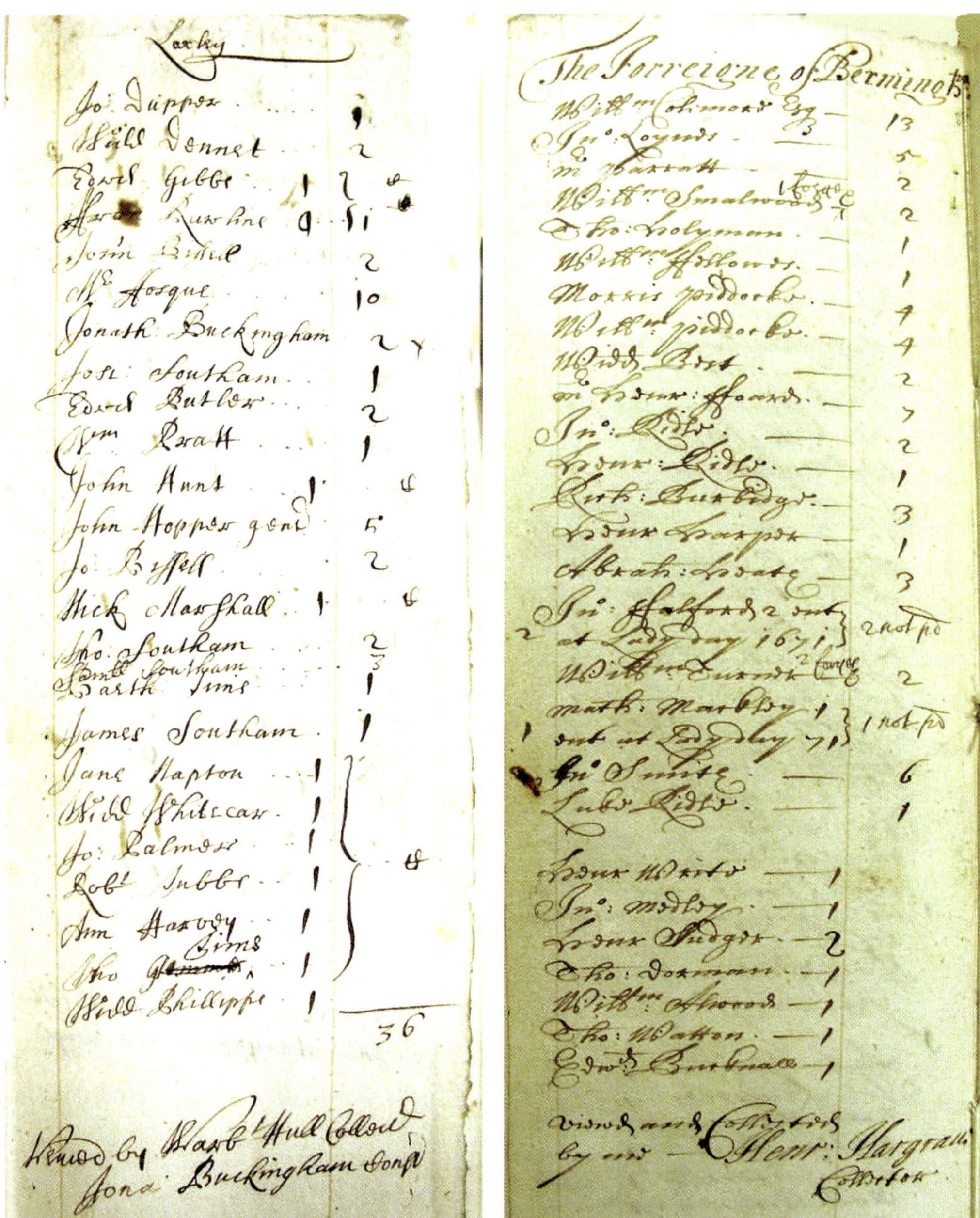

(a) Warberton Hull's return for Loxley in Stratford division, with his signature (WCRO, QS11/12, f. 20). The non-chargeable, marked with a 'C', were included in an exemption certificate.

(b) Henry Hargrave's return for the Foreign of Birmingham in Birmingham division, with his signature. (WCRO, QS11/22, f. 20v).

Figure 20 Two pages from the 1670 hearth tax returns in the hands of Warberton Hull and Henry Hargrave. The left-hand column records the non-chargeable and the right hand column the chargeable.

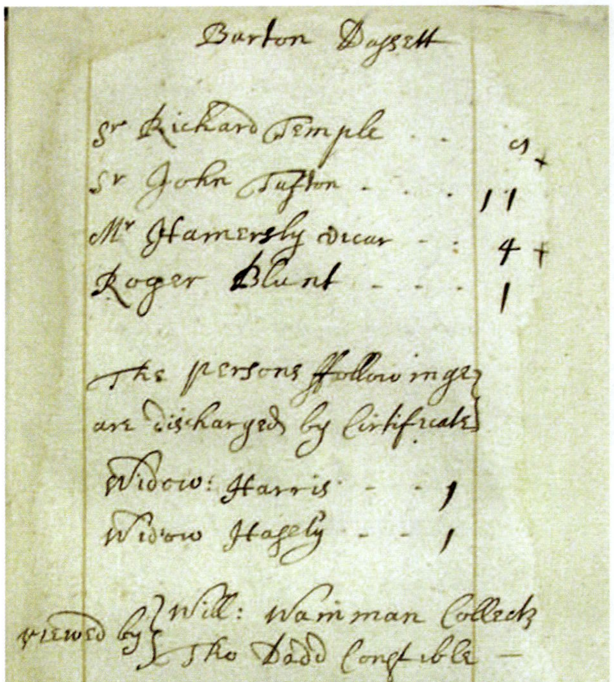
Burton Dassett
Sr Richard Temple . . 9
Sr John Tufton . . . 11
Mr Hamersly Vicar . : 4
Roger Blunt . . . 1
The persons followinge are discharged by Certificate
Widow: Harris - - 1
Widow Hagely - - 1
viewed by Will: Wainman Collect
Tho Dodd Constable —

(a) (above) John Newsham's return for part of Burton Dassett in Priors Marston division, including the 'signature' of its collector, William Wainman (WCRO, QS11/9, f. 7v).

(b) (left) William Wainman's return for part of Jury Street Ward, Warwick borough, with his signature (WCRO, QS11/7, f. 8v).

Figure 21 Extracts from the 1670 returns in the hands of William Wainman and John Newsham

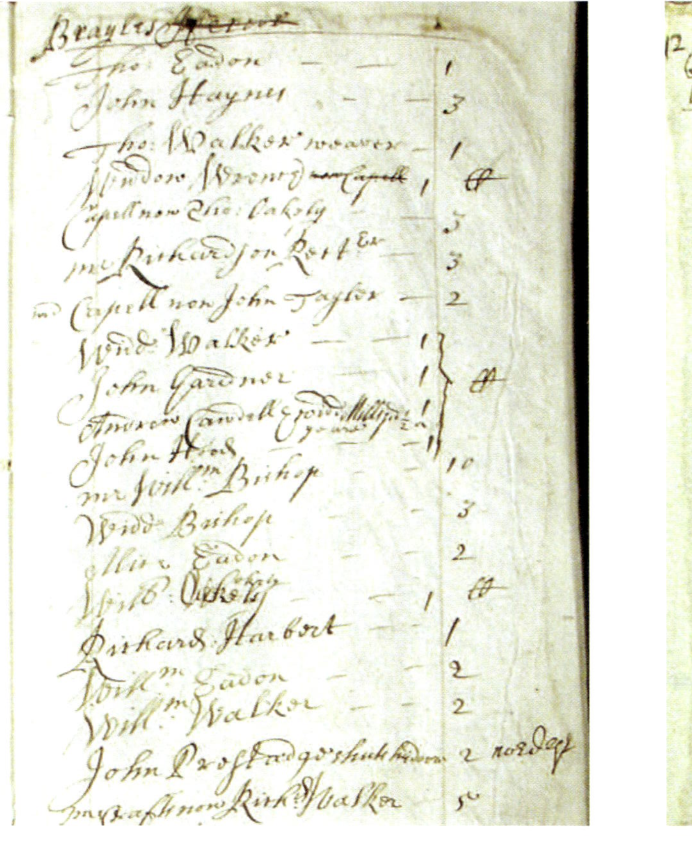

(a) Richard Samon's return for part of Brailes in Brailes division (WCRO, QS11/10, f. 2).

(b) Unknown scribe's return for part of Barston in Solihull division, amended and signed by Richard Samon (WCRO, QS11/20, p. 12).

Figure 22 Extracts from the 1670 returns in the hands of Richard Samon and an unknown scribe.

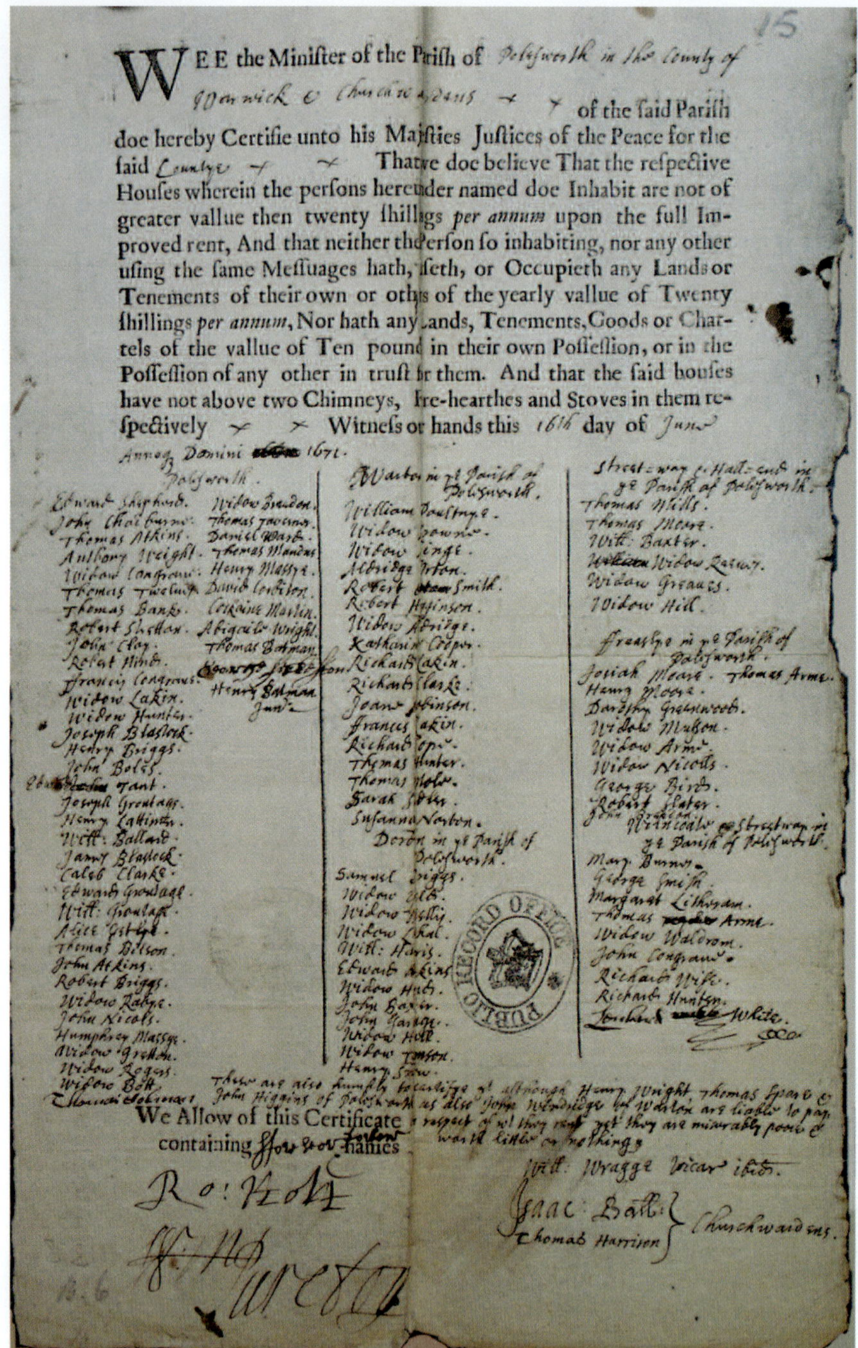

WEE the Minister of the Parish of Polesworth in the County of Warwick & Churchwardens of the said Parish doe hereby Certifie unto his Majesties Justices of the Peace for the said County That we doe believe That the respective Houses wherein the persons hereunder named doe Inhabit are not of greater vallue then twenty shillings *per annum* upon the full Improved rent, And that neither the person so inhabiting, nor any other using the same Messuages hath, useth, or Occupieth any Lands or Tenements of their own or others of the yearly vallue of Twenty shillings *per annum*, Nor hath any Lands, Tenements, Goods or Chattels of the vallue of Ten pound in their own Possession, or in the Possession of any other in trust for them. And that the said houses have not above two Chimneys, Fire-hearthes and Stoves in them respectively Witness our hands this 16th day of June Annoque Domini 1671.

Polesworth.

Edward Shepherd. John Chatburne. Thomas Atkins. Anthony Wright. Widow Congreave. Thomas Twelves. Thomas Banks. Robert Skelton. John Clay. Robert Hinds. Francis Congreave. Widow Lakin. Widow Hunter. Joseph Blastock. Henry Briggs. John Boles.

We Allow of this Certificate containing [illegible] names

There are also humbly to certifye yt although Henry Wright Thomas Spare & John Higgins of Polesworth as also John Wendridge of Warton are liable to pay in respect of wt they rent yet they are miserably poore & worth little or nothing.

Will: Wragge Vicar ibid.

Isaac Ball, Thomas Harrison — Churchwardens.

Figure 23 Printed exemption certificate for Polesworth, 1671 (TNA, E179/334/15).

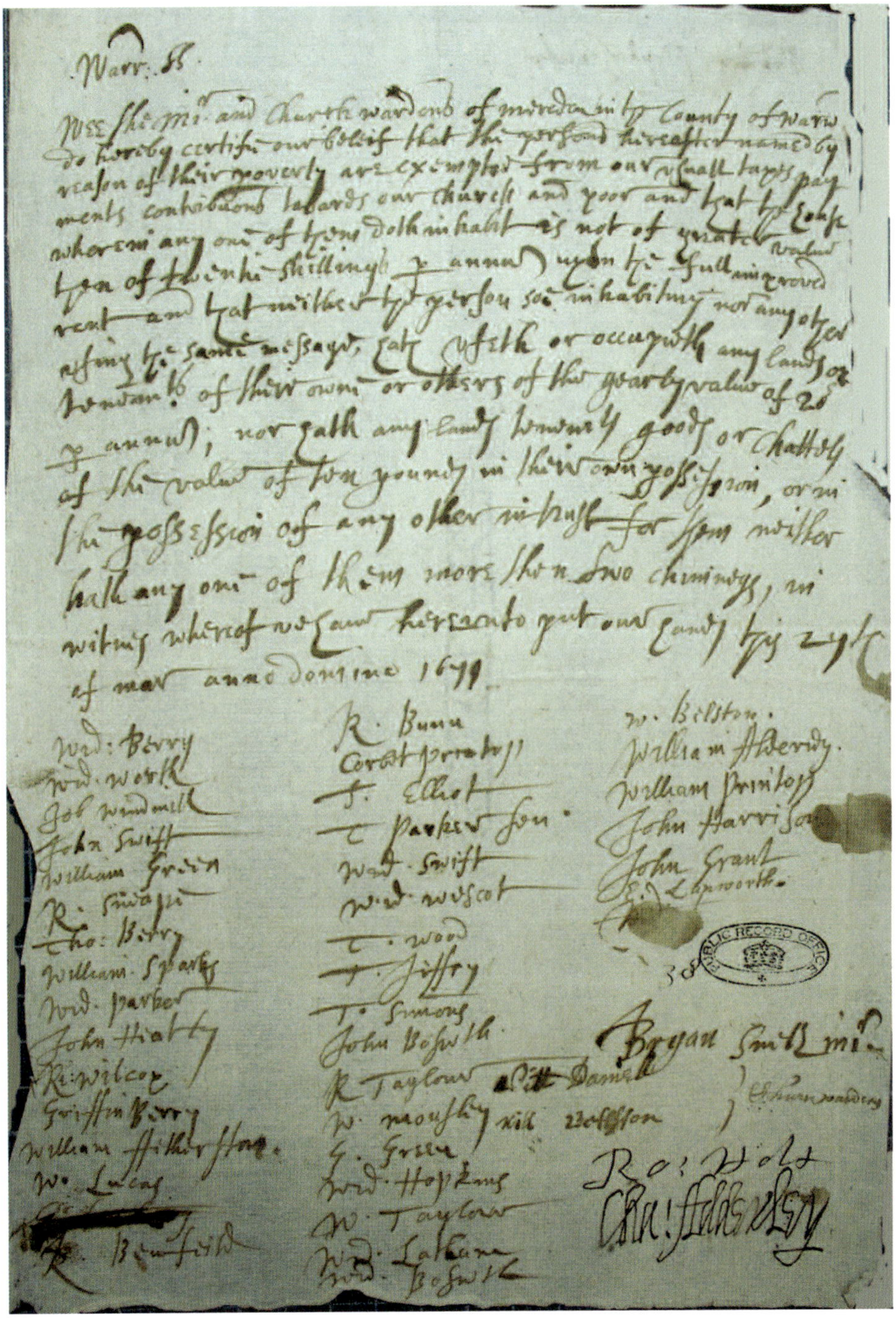

Figure 24 Hand-written exemption certificate for Meriden, 1671 (TNA, E179/347).

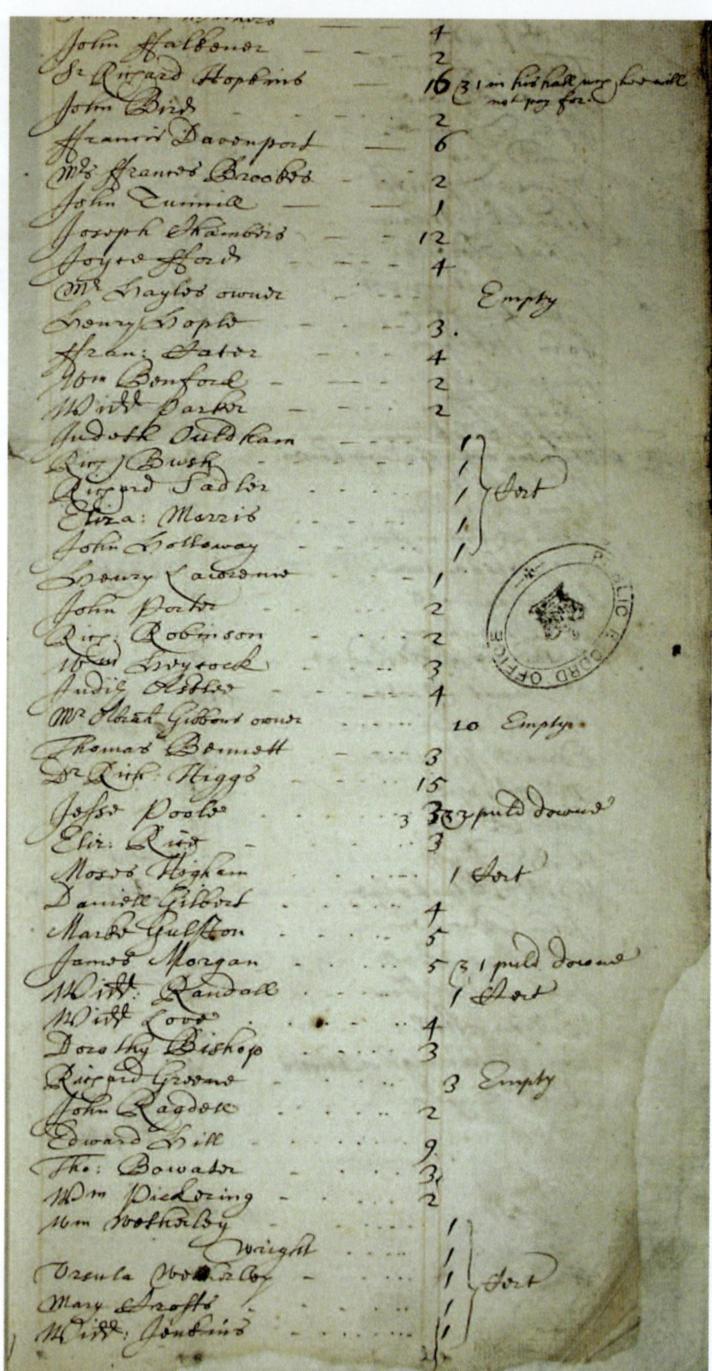

Figure 25 Part of the 1666 hearth tax return for Little Park Street Ward, Coventry (TNA, E179/259/9, f. 6). The left-hand column records those who had paid and the right hand column those who had not paid, whether certified exempt or not.

THE TRANSCRIBED DOCUMENTS

Warwickshire returns

The apparent uniformity of the 1670 Warwickshire hearth tax transcript disguises the fact that it derives from 17 different documents, based upon the high constables' divisions (Table 3, p. 31). The returns are printed here in the same order as the Warwick County Record Office's reference numbers, except for Atherstone and Birmingham divisions that were misarranged and so have been reversed. A few short sections in Hemlingford hundred have also been restored to their intended positions. The sequence of names within these transcripts follows the original returns apart from presenting the data in two groups of columns per page instead of one. For clarity, where a 'C' for 'certified' appears in the manuscript, it is now placed beside the relevant non-chargeable hearth number.

Warwickshire exemption certificates

The 41 exemption certificates printed here come from The National Archives and have been arranged in alphabetical order by hundred, division and parish. They have been chosen to provide the names for as many as possible of the 1,200 exempt householders who were either not named in, or omitted from, the 1670 hearth tax lists. However, everyone named in a certificate of a later date will not have been omitted from the 1670 lists. The two certificates for Avon Dassett and Brailes demonstrate how problematic attempts to identify all the non-chargeable can be.

All but three of these certificates were written on printed forms similar to the one transcribed for Tutnall and Cobley. They vary in length from nine to 365 names and from one to six columns. Here they are normally transcribed in three columns. As far as possible, all the names and numerals have been copied as written, apart from the signatories who have been omitted.

Coventry return

The 1666 return for Coventry, which was a separate county, is the start only of a much larger document in The National Archives that also covers Warwickshire. Its two numerical columns record those who had paid or not paid the hearth tax, in reverse order to the 1670 lists, where the non-chargeable come first. However, the paid and unpaid of 1666 must not be equated directly with the chargeable and not chargeable in 1670. Most of the unpaid entries in Coventry are followed by explanatory comments.

Editorial method

The following conventions have been applied to all the transcribed texts:

General

(a) [?] adjacent to a word or number indicates an uncertain reading.

(b) … (three dots) indicate words, letters or figures that are illegible or missing because the manuscript is damaged.

(c) <angle> brackets are used to indicate deletions, both with and without corrections. Thus <…> records an illegible deletion.

(d) (ordinary) brackets at the start or end of an entry indicate information that comes from the left or right hand margins respectively.

(e) [square] brackets denote editorial insertions, including some word expansions where the reading is uncertain.

(f) Data inserted from other hearth tax returns or exemption certificates are also given in square brackets but in [*italics*].

(g) Capitalization has been altered throughout in accordance with modern practice.

(h) Letters that were used interchangeably, such as 'i' and 'j' or 'u' and 'v', have been transcribed according to modern practice and not as in the original, e.g. 'oven' and not 'ouen'.

(i) A few common contractions have been expanded without comment, such as 'th' from 'y', and 'Christ' from 'X'.

(j) Annotations have normally been transcribed unaltered, apart from capitalization. Some common abbreviations have been expanded for clarity without indication, for example, from 'em' to 'empty', and 'unpd' to 'unpaid'.

(k) Similarly, missing 'e's have been inserted into words such as 'forg' and 'enterd'.

(l) Superscript letters are not reproduced as such.

(m) Page and folio numbers are inserted in square brackets at the appropriate place in the text. Continuation headings at the top of pages are ignored.

(n) Marks in the margin that are not readily intelligible, such as crosses, have been omitted.

Personal names

(a) Forenames and surnames have been transcribed as written, except for the relevant conventions above.

(b) [blank] indicates the absence of a forename and/or surname from the manuscript.

(c) Because the many different abbreviations and spellings used in status descriptions appear to be of no significance, most have been standardised in the transcript as follows: bart (baronet); esq (esquire); gent (gentleman); jun (junior); kt (knight); sen (senior). The various abbreviations and forms for widow in the original have been retained (vid, vidua, wid, widd).

(d) Punctuation after some abbreviated forenames and titles was applied very haphazardly in the original and so has been ignored in transcription.

Place names

(a) Place and house names are printed in bold.
(b) When their wording or spelling differs from the current version used by the Ordnance Survey, the latter is added in square brackets. However, minor entries, such as street names, are only supplemented in this way if they are not readily identifiable.
(c) Wherever possible, the contemporary parochial standing of each separate place is indicated. Only fully-independent chapelries with a minister and register of their own are described as such.

Totals

(a) [–] records the lack of a hearth total for an individual entry. Where a total for the same property can be supplied from another return, this appears in square brackets in [*italics*].
(b) The hearth totals for places that were enumerated separately are always placed below a line in the same column as its other figures, regardless of where they appear in the manuscript.
(c) Incorrect totals are supplemented by the correct figure in square brackets.
(d) Missing totals are normally supplied in square brackets, except in Brailes and Solihull divisions where they were rarely supplied.
(e) Running sub-totals at the end of a page have been omitted, as have other jottings and calculations in the manuscript.

Abbreviations

The following editorial abbreviations have been used:

C, cert = certified (exempt)
ch = chargeable
chap = chapelry
ex par = extra parochial
NC = not chargeable
par = parish
[X] = probable duplicate

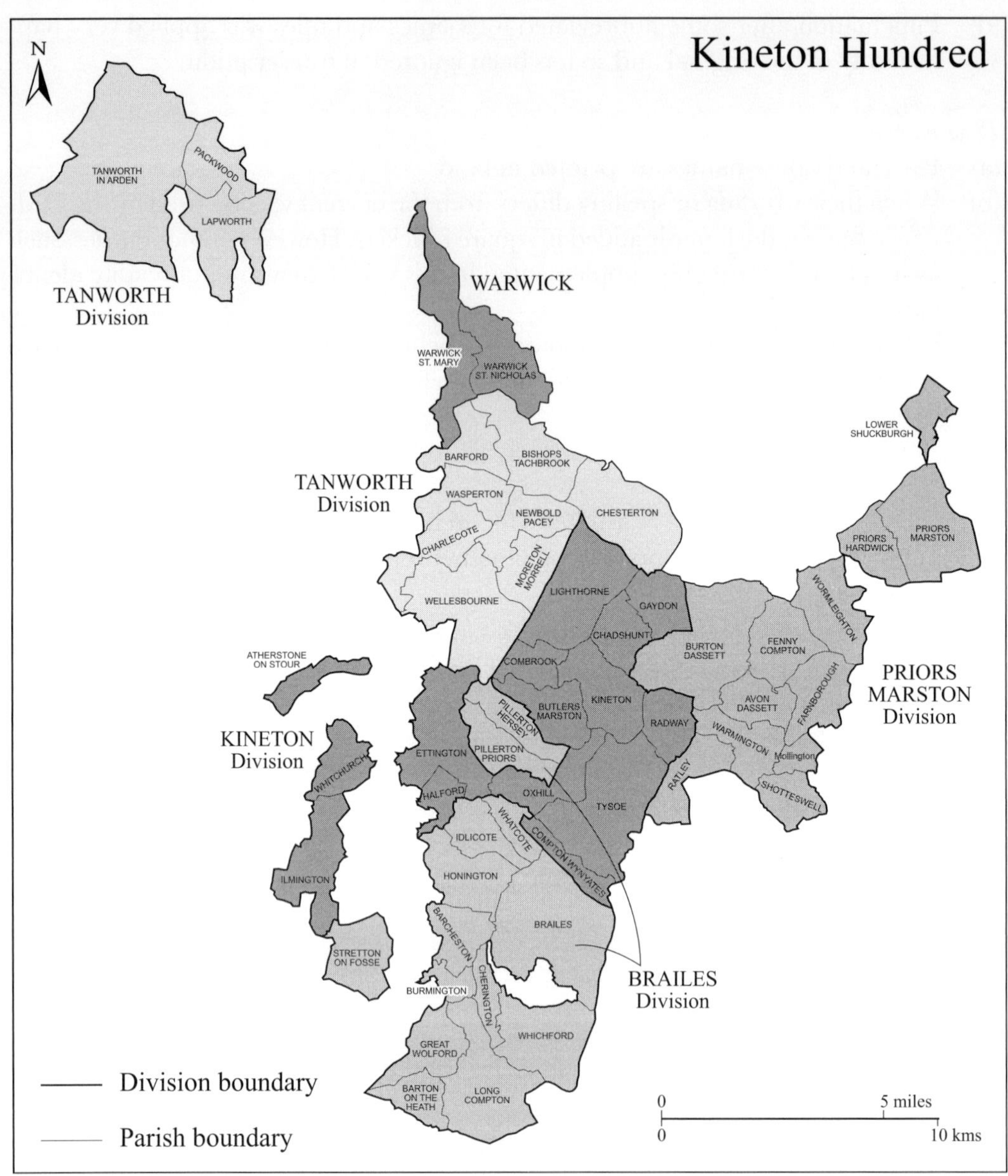

Map 14 Kineton Hundred with parish names.

Warwickshire Hearth Tax Returns Michaelmas 1670

Kineton Hundred

[WCRO, QS11/7]
[f. 1]
Warrwick Burrough
[Warwick Borough]
in Kineton Hundred and
in Kineton Division
[Warwick[1]]
1670
Exchequer Roles[2]
[written by William Wainman]
[f.1v: blank]

[f. 2]	[NC]	[Ch]
Warrwick [Warwick]		
Castlestreete Warde		
[in St Mary par]		
Robert Lord Brooke		47
In the vyneyeard[3]		2
Mr John Edes		10
Tho Marriott		4
Tho Marriott his voyd house		3
Wid Pippin	2	
Sam Wheeler		3
Will Lane		5
Mr Joyse		4
Godferey Mercy	1	
Joseph Blisset		3
James Jukes	1	
Samuell Gibbs	1	
John Jackson		3
Wid Bush	1	
Littel Dick	1	
Alice Chambers	1	
Edw Lee		2
Rich Knight	1	
Rich Hoddey	1	

	[NC]	[Ch]
Will Baggott		6
Wid Ridgley		1
Anthony Lane		5
Math Heywood	1	
Charles Emms		4
Cradock Fish	1	
Rich Peny		2
Rich Clarridg	1	
Edw Brasier		2
Wid Paine		2
Rob Warden	1	
Edw Sheapard		5
Will Felpes		2
[f. 2v]		
Will Perkes	1	
Wid Smith		1
Good Woster	1	
Will Williams		1
Edw Bromley one an oven		6
Wid Nickalls		3
Will Roe		3
Eliz Mosse		1
Tho Hurde		6
Will Fulkes		2
Tho Wincott		1
Rich Peny		2
Rob Millard		3
Will Kilbey	1	
Wid Kerbey		10
Will Stanley		5
John Far one a forge		4
		163

Veiwed by:
Will Wainman collector
Samuel Wheeller constable

1 Warwick borough was never part of Kineton division. In the 1660s it was grouped with Tanworth division before being assessed separately from 1670 onwards – see above p. 32.

2 'Exchequer Rolls' is a misleading description: all these returns are the county or Quarter Sessions copies and not the Exchequer duplicates.

3 Lord Brooke's vineyard or vine house at Warwick Castle was listed with 13 hearths in 1663 and 1664, but only four in 1665, when Styles, 'Hearth tax', p. xliii, suggested incorrectly that it had been demolished.

[f. 3]

High Streete Ward

[in St Mary par]

	[NC]	[Ch]
Stephen Allin		2
Rich Cumberlige		3
Wid Ashbey	1	
Wid Dunn		2
Rich Cumberlige his voyd house		3
Tho Watts		6
Tho Dadley		2
Mr Tho Craine		9
Georg Smith		2
Mr Mosses Holloway		20
Mr Tho Stratford		17
Tho Ebrall		2
Mr John Hipsley		18
Mr Hicks		9
Tho Overton		3
Rich Wincotte		2
Nick Morrell one a forge		5
Mr Tho Green one an oven		8
Alderman Vinor[1] / Alderman Vinor } both voyd		[*5,5*[2]] 10
An hospitall [*of the Earl of Leicester*[3]]		14
Math Copson		3
Math Copson		4
Tho Russell		3
Mr Combs voyd		4
Wid Smith	1	
Rich Sharp		1
Tho Harris		4
Margaret Hobdey		5
Fran Tuttle		2
John Leeke		2
Mr Rich Combey		7
Wid Tustin		1
Tho Gibbs		5

[f. 3v]

	[NC]	[Ch]
Mr Francis Eades		13
Mr John Welton one an oven		5
Rich Roe		2
Mrs Raynsford wid		10
Mr Tho Nickalls		2
Tho Maunder		4
Hen Lord		2
Georg Smith & John Thomas		4
Mr Edm Willson		4
Mr Edm Willson		2
Mrs Weale		6
Mr Babington		4
Mr Willson voyd		2
Anthony Blackford		3
Will Tong	1	
John Knib	1	
Rob Far		2
Jonathan Taylor		4
Tho Loe	1	
Wid Leg	1	
Wid Horsley	1	
Wid Clarke	1	
James Jewkes	1	
John Radill	1	
		247

Viewed by:
Will Wainman collector
and John Thomas constable

[f. 4]

Smith Street Ward

[in St Nicholas par]

	[NC]	[Ch]
Sir Henery Puckring voyd		13
Nath Stoughton esq		06
[*Richd*[4]] Moody one an oven		5
Georg Weale		6
John Yardley sen		3
Edm Makepeace sen		4
Edm Makepeace jun		4
John Neale		8
John Glover		2
John Medley		2

1 Sir Robert Viner was a very wealthy financier, who later became Lord Mayor of London. He was a major lender to the government and financial supporter of the farmers of the hearth tax from 1666 to 1669.

2 WCRO, QS11/24 (1671).

3 TNA, E179/259/9 (1666).

4 WCRO, QS11/24 (1671).

	[NC]	[Ch]
Will Mills		3
Will Willes		5
Math Tybats		1
Will Glover		2
Will Nickalls		4
John Tuckey		4
Will Glover		3
Nick Broughton		3
Tho How		2
Oliver Cross		3
Edm Makepeace		1
Mary Grascum		5
John Eyres	1	
Tho Glendall	1	
Tho Vennor	1	
Jonatham Tidingham		3
Edm King	1	
Renold Harris		2
Sir Hen Puckring voyd		2
Peeter Cartwright	<1>2	
Tho Whitway		2
John Rands & [blank] Moody		2
[f. 4v]		
Peeter Sheapard	1	
[*John*[1]] Dighley	1	
Simon Warner		3
Mich Willinger		2
Ralph Wilding	1	
John Colton		3
James Fell		1
John Hamp		1
Isack Twicross		2
Rob Broomwell		1
Rich Wotton		3
Will Rawbone		1
Mary Battes widd		1
Will Rippingham		4
Rich Hands		2
Rob Tantum		6
Peeter Gazey	1	

	[NC]	[Ch]
Tho Kemp		3
Will Gary	1	
John Savidg		2
Joseph Kerbey one an oven		3
Mary Grascum		3
John Davis		6
Mr John Warner		3
John Glover		3
Goody Robins	1	
John Willson		3
Edw Sharley	1	
Will Green		1
Lewes Rush		1
Edw Keen		2
Will Savidge		2
Wid Grisold		4
Will Wagstaff		3
[f. 5]		
Edw Barnecle		1
Wid Slaytor	1	
John Harris		3
Sam Robins	1	
Tho Borseley	<1>2	
Tho Basset		1
Will Watton	1	
John Brown	1	
Will Thomas		1
Leonard Izard	1	
Rich Moody		3
Sam Drayton		1
John Hunt	<1>2	
Mrs Griffin		4
Rich Banister		1
Mrs Weale voyd		1
John Wharton	1	
John Masters	1	
Fran Clarke	1	
Tho Lenton	1	
Tho Jeffcott		1
Mr Tho Glover [*minister*[2]]		5
John Green	<1>2	

1 WCRO, QS11/24 (1671).
2 TNA, E179/259/9 (1666).

	[NC]	[Ch]
Will Smith	1	
Wid Web	<1>2	
Will Williams	1	
Tho Free	1	
Edw Wisdome	1	
John Marcot	1	
Stephen Shatswell	1	
[*Wm*[1]] Johnson	1	
Rob Wiggs	1	
Will & John Smith	1	
Tho Griffin one a forge	<1>2	
		<184>
		191

Veiwed by:
Will Wainman collector
Isack Twycross constable

[f. 5v]

Bridg[e] **End Ward**

[in St Nicholas par]

	[NC]	[Ch]
Mr Charles Worthington		4
Georg Whartton		1
Georg Cattele		1
Hatton Adkins		2
William Tarvell		1
Hen Edmunds		2
Joseph Dingley		1
Jobe Bench one a forge		4
Hen & Wid Furnice		4
John Davis		1
Will Weale	1	
Walter Draper		1
John Phelpes		3
Hen Keen	1	
Tho Hill		1
Wid Wright	1	
John Carter	1	
Will Cattle		1
Wid Piggin		1
Tho Dowes		1
Rich Fort	1	
Joseph Gardner		1
Rich Fort & Hen Baker		2
Wid Jackson	1	
Tho Kemp		7
Rich Coulton		1
Daniel Hill		1
Jonas Higgens		2
John Kempcey		4
Hen Baker		2
Will Harris	<1>2	
[f. 6]		
Laruance Lee	1	
John Court		2
Rich Twicross		6
James Morrell	2	
Georg Perkins		1
John Rogers		5
John Hall	1	
Will Jeacocke	1	
James Beale		1
John Barret		1
Will & Fran Hobby	1	
Hen Tomes	1	
Tho Shatswell one a forge		2
Nick Tibbats	1	
Tho Spencer	1	
		067

Veiwed by:
Will Wainman collector
Henry Furnis constable

Saltisford Street Ward

[in St Mary par]

	[NC]	[Ch]
Three almes howses [*of Sir Henry Puckering*[2]]	4	
Will Jordain		4
Tho Dail	1	
Wid Pinch	1	
Will Brent		1
John Moore	1	

[f. 6v]

1 WCRO, QS11/24 (1671).
2 TNA, E179/259/9 (1666).

	[NC]	[Ch]
Sir Hen Puckring voyd		1
John Dunckley		2
Georg Hands sen		3
An almes howes [*with 4 rooms*[1]]	4	
Mrs Moore two of them flax ovens		3
Will Martin	2	
Tho Hogkins	2	
Wid Heath		3
Wid Green	1	
Wid Bury	1	
Wid Sumers	1	
Arther Budd	1	
Nick Gibbons	1	
Anthony Gately	1	
Will Casemore	1	
Elias Tomlinson	1	
Rich Wood	1	
Roger Witt	1	
Vall Harris		3
Mrs Elly		4
Sir Hen Puckring		36
Mr Charnock [*in Wedgnock Park*[2]]		7
Will Bromfeild	1	
Jobe Roodes		1
Wid Hadley		1
Tho Cooper	1	
Edw Wood	1	
Eliz Bodington	1	
Hen Winn	1	
Tho Gazey	1	
Steph Glendall	1	
[f. 7]		
Tho Barthellmear	1	
John West		1
John Hallford		5
Three little cott[ages] [*in the highway*[3]]	3	
Georg Hands jun		1
Humph Hands		2

	[NC]	[Ch]
Wid Robinson	1	
[*Tho*[4]] Clarke	1	
Rob Ratleife		1
John West		6
Wid Goodcheape		2
Wid Furnice	1	
Wid Miller	1	
Wid Dicans	1	
Joseph Deny	2	
Steph Taylor	1	
Bridget Furnice	1	
Mary Ashbey	1	
Tho Styles	1	
Georg Kerbey	1	
Rich Mumford	1	
Wid Harding	1	
Ann Larg	1	
Mary Chinn	1	
Isabell Hancock	2	
Wid Dunckley		1
Daniel Cross		1
Hen Smith		3
John Smith	2	
Rob Juons		5
Humph Jewkes		4
Roger Bird	1	
[f. 7v]		
[blank] Allet		1
Rob Briscoe	2	
John Briscoe	1	
A cott[age] in the high way	1	
Wid Far	1	
Rich Hurst		1
Mrs Margaret Yardley		10
Rich Mellowes	1	
Rob Gray	1	
Edw Brass	1	
Will Kerbey	1	
Will Squiers	1	
Joane Roe	1	
Will Lag	1	

1 TNA, E179/259/9 (1666).
2 TNA, E179/259/9 (1666).
3 TNA, E179/259/9 (1666).
4 WCRO, QS11/24 (1671).

	[NC]	[Ch]
Wid Hobkins	1	
Rich Tyso	1	
Nick Hall	1	
Dorothy Hewes	1	
Wid Moore	2	
Rich Beard	1	
Wid Leg	1	
Hen Vallentine		1
Will Burford		1
Hen Shackshaft	1	
Hen Winn	1	
John Kerbey	1	
Tho Clements	1	
Tho Bud [*in the parke*[1]]		3
Stephen Boulton esq		4
Wid Sherwood		10
Rob Pen empty		1
Oliver Cross	1	
Tho Cock Bread	1	
Wid Witt	1	
[f. 8]		
Math Busbey	1	
Tho Walker	1	
John Hudson [*in the parke*[2]]		2
Eliz Miller [*at Fane hill*[3]]		2
		137

Viewed by:
Will Wainman collector
John Dunckley constable

Jury Street Ward

[in St Mary par]

	[NC]	[Ch]
Fulke Grivell esq		14
James Prescott esq		12
David Rainboe		3
Mr Tho Eades		5
Rich Bird		6
Stephen Nickalls		4
John Vennor		11
Rich Asplin		4
Tho Hunt	3	
Nich Parris		3
Tho Glendall	2	
Tho Smith		6
Edw Typin	1	
Mr Rich Eades		9
Mrs Alice Weale		9
Charles Hicks		4
Mr Job Murcott		7
[f. 8v]		
Mr James Cooke		5
Josua Drake	1	
Tho Archer esq		13
John Garlick sen		6
John Garlick jun		3
Tho Heath Sam Coopk [sic]		4
Barnaby Buttler		1
Stephen Murcott		2
Clement Hobkins		2
Rich Hamcock	1	
John Swain		3
The maior for the courthouse		3
[*Widd*[4]] Wincott		2
		141

Veiwed by:
Will Wainman collector
John Garlick constable

Market Place Ward

[in St Mary par]

	[NC]	[Ch]
Mr Rob Heath		8
Mr Colemore esq		11
Mr Will Preston minister		7
Doctor Hollioke		8
Mr Martin [*schoolmaster*[5]]		5
Mr Smith & Sam Bodell		14
Mr Rich Aing		7
Wid Aing		2

1 WCRO, QS11/24 (1671).
2 WCRO, QS11/24 (1671).
3 TNA, E179/259/9 (1666).
4 TNA, E179/259/9 (1666).
5 TNA, E179/259/9 (1666).

	[NC]	[Ch]
John Jarvis		3
Hen Willson	2	
Rich Mumford		2
Tho Ashbey		1
Tho Clarridg		2
Mrs Allin wid		5
Mr Sumerton		11
Mr Georg Palmer		9
John Smith one an oven		5
Rich Penn	1	
Christopher Alsbury		5
Josua Pearkes two ovens		5
Wid Meades		4
Rob Ashbey	2	
Ann Ashbey	1	
Edw Chesley		2
Mr Yarwod		8
John Atturbury		2
Will How		6
Will Ashorne one an oven		3
Peeter Cartwright	2	
Mr Jobe Ramsford		7
Wid Hulbert	2	
Mr Tho Wise		5
John Fluellin	1	
Tho Hopkins		7
Tho Rush	2	
John Penny		1
Rich Hadley		6
Wid Melles		1
Martin Taylor one an oven		2
Wid Canthorne		3
Oliver Holliocke		1
Avory Swarbrook		4
[f. 9v]		
Rob Watts		5
Mr Charnock		9
Rob Whinnock		3
Tho Wall		2
Rich Rogers one an oven		3
Wid Lewes		4
John Hadley		4

	[NC]	[Ch]
Will Bucknall		2
Tho Sly		5
Will Gray		1
John Sharley	<1>2	
Rich Eades	1	
Dor Deacon		2
Tho Spencer		5
Georg Westbury		3
[*Henry*[1]] Mullin		3
Samuel Willes		3
Joseph Reeve		4
John Marten		5
Will Pestell		1
Tho Laine		4
Will Clarke		3
Will Clement one an oven		5
Wid Mathews	1	
Rich Hancock		1
Samuel Watts		1
Tho Py		1
Wid Pettaway	1	
Tho Hands		3
Edw Meao		1
Mr[s] Bridget Kerbey		8
Edw Harding		3
Wid Jackson		3
John Corpson voyd		2
John Meadley		3
[f. 10]		
Wid Griffin		4
Will Far a forge		1
Rich Willson		3
Rob Fox		7
Wid Dungon		4
Wid Clement		5
Will Routhwell		4
Wid Nickalls		5
John Avarn		1
Mr John Townsend		10
Rich Doleman		2
Peter Milward		1
Wid Neale	1	<1>0
Jobe Burt	<1>0	01

[1] WCRO, QS11/24 (1671).

	[NC]	[Ch]
Tho Deacon		6
Hen Waring one a forge		4
John Hadley		5
John Wescot		5
Georg Flower		3
Ann Cooper		<1>2
John Martin sen		4
John Meadley		3
John Sharley sen		3
John Sharley jun		2
John Westcott		2
Hen Johnson	2	
Rob Amplet 1 oven		3
John Tybats	1	
Josua Lord		1
Tho Hurst		1
Tho Roberts		2
Wid Knib	1	
Hewin Swan	1	
[f. 10v]		
John Fletcher	1	
John Ansich	1	
Rich Burnill	1	
		372
		[368]

Veiwed by:
William Wainman collector
Robert Fox, Tho Roberts } constables

West Street Ward
[in St Mary par]

	[NC]	[Ch]
Will Dewsbury		4
John Claridg sen	1	
John Garner	1	
Edw Wright	1	
Widd Elliots		1
Edw Morris	1	
Abraham Kining	1	
Rob Garner	1	
Wid Miller	1	
Wid Perkins	1	
Rich Garrat	1	
Rich Thomas	1	
Will Shakshaft	1	
Tho Cooper	1	
Wid Kerbey	<1>2	
Will Shakshaft jun	1	
Tho Cockbill		6
Will White	1	
Wid Turner	1	
John Tucky voyd		1
Rob Fish		1
[f. 11]		
Rich Harborne		3
Dor & Jane Prescott	1	
Tho Thomas	1	
Jonathan Brooks one an oven		3
John Hewes	1	
Math Lovet	1	
Wid Stanley	1	
Wid Winterington		2
Nick Faulkner		3
Miles Reading		2
Humph Morris	1	
Hen Palmer	1	
Rob Hodgkins		4
Rob Southam		2
Hen Faulkner		4
Wid Tackell	1	
Daniel Morrell		4
Fowell Buskin	1	
Hen Harper		2
Joseph Boss		4
John Cooper		4
Tym Smith		1
Tho Collins		1
Nath Cross	<1>2	
Mr Allet		4
Solloman Warner		3
[***Longbridge***[1]]		
Joseph Rands		2
John Abington		4

[1] WCRO, QS11/24 (1671).

	[NC]	[Ch]
Tho Sanders		5
Mr John Stanton		10
Mr John Stanton voyd		1
John Boyse		3
Tho Skidmore	1	
[*end of Longbridge*[1]]		
Tho Parsley		4
[f. 11v]		
John Cooper voyd		1
Rowland Palmer	1	
Jerimiah Harrison	1	
John Clarke	1	
Roger Hulbert		1
Tym Smith	1	
Hen Gibbens sen		1
Tho Sheens		2
James Rudge	2	
Luke Perkins	1	
Will Cleave		<1>2
Rich Harrisson	1	
Will Lea		1
Hen Gibbens jun		1
An almes man Hen More	3	
Will Walker	1	
Ralph Smith	1	
Wid White	1	
John Wedge	1	
Jobe Robinson		2
Wid How		5
John Causier	1	
Will Welden	1	
Tho Breedon	1	
Will Towne	1	
Wid Rush	1	
Tho Fisher		3
Will Hind		4
Eliz Handson	1	
Joseph Iron	1	
Hen Cole	1	
John Dadley		1
Will Jobe	1	
Sam Hammon	1	
Arther Henley	1	
[f. 12]		
John Scot	1	
James Fish	1	
John Yeates	1	
Edw Saunders	1	
Elias Creede	1	
John Whitfoot	1	
Goody Kilbey	1	
Wid Wharton	1	
W Huit	1	
Wid Wheal	1	
John Chapman	1	
John Sharley	1	
Christ Cox	1	
Tho Donkly		1
Rich Walker		2
Wid Prescot	1	
John Cooper	1	
Rich Heacock	1	
		112
		[115]

Viewed by:
Will Wainman collector
Tho Parsley constable

[WCRO, QS11/8]
[f. 1]

Kineton Hundred 1670
Kineton Division
Exchequer Roles

[written by John Newsham]
[f. 1v: blank]
[f. 2: list of place names has been omitted]
[f. 2v]

Lighthorne [par]

Will Mearce	2
Leonard Jeacox	1
Ephraim Hunt	2
William Smith	4

[1] WCRO, QS11/24 (1671).

	[NC]	[Ch]
Will Townsend		1
Will Hihorne		2
Widow Harbert		2
John Taylor		1
Tho <W>Sarton		2
John Maunton		2
Tho Greene		4
Widow Renalls		2
Leonard Jeacox		4
John Hanbut		2
Tho Flecher		2
Will Butcher		1
Tym Suffolke	1	
Micall Pardew		1
John Bradshaw		7
John Dod rector		5
John Mason		2
Tho Crowder		1
Tho Robinson	1	
Francis Ayres	1	
Widow Millner sen		1
<Will>Widow Milner jun	1	
Richard Kinge	1	
Will Halford	1	
John Lea		1
Charles Barloe with a forge		2
		054

Viewed by:
Will Wainman collector

[f. 3]

Gaydon [par]

	[NC]	[Ch]
Richard Burden		4
Robert Walker		1
Widow Kempe		1
John Kempe		1
Joseph White		1
Richard Shropsheire		3
Will Burrowes		3
John Randall		2
Nickolas Padmore	1	
Henrie Neale		2
Henrie Neall in a new house		1

	[NC]	[Ch]
John Smith		1
Tho Proofe	1	
Will Barloe with a forge		2
Tho Sumner		1
Richard Petipher		4
Widow Garlick		1
Richard Bostock		1
Richard Bottom		1
Richard Tasker		2
Widow Righton		1
John Tomkins		1
Will White		3
Richard Terrall		1
Will Beardes		3
Isabell Garrett		3
Will Davis		3
Richard Sumner		2
John Righton		1
Richard Bragg		2
Marie Haskew		1
Tho Bottom	1	
Francis Bottom	1	
Mr Keck		5
John Sabin		2
John Toley		1
William Davis		3
		064

Viewed by:
William Wainman collector
<Tho>Rihd Burden constable

[f. 3v]

Chadshunt [par]

	[NC]		[Ch]
Charles Newsham esq			13
Robert Clarke			2
William Loe			1
Will Taylor	1	C	
Allen Jordan	1	C	
Henrie Ward and a forge			1
Tho Burden			1
Sam Mills			1
Will Washbrook			1
Will Ward with a forge			2
Tho Ward			1

	[NC]	[Ch]
John Shropsheire		1
Will Richardes		1
Luke Shropsheire		1
Tho Baylis		<1>2
Henrie Lancaster		1
Allan Jardon sen		1
Tho Hanckes		1
Tho Burden		2
Leonard Armes		2
John Randoll		1
Widow Shropsheire		1
Will Smith		1
John Willkins	1	
		038

Viewed by:
Will Wainman collector
Henrie Lancaster constable

[f. 4]

Kineton Magna

[Great Kineton in Kineton par]

	[NC]	[Ch]
Richard Stanley	1 C	
Nathaniell Bratt	1 C	
Benjamine Renalds		1
Allexander Welch		1
Tho Hutchens et Eliza Townsend		3
John Butler		4
Widow Heacock		1
Widow Coales		2
Sam Bacon		4
Nathaniell Clark		2
Will Ashbey		1
Will Dunn sen	1 C	
Will Dunn jun		1
Sarah Wootten	1	
Nickolas Laurance		1
Tho Hancock		1
Richard Napton		1
Tho Wheeler		1
John West		1
John Chandler		1
Tho Chandler		1
Leonard Chandler		1
Nath Hiron	1	
Tho Smith		1
Widow Smith		1
Zacharie Penn		1
Will Rouse		1
George Wilkins		1
Will Orton Jonat Ordway		[*2,2*[1]] 4
John Lavender		1
John Dixon		1
Tho Dunn		1
Richard Wharum		1
Francis Hitchcox	1	
Widow Washbrooke	1	
[f. 4v]		
Jeffery Pricket	1 C	
Will Elliband	1 C	
Toby Norton		2
Tho Mearce with a forge		2
Mathew Hihorne		1
Ralph Spicer		2
Henrie Napton		1
Benjamin Renoldes		2
Will Norton with a forge		3
Richard Gibbs		1
John Hathaway with oven		4
Vall Hollifeild		1
Widow Adkins		3
Richard Ballad		2
Tho Elliott		3
Tho Renolds		3
Tho Prickett	1 C	
Widow Westburie	1 C	
Widow Pallmer	1 C	
Mr Russell vicar		3
John Bass		4
Tho Hyhorne		1
Widow Gibbs	1	
Will Worrall		2
Widow Wellingeton		1
John King for 2 houses		2
Lord Brooke		5
Widow Eaborne		2
Widow Hudson	1	

[1] WCRO, QS11/25 (1671).

	[NC]	[Ch]
Henrie Goodinge		2
Ellias Hornesby		2
Tho Coates		1
Edward Taylor		3
Tho Bannell	1	
Elizabeth Pearson	1	
[f. 5]		
John Washington	1	
Edward Courte	1	
James Hatrick		1
John Hardinge		1
John Lifely	1	
Tho Martley	1	
Edward Washbrooke	1	
Will Court with a forge		2
Tho Gloster		1
Widow Eaborne		1
Tho Durant		3
Tho Wharum		1
Richard Taylor		1
Will Cookes	1	
Henrie Haycock		1
Will Gilbert	1	
		111

Viewed by:
Will Wainman collector
Tho Durant constable

Kineton Parva
[Little Kineton in Kineton par]

	[NC]	[Ch]
Charles Bentley esq		15
Tho Faulkener		2
John Hathaway		3
John Ward	1	
An emptie poore cott[age]	1	
John Norton		1
Marie Richardson	1	
John Vincent		1
John Harris		1
Will Bidle		3
[f. 5v]		
Tho Norton		1
Moses Westly		2
Widow Savidge	1	
James Wale		1
Widow Rawbone		1
Humpherie Norton		1
Widow Rawbone		1
Tobias Norton		1
Francis Faulkener		1
Richard Ballard		1
Ralph Wisdome		1
John Adkins		1
Katherine Phettieplace		1
Humpherie Phettieplace		2
Will Savidge	1	
Edward Savidge	1	
Widow Cross		3
Will Christopher		1
Tho Crosby		2
John Norton sen		1
Margerett Sabin		1
Will Faulkener		1
John Hathaway		1
Robert Basely		1
John Westly		1
Henrie Savadge		2
		055

Viewed by:
Will Wainman collector
Tho Durant constable

[f. 6]
Compton Mordack et Brookehampton in Kineton Constablry
[***Compton Verney***[1] ex par with Lighthorne par[2]]

	[NC]	[Ch]
The Ladie Verney		21
In the mill		1
Anthony Garrett		1

1 WCRO, QS11/25 (1671).
2 *VCH*, v, p. 59.

	[NC]	[Ch]
[***Brookhampton***[1] in Combrook chap]		
John Bass		5
John Maudick		1
		029
Combrooke [Combrook chap[2]]		
Mr Waldron		3
Will Horner		2
Margerie Bever		1
Joane Clarke		1
Tho Gaunt	1	
Henrie Palmer	1	
Richard Ward	1	
Robert Sabin	1	
Tho Cooke		1
Will Righton	1	
Robert Powers		1
Widow Arne		1
Jonathan Taylor		2
John Morrell in 2 houses		3
Henrie Clarke jun		3
Tho Savidge	1	
Will Cross		1
John Grascock		1
[f. 6v]		
Francis Walker		1
Robert Baylis		3
Robert Hunte		2
Robert Chester		1
James Gosnell		1
John Gosnell	1	
Tho Gosnell		1
Henrie Clarke sen		1
Hugh Irons		1
Richard Kimnell with a forge		2
		033

Viewed by:
Will Wainman collector
Richard Kimnell constable

	[NC]	[Ch]
Butlers Marston [par]		
Richard Greeneway		2
John Capp		1
Charles Deaves		2
Ralph Greeneway		3
Ralph Ellis		4
Mr Richard Woodward		5
Will Greeneway		2
Richard Greeneway		1
Will Midleton		1
Will Marshall		3
Richard Collins		2
Will Austin		1
Richard Evitts		2
Widow Hutchens one forge		2
[f. 7]		
John Hudson		1
Tho Ward		1
Tho Napton		3
John Hooker		1
Mrs Abraham		7
Will Betts		1
John Byshopp		1
Edward Palmer		1
Widow Goode		1
John <W>Veale		3
Manasse Capp		4
Widow Welch	1 C	
Mr William Loggin		10
John Lent		1
Tho Deaves		1
Wid Lumbert	1	
Alice Redle	1	
Marie Hitchcock		1
John Bycar		1
John A<los>mos	1 C	
Robert Baylis	1 C	
		069

Vieued by:
Will Wainman collector
Richard Evits constable

1 WCRO, QS11/25 (1671).
2 Chapelry of Kineton parish.

	[NC]	[Ch]
[f. 7v]		
Radway [par]		
Mr Peck vicar		3
Edward Tomkins sen		2
Edward Tomkins jun		2
John Hyhorne		3
Will Palmer		4
Richard Mills		2
Henrie Hunt		1
Will Tomkins		3
Will Andrewes	1	
John Shutle	1	
Tho Goodwin gent		8
Tho Herritage sen		1
Thomas Heritage jun		1
Rich Palmer		2
Jerriemie Tomkins		1
Henrie Leevinge		3
Will Greene		1
Robert Greene	1	
John Heminges	1	
Ann Wheately		1
Fra[n]ces Sparkes	1	
Will Davis	1	
Richard Blaby		1
Walter Hunt		1
Robert Hihorne		2
Will Hunt		1
William Sparkes on the hill		1
Humph Pettipher		1
Will Warner jun		2
Walter Heritage		1
Will Hunt		1
Tho Hunt		1
Tho Usher		1
Simon Higgons		1
John Enock		1
[f. 8]		
Edward Tomkins jun		1
Tho Heritage		2
Tho Palmer		3
Edward Thomkins sen		2
Will Warner sen		2
Robert Herritage		1

	[NC]	[Ch]
John Higgons	1	
Widow Jefferis	1	
Tho Hancock	1	
Widow Waine	1	
		064

Viewed by:
Will Wainman collector

	[NC]	[Ch]
In Tysoe Constablry [and par]		
[Lower Tysoe]		
Westcott [Westcote]		
Mr Edward Loggins		5
John Pratt		1
Hardwick		
Richard Callway		5
Brixhill [Brixfield]		
Richard Mills		2
Widow Wayle		1
Edghill [Edgehill]		
John Lampett		4
Richard Simons		1
[f. 8v]		
Temple Tysoe [Lower Tysoe]		
Henrie Browne	1	
George Willkins	1	
Tho Seargent		1
Mathew Lifely		1
John Taylor		2
Mr Richard Willcox		4
James How		3
Will Cole		1
Richard Hunt		1
Will Richardes	1	
Tho Upton		<1>2
Will Herritage		1
Will Hanckes	1	
Humpherie Slade		3
Richard Walker		3
Widow Clarke		4
Tho Plombe	1	
Tho Tysoe		1
Edward Horseman	1	
Mr Richard Warner		5
John Betts		1

	[NC]	[Ch]
John Evans		1
Will Hunt	1	
John Newman	1	
John Rose		3
Roger Heminges		1
Richard Hihorne		3
Widow Pratt	1	
Widow Clarrage		3
Adrean Clarke		2
Martin Malins		3
Henrie Midleton		3
Edward Wyatts		1
[f. 9]		
Richard Chandler		1
Richard Morner		1
Tho Callow		5
Widow Callway		1
Will Midleton		4
		084

Viewed by:
Will Wainman collector
Martin Malins constable

Church Tysoe
[Middle Tysoe in Tysoe par]

	[NC]	[Ch]
Mr Henrie Clarke		4
Tho Walker		1
Joane Cox		1
Richard Hau<r>ton		1
Will Hyhorne		1
Tho Horseman		3
Jonas Malins		3
Tho Edmar		2
Mr Will Stevenage		4
Simon Betts		1
Richard Hammond		1
Anchor Kilby		1
Richard Appleby	1	
Richard Gaydon	1	
Henrie Kinge	1	
Will Newman		1
Edward Wilkins		1
John Wilkins		1
Nicklas Harris		1
Simon Hewins		3
Will Elliott		3
Nick Bennitt	1	
Tho Horsman		1
[f. 9v]		
Robert Endall of Roleright		1
Tho Widowes		1
Jonas Rymill		1
Robert Newman		1
Will Russell		1
Henrie Norton		1
Widow Jarvis		3
Widow Hitchcox	1	
Robert Newman		1
John Lagoe		1
Richard Hedon	2	
Henrie Tomkins	1	
Edward Wincott		2
Henrie Wilkins		1
[blank] Barnaby esq	1	
Tho Hewins with a forge		2
Tho Elliott		1
Tho Gibbs	1	
Robt Lightfoote		1
Widow Tomkins		3
Tho Wells		1
Joseph Hewes	1	
Henrie Newman	1	
Widow Clarke		4
Widow Smith	2	
Widow Eglington	2	
Robert Willkins		2
Robt Ratcliff	1	
Emanuell Ratlif	1	
Francis Clarke		1
John Calloway		1
Widow Ratnett		1
Elizabeth Midleton	1	
John Chamberline	1	
James Ludyate		1
[f. 10]		
Elizabeth Ward		1
Nath Clarke jun		1
Ann Midleton		1

	[NC]	[Ch]
Tho Bloxsom	1	
Will Hydon	1	
Tho Allen		1
		070

Viewed by:
Will Wainman collector
Martin Malins constable

Over Tysoe
[Upper Tysoe in Tysoe par]

	[NC]	[Ch]
Tho Townsend sen		2
Nick Tysoe		3
Tho Midleton		3
Tho Widowes		3
Tho Townsend now Hewins		2
Richard Bloxsom		2
Tho Malins		1
Tho Greneway		4
Henrie Leay		1
Nath Townsend		1
Will Hemmings with a forge		2
Marie Tasker		2
Tho Walker		1
Ann Wyate		3
Tho Darloe		4
Tho Ward		3
William <widow> Bradford		1
Roger Marshall		4
Tho Ward		1
Nickolas Vaurster		1
James Ratnett		1
Will Midleton		2
Will Rose		1
Tymothy Malins		1
[f. 10v]		
Daniell Grime		1
Nath Seargeant		1
Will Curtis		1
Francis Biggs		1
Robt Rose		1
Will Parker		1
John Miller		1
Lucie Howell	1	
Theophill Pastor		1
John Cradock		1
Rich Hitchman		1
John Hamon		1
Will Rose		4
Will Townsend		1
Mrs Archer		5
James Clarke		1
Ann Allen		1
		072

Viewed by:
Will Wainman collector
Martin Malins constable

Compton Viveat
[Compton Wynyates par]

	[NC]	[Ch]
James Earle of Northampton		26
Nick Styles		1
John Parker		1
Richard Bew	1	
		028

[f. 11]
Oxhill [par]

	[NC]	[Ch]
Sir Will Bromley kt		7
Mr Mees		6
Ursula Duncombe		2
Tho Walton		1
Edward Eadon		2
Anthoni Blackford		2
Walter Somerton with a forge		2
Walter Somerton jun		2
Will Herritage		1
Widow Blackford		3
Widow Eadon		1
John Blackford		1
Richard Blackford		1
Alice Moss		2
Will Walton		1
Tho Neale	1	
Will Randle		1
Widow Bradford	1	
Leo Davis		2
Will Berkinson		1
<N>Samell Killby		3

	[NC]	[Ch]
Tho Lightfoote		1
Will Townend		5
Henrie Clarke		2
Rich Townend		1
John Hancox		1
Henrie Nicolls		1
Rich Savidge	1	
Nathanill Savidge		2
Mr Henrie Gibbs		4
Will Marshall		1
John Nicolls		4
John Tenant		5
John Lightfoote		1
Daniell Wallton		2
[f. 11v]		
Robert Pilkington		1
Will Makepeace	1	
Richard Spicer	1	
John Rowdech	1	
Kemp Baggott	1	
Will Joanes	1	
		072

Viewed by:
Will Wainman collector
Anthony Blackford constable

Halford [par]

	[NC]	[Ch]
Mr George Granger		6
John Tubbs	1	
Tho Tomes		1
Tho Halford		3
Tho Salmon		1
Walter Tubbs		1
Robert Buller		1
Richard Higgins		1
Francis Langford	1	
Will Higgins		1
John Deane		1
Tho Blackburne		1
Isack Hauton		3
Phill Gardner		3
John Procter	1	
John Hamlins		3
John Hobbins		3

	[NC]	[Ch]
Mary Loynes	1	
Robt Gunn		1
[f. 12]		
Edward Masson		2
Tho Nibbs		1
Mr Will Halford		5
Mr Will Brent		4
Jane Dukes	1	
Ann Fearne	1	
Henrie Allibone	1	
Sibill Baylis	1	
Will Boyce	2	
Richard Dyer with a forge		2
Stephen Cox	1	
Francis Williams	2	
John Wills	<3>	3
Will Higges		1
Nick Harris		1
<…>Nick Spicer		3
Richard Feild		1
Will Boule	1	
		053

Viewed by:
Will Wainman collector
Tho Blackburne constable

In the Parish of Eadington [Ettington]

Fullreadie [Fulready]

	[NC]	[Ch]
Mr Tho Underhill		4
Nathaniell Smith		1
Nathaniel Blackford		1
Richard Page		1
Rich Merrall	<1>	1
Francis Sheffeild	1	
Margerie Woofe	1	
Edward Vincett	1	

[f. 12v]

Thorneton in Eadington [Thornton]

	[NC]	[Ch]
Sir Thomas Doleman		9

Eadington [Ettington]

	[NC]	[Ch]
Mr John Brent		5
Tho Kitchin		1

	[NC]	[Ch]
Francis Walker		1
Richard Lucas		1
Andrew Vincent		1
Jeffery Bavington		2
Will Heritage	1	
John Feild		1
Sam Lucas		3
<Tho> Will Handes		2
Edward Kanning		3
Francis et Tho Pallmer		3
Anthony Harrison		1
Tho Smith		4
Phill Halford		1
Widow Jackman		2
Richard Smith		1
Henrie Troley et [blank] Fowler		2
John Bacon		3
Widow Blackman		2
George Clarke		1
Tho Whitacer		1
Oliver More		1
Nick Hutchens		1
Widow Buckley		1
Will Rawlins		1
John Thorpe		1
Tho Bennitt		1
Tho Dickens		1
Will Sly		1
Christo Freeman		1
Robt Price		1
[f. 13]		
Widow Smith		3
John Sabill		1
Daniell Bickerton		4
Henrie Vincent		1
Edward Hill		1
Gabrill Pilkington		2
Edward Compton		1
Henrie Statum		1
Nick Wells		1
Joseph Rouse	1	
Will Lucas of Lamcott		4
Ellinor Williams	1	

	[NC]	[Ch]
Widow Kinge	1	
Widow White	1	
Gyles Clifton	1	
Edward Court	1	
<Tho> Edward Sly	1	
Widow Odell	1	
Robert Dickens	1	
Widow Pratt	1	
Tho Vincent	1	
Will Jones		1

Eadington Inferior

[Lower Ettington]

	[NC]	[Ch]
Mr Edward Crofftes		13
John Etheridge		1
John Willkins	1	
Robert Clifton		1
		107
		[103]

Viewed by:
Will Wainman collector

[f. 13v]

Ilmington cum membris

[Ilmington par with its parts]

	[NC]	[Ch]
Will Smith		1
Humpherie Hulston		3
Will Collicott		2
John Lydsey		2
Will Haselwood	1	
Sam Clarkeson		4
Widow Taylor	1	
Will Archer		1
Will Rose jun		1
Sir Henrie Capell		4
Will Southerne		1
Mr Swann		5
Nathaniell Rose		4
John Hixon	1	
Will Shorthasell		1
Daniell Willkins		2
Tho Bond		1
John Hurlestone		1
George Archer		1
John Paine		2

	[NC]	[Ch]
John Rose sen		2
Richard Archer	1	
Widow Driver	1	
Jonathan Pettie		1
Widow Sammon	1	
Simon Burmon	1	
Tho Bidle		1
Will Courte	<4>	4
Tho Price	1	
Will Carpenter	1	
John Gray		2
Widow Eadon		2
John Rose jun		2
[f. 14]		
Nick Saunder	1	
Sam Handy with a forge		2
Will Curtice		1
John Soley	1	
Francis Bull	1	
Will Rose jun		1
John Boyse	1	
Will Burrow	1	
Isack Peate		1
Widow Archer jun	1	
Will Rose sen		3
Widow Fleetewood	2	
Will Fleetewood	1	
John Rowney		3
Will Byshopp		2
<Will>Widow Baylis	1	
Will Sammon	1	
Paull Manners	1	
John Tysoe		1
Widow Allen		3
Nickolas Loe a forge		1
Will Reddle		2
Robert Sammon		1
Widow French		5
Rich Rose sen		1
Rich Rose jun		2
Rich Colldicoate sen		1
Walter Wells		2
Rich Edden		3
Tho Hurlestone		2

	[NC]	[Ch]
Rich Tidsdall		1
Tho Collicoate		1
Edward Eddon		3
Nickolas Turner	1	
John Collicoatt sen	1	
[f. 14v]		
John Rose		1
John Shakle		1
Rich Colldicoate jun		3
Rich Coldicoate sen		1
[4 lines deleted]		
Will Reddle jun		1
John Ballard	1	
Widow Coldicoate jun	1	
Edward Coldicoate		1
John Coldicoate		2
Tho Greogorie		2
Widow Archer sen		3
Will Cleaver	1	
Will Gray	1	
Will Neale		2
John Sammon sen	1	
John Samon jun	1	
John Coleman	1	
Samell Coldicoate		1
Widow Neale	1	
George Souther	1	
		110

[f. 15]

Fauscoate

[Foxcote in Ilmington par]

	[NC]	[Ch]
Mr Tho Clapton		1
Mr How		1
Mr Canninge		10
Will Churchhouse	1	
Christopher Coleman	1	
		012

Compton Scorphin

[Compton Scorpion in Ilmington par]

	[NC]	[Ch]
Mr John Palmer		11
Mr Will Vernon		4
Will Fleetewood		1
		016

Which Church cum membris
[Whitchurch par with its parts]

	[NC]	[Ch]
Mr Trapp rector		8
<Mr>Tho Marriott esq		7
Will Grivill		1
Rich Sammon		1

Brooton
[Bruton in Whitchurch par]

	[NC]	[Ch]
Will Hawkins		3
		020

[f. 15v]
Crimscoate
[Crimscote in Whitchurch par]

	[NC]	[Ch]
Mr George Underhill		4
Will Williams		1
Tho Slauler		1
Tho Williams		1
John Mills		2
Allen Lock		1
Richard Holtam		2
Cornelius Blackwell	1	
Widow Garner	1	
		012

Alston
[Ailstone in Atherstone on Stour par]

	[NC]	[Ch]
Mr John Browne		4
Henrie Bently		4
John Smith		2
Richard Wootten		1
Tho Jackson		2
Henrie Morrell		2
Tho Tybbett	1	
Will Parrett	1	
Will Buckley		1
James Smith	1	
		016

[f. 16]
Atherston [Atherstone on Stour par]

	[NC]	[Ch]
Mr James Hurdis		3
Jackson Morrell		7
Mr Wilkes		3
Tho Tysoe		1
Bartlemew Bennit	1	
Widow Banckes	1	
Mr Rice Yates		3
Tho Meades		1
		018

Wimston
[Wimpstone in Whitchurch par]

	[NC]	[Ch]
Widow Adams		1
John Tyms		2
Tho Pare		2
Tho Riland		3
John Etheridge		1
Widow Ryland		1
Richard Sammon		1
Nath Robins	1	
John Bolton	1	
Richard Sadler		1
Walter Nickolls	1	
Richad Meades	1	
John Hutchins	1	
John Barber	1	
Mathew Band	1	
		012

[WCRO, QS11/9]
[f. 1]
Priors Marston Divison 1670 in Kineton Hundred
[written by John Newsham]
[f. 1v: list of place names has been omitted]
[f. 2]
Neither Shugburgh
[Lower Shuckburgh chap[1]]

	[NC]	[Ch]
Edward Shaw		2
William Watson		1
Richard Shenton		1
Widow Butler	1	
Thomas Rawbone		1

1 Chapelry of Priors Hardwick parish.

	[NC]	[Ch]
Nick Goode		1
Thomas Feild		2
John Chatter		1
Widow Chatter		1
Jon Eales		1
Tho Tubb		1
Will Burnall	1	
Henrie Jackson		5
John Shaw	1	
George Duglas		2
Widow Maull	1	
Rich Shaw		2
Richard Allet		4
Tho Meale et [blank] Corrall	1	
Will Cleaver		2
Marie Watson	1	
Tho Chatter		1
Rich Willson	1	
James Everton	1	
Rich Willcox		1
Widow Steele		2
Sarah Noell	1	
Widow Watson	1	
Tho Shaw		1
Henrie Berrie		1
Joyce Hodges	<1>2	
Tho Genninges		1
Tho Goode		3
Joseph Taylor voyd		
Joh Colburne landlord	<2>	2
		039

Viewed by:
William Wainman collector
John Chatter constable

[f. 2v]

Priors Hardwick [par]

	[NC]	[Ch]
Robert Edmonds		2
John Masson		3
Richard Renall	1	
Ralph Warrin	1	
Widow Gardner	1	
George Knight		1
Widow Rainbow		2
Widow Jackson		1
Mr Kent rector		3
Will Palmer		1
George Feasie		2
Katherine<ll> Taylor		1
Will Heritage		5
Richard Bowers	1	
Wid Gubbins		3
Benjamine Goodwin		3
Nickolas Ellis		1
Widow Croffts	1	
Robert Clarke		1
Richard Washbrooke		3
Richd Rainbow		4
Francis Woodfall		2
Tho Budd		2
Will Heritage		2
Rich Pallmer		2
Thomas Fesey		3
Samuell Eberall		3
Widow Ebrall		1
Henrie Hinde		4
Barnard Bradshaw		1
Leonard Carter	1	
John Driver	1	
George Clarke		2
Will Bradshaw		3
[f. 3]		
Richard Heminges		2
John Elmore		1
		064

Viewed by:
Will Wainman collector
et Robet Edmond constable

Priors Marston [chap[1]]

	[NC]	[Ch]
Jon Petifer		3
Will Jeffs		1
Tho Nibb		1
Rich Davis		5
Widow Bythell		1
Widow Perrie		1

[1] Chapelry of Priors Hardwick parish.

	[NC]	[Ch]
John Bradshaw		2
Will Priest		2
Edward Bryon		2
Henrie Churchill		3
Will Churchill		2
John Meales		3
Tho Meales		3
Tho Barrett		6
John Glass		4
Tho Flower		2
Tho Hindes		5
George Edwards jun		3
John Blackford		1
Richd Key		1
Jobe Basely		4
Tho Blis		4
Tho Key jun		2
Tho Key sen		2
George Edwardes		1
Will Willis		3
John Wills		2
[f. 3v]		
William Spence		1
John Trusloe		1
Tho Jeffs		4
Rich Jeffs		2
Joseph Carpenter		1
Richard Malins		1
Mr West		5
Tho Haxford		1
Tho Bythill		2
Henrie Budd		1
Guyes Key with a forge		2
William Malins		1
Will Jefkins		2
Tho Wills		3
Tho Worrall		3
Jon Bythill		3
Widow Right		1
Tho Adkins		1
Henrie Bennett		1
Robert Bennitt		1
John Jeffkins		1

	[NC]	[Ch]
Widow Davis		1
Tho Bennett		1
Will Rainbow		2
Widow Allimon		1
Richard Bennett		1
Henrie Carter		1
Samuell Carter		<1>2
Tho Basely		4
John Allett		1
Rich Reeve		1
Henrie Petifer		1
Richard Flowers		1
Rich Carter		2
Widow Jeffes		1
[f. 4]		
John Bullen	1	
Will Butlin	1	
Will Perry		1
Marke Spence		1
Elizab Key		1
Henrie Key	1	
John Ballard	1	
Silvester Sammon	1	
Will Leason	1	
John Marriott	1	
John Rainbow		1
James Bythill		1
Wid Stacie	1	
John Churchill	1	
Micall Harrison	1	
Tho Burras	1	
Widow Graunt	1	
Edward Mould	1	
Robert Row	1	
John Mallin	1	
Richard Sleath	1	
Tho Compton	1	
John Price	1	
James Price	1	
Robt Bennitt	1	
Thomas Abbott	1	
Widow Clayton	1	
<...>William Handes	1	
James Winckles	1	

	[NC]	[Ch]
Allexand Herbert	1	
Widow Kineton	1	
William Carpenter	1	
Widow Tiffs	1	
Edward Welch	1	
[f. 4v]		
John Johnson	1	
Richard Sweateman		1
Richard Leedes	1	
Richard Rogers	1	
John Rogers	1	
William Jeffes	1	
		133

Viewed by:
William Wainman collector
Thomas Hawford constable

Wormelayton
[Wormleighton par]

	[NC]	[Ch]
The Earle of Sunderland		15
Mr Barford rector		3
Will Welch		3
Richard Welch		2
John Tibb		1
John Nicolls		2
Robert Chapman		1
Robert Withybed		1
Will Prist		1
John Grubb		1
Widow Wills	1	
Will Hastinges with a forge		2
Widow Shrewsburie	1	
Widow Lynell	1	
Widow Taff	1	
Widow Welch	1	
		032

Viewed by:
Will Wainman collector
John Grubb constable

[f. 5]
Fenicompton
[Fenny Compton par]

	[NC]	[Ch]
Mr Unitt rector		7
Mr George Wills		8
Mrs Katherine Smith		6
John Yonge		3
Widow Petifer		2
Jerimie Griffin		2
Tho Kinnell		2
Will Bass		2
Richard Nibb sen		1
Richard Nibb jun		1
George Baker		1
Edmond Clarke		2
George Nibb		2
Widow Hihorne <with> a forge		1
Tho Gray		1
Edward Freeman		1
Nick Duckett		1
John Potter		1
John Robertes		1
John Basely		1
Widow Tomkins		1
Tho Shersby		1
Richard Trimly		1
Vallentine Haynes		2
John Petipher		1
George Thomas		1
Richard Dodd		4
Mr Messenger		4
Nick Duckett		1
Widow Nibb sen		1
George Haynes	1	
Henrie Newman	1	
George Southam		1
Richard Basely		1
Richard Meacock		1
Tho Blick		2
[f. 5v]		
Richard Russell		1
Emptie house Widow Beasly		2
William Neale		5
John Edwardes		1
William Hihorne		2
Alice Haynes		1
Jonas Payne		1
John Warr		1

	[NC]	[Ch]
William Gray		1
Widow Tooly	1 C	
Henrie Petifer	1 C	
Thomas Bass		1
Will Westburie	1 C	
Samuell Harris	1 C	
John Johnson		1
Thomas Talbut	1	
Widow Meacock		1
John Bignall		1
Will Parker	1	
Widow Hihorne	1	
[indication that the next eight entries should be moved to the end of the parish]		
Widow Basely	1	
Widow Watts		1
<Widow>William Burrows	1	
Abraham Watts	1	
Obadiah Petipher		1
Robert Renolds		1
Tho Knibb		1
Will Gray		1
[f. 6]		
William Burrows	1	
John Bass jun		1
Richard Childes	1	
Tho Veares	1	
Widow James	1	
John Numan	1	
Richard Watts		1
Garrat Wilding	1	
Rich Watts sen	1	
Joseph Faulkes		1
Cristopher Clarke	1	
Nicolas Handes	1	
William Knibb jun		1
John Stock	1	
Widow Simkins	1	
John Auris	1	
Bridgett Bass		1
Widow Knibb	1	
Francis Robins	1	

	[NC]	[Ch]
Henrie Hodgetts	1	
Will Knibb jun		1
Will Whitehead	1	
William Barker	1	
Nicolas Kempe	1	
Richard Burrows	1	
Mathew Battes	1	
Henrie Griffin		1
John Paine	1	
		099

Viewed by:
William Wainman collector
John Potter constable

[f. 6v]

Knightcote in Burton Dassett Constablry [and par]

Robert Ladbrooke		4
Thomas Basely		1
Tho Dodd		3
Nathaniell Lidbrooke		3
Jona Lidbrooke		1
Richard Robinson		2
John Benson		3
Will Francklin		1
Robert Lydbrooke		2
Henrie N[i]calls		1
Mrs Drope		2
Mr Wagstaff		5
Richard Brookes		3
Thomas Warner		1
John Aleworld		1
Marie Lydbrooke		2
Edward Leaborne		3
Thomas Yeardly		2
Will Enock		3
Francis Beesby		1
Nathaniell Adams		1
Thomas Nason		1
Richard Walgrave		1
Bartho Lewis		1
John Meacock	1	
Tho Harris	1	
Widow Holtum	1	

	[NC]	[Ch]
Widow Tallett	1	
John Williams	1	
Tho Rice	1	
Richard Grant	1	
Widow Rice et Tho Rice	1	
Hierom Gillett	1	
		048

Viewed by:
Will Wainman collector
Tho Dadd constable

Northen in Burton Dassett Constablry
[Northend in Burton Dassett par]

	[NC]	[Ch]
Thomas Makepeace		2
Will Queeny		4
Mr John Unitt		6
Robert Freeman		1
Widow Whitehead		1
Mr Palmer et Will Baylis		6
Mr Willam Bradshaw		6
Mr Bradshaw in his empti house		1
Tho Allebone		3
Mathew Clarke		2
Will Norman		1
Tho Miller		1
John Allebone		2
Edward Graunt		1
Richard Baylis		2
Widow Bloxsum		2
John Lydbrooke		3
Mr John Unitt		1
These persons following are discharged by cirtificate		
Tho Rose	1	
John Baylis	1	
Sarah Jeffes	1	
Widow Bass	1	
Edward Gee	1	
William Bull	1	
Simon Gibbs	1	
Will Tooley	1	
Henrie Hitchman	1	
Tho Gibbs	1	
		045

Viewed by:
Will Wainman collector
Tho Dadd constable

[f. 7v]
Burton Dassett [par]

	[NC]	[Ch]
Sir Richard Temple		8
Sir John Tufton		11
Mr Hamersley vicar		4
Roger Blunt		1
The persons followinge are discharged by cirtificate		
Widow Harris	1	
Widow Hasely	1	

Viewed by:
Will Wainman collector
Tho Dadd constable

Dasset parva in Burton Constablry [Little Dassett in Burton Dassett par]

	[NC]	[Ch]
Francis Neale		7
Baruck Tusten		3
Benjamin Tyner		2
Widow Smith		2
Richard Hancock		1
Will Whitehead		1
<Widow Tyner>		
The persons followinge are discharged by legall cirtificate		
Francis Yarrow	2	
Widow Tyner	1	
Widow Pellett	1	
		040

Viewed by:
Will Wainman collector
Tho Dadd constable

	[NC]	[Ch]
[***Part of Radway in Burton Constabulary***[1] and Radway par]		
[*John Petipher*		*3*]
[*Robt Palmer*		*2*]
[*Wm Hunt*		*2*]
[*Henry Hunt*		*2*]
[*Wm Hunt*		*1*]
[*Wm Enock*		*1*]
[*Richd Sparkes*		*1*]
[*Alice Ball*		*3*]
		[*15*]

[f. 8]

Avon Dassett [par]

	[NC]	[Ch]
Mr Richard Woodward sen		8
Mr Staunton rector		8
Mr Woodward		1
John Batchelor		1
Daniell Neale		4
John Batchelor		2
<Nick>John Batcheler		1
Widow Dod		2
Tho Dod		2
John Dod		1
Edward Kimnell et Wid Perkin		5
Tho Rose		3
John Rawlins sen		1
John Batchelor sen		2
Richard Kimnell		2
Francis Perkins		2
Henrie Lynnett		3
Phillipp Perkins		3
Robert Renall		1
John Stickley		1
Henrie Dod		3
Richard Glover		1
Jon Rawlins jun		1
Leonard Perkins a forge		1
Mr Richard Woodward jun		5
John Tynsill		1
Will Sharpe		1
These persons following are discharged by legall cirtificate		
Widow Walker	1	
Tho Petipher	1	
Richard Hancock	1	
Widow Phipps	1	
Elizabeth Smith	1	
Jon Smith	1	
Tho Gibbs	1	
Will Round	1	
		066

Viewed by:
Will Wainman collector
John Batchelor constable

[f. 8v]

Farmebrough

[Farnborough par]

	[NC]	[Ch]
George Rawleigh esq		11
Mr Tho Stanton		4
Mr Osburne		2
Widow Davis		1
Mr Christopher Rawleigh		4
Widow Brock		3
John Greenwod		1
Will Davis		1
Mr Will Wagstaff		8
John Freckleton		4
Tho Greenwood		1
Tho Grenewood in new house		1
Widow Gardner		1
Martin Rawbone		2
John Ealkes		1
George Nibb		2
Mr Richard Unitt		4
Tho Deakins		1
Will Durie		1
Widow Hickson		1
Mr Withyfords emptie house		4
Mr Wilkes emptie house		1
Will Rawbone		2
Widow Dumbleton		1
Micall Corbett		2

1 Data inserted from WCRO, QS11/26 (1671).

	[NC]	[Ch]
The persons following are discharged by legall cirtificate		
Will Wells	1	
Simon Haydon	1	
John Haydon	1	
George Glover	1	
Will Glover	1	
John Worsely	1	
Widow Corbett	1	
[f. 9]		
Leah Davis	2	
Widow Tarver	2	
Tho Cleaton	1	
John Howes	1	
George Beare	2	
Tho Cawdwell	1	
John Austin	1	
John Browne	1	
Tho Kinge	1	
Will Denton	1	
Bridgett Sabin	1	
		064

Viewed by:
William Wainman collector
William Davis constable

Mollendton
[Mollington in Cropredy par]

	[NC]	[Ch]
Mr Ambrouse Holbech		10
Mr John Gorsteloe		6
Nick Downes		3
George Gardner		2
John Bull		2
Rich Childes		1
Richard Gullifer		3
Will Robins		1
John Knight		2
Richard Sandiford sen		1
Samuell Knight		2
Marie Benfeild		3
Will Tyms		1
John Childes		3
The persons followinge are discharged by cirtificate		
Rich Stainton	1	
Rich Corbett	1	
Elizabeth Coleman	1	
John Stanton	1	
Rich Sandiford jun	1	
		040

Viewed by:
Will Wainman collector
John Child constable

[f. 9v]
Shatswell [Shotteswell par]

	[NC]	[Ch]
Mr Coleman <vicar>sen		<2>3
Mr Grivill vicar		2
William Arnall		2
Edward Brayne		1
Tho Phipps with 2 forges		4
Will Tibbitts		1
Widow Bedford		1
Widow Beck		2
John Abbitt		1
Richard Pratt		3
Tho Pratt		1
Tho Perkins		8
Mathew Coleman		1
John Abbitt jun		1
Stephen Hix		1
Widow Petipher		1
John Gibbs		1
John Bagley		1
Widow Pratt		1
Joseph Grime		1
Will Pratt		2
Will Coleman jun		2
Samuell West		2
Simon Jud		1
Francis Petipher		3
Tho West		3
Will Coleman		1
Richard Bannell		1
Widow Gaskin		1
Edward Randle		1
Will Spurrier		3
Widow Pratt		1

	[NC]	[Ch]
Ann Carter		1
Will Rose		3
[f. 10]		
Widow Grivill		1
Peeter Davis		2
Tho Basely		3
Edward Grivill		1
The persons following are discharged by legall cirtificate		
Edward Gregorie	1	
Will Basely	1	
Will Harris	1	
Will Rose alias Peter Kerry	1	
Hester Miller	1	
Robert Iszard	1	
Jonas Kinge	1	
Tho Kendrick	1	
John Clarrage	1	
John Francis	1	
Richard Westburie	1	
Widow Harwood	1	
Widow Freeman	1	
Tho Freeman	1	
Christopher Freeman	1	
<Widow Grivill>		
Widow and Thomas Bowers	1	
Elizabeth Harwood	1	
		069

Viewed by:
Will Wainman collector
Edward Braine constable

	[NC]	[Ch]
[f. 10v]		
Warmeington et Arlescoate[1]		
[Warmington par]		
Mr John Wootton		7
Mr Anthony Petipher		6
Mr Will Goodwin[2]		7
Richard Judd		3
Christopher Ward		1
John Collins		3
John Catch		1
Tho Bennitt		3
Simon Cotterill		1
Micall Hancock		4
Simon Davis		2
Uriah Faulkener		1
Tho Perkins		2
Mathew Gaskin		1
Richard Heminge		2
John Tue		5
John Hill		1
Simon Davis jun		1
Richard Rose		1
Richard Rawbone		1
Widow Gaskin		1
Tho Collins		1
Tho Joyles		1
Anthony Bugby		1
Richard Burrows[3]		5
John Hinton		1
Tho Enock[4]		4
Will Wharum[5]		3
Widow Paris		1
Edward Walker		6
John Perkins		1
John Judd		1
John Wareinge		2

1 Arlescote was enumerated separately in 1664 and 1665, with six and five entries respectively, but not from 1666 onwards. These data, however, make it possible to identify all the Arlescote entries in 1666 and 1670, as indicated here. The fluctuating total was caused by the entry for Richard Burrows being listed sometimes as two households (senior with one hearth and junior with four). In 1670 William Wharum had replaced Peter Davis senior: WCRO, QS11/5 (1664); TNA, E179/259/10 & 9 (1665 & 1666).

2 In Arlescote.

3 In Arlescote.

4 In Arlescote.

5 In Arlescote.

	[NC]	[Ch]
[f. 11]		
Elizabeth Huggins		3
Will Clarridge		3
Marke Legg		2
Widow Astell		1
Robert Harrison		1
Ann Bradford		1
Widow Perkins		1
Richard Hill		1
Richard Gaskin		1
<West>Will West		1
Peter Davis		1
Richard Thorpe		3
Henrie Huggins		1
John Davis sen		1
Leonard Perkins with a forge		2
Joseph Draper		1
Richard Puller		1
		106
These persons followinge are discharged by legall cirtificate		
Tho Hopcroft[1]	1	
Will Draper	1	
Allexander Bradford	1	
Tho Heritage	1	
Marie Mawson	1	
Tho Welchman	1	
Jonas Tombes	1	
Robert Joyle	1	
Katherine Walker	1	
John Joyles	1	
Three poore cottages	3	

Viewed by:
Will Wainman collector
John Collins constable

	[NC]	[Ch]
[f. 11v]		
Ratley et Upton [Ratley par]		
[***Upton***[2]]		
John Danvers esq		11
Edward Coleby		2
[***Ratley***[3]]		
Mr Tho Walker		11
Mr Tho Lewis		6
John Burrows gent		5
Simon Lucas		3
Neven Usher		2
Will Hitchcock		<2>4
John Lambe		2
Mr Tho Lewes		2
John Harris		2
Tho Hitchcock		3
John Archer		1
Mr Lewis		5
Richard Archer		1
Tho Neale		1
Tho Weaver		1
Mr Walker		1
Henrie Blackman	1	
Mr Tomkins		3
Richard Burrows		3
Will Jenninges		1
Mannas Herritage		2
Robert Heritage		1
John Herritage		1
Richard Tomkins		<2>3
		077
[f. 12]		
The persons following are discharged by legall cirtificate vizt		
John Russell	1	
Will Cooper	2	
Henrie Blackman	1	
Francis Genninges	1	
Richard Denny	1	
Will Bucknell	1	
Ellianor Weaver	1	

1 In Arlescote.
2 WCRO, QS11/49 (1674).
3 WCRO, QS11/26 (1671).

	[NC]		[Ch]
Will Archer	1		
Thomas Russell	1		
Will Bray	1		

Viewed by:
William Wainman collector
Thomas Hitchcock constable

Examined and subscribed per me
William Wainman collector

[WCRO, QS11/10]
[f. 1]
Kineton Hundred
Brayles [Brailes] **Division**
Anno 1671
Exchequer Roles
received 24 Nov 71
[written by Richard Samon]
[f. 1v: blank]
[f. 2]
Brayles <Inferior>
[Lower Brailes in Brailes par]

	[NC]		[Ch]
Tho Eadon			1
John Haynes			3
Tho Walker weaver			1
Widdow Wrench <now Capell>	1	C	
Capell now Tho Oakely			3
Mr Richardson rector			3
Wid Capell now John Tayler			2
Widd Walker	1	C	
John Gardner	1	C	
Andrew Cawdell & Widd Mills paid ½ a yeare	1	C	
John Hood	1	C	
Mr Willm Bishop			10
Widd Bishop			3
Alice Eadon			2
Will <Oakely> Okely	1	C	
Richard Harbert			1
Willm Eadon			2
Willm Walker			2
John Prestadge shuts his doore (noe dest[ress])			2
Isac Crafts now Richd Walker			5
John Herbert			1
Miles Tennant			1
John Hall			3
Tho Mills			2
Tho Middleton			4
Tho Midletons empty			3
James Rymill			3
Edward Alexander			3
John Whight			3
Richard Godson			2
Robt Porter			1
Bradshaw Tayler			1
Richard Walker			4
Lawrence Walker	1	C	
Eliz Styler	1	C	
Widd Collins	1	C	
Robt Purham empty	1	C	
Widd Thornitt	1	C	
Jno Haynes now Jno Lumbert			1

[f. 2v]

	[NC]		[Ch]
Walter Hennings	1	C	
Tho Brewer			1
Ralph Prestadge			1
Willm Albury	1	C	
John Upton	2	C	
John Prestadge	2	C	
Ed Humphery	[-] [*1*	*C*[1]]	
Will Prat	1	C	
James Gardner	1	C	
Widd Napton	1	C	
Will Hunt	1	C	
Geo Pettaway			1
Will Harbert	1	C	
Tho Humphery			1
Widd West	1	C	
Will Gardner	1	C	
Widd James	1	C	

1 WCRO, QS11/27 (1671).

	[NC]		[Ch]
John Johnson	1	C	
Tho Parker			3
Tho Wells			1
Richard Hancock			1
John Marshall			1
Mary Saull	1	C	
Ralph Shurly			1
Edwd Banister			1
Willm George			1
Widd Hancock	1	C	
Will Rymill (refuseth to pay)	1		
Francis Capell sen			5
Jno Becket			1
John Allin with an oven			2
Henry Cockbill	<1>		1
Natt Smith	<1>		1
Robt Hone	<1>		1
Tho Taylor			1
Widdow Moore	1	C	
Tho Eadon			1
Richard Eadon			1
John Eadon	1	C	
[f. 3]			
Roger Marshall			2
Tho George			1
Willm Rymill			2
James Chadborne	1	C	
John Bryon	1	C	
Will Whiting			1
Widd Browne			2
Francis Capell jun			4
Will Aston	1	C	
Tho Rymill			1
John Cockbill			1
Walter Gregory	1	C	
Will Hancock	1	C	
Ralph Harrison	1	C	
Francis Shurly 1 new built			5
John Bishop			1
Mary Laude	1	C	
Richard Bishop			1
Gerrard Whiting	1	C	

	[NC]		[Ch]
Willm Saull	1	C	
Tho Freeman	1	C	
Widd Wrench	1	C	
Widd Brickerstaffe void	1	C	
Tho Bishop	1	C	
Willm Carter	1	C	
Widd Hancock empty Wm Rymill landlord refuseth to pay			1
John Hall empty refuseth to pay			2
Robt Eadon	1	C	
Kath Cleadon alias Tayler	1	C	
Willm Hemings	1	C	
Michaell Phillips	1	C	
Tho Jennings	1	C	
John Haynes	1	C	
Chemscotte [Chelmscote]			
Willm Somerford			2
Richard Pilcanton	1	C	
[***Upper Brailes***[1]]			
Richard Workeman			3
Charles Allin			1
John Hitchcock			1
Tho Ward			2
Richard Mills			1
[f. 3v]			
More of Brayles Superior			
[Upper Brailes]			
Willm Cockbill			1
John Okely			2
Geo Wyott			3
Will Eadon jun			2
James Lumbert			1
Willm Eadon 1 a forge			2
Richard Eadon			2
Tho Napton			2
Tho Wells			1
Richard Walker			4
Antho Bishop			1
Geo Stock			3
Willm Powell			3
Richard Watkins			1
Edwd Davis			3

[1] WCRO, QS11/27 (1671).

	[NC]	[Ch]
Tho Walker		1
Tho Stock		2
Tho Rose		2
John Cockbill		2
Gregory Luke	1 C	
Marke Johnson		2
Phill Mumford		2
Katherine Litchcock		2
Tho Luckefeild		1
Widd Nickalls		2
Willm Baldwin		3
John Corbett		1
Willm Wilden		1
Mr John Okely		3
Robt Davis		2
Tho Walker jun		4
Tho Woodley	1 C	
James Mumford	1 C	
Tho Crafts	1 C	
Willm Cox	1 C	
Richard Blackman	1 C	
Willm Bradley	1 C	
Willm Wood		1
James Cooke		1
Tho Robinson		1
John Mumford	1 C	
Widd Perkinson		1
[f. 4]		
Nick Perkinson	1 C	
Willm George	1 C	
Jone Bumpass	1 C	
Widd Spicer	1 C	

Winderton [in Brailes par]

Tho Cole		1
Will Swarbrooke		2
Mr Natt Hill		5
John Wilkes		1
James Stocke		1
John Kilby		1
Richard Greenhill		1

	[NC]	[Ch]
Tho Greenhill		1
Simon Gibbs		2
Richard Wilkes		1
Richard King		1
Richd Hone	1 C	
Richd Wilkes ante		1
Widd Wilkes		1
Richard Capell		2
Edwd Leakins		3
Will Bishop		1
Jos[ia]s Phillips		1
John Tayle	1 C	
Esay Walker	1 C	
John Pettaway new built	[–] [*1* *C*[1]]	
Willm Kilby	1 C	
John King	1 C	
John Beard	1 C	
		26

[£]3 - 13s - 0
memento Jno Wells paid for
5 ½ year[s] 5s
[ff. 4v, 5 blank]
[f. 5v]

Cherrinton [Cherington par]

Jeffery Court	1 C	
Mr Anthony Dickins		3
Richard Adams		1
Nick Webb		1
Edwd Day		3
Willm Neale	1 C	
Tho Gardner	1 C	
John Houlton		2
Widd Cladon	1 C	
Richard Barrat	1 C	
Mrs Mansell		3
Widd Curtis	1 C	
Stephen Garrat		2
Willm Sly	1 C	
Dorothy Sly vidua		1
Tho Day		3
Willm Stock		3
John Masson		1

[1] WCRO, QS11/27 (1671).

	[NC]		[Ch]
Willm Bishop sen	1	C	
Willm Bishop jun	1	C	
Willm Turner			2
Willm Steele			1
Mr Smith rector			5
Willm Tiddiman			1
Willm Brewer 1 a forge			2
John Webb			1
Robt Cutts	1	C	
Tho Tayler			2
Willm Meades			2
Tho Masson			2
Widdow Masson			1
Tho Neale	1	C	
Edwd Stout			2
John Petty			3
John Hyerne			1
Widd Webb			1
John Webbs empty			1
[f. 6]			
Tho Claridge	1	C	
Robt Curtice			2
Tho King			2
Widd Hawkes	1	C	

Whichford [par]

	[NC]		[Ch]
Widd Bradly	1	C	
Tho Sondledoum			2
Richd Gearing	1	C	
Edwd Hyern			2
Richd Wincott			3
John Tymmes			2
Tho Tymes			2
John Wakeman			4
Nick Harrison			2
Willm Ellins 1 a forge (vir[?] poore noe des[tress])			3
Richd Masson			1
Valentine Emitts			2
John Wells			2
Richd Harris	1	C	
Henry Harrison			1
John Davis			1
John Hitchman			1
Leonard Harris	1	C	
Widd Watts	1	C	
Alice Smith	1	C	
John Wilkins	1	C	
Walter Herings	1	C	
Tho Taylor	1	C	
Mr Watkins rector			8
Mrs Mary Oldish			9
Anthony Lampet			3
Tho Clarke			2
Willm Bury			3
Robt Rous			3
Rich Awebury			2
Willm Rous			3
[f. 6v]			
Tho Hitchman			1
Will Ryshall	2	C	
Henry Baker			3
John Jones			3
Mary Slaughter paid a yeare			1
Robt Wincott jun			2
John Slaughter sen	1	C	
Robt Taylor	1	C	
Widd Pettifer	2	C	
Willm Hitchman	1	C	
Willm Rous			1

Astcott
[Ascott in Whichford par]

	[NC]		[Ch]
Hump Whight			7
Richd Aynge			3
Willm Browne			1
Wm Aynge			2
Robt Slaughter			4
John Fraine			3
John Tymes			3
Tho Harris			1
Rich Hyott l[andlord]			3
Widd Fraine			1
Richd Adams			3
Richd Walker			2
John Archer			2

	[NC]	[Ch]
Tymes Archer		2
John Bury jun	1 C	
Tho Bull		2
John Grafton		1
Willm Carter		1
Tho Gibbs		3
John Sturch		3
John Bury sen		4
Tho Wheeler	1 C	
John Leadbeater	1 C	
Widd Crobey	1 C	
[f. 7]		
John Argent	1	
Henry Pettifer	1	
James Fraine	1	

Stouerton

[Stourton in Whichford par]

	[NC]	[Ch]
Richd Crafts		1
Richd Bishop		4
John Rous		4
Walter Webb		4
Mr John Johnson		3
Josuah Slaughter		1
Josiah Jackman		3
John Garrat		1
Richd Taylor		1
Richd Taylor		1
Robt Shaw		4
Richd Wakemen		5
Willm Webb		1
John Blackman		1
Nick Sturch		2
Richd Sturch		1
Richd Katchby	1 C	
Willm Wells		2
Wm Slaugter		1
Wm Gibbs		1
Jno Hews		1
Edwd Godson	1 C	
Jno Webb		2
Hen & Edwd Tymes		2
Richd Baldwin		2

	[NC]	[Ch]
John Ratford	1 C	
Edwd Lock	1 C	
John Shepheard	1 C	
Tho Barrat	1 C	
Tho Ward	1 C	
John Webb jun	1 C	
Wm Gibbs paid ½ a yeare		1

Weston Pallace

[Weston in Long Compton par]

	[NC]	[Ch]
Ralph Sheldon esq		38

[f. 7v]

Long Compton [par]

	[NC]	[Ch]
Tho Hunt		8
Nich Brayn		4
Tho Brayn		4
Will Beale sen		1
Richd Tymes		3
Richd Sallis		1
Widd Rous		1
Jno Harris of Nether end		1
John Arkell		2
Anne Nevell widdow		3
Richard Young		2
Andrew Brew		1
Henry Slaughter		1
John Taylor		1
Widd Miles		<1>2
John Hunt		1
Tho Hunt		1
Mary Grevill		1
Richard Rous		2
Wm Tombes		2
Widd Widdows		1
Robt Wells		1
John Walker		3
George Wheeler		3
John Harris		1
Edwd Crossly		2
Eliz Matthews		1
John Blizard		1
Edward Raysell		1
Richard Bullard		3

	[NC]	[Ch]
Will Corall		3
John Buller		3
Walter Walford		2
Henry Gibbs		1
Tho Hews		3
Tho Blizard		1
Willm Buller		2
[f. 8]		
Richd Wilcox		1
Henry Hunt		3
Richard Haydon		3
Robt Joyner		2
Mr Tho Sheppard		4
Widd Joyner	1 C	
Nick Clarke		1
Robt Corke		1
Widdow Hankes		3
Richd Fowler		1
John Harris		1
Edwd Young		3
Richd Davis		3
Widd Lambert		2
Widd Hewes		1
John Skey		2
Will Beale jun		1
Robt Wheeler		1
Mr Edwd Smalbone		4
John Harris		3
Antho Rawlins		3
Richd Rawlins		3
Robt Hydon		5
John Joyner		2
Antho Braine		3
Matt Herbert	2 C	
Mr Hawkins		6
Edwd Oliver		2
Jno Crosse	1 C	
Wm Currall		1
Wm Beale sen		1
Nich Geery		1
Tho Basely		1
Robt Wheeler jun		1
Samson Simes		1
30 poore people certified for	30	

	[NC]	[Ch]
[f. 8v]		
Barton on the Heath [par]		
Nick Overbury esq		18
Richd Parris		6
Nick Overbury esq		3
Mr George Stratford		7
Mr John Dover		12
Mr Briske rector		5
Mr John Lambert		4
John Kerry		3
Tho Bentley		2
George Phelps		4
Willm Neale paid a yeare		2
Antho Robins		3
Tho Lane		1
John Ward		2
Robt Ward		2
Richard Freeman		2
Richd Dupper	1 C	
John Hall	2 C	
John Beck	1 C	
Willm Shurly	1 C	
Richd Brown	1 C	
Elizabeth Compton	1 C	
John Jobson	1 C	
Richd Cox	1 C	
Widd Meades	1 C	
Lawrence Hands		2
Henry Savidge	1 C	
Eliz Tydmonds	1 C	
Richard Widdowes	1 C	
Tho Widdows	1 C	
Great Woolford		
[Great Wolford par]		
Mr Tho Keyt		7
Mr Edwd Okely		8
Mr Smith rector		3
Robt Hobbs		1
Anne Wakeman		1
Edwd Parson		2
Willm Randle		2
[f. 9]		
Lot Keyt		4

	[NC]	[Ch]
Richard Barrat		2
Wm Greene		1
Wm Muffin		2
Tho Shepheard		1
John Durham		1
Henry Cooper		2
Anthony Newell		2
John Rose		2
Richd Rose		1
Wm Rose		1
Richd Clemand	1 C	
Richd Dyer one a forge	2 C	
Widd Granger	1 C	
Robt Browne	1 C	
Willm Dyer sen		4
Wm Dyer jun 1 a forge		2
John Randle		3
John Hind	1 C	
Willm Durham	1 C	
John Barrat		1
Widd Hobbs		1
Tho Shortland		2
Tho Mullis	1 C	
Widd Lardin		1
John Trueby		1
Widd Powell	1 C	
Edwd Durham	1 C	
Widd Greene	1 C	
Widd Durham	2 C	
Richd Newell		2
Richd Gery	1 C	
Widd Huntly	1 C	
Widd Hewins	1 C	
Richd Huntly	1 C	

Litle Woolford
[Little Wolford in Great Wolford par]

	[NC]	[Ch]
Hastings Ingram esq		11
Mr Richd Randell		8
John Burridge		1
Tho Sheldon		1

[f. 9v]

	[NC]	[Ch]
Wm Sheldon		1
Wm Okely		1
Antho Okely		1
Tho Okely	1 C	
John Smith		1
Richard Hall		1
John Cooper		1
Robt Sheldon		3
Richd Rolewright		3
Wm Gardner		1
Robt Blackburne		2
John Rowlwright		4
Richd Bromly		1
John Walker		3
Tho Tayler		1
Widd Buckland		2
Robt Sherly sen		1
Wm Shakell	1 C	
Widd Taplin	1 C	
Wm Slater	1 C	
Jonathan Tomkins		1
Morris Shepherd		1
Richd Thacker		1
Geo Weale		1
Francis Trevors	1 C	
Edwd Fry	1 C	
Moses Webb	1 C	
Tho Hyerne	1 C	
Richd Petty	1 C	
Paul Robins	1 C	
John Andrews		1
Wm Claridge		1
John Mullis	1 C	
Katherine Bradley	1 C	
James Sumerton 1 forge		2
Richd Browne	1 C	
George Widdows	1 C	
Robt Gardner	1 C	

[f. 10]

Burmington [par]

	[NC]	[Ch]
Mr Wm Randle		7
Robt Beale		2
Michaell Gray		4

	[NC]	[Ch]
Matt Tombs		2
Richd Hemnnings 1 forge		3
Richd Stickly		1
Henry Sandele		1
Robt Tombs		1
Wm Hall		1
Wm Heydon		1
John Hyernes		2
Joyles Tombes		1
Tho Currier		1
Danll Blackford		1
Wm Whatcock		3
Widd Williams	1 C	
Widd Franklin	1 C	
George Griffin	1 C	
John Fry	1 C	
John Mullis	1 C	
John Masson	1 C	
John Hodgekins	1 C	
Wm Hitchcocks	1 C	
Trubshaw Stiles		1
John Warner	1 C	
Robt Tombs noe distresse	1 C	
Richd Amsdon		1
Anthony Hart	1 C	

[f. 10v]

Stretton Super Faus

[Stretton on Fosse par]

	[NC]	[Ch]
Henry Hickes rector		6
Tho Proctor		5
Mr Robt Purser		10
Tho Keck		3
Edwd Gibbs		3
Edmd Gibbs		2
Wm Gibbs sen		1
Wm Gibbs jun		4
Richd Gibbs sen		1
Richd Gibbs jun		2
John Purser		3
Tho Cotterell		4
Richd Pancridge		1
Widd Crafts		2
Tho Plefts		3
John Humphereyes		3
Wm Leey		2
Robt Long		2
Tho Padock		1
Danll Keyt	1 C	
Wm Whight		1
Richd Long sen	1 C	
Richd Long jun	1 C	
John Long	1 C	
Tymothy Miles		1
John Salter	1 C	
George Sands	1 C	
Joan Gibbs	1 C	
Valentine Rawlins	1 C	
Widd Gibbs	1 C	
Richard Proctor		1
Francis Greenaway		2
John Townesend sen		2
John Townesend jun	1 C	
Richard Sliser		1

[f. 11]

	[NC]	[Ch]
Richd Tayler		1
Widdow Bentley		1
Tho Clarke	1 C	
John Savidge	1 C	
Henry Bayles	1 C	
Henry Enston	1 C	
John Ward		1
Tho Berry	1 C	
John Dyer 1 a forge		2
Tho Hewes		1
Wm Gibbs		1

Willington

[in Barcheston par]

	[NC]	[Ch]
Mr Brunt		6
Widd Freeman		6
James Ashfeild	1 C	
Wm Allen		1
Robt Edlington	1 C	
Nick Horton	1 C	
John Williams	1 C	
Joane Hewet	1 C	
Will Souldern	1 C	

	[NC]	[Ch]
John Martin	1 C	
Widd Hall	1 C	
Anthony Amsden		3
Mrs Colburne		2
John Ashby paid a year		4
Richd Goodwin		2
Richd Goodwin		1
Richd Hancock		1
Mr Henry Joans		4
John Humphreys		3
Stephen Thornit		1
Margery Hunt	1 C	

[f. 11v]

Barcheston [par]

	[NC]	[Ch]
Ralph Sheldon esq		5
Mr Hornit rector		6
John Wedge		1
Henry Turner		1

Honington [par]

	[NC]	[Ch]
Tho Gibbs esq now Mr Parker		17
Tho Fearne		2
Widd Curtis		1
Widd Potter	1 C	
Rowland Harris vicar		2
Tho Troley		1
Wm West		1
John Williams	1 C	
Matt Kent		1
Tho Morley 1 forge	2 C	
Richd Hancock		2
Tymothy Marshall		1
Widd Millington	2 C	
Henry Watton		3
Richd Watton	2 C	
Tho Bevington		1
Luke Gascoigne	2 C	
Ellis Adams		6
Willm Brandis		3
George Adams		2
Jeff Benington		2
Richd Wells	1 C	

	[NC]	[Ch]
Will Tombes		2
Robt Gibbs <with> an oven		1
Christfr Hands		1
Wm Curtis		1

[f. 12]

	[NC]	[Ch]
Arris Davis		1
Wm Cooper		2
Robt <W?>Neale		1
Nick Kenton sen		3
George Morrell	1 C	
John Walford		3
Willm Courtis		8
Henry Collins		1
Tho Hands	1 C	
Richd Bumpas		1
Widd Durham		1
Willm Morrall	1 C	
Widdow Ward		2
Richd Sturch	2 C	
Nick Tompkins	1 C	
Richd Durham	1 C	
Widd Peate	1 C	
Stephen Quinton		1
Hugh Burmingham		1
Hugh Troley	1 C	
Ralph Cleaton	2 C	
Hump Wright		1
Mary Johnson	1 C	
Fran Cooper	1 C	
Widd Eadon	1 C	
Robt Kinton	1 C	
Robt Gibbs	1 C	

Idlicoate [Idlicote par]

	[NC]	[Ch]
Sir Wm Underhill		15
Mrs Dorothy Underhill		4
Mrs Dorothy Underhill		7
Mr Rudd new built paid ½ year		4
Mr Jos[ia]s Brookes minister		3
Will Walton		1
Henry Ellis		2
John Smith		2

[f. 12v]

	[NC]	[Ch]
Widd Gibbs		2

	[NC]	[Ch]
Marke Marshall		2
Christfr Brandis 1 forge		2
John Wilson		1
Richd Adams	1 C	
Tho Tarver		1
Widd Lepington		4
Hump Sumner	1 C	
Matt Cradock	1 C	
Tho Tant	1 C	
Widd Hill	1 C	
John Turbit	1 C	
Tho Blackman	1 C	
George Blackman	1 C	
Whatcoate [Whatcote par]		
Mr Rowland Arris		3
Richd Davis		2
Michaell Mitchell		1
Erasmus Pilkington		1
Tho Westley		1
Willm Tayle		1
Wm Chamberlaine	1 C	
Tho Savidge		1
Widd Stickly		1
Tho Nicholles		1
George Marshall		2
Wm Wyatt		2
Henry Courtis		1
Widd Neale		1
Will Banbury		3
John Bull		1
Gabriell Pilkinton		2
Richd Nickalls		1
[f. 13]		
Richd Wells		2
John Neale		2
Matt Bryan		1
Will Tayler	1 C	
Wm Hickes 1 not finisht		1
Eliz Saile vidua		1
Richd Davis		1
Wm Wind	1 C	
Wm Sumner	1 C	
Alex Pilkington		1

	[NC]	[Ch]
Pillerton Priors [par]		
Widd Walker		1
John Vincent		1
Tho Smith		1
Wm Smith jun		1
John Clarke		1
Jno Ellebond		1
John Wing		3
Wm Smith sen l[andlord]		1
Tho Baseley		1
Wm Smith sen		2
John Gardner		4
Wm Sambidge		6
John Soeden		1
Tho Neale		2
Eliz Prophet		1
Ralph Adams		2
Widd Walgrave		1
Ralph Ellis		3
John Moore		2
Wm Bayles	1 C	
Richd Bond		1
[f. 13v]		
John Earle	1 C	
Tho Whitelsey	1 C	
Widd Neale	1 C	
Wm Hutchins		1
John Smith	1 C	
Arthur Moore		1
Willm Atkins	1 C	
Pillerton Hersey [par]		
Richd Stukely		1
Isaack Smith		1
Willm Phillips		1
Widd Hierne		1
Tho Trimnell	1 C	
Willm Sable		1
Miles Gibbs		1
Widd Cox	1 C	
Humanitas Jackson		4
Humanitas Jackson		2
Tho Ward esq		3
Henry Reeve		3

	[NC]	[Ch]
Mr Allen Smith		5
Mr John Mothershed paid 1 yeare		1
Henry Smith		1
Francis Palmer		3
Francis Hancocks		2
Edwd Phillips		3
Richd Hancocks 1 a forge		2
Tho Reeve		4
Hugh Bradford		1
Nick Hutchins		1
John Davis	1 C	
Simon Richardson	1 C	
[f. 14]		
Nick Kilbey	1 C	
Alex Leigh		1
Widd Simkins	1 C	
Andrew Reeves		1
Richard Davis	1 C	

This division viewed by me
Will Wainman collector

[WCRO, QS11/11]
[f. 1]

Kineton hundred
Tanworth Devission

[written by William Wainman]
[List of place names written by John Newsham has been omitted]
[f. 1v: blank]
[f. 2]

Chesterton [par]

[***Kingston***[1]]

	[NC]	[Ch]
Rich Varney sen esq		6
Mr Bradshaw		4
Rich Varney jun esq		16

[***Chesterton***[2]]

	[NC]	[Ch]
Rob Snoake		5
Rich Ladbrook		2
James Budd		2

	[NC]	[Ch]
Rob Ablin		1
Barnby Parker		2
John Bosse	1	
Tho Harwood		3
Rich Gibbs		1
Walter Palmer		1
Walter Batcheller		1
Miles Cottrell		1
The Lady Peto empty cott[age]		1
Wid Robinson	1	
John Palmer		1
Wid Lock	1	
Will Lock		1
Wid Willes	1	
Hen Juanes	1	
Rich Willson	1	
		048

Veiwed by:
William Wainman collector
William Lock constable

[f. 2v]

Morton

[Moreton in Moreton Morrell par]

	[NC]	[Ch]
Rich Right		3
Rich Haukes		2
Tho Gilbert		1
Will Washbroke	<1>2	
Will Hopkins		2
John Web		1
Will Overton		2
Tho Washbrooke	1	
The parssnidg house		2
Mr Hen Lees		3
Tho Seeley		1
Rich Hanks		1
Tho Bannell		1
John Burdon	1	
Sillvanus Hunt		2
The Lady Harvey		12
Gregory Greene		1
Wid Taylor	1	

1 WCRO, QS11/47 (1674).
2 WCRO, QS11/47 (1674).

	[NC]	[Ch]
The Lady Harvey voyd		1
Margaret French		1
Adrian Tanton	1	
Tho Wiggin	1	
		036

Veiwed by:
William Wainman collector
John Saile constable

[f. 3]
Morrell
[***Moreton***[1] Morrell
in Moreton Morrell par]

	[NC]	[Ch]
Rich Hunt		3
Ursila Sayle	<1>2	
John Sayl		2
Rich Brows one a forge		2
John Whit		3
Tho Smith		2
Roger Griffin	1	
Ann Palmer	1	
		012

Veiwed by:
Will Wainman collector
John Saile constable

Newbold Pacey [par]

	[NC]	[Ch]
Mr Edw Greene		9
Rich Blick	1	
Hen Harbert		1
Eliz Halfpeny	1	
Rich Burden	1	
Mr Smith		7
Mr Smith voyd		1
James Hurdis	1	
Mr Hunter rector		6
Will Izard		1
		025

Ashorne
[in Newbold Pacey par]

	[NC]	[Ch]
Hen & John Spicer		6
John Wallin		1
John Chapman	1	
Humph Muckley one a forge	2	
Rich Button	1	
John Gibbs		1
John Ellet		2
Michael Tombs		2
Hen Bredon	1	
[f. 3v]		
Rich Tomkins	1	
John Halls 2 houses		2
Wid Southam		1
Will Fairman		2
John Bafford		1
Joseph Hobbins		2
Laurance Sandish		3
Rich Pettestone		1
		024

Veiwed by:
Will Wainman collector
John Hall constable

Bisshopps Tachbrooke
[Bishops Tachbrook par]

	[NC]	[Ch]
Wid Jeacocke		1
Rob Kining		1
Rich Savidg voyd		1
Mr Savidg voyd		1
Mr Booth		7
Edw Reading		1
Rich Weale		1
Wid Meades	1	
Mr Rich Savidg		2
Hen Whithead		1
Daniel Ayres		3
Eliz Reading		1
Will Commander		2
Mr John Coles		3
John Reading		1
Wid Reading		3
John Ashton		1
Wid Hurdis	1	
Dor Commander w[id]		1
James Rawlins		1

[1] WCRO, QS11/28 (1671).

	[NC]	[Ch]
John Wagstaff esq		4
[f. 4]		
Edw Commander		1
John Hemings one a forge		2
Will Tubs		1
Fulke Hurdis		1
Abraham Reading		1
Tho Reading		1
Samuel Commander		2
James Hurdis		1
John Ayers		1
Rich Reading		1
John Shakespeare		1
Mr Will Savidg		3
Tho Hurdis		1
Mr Lees		3
Edmund Abotts		4
John Overton sen		2
John Overton jun		1
Jobe Hobbins		1
Rich Rawlins		1
Hen Kempe		1
Wid Powers	1	
Tho Collins	1	
Tho Tomlins	1	
Rob Joanes	1	
Hen Greene		3
Tho Lea	1	
Tho Rawlins	1	
Rich Hall	1	
Tho Wharram	1	
Roger Reading	1	
Susana Robinson	1	
Tho Wharram jun	1	
Will Reading	1	
Will Jackson	1	
Ann Hurdis	1	
Mary Allbone	1	
Hen Reeve	1	
		069

Veiwed by:
Will Wainman collector
Samuel Commander constable

	[NC]	[Ch]
[f. 4v]		
Barford [par]		
Tho Smith sen		1
Clement Dyson	1	
John Clark	1	
Rich Clark	1	
Mr Spier voyd		3
Edw Prestadg		2
John Cockbill		2
John Hopkins		1
Edw Hobley		1
Will Hockley	1	
Tho Smith jun		1
Fran Clarridg	1	
Emery Smith one a forge		2
Ben Spier	1	
Eliz & Alice Standley		1
Rebeck James	1	
Mrs Handy		1
Mary Whiteridg		1
Tho Rogers		1
Tho Buttler	1	
Rich Banbury		1
Ann West	1	
John Weale		1
Will Bell	1	
Tho Blick one of them a forge		2
Joane Blick		2
Ann Whiteridg		2
Rob Cooper		1
Tho Greenway		<1>2
Hugh Cross		1
James Hunt	1	
Wid Meades	1	
Will Ryland		1
Rob Dunn		1
Tho Rogers	1	
Mr Lord		3
[f. 5]		
John Ward		1
James Heacock		1
Tho Phillipps		1
Joane Trumper	1	
Edw Dunn	1	

	[NC]	[Ch]
Andrew Dunn		2
Mr Rich Spier		5
Mr John Dunn jun		3
Tho Ward esq		9
Mr Wards 2 voyd houses		2
John Tomson	1	
Tho Dunn		1
Heugh Cross	1	
Edw Slaughter		1
Edw Rimell		1
Wid Ball	1	
Rich Butler	1	
Wid Butler	1	
Mr Dugard rector		6
Anthony Chamberlin		1
Joseph Dyson	1	
The mill house		3
John Dunn sen		1
Rich Odell		1
Rob Fearfax		2
Embry Blick		1
Alice Hobkins	1	
Joane Fox	1	
Mr Rich Fearfax		5
Will Hurd	1	
Will Wallsgrave		4
Tho Harvey	1	
Will Dunn		1
Fran Brokes	1	
Wid Massor	1	
[f. 5v]		
John Pain	1	
John Wharram	1	
Wid Hurd		1
		087

Veiwed by:
William Wainman collector
Andrew Dunn constable

Wasperton [par]

	[NC]	[Ch]
Mr Doolittle		3
Mr Warner		6
Joseph Saunders		1
Mr Laurance		2
Sanuell Johnson		1
Will Launder		1
Will Hoper		1
Sir Simon Phanshaw 3 voyd houses		5
Will Bury	1	
John Beane	1	
Tho Palmer		1
Wid Greene	1	
Wid Tandey & Will Tomson	2	
Wid Ball	1	
Rob Heacock one a forge		2
Kath Woodward	1	
Rich Harris		1
Heathcott [Heathcote]		
John Seeley		3
		027

Veiwed by:
William Wainman collector
James Laurance constable

[f. 6]
Charlecoate [Charlecote par]

	[NC]	[Ch]
Rich Lucy esq		42
Rich Hinton		1
Georg Hunt	1	
Rich Laurance vickar		3
Rich Knight		2
John Tasker	1	
Georg Francis		3
Hen Sands		2
Wid Mason		2
Eliz Cornehill	1	
Rob Sands		1
Mr Will Laurance		4
John Dunkley	1	
Laurance Keyt	1	
Tym Seeley		2
John Palmer		1
Jonathan Bacon		2
Will Thomson	1	
Wid Edwards	1	
		065

Veiwed by:
Will Wainman collector
Georg Hunt constable

Welsborne Hastings

[in Wellesbourne par]

	[NC]	[Ch]
Wid Payne	1	
Mr Tho Jackson jun		<1>2
Rich Rose		2
Georg Tomkins		1
Mr Rob Joanes rector		4
Tho Hyman		5
Will Bradford		2
[f. 6v]		
Peeter Gasze		1
Rich Jackson		<1>2
Rich Maggett	1	
John Odell	1	
Wid Pain	1	
Joane Palmer		1
Wid Savidg	1	
Tho York		1
Nath Jackson		3
Mr John Hopper		3
Tho York jun		1
Mr Clark		4
Tho Jackson sen		3
Abraham Eades		1
Wid Batts	1	
Tho Meacock	2	
Will Whitaker sen		1
Will Whitaker jun		1
John Ryley		3
Wid Ryley		3

Newbald in Welsborne Constablery

[Newbold in Newbold Pacey par]

	[NC]	[Ch]
Anthony Odell	1	
Samuell Jackson		1
Ann Harris	1	
Wid Wall	1	
John Batcheler	1	
Wid Canning	1	
John Robins	1	
Wid Bennet	1	

[f. 7]

Welsborne Montfort

[Mountford in Wellesbourne par]

	[NC]	[Ch]
Mr John Vener		5
Will Nason	1	
Mr John Francis		3
Tho Askell		1
[blank] Ward	1	
Wid Greenway	2	
Mrs Margery Boyce		8
Mr Tho Nasson		4
Edw Sabin		2
Will Wilkes	1	
Rich Collins	1	
Tho Tomkins		1
Rich Hopkins		2
Lettice Gibbs	1	
John Hyerne		1
Tho Hyerne		1
Wid Bull	1	
John Hill	1	
Goerg Bastock	1	
Tho Hopper	1	
John Bastock	1	
Moses Herritage	1	
Mr Samuel Aleworth		6
Edw Ward	1	
Rebecka Cleave		3
John Neuton		3
Tho Rousham		1
Tho Hall	1	
Sam Jackson		2
Hen Collins		2
Edw Nasson		1
John Nasson one a forge		2
Hen Herritage		1
Hen Herritage voyd		1
Mr John Eades		8
[f. 7v]		
Will Reeve		1
Wid Hopkins	1	
John Blunt	2	
Rich Askell	1	
		104

	[NC]	[Ch]
Veiwed by:		
William Wainman collector		
John Rily constable		

Walton Mordack et Duell
[Walton Deyville in Wellesbourne par]

	[NC]	[Ch]
Mr John Askell		5
Leonard Ward	1	
John Burd	1	
Wid King	1	
Rich Rose		2
Tho Roberts		1
John King	1	
Wid Whiteker	1	
John Hastings		1
Will Neuton	1	
Tho Haynes		1
Tho Hopper	1	
Fridsweed Greenaway w[id]	1	
Mr John Askell		10

[f. 8]
Kingswood Brooke
[in Lapworth par]

	[NC]	[Ch]
John Greene		5
Barth<elemew[?]> Roadway		1
Will Duncalfe		4
Rich Sly		2
Will Brooke	1	
Roger Stanley		1
Edw Clark one a forge	2	
Joan Fisher wid		2
Will Twicroft		1
John Duchman	1	
Will Graffton		3
Will Cottrell		1
Anthony Bird	1	
Tho Slyland		2
James Leeke	1	
Wid Robins	1	
		042

Veiwed by:
William Wainman collector
John Rily constable

[f. 8v]
Lapworth [par]

	[NC]	[Ch]
Will Whatley		2
Rich Clark		1
Rich Greene		1
Edw Ledbury		2
Mrs Ealley voyd		2
John Whitefoote	1	
Mrs Eally voyd		1
Will Lea		4
Tho Killcup		1
John Camden		3
Wid Werret	1	
Tho Taylor	1	
Hump Shakespeare		1
Wid Rutter	1	
Hen Shakespear & Tho Sly		4
John Price		2
Wid Lilly	1	
Susana Brookes		1
Edw Green		1
John Robins		4
Caley Buffrey		2
Georg Glover		1
Rob Twicrofft		2
Mrs Moumford w[id]		5
Hen Hauthorne		1
John Smith		1
John Kendall		1
Tho Sanders		2
Tho Hall		4
John Palmer	1	
John Raulins	1	
John Morrill	1	
Wid Dy	1	
Tho Shatchwell	1	
Mr Will Askew		4
[f. 9]		
Mr Powell rector		4
Math Maggett		2
Uriah Waring		1
Will Peaton	1	
Humph Ince	1	
Edw Lukeman	1	
Nick Tice	1	

	[NC]	[Ch]
Tho Clarke		1
John Pary	1	
Tho Barrat		1
Mr John Askew		6
Isacake Greene		1
Dor Mumford		3
Tho Adkins		2
Wid Arnell		1
Mr Tho Underhill		3
Will Lewis one a forge		2
Hen Hopkins		2
Joseph Robinson		3
Lazar Bossard	2	
Tho Sergent		3
Tho Cranmore		4
Will Marshall		2
James Cleadon	2	
Soloman Weekes	1	
Tho Benford		1
Edw Hill		1
Edw Hobby one a forge	<1>2	
Tho Allin		1
Fran Grissill		2
Rich Petoe	1	
Dorotthy Killcup	1	
Rob Weekes	1	
John Palmer	1	
Georg Hollioake	1	
John Ward	1	
Ann Wheeler	1	
Wid Gardner		1
		100

Veiwed by:
Will Wainman collector
Tho Hall constable

[f. 9v]
Packwood [par]

	[NC]	[Ch]
Tho Fetherston esq		10
Fran Parker	1	
Fran Lockyear		1
Tho Wheeller	1	
Georg Whitfoot		2
John Palmer		1
Embrey Blick		1
Hen Tafft		1
Tho Tafft		2
Wid Dadeley		1
Will Wootton		1
John Satchwell		2
John Bradnock		1
John Ellet	1	
Ann Sadler	1	
John Webb		1
Elinor Williams	1	
Tho Feild	1	
Margarett Gibbs	1	
Tho Twicross	1	
John Bayley	1	
Rob Ross		2
Tho Ossiter	1	
John Green	1	
Mr Hen Porter		6
Rich Barnet	1	
Edw Barnet	1	
Eliz Ash	1	
Mary Chatterley	1	
Grace Gibbs		1
John Far		3
Ann Ash	1	
Humph Buttler		1
Tho Green		1
Fran Hayward		1
Wid Ashbey	1	
[f. 10]		
Tho Green		2
Wid Sergent	1	
Will Dent		1
Alice Preist		1
Tho Green one a flax oven		4
Will Evans		1
Hen Bellamy 2 of them forges		4
John Jorden		1
John Walton		1
Mary Allin	1	
John Radford	1	
Will Troath	1	

	[NC]	[Ch]
John Radford	1	
John Woodward	1	
Rich Benford		2
Edm Alesbury		2
Fran Alesbury		3
Wid Wheeler	1	
Will Shakespear	1	
John Price	1	
Wid Ellot	1	
Wid Feild		1
Will Hitchcock		2
John Sly		3
John Lakings		1
Rich Smith		3
John Davis		1
		072

Veiwed by:
Will Wainman collector
Embry Blick constable

[f. 10v]
[Tanworth in Arden par]

Tanworth one [on] **the Heath Side**

	[NC]	[Ch]
Mr Tho Osburne		7
Tho Withiford		2
Wid Jackson		2
Wid Kettel		1
Mr Archer voyd		1
Hugh Izard	1	
Wid Willson	1	
Tho Burd		1
Tho Saunder		1
Wid Twist	1	
Wid Biddle	1	
Hen Bristo	1	
John Glover	1	
Wid Lea	1	
Wid Robinson	1	
Wid Brown	1	
Rob Cubbidg	1	
Will Bossard	1	
Will Cranmore	1	
John Wooleston		1
Mr John Biddle		4

	[NC]	[Ch]
Georg Evans	1	
Georg Hemings		2
Edm Alesbury	2	
John Burley		1
Tho Wood		1
Lauranc Heaword	1	
Wid Lansdail	1	
Wid Fetherston	1	
Wid Hitch	1	
Wid Gregg	1	
Tho Ward		1
Tho Green a flax oven		1
Mr Tho Parson		4
Tho Whitemore		2
[f. 11]		
Tho Anderton		2
Tho Taylor		2
Wid Ross		2
Humph Cotterill		3
John Arnall		1
Rich Kettel		3
John Morgan	1	
Tho Cort		1
Fran Anderton		2
Jacob Watton		3
Tho Simonds		1
Will Withiford		1
John Plumb		1
Wid Withiford	1	
Tho Camden		1
Jobe Freeman		3
John Row	1	
Rich Deely		1
Will Deely	1	
Wid Preety one a forge	2	
Will Preety		1
Peeter Benford		1
John Slaughter		3
Wid Ashford	1	
Tho Bissell		1
Tho Marsson	1	
Tho Bennit	1	
Wid Johnson	1	
Georg Battes		2

	[NC]	[Ch]
Mrs Wills		2
John Bitterston	1	
Tho Bitterston	1	
Edw Hinkley		1
Wid Abbot	1	
John Davis		2
[f. 11v]		
Tho Minor		1
Mr Pool Feild		5
Will Terry		2
Rich Britten		1
Rob Heacock		1
John Haxter		1
Edw Heacock		1
John Wheeler	1	
Eliz Weekes	1	
Rich Arnall	1	
Edw Hickman	1	
Wid Clarke	1	
Wid Benton	1	
John Bunn		1
Hen Hawthorne		1
Will Griffin	1	
Nick Arnall		1
Edw Avery	1	
Edw Lansdale	1	
Will Cottrell		4
Will Ward		1
John Smith		1
Mr John Browne		6
John Bayles		1
Tho Whatley	1	
John Wheeler		1
Edw Cottrell		2
Elias Weekes	1	
John Bissell		1
Tho Simonds sen		1
John Terry		1
Baldwin Woodcock	1	
Mr John Everitt		1
Rob Phillipps		1
John Greaves		1
Will Bird	1	

	[NC]	[Ch]
Rich Essex		1
Fran Bellamy	1	
[f. 12]		
Mrs Taylor		1
Wid Wheeler	1	
John Leakins		1
Tho Fullford		3
John Stuart		1
Mr Carter rector		1
Rich Brockington		1
John Wild	1	
Fran Houlder		1
Edw Wheatley	1	
Mr Tho Greene		3
Tho Fullford sen	1	
Tho Ebrall	1	
Edw Killcupp		1
Edw Clark		2
Wid Davis	1	
John Wheatley		2
John Sweatkins		1
Will Baker		1
John Brookes		2
Mary Walker w[id]	1	
Rich Heayes	1	
Ann Weekes		1
Rich Bradbury		1
John Britton		2
Tho Kempsey sen	1	
Edm Chipman		1
Will Whatley	1	
Tho Courte		1
Wid Weale	1	
Ann Sanders	1	
Tho Sarson		3
Tho Kempcey		1
Rich Abbott	1	
John Barton		2
John Sergent		1

[f. 12v]

The Clay sid[e] **of Tanworth**

John Bennet		2
Will Chambers		2

	[NC]	[Ch]
Mr Will Millard		3
Ros Gilbert	1	
Will Loe		1
Hen Doeley		1
John Clarke		3
Tho Cotterell		2
Hen & Wid Hunt		1
John Greeves		1
Rich Bennet		1
Tho Mathewes		1
Christ Feild	1	
John Bissell		1
Wid Poole		1
Hen Harris		2
Rich Palmer		4
Jonathan Weale		2
Rob Cranmore		1
Clement Webb		4
Tho Archer esq		14
Hen Williams		3
Hen Benford		1
Rob Johnson	1	
Wid Court		2
Edm Knight		1
Hen Baker		1
Wid Court		2
Georg Lee	1	
John Tyso		1
Elias Berry	1	
Nick Eades		1
Hen Ward one a forge		3
John Court		2
Stephen Rogers		1
Tho Townsend		3
[f. 13]		
Tho Read	1	
Tho Nash		1
Mr John Walker		7
Will Nickalls		2
Wid Wheeller		3
Will Lea		1
John Feild		1
Will Feild		1
Mr Will Hurlstone		3

	[NC]	[Ch]
Humph Lea		2
Wid Feild		1
Will Gilbert	1	
Tho Sly		1
Gabrill Lee	1	
Wid Hunt		2
John Lea		6
Georg Freeman voyd		1
John Lea voyd		1
Barth Austin		1
Rich Deane		1
Hen Hyott voyd		2
Wid Carter	1	
Wid Chambers		5
Mr Hen Hunt jun		2
Fran Cooper		3
Tho Lindon	1	
Rich Court		1
John Morris	1	
Rich Dalffin	1	
Rich Whatley	1	
Tho Millard	1	
Rich Brandbury		1
John Griffin		1
Joseph Meare		3
Mr Hodges rector		4
Rich Bushill		1
Will Suter	1	
[f. 13v]		
John Wagstaff		1
Edw Lyndon	1	
Wid Arnell	1	
Rob Bradnock one a forge		2
John Collins		1
Rich Browne		1
Rich Waring		1
Will Wild	1	
John Astley		3
Mary Davis	1	
Tho Parsons	1	
Tho London		1
Rich Edwards		1
Will Heath	1	
Edm Parkes		1

	[NC]	[Ch]
Edm Yardley		1
Rich Slow		3
Wid Barker	1	
John Bauldwin		1
Wid Powel	1	
Hen Willams	1	
Rich Ashbury		1
John Bauldwin		1
Edm Barker	1	
Rich Brockhurst	1	
Fran Johnson	1	
Edm Yardley jun		1
Wid Carter	1	
Rich Slow		2
Alice Hyan	2	
Humph Watton	1	
Hen Chambers one a forge	2	
Rob Faulkes		1
Rich Lea		1
Gilbert Hill		1
Edw Wilkes	1	
[f. 14]		
Mr Edm Willson		3
Samuell Handy	1	
Humph Powell	1	
Nick Goyles	1	
John Crandon	1	
Will Crandon	1	
Wid Payn	1	
Christ Court		2
Rich Brinton	1	
Wid Wheeler	1	
Tho Tybbins		1
Tho Farmer		1
Ben Taverner	1	
John Wheeler		1
Edw Hyot		1
Will Faulkes		1
Rich Eades		1

	[NC]	[Ch]
Tanworth Towne		
Mr Rob Adams		4
Fran Dooley	1	
Ed Colman	1	
John Woodhous	1	
Sam Wheeler	<1>2	
Tho Masters		2
Edm Normundsel		2
Hen Wheeller one a forge	2	
Will Lea	1	
Ann Bagger	1	
Margaret Rawlins	1	
Mary Gossage	1	
Wid Lea		3
[f. 14v]		
Humph Fitter		2
Anthony Briscoe	1	
Will Briscoe	1	
Wid Horton	1	
Hen Hunt	1	
Will Perkins	1	
Tho Smith	1	
Georg Howes		2
Tho Lewis		1
Wid Stanfeild	1	
Wid Beasley	1	
		[322]

Veiwed by:
Will Wainman collector
John Bennet constable

Examined and subscribed
by Will Wainman collector

The tot[al] is 312
25
337 [322]

Barlichway Hundred

[WCRO, QS11/12]
[f. 1]
Barlichway Hundred
Stratford Division
1670
Exchequer Roles
[written by Warberton Hull]
[f. 1v: blank]
[f. 2: list of place names has been omitted]
[f. 2v: blank]
[f. 3]
Stratford Super [upon] **Avon**
[borough in Stratford upon Avon par[1]]

High St Ward

	[NC]	[Ch]
Mr John Willmore sen		2
Mr John Willmore jun		5
Peetter Holland		4
John Capp with a forge		2
Edwd Rogers		3
Laur Harwood		5
John Woolmer		3
Mr Wm Lyndon		4
Edwd Smith		4
Mr Michll Johnson		5
Tho Shackle		7
<Tho>Wm Hickcox		5
Robt Ingram		3
Wm Myles		2
Wm Martin		6
Mr Rich Lambert		5
Fran Hadock		3
Mr Rich Courte		5
John Tante		3
John Noble		5
Tho Nasson jun		3
Edwd Ingram		2
Mr Hunt		6
Rich Whiston		4
Mr Goodridge		2
John Aynge		4
Jonath Newbery		6
Tho Mills		5
Edwd Baker		3
Rich Sturley		5
Mary Hammon		4
		125

[f. 3v]

Church et Chappell St Ward

	[NC]	[Ch]
Mr Tho Tayler with an oven		8
John Loach alias Richard		3
Widd Hathaway		2
Eliz Tomlins		3
Widd Bromley		3
Rich Canning		3
Mr Oldfeild		<3>10
Edwd Palmer	1 C	
John Nickall	1 C	
Isabll Norton	1 C	
Rich Masson	1 C	
Peettr Hall	1 C	
Ann Ward	1 C	
Alice Mace	1 C	
Ann Times	1 C	
Ann Haynes	1 C	
Widd Bridges	1 C	
Tho Dide	1 C	
Robt Baker	1 C	
Wm Smith		2
Alice Harret		2
Ann Crick	1 C	

1 Old Stratford was originally the name applied to that part of the medieval parish of Stratford upon Avon which lay outside the borough bundary as defined, c. 1196. Subsequent references confirm that Stratford upon Avon remained the accepted name for the whole parish well into the early modern period and is the term that has therefore been used to define it here. It does become apparent, however, that by the late eighteenth century, the term Old Stratford was sometimes used as an alternative name for the whole parish and that is how it was described in the census abstracts from 1801, thus explaining its use in *VCH*, ii, p. 185, and the *Phillimore Atlas*, p. 242 and map 35.

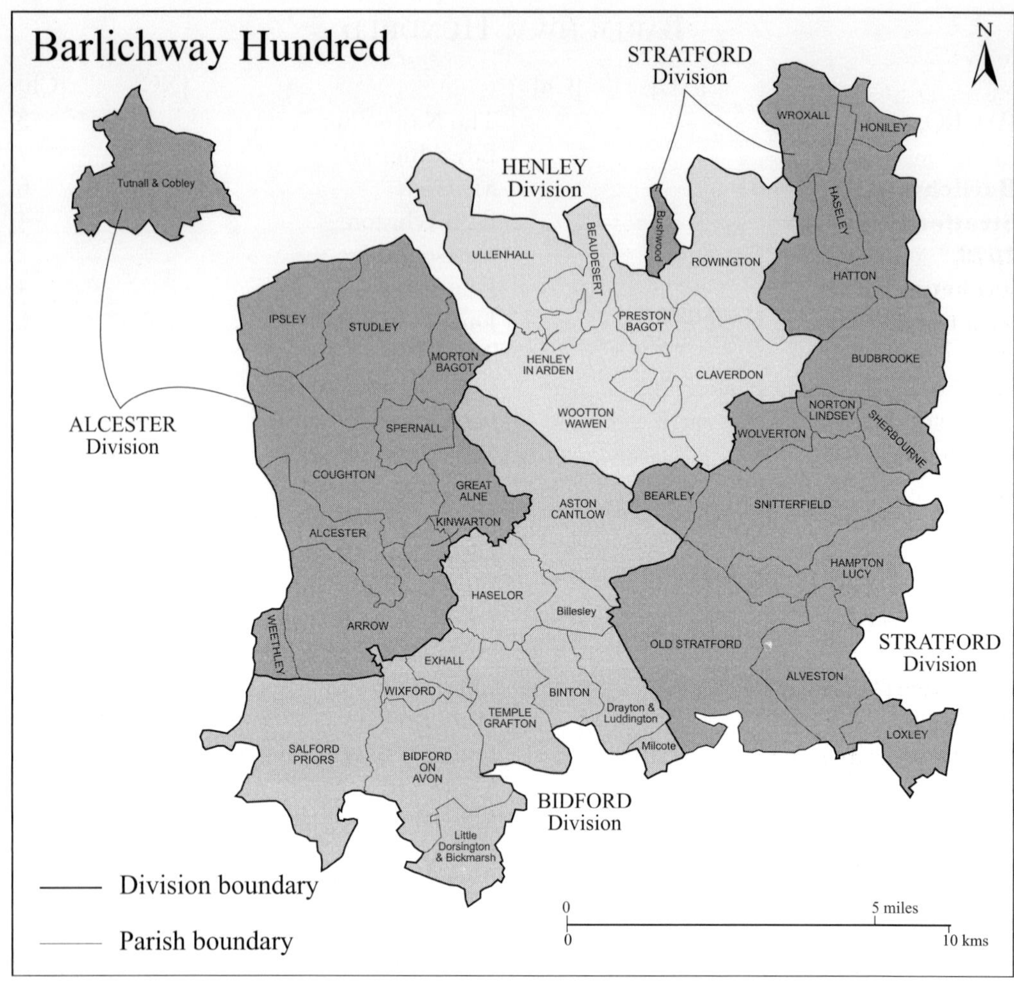

Map 15 Barlichway Hundred with parish names. Detached parts of parishes and subsidiary parts of those in other divisions are named in lower case.

	[NC]	[Ch]
Tho Ludyate	1 C	
Mr Rich Hunte empte		1
Edwd Lord with an oven		3
Phillip Edmunds	1 C	
Mary Walford	1 C	
Math Tredwell	1 C	
Rich Smart	1 C	
<Edwd>Eliz Maunder	1 C	
Mr Rich Hunt		6
Rich Loach		3
Tho Nason sen		2
Rich Baker		1
Joseph Smith Jo More		3
[f. 4]		
Rich Phillipps		4
Samll Wright	1 C	
Joseph Lea	1 C	
Rich Bromley		1
John Berry		4
Joseph Phillipps		9
Edwd Coleman	1 C	
John Saunders	1 C	
Rich Darke	1 C	
Jo Morris	1 C	

	[NC]		[Ch]
John Roger	1	C	
Rich Harding	1	C	
Robt Tayler	1	C	
Mary Smith	1	C	
Kath Woodward	1	C	
Tho Hewson	1	C	
Hen Wright	1	C	
Eliz Finch	1	C	
Rich Darke sen	1	C	
Widd Covill	1	C	
Wm Fosque	1	C	
Abrah Bayley esq			10
Hen Freeman			3
David Ward			1
Wm Castle			1
Rich Bromley			1
Widd Courte	1	C	
Nath Roberds	1	C	
Ann Bromley	1	C	
Rich Bartlet			5
Wm Ward	1	C	
John Smith of Blackwell emptie three emptie cott[age]s			<1>3
<Mr>Hen Goodwin			1
John Harding	1	C	
Tho Rawlins esq			8
John Weston	1	C	
[f. 4v]			
Mr Rawlins a cottage			1
Wm Amos	1	C	
Tho Kanning	1	C	
Mr Wm Challenor			4
Mr Hen Cale			2
Tho Townsend			2
Wm Mills	1	C	
Rich Gibbons	1	C	
John Fisher	1	C	
Tho Walton	1	C	
Wm Tibbotts	<1>0	<C>	2
Rich Walton	1	C	
Widd Bridges	1	C	
Widd Broome	1	C	
Phillipp Doyde			3
Widd Smith	1	C	

	[NC]		[Ch]
Robt Biddle			3
Widd Earle			1
John <…>Walter	1	C	
Samll Morrell with an oven			4
Mr Ward minester			8
Mr John Trapp			5
Twelve almes houses	12		
			141

Sheep St Ward

	[NC]		[Ch]
Rich Millman empte	1	C	
A cottage towne empte	1	C	
Wm Tayler	1	C	
Tho Loves	1	C	
Tim Nix	1	C	
Widd Savidge	1	C	
Widd Edkins	1	C	
Geo Winson	1	C	
Tho Southam [of] Loxley a cottage empte	1	C	
[f. 5]			
Rich Adkins	1	C	
Danll Masson	1	C	
Robt Gibbes	1	C	
Mary Walford	1	C	
Fran West	1	C	
Geo Pye	1	C	
<Geo>Josp Brandon	1	C	
Hen Hall	1	C	
Rich Shelvinton	1	C	
Hen Hudson	1	C	
Edwd Cleaver	1	C	
John Perkins			2
Wm Loach	1	C	
Margt Love	1	C	
Robt Rawbone	1	C	
Widd Loydes	2	C	
Rich Symkins			3
Wm Durham			4
Mr Rich Broune			3
Geo Adkins			2
Rich Mills emptie	2	C	
Tho Scriven			4
John Spratt			5
Wm Capp with a forge			2

	[NC]	[Ch]
John & Phill Bridges		2
Widd Washbrook		1
<Hen?>John Veale		1
John Knight		3
Edwd Harford	1 C	
Rich Smarte	1 C	
Widd Tradwell	1 C	
John Joanes	1 C	
Abrah Tibbits		2
Ann Mills		2
<Robt>Rich Hall	1 C	
A cottage belonging to the poore of Clifford emptey	1	
[f. 5v]		
Rich Durley	1 C	
Mary Walford sen	1 C	
John Plumer	1 C	
Marke George	1 C	
Wm Newbery	1 C	
Alice Atwood	1 C	
Wm Stephens	1 C	
Robt Cornmill	1 C	
Samll Hemings	1 C	
Margt Maries	1 C	
Robt Baker	1 C	
Mary Duty	1 C	
John Smith	1 C	
Fran Millard	1 C	
John Veale	1 C	
Joyce Smart	1 C	
Hen Bridges	1 C	
Elinor Aynger	1 C	
Danll Bearde		1
Ann Trapp		1
Hew Tew	1 C	
Tho Hyat	1 C	
Alice Shelfeild	1 C	
Mr Woolmer jun		4
Robt Fitcher		2
Rich Loach		2
Mary Porter	1 C	
Wm Johnson		1
Rich Johnson	1 C	
Geo Winston	1 C	

	[NC]	[Ch]
<Geo>Rich Moore		1
John Grey	1 C	
John Baxter		1
Widd Webb	2 C	
Tho Palmer	1 C	
Wm Hornbey	1 C	
[f. 6]		
Walter Davis		2
Wm Greenway		3
Gilbert Dewley with an oven		6
Peetr Frensham		6
Widd Jordaine		2
Leonard Dawson		2
Rich Dawkes		1
<Jos>Tho <Brandon>Loe		2
Benj Beadam		2
Allex Price with an oven		3
Nick Ingram		3
<Tho Lee>		
John Randle	1 C	
Elinor Edley	1 C	
Kath Day	1 C	
Rich Moore emptie	1 C	
Rich Drewry	1 C	
		081

Wood Street Ward

	[NC]	[Ch]
<Mr> Hen Tomlins		4
Mr Danll Masson		3
Robt Wootton		1
Wm Jakeman		4
Wm Jakeman a cott[age]		1
John Nasson	1 C	
Tho Aynge		4
Tho Veale		2
Adam Atkins		5
Jo & Judeth Webb with a forge		3
Widd Mayo	1 C	
John Marshall	1 C	
Wm Mayo		3
John Copland		1
[f. 6v]		
Tho <Copland>Carless		3
Symon Horne emptie		1
Simon Horne		2

	[NC]		[Ch]
Rich Chamberlaine			1
Samll Houltam			1
Hen Mace	1	C	
Tho Kerke	1	C	
Marth West	2	C	
Tho Mills			3
Rich Lord			3
John Edwards			1
Kath Loach	1	C	
Widd George	1	C	
Rob Hall			1
Mr Tho Hill			3
Anth Bell			2
John Moore			1
Tho Myles with a forge	2	C	
Tho Hickcox			4
Roger Dawley			3
John Smith			1
Rich Hemings	<1>2	C	
Samll Scriven			2
Tho Edwards			<3>2
Humpr Wood			3
Margt Rogers	1	C	
Lettice James			1
Leonard Tybrell			2
Eliz Jakeman			1
Mr Rich Smarte			5
Widd Ward	1	C	
Widd Cooke	1	C	
Edwd Roberds			2
Tho Hatheway	2	C	
Tho Edwards			<2>4
[f. 7]			
Widd Wright			2
Widd Clarke			1
Clemt George			1
Step Sitch			1
John Lock	1	C	
Tho Finch	1	C	
Alice Atkins			6
Hugh Wakfeild			1
Rich Wake			2
Rob Rede	1	C	
Edwd Jordaine			1

	[NC]		[Ch]
Geo Hanoway			1
Lewis Clark	1	C	
John Hemings	1	C	
Sus Gunn			1
Hen Borrowston	1	C	
Robt Cooper	1	C	
Widd Sabell	1	C	
Tho Green			4
Tho Huntbatch			1
Symon Cale			4
Alice Spiers			1
Edwd Staples			3
Edwd Howes			3
Tho Ward			1
Samll Hewes	1	C	
John Biddle	1	C	
John Freeman			3
Mr Rich Jackson with an oven			<3>4
Widd Rutter			3
Widd Hunte			3
Sus Ingram			1
Widd Handes			3
Math Blackford			2
Rich Hall	1	C	
Leo Edgerton	1	C	
James Tayler	1	C	
			130
			[136]

[f. 7v]

Henley Street Ward

	[NC]		[Ch]
Mr Jo Careless			3
Ann Walker			3
Rich Ward			1
Mr John Bradley			3
Mrs Mary Beane			3
Mary Mullinux			1
Wm Hall			1
Rich George	1	C	
Mr Wm Atwood			2
Mr Step Edkins			2
Rich Kings	1	C	
Jos Cole with a forge	2	C	
James Tranie empte			2
Joane Hornobey	1	C	

	[NC]	[Ch]
James Tranie		2
John Tomes		6
Geo Heart		1
Walter Gillkes	1 C	
<J>Geo Hearte emptie	1 C	
Mr Horne mayor }		6
His emptie }		2
Mr Hen Harbadge		11
Tho George		1
John Hornoby with a forge	2 C	
Geo Masson	1 C	
Rich Peacock		3
John Smith		4
Kath Barton	2 C	
Rich Sitch	1 C	
Tho Cleaver		1
John Hunt	1 C	
John Bentley	1 C	
Wm Harding	1 C	
Robt Ward	1 C	
[f. 8]		
John Cooper		1
Tho<. . .> Holmes	1 C	
Rich Joyles	1 C	
Geo Cooper jun	1 C	
Geo Cooper sen	1 C	
Rich Cooper	1 C	
Widd Sharnock	1 C	
Edwd Pidgeon	1 C	
Widd Giles	1 C	
Fran Aynge	1 C	
Fran Mullinux		2
Clemt George sen		3
Mary Wheeller	1 C	
John Cooper		1
Nath Lord	1 C	
John Mumford	1 C	
Jonath Southam		1
Clemt George jun		3
Rich Warrin	1 C	

	[NC]	[Ch]
Eliz Ingram	1 C	
Geo Southerne		2
Geo Johnson	1 C	
<John>Ann Young	1 C	
Mary Deaves	1 C	
Wm Benson		[-] [*1*[1]]
Margt Deram [}]	[-] [*1 C*[2]]	
Widd Gurman [}]		
Elinor Feild	1 C	
Margt Griffin	1 C	
Mary Masson	1 C	
<Castle>Joane Hornaby	1 C	
Tho Wotton with 2 ovens		6
Widd Hicks		1
Tho Aynge		1
Wm Cooper	1 C	
Fran Barton	1 C	
		079

[f. 8v]

Bridge Street Ward

Mr Edwd Green		10
Mr Izard		4
Charles Hopkins		4
Benj Joane		1
John Sharpe		3
Robt Sharpe		4
John Rogers		4
Symon Cole with 2 forges		4
Christpher Waring with 1 forge		3
Alice Cooksey		[-] [*2*[3]]
Tho Ludyate		1
John Cleaver		2
Alice Kanning		4
John Wood	1 C	
{ Michll Palmer with a forge		5
{ Mich Palmer per Moodey ho[use]		2
Fulke Sellers		4
Math Collet with an oven		5
Wm Higgins		3
Arthur Lane		2
Mr Fran Halford		7

1 WCRO, QS11/41 (1673).
2 WCRO, QS11/41 (1673).
3 WCRO, QS11/41 (1673).

	[NC]	[Ch]
Ann Ashfeild		4
Mr Joane		3
John Miller		2
Hen Davis		1
Geo Cooper	[-] [*2 C*[1]]	
Mr Iston emptie		1
Wm Horne shoomaker		3
Tho Smith		1
Rich Smith		6
John Moore		1
Robt Moore		2
John Boulton		6
Wm Horne sergent		3
Edwd Petway		2
Hen Caudrey		1
Wm Biddle	[-] [*2 C*[2]]	
		108

Veiued by:
Warberton Hull collector
Hen Izard & Charles Hopkins } constables

[f. 9]

Ould Stratford et cum membris

[Old Stratford constablery with its parts in Stratford upon Avon par]

[***Old Stratford***[3]]

	[NC]	[Ch]
Capt Swann		11
John Ashley	1 C	
Edwd Hawkins	1 C	
Tho Smith		2
Wm Combes esq [*in the college*[4]]		15
John Harwood	1 C	
Avery Sandes	1 C	
Humpr Allin	1 C	
Edwd Rudge	1 C	
Mr Fran Watts		6
Mr Edwd Hudson		2
Wm Combes esq empte		9
Tho Rogers		<3>4
Widd Penie	1	
Mr Rich Bartlet		4
Widd Bayles		3
Robt Southerne		2
Mary Juanes	1 C	
John Nickalls	1 C	
Alice Capp	1 C	
Edwd Dorcasley	1 C	
Widd Turbutt	1 C	
Rich Hopcraft	1 C	
Nick Latham	1 C	
Robt Lock	1 C	
Widd Huntley	1 C	
Widd Eadon	1 C	
Edwd Bentley	1 C	
John Weaver	1 C	
Wm Blackford	1 C	
Tho Tomlins	1 C	
Math Knibb	1 C	
John Gibbins	1 C	
John Turbut	1 C	
Barth Turbut	1 C	
Rich Prescott	[-] [*1 C*[5]]	
Edwd Hewson	[-] [*1 C*[6]]	
		058

[f. 9v]

Shottrey in Old Stratford

[Shottery in Old Stratford constablery]

	[NC]	[Ch]
John Jorne		1
John Wells		2
Jo Sitch		1
Rich Wayne	1 C	
John Burman	1 C	
Rich Peace	1 C	
James Tysoe	1 C	
Widd Maunder	1 C	

1 WCRO, QS11/41 (1673).
2 WCRO, QS11/41 (1673).
3 WCRO, QS11/41 (1673).
4 TNA, E179/259/9 (1666).
5 WCRO, QS11/41 (1673).
6 WCRO, QS11/41 (1673).

	[NC]	[Ch]
Wm Turbut	1 C	
Tho Burman jun	1 C	
Edwd Lane	1 C	
Jo Spiers	1 C	
Tho Wedge	1 C	
Widd Barman sen		3
Jo Richardson		2
Tho Horne		2
Jo Perkes	1 C	
Widd Tayler	1 C	
Wm Ardway	1 C	
Rich Hadoway		3
Edwd Hadoway with a forge		<2>3
Rich Tarver	1 C	
Step Loe		1
Samll Barber		2
Jo Barber		3
Jo Smarte	1 C	
Luke Barloe	1 C	
Edmd Sitch		2
Rich Wayne	1 C	
Leo Courte	1 C	
Jo Cottrell		1
Allex Edkins	1 C	
Edwd Baker	1 C	
Hump Butler	1 C	
Fulke Sands	1 C	
Wm Burman jun		3
[f. 10]		
Mr Barnard		5
Mr Samll Tyler		5
Tho Spiers		2
Mr Rich Queeney		7
John Earle		2
		030
		[50]

Bisshopton in Old Stratford [Bishopton in Old Stratford constablery]

	[NC]	[Ch]
Wm Smith		3
Sym Horne jun		2
Rich Spiers		3
Mr Green		3
Wm Horne		2
Rich Hawting	1 C	
Tho Horne		2
Eliz Harrison	1 C	
Jo Tayler	1 C	
Symon Ball		1
Widd Aynge		3
Edwd Sargent	1 C	
Jo Freeman		2
Jo Walker	1 C	
		021

Clopton [in Old Stratford constablery]

	[NC]	[Ch]
Sir Jo Clopton		14
Jo Harris		4
Widd Kinge	1 C	
		18

Welcombe [in Old Stratford constablery]

	[NC]	[Ch]
Wm Combes esq		6
Widd Hurst } <Rich Phillipps> }		1
Robt Whittell	1 C	
		7

[f. 10v]

Bushwood in Old Stratford [constablery]

	[NC]	[Ch]
Tho Glover		3
Robt Owin		1
Ann Jeffes widd	1 C	
Jo Whitfoot		4
Samll Bullock		2
[blank] Bull	1 C	
Tho Merrall	1 C	
Edwd Sadler	2 C	
Nick Higgins	1 C	
Wm Bann		1
Zach Woollington	1 C	
Eliz Satchwell	1 C	
Widd Purden	1 C	
Edwd Wheeller	1 C	
Samll Jeffes	1 C	
Tho Jucs	1 C	
Hen Griffin	1 C	

	[NC]	[Ch]
Tho Hewes	1 C	
		11

Bridge Towne in Old Stratford [constablery]

	[NC]	[Ch]
Walter Miller		2
Avery Miller		2
Jo Miller		2
Wm Bradforde		4
Robt Saunders	1 C	
Samll Cox		3
Rich Francklin	[-] [*1 C*[1]]	
Wm Joanes		1

Ryen Clifford in Old Stratford
[Ruin Clifford in Old Stratford constablery]

	[NC]	[Ch]
Mr Watts emptie		2
Mr Fran Watts		6
		22

Veuied by:
Warberton Hull collector
& Samll Barber constable
for Old Stratford

[f. 11]
Shirbourne [Sherbourne par]

	[NC]	[Ch]
Mr Patchell Ayres		6
Hen Rogers		6
Widd Meades		1
Widd Asplin		3
Jo Hawkes		2
Wm Butler		2
Jo Walter	1 C	
Widd Blick		2
Rich Spencer jun		2
Widd Ellott		1
Widd Baldwine		1
Widd Bastocks		1
Tym Randall	1 C	
Tho Harvey		1
Wm Oakeley		1
Rich Knibbs		1
Jo Woolmer		1
Thomas Blicks		2
Jo Fox		1
Mr Lucie emptie		1
Wm Turner	1 C	
Jo Cookes	1 C	
Lucy Asplin	1 C	
Tho Butler		1
Andrew Hickes	1 C	
Widd Carter	1 C	
Widd Bradshaw	1 C	
Widd Bickerstaff	1 C	
Tho Morrell		3
Rich Fletcher	1 C	
Wm Hawkes		1
Edwd Riddle	1 C	
Widd Alcox	1 C	
Rich Morrell with a forge		2
Robt Haynes	1 C	
Tho Gilk		1
[f. 11v]		
Widd Joanes		1
Wm Merry	1 C	
Jo Hudson		1
Widd Blicke	1 C	
Wm Bakcon	1 C	
Widd Neway	2 C	
Wm Bayles		1
Wm Wharram	1 C	
		46

Shrowley
[Shrewley in Hatton par]

	[NC]	[Ch]
Tho Younge		4
Rich Allesbury		2
Nath Hill		3
Tho Edwards		3
Widd Waite		3
Wm Ebrall		3
Rich Hunt		2
Ralph Nickline		2
Rich Maycocke		1

[1] WCRO, QS11/41 (1673).

	[NC]	[Ch]
Christpher Arnall		1
Wm Feasley		1
Jonas Haynes		1
Wm Ebrall		2
Wm Doglas		1
Wm Toney		1
Widd Price		1
Tho Bonds		1
Hen Chin		1
Jos Williams		2
Roland Blackford	1 C	
Math Anstey		3
[f. 12]		
Hen Masser	1 C	
Rich Blackford	1 C	
Mary Price	1 C	
Jame Rue	1 C	
Wm Haycocks	1 C	
Ann Cox alias Cookes	1 C	
John Cox sen	1 C	
Jo Cox jun	1 C	
Nick Cox	1 C	
Rich Cox	1 C	
Rogr Hoggins	1 C	
Fran Bryery	1 C	
Jo Price	1 C	
Wm Sable alias Edwards		2
		40

Beusall
[Beausale in Hatton par]

	[NC]	[Ch]
John Ward	1 C	
Abrah Carpenter	1 C	
Widd Eatton	1 C	
Samll Hill		1
Hump Rodes		1
Wm Hutchins		1
Wm Whitheade		1
Jo Blicke	1 C	
Tho Scarlet	1 C	
Jos Mason		1
Samll Parson		1
Wm Hill		2
John White		1
Jo Jeffreys		1
Jo Butler		2
Jo Hope		1
[f. 12v]		
Rice Brookes		4
Wm White sen		2
Nath Walforde	1 C	
Jo Blicks		1
Wm White		2
Jos Guyes		2
Abrah Carpenter	1 C	
Widd Wells	1 C	
Widd Floyde	1 C	
Tho Banister		1
Wm White jun	2 C	
Jo Bree		3
Nick Kinge		1
Jo Browne	1 C	
Tho Renalls	1 C	
Anth Wills	1 C	
Widd Burrowes		1
Rich Casemore	1 C	
Jo Gibbs	1 C	
Tho Roberds	2 C	
Nick White	1 C	
Jo Tayler	1 C	
Widd Williams	1 C	
Widd Stoakes	1 C	
Jo Roades		1
Samll Copp		2
		33

Veiued by:
Warberton Hull collector
Samll Parsons constable

[f. 13]
Wroxall [par]

Sir Rogger Burgame bart		22
Jo Patston		2
Jo Smith		2
Mr Jo Baker		2
Edwd Dormer		2
Jo Ellice		2

	[NC]	[Ch]
Tho Saunders		2
Widd Dry	1 C	
Wm Jephkine	1 C	
Wm Fisher & Mrs Staunton widd		6
Tho Morris		1
Samll Griffin sen	1 C	
Rich Clare		1
Samll Grisward jun		2
Wm Smith		1
Wm Tibbotts		2
Jos Gayes	1 C	
Tho Fownes		4
Hen Courte		3
Tho Courte		1
Jo Sharpe	1 C	
Jo Stanley		2
Abrah Carter		2
Tho Saunder	1 C	
Robt Shackspeire		2
Edwd Saunders		2
Wm Giurdler		2
Wm Halford		1
Tho Girdler		1
Jo Heath with an oven	2 C	
Ann Co<x>okes	1 C	
		67

Veiued by:
Warberton Hull collector
Wm Fisher constable

[f. 13v]

Huneley [Honiley par]

	[NC]	[Ch]
Mr Sim Dingley		14
Samll Winters		4
Widd Terry		<3>1
Greg Barnecle		3
Widd Clarke		1
Jo Jeacox		2
Tho Nelson		1
Tho Roberts	2 C	
Wm Mynors sen		3
Wm Tayler		1
Rich Powell		1
Rich Willeford	1 C	
Jo Faulkner	1 C	
Geo Barnecle		1
<Daniell Cope>		<1>0
Mr Tho Hawkes		1
James Simons	1 C	
Widd Ludforde	1 C	
Mr Burgame l[andlord] emptie		1
		34

Hasley [Haseley par]

	[NC]	[Ch]
Clemt Frockmorton esq		16
Widd Dingley		4
Nick Oddams		2
Math Smith		2
Edwd Masters		1
Ann Walford	1 C	
Mary Ebrall widd	1 C	
Wm Bull	1 C	
Hen Heath		1
Geo Bryeres		2
[f. 14]		
Edwd Priste		1
Wm Terrall	1 C	
Alice Oddams		1
Jo Cottrell		2
Hugh Palmer		4
Widd Lovet	<1>0	1
Eliz Wright	<1>0	1
Edwd Dorman	1 C	
Widd Tayler	1 C	
Luke Rodgers	1 C	
Widd Roades	1 C	
Widd Richardson		1
Doctr Amersley		2
Wm Cornwell	1 C	
Tho Watson	1 C	
James Richardson	1 C	
Wm Wright	1 C	
Hen Whithead		1
Margt Richardson		1
Jo Walford jun	1 C	
Kath Rawbone	1 C	
Jo Whithead		1
Jo Walford sen	1 C	

	[NC]		[Ch]
Widd Hobbins	1	C	
Widd Browne	1	C	
Jo Shaw	1	C	
Tim Roberts			1
Samll Green			1
Wm White			2
Jane <Raur>Laurence	1	C	
			48

Veiued by:
Warberton Hull collector
Hen Heath constable

[f. 14v]

Hatton [par]

Tho Whitheade			1
Jane Crane			4
Tho Clarke			7
Nick Odams			2
Tho Search			3
Hen Ballard	2	C	
Jo Bellaway			2
Wm Smith	1	C	
Mr Dingley [&] } Jo Averne }			2
Wm Robards with a forge			2
Samll Price			1
Edwd Fox			1
Jo Dadley			2
William Alleband			1
Jo Winsper			1
Wm Packer			1
Nick Wright			1
Tho Lewis			1
Rich Clare	1	C	
Robt Shaw			1
Wm Richardson			1
Tho Edwards			2
Rich Harris			1
Wm Shaw	1	C	
Math Cox	1	C	
Wm Smith	1	C	
Fran Weale	1	C	
Rich Adkins	1	C	

	[NC]		[Ch]
David Carpenter	1	C	
Math Basley	1	C	
			37

Veiued by:
Warbt Hull collector
Tho Edwards constable

[f. 15]

Norton Linsey

[Norton Lindsey par]

Mr Rich Phillpott			5
Fran Hayate			1
Jo Bissell			1
Tho Findall			1
John Bayles			1
Edwd Rogers			1
Wm Easell			1
Tho Higgins			4
Wm Rennalls			1
Sibll Walford	<1>0		1
Roger Harrison			1
Tho Rogers			1
Hen Richardson			2
Tho Findall			1
Math Blick } Rich Halpeney }			2
Widd Wrighton			1
Hen Collice			1
Baptistay Hewes	1	C	
Jo Hewit	1	C	
Nathll Brockles	1	C	
Rich Eassell	1	C	
Tho Blawell	1	C	
Tho Jornes	1	C	
Wm Petty	1	C	
Wm Blick	1	C	
Joane Townesend	1	C	
Wm Ragg	1	C	
			26

Veiwed by:
Warbt Hull collector
Wm Phillpott constable

	[NC]	[Ch]
[f. 15v]		
Budbrooke [par]		
Tho Mills		1
Tho Wootton		1
Jo Tuckey		1
Nick Whitheade		2
Barth Heath		1
Robt Neale		3
Mr Hewes		3
<Jo>Hen White	1 C	
Roger Paine		1
Edwd Overton		2
		15
Veiued by:		
Warbt Hull collector		
Tho Harvey thirdbrough		
Hampton Curley alias one the hill [Hampton on the Hill in Budbrooke par]		
Tho Wright	1	
Wm Wilson		1
Rich Edwards		2
Ralph Blick sen		1
Wm Webb		1
Widd Parker	1 C	
Rich Tydmouse		1
Thomas Pitcher	1 C	
Tho Masters sen		1
Rich Abbington	1 C	
Widd Skidmore		1
Wm Green		1
Anth Walker	1 C	
Ralph Blick jun		1
Wm Lee emptie	1 C	
James Masters		2
Tho Masters jun		2
Mr Jo Tooney		6
Mr <…>Tho Fairfax		3
[f. 16]		
Edwd Billington	1 C	
Samll Hewet	1 C	
Wm Lea emptie	1 C	
Wm Mills		1
Tho Edwards		1
Jo Sable	1 C	
Wm Edwards jun		1
Widd Edwards sen	1 C	
Fran Blabey		1
Robt Tidmouse		1
Mrs Dormer widd		16
		44
Veiued by:		
Warbt Hull collector		
Tho Harvey thirdbrough		
Hampton Lucy [par]		
Robt Wootton		1
Jo Fenton	1 C	
Ann Oakeley	1 C	
Rich Hinton		1
Wm Ward		1
Tho Hawkes		2
Marg Doolittle		4
Rich Tue		1
Wm Hill		1
Wm Hawkes carpenter	1 C	
Robt Hemings with a forge		3
Jo Marston		1
Tho Fauster		4
Tho Gibbs		2
Mary Lynes	1 C	
Jo Warde	1 C	
Andrew Taunte	1 C	
Widd Adams		2
[f. 16v]		
Mary Clarke		1
Rich Shackelton		1
Jo Boulton	1 C	
James Laurence		2
Mr Wm Watts		3
Mr Roggers rector		7
Robt Mathews		2
Rich Johnson		1
Widd Wootton	1 C	
Cresence Stichbury	1 C	
Jo Jackson		1
Widd Bickley		2

	[NC]	[Ch]
Jo Aynge		1
Wm Hawkes	1 C	
Rich Drew sen		2
Widd Marston		1
Widd Simcox		1
Tho Simcox	1 C	
Wm Tue		3
Tho Cooke		1
Wm Eadon		1
Tho Ward	1 C	
Widd Fran Ward	1 C	
Ann Kerkham		1
Widd Griffin	1 C	
Wm Kerkham	1 C	
Edwd Craftes gent		2
Adam Hawkes		3
Hen Allebone		3
Tho Aston		1
Michll Odell		1
Jo Turner		1
Mr Edwd Cookes		5
Ann Rea	1 C	
Jo Meades		5
Ralph Calloway		3
		78

Viued by;
Warbt Hull collector
Wm Tue churchwarden

[f. 17]

Alveston et Tidington

[Alveston par]

[***Alveston***[1]]

	[NC]	[Ch]
Wm Weaver		1
Mr Rich Craftes		8
Mr Groves		3
Tho Townsend		3
Tho Dennet		2
Hen Treene		2
Tho Skinner with a forge		2
Rich Hastings		1
Allex Townsend		3
Tho Cale		1
Mr Lane		1
Jo Scarlet		2
Tho Baker		1
Tho Browne		1
Edwd Ash	1 C	
Sarah Alcox		1
Rich Aynge jun		2
John Ladbrooke		2
Tho Hyerne		3
Jo Walton	1 C	
Jo Smith		1
Rich Aynge sen		2

Tidington [Tiddington]

	[NC]	[Ch]
Rich Bisshopp esq		9
Wm Goodwin		2
Mr Cherriton		2
Tho Higgins		2
Edwd Lord		2
Rich Heritage		1
Tho Harte	1 C	
Wm Hurdice		3
Wm Hinde		4
Tho Baker		1
Wm Baker		1
Jo Lord		4
Avery Edwards		3
Mr[s] Mary Faulkner		3

[f. 17v]

	[NC]	[Ch]
Wm Aynge		2
Tho Compton		2
Wm Weaver emptie		1
John Smith sen	1 C	
Tho Ashbourne		1
Jos Weaver		1
Jo Smith		1
Jo Ludford		2
Samll Hunt	1 C	
Widd Miller	1 C	
Rich Wells	1 C	
Clemt Hornton	1 C	

1 TNA, E179/259/9 (1666).

	[NC]		[Ch]
Marg Blackwell	1	C	
Hen Hancock	1	C	
Widd Horton	1	C	
Widd Bilson	1	C	
Tho Gilkes	1	C	
Jo Gilkes	1	C	
Jo Blithe	1	C	
Rich Bellamy	1	C	
Widd Poyner with a forge	2	C	
Wm Downing	1	C	
Edwd Plumm	1	C	
Rich Baker	1	C	
Phill Harris	1	C	
Rich Gilkes	1	C	
Zach Lord	1	C	
Widd Thornell	1	C	
Math Hall	1	C	
Wm Morris	1	C	
Ann Morrell			1
Widd Morrell	1	C	
Wm Robins	1	C	
Widd Jobe	1	C	
Widd Wells	1	C	
Rich Lord			1
			91

Viued by:
Warbt Hull collector
Rich Hastings constable

[f. 18]

Bearley in the Parrish of Sniterfeild [Bearley par[1]]

Mr Rich Moskell	3
Geo Scarlet with a forge	2
Widd Browne	1
Geo Holland	1
Wm Charles	1
Wm Mace	2
Anth Floyde	1
Tho Perkes	4
Jo Mussin	1
Wm Ryland	<1>2
Geo Seeley	1 C
Jo Seeley	1 C
Tho Bromley	1 C
Wm Cottrell	1 C
John Hickcocke	1 C
Widd Carless	1 C
Jo Perkes	3
	<91>
	21

Woolverton in Sniterfeild Counstablery [Wolverton par]

	[NC]		[Ch]
Mrs Alice Staunton			4
Widd Buxston	1	C	
Mr Sturch Walford			7
Mr Jo Kent			4
Tho Walford			3
Geo Cleaver			1
Christpher West			1
Edwd Soeden			1
Tho Sanbidge			2
Tho Townsend			1
Tho Cleaver			1
Tho Eades			1
[f. 18v]			
Tho Creed			1
Mrs Staunton emptie			1
Dorothy Stanton			1
Mary Creed			1
			30

Sniterfeild [Snitterfield par]

Tho Coventrey esq	28
Mr Nath Cookes	3
Mr Rich Hunte	<3>4
John Sheepye with a forge	2
Wm Meades of the brook	2
Jo Bracy	2
Hen Smith	3
Widd Hanckhorne	2
Jo Elvins	1
Hugh Meades	1

[1] Bearley was a separate parish.

	[NC]	[Ch]
Hen Tomes		1
Rich Reading		1
Jo & Tho Meades		2
Eliz Corbet		3
Jo Tidmouse & Robt Merce		2
Samll Perkes		3
Jo Hill		1
Wm Carr		1
Jo Harbidge		2
Widd Bayley		2
Geo Pettaway		1
Widd Bray		1
Hen Walker		3
[f. 19]		
Wm Meades in the lodge		3
Fran Browne		2
Hump Wheatley		2
Rich <Reading>Tomes		2
Edwd Bromley		6
Mr Evins vicker		4
Robt Harvey		2
Ellis Morrick		1
Jo Leaper		1
Wm Meades }		4
Tho Raulins }		4
Jo Goodridge	1 C	
Rich Hewes	1 C	
Wm Bedforde	1 C	
Wm Woodward	1 C	
Widd Terry	1 C	
Tho James	1 C	
Robt Dutton	1 C	
Tho Procter	1 C	
Widd Pardue	1 C	
Wm Graunt	1 C	
Samll Morrick		1
Jo Merce	1 C	
Tho Jerkins	1 C	
Jo Elson	1 C	
Jo Dutton	1 C	

	[NC]	[Ch]
Mr Jo Meades		4
Goody Whittle	1 C	
Jos Bickerstaff		3
Hen Corbit with a forge		2
Widd Harpur		1
Wm Dunn		1
Wm Dutton	1 C	
Jo Piggeon	1 C	
Kath Meades	1 C	
Tho Bedford	1 C	
[f. 19v]		
Sus Pardue	1 C	
<M>Sarah Pardue	1 C	
Wm Chapman	1 C	
Bridget Sumnors	1 C	
Jo Sumners	1 C	
Hen Sumners	1 C	
[Fulbrook ex par[1]]		
Norbrooke [Northbrook]		
Joseph Bennet		4
Priery land [Briery Land]		
Tho Loe with a forge		3
Edwd Willmore		1
Andrew Reeve		1
		123

Viued by:
Warbert Hall [sic] collector
Fran Browne constable

[f. 20]

Laxley [Loxley par]

	[NC]	[Ch]
Jo Dupper		1
Widd Dennet		2
Edwd Gibbs	1 C	
Fran Rawlins	<1>0 <C>	1
John Bissell		2
Mr Fosque		10
Jonath Buckingham		2
Josi Southam		1
Edwd Butler		2
Wm Pratt		1

[1] A dispute from 1656 over the payment of the poor rates by the inhabitants of the defunct parish of Fulbrook was settled finally in favour of Snitterfield (*VCH*, iii, pp. 91–2).

	[NC]		[Ch]
John Hunt	1	C	
John Hopper gent			5
Jo Bissell			2
Nick Marshall	1	C	
Tho Southam			2
Samll Southam			3
Barth Tims			1
James Southam			1
Jane Napton	1	C	
Widd Whitecar	1	C	
Jo Palmer	1	C	
Robt Tubbs	1	C	
Ann Harvey	1	C	
Tho <Gemmes?>Tims	1	C	
Widd Phillipps	1	C	
			36

Veuied by:
Warbt Hull collector
Jona Buckingham constable

[f. 20v]

Neather Norton

[Lower Norton in Budbrooke par]

Tho Woolmer			2
Jo Merce	1	C	
Tho Rennalls	1	C	
Tho Sheldon			<3>2
Edwd Hopkins			2
Clemt Deusbury			1
Widd Tiller			1
Lau Francklins	1	C	
Rich Halpeny			1
Widd Dewkes	1	C	
Mrs Woodward			4
Tho Hargrave			2
Rich Hargrave			3
Andrew Reeve			1
Hugh Aderston	1	C	
Widd Hewet	1	C	
Eliz Morgams	1	C	
Rich Green	<1>0	<C>	1

	[NC]		[Ch]
Widd Hinde	1	C	
Widd Wickley	1	C	
Robt Johnson	1	C	
			20

Veuied by:
Warbt Hull collector
Tho Hargrave thirdbrough

[WCRO, QS11/13]
[f. 1]

[The Hundred of Barlichway]
Henly [Henley] **Division**
Exchequer Roles
Anno 1670

[written by Warberton Hull]
[f. 1v: blank]
[f. 2: list of place names has been omitted]
[f. 2v: blank]
[f. 3]

Ullinghall [Ullenhall chap[1]]

John Lea			1
Rich Eades			1
Fran Parker			1
Mr Wm Dimack			1
Widd Woodward			1
Hen Feilde			2
Hump Damm			2
Rich Russell			2
Mrs Kath Green			4
John Morris			3
Wm Maunder			5
Rich Hurleston			2
John Knight			6
Alice Poole d[ead?]	1	C	
Hum Morris	1	C	
Geo Smith			1
John Courte			3
Hump Fairfax			3
Samll Preston	1	C	

1 Chapelry of Wootton Wawen parish.

	[NC]	[Ch]
Tho Smith tanner		2
Wm Baker		1
Eliz Lea		2
Fran Cooper		1
Wm Courte		1
Hump Asbaston		1
Hen Bradnock		2
Hann Clarkson		1
Wm Smith		<1>2
Fran Darby	1 C	
Wm Poole	1 C	
Wm Bearde	1 C	
Fran Higland	1 C	
Rich Littleford	1 C	
Jeffrey Poole	1 C	
[f. 3v]		
Wm Bryan		1
Hump Bayles	1 C	
Rich Asbaston	1 C	
Jo Coles	1 C	
Wm Wise	2 C	
Hump Morris	1 C	
Edwd Cooper	1 C	
Barth Clarke	1 C	
<Edwd?>Hen Lee	1 C	
Wm Parker	<1>2 C	
John Symonds	1 C	
Tho Hemings	1 C	
Edwd Pritchet	1 C	
Symon Smith	1 C	
Rich Taunton	1 C	
John Crune	1 C	
		52

	[NC]	[Ch]
Wootton Wawin et Province		
[Wootton Wawen par]		
[***Wootton Provost***[1]]		
Tho Moore gent		3
Jo Jennins	1 C	
Rich Pitman		1
John Millard		3
Mr Fran Ashenhurst vickar		3
<…>Edwd Egelston		2
Tym Mascall		2
Widd Johnson	1 C	
Roger Hopkins		1
Widd Perkins	1 C	
John Harrisson		1
John Tomson		1
Rogr Francklin		1
Rogr Shalle	1 C	
[f. 4]		
[***Wootton Wawen***[2]]		
The Lord Carrington		22
Fran Howes		1
Wm Grassingham		2
Hen Bryan with a forge		2
John Moult <with a forge> }		2
Rich Biddle with a forge }		4
Edmd Jobe		1
Widd Jobe	1 C	
<…>Robt Houltham		1
Tho Fisher sen		1
Jo Cale sen		1
Isable Corbit		1
Jo Cale jun		1
Jos Jobe	1 C	
Margt James	1 C	
Math Browne		2
Bradshaw Tayler		2
<Wm>John Tomson		[-] [*2*[3]]
Wm Clement	1 C	
Tho Houlder		1

1 TNA, E179/259/10 (1665). This was a manor held by the Provost and Scholars of Kings College, Cambridge, since 1443, when it contained a priory (*VCH*, iii, p. 198). The name 'Wootton Province', which also appears in the returns for 1673 and 1674, would seem to be a corruption of 'Provost'.

2 WCRO, QS11/53 (1674).

3 TNA, E179/259/9 (1666).

	[NC]		[Ch]
Tho Holland			1
Hen Johnson			1
James Aston gent			3
Wm Hopkins	<1>0		1
Jo Corbet			2
Widd Price			1
Geo Price			1
John James	1	C	
Tho Fisher			1
Edwd Grissould			1
Math Peatoe			1
Fran Howes			1
Geo Petford	1	C	
Wm Bradley	1	C	
Wm Beadley	1	C	
[f. 4v]			
Widd Hemings	1	C	
Samll Lane			1
Jo Andrews	1	C	
Eliz Browne	1	C	
Isaack Lowen	1	C	
Geo Shaw	1	C	
Margt Jennings	1	C	
Eliz Wheeller	1	C	
Edston [Edstone]			
Wm Summervill esq			13
			90

[***Edeston***[1]]

[*John Hawks*			*1*]
[*Timothy Sutton*			*1*]
[*William Procter*			*1*]

Henley in Arden [chap[2]]

	[NC]		[Ch]
Samll Perkins			2
John Trapp with an oven			2
John Symonds sen	1	C	
Widd Poole	1	C	
Nick Neale			1
Wm Pretty	2	C	
Geo Pitford	1	C	
Jo Morrell			5
Wm Beasley	1		
Jo Packwood			1
Wm Hobday			1
Wm Turner	1	C	
Tho Harrison	1	C	
Rich Mayner	1	C	
Alice Parker	1	C	
Job Beasley	1	C	
Hump Grasingham	2	C	
Math Bird			3
Mr Ingram emptie			1
Rich Harrison	1	C	
Rich Gresingham	1	C	
Edwd Grasingham	1	C	
[f. 5]			
Ushell Harrison mill			1
Rich Packwood	1	C	
Widd Morris	1	C	
Widd Trinings	1	C	
Jo Fitters			1
Mr Jo Horsley			2
Jo Higgins	1	C	
Hump Lacey	1	C	
Vall Beasley	1	C	
Robt Davis	2	C	
Wm Turner	1	C	
Wm Arnold			1
Wm Mayner	1	C	
Widd Clauson	1	C	
Foure almes houses	4	C	
Jo Symonds	2	C	
Jo Hemings			4
Jo Mayner	1	C	
Math Saunders			3
Jo Hemings	1	C	
Jo Cooper with an oven			4
Tho Cooper			5
Wm Handey			2
Tho Williams			2
Rogr Morris	1	C	
Wm Knight	<1>0		1
Tho Freeman			2
Avery Phillipps with a forge			2

1 Data inserted from TNA, E179/259/10 (1665).
2 Chapelry of Wootton Wawen parish.

	[NC]		[Ch]
Ralph Smith	1	C	
Rich Mills	1	C	
Jo Corbitt			1
Rich Kerby			2
Fran Pinchbach	1	C	
Robt Handey			2
Wm Horsley			2
[f. 5v]			
Tho Haynes with an oven			3
Geo Haynes			1
Jo Haynes with an oven			3
Widd Parker	2	C	
Peettr Wheatley	2	C	
Edwd Mayner	1		
Math Walford			1
Wm Garrett	1		
Roger Ward			1
Tho Bennet	1	C	
Phill Hollioke	1	C	
Jo Clarke			1
Anth Freeman	1	C	
Rich Bradley	1	C	
Nick Garner	1		
Peetr Lewis			1
Jo Hobday	2		
Robt Handey			1
Wm Warde			1
Wm Hide			1
Wm Howman	1		
Tho Ward			1
Joh Harpur			1
Abrah Bennet	1		
Wm Hewes			2
Ann Baker	1		
Rich Beasley	1		
Robt Barker	1		
Rich Bennit	1		
Jo Chaire	1		
Widd Price	1		
Jo Jennings			1
Fran Clarkson	1		
John Ward			1
Ann Whestons	1		
Jo Milles	1		

	[NC]		[Ch]
[f. 6]			
Robt Wheatley	1	C	
John Edwards	1	C	
Joseph Ashbey	1	C	
Hump Hopkins			1
Jo Hobday			1
Hen James	1	C	
Widd Cooper	1	C	
Hump Edkins	1	C	
Mary Edkins	1	C	
Wm Harpur			1
Abrah Price	1	C	
Wm Harpur emptie			1
Tho Stocke			1
Joane Brookes widd landlord			1
Mr Symon Kempson			6
Widd Cole	1	C	
Geo Ward			3
Wm Cooper with an oven			5
Tho Mayner	1	C	
Tho Walford	1	C	
Dorth Everet	1	C	
Jo Jennings			2
Widd Knoles	1	C	
Mr Rich Holmes			5
Joseph Pinchback	2	C	
Ralph Cluff	1	C	
Fran Baker			2
Ann Brittaine	1	C	
Rogr Hollioke	1	C	
Wm Garald jun	1	C	
Roger Skelleton	1	C	
Eliz Brewer	1	C	
Jo Hopkins			2
Wm Wheston			2
Wm Joanes			4
[f. 6v]			
Rich Horsley			1
Tho West			2
John Faulkes			2
Fulke Wheatley			6
John Egelston	1		
Wm Haynes			4
			125

	[NC]	[Ch]
Rowington[1] [par]		
Wm Bryers		4
Jo Tybitts		4
Rich Ballard		4
Edwd Queeney	1 C	
Wm Walton	1 C	
Widd Harris	1 C	
Tho Powell	2 C	
Gregr Garrat	1 C	
Mr Robt Tybitt		5
Clemt Averne		1
Rob Smith		4
Robt Capp		3
Wm Darby	1 C	
Widd Shackspeire	1 C	
Jo Saunders	1 C	
Rich Smith	1 C	
Tho Slye		1
Math Masson		2
Wm Green		1
Tho Harbert	1 C	
Eliz Blunt	1 C	
Jo Clarke		1
Edwd Tybitts		3
[f. 7]		
Edwd Wright		1
Jo Knight		4
Rogr Purden	1	
Jo Peatoe	1	
Nick Farcey	1	
Jo Cookes	1	
Jo Mollrey landlord emptie		1
Robt Tayler		3
Jo Tybitts		3
Mr Samll Hill		5
Mr Feild vicker		5
Tho Burfrey	1	
Clement Lucas		1
Jo Dale	1	
Edwd Kings	1	
Tho Renalls	1	
Wm Dale	1	
Jo Chinn	1	
Wm Lucas		2
Rich Averne	1	
Wm Shackspeire		3
Tho Shackspeire		2
Mr Wm Saunders		3
John Palmer		5
Mr Raulins		4
Mr Rich Mould		1
Mr Wm Cooper		3
Jo Milbourne sen		1
Mr Jo Milbourne		4
Mr Milborne		1
Geo Rounde	1	
Robt Lovet		1
Alice Collins widd	1	
Samll Cooke	<1>0	1
Widd Hill	2	
[f. 7v]		
Mr Jo Harvey		4
Widd Parr	1 C	
Jo Blithe	1 C	
Dorothy Thomas	1 C	
Wm Sparry		2
Mr Robt Atwood		7
Tho Symonds		3
Michll Griffin	2 C	
Tho Blick		1
Wm Benford jun		2
Wm Benford sen	1 C	
Tho Cooper weaver		1
Mr Roberts		5
Tho Tybitts		3
Nathll Rouse		3

[1] Rowington was subdivided into seven ends, which are indicated only for the chargeable in the return for 1665 (TNA, E179/259/10). However, despite being listed in a somewhat different order in 1670, all but a few names can be located here with reasonable certainty as follows: Turners End (first 11 names), Rowington End (32 entries from R. Capp), Mouseley End (six from W. Shackspeire), Lowson End (probably 13 from W. Cooper), Finwood End (12 from W. Sparry), Poundley End (20 from T. Shackspeire), Lowson End (12 more from W. Shackspeire), Pinley End (seven from Widow Collice), Lowson End (three more from M. Ansley), Mouseley End (one more T. Cooper), Turners End (10 more from L. Cooper) and finally four unplaceable cottages.

	[NC]	[Ch]
Widd Eaton		3
Tho Shackspeire		2
Widd Horsey emptie	1 C	
Tho Biddle	1 C	
Roger Jennings		2
Widd Shipton	1 C	
Wm Rennalls	1 C	
Wm Blunt	1 C	
Wm Walton	1 C	
Rich Sparry	1 C	
Wm Suter		7
Clemt Russell		4
Wm Saunder		1
Wm Smith		4
Benj Reeve		2
Nath Rouse		2
Jo Baker	1 C	
Ralph Gilbert		2
Rich Cooper	1 C	
Rich Smith	1 C	
[f. 8]		
Coll Colmer landlord		2
Wm Shackspeire		4
Samll Walford		4
Widd Wharrat		2
Wm Reeve		1
Tho Reeve		5
Jo Parson	1	
Fran Grissould		2
Eliz Grissould		2
Robt Bird	1	
Walter Woolson		2
Tho Rogers		2
Hen Wigson		2
Widd Collice		2
Widd Wakeman	1	
Samll Woodward		3
Mr Hen Cookes at the abbey		3
Mrs Cookes widd		3
Ann Burges		1
John Grisswell		1
Math Ansley		1
Hen Coleman		2
Widd Birde		3

	[NC]	[Ch]
Mr Tho Cooper		6
Lau Cooper with a forge		3
Fridrick Vanstanwick	2	
Jane Greathead	1	
Rich Price		1
John Cooper	1	
Mr Rich Beaton		9
Tho Smith		2
Widd Browne	1	
<…>Michll Dale	1	
John Price		3
Foure poore cott[age]s	4	
		217
		[218]

[f. 8v]

Budesert [Beaudesert par]

	[NC]	[Ch]
Mr Warkman rector		4
Wm Edmonds		3
Kath Eales		1
Robt Maines	1 C	
Gabrell Kemberly	1 C	
Widd Grasingham	1 C	
Widd Green	1 C	
Widd Harris	1 C	
Joseph Morteboys		2
Hump Rogers		1
Robt Baker		1
Robt Cranmore		2
Rich Hawithorne		1
Wm Lumbert		1
Tho Cooper		1
Wm Reeve		1
Geo Saunders		<1>2
Tho Morris	2 C	
John Dutridge	1 C	
Mary Stanfeild	1 C	
John Dewes	1 C	
Tho Etkins	1 C	
Humpr Hawthorne	1 C	
John Hawthorne	1 C	
Judy Hawthorne	1 C	
Tho Brown	1 C	
		20

	[NC]	[Ch]
[f. 9]		
Claverdon cum membris		
[parts of Claverdon constablery[1]]		
Whitley Aspley Fordhall et Sunger Farme[2]		
[***Whitley***[3] in Wootton Wawen par]		
Mr Tho Goodwin		4
Widd Courte		3
Mr Tho Rogers		1
John Banister		1
Fran Brittaine	1 C	
Widd Bellomy	1 C	
Tho Rogers		1
Wm Buckley	1 C	
[***Forde Hall***[4] in Ullenhall chap]		
Capt Dobins		7
[***Aspley***[5] in Ullenhall chap]		
Geo Freeman		1
Mr Edward Morgain		3
Christpher Courte		4
John Lea		2
Tho Cottrell landlord with 1 oven		2
Geo Ward miller		2
Tho Feild	1 C	
Tho Causier	1 C	
Widd Causier	1 C	
		31

	[NC]	[Ch]
Langley [in Claverdon par]		
Edwd Whithead		1
Edwd Rogers		2
Tho Phillipps		2
Robt Smitton		1
Math Edwards		1
Edwd Elvins		1
Wm Meades		1
Mr Hugh Walford		4
Wm Phillipps		1
Tho Winmill sen		1
James Seyley	1	
Humpr Dyer	2	
John Roger		4
Jo Howes	1	
[f. 9v]		
Wm Gibbs sen	1 C	
Wm Gibbs jun	1 C	
Tho Winmills jun		1
Wm Hopkins		<1>2
Mary Archer		<1>2
Mr Robt Heath		1
Widd Gibbs	1 C	
Widd Dewsbury	1 C	
Tho Baggott	1 C	
Tho London	1 C	
John Williams	1 C	
Rich Winmills	1 C	
		25

	[NC]	[Ch]
Claverdon [par]		
John Walker		3
John Moore		1
Mr Parker emptie		1
Mr Wm Parker		4
Mr John Cheward		2
Tho Reason		4
Christpher Graffton		2
Robt Hopkins		1
Tho Ward		1
Tho Desbury	1 C	
John Parker		<4>1
Clemt Robins		3
Wm Staples		4
Tho Walford jun		2
Wm Dyson	1 C	
Math Walford sen		5
John Edwards		2
Robt Smitten		1
Wm Findall		1
John Haynes		1

1 WCRO, CR1741/13/20.
2 The entry for Songar Farm, in Claverdon parish, has not been identified.
3 TNA, E179/259/9 (1666).
4 TNA, E179/259/9 (1666).
5 TNA, E179/259/9 (1666).

	[NC]	[Ch]
[f. 10]		
Mr Samll Parker		5
Robt Ryland		1
Tho Hobday		3
Peetter Lucas		1
Tho Reason		1
Hugh Townsend		1
John Hancox		1
Peetter Manton		1
Edwd Powers		1
Widd Ansell		1
Sir Tho Spencer bart		3
John Parry		2
Mr Rowley		1
Roger Cox		2
Mr Tho Higgins		5
John Savidge		1
Sarah Rose		1
Wm Smith		2
Clemt Rogers		1
John Brockless		<4>2
Wm Welch		<2>3
Hen Saule		2
Robt Howes		1
Widd Griswell		2
Widd Moore	1 C	
Rich Patford	1 C	
Mary Joyce	1 C	
Eliz Hobday	1 C	
John Biddle	<1>0	1
Mr Tho Pelkinton vickar		2
Widd Ainge	1 C	
Widd Barley		1
Widd Joanes	1 C	
Rich Symonds	1 C	
Kath Coles	1 C	
[f. 10v]		
John Morris	1 C	
Widd Beardes	1 C	
Tho Knight	1 C	
Edwd Joanes	1 C	
Tho Biddle	1 C	
Mary Loe		1
		088

[f. 11]

Preston Baggott

[Preston Bagot par]

	[NC]	[Ch]
Mr Rich Willson minister		3
Mr Rich Williams		4
Mr Robt Randall		4
Mr Andrew Griffin		2
<Mr> Clement Clarke		2
Widd Yeates		1
John Eales		1
Jerimiah Robbins		3
Edwd Boult		1
John Rogers	1 C	
Tho Gibbs	1 C	
John Williams	1 C	
Fran Britten	1 C	
Humpr Benton	1 C	
Hen Rogers	1 C	
		21

[WCRO, QS11/14]

[f. 1]

The County of Warwick

[**Barlichway Hundred**]

Bitford Devission

[Bidford Division]

[written by Warberton Hull]

[f. 1v: blank]

[f. 2: list of place names has been omitted]

[f. 2v]

Little Dossington et Bickmarsh

[in Welford par]

[***Little Dorsington***[1]]

	[NC]	[Ch]
John Miller		2
James Elvins		1
John Houltham		1

1 WCRO, QS11/40 (1673).

	[NC]	[Ch]
John White	1 C	
[***Bickmarsh***[1]]		
Edwd Griffin esq		5
		[9]

Willmcott in the parrish of Aston Cantloe
[Wilmcote in Aston Cantlow par]

	[NC]	[Ch]
Jobe Attwood		1
Mr Anth Smith		4
Geo Perkes		2
Robt Gibbs		2
John Smith		2
Edwd Harrat		2
Tho Scarlet		3
Wm Edkins		2
Tho Gaulter		1
Adam Adkins		2
John Halford	1	
Samll Edkins	1	
		21

Exall [Exhall par]

	[NC]	[Ch]
Mr Kerke minester		8
Tho Mallins		6
John Lane		2
Robt Burston		1
Widd Lamley		1
Mr Morris Walsingham		2
Anth Wise		1
Tho Parr		1
Widd Mills		2
[f. 3]		
Ann Heath	1 C	
Eliz Groves	1 C	
Tho Goodwin with a forge		3
Jobe Jakeman	1 C	
John Grimet	1 C	
Wm Mauncell	1 C	
		24
		[27]

Wixford [par]

	[NC]	[Ch]
Mr Fran Bickerton		18
Wm Sturdy	1 C	
Morris Allin	1 C	
Widd Oakley	1 C	
Widd Kiffin	1 C	
Rich Mills		2
Tho Reasin	1 C	
Robt Allin		2
John Medley		1
Wm Allin		6
Anth Russell	1 C	
Wm Garrat		2
Geo Parker		3
Wm Snedwell		1
Wm Hyham		1
Tho Wharram	1 C	
Widd Harris	1 C	
Tho Carter with an oven		3
Hen Roberts	1 C	
Widd Edkins		1
Christpher Roberts	1 C	
<Widd>Richd Page		1
Rich Haynes	1 C	
		41

[f. 3v]
Broome Regis in the Parrish of Bitfod
[Kings Broom in Bidford on Avon par]

	[NC]	[Ch]
Tho <Chap>Carter		3
Edwd Chapman sen		2
Fran Chapman		2
John Shaller		2
John Quoyner		2
John Chaman jun		3
Alice Searche		2
Tho Roberts		1
Tho Harris	1	
Wm Bartlam	1	
Tho Warrington	1	

[1] WCRO, QS11/40 (1673).

	[NC]	[Ch]
John Garrett		2
Rich Garret with a forge	[-] [*2*[1]]	
John Bent	1	
Wm Tayler		1
John Layton	1	
Wm George	1	
Hen Lett	1	
Widd Houltam	1	
Roger Bayles	1	
Wm Bayles	1	
Tho Layton	1	
Jo Layton jun	1	
Widd Chapman	1	
Tho Morris	1	
Roger Knight	1	
Wm Shutter sen	1	
Robt Williams	1	
Widd Roberds	1	
Fran Peares		2
Wm Layton	1	
Widd Robbins	1	
Hen Harwood	1	
John Leasey	1	
Hen Layton	1	
Wm Reddle dead	[-] [*1*[2]]	
John Layton	1	
Humpr Wright	1	
[f. 4]		
Math Layton	1	
Edwd Grimet	1	
Rich Elston	1	
John Gray	1	
Edwd Saunders	1	
Rob Shaller		1
Wm Leonard	1	
Wm Suter jun	1	
Wm Kinsin	1	

	[NC]	[Ch]
John Stanley	1	
		23

Viued by:
Warberton Hull collector
John Stanley thirdbrough

Temple Grafton

[***Billesley*** ex par[3]]

	[NC]	[Ch]
Sir Charles Lee		25

[***Temple Grafton*** par]

	[NC]	[Ch]
Margt Sheldon		4
John Asplin		8
Mr Fran Halford		7
Tho Phillipps		7
John Appleby		5
<…>Arth[?] James		3
Robt Fairfax with a forge		2
Michll Goodrich		4
Tho Henley		1
Wm Harris		1
Wm Walker		1
John Godfrey		1
Rich Biddle		1
Wm Walker		1
John Appleby		1
Widd Sale		1
Ralph Wagstaff		1
Wm Biddle jun		1
Tho White jun & Wm Adkins		2
Fran Boult		3
[f. 4v]		
Ann Rowley	1 C	
Geo Tayler	1 C	
Symon Herne		1
Mr Tho Sheldon		3
Tho White sen	1 C	
Rich Edwards	1 C	
Mr Tho Sheldon		7

1 TNA, E179/259/9 (1666).

2 TNA, E179/259/9 (1666).

3 In 1670 Billesley consisted of a single manor house, which contributed to Temple Grafton's poor rates. Although technically still a parish, its church was in ruins until it was rebuilt in 1692 and it had no incumbent or parish register so that it is treated here as extra parochial (*VCH*, iii, pp. 58–61).

	[NC]		[Ch]
John Joanes	1	C	
Geo Walker	<1>0		1
Margt Walker	<1>0		1
Margt Wise	1	C	
Eliz Hawkes	1	C	
John Chesley	1	C	
Tho White sen emptie	1	C	
Morris Applebye with a forge			2
John Sparrow	1	C	
Eliz Harret	1	C	
Margr Widdowes	1	C	
Math Biddle	1	C	
Mary Tayler	1	C	
Widd Salter	1	C	
Rose Edkins	1	C	
Joane Hawkes	1	C	
Fran Skiner	1	C	
Ann Jennings	1	C	
			95

Viued by:
Warberton Hull collector
Ralph Wagstaff constable

[f. 5]

Bitford cum membris

[Bidford on Avon par and parts]

The Grange

	[NC]		[Ch]
Mr Tho Cookes			9
John Slater			1

Burnets Broome et Barton

[in Bidford on Avon par]

[***Burnells Broom***[1]]

	[NC]		[Ch]
Rich Bennit	1	C	
Rich Satchwell	2	C	
Margt <C>Bundle	1	C	
Sir Fullware Skipwith			15
Edwd Oakley			1
Wm Penn	1	C	
Widd Berry	1	C	
Rich Blundell	1	C	
John Queeney	1	C	
Hugh Joanes	1	C	
Wm Harris	1	C	
Tho Goreing	1	C	
John Garret			2
Mary Garret			1
Tho Alcock			1

Barton

	[NC]		[Ch]
John Allexander			1
John Peetters	1	C	
Tho Tayler	1	C	
Rich Tapping sen	<1>		1
Wm Willmore	1	C	
Widd Slater	<1>		1
<Tho>Peetr Staunley	1	C	
John Cannings	1	C	
Widd Bennit	1	C	
Ursula Joanes	1	C	
John Walker	1	C	
Tho Goodman sen with a forge			2
Tho Harris	1	C	
John Payton			2
John Hemings	1	C	
Rich Payton			2

[f. 5v]

	[NC]		[Ch]
Tho Harbidge			1
Wm Millard			1
John Saunsam			1
Fran Handey	1		
Rich Handey	1		
Fran Tarpley	1		
Tho Goodwin jun	1		
John Bennet	1		
Mrs Margt Harwood			3
Widd Rascall	1		
Jo Payton jun			3
			48

Bitford Towne

[Bidford in Bidford on Avon par]

	[NC]		[Ch]
Geo Bayles			1
Christpher Collice			1
John Russell			2

[1] WCRO, QS11/40 (1673).

	[NC]	[Ch]
Mr Wm Collins vickar		2
Edwd Grimet		1
Rich Bucher		1
Widd Handy	1 C	
Rich Bayley	1 C	
John Grimet	1 C	
Jobe Russell	1 C	
Widd Mills	1 C	
Ann Brandon		1
Fran Millard		3
Tho Gardner		1
Mr Keck		3
Mr Jo Ipsley		1
Rich Pagget with a forge		2
Fran Leaton	1 C	
Kempe Able	1 C	
[f. 6]		
John Millard		7
Wm Holmes jun		1
Robt Millard with an oven		3
Aurth Ingran	1 C	
John Burden		2
Tho Harwood		1
Sym Hill	1 C	
Anth Gillam		2
Martin Higgins		1
Rich Williams	1 C	
Peetr Haynes		2
Rich Broome		1
Mary Joanes	1 C	
Tho Minte	1 C	
John Tayler	1 C	
Margt Bayles	1 C	
Tho Hawkins		1
John Beaman	1 C	
Eliz<...> Joanes	1 C	
Tho Sharpe	1 C	
Baraby Trimnell	1 C	
Wm Grett	1 C	
Wm Ashfeild	<1>0	1
John Tobey	1 C	
Alice Bayles widd	1 C	
Jeffrey Grimett	1 C	

	[NC]	[Ch]
John Baker	1 C	
Rich Ingram	1 C	
Tho Chapman	1 C	
Tho Bayles	1 C	
Edward Smith		1
Tho Butler	1 C	
Tho Blundell	1 C	
Silvanus Busshell		1
Tho Freeman	1 C	
John Harris	1 C	
[f. 6v]		
John Woodward	1	
Tho Alcock	1	
Edwd Palmer	1	
Step Miller		2
Robt Baldwin	1	
Eliz Hemings	1	
		45

Moore Cleave in Bitford
[Marlcliff
in Bidford on Avon par]

	[NC]	[Ch]
<Edwd>Wm Emmes		3
Wm Gillman		1
Rich Pettipher		4
Rich Gossoe		1
Wm Godffrey		1
John Godsoe	1	
John Browne	1	
Edwd Harbidge	1	
John Harbidge	1	
Rich Mumford	1	
Eliz Charlet	1	
Clemt Ayres		1
Wm Tappin	1	
Sus Layton	1	
John Daunce	1	
Rich Saulter	1	
Ann Roberts	1	

Veiued by:
Warberton Hull collector
John Saunsom constable

	[NC]	[Ch]
Millcott		
[Milcote in Weston on Avon par]		
Tym Howes		1
Mr Geo Peacock		1
Barth Edwards		1
Tho Bickerstaffe		1
Mr John Fathom		5
		20

[f. 7]

	[NC]	[Ch]
Binton [par]		
Mr Sheepard minister		4
Mr Rich Kempson		5
Mr Tho Walford		4
Rich Jakeman		5
Tho Mallins & Widd Jakeman		4
Tho Hill		1
Avery Mills		2
Symo Page		1
Wm Hobin jun with a forge		2
Tho Mosley		1
Hugh Walker		3
Brace Fairfax		1
Tho Allins		1
Tho Badson		1
Robt Shalcton		1
Tho Walford		2
Tho Badson		1
Walter Fouller	1 C	
Hugh Tayler	1 C	
John Richardson	1 C	
Tho Richardson	1 C	
Rich Beardes	1 C	
Tho Petteford		1
Widd Badson	1 C	
<Widd Jakeman> mistake		<1>
Tho Hill		1
		<42>
		41

[f. 7v]

	[NC]	[Ch]
Drayton et Ludington		
[in Stratford upon Avon par]		
[***Drayton***[1]]		
Wm Goff		2
Eliz Hill		2
Hugh Millard		4
Avery Edwards		3
Wm Fletcher		1
[***Luddington***[2]]		
Tho Harris		1
Wm Eadon		2
The Lord Conway		1
Fran Fletcher		1
Wm Mosley		3
Fran Tarver		4
Tho Riddle	1 C	
Giles Roberts		1
Wm Smarte		2
Tho Cookes		1
John Barloe		3
Nick Harris	1 C	
Geo Wilkes		1
Steph Altrey	1 C	
John Archer	1 C	
Widd Townsend	1 C	
Tho Davis		1
Jeff Hudd	1 C	
Step Waring	1 C	
Barth Holmes		1
John Handy	1 C	
Tho Oakley	1 C	
		34

[f. 8]

	[NC]	[Ch]
Sallforde Abbotts		
[Abbots Salford in Salford Priors par]		
Wm Stanford esq		16
Mr Edwd Stanford		4
John Haywood		3
Tho Chamberlin		2

1 WCRO, QS11/5 (1664).
2 WCRO, QS11/5 (1664).

	[NC]	[Ch]
Fran Sorrell		2
Nick Marshall		2
Tho West		2
John Reede		2
Widd Andrews		2
Wm Bromley	1 C	
Wm Hyerne	1 C	
Joseph Yardley		2
Edwd Aston	1 C	
Rich English	1 C	
Widd Maunder	1 C	
Geo Hyorne		1
Fran Forde	1 C	
Josep Parnell	1 C	
John Griffin	1 C	
Widd Sheepey		1
Rich Hopkins	1 C	
Anth Welch jun	1 C	
Joseph Cooper	1 C	
Anth Welch sen	1 C	
John Sturdy	1 C	
John Willis	1 C	
Tho Hyorne	1 C	
Widd Hyorne	1 C	
Rich Hyorne	1 C	
John Hawkes	1 C	
		39

[f. 8v]

Sallford Pryors

[Salford Priors par]

	[NC]	[Ch]
Mr Charles Hatt		8
Robt Doubty		1
Tho Widd sen		2
John Poole		1
Tho Doubty		1
Rich Edgwick		1
Mr Sym Clarke		5
Geo Brittaine		2
Rich Walford		3
Widd Houltam		2
Fard Stephens		2
Widd Jelfes		1
John Robins		1
Widd Sorrell		1
Widd Rawlins		5
John Huband		2
Nick Harris		2
Wm Yeates		2
Wm Savidge		<2>3
Alice Harrison		2
John Johnson sen }		1
Nick Johnson }	1 C	
Tho Shrives <…>	<1>0	1
John Staples		1
Robt Widdowes		1
Charles Benet gent		3
John Harris		2
Walter Gibbs		1
Tho Baker		1
Widd Abell		1
Tho Swatman		2
Anth Lee		2
Tho Swatman		1
Anth Walker		3
Paull Cox		2
[f. 9]		
Paull Cox		1
Symon Brittain		3
John Hobbin		2
Widd Emmes		2
Rich Bennet		2
Geo Sorrill		1
Widd Edgwick		1
Andrew Stephens		1
Edwd Rawlins		1
Rich Warington		1
Wm Wheeller		1
John Spratt		1
John Tysed		2
Tho Jew		1
Charles Bradshaw	2 C	
Hen Clarke		1
Myles Fairfax	1 C	
Rich Welch	1 C	
Joyce Coney	1 C	
John Biddle	1 C	

	[NC]		[Ch]
Sir Fullwar Skipwith			2
Wm Phillipps	1	C	
Wm Haynes	1	C	
John Haynes	1	C	
Tho Atwood	1	C	
John Hawkins	1	C	
Margt Twitty	1	C	
Widd Doubty	2	C	
John Ivans	1	C	
John Jennings			2
Robt Widd sen			1
Tho Widdowes	1	C	
Tho Doubtys sen	1	C	
Fran Knight	1	C	
Widd Houltham	1	C	
[f. 9v]			
John Jene	1	C	
John Warington			1
Tho Warmington			1
Rich Haughton	1	C	
John Wilson	1	C	
Geo Brewer			1
Fran Chanch	1	C	
Widd Hawton	1	C	
Tho Bissell	1	C	
Edwd Rawlins	1	C	
Widd Badsey	1	C	
John Sheldon	1	C	
Peetter Marshall	1	C	
Widd Hawton	1	C	
Widd Russell			1
Tho Partington	1	C	
Rich Cottrell	1	C	
Doroth Hopkins	1	C	
Joseph Clarke	1	C	
Widd West	1	C	
Edwd Morris	1	C	
Miles Fairfax	1	C	
Tho Tarbut	1	C	
John Howard	1	C	
Rich Bennet jun	1	C	
Wm Marshull	1	C	
Wm Horton	1	C	
Wm Woodland	1	C	

	[NC]		[Ch]
Samll Fox	1	C	
Joane Page	1	C	
Peetter Marshull	1	C	
Tho Horton	1	C	
Wm Walford			2
			102
			[101]

[f. 10]

Newnham in Aston Cantloe parrish

	[NC]		[Ch]
Clemt Etkins sen			3
Edwd Atwood			2
Clemt Etkins jun			2
Jo Garrat			1
Rich Bartlam			1
Jos Perkes			3
Widd Dixson			3
Avery Fullwood			1
John Fariner			1
John Green			2
Robt Edkins	1	C	
Geo Jenks			1
Eliz Mace			1
Widd Evans	1	C	
Widd Garrat	1	C	
James Farrin	<1>0		1
			22

Aston Cantloe Towne

[Aston Cantlow]

	[NC]		[Ch]
Mr Tho Green clark			1
Tho Whyam			1
John Sutton			3
Rich Belcher			1
Wm Knight			1
Widd Whyam			<2>1
Widd Atwood			2
Widd Hemings			<1>2
Widd Anderston			1
Joseph Edkins			3
Widd Wheyam			2
Hen Bartlam			1
John Poole			1

	[NC]	[Ch]
Hen Maunder		2
John Perkes		1
Robt Hopkins		1
Rich Clarke		1
[f. 10v]		
Christpher Cox		2
Robt Morrell		1
John Clarke	1 C	
Humpr Glenn		1
Wm Bushell		1
Hen Fairfax with a forge	2 C	
Robt Bartlam	1 C	
Wm Symonds	1 C	
Samll Aston	1 C	
Elinor Bradshaw	1 C	
John Fell	1 C	
Tho Ellock	1 C	
John Fullwood	1 C	
Rich Cutler	1 C	
Robt Hopkins	1 C	
Phill Cartwright	1 C	
Robt Maunder		1
John Farin	1 C	
Eliz Mills	1	
Rich Carless	1	
Rich Buckley	1	
Widd Harrison	1	
Wm Younge	1	
Widd Younge	1	
Tho Kinge	1	
		31

[f. 11]

Alne Parva in Aston Cantloe
[Little Alne in
Aston Cantlow par]

	[NC]	[Ch]
Mr Geo Fullwood		6
Wm Davis		2
Anth Gibbs		3
John Green		3
Rich Houltham		1
John Fosrley		2
Geo Harison		1
Fran Darbey with a forge	2 C	
Geo Moore		1
Tho James		1
Step Symons		1
John Hanckes	1 C	
John Ginkes	1 C	
		<19>
		21

Shelfeild in the same parish
[Shelfield in
Aston Cantlow par]

	[NC]	[Ch]
Geo Skiner gent		10
Robt Fullwood		3
Eliz Houltham		1
Rich Ingram		1
John Bartlam		1
Wm Joyce		1
Wm Smith		2
Jos Fielde		2
Mich Sabell		2
Edwd Perkes		1
Mary Cottrell	1	
<…>Humpr Page	1	
Wm Swift	1	
John Wood	1	
John Cooke	1	
Mark Hunte	1	
Lau Faulker		1
Roger Gee		1
Wm Hill		1
[f. 11v]		
Tho Fullwood	1	
John Fullwood	1	
Mr Skiner pro Hunt		3
		30

[f. 12]

Hasler [Haselor par]

	[NC]	[Ch]
Edwd Hemings sen		2
Edwd Hemings jun		2
Fran Gibbs		2
Wm Fairfax with a forge		2
Anth Mills		1
Tho Feild		2

	[NC]	[Ch]
Hen Hemings		1
Robt Petford jun		1
Robt Petford sen		1
Rich Gibbs		3
Hen Lane		2
Robt Mills		2
Geo Hemings		2
Geo Baker		1
Hen Hemings		1
Robt Feild		1
Wm Reason		1
Geo Hemings		2
Wm Breirley		1
Edwd Smith		2
Wm Haweks		1
Rich Gibbs weaver		1
Ann Gibbs	1 C	
John Gibbs		1
John Gibbs shoomaker		1
Ann Baker	1 C	
Tho Preston	1 C	
Robt Feild	1 C	
Fran Breirly	1 C	
Edwd Grisswell	1 C	
Eliz Green	1 C	
Step Dunsmer	1 C	
Hen Rennall	1 C	
John Feilde		2
[f. 12v]		
Joseph <Feild>Cooke	1 C	
Wm Whatcott	1 C	
Roger Knight	1 C	
Tho Oaty	1 C	
Ann Feild widd	1 C	
Joane Feilde widd	1 C	
Widd Wescott	1 C	
Widd Cooper	1 C	
Tho Lane		2
Geo Heming		2
Rich Gibbs		2
Hen Parsons		4
Tho Parsons		1
Rich Parsons		2
Mary Reason		1
Edwd Lane		1
Clemt Dauson with a forge	2 C	
Wm Joanes		1
Tho Myles		1
Edwd Winter	1 C	
John Clayton sen	1 C	
John Clayton jun	1 C	
Hen Feilde		2
Tho Crow		2
		58
		[59]

[WCRO, QS11/15]
[f. 1]

Barlichway Hundred
1670
Allcester Devission
[Alcester Division]
[written by Warberton Hull]
[f. 1v: blank]
[f. 2: list of place names has been omitted]
[f. 2v: blank]

[f. 3]	[NC]	[Ch]
Kinwarton [par]		
Mr Cudworth minester		6
Jeffrey Hopkins		6
Hump Egiock		2
Edmd Eades		3
Kath Crowley		1
Geo Croweley		1
Geo Brandon		3
Hen Watson		1
Geo Kinsell	1 C	
Samll Bennet	1 C	
Simon Kinsell	1 C	
John Crowley	1 C	
John Myles	1 C	
Widd Archin	1 C	
		23

Veiued by:
Warberton Hull collector
Geo Brandon constable

	[NC]	[Ch]
Arrow [par]		
Widd Fidgit	1 C	
John Burker	1 C	
Addam Neale		2
Humpr Tombs		1
Widd Cluff	1 C	
Tho Feild		3
Wm Churchley		2
Wm Yeates		1
Ralph Ampson		2
Wm Roberts with a forge		2
Tho Bewford		1
(a new ho[use]) The Lord Conway		20
Tho Hemings	1 C	
Tho Restall	1 C	
Samll Case		1
[f. 3v]		
Mr[s] Alice Walford		2
Mr Tho Wilson minister		5
Step Stringer		1
John Rice	1 C	
Anth Camden		1
Widd Hemings		1
Hen Tombes		3
Tho Pidgeon		1
Edwd Holmes emptie		2
John Roberts	1 C	
Tho Mills		1
Hugh Dipple	1 C	
John Mercer	1 C	
Mary Hyerne	1 C	
Ann Rowbery	1 C	
		52

	[NC]	[Ch]
Oversley [in Arrow par]		
Mr Rich Kempson		5
Mr Symon Wake		4
Rich Jelson		2
Tho Heywood jun	1 C	
Phill Showell with a forge		2
Wm Ward	1 C	
Rich Ferris		1
Widd Wakeman	1 C	
John Curtice	1 C	
Rich Aston	1 C	
Isbell Selvester	1 C	
Wm Higgins		2
[f. 4]		
Wm Clementager	1 C	
Widd Newsham	1 C	
Widd Hyerne	1 C	
Hen Harbage	1 C	
Peeter Watters		4
Ann Heywood	1	
Mrs Alice Wareing		5
Widd Aston		1
Tho Richardson		1
Alice Bruce		2
Wm Heatley	1 C	
Tho Haywood sen	1 C	
Cornel Cox		1
Geo Allen		5
Widd Hawood	1 C	
Edwd Kempson	2 C	
Wm Laurence		1
Antho Laurence	1 C	
		36

Veiued by:
Warberton Hull collector
Rich Jelson constable

	[NC]	[Ch]
Weethley [chap[1]]		
Widd Emms		2
Tho Emms		1
Jerim Francis	1 C	
Edwd Gee		1
Wm Gilbert	1 C	
Wm Parker		2
Mr Fosque		5
John Blicke		1
Robt Harris		1
Widd Moore	1 C	
John Clarke	1 C	
Roger Smarte	1 C	

[1] Chapelry of Kinwarton parish.

	[NC]		[Ch]
Fran Deacon	1	C	
Widd Dixson	1	C	
Hen Ferras	2	C	
			13
[f. 4v]			
Alcester [par]			
John Asperlin			2
Widd Parr	1	C	
Hen Boyer	1	C	
Wm Asperry			1
Edwd Charlett			1
Jeff More			2
Jo Pursser	1	C	
Walter Moore			3
Widd Howes	1	C	
John Harrington	1	C	
<Ed>Hen Boulton	1	C	
John Boulton	1	C	
Tho Sutter	1	C	
Eliz Boulton	1	C	
Widd Page	1	C	
Tho Palmer	2	C	
Widd Pare sen	2	C	
Rich Bucher			1
Rich Stephens	1	C	
Widd Hewes	1	C	
Wm Searche	1	C	
Phill Dale			1
Rich Bridges emptie			1
John Newman			1
Widd Dixson	1	C	
Widd Eaton	1	C	
Widd Hayes	1	C	
John Cox			1
Jo Oakley	1	C	
Fran Howell	1	C	
Wm Stacey			3
John Allen			2
John Massam	1	C	
Edwd Wootton	2	C	
Geo Phillipps	2	C	
[f. 5]			
Mary Frost	1	C	
Wm Camden	1	C	

	[NC]		[Ch]
Tho Dale	1	C	
Wm<Peas…> Reading	1	C	
Roger Shaller	1	C	
Rich Reading	1	C	
Widd Shaller	1	C	
Widd Eades	1	C	
Widd Joans	1	C	
Wm Percefeild	1	C	
Joane Stephens	1	C	
Ann Brookes	1	C	
Tho Rounde jun			3
Wm Ravon with a forge	2	C	
Tho Shaller	1	C	
Fran Smith a forge			1
Josp Price			4
John Garrat	1	C	
Edwd Boyer			2
Hen Wagstaff	1	C	
Samll Jennings			2
John Dewes			1
Wm Hawthorne			3
Rich Jennings glover			2
Rich Jennings barber			3
Ann Ward			1
Elisha Johnson			3
Caleb Godffrey			2
Hen Kinge			2
Rich Tayler			3
Mr Math Bridges			5
Tho Bucher			2
Rich Dewes			1
Benj Jennings			2
<Richard>Edwd Johnson			1
Robt Brookes			5
[f. 5v]			
Fran Parker			3
Wm Rennall			4
Mr Math Crabb			5
Mr John Hunt			4
Mr Tounge clark			4
Geo Tounge with 1 oven			4
Geo Throgmorton	1	C	
Calebe Oakes	2	C	
Geo Harpur	2	C	

	[NC]	[Ch]
Wm Miles		2
Sus Whistle		2
Ann Palmer	1 C	
Joane Green	1 C	
Wm James		2
Jos Spencer with 1 forge		3
James Pickard		2
Thomas Lucas		3
Humpr Coles		2
The towne hall		1
Widd Wheeller		2
Tho Pickard		3
Step Rounde		6
Mr Rounde emptie		5
Edwd Scriven		2
Wm Parker with 1 oven		4
Geo Salmon		2
Edwd Hyern		2
John Bovey		1
Ellinor Clements	1 C	
Widd Morris	1 C	
John Bridges		2
Wm Parker emptie		1
Mr Simon Bellers		4
Hen Dobbins & Hen Tilsley		3
Hen Churchley	1 C	
Math Followay	1 C	
[f. 6]		
Jose Walker		1
Wm Tofte		1
Nick Boulton		2
Widd Whistle		1
Step Stringer et John Tayler		2
Rich Cristopher	1 C	
Widd Green	1 C	
Geo Whistle	1 C	
Elner Birchley	1 C	
John Stanton	1 C	
Widd Cartwright	1 C	
John Launder	1 C	
Hester Whistle	1 C	
Widd Minniger	1 C	
Widd Tilsley	1 C	
Tho Rogers	1 C	

	[NC]	[Ch]
Arthur Lagoe	1 C	
John Dolefeild	1 C	
Hen Goodred		1
Wm Whistle		3
A house new builte		[-]
Josiah Rogers		1
Widd Hawood	<1>0	1
Widd Kanning		1
Widd Lagoe	1 C	
Rich Boulton	1 C	
Charles Bellars		1
John Dale		1
Mr Rich Beale		2
Edwd Bradley		2
Mrs Green		4
Mrs Mary Price		4
Step Bradley with 1 forge		5
Mr Lilly	1	
<Christpher Dewes> Wm Hopkins		<1>2
[f. 6v]		
John Whoman		3
Anth Charles		2
Rich Chalter		2
John Eades		2
Tho Tounge with 1 oven		3
Mr Tho Smith		2
Mrs Garner		4
John Boovey		2
Wm Harris	1 C	
Edwd Dolefeild	1 C	
David Berry	1 C	
Widd Hayles	1 C	
Three poore cott[age]s	3 C	
Tho Chalter jun	1 C	
John Ravon	1 C	
Edwd Hall	1 C	
Ann Johnson	1 C	
Charles Palmer	1 C	
Wm Johnson	1 C	
Fran Hayles		1
James Atwood		1
Ann Trindall	1 C	
Widd Cox	1 C	
Eliz <…>Baldwin	1 C	
Mary Gardner	1 C	

	[NC]	[Ch]
Widd Dingley	1 C	
Widd Emmes	2 C	
Joseph Wheeller		2
Rich Christopher		2
Mr John Hun<d>t		2
Rich Dews		1
John Mathews		4
John Cannon		1
Rich Ravon		2
Tho Leatherland		1
[f. 7]		
Hen Heming		1
Tho Quinton		1
John Taplin	1 C	
Mr Jos Wheeller shopp		1
Samll Johnson		1
Hen Cox	2 C	
Tho Felstead		1
Tho Francklin		1
Wm Heming	1 C	
Tho Ravon	1 C	
Widd Maning	1 C	
Tho Haynes with a forge		2
Eliner Johnson	1 C	
Robt Johnson	1 C	
Widd Feilde	1 C	
John Swann	1 C	
Widd Battersby	1 C	
Widd Horton	1 C	
John Joanes		2
Roger Handes et Wm Tibbs with 1 oven		2
Rich Adkins	2 C	
Tho Lineger	1 C	
Edwd Jennings	1 C	
John Harpur	1 C	
John Davis		1
Tho Hyerne		1
Wm Seavern		1
Tho Cox with 1 oven		3
Edwd Houltham		1
Ralph Moreton	1 C	
Wm <…>Ravon	1 C	

	[NC]	[Ch]
John Broome		2
Kath Ireland	1 C	
John Beele	1 C	
Wm Voughon		2
[f. 7v]		
Mary Shriffe	1 C	
Geo Ireland 2 houses		2
Wm Bromwell	1 C	
Tho Binder	1 C	
John Sedge	1 C	
Widd Hewes	1 C	
Jos Skinner	1 C	
Roland Bridges	1 C	
Widd Dale	1 C	
Isaack Hawood	1 C	
Widd Ainge	1 C	
Edward Oakes	1 C	
The scoole		1
Tho Unckells		1
Hen Boyer	1 C	
Alice Bridges	1 C	
Eliner Chaire	1 C	
Widd Brownell	1 C	
John Hemings	1 C	
Fulke Tounger	1 C	
Mary Phillipps	1 C	
Tho Shriffe	1 C	
Widd Brookes	1 C	
Tho Joanes	1 C	
Edward Scruby	1 C	
Mr Edmd Joanes		2
Mr Tho Rounde sen		8
Nick Leake		2
Mr Geo Kempson		4
Mr Tho Mathews		4
Widd Ward emptie		1
Kath Dickeson	1	
John Glover		1
Tho Allin		3
Mr Wm Winsloe		3
[f. 8]		
John Dingley		1
Tho Armes		1
Tho Rounde jun		[-] [*1*[1]]

[1] TNA, E179/259/9 (1666).

	[NC]	[Ch]
Robt Kanning		4
Edwd Hyerne		1
Rich Perkhouse		3
Edwd Harpur		3
Cornll Cox		1
Mr Jo Yarnall		4
John Gibbs		3
Widd Roberts		1
Barth Eades		1
Joane Parr		1
Tho Eades with 1 oven		5
Wm Allin		2
John Niblet		1
Edwd Crow		2
Mr Charles Johnson [*at Beauchamp Court*[1]]		8
Mr Fran Bridges		9
Mr Wm Dewes		5
Widd Geary		1
Widd Aston		2
		332
		[331]

Veiued by:
Warberton Hull collector
John Joanes constable

[f. 8v]

Alne Magna [Great Alne par]

	[NC]	[Ch]
John Throgmore gent		8
John Atwood gent		5
Wm Davis		4
Tho Watts		3
Mr Tho Dunn emptie		3
John Garner		2
John Symonds		2
Tho Clarke		4
Mrs Green widd		5
Widd Hobbins		1
John Mordick		1
Hen Bickerton		3
Fran Greenhill		1
Fran Harband		1
Humpr Whyam		1
Humpr Dewes		1
John Marshall		2
Tho Bickerton jun		1
Geo Sale		2
John Greenhill <emptie>		1
John Greenhill		3
Widd Atwood		1
Tho Bickerton sen		1
Mr Edwd Atwood		1
Tho Green		1
Robt Staples		1
John Houltam with 1 forge		3
Edwd Cockbill with 1 forge		2
Mrs Green emptie		1
Rich Edkins	1 C	
Tymoth Hemings	1 C	
Rich Williams		1
Wm Maunton		1
Nick Hemings	1 C	
Tho Hopkins		1
Edwd Phillipps	1 C	
Margt Cooper	1 C	
[f. 9]		
John Williams	1 C	
Rich Howlet	1 C	
Rich Green	1 C	
Eliz Green	1 C	
John Hopkins	1 C	
Geo Parsons	1 C	
Geo Green <sen>jun		1
John Boulton	1 C	
Robt Staples		1
John Countenance	1 C	
John Scarlet	1 C	
Edwd Marshall		1
Widd Mancell	1	
Tho Watts		1
Rich Edkins	1	
Widd Snedwell		1
		73

Viued by:
Warberton Hull collector
Wm Greenhill constable

[1] TNA, E179/259/9 (1666).

	[NC]	[Ch]
Coughton Magna		
[Coughton par]		
Sir Fran Throckmorton		37
Mr Fran Reeve <gent>		7
Mr[s] Smith widd		10
Mr Josep Bewley		1
Mr Wm Ducket		3
Wm Roberts with 2 forges		3
Step Saunders		2
Mr Rich Dewes		3
Jos Houghton		2
Robt Hinton [*at mill*[1]]		1
Morris Walsingham		4
Blannch Haughton		1
Mr Benj Tomlins		2
Steph Street		1
Wm Benet		1
Rich Wright		1
[f. 9v]		
Rich Parson		1
Hen Hinton		1
Rich Loxley		1
Mr James Watts		3
Tho Hewman		2
James Palmer		2
John Hasell		1
Wm Saunders		1
John Parker	1	
Rich Horne	1	
Rich Mills	1	
Mary Wheeller	1	
Geo Chambers	1	
Wm Smith	1	
Rich Morgam	1	
Geo Parker	1	
Rich Aston	1	
John Morton	1	
Edwd Bromley sen	1	
Robt Dale	1	
Wm Parker	1	
Joyce James	1	
Rich Parsons	1	

	[NC]	[Ch]
Tho Bromley	1	
Rich Aston jun	[-] [*1*[2]]	
		<81>
		91

[f. 10]

	[NC]	[Ch]
Samborne in Coughton Parrish		
[Sambourne]		
Rich Laurence		2
Fran Whatley		5
Hugh Hopkins		4
Alice Hopkins widd		1
John Roppier		3
Mary Haynes		1
Wm Leadbury		1
Edwd Joanes		1
John Battin		1
Tho Perkes		1
Eliz Biddle		1
Wm Baund		<1>6
John Fewster		2
Alice Harris		1
John Leadbury		1
Fran Masson		6
John Williams		4
Jo Challingworth		3
John Hill		2
Anth Palmer		1
Widd Eades		2
John Reeve		4
Tho Woolson		3
Widd Chambers		1
Anth Chambers		3
Hen Sheepard	1 C	
Hugh Arrowsmith		3
Rich Harrison	1 C	
Roger Green	1 C	
John Hawkins		1
Fran Large		1
John Chambers		1
John Tayler		1
Edwd Joanes		4

1 TNA, E179/259/9 (1666).
2 WCRO, QS11/42 (1673).

	[NC]	[Ch]
Rich Wicket		2
[f. 10v]		
Wm Parsons		1
Wm Marshall		1
Rich Parker		1
Geo Eades		1
Tho Haynes		3
Robt Haynes		1
Tho Whoman		2
Wm Shrive		1
Tho Straine		2
Hen Mills		2
Robt Hunt		1
Fran Parson widd	1 C	
Edwd Witheford	[-] [*1*[1]]	
Jo Biddle	1 C	
Geo Boulton	1 C	
Rich Mills	1 C	
Hen Kinsell	1 C	
Geo Smith		1
		90

Morton Baggott

[Morton Bagot par]

	[NC]	[Ch]
Mr John Holliock		4
Mary Walford widd		1
Geo Green	1 C	
Clemt Drinkwater	1 C	
Christpher Mordick		3
Mr Edwd Tayler		4
John Myles		1
Mr Wm Holliacke sen		6
Tho Smith		5
Tho Cooper		1
Wm Handes	1 C	
Christpher Mordick emptie		<1>2
[f. 11]		
Mr John Goodwin		2
Mr Tho Holliock		4
Walter Woodward		1
Anth Miller		1
John Miller	1 C	
Tho Ward		2
Tho Bote	2 C	
Ann Hall	1 C	
Jo Mordick	1 C	
Wm Shottrey	1 C	
Wm Green	1 C	
Tho Sutton	1 C	
Geo Gibbs	1 C	
John Maddock	1 C	
Mary Tyner	1 C	
Rich Jackson	1 C	
Tho Berry	1 C	
Phillipp Houlder	1 C	
Ann Woodward	1 C	
John Ingram		3
Widd Paylin		1
John Bartholomew		2
Hen Fairfax		3
Lord Carington in the lodge		7
Fran Manning	1 C	
John Miller	1 C	
Mary Ryland	1 C	
Widd Drinkwater	1 C	
		53

Veuied by:
Warberton Hull collector
Edwd Tayler constable

[f. 11v]

Spernall [par]

	[NC]	[Ch]
Widd Ryland		1
Geo Parsons gent		6
Fran Hemings		4
Mary Parker		4
Tho Wigget		3
Geo Hollice		2
Rich Ingram		3
Edmd Viz	1	
John Parson gent		2
Tho Milburne		1
Rich Price		1
Tho Hopkins		1
Rob Gaile		5

1 WCRO, QS11/42 (1673).

	[NC]		[Ch]
<Rich>Hen Hancock			1
Widd Price			3
Tho Hollier	1	C	
			37

Studley [par]

	[NC]		[Ch]
Edwd Millard			1
John Hemings			1
Rich Binton with a forge			3
Tho Holliock			4
Widd Kendrick	1		
Adam Fulwood			2
John Ayres			3
Margt Courte			2
Alice Feild			1
James Westrupe			1
Wm Ayres			1
Wm Hemings	1	C	
Rich Lee with a forge			2
Tho Cooper			3
Jo Townsend			3
[f. 12]			
John Milton			1
Rich Wilson			1
Tho Perkins			3
Ralph Steward			2
John Turner			1
John Banckes			2
Rich Dewes			2
Hen Barr			2
The Lady Knotsford			9
Anth Gibbs			3
Wm Moore			1
Widd Straine			3
John Berry	1	C	
Tho Dewes	1	C	
Laurence Green	1	C	
Christpher Kiffin	1	C	
Tho Smith	1	C	
John Andrews	1	C	
Rich Dauley with a forge	2	C	
Wm Tranter	1	C	
Wm Hitchcox	1	C	
Tho Broxson	1	C	
John Bascott	1	C	
Alice Gibbs widd	1	C	
Tho Gibbs	1	C	
Wm Dewes	1	C	
Tho Hopkins with a forge	2	C	
Jo Kings			1
John Joanes	1	C	
John Hobday	1	C	
Tho Wedgbury sen	1	C	
Tho Wedgbury jun	1	C	
Hen James	1	C	
Fran Haynes	1	C	
Roger Turner	1	C	
John Dewes	1	C	
[f. 12v]			
John Rauson	1	C	
Rich Phipps	1	C	
Tho Harris	1	C	
Robt Mott	1	C	
Merrell Haynes	1	C	
Mary Blackford	1	C	
Winsford Finde	1	C	
Tho Tayler	1	C	
Tho Parker	1	C	
John Clarke	1	C	
Hen Mathews			4
Tho Hurst			1
Wm Robins			2
Widd Rooke	1	C	
Tho Wilson			1
Mich Parr			4
Wm Blick sen			1
John <Feild>Shawe			1
Mr Edwd Feild emptie			1
Widd Corke	1	C	
Walter Parker			1
Wm Parr jun			1
Wm Courte			1
Rich Blackford			1
Edmd Feild	1	C	
Widd Gaudey	1	C	
Fran Hanson			1
Tho Savidge	1		
Widd Atwood	1		
John Holliock			3
Hen Gauderton			2

	[NC]		[Ch]
John Sturdey			1
Wm Holliock			4
Mr Edwd Chambers			5
Widd Harpur	1	C	
Wid Wheeller	1	C	
Wm Parson	1	C	
[f. 13]			
Mr Edmd Courte			5
Skilts[1] Ralph Sheldon esq			26
Tho Phillipps	1		
John Lewis			1
Widd Tanner	1	C	
Joyce Rogers	1	C	
Phill Rogers	1	C	
Wm Faune			1
Edmd Farmer			1
Leo Coppage			1
Anth Wall			1
Rich Hunt			1
Wm Blicks jun			3
Widd Whatley			1
Robt Willis	1	C	
Eliz Hunt			1
Wm Baker gent			6
Tho Boulton sen			2
Tho Willis			1
Mr Jos Potter vickar			1
Wm Shrine	1	C	
Mr John Phillipps			9
Wm Cale			1
John Biddle			1
Hen Elbanck			1
John Griffin			1
Anth Harpur	1	C	
John Harpur	1	C	
John Stock	1	C	
Wm Rauson	1	C	
Tho Kempe	1	C	
Edwd Haynes	1	C	
Jo Corke	1	C	
			158

Viued by:
Warberton Hull collector
John Turner constable

[f. 13v]

Ipsley [par]	[NC]		[Ch]
The Lady Huband			20
Mr Tho Wilde			<14>12
Mr Roger Bird [*clerk*[2]]			4
Mr Rich Walford			2
Mr John Cheston			2
Wm Holliock			3
Sir Jo Huband			1
Wm Bant			2
Wm Mills			2
Wm Bant			1
John Jackson			3
Mary Court			1
<…>John Hewster			5
John Lewis			1
Robt Boulton			2
John Melton			1
John Johnson			1
Widd Timbrill			3
Hump Shackspire			2
John Mace			2
John Tayler			1
Robt Causier			1
The Lady Huband emptie			1
Wm Hurleston			2
Tho Hemings			2
John Bardwin			3
Abrah Fisher			1
Widd Sheward			1
John Moore			4
Wm Durling	1	C	
Anth Bumpas			1
Mr Marshall			3
Abrah Fisher			1
Jo Millington	1	C	
Widd Lewis	1	C	
Alice Tymbrill	1	C	

1 Skilts was the name of Ralph Sheldon's house.
2 TNA, E179/259/9 (1666).

[f. 14]

	[NC]	[Ch]
John Boroughes	1 C	
Tho Johnson	1 C	
John Clarke	1 C	
Tho Elloway	1 C	
Widd White	1 C	
Edwd Causier	1 C	
Widd Wedgbury	1 C	
John Turner	1 C	
Laurence Hanley	1 C	
Cornelus Bradwin	1 C	
Rich Millington	1 C	
Wm Hewkins	1 C	
Widd Tayler	1 C	
Widd Childes	1 C	
John Hantlow	1 C	
Tho Palmer	1 C	
Joane Cottrell	1 C	
Widd Parr	1 C	
Ann Moore dead		[-]
Trustam Peirce	1 C	
		91

Veiued by:
Warberton Hull collector
Wm Bante constable

[f. 14v]

Tutnell et Cobley
[Tutnall and Cobley in Tardebigg par]

	[NC]	[Ch]
The Lord Winser		10
Widd Bumpas		2
John Wild		1
Widd Wheeller }		2
John Johnson }		1
Rich Payton		5
Rich Button	1	
John Harrison		4
Mr John Cheward		4
John Dunn		1
Hen Willis		4
Hen Cheward		2
Mr Hen Hickman		5
Rich Deriton		1
Joseph Freeman		1
Widd Wasell		2
John Payton		1
Tho Wilkes		2
Rich Moore		4
Rich Mence		4
Wm Bell		4
Widd Derriton		1
John Edmonds		1
John Payton		1
Fran Hemings		1
Rich Ashwell		1
John Bracy		2
John Lilly		2
Wm Staples		<1>3
Rich Eales cooper		1
Wm Horton		2
Wm Davenporte		1
The Lord Winsor a cottage		1
Wm Wood		1
Hen Palmer & }	1 C	
Widd Loxley }	1 C	
[f. 15]		
Martin Cocket		2
Walter Abbott		1
Geo Hunt		3
John Steele		2
Mr Hodge minister		2
Fran Chapman	1 C	
Wm Cooksey		1
Tho Lewis	1 C	
<Wm>Mich Jordaine	1 C	
John Kendrick	1 C	
John Baker	1 C	
Wm Shell		2
Wm Dunn	1 C	
Humpr Walker		1
Fran Peaton		2
		95
		[94]

Veiued by:
Warberton Hull collector
John Harrison constable

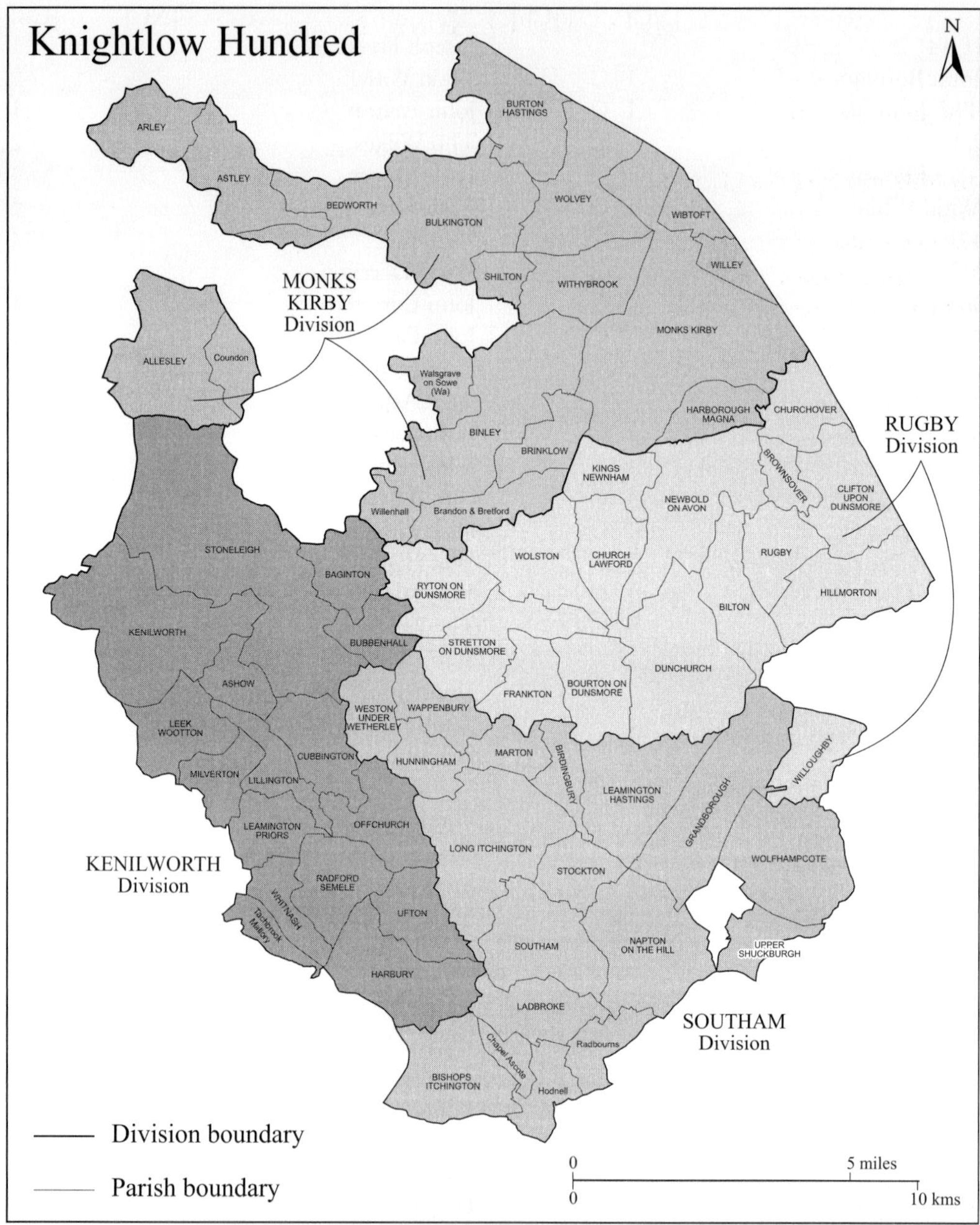

Map 16 Knightlow Hundred with parish names. Detached parts of parishes and subsidiary parts of those in other divisions are named in lower case.

KNIGHTLOW HUNDRED

[WCRO, QS11/16]
[f. 1]
Knightloe [Knightlow Hundred]
1670
Rugby [Division]
Exchequer Roles
[written by Warberton Hull]
[f. 1v: blank]
[f. 2]
Franckton [Frankton par]

	[NC]	[Ch]
Wm Biddulph esq		9
Hen Flemwell	1 C	
Wm Stockton with 1 oven		3
Edwd Buckingham		2
Wm Reeve		2
Jo Terry		2
Emptie house Mr Biddulph		4
Wm Boddington		1
Math Morrell		1
Ann Burman	2 C	
Mrs Byker		6
Tho Welch		2
Geo Clarke	1 C	
Wm Milles		1
Danll Flower	1 C	
Tho Constant		1
Wm Seale	1 C	
Christian Good		2
Robt Archer	1 C	
Tho Flemwell		1
Jo Warde		2
Mr Berriman rector		3
Jo Wallis		<1>2
Jo Busbey		1
Rich Patch	1 C	
Edwd Harralld		<4>3
Wm Baseley	2 C	
Jo Fleckham		1
Rich Copland		2
An emptie cottage R Copland		1
Kath Hinson	1 C	
Joane Wilkins	1 C	
Christ Fulhurst	1 C	
Emptie cottage	1 C	
		52

Veiued by:
Warbt Hull collector
Jo Terry constable

[f. 2v]
Ryton Super Dunsmer
[Ryton on Dunsmore par]

	[NC]	[Ch]
Robt Spencer		3
Jo Randall		1
Attorell Hill	2 C	
Wm Wigson		1
Jo Arnald		1
Joane Benson	1 C	
Rich Hall	1 C	
Hen Smith		5
Wm Clarke		1
Jo Baker	1 C	
Fran Wills		1
Emptie cottage	1	
Jo Amplett		1
Mary Lapworth	2 C	
Robt Paggett		1
Wm Lapworth sen		2
Tho Lapworth jun		1
Samll Wride		1
Wm Mathews		1
Jo Paggett		1
Samll Turner		1
Hen Yeates		1
Wm Jeffcott	1 C	
Mrs Eliz Dilkes		8
Ralph Good		2
Rogr Smith		1
Wm Lapworth jun		2
Wm Wills		4
Emptie cottage	1 C	
Robt Burnabey	1 C	
Jo Pagget	1 C	
Math Browne	1 C	

	[NC]		[Ch]
Wm Ryley			1
John Amphlett			1
Rich Daffarne	1	C	
Tho Bradley			1
Widd Arnall	1	C	
Ann Miller			1
Emptie cottage	1	C	
Widd Yeates	1	C	
[f. 3]			
Tho Jeffcott			1
John <F>Phillipps			2
Rich Talbut			3
Rich Randall			1
Jo Burton			2
Tym Gamm			1
Jo Bullock			2
			56

Veuied by Warbt Hull collector

Stretton Super Dunsmer et Princthorpe

[Stretton on Dunsmore chap[1]]

[***Stretton on Dunsmore***[2]]

	[NC]		[Ch]
Emptie cottage	1		
Mr Jo Elkinton			4
Wm Watson			7
Jo Bromage	2	C	
Wm Sathwell	1	C	
Tho Stockton	1	C	
Rob Foster			1
Jo Spier			1
Wm Cheatton	1	C	
Tho Ayres	1	C	
Robt Johnson			2
Rich Spiers			1
Robt Barnecle	1	C	
Jo Constant	1	C	
Wm Paggett			1
Bridgett Beale	1	C	
Widd Kilbey	1	C	
Wm Webb			1
Mr Tho Harbert			8
Tho Higgs emptie			2
Tho Bacon	1	C	
Jo Burton a forge			1
Emptie cottage	1	C	
Widd Bayley	1	C	
John Ostler jun			1
Widd Kibble	1	C	
Jo Woolston			2
Stanley Johnson			1
Wm Browne			1
Edwd Moore			1
Rich Ostler			1
[f. 3v]			
Tho Goadbey	1	C	
Tho Watson	1	C	
Edwd Deltworth	1	C	
Wm Malling	1	C	
Edwd Lole	1	C	
Samll Watts	2	C	
Emptie cottage	1	C	
Ann & Ursu Glover	2	C	
Hen Mathews	1	C	
Jo Pegg			1
Wm Preist			1
Wm Boddington			<1>2
Rich Higgs			3
Fran Bartlett			1
Tho Everton	1	C	
Widd Johnson with an oven			<1>2
Jo Russell			1
Widd Everton	1	C	
Tho Russell			1
Emptie cottage	1	C	
			48

Veuied by Warbt Hull collector

Princthorpe

[Princethorpe in Stretton on Dunsmore chap]

	[NC]		[Ch]
Wm Green & Tho Lapworth			2
Mr Wm Chamberlaine			8

[1] Chapelry of Wolston parish until 1696 (*VCH*, vi, p. 244).

[2] WCRO, QS11/43 (1673).

	[NC]		[Ch]
Mr Wm Davis			2
Edwd Lole			1
Rich Dillers			1
Tho Austin			1
Wm Hall			1
Rich Saunder emptie			1
Edwd Astley	1	C	
Edwd Stonley			1
Rich Saunders			2
Hen Odams			1
Tho Underwood			1
Mrs Eliz Benskin			6
Wm Winmills with a forge			2
Edwd Green			1
Widd Burges	1	C	
Tho Underwood	1		
			31

Veuied by:
Warbt Hull collector
Wm Winmills constable

[f. 4]

Boreton et Dracott

[Bourton on Dunsmore par]

[***Bourton***[1]]

	[NC]		[Ch]
Mr Wm Worcester			6
Tho Waring			2
Jo Rose			2
Jos Smith			1
Jo Porter	1	C	
Ambross Masson	1	C	
Mr Gilbert rector			6
Wm Currall jun			1
Rich Flower			2
Wm Currall sen	1	C	
Emptie house			7
Widd Adkins	1	C	
Tho Worcester			1
Jo Hagle	1		
Wm Master	1		
Rich Hill			2
Bridgett Sedgley			1
Jer Saunders			2
Rebeck Portter			2
Widd Harris			1
Tho Flemwell			2
Edwd Flemwell	1	C	
Jo Flower	1	C	
Wm Walton	1	C	
Edwd Barton	1	C	
Mary Maw	1	C	
Tho Bradley	1	C	
			38

Draycott

[Draycote in
Bourton on Dunsmore par]

	[NC]		[Ch]
Mr Geo Flower			3
Mr Wm Harris			5
Wm Reeve			2
Tho Woolfe			1
Samll Masson			2
Geo Masters			1
Hen Smarte			1
Tho Johnson			2
Jo Benson			1
Edward Bradwell			1
Jo Waring			1
Wm Good	1		
Tho Walker			2
Rich Waring			2
[f. 4v]			
Jo Harbert	2	C	
Mary Hobley			1
James Wright			3
Hen Johnson			2
Jos Waring			1
Rich Benson	1	C	
Jo Blythe	1	C	
Jo Harbert	1	C	
Jo Walton with a forge	2	C	
Rich Bartlet	1	C	
Robt Johnson	1	C	
Wm Mann	1	C	
			31

Veuied by Warbt Hull collector

[1] WCRO, QS11/57 (1674).

	[NC]	[Ch]
Dunchurch et cum membris		
[Dunchurch par and parts]		
[***Dunchurch***[1]]		
Jos Bassett		3
Tho Edwards		4
Widd South	2 C	
Hen Gupwell		2
Mary Morris		3
John Starr		6
Jo Pitts		8
Jo Stanfeild		1
Tho Stanfeild Pettr Malling		3
Jo Mathews		1
Tho Shaw		1
Mr Price rector		4
Rich Cammis		2
Jo Worsester		10
Wm Collings		2
Jo Webb		1
Widd Webb		1
Mr Nick Byker		5
Jo Bradshaw		2
Robt Bassett		1
Widd Edwards		3
Jo White		2
Edwd Hyerns		4
Jo Lockington		3
Jo Wilkinson	1 C	
Jo Flemwell with a forge		2
Widd Watts	1 C	
<Widd>Rich Busswell		2
Mr[s] Joane Harrison		6
[f. 5]		
[***Cawston***[2]]		
Fran Boughton esq		16
Rob Hartell	1 C	
Edwd Bradshaw		1
[*end of Cawston: more of Dunchurch*[3]]		
Jeff Ostler	1 C	

	[NC]	[Ch]
Jo Johnson	1 C	
Edwd Killpach	1 C	
Hen Lucas	1 C	
Tho Godard	1 C	
Joane Garfeild	1 C	
Fran Partington	1 C	
Edwd Edwards	1 C	
Rich Smith	1 C	
Mary Gulliver	1 C	
Tho Jennings	1 C	
Ussiby Gilbert	1 C	
Charles Roe	1 C	
Jo Jennings	1 C	
Hen Browne	1 C	
Sams Guttridge	1 C	
Wm Symonds	1 C	
Widd Goffe	1 C	
Widd Powers	1 C	
Elli Tansor	1 C	
Jo Hutchins	1 C	
Geo Treapas	1 C	
Widd Smith	1 C	
Widd Whinges	1 C	
		99
Tafte [Toft in Dunchurch par]		
Jo Harrison		1
Wm Smith		4
Abrah Barrs		3
Jo Blackwell		1
Aurth Faulkes		3
Ann Edwards	1 C	
Jo Smith		3
J Lucas		2
Hen Jenkins		2
Tho Roe	1 C	
John Wright	1 C	
		19
Thurlesston		
[Thurlaston in Dunchurch par]		
Hen Powers		5
Mary Faulkes Hen Foster	2 C	<2>0

1 WCRO, QS11/43 (1673).
2 WCRO, QS11/43 (1673).
3 WCRO, QS11/43 (1673).

	[NC]	[Ch]
Nick Smarte		1
John Lester		2
Jo Gupwell & Wm Harris		3
Tho Smith		2
[f. 5v]		
Phill Morris		2
Tho Sherwood		2
Wm Bromfeild		1
Wm Collins		1
Jo Bennett & his son		3
Tho Butler		2
Widd Adkins	1 C	
Wm Sale		2
Tho Farndon		2
John Adkins		2
Abra Barres sen		3
Rich Barnwell		1
Hen Edmunde		1
Jo Bennett		1
Rich Sale		1
Mr Hump Clarke		5
Rich Barnecle		2
Widd Barres		1
Jo Smith		1
Robt Barton		1
Rich Lucas		2
Jo Reeve		1
Edwd Smith		2
Jo Edmunds		1
Wm Smith		1
Tho Goodwin	1 C	
Edward Farndon		2
Tho Waring		1
Walter Burton		1
Jo Wesbury	1 C	
Hen Grubb	1 C	
Wm Picke	1 C	
Tho Morgan	1 C	
Jo <Sargent>Farndon	1 C	
Widd Sargent	1 C	
Jo Picke	1 C	
Eliz Barnecle	1 C	
Sarah Mills	1 C	
Rob Shaw	1 C	

	[NC]	[Ch]
Mary Watson	1 C	
Widd Hawgood	1 C	
Jo Coles	1 C	
Jo Batnett	1 C	
Hen Farndon jun	1 C	
Nathll Oxon	1 C	
[f. 6]		
Nick Green with a forge	2 C	
Tho Barnecle	1 C	
Ann Edmunds	1 C	
Geo Basterd	1 C	
Widd Goode	1 C	
Rich Calloway	1 C	
Hen Farndon sen	1 C	
Rich Wilcox	1 C	
Wm Goode	1 C	
Widd Bossworth	1 C	
Widd Garrett	1 C	
Fran Eales	1 C	
Rich Smith	1 C	
Hen Westbury	1 C	
Rich Percy	1 C	
		58

Veiued by:
Warberton Hull collector
Abrah Barres constable

Willoughby [par]

Tho Clarke esq	12
Mr Jo Hawton	7
Geo Clarke	1
Peettr Tustin	4
Tho Bodell	1
Mary Clarke	1
Jo Watson	1
Rob Worrall	1
Clemt Clarke gent	4
Hen Clarke	1
Jo Adson	1
Hen Thomas	1
Edwd Watson	3
Robt Cross	1
Mr Beale minister	4
Hen Tarlesston	2

	[NC]	[Ch]
Widd Maleing		1
Tho Marriott		1
Edwar Russell	1 C	
Jo Cooper	1 C	
Rich Bassett	1 C	
[f. 6v]		
Widd Barnecle	1 C	
Wm Harris	1 C	
Nath Fleckham	1 C	
Robt Murcott		1
Widd Borowes	1 C	
Tho Garrett	1 C	
Jo Arlige	1 C	
Wm Gardner	1 C	
Wm Trepas with a forge	2 C	
Jo Aris		2
Widd Pobbins		2
Jo Clarke gent		2
Widd Smith		1
Tho Watson de belch		1
Jo Lee		1
Tho Clarke gent		3
Jo Watson		2
Robt Chamberlaine		1
Mr Tho Watson sen		2
Mr Tho Watson jun		2
Wm Glenn		2
Tho Clarke esq emptie		3
Jo Tuckey	2 C	
Jo Downes	1 C	
Widd Bodell		1
Tho Wareing		1
Wm Jackson	1 C	
Ann Steele	1 C	
Eliz Smith	1 C	
Two emptie cottages	2 C	
		74

Veuied by:
Warberton Hull collector

Hillmorton [par]

	[NC]	[Ch]
Wm Bustard	1	
Wm Watts		2
Jo Gumley		1
Widd Hambleton		1
Christ Wildbore	1 C	
Rich Hurley		1
Tho Compton		3
Wm Kimble		1
Barth Sheepey		1
[f. 7]		
Robt Smith	1 C	
Robt Daulton		1
Rich Knott	1 C	
Jane Bromidge	1 C	
Jo Satchwell		1
Jo Blockley		1
Tho Cave		1
Clemt Perkins		1
Tho Chamberlaine	1 C	
Wm Andrew		5
Widd Church	1 C	
Mr Norton minister		2
Rob Harris	1 C	
Rich Robins	1 C	
Mary Porter	1 C	
Wm Ward		2
Jo Hyerne		2
Rich Hurley		1
Wm Hore	1 C	
Jo Cobley	1 C	
Tho Odams	1 C	
Wm Cobley	1 C	
Geo Harris	1 C	
Rich Meverley	1 C	
Wm Dawson	1 C	
Sarh Dixson	1 C	
Vincent Hurley	1 C	
Jo Lampton	1 C	
Edwd Garratt	1 C	
Mary Joynes	1 C	
Jeffery Hurley	1 C	
Tho Porter		1
Tho Orton	1 C	
James Green	1 C	
Wm Chamberlaine	1 C	
Widd Combes	1 C	

	[NC]	[Ch]
Jo Causier		1
Jo Budcock		2
Wm Cattle		1
Jo Carvell		1
Tho Bird		1
Jo Clarke	1 C	
Jo Compton		2
Hen Harbert		2
Geo Harbert		2
[f. 7v]		
Jo Wilson sen	1 C	
Jo Wilson jun		1
Jo Porter	1 C	
Jo Watts		1
Jo Bottrell	1 C	
Jo Collesson		1
Widd Cryer	1 C	
Wm Sawbridge		2
Tho Clarke		2
Jo Satchwell		2
Tho Walton		1
Tho Hollowell		1
Rich Prockter		1
Jo Abotts with an oven		3
Luke Bradshaw		2
Wm Odams		2
Jo Francis		2
Rich Kinch		1
Rich Syddon		5
Wm Bottrell	1 C	
Edwd Boddington		1
Mr Rich Pettipher		4
Widd Bassett	1 C	
Wm Satchwell		1
Jo Smith laborer		1
Jo Smith blinde	1 C	
Wm Smith		1
Eliz Harrison		2
Widd Page	1 C	
Lett Smith	1 C	
Mr Edwd Bromidge		6
Wm Chattwell		1
Widd Walton		1
Randall Marriott 2 houses		3

	[NC]	[Ch]
Wm Bullock		1
Rich Smith		2
Ralph Tulley		1
Jo Satchwell		1
Jo Cryer		2
Edwd Perkins sen		1
Robt Harding with 1 oven		4
Jo Twigger		1
Emptye cottage	1	
Wm Cave		3
Geo Smith	1	
Wm Sherman		2
[f. 8]		
Rich Sydon		5
Rich Luke with two forges		4
Mr Tho Marriott		4
Edwd Perkins jun		2
Tho Barrow		2
John Smith weaver		1
		126
		[124]

Veiued by:
Warberton Hull collector
Wm Smith constable

Cliffton
[Clifton upon Dunsmore par]

	[NC]	[Ch]
Mr St John Cave		8
Geo Green with a forge		2
Wm Shittlewood		1
Widd Southam		1
Math Newton		1
Mrs Harvey widd		7
Mr Weaver rector		4
Wm Higgs		1
Wm Sallesbury	1 C	
Jo Pinchbacke		1
Jo Wright	1 C	
James Higgs		4
Johnson Higgs		3
Edwd Barford		1
Widd Sedgley		1
Rich Radbourne		4
Jo Perkins		2

	[NC]	[Ch]
Mr Wm Wright		3
Geo Cooper	1 C	
Geo Houltam		2
Jo Fossell		2
Fran Ruffheade		1
Tho Tue		2
Step Sutton		1
Mary Hewett		3
Edwd Cooper		3
Tho Sedgley		2
Mary Clarke		1
Mr Jo Barford		4
Sym Tarsey		2
[f. 8v]		
Hen Harrald		1
Hen Meades		1
Rich Andrews		1
Widd Andrews		2
Widd Bennett	1 C	
Edwd Bennett	1 C	
Rich Shittlewood	1 C	
Rich Hewett	1 C	
Wm Samson	1 C	
Edwd Ashmore	1 C	
Jo Watkins	1 C	
Widd Perkins	1 C	
Widd Woodward	1 C	
Widd Hayles	1 C	
Geo Hyam	1 C	
Edwd Gardner	1 C	
Sarah Hartherley	1 C	
Hen Harrald		1
		73

Newton et Biggen in Cliffton Parrish

[Newton and Biggin in Clifton upon Dunsmore par]

Mrs Dorothy Only widd		5
Mr Wm Martin		4
Jo Crofts		1
Wm Howkins		3
Wm Elkson		1

	[NC]	[Ch]
Tho Ostler	1 C	
Rich Chamberlane		<3>2
Widd Adnett		3
Edwd Stapples	1 C	
Wm Pratt		2
Hen Pratt		2
Hen Gibson		1
Jo Gibbs	1 C	
Hen Collins	1 C	
Tho Staples		1
Wm Haskes	1 C	
Tho Strange		2
Wm Letts with a forge	2 C	
Robt Shittlewood	1 C	
Wm Watson		3
Rich Smart		1
Widd Butler		1
<Widd>Will Bassett		1
Widd Clement		1
Widd Adkins		1
[f. 9]		
Eph Howlett	1 C	
Randll Aman	1 C	
Wm Aman	1 C	
Jo Clement		2
Joane Birde	1 C	
Jo Pratt		2
Tho Chamberlaine		1
Tho Brawnson		1
		41

Brownsover [chap[1]]

Mr Wm Willington		3
Mr Tho Pettifer		4
Mr Edwd Bassett		3
Mr Tho Robins		2
Wm Howkins		2
Rich Clarke		2
Wm Sawbridge		2
Hen Lorde }		2
Edwd Lorde }		1
Arth Sedgley		1
Edwd Webb		2

[1] Chapelry of Clifton upon Dunsmore parish.

	[NC]	[Ch]
Robt Harrald		1
Nick Wright		1
Geo Butler		1
		27

Veiued by:
Warbt Hull collector
Rich Chamberlaine constable

Bilton [par]

	[NC]	[Ch]
Rich Boughton esq		12
Jo Leigh esq		5
Mr Jo Tante		2
Geo Arden	1 C	
Widd Cotton	1 C	
Robt Hestley		1
Tho Blockley	1 C	
Joane Steane	1 C	
Treen Walkers		1
Wm Dixens	1 C	
Jo Selvidge		1
[f. 9v]		
Mr Tho Watmore minister		1
Eliz Everton	1 C	
Widd Green	1 C	
Wm Badson		2
Jo Keen		1
Jo Smith		1
Mr Rich Hinde		2
Rich Smith		1
Widd Palmer	1 C	
Tho Arden		1
Rob Marloe		1
Edwd Harris	1 C	
Fran Coles	1 C	
Jo Coles	1 C	
Edwd Adkins	1 C	
Widd Ardingworth	1 C	
Danll Smith	1 C	
Fran Tommes	1 C	
Widd Loley	1 C	
Rich Seale	1 C	
Eliz Wills	1 C	
Jas Cooley emptie		1
Widd Sneade	1 C	
Anth Buggs	1 C	
Widd Basterd	1 C	
Robt Hill	1 C	
Wm Elliott	1 C	
Lettice Roggers		1
Widd Benn	1 C	
Jo Molling	1 C	
Hen emptie cottage	1 C	
Ewd White	1 C	
Tho Buttres	1 C	
Rich Palmer		1
Wm Kinge	1 C	
Hen Newbold	1 C	
Faulkes Newbold		4
Fran Enos		2
Jo Clarke		2
Humpr Perkins		2
Jo Perkins		1
Danll Hamond		1
Hump Green	1 C	
Robt Staple		1
[f. 10]		
Jo Palmer		1
Mr Boughton emptie		3
Jonath Enos		1
Wm Eales		1
Arth Adams		1
Widd Sedgley	1	
Tim Arne	1	
Jo Green	1	
Samll Morris	1	
Augt Franklin	1	
		55

Veiued by:
Warberton Hull collector
Rich Palmer constable

Woolston et Marston
[Wolston and Marston
in Wolston par]

	[NC]	[Ch]
Mr Gorton minester		6
Robt Bearson		2
Rich Hancock	1 C	
Samll Goodman		1

	[NC]	[Ch]
Widd Smith	1 C	
Hump Darne		2
Jo Lord		2
Satchwell Phillipps		1
Tho Ward		1
Jo Farndon		2
Jo Pearson		1
Wm Francis	1 C	
Robt Wilton		1
Hen Woster		1
Jo Sutton		1
James Watson		1
Tho Chades		1
Tho Sheafe	1 C	
Rob Soeden	1 C	
Th Woolfe	1 C	
Mr Tho Powell		4
Tho Handes		1
Christp Burton		1
Sir Peettr Wentworth		13
Rob Rore	1 C	
Wm Burton	1 C	
Jo Carter		1
[f. 10v]		
Hump Cox		1
Widd Oakley	1 C	
Eliz Anstey	1 C	
Tho Roote 2 houses		2
Hugh Hinton		2
Wm Edwards		1
Wm Adkins		1
Wm Rose		2
Jo Yeates		1
Jo Tomkins		1
Jo Perkins		1
Clemt Priste		1
Wm Harbert with a forge		3
Jo Hancox		1
Samll Harding		2
Jacob Carter		1
Rich Warde		11
Eliz Bussell		1
Rich Lickorish		4
Zach Elkinton		2
Wm Hookes		2
Edwd Bates		2
Widd Smith		1
Jo Dyson Jo Skellett		2
Jo Arne	1 C	
Nick Everton		1
Edwd Smith	1	
Wm Griffin	1	
Jo Bossworth	1	
Augt Fretter	1	
Moss Ward	1	
Martin Beaseley	1	
Barth Smith } Mary Carter }	2	
		89

Veuied by:
Warbert Hull collector
Zach Elkington constable

[f. 11]

Churchover [par]

	[NC]	[Ch]
Robt Tue		1
Rich Boddington		2
Wm Chapman		4
Wm Smith		2
Wm Wright sen		2
Rogr & Alice Wright		1
Jos Blockley jun		1
Wm Clarke		1
Rob Webb		1
Tho Bretfeild		1
John Frost		1
Jo Blockley sen		2
Mr Marshall minister		3
Geo Collidge with a forge		2
Wm Essex	1 C	
Rich Satchwell	1 C	
Mary Webb	1 C	
Mary Baske	1 C	
Wm Cotes	1 C	
Jo Frost	1 C	
Robt Tayler	1 C	
Jo Knight	1 C	

	[NC]	[Ch]
Tho Frost	1 C	
<Jo>Widd Baseley	<1>0	1
Tho Pilgrim		1
Rich Nobbs	1 C	
Tho Limber		1
Christpher More		1
Mr Wm Dixall		7
Widd Bill		3
Jos Steane		1
Jo Bill emptie		2
Jo Collidge		1
Mr Rich Baseley		3
Wm Page		1
Hen Collidge		1
Edwd Hyatt		6
Wm Ballard		1
Tho Mounte with a forge		2
Eliz Godard	1	
Emptie house		1
[f. 11v]		
Jo Wilkinson		1
Jo Smith		1
Widd Baseley		1
Wm Gibson		1
Tho Randall	1 C	
Tho Godard	1 C	
Jo Gilbert	1 C	
Tho Wright		1
Tho Blockley	1	
(new …) Edwd Cave		4
Cotton [Coton] **house**		
Wm Dixall esq		10
		76

Veiued by Warberton Hull collector

Newbold Super Avon
[Newbold on Avon par]

	[NC]	[Ch]
Mr Walker vicker		6
Robt Francis		3
Wm Francis		3
Rich Francis		3
Tho Only		2
Jo Adnett		2
Widd Legson		3
Jo Only		4
Sus Walker widd		3
Jo Francis		1
Jo Overton now Hoult		2
Hen Smith		3
Tho Walker		1
Jos Downes		4
Jos Ashborne	1 C	
Rich Hawkes jun	1 C	
Wm Satchwell	1 C	
Rich Walker sen	1 C	
Jo Heacock	1 C	
Wm Smith	1 C	
Wm Marston	1 C	
Widd Stephens	1 C	
Christpher Francis	1 C	
Wm Hawforde	1 C	
[f. 12]		
Widd Green	1 C	
Jo Foster	1 C	
Geo Smith	1 C	
Wm Lagoe		1
Widd Hawkins	1 C	
Margt Terry	1 C	
Tho Howkins	1 C	
		41

Harbury Parva in Parrish
[Harborough Parva
in Newbold on Avon par]

	[NC]	[Ch]
Tho Busshell		2
John Leatherland		2
Tho Plant		3
Jo Perkins		1

Cosford
[in Newbold on Avon par]

	[NC]	[Ch]
Tho Carter		3
Charles Webb	1 C	
Wm Webbe		1
Mr Wm Steane		4
John Bill jun		1
Mr Rich Steane		5
Jo Morris	1 C	
Charles Beasley	2 C	
Jo Bill sen	<4>	4

	[NC]	[Ch]
Oliver Baggott	1 C	
Jo Marttin	1 C	
Edmd Mathews	1 C	
Tho Steane		2
Wm Mathews	2 C	
Tho Baggott	1 C	
Tho Steele		1
Rich Porter		2
Wm Bennett emptie		1
Nick Danll		1
		33

Veiued by:
Warbt Hull collector
Wm Steane

[f. 12v]

Longe Lawford
et Little Lawford
[in Newbold on Avon par]
[***Long Lawford***[1]]

	[NC]	[Ch]
Danll Varnum	1 C	<1>
Peettr Grimsley		1
Robt Edkins emptie		1
Nick Webb with an oven		2
Widd Webb		2
Wm Cox		2
Jo Shorte		2
Tho Adkins	1 C	
Wm Bucknell		1
Nick Webb jun		1
Mr Jo Only		3
Dorothy Smarte		1
Edwd Burton jun		2
Mary Walker Alice Begg	1 C	
Nick Adkins		1
Fran Smarte	1 C	
Tho Thruston		1
Benj Essex		1
Wm Essex		1
Hen Colles	1 C	
Tho Sneath		1
Rob Adkins sen		1
Rich Sachwell		1
Widd Bassett	1 C	
Jo Pratt		1
Jo Bagshaw		1
Mr Tho Onley		3
Jo Bowers	1 C	
Tho Townsend		2
Edwd Jeeland		2
Tho Hartopp		1
Mr Robt Croft		4
Jo Joanes		1
Rich Webb		2
Tho Marsson with a forge		2
Tho Boyes		1
Edwd Burton sen		1
Widd Heycox	1 C	
Tho Only new built		[-]
Widd Craft	1 C	
Robt Adkins jun		2
Widd Adkins		1

[f. 13]

	[NC]	[Ch]
Christpher Chattwell		2
Wm Butler	1 C	
Widd Bateman	1 C	
Jo Ball	1 C	
Widd Gilman	1 C	
Wm Perkins	1 C	
Geo Mathews	1 C	
Tho Renn	1 C	
Wm Bucknell	1 C	
Wm Rorhead	1 C	
Rich Silvester	1 C	
Jo Dyson		1
Tho Porter	1 C	
Widd Perkins	1 C	
Widd Hampton	1 C	
Little Lawforde		
Sir Edwd Boughton bart		22
		52
		[74]

Veiued by Warbt Hull collector

[1] WCRO, QS11/43 (1673).

	[NC]	[Ch]
Newnham Regis et Church Lawford		
[***Kings Newnham*** par[1]]		
Rob Leigh esq		17
Benj Arnall		2
Sus Sedgley		2
Lau Worth		2
Jo Harris		2
Jo Skinner		1
Mr Rich Warde		3
Wm Adkins		1
Wm Adkins jun	1 C	
Widd Cotton	1 C	
Widd Daniell	1 C	
Church Lawford [par]		
Mr Edwd Wright		5
Jo Garfeilde		1
Rich Bende		1
Tho Bende		1
Geo Cotton		1
Rich Oliver		1
Rob Mathews	1 C	
Samll North		1
[f. 13v]		
Cfpher Moore		1
Danll Doulton		1
Emptie House		4
Robt Bradford		1
Tho Moe		1
Tho Bird with a forge		2
Mrs Lester widd		3
Robt Wamsley		2
Mr Rich Hutchinson		5
Nick Herbert		1
Wm Phillipps		1
Wm Coles		1
Robt Garfeild		1
Widd Saunson		1
Rich Hill	1 C	
Hen Doulton		1
Alice Bonde		1
John Doulton jun	1 C	

	[NC]	[Ch]
Moss Moore	1 C	
Tho Pulves	1 C	
Tho Reade	1 C	
Barnaby Hall	1 C	
Tho Doulton	1 C	
Widd Aspley	1 C	
Margt Perkins	1 C	
Widd Cox	1 C	
Jo Doulton sen	1 C	
		090
		[68]
[f. 14]		
Rugby [par]		
Mr Tho Langley		8
Luke Barroe		4
Marmaduke Faulkes		3
Wm Houlden		2
Mr Samll Newton		4
Mr Wm Boyce		3
Mr Wm Tilghman jun		5
Phaskey Barnwell		1
Rich Clarke	1 C	
Wm Lathbury	1 C	
Jo Ladbrooke	1 C	
Mich Kidney		2
Robt Only		2
Mrs Millecent Tilghman		12
Jo Bisshopp		3
Wm Robinson		2
Mrs Burnabey widd		12
Tho Cliffton }		1
Emptie cottage }		1
Ralph Alsopp		1
Widd Smith		1
Jo Bradshaw		1
Fran Green with a forge }		2
Hen Gamage }		1
Jo Green with a forge		3
Walter Flett jun	1 C	
Jo Kinge		1
Jo <Rooke>Poole		1
Jo Sale jun	<2>1 C	
Widd Green		1

[1] WCRO, QS11/43 (1673).

	[NC]	[Ch]
Jo Wright	1 C	
Mr Rob Craftes		1
Christpher Higgins		1
Jo Harford		1
Edwd Faulkes		2
Tho Bacon		4
Jo Moore		1
Rich Stretton	1 C	
Nath Bacon		4
[f. 14v]		
Jo Chebsey sen & jun		3
Rich Eales sen		1
Rich Eales jun		1
Rich Eales emptie		1
Jo Seftton		3
Jobe Ladbrooke		2
Widd Cooper	1 C	
Isa Ladbrooke	<3>0	3
Eliz Heayford wid		3
Rich Hobdey		2
Rich Webb		3
Jo Shell		4
Tho Gabrill		3
Tho Goodley sen		3
Isa Cowley		2
Tho Tracser		3
Tho Nickall		<2>1
Tho Blizard		1
Mr Rich Elbrowe		6
Widd Nickalls 2 houses		2
Jo emptie cottage		1
Jo Mayo		3
Wm Joyner		2
Widd <Taunte>Webb		3
Tho Taunte	1 C	
Josi Alloway		2
James Sale emptie	1 C	
James Sale jun	1 C	
Rich Harris	1 C	
Edwd Harris		3
Joyce Baggott		4

	[NC]	[Ch]
Tho Gettling jun		1
Wm Lee		1
Wm Chebsey		3
Mary Newbold with a forge		2
Mr Tho Shaw minister		5
Jos Bisshopp sen		3
Jos Bisshopp jun		2
[f. 15]		
Rich Bisshopp		1
Jo Waring		1
Eliz How	1 C	
Edwd Penn		1
Tho Currall	1 C	
Wm Green		1
Fran Marriott		1
Mrs Mary Newton		3
Mr <Jo>Edwd Howe		6
Mr Edwd Berry		4
Jo Lett		1
Mr Knightloe Harrisson		6
Tho Tooley jun		5
Rogr Ravon		4
Jo Hall		3
Mr Wm Heyford jun		2
Wm Cooke with a forge	2	
Jo Baggott		4
Tho Joanes		1
Tho Egells		1
Hen Pindes		1
Wm Currall sen	1 C	
Jo Francis	1 C	
Jo Green emptie refuseth to pay		[-] [*1*[1]]
Edwd Joanes		1
Hump Davis	1 C	
Wm Haws	1 C	
Tho Bassnett		2
Tho Bates		1
Edwd Bates		2
Walter Flett		1
Geo Cotton		1
Saml Baker		1
Tho Ambross with a forge		2

1 WCRO, QS11/43 (1673).

	[NC]		[Ch]
Samll Danniell			3
Edwd Terry			1
Wm Rugby			2
[f. 15v]			
Edwd Beavon			3
Mr James Leavett			6
Wm Heyford sen			1
Mr Samll Cravon			3
Mr Harpur & Mr Holliman			6
Rich Stoakes			1
Ralph Horsley	1	C	
Wm Satchwell	1	C	
Tho Wright	1	C	
Jo Randes	1	C	
Wm Prince	1	C	
Tho Frost sen	1	C	
Mary Cooper	1	C	
Mary Marshall	1	C	
Hen Gamage	1	C	
Abigll Shelly	1	C	
Wm Mounckes	<1>[1]		1
Tho Russell			1
Widd Kerkton	1	C	
Edwd Wright	1	C	
Tho Buntin	1	C	
Rich Woodford	1	C	
Forty cottages[2]	[40]	C	
			259
			[258]

Veiued by:
Warberton Hull
Jo Green constable

[WCRO, QS11/17]
[f. 1]
Knightloe [Knightlow Hundred]
Southam Division
1670
Exchequer Roles
[written by Warberton Hull]
[f. 1v: blank]

	[NC]		[Ch]
[f. 2]			
Southam [par]			
Mr Samll Andrews			6
Mr Tho Hanslopp			6
Rich Bicknall with a forge			7
Robt George emptie			3
Wm Butler			2
Mary Turner	1	C	
Widd Spicer	1	C	
Tho Judkin	2	C	
Mr Robt Hinslopp & Tho Craftes			8
Rich Budd			2
Wm Arch			2
Wm Gilbert	1	C	
(poore) John Turner with a forge	3		
Widd Winmills			3
Widd Banbury	1	C	
Rich Maunton	1	C	
Tho Corbitt			3
Tho Rascall emptie			1
Tho Turner emptie			1
Wm Doster			1
Margr Cox emptie	1	C	
Hen Stallworth			1
Mr Rowland Jackson			2
Samll Tipler			2
Rich Wootton	1	C	
Nath Arnall with 1 oven			4
John Mills			1
Wm Beasley	1	C	
Mary Cox	1	C	
Rich Bryan			1
Robt Rose sen			2
Edwd Horne	1	C	
Rich Goodwin			2
Jo Good	1	C	
[f. 2v]			
John Williams	1	C	
John Mariott			1
Widd Hyam	1	C	

1 Not deleted in the manuscript but a chargeable hearth is more consistent with the total given.
2 Described as: '40 misserable poore cotts not worth taking notice of' in TNA, E179/259/9 (1666).

	[NC]		[Ch]
Wm Chester	1	C	
Rich Pettifer	1	C	
Widd Jackson	1	C	
Eph Benson	1	C	
Rob Browne	1	C	
Widd Good	1	C	
Wm Wright	1	C	
John Freeman	1	C	
Wm Chetwin jun			2
Robt Betts			3
Rich Freeman	1	C	
Hen Edmunds emptie			<1>2
Tho Edmunds & Hen Wiblin }			2
Robt Edmunds gent			4
Robt Woodfall			4
Widd Edmunds			1
Robt Gibbons			1
Hen Good			2
Wm Queeney			1
John Procter			1
Elish Wright			1
Tho Wallis			1
Jonas Robinson			1
Robt Spicer			2
Hen Spicer			1
Robt Hill a forge	1	C	
Rich Ryndon			3
Ann Cornish widd			2
Wm Daniell			2
Rich Newcombe			2
Jonath Ebrall			1
Isabell Cornish widd			4
Prisll Hall widd			1
Margr Ludloe			3
[f. 3]			
Joane Cole widd	2		
Tho Wills			2
Jonath Wye			1
Wm Goffe	1	C	
Tho Freeman	1	C	
Tho Basley	1	C	
Widd Lyndon in 2 houses			10
Widd Lade	1	C	

	[NC]		[Ch]
Wm Goode	1	C	
Wm Kinge	1	C	
Rich Lindon emptie			2
Mrs Sarah Cheston			2
Mr Jo Chebsey			9
Judeth Hill widd			3
Widd Perry	1	C	
Widd Webb	1	C	
Wm Heaywarde	1	C	
Rich Bryan emptie			1
Widd Cox	1	C	
John Edmunds	1	C	
Rich Worrall	1	C	
Wm Sharman	1	C	
Mr Nick Hanslopp sen			5
Jos Julian	1	C	
John Furloe			1
Wm Marsh			3
Tho Welch			2
Tho Marsh			2
Fran Betts			3
Mr Nick Hanslopp jun			5
Hen Biddle	1	C	
Fardin Gibbons			2
Edwd Rose			2
Hugh Avorne			1
Eliz Jeffcot emptie			1
Robt Wootton			1
John Mumford			1
[f. 3v]			
Mr Tho Coleburne			5
Fran Cox	1	C	
Widd Castle	1	C	
Tho Clarke	1	C	
Eliz Jeffcote			2
Tho Stalworth	1	C	
Widd Sheepard			1
Wm Barnecle			1
Tho Queeney jun			1
Clemt Betts			4
Rich Queeney with a forge			2
John Brayfeild			2
Tho Chetwin			2
Robt Marsh			1

	[NC]		[Ch]
Robt George			4
Geo Worrall	1	C	
Samll Lord			2
Hen Pitcher	1	C	
John Lorde			3
John Procter			1
Geo Tomes	1	C	
Tim Mordick			1
Abra Clarke	1	C	
Widd Wright	1	C	
Tho Gibbs	1	C	
Danll Lee	1	C	
Sy Julian	1	C	
			199

Veiued by:
Warberton Hull collector
Tho Chetwin constable

Napton Super Mountain
[Napton on the Hill par]

	[NC]		[Ch]
Hen Tayler			2
Tho Tue			1
Ann Baker			1
Eliz Hewes			1
Math Biddle	1	C	
Rich Loe	1	C	
Winefride Clarke	1	C	
John Kiteley	1	C	
Wm Clarke	<1>0		1
Tho Horley			1
Ann Horley			1
Tho Trusloe			2
Wm Hews			1
Cottage emptie	1	C	
John Sedgley			1
John Biddle sen			2
Wm Clarke			2
Widd Clarke			1
John Prophett			1
John Sheasbey jun			1
John Trusloe sen			1
Arth Holloway			1
Rich Makepeace			2
Robt Hunte sen			1
Rich Makepeace empte			1
Tho Hall			1
Tho Eales	1	C	
Tho Allebone & his mother			2
Rich Prophett			1
Wm Pywell			2
Mr Tho Weale			6
Wm Collins			2
John Kenning			1
Samll Simson			1
Robt Baker			1
Wm Makepeace			1
John Trusloe jun			2
[f. 4v]			
Wm Greenway			1
Mr Hen Walker minester			2
Edwd Smarte jun			2
Tho Alsoppe			1
Tho Hyorne with a forge			2
Tho Garret with an oven			3
Nick Letts with 1 oven			3
Rich Price			1
Tho Knight			1
Tho Hixson			1
John Mallins	1	C	
Hen Prophett			1
John Barnecle	1	C	
Wm Houltam	1	C	
John Barnes			1
Rich Hall			1
Rich Hall emptie			1
Wm Sheepard			1
John Sheepard			1
Tho Dadeley sen			1
John Collins			1
Edwd Smarte sen			1
Wm Cleaver			2
Geo Mayo			1
Rich Basswell			2
Wm Gardner			1
Fran Treadwell sen			1
Mr Edwd Griffin			3
John Barnes emptie			1
Mrs Loe			2

	[NC]	[Ch]
Hen Wright		1
Tho Taft		1
Wm Markham		1
Wm Adkins	1 C	
Fran Treadwell jun		2
Geo Tayler		1
[f. 5]		
Tho Taft		1
Nick Goode		1
Martin Gline		2
Tho Partridge		1
John Adkins		1
Wm Raynbowe jun		2
Tho Treadwell		1
John Sheasbey		1
Wm Smith		1
Wm Jackson		1
John Bryan		3
Tho Dadley jun		1
Geo Clarke & Isble Minster		5
Tho Orton		2
John Taft	1 C	
Nick Harwood		1
John Powell with a forge	2 C	
John Goode		1
Rich Tomkins emptie		1
Tho Garrett		2
Mary Harwood		1
Hen Markham		1
John Soden		1
Tho Wright		4
Tho Perry		1
John Sheasbey sen	1 C	
Wm Reasbey		1
John Gibbon		1
Rich Marriot		1
Rich Thornton		1
Wm Prophett		2
Widd Garrett		2
Anckor Baker		1
Rich Barret		1
Wm Goode		1
Rich Hyerne		1

	[NC]	[Ch]
Tho Pratt	1 C	
Rich Cleaver sen		1
Tho Carpender		1
[f. 5v]		
Joane Jeffkins widd		1
Tho Gibbons		4
Wm Garrett		1
Rich Cleaver		2
Wm Raynboe jun		4
Edwd Whitheade	1 C	
Wm Raynboe		1
Hen Pigstock	1 C	
Fran Barnett	1 C	
Wm Barret	1 C	
Olliver Maxfeild	<1>	1
James Marriot	1 C	
Moss Breedon		1
Geo Renall		1
Wm Griffin	1 C	
John Nasbey	1 C	
Tho Mallins	1 C	
Peettr Beaver	1 C	
Rich Hyerne	1 C	
Wm Mallins	1 C	
Sus Powell	1 C	
Robt Hurst	1 C	
James Tidman	1 C	
John Biddle jun	1 C	
Tho Budd	1 C	
Hen Budd	1 C	
Widd Horley	1 C	
Widd Hixson	1 C	
Wm Harwood	1 C	
Robt Nasbey	1 C	
Wm Mortiboyes	1 C	
Robt Trippas	1 C	
Wm Makepeace	1 C	
Robt Talbutt	1 C	
Wm Treadwell		1
		157

Veiued by:
Warberton Hull collector
Tho Allebone constable

[f. 6]

Stockton [par]

	[NC]	[Ch]
Fulck Mollchar		2
Mr Edwd Pilkinton		9
Mr Wm Crooke		4
Wm Goode		2
Edwd Gibbons		2
Tobias Over		2
Hen Eales		2
Tho Wright		1
Rich Watts		1
Wm Perry		1
Wm Terrall		1
Hen Simonds	1 C	
<Alice>Fulck Mollcher jun		4
John Simonds		1
Rich Turner		1
Mary Mills widd		2
John Overs emptie		1
Ralph Hill	1 C	
Hen Turner		2
James Tidman	1 C	
John Harris		2
Hen Eales emptie		1
Tho Eales	2 C	
Wm Cleaver		1
Tho Bent with a forge	2 C	
Tho Smith	1 C	
James Masson	1 C	
Tho Terrell	1 C	
Tho Hyerne	1 C	
Widd Turner	1 C	
Rich Simonds	1 C	
Widd Cox	1 C	
Widd Gibbs	1 C	
Sus Robbinson	1 C	
Widd Treene	1 C	
John Bent	1 C	
Ann Perry	1 C	
Jo Weale	1 C	
Sus Terrell	1 C	
Sy Wilcox	1 C	
Alice Queeney	1 C	
Eliz Cleaver	1 C	
		42

Veiued by:
Warberton Hull collector
Wm Terrall constable

[f. 6v]

Woolfhampcote et Neathercote Sawbridge & Flecknoe

[Wolfhampcote par]

[***Sawbridge***[1]]

	[NC]	[Ch]
Tho Butler		1
Robt Lucas		1
John Eales		1
Rich Saunder		1
Tho Wilkins		1
Wm Childes		2
Mr Robt Cleaver		4
Tho Hill		1
Tho Curtice		2
Rich Graunte		1
Wm Graunte		1
Hen Nowell		1
Rich Cross		3
Mr Wm Basley		2
Hen Goode		1
Mr Tho Cleaver		5
Wm Holmes		2
Mr Robt Clarke		2
John & Ann Graunt		1
Rich Marchart	1	
		33

Nethercot

[Nethercote in Wolfhampcote par]

	[NC]	[Ch]
Tho Queeney		2
Walter Watson		4
Robt Enfeild		3
Tho Shaw		2
Mr Jo Clarke		1
Mrs Eliz Clarke		6

[1] WCRO, QS11/56 (1674).

	[NC]		[Ch]
Ovencott [Wolfhampcote]			
Mr Tho Bateman			4
Mr Tho Clarke			4
Mr Jo Vale vicker			1
Wolfhampcote et Flecknoe			
[Flecknoe in Wolfampcote par]			
Hen Tomkins & his mother			3
Hen Goode			1
Hen Goode jun			2
Wm Masters jun			1
Ann Goode widd			1
John Webb			2
Hen Denney			1
[f. 7]			
Eliz Goode widd			2
Rich Shenston			1
John Craftes			1
Edwd Still			1
Tho Rawbone			1
John Masters sen			2
Eliz Thornicraft			1
Edwd Thornicraft with a forge			2
Tho Sadler			2
Edwd Shenston			2
Tho Worsley	1	C	
Geo & Tho Smith			2
Wm Smith & Edwd Rawbone			3
Mr John Arnall sen			4
John Masters jun			1
Hen Loute			1
Wm Masters sen			2
Tho Webb			2
Widd Shenston jun			1
John Arnall jun			2
Tho Shaw			2
Rich Masters sen			2
Tho Shenston			1
Nick Masters jun			3
Jos Sutton			1
Tho Masters			1
Nick Goode			1
Robt Webb			1
Math Arnall			3
Rich Sheasbey	1	C	
Rob Sherwood	1	C	
Rich Cleaver emptie			1
Cottage emptie	1	C	
Rich Denny	1	C	
Ussaby Holmes	<1>		2
Widd Bucknell			1
Robt Curtice			1
Geo Browne			1
[f. 7v]			
Eliz Allibone	1	C	
Eliz Wheatley	1	C	
Jo Hindes	1	C	
Nath Bucknell	1	C	
Mary Worrall	1	C	
Sarh Watson	1	C	
Jo Cleaver	1	C	
John Grosbey	1	C	
Alice Kerke	1	C	
Eliz Queeney	1	C	
Sarah Yardley	1	C	
			92

Veuied by:
Warberton Hull collector
Tho Queeney constable

	[NC]		[Ch]
Granborough et Woolscott			
[Grandborough par]			
[***Woolscott***[1]]			
Mr Robt Radburne sen			3
Mr Tho Adkins			2
Sarh Steele	1	C	
Jo Burman			2
Jo Biddle			2
Mr Wm Adkins			4
Mr Rob Radburne jun			4
Mr Edwd Beale			6
Hen Shaw			3
Wm Radburne			2
Mr Christpher Tilly			2
Edwd Radburne			2

1 TNA, E179/259/9 (1666).

	[NC]	[Ch]
Mr Rich Heawood emptie		6
Tho Enock		1
[***Grandborough***[1]]		
Jo Shaw		1
John Farndon		1
Mr Harvey emptie		1
Ann Walton	1 C	
Wm Mayo	<2>	2
Robt Shenton	<2>	2
Jos Eales	1 C	
[f. 8]		
Baruck Basley		2
Margt Edwd	2 C	
Samson Prist		1
Hen Benston		2
Mr Tho Clarke		3
Mrs <Widd> Hill widd		8
Tho Towne		2
James Higgs		1
Jo Walter		2
Jo Woodfall		2
Wm Smith		1
Rich Curtice		1
Tho Allard	1 C	
Nick Smith		1
Edwd Allarde		2
Rob Radburne		1
Jo Bale	1 C	
Jo Addams		1
Tho Radburne		1
Edwd Geas		2
Jo Smith emptie		2
Tho Hewit		1
Anth Allebone		1
Jo Burman		1
Jo Jackson		1
Robt Woodfall emptie		2
Rich Hancock		1
Alice Wilcox	1 C	
Tho Southam	1 C	
Nath Newbold		2
Mr Rich Beale		3
Jo Odams		4
Wm Wilcox		2
Rich Gardner		2
Jo Hewet		1
Wm Collet	1 C	
Rich Green	1 C	
Wm Garfeild	1 C	
[f. 8v]		
Jo Turner	1 C	
Wm Roades	1 C	
Rich Eales	1 C	
Widd Barnecle	1 C	
Sus Heycock	1 C	
Emptie cott[age]	1 C	
Mrs Davis		1
Rob Cox	1 C	
		<122>
		103

Veiued by:
Warberton Hull collector

Lemington Hastings cum membris

[Leamington Hastings par and parts]

	[NC]	[Ch]
Mr Tho Mathewes in the mannor house		11
Eliz Mathews widd		2
Mr Allington minister		4
Mr Tho Mathews pro Colebourne		2
Rich Twigger		2
Wm Heycock		2
Jo Mathews		5
Jo Mann		1
Tho Parson with a forge		2
Eliz Walforde	2	
Tho Mann		1
Widd Biddle	1 C	
Widd Blithe	1 C	
Widd Barton	1 C	
Wm Tomkins	1 C	

[1] TNA, E179/259/9 (1666).

	[NC]		[Ch]
An almes house	6	C	
Ann Tarsey	1	C	
Rich Twigglor	1	C	
			32

[f. 9]

Hill in Lemington Hastings [par]

	[NC]		[Ch]
Ann Masson widd			2
Jo Masson			1
Tho Buswell			2
Phillipp Hewett			2
Hen Bliss			2
Tho Headon			4
Widd Pedler			1
Hen Busswell			1
Zephany Binley			3
Math Over	1	C	
Jo Tayler	1	C	
Tho Hawton	1	C	
Widd Cooper			1
Addam Oakley	1	C	
Tho Tuckey	1	C	
Rich Cleaver	1	C	

Hardwicke in Lem

[Kites Hardwick
in Leamington Hastings par]

	[NC]		[Ch]
Hen Biddle gent			4
Wm Smith			3
Wm Cleaver			2
Hen Watson			2
Widd Cleaver			1
Tho Hintch			2
Rich Goode			1
Hen Bliss	1	C	
Rich Over	1	C	
Geo Bell	1	C	
Rich Allebone	1	C	
Rich Wheeller	1	C	
Tho Drewrey	1	C	
			34

[f. 9v]

Bradwell in Lemington

[Broadwell
in Leamington Hastings par]

	[NC]		[Ch]
Edwd Barton	1	C	
Mr Edmd Clarke			4
Hen Flackham	<1>0		1
Widd Whithead	<1>0		1
Jo Over sen & jun			2
Amy Tarsey	1	C	
Geo Benson			1
Wm Ayres			1
Rich Williams			1
Andrew Pedley			1
Rich Cox			1
Nick Jolly	<1>2	C	
Rich Over			2
Wm Chitham	1	C	
James Over			2
Hen Smith	1	C	
Math Over			4
Rich Fleckham	1	C	
Robt Turner	1	C	
James Over			2
Jo Harding			1
Rich Pedley			1
Tho Jackson			1
Hen Benson			2
Han Smart			2
Cottage emptie	2	C	
David Ryland			2
Rich Russell			2
Jo Harwood with a forge			2
Samll Benson			1
Ann Tarsey	1	C	
Tho Nickalls	1	C	
Cottage emptie	1	C	
Jos Turner	1	C	
Wm Drewrey	1	C	
Wm Busswell	1	C	
Jo Mann	1	C	
Jos Turner	1	C	
Margr Gilly	1	C	
James Scotton	1	C	
Hen Mann	1	C	
John Mawson	1	C	
			37

Veuied by:
Warbt Hull collector
Zeph Binley constable

	[NC]	[Ch]
[f. 10]		
Birdingbury [par]		
Charles Leigh esq		19
Mr Cookes rector		4
Wm Bayes		2
Hen Harbert		1
Tho Reeve		2
Hen Underwood		1
Jo Harbert with an oven		3
Geo Cooke		5
Marke Abbott		1
Hen Jeffcott		2
Tho Browne		2
Nath Worrall		1
Tho Morgan		1
Hen Handes		1
Wm Miller		2
Jo Botson		1
Tho Willmills with a forge		2
Jo Neale		1
Jo Cooke		3
Eliz Smith		1
Benj Chapman		1
Edwd Eyers Jo Hudson	1 C	
Jo Johnson Sybell Deny	1 C	
Jo Elmes	1 C	
Ann Chitham	1 C	
Ann Russell	1 C	
Joane Gibbs	1 C	
In Marton Parrish		
Wm Kingerley	1 C	
Wm Satchwell	1 C	
Nick Masters	1 C	
Joane Clarke	1 C	
Edwd Foster	1 C	
Rich Tomson	1 C	
Jo Tayler	1 C	
Jo Satchwell	1 C	
		056

Veiued by:
Warbt Hull collector
Tho Browne constable

	[NC]	[Ch]
[f. 10v]		
Marton [par]		
Mr Wm Smith vicker		3
Mr Tho Walter		5
Mr Edwd Walter		5
Tho Bennett		3
A cottage emptie	1	
Rich Goode		2
Jo Borsley		5
Mr Edwd Walter empte		2
Widd Sibley		3
Jo Radburne		1
Robt Little		1
Jo Byton		1
Tho Goode		2
Rich Warde sen		1
Widd Borseley		2
Elias Walter gent		3
Wm Wootton		1
Robt Jeffes		2
Jo Jeffes		1
Wm Jefcott		2
Wm Goode		1
Wm Faulke		2
Rich Scotton	1 C	
Ann Hawes	1 C	
Edwd Warde	1 C	
Rich Warde	1 C	
Jo Jeffes	1 C	
Ann Rollesson	1 C	
Widd Evans	1 C	
Abig Rattnett	1 C	
Hen Ash	1 C	
Hen Andrewes	1 C	
Rich Wright	1 C	
Tho Mathews with a forge		2
Widd Robbinson	1 C	
Tho Ward	1 C	
Eliz Harris	1 C	
Jo Scotton	1 C	
Jo Morris	1 C	
Widd Garlick	1 C	
Ann Ash	1 C	
Rich Clarke		1
		51

	[NC]	[Ch]
Veuied by:		
Warbert Hull collector		
Tho Little constable		

[f. 11]

Ethorpe

[Eathorpe in Wappenbury par]

	[NC]	[Ch]
Mr Jo Westley		9
Mr Jo Allcott		7
Mr Rich Roggers		4
Rich Cosley	1 C	
Tho Steane gent		2
Ann Griffin		2
Nick Benson		1
Rob Stoney		1
Rich Hindes		1
Wm Atwood	1 C	
Jo Stiffe	1 C	
Tho Fanlowes	1 C	
Wm Milles		1
Rich Batcheller		1
Jo Bissell with a forge		<1>2
Widd Gibbs	1 C	
Wm Green	1 C	
Widd Westley	1 C	
Tho Letts	1 C	
Wm Darby	1 C	
Tho Mix	1 C	
Goodman Jorden	1 C	
Edwd Steane		1
		32

Veuied by:
Warbt Hull collector
Robt Stoney constable

Wappenbury [par]

	[NC]	[Ch]
Mr Tho Cussheth		6
Mr Tho Irland in 2 houses		[*2,5*[1]] 7
Widd Handey		2
Hen Banbury		2
Wm Ebrall		2
Jo Haw		2
Rich Hewet	1 C	
Elinor Parker		1
Tho Kellum		2
Wm Kyte		1
Edwd Wimbleton & Jo Handes		2
Wid Spencer	1 C	
Tho Andrews	1 C	
		27

Veuied by:
Warbt Hull collector
Tho Kellum

[f. 11v]

More of Wappenbury

	[NC]	[Ch]
Tho Harman	1 C	
Jo Steele	1 C	
Wm Kinge	1 C	
Step Rawbone	1 C	
Wm Tayler	1 C	

Weston Subter Weathley

[Weston under Wetherley par]

	[NC]	[Ch]
Mrs Morggan widd		20
Jo Bissell with a forge		2
Mr Mulliner		2
Widd Ebrall	1 C	
The vickeridge house		3
Jo Roe		2
Tho Maine		2
Tho Hayward		1
Eliz Mayne & Alice Murcott } emptie		2
Rich Chaplin	1 C	
Tho Fell	1 C	
Kath Corbett	1 C	
Tho Tobeard		3
Robt Shaw		1
Danll Maine		2
Jos Cornborough with 1 oven		3
Jo Fauster	1 C	
Samll Manning		4
Tho Whitheade		2

1 WCRO, QS11/44 (1673).

	[NC]		[Ch]
Rob Gibbard			3
Sir Wm Curtyne emptie			1
Tho Gumbole	1	C	
Wm Shreade	1	C	
			53

Veuied by:
Warbt Hull collector
Tho Whitheade constable

[f. 12]

Huningham [Hunningham par]

	[NC]		[Ch]
Tho Cox sen & jun			3
Tho Satchwell sen			1
Tho Satchwell jun	1	C	
Widd Amplett			1
Jo Barnard			3
Jo Symonds	1	C	
Jo Odell			1
Widd Tayler	<1>2	C	
Jo Draper	1	C	
Wm Ayres			1
Widd Pratt			2
Wm Adkins			2
Jo Adkins	1		
Jo Maine			2
Hen Jeffrey			1
Tho Tayler			3
Widd Compton			1
Abra Gascoyne	1		
Tho Birde			1
Tho Terrall with a forge			3
Widd Bovey			2
Hen Marson			1
Joseph Vennors gent			10
Widd Westley	1		
Tho Barnes	1		
Sus Lee	1		
Jo Perkins	1		
Sus Russell	1		
Tho Dolton	1		
			38

Veuied by:
Warbt Hull collector
Tho Birde constable

[f. 12v]

Itchington Longa et Bascott
[Long Itchington par]

	[NC]		[Ch]
Jo Overton			2
Rich Kendrick			1
Jo Yeates alias Overton	1	C	
Robt Raynbowe			<1>3
Jo Bromidge			1
Edwd Garland			1
Robt Cleaver			2
Tho Yeates	1	C	
Mrs Bird widd			4
Nath Overton			1
Tho Webb			1
Edwd Goode			2
Tho Tomson	1	C	
Geo Mills	1	C	
Robt Tomson	1	C	
James Alsoppe			1
Widd Smith	1	C	
Tho Wilson	1	C	
Samll Pratt			1
Wm Watts			5
Ralph Pratt			1
Edwd Skidmore	1	C	
Roger Overton	1	C	
Widd Deire	1	C	
Widd Roberts			1
Widd Furloe	1	C	
Edwd Boulton	1	C	
Nath Duglas	1	C	
Hen Lynes alias Reade			1
Jo Vickers	1	C	
Tho Baker			2
Tho Waring	1	C	
Hen Bodington	1	C	
Jo Hanslopp	1	C	
Tho Wigley	1	C	
Tho Banbury			<1>2
Rich Raynboe			1
Mr Roe minister			3

[f. 13]

	[NC]		[Ch]
Jo Lynes alias Reade			2
Samll Cleaver			4

	[NC]		[Ch]
Mr Tho Bossworth			4
Math Masson			2
Jo Mathews with a forge			3
Tho Roadknight			1
Wm Roadknight			1
Geo Butler	1	C	
Robt Garrett			3
Tho Roberts jun	1	C	
Tho Fowler	1	C	
Jo Dewes	1	C	
Nath Reeve			2
Tho Harley			1
Jo Vickers			1
Jo Noone			1
James Johnson			2
Martin Knight			2
Robt Garrett			2
Edwd Goode sen			1
Widd Baker	1	C	
Wm Watts emptie			1
Mary Cox	1	C	
Wm Wilson sen	1	C	
Wm Wilson jun	1	C	
Wm Muston			1
Widd Coyne	1	C	
Tho Lynes alias Reade	1	C	
Tho Morrell	1	C	
Eliz Heacock	1	C	
Edward Allin	1	C	
Ann Terrall	1	C	
Rob Summers	1	C	
James Isaacke	1	C	
Jo Allin	1	C	
Robt Carter	1	C	
Alice Middleton	1	C	
Clemt & Margt Smith	1	C	
Tho Wigley sen	1	C	

[f. 13v]

Bascott et Stonythorpe in Itchington

[Bascote and Stoney Thorpe in Long Itchington par]

[***Stoney Thorpe***[1]]

	[NC]		[Ch]
Mr Ambross Holbech			10
The mill			1

[***Bascote***[2]]

	[NC]		[Ch]
Nath Cox			8
James Tidman			1
Tho Frankton			2
Jo Hobbey			1
Jo Budd			2
Widd Heycock			1
Jos Hobley			1
Geo Jeffes			2
Tho Gibbons			1
Rich Hobley			2
An emptie house Bankes landlord			1
Hen Harper			1
Jo Boulton			2
Robt Eales	1		
Rich Overton			3
Arthr Mosley			1
Jo Fyfeild			1
Widd Cooke	1	C	
Tho Wright	1	C	
Robt Barnecle	1	C	
Rich Renall	1	C	
Edwd Renalls	1	C	
Rich Marshall	1	C	
Eliz Baker	1	C	
Phill Hopkins	1	C	
Eliz Wells	1	C	
			111

Veuied by:
Warbt Hull collector
Geo Jeffes constable

[1] TNA, E179/259/9 (1666).
[2] TNA, E179/259/9 (1666).

	[NC]	[Ch]
[f. 14]		
Itchington Episcopall		
[Bishops Itchington par]		
Tho Collins		15
Jo Tarver		1
Wm Browne		1
Mr Tho Kings		6
Nath Shrewsbury	1 C	
Mr Jo Beale		3
Tho Yeomans		1
Mr Hunt vicker		5
Tho Rounde		1
John Slacker	1 C	
Jo Cornish	1 C	
Samll <Cornish>Tomson		2
Jo Wright		1
Widd Penn	1 C	
Rich Penn	1 C	
Rich Tomkins		1
Rich Smith	1 C	
Wm Tomkins		3
Tho Tomkins		2
Rich Watts		1
Wm Webb		2
Geo Pearson		1
Rob Harris emptie		1
Math Randle with a forge	2 C	
Wm Wiggin		2
Rich Worrall	2 C	
Jos Lewis		1
Tho Anesley		1
Danll Smith		1
Hen Pettifer	1 C	
Edwd Pearson	1 C	
Math Cookes		1
Mrs Dyana Avery		6
Mr Avery emptie		<1>2
Jo Worrall		2
Wm Poole jun		1
Math Poole		2
Wm Robinson	1 C	
Wm Watts	1 C	
[f. 14v]		
Tho Smith jun	1 C	
Rich Preist		1
Tho Smith sen		2
Mr Edwd Tomkins		3
Widd Tomkins		1
Sus Pettifer	1 C	
Widd Trippas	1 C	
Anth Robbinson		1
Wm Mearse		1
Jo Hixson		2
Robt Rowsham	1 C	
Jo Winkley		1
Wm Varnum	1 C	
Tho Woodfall	1 C	
Joyles Marshall		3
Robt Harris		1
Tho Coales	1 C	
		82

Veiued by:
Warbt Hull collector
Tho Tomkins constable

	[NC]	[Ch]
Ladbrooke [Ladbroke par]		
Rich Gill		3
Mr Robt Edmunds		2
Mr Wm Cooper		3
Mr Smith emptie		2
Jo Harwood		1
Widd Hancox		1
Jo Rawbone		1
Ann Wasington		1
Barth Kinge		1
Jo Oldfeild		1
Jo Hancox		1
Tho Smallbone		3
Wm Avery		1
Sir Wm Palmer emptie		2
Mr Smith rector		6
Hen Spraggott		1
Sir Wm Palmer in the farme		5
[f. 15]		
Mr James Graunte		5
The ould farme		1
Edwd Smalbone		1
Edwd Harwood	1 C	

	[NC]	[Ch]
Rich Highorne		1
Robt Rascall		2
Widd Puncker		2
Abbrah Wride		2
Wm Ward		2
Wm Kenning		3
Rich Staunton		2
Hen Stickley	1 C	
Nick Squires		1
Tho Chebsey		3
Jo Kench		3
Wm Gibbons	1 C	
Robt Harwood		1
Jo James sen	1 C	
Samll Maine	1 C	
Jo Kenning		1
Margt Tayler	1 C	
Ephrim Mumford	1 C	
Cottage emptie	1 C	
Robt Hudson	1 C	
Margt Lucas	1 C	
Peettr & Tho Croper	1 C	
Anth Lane		1
Rich Hurdie	1 C	
Tho Belcher	1 C	
Tho Pearson	1 C	
Eliz Dixson	1 C	
Wm Etkins	1 C	
Robt Lucas	1 C	
Eliz Betts	1 C	
Antho Rascold	1 C	
Jo & Wm Driver	1 C	

	[NC]	[Ch]
Mr Tho Hewett		3
		69

Veiued by:
Warbt Hull collector
Wm Cooper constable

[f. 15v]

Hodnell: Ascott, Watergall, Radburne

[***Hodnell***[1] ex par with Fenny Compton par[2]]

	[NC]	[Ch]
Sarah Nix		3
Rich Kinge		2

[***Chapel Ascote***[3] ex par with Napton par[4]]

	[NC]	[Ch]
Tobias Leeke		2

[***Watergall***[5] ex par with Fenny Compton par[6]]

	[NC]	[Ch]
Tho Watson		7

[***Radbourn***[7]]

[Radbourne ex par with Napton par[8]]

	[NC]	[Ch]
Symon Goode		3
Mr Jo Colburne		2
Rich Gillman	1 C	

Shuckbrugh Superior

[Upper Shuckburgh par]

	[NC]	[Ch]
Robt Harvey esq		22
Anth Bagley		1
Tho Gent		1
Wm Hodge		1

1 WCRO, QS11/44 (1673).
2 Hodnell and Watergall were officially attached to Fenny Compton parish by the archbishop of Canterbury in the 1640s and subsequently rated with it (*Quarter Sessions*, ii, p. 194; vii, pp. 150, 160, 209). Hodnell included Wills Pastures, which was uninhabited and was sometimes called Lower Hodnell (Youngs, *Guide*, ii, pp. 446, 456).
3 WCRO, QS11/44 (1673).
4 Chapel Ascote was rated towards the poor of Napton parish in 1651 (*Quarter Sessions*, iii, p. 50).
5 TNA, E179/259/10 (1665).
6 Watergall was attached to, and rated with, Fenny Compton parish from the 1640s onwards (see note 2 above).
7 TNA, E179/259/10 (1665).
8 Upper and Lower Radbourne were rated towards the poor of Napton (*Quarter Sessions*, iii, p. 50). They were not identified separately in any hearth tax return after 1663, when William Goode was recorded with two hearths in Upper Radbourne and Ezekiell Pargitor with three in Lower Radbourne (WCRO, QS11/1).

Shuckbrugh Infferior
[more of Upper Shuckburgh par[1]]

	[NC]	[Ch]
Samll Cleaver		1
Tho Feild		1
Rich Steele		1
Cottage emptie	1 C	
Robt Stockley		1
Rich Forde		1
Widd Worth	1 C	
Mart Brookley	1 C	
Samll Cleaver emptie		1
Jo Benson		1
Widd Green	1 C	
Widd Hodge	1 C	
Jo Spicer	1 C	
John Glenn	1 C	
Tho Sheasbey	1 C	
		51

Veiued by:
Warberton Hull collector
Samll Cleaver constable

[WCRO, QS11/18]
[f. 1]
The County of Warwick
Knightloe [Knightlow] **Hundred**
Kennellworth Devission
[Kenilworth Division]
1670
Exchequer Roles
[written by Warberton Hull]
[f. 1v: blank]
[f. 2]
Ashoe [Ashow par]

	[NC]	[Ch]
Mosses Robinson }		1
Tho Jecocke }		2
Tho Clarke		1
Tho Gibbs		1
Tho Keen		1
Wm Weale		3
Widd Timm		1
Lau Clarke		1
Jo Gibbs		2
Jo Eborne		3
Mr Allestrey clark		3
Jo Cole		1
Rich Hobday		2
Jo Jecocke		2
Tho Smith		1
Wm Hanscott		1
Rich Pratt		1
Tho Jeacock emptie		2
Kath Dyto	1	
Widd Hollioake	1	
Widd Beards	1	
Mary Blasson	1	
Widd Elbancke	1	
		29

Veiued by:
Warbt Hull collector
Tho Gibbs constable

[f. 2v]
Stoleigh [Stoneleigh par]

	[NC]	[Ch]
Tho Lord Leigh		70
His emptie house		9
Mr[s] Robinson widd		3
Widd Buckerfeild		1
Edwd Phillipps		2
Jo Hudson		1
Rich Grisould		1
Wm Kingston		1
Ann Hewett		1
Widd Smith with an oven		2
Eliz Wheeller		1
Robt Faulkner		2
Mr Agbrowe clark		4
Tho Alliott }		1
Patience Elliott widd }	1 C	
Edwd Hall with a forge		2
Geo Cross		2

[1] This heading for Lower Shuckburgh is a mistake: all these entries were in Upper Shuckburgh (see p. 10 above and *VCH*, vi, p. 215).

	[NC]		[Ch]
Rich Flavell			1
Edwd Sturton			1
Hen Phillipps			3
Wm Alliott			1
Tho Garratt			2
Rich Tim			1
Edwd Adington			1
Widd Mayo			3
Geo Whitmore			1
Christpher Brookes			3
Tho Jarvise			2
Widd Garvice	1	C	
Tho Garnett	1	C	
Tho Usley	1	C	
Rich Whitheade	1	C	
Edwd Godard			1
Tenn almes houses	10		
Hump Dixson	1	C	
Fran Whitmore			1
Jo Evans	1	C	
Tho Ladbrooke	1	C	
Jo Clarridge	1	C	
Jo Lockwood	1	C	
Jo Jordane	1	C	
Wm Worth	1	C	
			124

[f. 3]

Flechamstead in Stonl Par

[Fletchamstead]

	[NC]		[Ch]
The mannor house			22[1]
[*William Meighs*[2] *5*]			
[*Mr Robt Crafts* *7*]			
[*Griffin Lewis* *5*]			
[*Rich Smith* *2*]			
[*The Lord Leigh* *3*]			
Rich Kimberley	2		
Mrs Oxwick			7
Mr Jo Tayler			10
Rich Barrs			2
Rob Jessey			1
Jo Barres			1
Hugh Hassell			1
Eliz Barnecle			3
Tho Slye			1
Wm Lynes			1
Samll Hydon			1
Rob Salmon			1
Ursu Slye	1	C	
Fran Jacey	1	C	
Rich Cannon			1
Mary Smith	1	C	
Jo Turner	1	C	
Eliz Benson	1	C	
<…>Thomas Billers	1	C	
Two emptie cott[age]s	2		
Eusta Salmon			1
Rich Nightingale			1
Emptie cottage	1		
Rich Boulte			2
Margt Price			1

Cryfeild

[Cryfield in Stoneleigh par]

	[NC]		[Ch]
Jo Hartley gent			4
Rob Scott	1	C	
Wm Dale			3
Jo Hartley for Milborn grange			4

Starton

[Stareton in Stoneleigh par]

	[NC]		[Ch]
Tho Mallin			2
Wm Castle			1
Widd Barber			1
Jo Gibbs			1
Hump How			2
Wm Whitmore			1
Tho Middleton			2
Wm Hurlbert			3
Tho Casmore			2

1 Styles, 'Hearth tax', p. xliii, states incorrectly that this house was demolished in 1665. In 1666 it was recorded as 'Tho Flint esq and tenants 19' (TNA, E179/259/9).

2 Data inserted from TNA, E179/194/338 (1671). This badly damaged return recorded the manor house as sub-divided into these five households. It then had a total of 23 hearths, with Richard Smith's liability raised from two to three hearths.

	[NC]		[Ch]
Edwd Copland			1
Ann Lynes			1
Tho Russell			2
[f. 3v]			
Canley in Stonleigh Parrish			
Jos Symcox gent			6
Bazill Holbech			7
Sus Nickall			1
Steep Hanckhorne			3
Tho Gibbs			2
Mr Math Stacey			2
Tho Bagshaw			1
Jo Smarte			1
Edwd Lea			1
Tho Brookes			1
Rich Tym			1
<Tho>Wm Brookes			1
Hen Godard	1	C	
James Godard	1	C	
Hurst [in Stoneleigh par]			
Zach Groves			3
Jo Alliott			2
Jo Williams			3
Tho Craftes			3
Jo Lockington			1
Jo Cooke			1
Jo Smarte			2
Edwd Lee			1
Peettr Mills with a forge			2
Rob Adams			1
Fran James			1
Edwd Biddle			1
Finham [in Stoneleigh par]			
Tho Stringfeilde			1
Tho Faulkner			2
Step Cross	1	C	
Mr Jo Holbech			8
Nath Bond	1	C	
Jo Manns			1
Jo Driver	1	C	
Tho Cross	1	C	
Mr Jo Downes			6
Gregr Arnoll			2
Widd Driver			1

	[NC]		[Ch]
Edwd Perkins			1
Hill [in Stoneleigh par]			
Rich Snell			4
Tho Whitmore			1
Jo Gamball			2
Samll Mervell			2
Rich Russell			1
Tho Grissould			1
Hen Phillipps			1
Tho Grissould jun			1
Wm Driver	1	C	
			170

Veuied by:
Warbt Hull collector
Hen Phillipps constable

	[NC]		[Ch]
[f. 4]			
Bubbinhull [Bubbenhall par]			
Gelly Adkins			1
Wm Sherrington			2
Wm Priste			2
Hen Adkins			2
Rich Louke			3
Mrs Draper widd			5
Jo Lapworth			1
Tho Robinson			3
Ann Roberts			2
Danll Adkins			2
Hen Lapworth			2
Jo Lapworth			4
The vickeridge			2
Tho & Jo Mudiman			2
Hen Snowe			1
Widd Wigson			1
Wm Boughton esq			5
Rich Powers			2
Wm Edwards			1
Widd Green	1	C	
Jo Draper			4
Leo Sherrington			3
Geo Foscett	1	C	
Jo Busbey	1	C	
Rich Hands			1
Edwd Norton	1	C	

	[NC]	[Ch]
Wm Benson	1 C	
Tho Norton		1
Jo Hall	1	
Tho Geeys	1	
Hugh Danporte	1	
Tho Pilkington	1	
Tho Mathew	1	
Jo Hinson	1	
Jo Lapworth sen	1	
		52

Veiued by:
Warbt Hull collector
Leo Sherrington constable

[f. 4v]

Bagington [Baginton par]

	[NC]	[Ch]
Sir Wm Bromley kt of the Bath		13
Luke Webster		2
Jo Walton		1
Tho Blaxley		2
Jo Bass		4
Mrs Abell widd		8
Mr Tho Lane		6
Wm Treen		2
Wm Wootton	1 C	
Ralph Hassell	1 C	
Bonaventure Dafforne		3
Tho Wilkinson		<2>3
Rich Russell		<3>2
Wm Green		1
Wm Hewcombe }		2
Wm Parker }		1
Tho Orton		1
Mr Cross rector		4
Wm Shaw		2
Rich Walker		3
Samll Wride		2
Is Carter		1
Step Sturton		1
Tho Dykes		1
Tho Stringer		1
Kath Wilkinson		1
Widd Adkins }	1 C	
Jud Adkins }	1 C	

	[NC]	[Ch]
Rob Barber	1 C	
Wm Sturton		1
Widd Toones	1 C	
Eliz Gelly	1 C	
Goody Gibbs	1 C	
Tho Gibbs		1
Fran Nickalls	1 C	
		67
		[69]

Veiued by:
Warbt Hull collector
Jo Walton constable

Cubbington [par]

	[NC]	[Ch]
Jo Ladbrooke		3
Tho Berry		1
Ralph Page		1
Wm Arnall	1 C	
Wm Garlick		2
Bennett Twitty sen		1
Nick Boddington		4
Nick Bonde		1
Robt Taft		1
Wm Fell jun		1
Hump Stratford jun		1
Emptie cott[age]	1 C	
Hen Stratforde	1 C	

[f. 5]

	[NC]	[Ch]
Hump Stratford sen with a forge		2
Jo Cox		2
Jo Salmond		1
Tho Jecock		1
Widd Welton		<1>2
Tho Parssons		5
Geo Warner		4
Wm Onley		1
Jo Rennalls		1
Tho Wootton		1
Widd Hodgkins		1
Tho West		1
Tho Russell sen		3
Tho Russell jun		3
Jo Murcott gent		3

	[NC]	[Ch]
Jo Lapworth jun	1	
Nick Wigg		3
Jo Hindes		5
Wm Fell sen		1
Rich Westley		3
Mr Andrew Murcott		5
Mr Harpur vicker		3
Tho Edwards		1
Tho Rouney		1
Tho Kinge with an oven		<1>2
Martin Garner		1
Mrs Albeny Grisould widd		8
Phillipp Wootton		2
Wm Love with a forge	2 C	
Widd Clarke	1 C	
Geo Flower	1 C	
Alex Welton	1 C	
Wm Roe	1 C	
Jo Dickens	1 C	
Emptie cottage	1 C	
Widd Clarke	1 C	
Alice Borton	1 C	
Rich <…>Handes	1 C	
Jo <Lapworth>Ladbrook jun	1 C	
Am Everton	1 C	
Abrah Newbrey	1 C	
Edwd Walker	1 C	
Hen Adkins	1 C	
Abrah Lapworth	1 C	
Alice Green	1 C	
Tho Watson	1 C	
Geo Stratforde	1 C	
Eliz Wright	1 C	
Widd Lapworth	1 C	
Widd Green	1 C	
Jo Lapworth sen	1 C	
Jos Morrell	1 C	
Rich Dickins	1 C	
Wm Winkell	1 C	
		80
		[82]

Veuied by:
Warbt Hull collector
Tho Parsons constable

[f. 5v]

Milverton [par]

	[NC]	[Ch]
Edmundcote house		10
Tho Middleton		2
Jo Boddington		4
James Millington		1
Jo Ladbrooke		6
Jo Clarke		1
Isa Buyfoye		3
Rich Gibbs		1
Ruth Tompson		1
Tho Masters		2
Widd Rowney 2 houses		2
Jo Newton		1
Jo Rowney		2
Wm Warde		3
Widd Steele	1 C	
Widd Hodgkins		1
Wm Webb		1
Jo Cross		1
Geo Sparkes		1
Hen Townsend		1
Jo Morrill		1
Anth Garrett		1
Tho Ward a forge		1
Tho Keen	1 C	
Hen Keen	1 C	
Mary Morrell	1 C	
Jo Barton	1 C	
Math Keen	1 C	
		47

Veuied by:
Warbt Hull collector
Geo Sparkes constable

Lillington [par]

	[NC]	[Ch]
Mr Eedes clark		2
Allex Dawkes		2
Tho Eborne		2
Eliz Nickalls		2
Fran Robins		2
Abrah Eborne		2
Jo Robins		2
Jo Arnall		2

	[NC]		[Ch]
Wm Harding			2
Ruth Geaydon			1
Widd Browne			1
Jo Wells jun			1
Jo Wells sen	1	C	
Hen Buckerfeild			1
Rich Boseley			2
Widd Suffolke			1
John Browne			1
[f. 6]			
Geo Warner			<2>1
Hump Nickalls			<1>2
Rich Hewett			1
Mrs Granger			1
Tho Clarke			1
Edwd Hudson	1	C	
Jo Joynes			1
Rich Prophett	1	C	
Widd Umbers	1	C	
Fran Pinchback	1	C	
Geo Newbrey	1	C	
Ann Julian	1	C	
Wm Rawbone	1	C	
Jo Boseley	1	C	
Rich Battrum	1	C	
Wm Bromidge	1	C	
Jo Chipman	1	C	
Tho Westley	1	C	
Tho Wilson	1	C	
Rich Pinchback	1	C	
Tho Witheford	1	C	
Tho Pinchbacke	1	C	
Nath Marston with a forge	2	C	
			33

Veiued by:
Warberton Hull collector
Rich Boseley constable

Leeke Wootton [Leek Wootton par]

	[NC]		[Ch]
Edwd Gilbert			1
Rich Gilbert	1	C	
Step Perry			1
Wm Raulins			1

	[NC]		[Ch]
Robt Davis sen			2
Widd Emmes	1	C	
Jo Dunton			1
Wm Smith with a forge			3
Tho Raulins			1
Rich Rawlins			1
Jo Boddington			1
Hen Saunders			1
Ann Collice			1
Hen Gupwell			1
Tho Sadler			1
Step Perry			3
Tho Dale			1
Tho Smith			1
Jo Hanckhorne			1
[f. 6v]			
Wm Smith & Ann Cooper			2
Widd Bird			1
Jo Tayler			1
Robt Smith with a forge			2
Jo Smith			2
Widd Phillipps			1
Widd Masters			1
Rob Smith masson			1
Mr Chamberlaine clark			5
Mrs Holbech at the grange			6
Widd Reading	1	C	
Sus Ellis	1	C	
Tho Baker	1	C	
Rich Dale	1	C	
Rich Phillipps	1	C	
Hugh Boulton	1	C	
Robt Dale	1	C	
Jo Fox	1	C	
Hen James	1	C	
Widd Perry	1	C	
Jo Jeacock	1	C	
			44

Hill Wootton
[in Leek Wootton par]

	[NC]		[Ch]
Wm Beard			1
Widd Welton			1
Jo Eborne			2
Wm Randes			1

	[NC]	[Ch]
Wm Raulins		1
Jo Knibb		1
Fran Knibb		1
Jo Smith		1
Edwd Page		1
Nick Smith		1
Edwd Freeman		1

Woodcotts et Woodlouse
[Woodcote and Woodloes in Leek Wootton par]

	[NC]	[Ch]
Jo Purden		2
Emptie house	1	
Rob Davis		2
Tim Basford		1
Mrs Chamberlane		4
Tho Merriden		1
		22

[***Guys Cliffe***[1]]
[*emptie Mr Somervile landlord*[2] *11*]

Veuied by:
Warberton Hull collector
Fran Knibb constable

[f. 7]
Lemington Pryors
[Leamington Priors par]

	[NC]	[Ch]
Geo Gumley		1
Rich Sharpless		1
Tho Nasbey 2 houses		3
Wm Cartwright sen		1
Edwd Rawbone		1
Tarry Wills		3
Jo Smith jun	1 C	
Alice Anderton	1 C	
Jo Burhill	1 C	
Jo Overton	2 C	
Tim Ellis	1 C	
Geo Hall with an oven		4
Wm Cartwright jun		2
Jo Only gent		1
Robt Laurence		1
Mich Sumners		1
Tho Pratt		1
Wm Boddington		1
Robt Johnson	1 C	
Rich Cartwright		1
Jo Ward		1
Step Sumners		1
Mr Edwd Farr rector }		2
Widd Jackson }		
Jo Grissould	1 C	
Jo Gardner	1 C	
Jo Swifte	1 C	
Rich Only gent		4
Jo Lee gent		4
Tho Cartwright		2
Tho Savidge gent		5
Widd Bates		1
Samll Clarke gent		1
Wm Grissould with a forge		2
Geo Collins	1 C	
Jane Hanckhorne	1 C	
Edwd Rawbone		3
Mr Edwd Wills		5
Wm Only		1
Geo Ebron		3
Eliz Sumners	1 C	
Rob Middleton		1
Walter Rose	1 C	
Wm Bingham	1 C	
Wm Purden		1
Rich Smith	1 C	
Blaunch Hurst	1 C	

[f. 7v]

	[NC]	[Ch]
Rich Walker	1 C	
Jo Anderton	1 C	
Wm Stoney	1 C	
Ann Blythe	1 C	
Widd Meades	1 C	
Wm Willinges	1 C	
Jud Maunton	1 C	

[1] Guys Cliffe was extra parochial, but Guys mill nearby lay in Leek Wootton parish (*VCH*, viii, pp. 442–3, 534).
[2] Data inserted from WCRO, QS11/30 (1673).

	[NC]		[Ch]
Widd Jackett	1	C	
Rich Penn	1	C	
			57
			[59]

Veiued by:
Warberton Hull collector
Tary Wills constable

Ufton [par]

	[NC]		[Ch]
Jo Westley			1
Wm Wilson			2
Tho Wilkins			2
Wm Pratt			2
Wm Noone			1
Jo Pratt			1
Geo Colburne gent			3
Jobe Radford			2
Wm Latimer			2
Widd Pratt			2
Widd Garrett	2	C	
Wm Heycock			1
Rich Judd			2
Wm Wills			1
Rich Mayo			1
Jo Jeacock with a forge	2		
Jobe Franklon			1
Widd Tayler			4
Widd Bradley			1
An emptie house			1
Tho Turner			3
Tho Tew			2
Rich Basley			2
Tho Hopkins			1
Widd Hodgkins	1		
Widd Copland	1		
Tho Rainbowe	1		
Widd Colman	1		
Mary Lee	1		
Tho Miller	1		
Jo Bates	1		
Samll Edgerton	1		
			38

Veiued by:
Warberton Hull collector
Wm Noone c[onstable]

[f. 8]

Harberbury [Harbury par]

	[NC]		[Ch]
Widd Mann			1
Tho Mann	1	C	
Rich Tayler			1
Walter Ward			1
Phillipp Morgan			1
Hugh Dunckley			1
Geo Jornes	1	C	
Wm Penn & Mrs Cleaves			3
Tho Mann masson			3
Jo Jeacocke			1
Wm Gibbs			1
Rich Copland			1
Anth Spragott			2
Tho Mills			1
Tho Danford			1
Tho Barnecle			1
Mrs Cookes widd			4
Jo Gumley			1
Wm Reading			1
Hen Harley			1
Rich Jackson			1
Rich Sabill			1
Tho Ivan chandler	1	C	
Mr Cooke claricus [clerk]			2
Edwd Mills			2
Jo Milloway jun			2
Tho Eborne			2
Rich Biddle			3
Jo Dickins			1
Robt Hodges			1
Wm Lucas jun			1
Samll Calloway			1
Eliz Blyth	1		
Jo Childs			1
James Hampe			1
Jo Odell			1
Mr Samll Hyott			2
Hen Neale			1
Rob Warde			2
Tho Porter			1
Jo Stickley			1
Benj Turvell			1
Jo Rennall			1

	[NC]	[Ch]
Tho Sabill		2
Edwd Watts		1
Samll Radford		2
Anth Mayo		1
[f. 8v]		
Jo Farmon		1
Mr Tho Green		4
Margt Wright		1
Wm Faulkes		1
Jo Coles		1
Mrs Christ Cookes widd		5
Wm Farmon sen		1
Widd Bonde		1
Widd Compton		1
Ralph & Jo Dafforn	2 C	
Rich Gibbs		1
Ann Haxford		1
Jos Evans		2
Rich Tomkins		2
Tho Goodin		1
Jo Stonleigh		1
Hen Shuckbrough esq		8
Jo Jeffes		1
Tho Copland		1
Robt Evons		1
Geo Mills		1
Edwd Pratt		1
Wm Harbert		1
Mr Rob Archer		3
Tho Garlicke		1
Widd Beasley	1 C	
Jo Mills		4
James Hampe with a forge		2
Rich Hoofe	1 C	
Jo Cooper		1
Wm Coles		1
Rob Coles		1
Wm Warde		1
Edwd Mann		3
Widd Russell		1
Wm Walker		1
Rich Neale		2
Jo Woodfall		1
Samll Radford		2

	[NC]	[Ch]
Jo Sproson		1
Widd Wilson	1 C	<1>
Robt Penn		1
Tho Cox		1
Jo Wincott		1
Widd Powers		1
Edwd Enocke		1
[f. 9]		
Wm Walker		1
Tho Maunton	1 C	
Wm Hyerns		1
Jos Cutty	1 C	
Widd Mayoe	1 C	
Tho Crabden	1 C	
Eliz Ward		1
Jo Palmer		1
Jo Petty	1 C	
Tho Barnes	1 C	
A cottage emptie	1 C	
Hen Chebsey		1
Tho Knibb	1 C	
Rich Roe	1 C	
Widd Lucas	1 C	
Mary Wincott	1 C	
Widd Freeman	1 C	
Samll Tidmouse	1 C	
Jo Lapworth	1 C	
Wm Freeman	1 C	
Geo Whitheads	1 C	
Wm Hanson	1 C	
Widd Meacocke	1 C	
Jo Spragott	1 C	
Widd Heywood	1 C	
		134

Veuied by:
Warberton Hull collector
Benj Turvell constable

Whitnash [par]

Mr Hen Chamberlaine	5
Tho Evans	5
Tym Jackson	5
Widd Mollrey	3
Wm Boddington	1

	[NC]		[Ch]
Wm Penn			2
Jo Everton			1
Widd Everton			1
Tho Stoakes			1
Mary Boddington			1
Robt Bodding			2
Jo Freeman jun			2
Jo Freeman sen			1
Tym Cornbrough			1
Job Everton			1
Mr Tho Chamberlane			2
Mr Kent emptie			3
[f. 9v]			
Abig Everton widd			1
David Buffrey			1
Tho & Eliz Bodington			2
Clemt Comebey			2
Rich Summers	1	C	
James Everton	1	C	
Tho Savidge	1	C	
Jos Wright	1	C	
Hump Poultney			1
Martha Olliver	1	C	
Wm Monton			1
			45

Veuied by:
Warberton Hull collector
Tho Stoakes constable

Tachbrook Mollrey
[Tachbrook Mallory
in Bishops Tachbrook par]

	[NC]		[Ch]
Jo Rouse esq			14
Mr Trible clark			3
Jo Radburne			2
Rich Cookes			2
Edwd Reading			1
Wm Kaninge			1
			23

Veiued by:
Warberton [Hull] collector
Edwd Reading constable

Radford Symely
[Radford Semele par]

	[NC]		[Ch]
Fran Fisher esq			12
Mr Jo Barton clark			3
Rich Hixson			2
Tho Lewis			1
Wm Merrall			1
Gabrll Stonleigh	1	C	
Eliz Neale	1	C	
Danll Whitheade			2
Widd Smith & Sus Walton }			2
Ann Bicknall }			1
Widd Copland	1	C	
Jo Cooper	1	C	
Tho Davis			1
Jo Yardley			2
Jo Bicknall with a forge	2	C	
[f. 10]			
Tho Davis			1
Jo Whitheade sen 2 houses			2
Nath Cox			3
Fran Twicross			1
Jo Norton sen			1
Rich Marston			1
Tho Marston			1
Tho Faulkes			1
Widd Moulton	1	C	
Jo Adkins			2
Jo Garner			1
Wm Cox			1
Tho Clarke			1
Robt Whitheade			2
Widd Carter	1	C	
Widd Green	1	C	
Tho Adkins			3
Jo Norton			1
Jo Whithead jun			2
Tho Badcock			1
Jo Boddington			2
Widd Walton			1
Robt Copland			1
Wm Wells	1	C	
Jos Bennett	1	C	
Hen Norton			2

	[NC]	[Ch]
Widd Jeacocke		2
Jo Goode		1
Hen Eaton		1
Jo Jeacocke		1
J Bukley gent		5
Josi Townsend gent		3
Tho Whitheade		1
Jo Smith		2
Edwd Phelpes		1
Mosses Badcocke		1
Jo Clarkson	1 C	
Tho Langley	1 C	
		76

Veuied by:
Warbt Hull collector
Tho Faulkes constable

[f. 10v]

Offchurch [par]

	[NC]	[Ch]
Sir Jo Knightley		14
Edwd Heyley		2
Tho Hope	1 C	
Robt Russell emptie	1 C	
Hen Jeacocke	1 C	
Edwd Hands		1
Widd Gregory		1
Emptie cottage	1 C	
Mr Palmer minister		3
Widd Page	1 C	
Alice Gibbs	1 C	
Wm Brobson		1
Jo Garner emptie	1 C	
Wm Handes		1
Tho Rawbone		1
Emptie cottage	1 C	
Arthur Lane	1 C	
Jo Russell	1 C	
Tho West		1
Wm Hayles		1
Tho Page		1
Jo Baker	1 C	
Widd Abbott		1
Mr Tho Lees		2
Jo Newton empte	1	
Rob Greenhill		1
Eliz Barthollomew		1
Wm Page		2
Eliz Cox	1 C	
Jo Wright	1 C	
Jo Fox		1
Rich Bradley		1
Edwd Arnall	1 C	
Fran Eborne	1 C	
Tho Luther	1 C	
Wm Russell	1 C	
Tho Horsman	1 C	
Jo Ratnell	1 C	
Widd Whatley	1 C	
Tho Barnett		2
		38

Veuied by:
Warbt Hull collector
Tho Rawbone constable

[f. 11]

Kennellworth the Augmentacon[1]
[Kenilworth Augmentation in Kenilworth par]

	[NC]	[Ch]
Robt Wells	2 C	
Wm Moore		1
Wm Button		1
Rich Burtonwood		2
Jo Reade		4
Tho Overton		1
Phill Cole		1
Robt Johnson		3
Joseph Drewry with an oven		6
Rich James		1
Vall Lee		1
Mr Wm Dunton		2
Mr Abell		6
Tho Avery		1
Jo Norton		3
Tho Whitmore	1 C	

1 Kenilworth parish was divided between two manors administered separately for the poor law. Augmentation was originally the Abbey manor and the Duchy (of Lancaster) the Castle manor.

	[NC]		[Ch]
Wm Glover	1	C	
Widd Moore	1	C	
Rich Heyfeild	1	C	
Rich Lee			1
Tho Boss	1	C	
Rogr Longdon	1	C	
Widd Middleton			1
Alice Fruterer	1	C	
Hen Smith	1	C	
Wm Mouncke			1
Tho Lee	1	C	
<Ge> Mrs Birde widd			1
Jo Lee	1	C	
Jo Wayle			1
Wm Smith			1
Wm Spencer			1
Wm Johnson			1
Is Banbury			1
Geo Salmon			1
Tho Cole			5
Widd Tapping	1	C	
Tho Chaplin	1	C	
Tho Lee			1
Widd Cox	2	C	
Tho Benson			4
Widd Dale			4
[f. 11v]			
Widd Wiggins	2	C	
Widd Gibbs downe	1	C	
Jo Ballard alias Bryan			1
Jo Norton empte	<2>0		2
Widd Roaden	2	C	
Ann Goffe	1	C	
Rogr Mills			1
Sarah Gibbs	1	C	
Wm Gardner with a forge			3
Edwd Heacocke			4
Mr Tho Mann			5
Mrs Phipps			6
Hen Bullock	1	C	
Wm Whitmore			1
Tho Sitch			1
Nath Winmill			1

	[NC]		[Ch]
Edwd Norton poore	1		
Rich Weale			1
Jenkins Jones			1
Emptie cottage	1		
Tho Lapworth			1
Jo Hodgkins empte	1		
Jo Featherston			2
Jo Yardley			1
Geo Clement			1
Jo Fox			1
Geo Salmon			4
Rich Bull			3
Nick Sly with an oven			3
Widd Yeates			1
Tho Wallis			2
Mrs Lee widd			3
Wm Wright			3
Hen Hearte			2
Mr Paulett			5
John Waites			1
Rich Sheepard			1
Anth Powers empte			2
Step Mather			1
Lewis Wright			1
Jo Burman			1
Rich Miller			1
[f. 12]			
Rich Greetham	1	C	
Jo Button			1
Dor Shackspeire	1	C	
Rich Hancox			1
Adrian Ayres			1
Wm Lee	1	C	
Wm Smith	1	C	
Edwd Longe			2
The vickeridge			2
Ann Slye			1
Wm Parker	1	C	
Samll Aires gent	<6>		6
Mr Rob Price			8
Rich Dorswood with a flax oven			3
Hen Robinson			6
Jo Averet			1
Wm Brookes			1

	[NC]		[Ch]
Lau Goss	1	C	
Wm Joyce			1
Eliz Clement	1	C	
Wm Pearcy	2	C	
Math Ambler	1	C	
Wm Goss	1	C	
Rob Campion	1	C	
Wm Chaplin	1	C	
Tho Bullock & Tho Chaplin	2	C	
Step Glay	1	C	
Widd Glay	1	C	
Wm Glay	1	C	
Jo Glay	1	C	
Sarh Whitheade	1	C	
Tho Arlidge	1	C	
Jo Brittain	1	C	
Hestr Hall	1	C	
Widd Scott	1	C	
Two almes houses	2	C	
Geo Glay	1	C	
Mary Rose	1	C	
Jo Sutton	1	C	
Tho Harpur	1	C	
Wm Heath	1	C	
Tho Clouston	1	C	
Jo Miller	1	C	
Widd Clement	1	C	
Robt Parr	1	C	
Widd Lunn	1	C	
Hen Miller	1	C	
[f. 12v]			
Jo Williamson	1	C	
Jo Ward	1	C	
Wm Dunn butcher			1
Alice Sherwin	1	C	
Jo Barr	1	C	
Geo Yeates	1	C	
Wood mill			2
Jo Allisbury	1	C	
Wm Goss	1	C	
			161

Kennellworth the Dutchey
[Kenilworth Duchy
in Kenilworth par]

	[NC]		[Ch]
Mr Olliver Paulett			8
Mr Jo Handes			6
Mr Jo Mallrey			6
Tho Dormon			4
Mr Jo Bree			3
Tho Rogers			1
Jo Skellington			3
Edwd Raulins <with> a forge downe			<2>1
Hen Marshe			1
Christpher Davis			4
Rich Pettipher			1
Geo Hinde			2
Jos Watts			4
Tho Busswell			<2>3
Mr Jo Clifton			4
Robt Cartwright			1
Wm Arnall			1
Geo Tayler with an oven			3
Widd Kanning			3
Tho Hancox			1
Tho Roades			2
Hen Bryan			1
Mr Deacon			5
Wm Johnson			4
Rich Adams	1	C	
Fran Houltam			2
Jo Stafford	1	C	
Wm Mathews			2
[blank] Faulkner			1
Wm Harpur			1
Selethiell Hill			1
Edwd Avery			1
[f. 13]			
Adrian Harte with a forge			2
Jo Paine	1	C	
Wm Robins	1	C	
Sus Corbitt	1	C	
Widd Granger			1
Jo Neway			1
Geo Blicke }			1
Tho Butler }	1	C	
Tho Pilgram	1	C	
Jo Courte	1	C	
Tho Dytoe with a forge	2	C	

	[NC]		[Ch]
Jo Parden	1	C	
Wm Wagstaff			1
Tho Rabin	1	C	
Hump Ansill	1	C	
Edwd Bullocke	2	C	
Jo Bullocke	1	C	
Geo Butler	1	C	
Alice Francklin	1	C	
Rich Bayley }			2
<Rich>Jo Butler }	2	C	
Jo Davis			3
Wm Atterbury			1
Rich Gibbs	1	C	
Mrs Danporte			1
Tho Betty			1
Rich Betty			1
Tho Bettey sen	1	C	
Jo Brayne			1
Mrs Cooke widd			3
Jo Bullocke	2	C	
Rich Walker	2	C	
Jo Leeson	2	C	
Jo Banbury	1	C	
Rich Bellamy 2 houses			2
Mr James Chapman minister			6
Mr Tho Boucher			4
Jo Hancocke	1	C	
Wm Lane & Tho Richards			4
Widd Pratt			1
Widd Cross	1		
Tho Williams			1
Fran Bullocke			2
Rob Boate			1
Mr Smith			4
Hen Bullocke			1
Hen Bennet			1
[f. 13v]			
Danll Kinge			3
Tho Grissould			1
Widd Cleadon			1
Wm Huntington	1	C	

	[NC]		[Ch]
Edwd Tybitts	1	C	
Wm Lucas	1	C	
Margt Harwood	1	C	
Jo Wallis	1	C	
Rich Collice	1	C	
Jo Jeacocke	1	C	
Hen Phillipps	1	C	
Tho Petty			1
Nick Tymms			1
Samll Randes			1
Hen Drake			1
Jos Tyrer			1
Tho Harborne with a flax oven			4
Fran Cradocke	1	C	
Marke Mann			4
Mrs Ann Granger			6
Edwd Kecke	1	C	
Tho Eborne emptie			1
Nick Tymms	1	C	
Jo Price			1
			152

Veiued by:
Warberton Hull collector
Rich Hancock constable

[WCRO, QS11/19]
[f. 1]
Knightloe [Knightlow Hundred]
Monkes Kerby
[Monks Kirby Division]
1670
Exchequer Roles
[written by Warberton Hull]
[f. 1v: blank]
[f. 2: second title page, omitted here]
[f. 2v]
Astley [par]

Christpher Merry	18
Tho Hancock	1
The vickeridge emptie	[-] [2[1]]
Jo Ballard	2

[1] WCRO, QS11/29 (1673).

	[NC]	[Ch]
Jo Herbert		3
Tho Hanckesson		1
Tho Mann		1
Wm Ballard		1
Abra Masser		1
Jo Brookes		2
Michll Swift		1
Tho Granger		1
Widd Webb		1
Abrah Younge empte		1
Eliz Wilkinson		1
Tho Hall		1
John Veare		2
Jo Stone		2
Jo Harbert		1
Christpher Lucas sen		2
Christpher Lucas jun		2
Tho Avery		1
Hen Townsend		1
Widd Hewett		2
Samll Partridge	2 C	
Mr Edwd Saunders		3
Jose Veare sen		4
Tho Wale		3
Jos Veare jun		4
Mr Rich Bayley		7
Danll Hinckley empte		2
Jo Clarke		2
Tho Satchwell		1
Jos Breedon		1
Tho Nasbey		1
Steph Wheatley		3
Samll Chesshire		1
Wm Lucas		4
Rob <Guye>Yell		2
Step Whatley		1
Samll Kelsey		2
Abrah Younge		2
Wm Guye		1
[f. 3]		
Mary Guye	1 C	
Widd Hall	1 C	
Widd Clarke	1 C	
Widd Foster	1 C	

	[NC]	[Ch]
Jo Chamberlaine	1 C	
Tho Clarke	1 C	
		93

Veiued by:
Warberton Hull collector

Arley [par]

	[NC]	[Ch]
Jo Harris		1
Mr Skeffington Broome		2
Widd Tompson		1
Tho Shackspeare		4
Christ Hancocke		1
Ann Steele		2
Mr Sherrard rector		3
Mrs Sadler widd		12
Ralph Gee		2
Wm Wrighte		1
Walter Butler		2
Widd Hancock empte		1
Fran Turner		3
Mr Rich Rose		4
Jo Becke		2
Fran Murwood		1
Wm Damms		1
Mr Rich Avery		4
Rich Clarke with a forge		2
Danll Hill		2
Wm Hall		2
Rich Terry		2
Tho Shaw		3
Wm Todd		2
Fran Tarton		1
Rich Hewett		2
Ballard Townsend		2
Wm Orton		2
Rich Mills with a forge		3
Tho Veare	1 C	
Jo Nixson	1 C	
Fran Carver	1 C	
John Fennell	1 C	
		70

Veiued by:
Warberton Hull collector

[f. 3v]	[NC]	[Ch]
Allesley [par]		
Tho Flint esq		7
Jo Hay		4
Wm Grindon		2
Wm Wheeller		3
Rich Masson		1
Robt Gardner }		2
Wm Underwood }		2
Rich Eborne		5
Mr John Hickes rector		5
Tho Moor		4
Geo Timms		2
Sus Keey		1
Wm Hancock		2
Widd Adams with a forge		5
Mr Tho West		2
Hen Timms	2 C	
Widd Swame		8
Samll Clarke esq		9
Rich Southerne		9
Widd Launte		3
Widd Hope	1 C	
Wm Hill		3
Tho Launte		4
Tho Docker		1
Widd Jennings		1
Edwd Eales		1
Samll Smith		2
Tho Nickalls		1
Tho Wall		2
Robt Stone		4
Hump Doleman		1
Major Rawbone		2
Hen Clement		1
<Edwd>Hen Casemore		2
Rich<L> Kenning		1
Arth Miller		3
Rich Gibbs		1
Mr Jo Tayler		4
Mr Wm Smith		4
Mr Tho West		3
Allex Latham		2

[f. 4]	[NC]	[Ch]
Mr Hall		5
Robt Adams with a forge		2
Mr Fran Blyth		8
Wm Meighes		1
Mr Blyth emptie		1
Tho Harpur		1
Jo Orton		1
Tho Edwards		5
Widd Harpur		1
Hen West	1 C	
Jo Wood		1
Wm Harpur		2
Wm Hide		1
James Cooper		1
Fran West		2
Eliz Woode		1
Tho Cleavsley		1
Tho West with a forge		5
Edwd Hackney		1
Jos Wall		1
Jo Walker		1
Tho Newcomb		1
Wm Chesterfeilde	1 C	
Mary Jackson		2
Tho Ingram		4
Edwd Basforde		3
Widd Overton		1
Rich Ebron hatter		2
Jo Bacon		4
Ann Floyde		1
Jobe Chetwin		1
Jo Nickall jun	1 C	
Hen Walker		1
Jo Craftes		12
Widd Avery		3
Mary Bradway		1
John Plumpton		1
James Haynes		1
Wm Ebron		5
Wm Davis		1
Mr Tho Launder		5
Hen Haynes	1 C	
Wm Smith		1

	[NC]		[Ch]
[f. 4v]			
John Jackson			1
Widd Newcombe			1
Jo Smith			1
Wm Bates			2
Ann Oldner			2
Tho Packwood			1
Tho Wright			1
Wm Oughton			1
Jo Handes			3
Wm Hawty			1
Rich Perkins			1
Wm Geyes			1
Tho Mann emptie			2
Tho Hobins	1	C	
Widd Fisher	1	C	
Edwd Pywell	1	C	
Wm Deacon	1	C	
Jo Mathews	2	C	
Widd Hyott	1	C	
Hump Farmer jun	1	C	
Hump Farmer sen			1
Hump Tayler	1	C	
Peetter Deacon	1	C	
Nick Tompson			1
Robt Ginkins	1	C	
Wm Wheeller			2
			233

Veiued by:
Warberton Hull collector
Jo Orton constable

Coundon
[in Coventry Holy Trinity par]

	[NC]		[Ch]
Tho Cleaver			1
Ann Showell			1
John Dagley			1
Jo Handes			1
Hen Symson			1
Tho Higginson			1
Leo Robinson emptie			1
Mr Abrah Boone sen			4
Mr Abrah Boone jun			7
Mr Samll Clarke			4

	[NC]		[Ch]
[f. 5]			
Margt Randoll			1
Ralph Ingram			1
Roger Astley			1
Wm Oldner			2
John Guest			1
Tho Chatterne			2
Jo Hatton			2
Tho Perkins	1	C	
Robt Harrisson			1
Tho Price			1
Gilbert Higginson			2
Wm Tuter	1	C	
Rich Warring	1	C	
Widd Garrat	1	C	
			36

Veiued by:
Warberton Hull collector
Tho Price constable

Bedworth [par]

	[NC]		[Ch]
Tho Darleston	1	C	
Jo Martin	2	C	
Margt Nibb	1	C	
Rich Garner	1	C	
Joane Stonley	1	C	
Hen Bunney	1	C	
Luke Shatswell	1	C	
Jo Hopkins	1	C	
Rich Daslington	1	C	
Wm Bradbury	2	C	
Hen Wise	1	C	
Robt Wise			1
Jo Yeates	2	C	
Rich Floyde	1	C	
Tho Bradbury	1	C	
Edwd Hurst			1
Alice Garner	1	C	
Hen Acers	1	C	
Tho Wood	1	C	
Hen Buswell			1
Joane Stonley	1	C	
Geo Stone			1
Margr Yeates	1	C	

	[NC]	[Ch]
Geo Bunney	1 C	
An emptie cottage	1 C	
Jo Garner		1
[f. 5v]		
Ralph Amersley	1 C	
Tho Bunney	1 C	
Tho Chettwin	1 C	
Josi Harvey	1 C	
Alice Southerne	1 C	
Widd Parson	1 C	
Eliz Ball	1 C	
Geo Ball	1 C	
Hen Burcott	2 C	
Jo Hamersley jun	1 C	
Geo Paule	1 C	
Christpher Burcott		1
Wm Southerne	1 C	
Tho Marson empte	1 C	
Wm Wilson	1 C	
Jo Lee	1 C	
Wm Ballard		1
Saunder Richardson	1 C	
Jo Friswell	1 C	
Geo Allcott		1
John Clarison	1 C	
Rich Darlesson	1 C	
John Clarisson	1 C	
Jo Lyndon with a forge		2
Wm Mathews		1
Mary Mathews	1 C	
Eliz Payne	1 C	
Jo Southerne	1 C	
Edwd Warriner	2 C	
Wm Lee		1
Jo Mathews	1 C	
Robt Mann	1 C	
Robt Smith	1 C	
Eliz Bradley	1 C	
Ann Chattell	2 C	
Ann Peares	1 C	
Tho Reader	1 C	
Jo Peares	1 C	
Kath Richardson	1 C	

	[NC]	[Ch]
Tho Bostridge	1 C	
Jo Mathews sen	1 C	
Robt Friswell		1
Andrew Friswell	1 C	
Widd Joanes	1 C	
Jo Wagstaffe	1 C	
Rich Dyer	1 C	
[f. 6]		
Mary Smith	1 C	
Wm Baker	1 C	
Eliz Page		1
Sir Jo Newdegatte empte		1
Tho Orton		2
Jo Haywood	1 C	
Jo Shaw	1 C	
Widd Saunders	1 C	
Hump Hanbury		2
Jobe Harvey	1 C	
Jo Eales	1 C	
Geo Hickman		2
Hen Joanes	1 C	
Step Lewis	1 C	
Widd Moore	1 C	
Joane Mathews	1 C	
Tho Carrey	1 C	
Eliz Wilcox	1 C	
Alice Moore widd	1 C	
Sar Allin	1 C	
Robt Walker	1 C	
Widd Johnson	1 C	
Jo Joanes	1 C	
Tho Dingley	1 C	
Hester Birde widd	1 C	
Alice Johnson	1 C	
Rich Kempe	1 C	
John Jewish	1 C	
Steph Page	1 C	
Ann Hanson	1 C	
Eliz Hill	1 C	
Jo Johnson & [blank] Mathews		1
Jo Greaves		2
Widd Wilson		1
An emptie house		2
Wm Brotheres		1

	[NC]	[Ch]
Wm Jackson		1
Jo Newton	1 C	
Tho Heathcock	1 C	
Mary Townsend	1 C	
Roger Murcott	1 C	
Jo Randell		1
Joane Selvey	1 C	
Wm Boggs		1
<Ed>Emptie cottage	1 C	
Widd Hampe	1 C	
Widd Hatt	1 C	
Rich Wood		1
[f. 6v]		
Tho Townsend	1 C	
Wm Quattrine	1 C	
Ustacy Loxley	1 C	
Widd Hewett	1 C	
Jobe Smith	1 C	
Mr Chamberlayne minister		4
Tho Kelly		2
Edwd Morton	1 C	
Wm Morton	1 C	
Widd Duell	1 C	
Jo Wootton	1 C	
Emptie cottage	1 C	
Widd Dyer	1 C	
Wm Stanley	1 C	
Robt Townsend	1 C	
Geo Dawkins }		1
In an emptie house }		1
Tho Musson		1
Eliz Sneade	1 C	
Jo Yeates	1 C	
Jo Sneade	1 C	
Jo Starkey		1
Robt Savin	1 C	
Widd Longdon	1 C	
Tho Satchwell jun		1
Jos<…> Stapels	1 C	
Edwd Staples	<1>	1
Tho Satchwell	1 C	
Jo Theane	1 C	
Tho Merry		1
Jo Warring		1

	[NC]	[Ch]
Widd Cookes	1 C	
Goodm[an] Smith	1 C	
Widd Holmes	1 C	
Tho Daniell Widd Hampe	2 C	
Mr Fishers tennant		1
Rich Harberd		1
Jane Harvey	1 C	
Rich Tayler		1
Geo Goodley	1 C	
Rich Brookes		1
Geo Newton		2
Rob Lucas		6
Hump Hanbury sen		4
[f. 7]		
Margr Wheatley	1 C	
Widd Mathews	1 C	
Margr Richardson	1 C	
Jo Ryley	1 C	
Widd Smith	1 C	
Hen Page	1 C	
Jo Smith	1 C	
Rich Wilson	1 C	
Widd Page	1 C	
Wm Kellum	1 C	
Wm Reade	1 C	
Tho Masson	1 C	
Sar Green	1 C	
Wm Meeke sen		1
Wm Wilson	1 C	
Wm Meekes jun	1 C	
Jo Meakins	1 C	
Jo Knight	1 C	
Tho Greasley	<1>2 C	
Hen Pickerin	1 C	
Tho Page sen	1 C	
Robt Brookes empte	1 C	
Rich Mother	1 C	
Widd Cleaver	1 C	
Wm Pickerin	1 C	
Tho Odams	1 C	
Tho Reader jun	1 C	
Dor Reader	2 C	
Jo Williams	1 C	
Rich Woolverston	1 C	

	[NC]		[Ch]
Gabrill Reader	1	C	
Widd Payne	1	C	
Leo Rayson	1	C	
Tho Borrowes	1	C	
Rich Robinson			1
Jo Ratleiffe	2	C	
Jo Johnson			1
Tho Peares	1	C	
Abra Moore	1	C	
Edwd Heaywood			1
Widd Willcox	1	C	
Nick Ballard			1
Zach Lynney	1	C	
Jo Carrey	1	C	
Tho Moore	1	C	
Tho Lucas			1
Roger Johnson	1	C	
[f. 7v]			
Widd More	1	C	
Wm Hartopp	1	C	
Anth Smith	1	C	
Edwd Savidge	1	C	
Vall Drake	1	C	
Eliz Butler	1	C	
Jo Hartopp	1	C	
Tho Perkins	1	C	
Tho Neale	1	C	
Vall Drake			1
Geo Johnson	1	C	
Jo Pickard	1	C	
Eliz Harrisson	1	C	
Fran Pearcey	1	C	
Rich Jewes	1	C	
Geo Johnson jun	1	C	
Rich Mathews	1	C	
Wm Harrisson	1	C	
Thurston Robbinson	1	C	
Edwd Dewes jun	1	C	
Mary Fryer	1	C	
Rich Smith	1	C	
Jo Crosland	1	C	
Jo Crachley	1	C	
Jo Ayers	1	C	

	[NC]		[Ch]
Wm Pace	1	C	
Emm Savidge	1	C	
Jo Johnson	1	C	
Isaa Moore	1	C	
Edwd Dewes sen	1	C	
Vall Harrison	1	C	
Jo Harrisson	1	C	
Tho Stratford	1	C	
Robt Friswell jun	1	C	
Wm Lythall	1	C	
Hugh Lyney	1	C	
Priss Stanforde	1	C	
Geo Mathews			1
Rich Howlett			1
Humpr Hanbury jun	1	C	
Tho Beneford	1	C	
Hen Poole	1	C	
Widd Garner	1	C	
Wm Rotherum			1
Hen Rotherum with a forge	2	C	
Wm Pearce	1	C	
Ann Warde	1	C	
Jo Cox	1	C	
[f. 8]			
Mr Fran Saunders			2
Widd Basford	1	C	
Geo Lee			1
Hen Stonleigh	1	C	
Hen Lee	1	C	
Ralph Gulliver			1
Hen Martin			1
Edwd Benes			1
Ann Bascer	1		
Widd Smith	1		
Widd Ward	1		
Widd Lambe	1		
Jane Ayers	1		
Mary Shirley	1		
Hester Bird	1		
Eliz Hill	1		
Alice Poole	1		
Jane Pickerin	1		
Widd Stonleigh	1		
Mary Yeates	1		

	[NC]	[Ch]
Ann Edge	1	
Ann Kennellworth	1	
		78

Veiued by:
Warberton Hull collector

Bulkington [par]

	[NC]	[Ch]
Geo Purifoy esq		11
Jo Bass		1
Jo Smith		1
Tho Jeffcott		1
Wm Musson		2
Jo Scotton with a forge		3
Abra Drew		2
Tho Goodacer		1
Tho Wright		1
Jo Lole		3
Wm Rogers		1
Jos Rogers		1
Rich Smith		1
Charles Smith		1
Jo Chesshire		2
Danll Corrall	1 C	
Hugh Mervin		1
Tho Bennett		3
Obid Butler		1
[f. 8v]		
Abrah Ballard		1
Jonathan Lagoe emptie		1
Tho Satchwell		1
Jo Gammage with a forge		3
Rich Jenkins		2
Tho Birddett		1
Samson Mervin		2
Jo Birditt		1
Samll Beamish		1
Tho Warde & his mother	1 C	
Jo Tayler		1
Jo Prowett		1
Nick Dabbs		2
Jo Wale gent		4
Rich Tayler		1
Jo Goulden		1
Jo Lee		1
Mr Holloway <rector>vicker		3
Jos Jeffcott		1
Jo Belcher	1 C	
Samll Mervin landlord		1
Margt Goodbey	1 C	
		66

Veiued by:
Warberton Hull collector

Weston in the same Parrish
[Weston in Arden
in Bulkington par]

	[NC]	[Ch]
Jo Scotton		2
Tho Harris		2
Rich Wallin		1
Jos Lole		1
Nath Allin		1
Tho Tayler		2
Wm Reeve & [*Widd*[1]] Tompson		2
Obed Perkins		<1>2
Samll Slingsbey		<1>2
Neh Clarke		2
Mr Wright }		8
Wm Walton }		1
Tho Hipwell		1
Alice Skinner		1
Moss Norman		1
Tho Richardson		2
Jo Richardson		2
Wm Johnson		1
Benj Lester		1
Jo Gee		2
Wm Walton	1 C	
Nehe Bassett	1 C	
		37

[f. 9]
Wrighton in Bulkinton
[Ryton in Bulkington par]

	[NC]	[Ch]
Jo Lee	2 C	
Wm Crabb		1
Jo Clare		2
Wm Tayler sen		2

[1] WCRO, QS11/29 (1673).

	[NC]	[Ch]
Edwd Wise		1
Robt Steane		1
Rich Butlin		1
Jerimiah Drought		1
Lidiah Lole		1
Wm Lole jun		2
Jo Masson		1
Widd Perkins		1
Levi Cooper		3
Han Tavernor	1 C	
Jonath Lagoe		1
Edwd Phipps		3
Jo Dixson		2
Robt Hipwell		1
Rich Barley		1
Jo Tayler emptie		2
Rob Townsend	1	
Geo Hayre	1	
		27

Bramcott in the same Parrish
[Bramcote in Bulkington par]

	[NC]	[Ch]
Jo Warner		2
Geo Floyde		2
Tho Draught		1
Tho Ryley		1
Jo Oakeley with an oven		2
Rich Wright		1
Wm Webster		1
Sebastin Webster		1
Robt Little		1
Tim Cornborough		2
Jo Woolfe		2
Jo Tayler		1
Jeff Walton		1
Wm Hewett		3
Tho Day	1 C	
Hen Sabin		1
Jo Bayley		2
Widd Stockton	1	
Wm Green	1	
		24

[f. 9v]

Marston Jabett in Bulkington parish

	[NC]	[Ch]
Mr Rich Walter		2
Jonath Perkins		3
Mr Robt Johnson		4
Geo Hardiman		1
Tho Goadley	1 C	
Jo Compton		1
Tho Abbott	1	
Wm Bonde		1
Mr Wm Perkins		7
Tho Moore		3
Tho Lagoe		2
Mart Bonde		2
Tho Perkins		2
Peettr Cooke		3
Tho Goodacer	1 C	
Lau Clewes	1 C	
Nath Whetston	1 C	
Christpher Ballard	1 C	
Widd Adams	1 C	
Robt Moore	1 C	
Ann Abbott	1 C	
		31

Veiued by:
Warberton Hull collector

Burton Hastings [par]

	[NC]	[Ch]
Wm Masson		1
Wm Bright		1
Sarah Baker		1
Mich Thrussell		1
Eliz Wanley		1
Rich Warden	2 C	
Wm Ellis with a forge	2 C	
Mr Tho Copson		5
John Spier 2 houses		5
Hen Wattenbury		1
Wm Watkins		2
Rich Gallard		2
Hen Mayne		3
Mr Wm Wise		5

	[NC]	[Ch]
Wm Garrat }		2
Widd Garrat }	1 C	
Edwd Brookes		3
Tho Rauson	2 C	

in this towne is left out
[*Samll*] Spiers: [*2*[1]]
[*Rich*] Adnett: [*3*[2]]
[*Will*] Warner: [*2*[3]]
7 hearthes

[f. 10]

Hide Pasture & Stretton Fields in the Parrish of Burton Hastings

[Hydes Pastures in Hinckley par and Stretton Baskerville ex par with Burton Hastings par[4]]

	[NC]	[Ch]
Rob Ball		1
Wm Whitmore		1
Widd Whitmore	1	
Robt Kever		1
Smll Good		1
Rich Miller		1
		38

Veiued by:
Warberton Hull collector
Mr Rich Wise constable

Combe Abbey

[Combe Fields ex par with Binley par[5]]

	[NC]	[Ch]
Wm Earle of Cravon in the mannor house & lodge		51
Isa Gibson esq		7
Edwd Crooke		<1>2
Wm Soeden		<1>2
Wm Pace		2
Rich Mobbs		2
Danll Weale		1
<Danll>Jo Watts		1
Nathll Pace		1
Rich Bentley		1
Mr Geo Cox		1
Mr Gilbert		1
Jonath Ballard		1
Jo Gammage		1
		74

Veued by:
Warberton Hull collector

Binley [par]

	[NC]	[Ch]
Jo Shires		3
Rich Carless		1
Hugh Wildey		4
Mary Wildey	2 C	
Mr Hen Butler		5
John Button		3
Mr Tho Sleighmaker		4
Rich Flavell		2
Godff Well	1 C	
Widd Overton		2
Rich Overton		2
Mich Asborne		1
Robt Cheaney		1
Tho Wale		4

[f. 10v]

	[NC]	[Ch]
Wm Younge	1 C	
Jo Queeney		1
Rich Barker		1
Mary Bucknell		1
Widd Skegg		1
Eph Gee		3
Samll Streete	1 C	
Widd Cheaney	1 C	
Rob Warde	1 C	

1 WCRO, QS11/29 (1673).
2 WCRO, QS11/29 (1673). Adnett's former house was assessed for five hearths in 1673, but, to preserve the overall total of seven in 1670, only three have been entered here.
3 WCRO, QS11/29 (1673).
4 These two places cannot be distinguished separately (*VCH*, vi, pp. 120, 240).
5 WCRO, DR132/1. The parish registers for Binley record various burials and baptisms for the inhabitants of Combe Fields from 1670 to 1680.

	[NC]	[Ch]
Rich Gees	1 C	
<R>Nick Heayes	1 C	
Edwd Evans	1 C	
Hen Paine	1 C	
Samll Joyce	1 C	
		39

Veiued by:
Warberton Hull collector
Hugh Wildey constable

Willinhall
[Willenhall in Coventry Holy Trinity par]

	[NC]	[Ch]
Sir Jo Hayles bart		9
Mary Treen		5
Rich Whitmore		3
Jo Grimson		2
Widd Hassell		3
Samll Wride		2
Robt Hassell		2
Mary Treen emptie		1
And Warner		1
Anth Burbage		2
Mary Treen		2
Tho Wilkinson with a forge		2
Mary Freeman	1 C	
Constantine Eales	1 C	
Nath Nickalls	1 C	
		34

Veuied by:
Warberton Hull collector
Robt Hassell constable

[f. 11]
Sow alias Sougrave
[Walsgrave on Sowe par: part[1]]

	[NC]	[Ch]
Joane Keene	2 C	
Jar Busswell		1
Mr Jo Symonds		3
Rich Bennion		2
Wm Daulton		1
Mrs Purifoye		6
Christpher Hooke		6
John Hurst		1
Hen Wright		4
Mrs Purifoy emptie		2
Wm Billinsley		2
Jeff Garratt		2
Wm Hutchins		1
Wm Hancock		3
Tho Harbert	2 C	
Jo Large		2
Kath Hextall		2
Rich Payne		2
Wm Godson		1
Tho Lucas		1
Hum Wale		1
Rich Shellett	1 C	
Rich Boddington		1
Danll Masson		2
Tho Gennings		1
Tho Busbey		1
Rich Masson		2
Rich Phipps		2
Tho Eales		6
Martin Killesley	1 C	
Wm Phillipps	1 C	
Wm Jordaine	1 C	
Widd Green	1 C	
Rich Gouldley	1 C	
Jo Arnall	1 C	
Tho Goode	1 C	
Tho Berry	1 C	
Margt Peattoe	1 C	
		58

Veiued by:
Warberton Hull collector
Tho Eales constable

[f. 11v]
Willey [par]

	[NC]	[Ch]
Mr Isham		6
Mr Flower minister		4

[1] The rest of the parish was in the County of Coventry.

	[NC]	[Ch]
Geo Smart jun	1 C	
Wm Wright		2
Ralph Tompson		3
Geo Holliock		1
Edwd Carter		2
Mary Steane		3
Jo Wright		1
Jo Enock		2
Wm Butler		1
Roland Upingham	1 C	
Jo Sturdivant		1
Danll Symonds		2
Edwd Bird with a forge		2
Alice Heywood		1
Rich Browne	1 C	
Wm Symonds		1
Emptie cottage	1 C	
Jo Leney	1 C	
Jo Johnson		1
Geo Smarte sen	1 C	
Rich Wright		2
Jo Gardner	1 C	
Edwd <Wright>Warde	1 C	
Bazill Scotton	1 C	
Mary Reeve	1 C	
Rob Birde	1 C	
		35

Veuied by:
Warbrt Hull collector
John Johnson constable

Wibtoft [chap[1]]

	[NC]	[Ch]
Mr Jo Fairfax		4
Wm Stretton		4
Wm Gilbert		4
Mr Ralph Winterton		4
Nath Reeve		3
Wm Douse		2
Wm Wakefeild emptie		1
Wm & Eliz Wakfeild		2
Mr Jo Fairfax emptie		1
Tho Ballard		2
Hanll Gilbert	1 C	
Sibill Gilbert		1
Tho Smith		1
Edward Birditt		5
Jo Haynes	1 C	
Nick Gilberte	1 C	
Jo Thornton	1 C	
Geo Mervin	1 C	
		34

[f. 12]
Withebrook [Withybrook par]

	[NC]	[Ch]
Mr Ambross Paggett		5
Jo Fritter		1
Mr Geo Cox		6
Mr Pettr Swane		3
Tho Hunte		3
Wm Compton	1 C	
Geo Hynman		<1>2
Wm Pegg		1
Wm Wilson sen		1
Tho Compton		2
Rich Springerfeild		2
Rich Laxson		2
Wm Jeffcott		2
Wm Wilson jun	2 C	
John Broughton		2
Tho Dunckley		1
Tho Wilson		1
Fran Lovett		2
Tho Laxson		2
Widd Wilson		1
Bazill Green		1
Rich Smith		1
Mr Jo Swanie		4
Widd Watkins		2
Ann Broughton		2
Jos Beesley		2
Tho Cheaney		1
Tho Hilliard		1
Jo Knoles	1 C	
Michll Woodburne		1

1 Wibtoft was a chapelry of Claybrooke parish in Leicestershire.

	[NC]	[Ch]
Mary Gallard	1 C	
Jo Masson		1
Wm Smith	1 C	
Wm Cooper	1 C	
Tho Masson		2
Danll Pettipher		1
Wm Goulding		2
Mr John Ward		5
Tho Smith	1 C	
Jo Wilson	1 C	
Amy Russell	1 C	
Widd Wormlayton	1 C	
Tho Chadwell		2
John Smith		2
Wm Walton		1
Robt Rautherum		1
Sarh Needham	1 C	
Widd Smith	1 C	
Tho Whinge	1 C	
		71

Veiued by:
Warbt Hull collector

[f. 12v]

Woolvey [Wolvey par]

	[NC]	[Ch]
Charles Conquest esq		8
Jo Tuckey		1
Rich Clare		1
Rob Phinney		1
Wm Foxson sen with an oven		4
Wm Warner		2
Wm Smith with a forge		3
Rich Warner with an oven		3
Rich Hill		1
Mr Smalbrooke		11
Mr Fitch		4
Rich Plover		1
Jo Johnson	2 C	
Jo Cross		1
Tho Payne emptie	<1>0	1
Geo Bratford		1
Jo Aske		2
Edwd Holles with a forge		2
Wm Beebey		1
Mary Grindon with an oven (poore)	3	
Rich Loveday		1
Edwd Baggott	1 C	
Charles Wilson	1 C	
Wm Whitheade		1
Tho Stockton jun		2
Rich Orton		1
Rich Day		1
Jo Spencer		1
Tho Townsend		1
John Scotton		2
Wm Farndon		1
Tho Browne		2
Wm Saunders		1
Tho Spencer		1
Wm Toone		4
Edwd Scotton		1
Mr Fitch emptie		1
Wm Hellis		1
Tho Adnett		1
Rob Scotton		2
Rich Plover emptie	1 C	
Mr Fitch emptie	1 C	
Mr Houlden emptie		2
Wm Randolph	1 C	
Mr Walker minister		3
Rich Laxson		1
Jo Taverner		1
		80

[f. 13]

Smockington in Woolvey Parr

	[NC]	[Ch]
Jo Myles		8
Rich Cooke		3
Jame Wigley	1 C	
John More		1
Hen Gilberte		1
Nick Abbott		2
Charles Nickall with an oven		3
Widd Webster		1
John Dunckley		1
Mary Dunckley	1 C	
John Howne	1 C	

	[NC]	[Ch]
Wm Saunders jun	1 C	
Wm Davis	1 C	
Jo Randall	1 C	
Nick Whitmore	1 C	
Widd Lovday	1 C	
Tho Brookes	1 C	
Wm Adkins	1 C	
Widd Perry		1
Jo Hearsley		1
Wm Wilcox		1
Jo Macham	1 C	
Barth Mutton	1 C	
Math Blacke	1 C	
Jonath Clare	1 C	
John Perry		1
Ann Coopper	1 C	
Mary Bryan	1 C	
Tho Bonte	1 C	
Mary Tomalin	1 C	
Edwd Aucott	1 C	
Hen Plover	1 C	
Jo Collins	1 C	
Widd Raulins	1 C	
Jo Farndon	1 C	
Rich Beebey		1
Tho Baker	1 C	
		25

Veiued by:
Warberton Hull collector
Robt Scotton c[onstable]

[f. 13v]

Mounckeskerby

[Monks Kirby par]

	[NC]	[Ch]
Mr Stapleton rector		4
Mr Rich Rose		4
An emptie house Earle Denby		[-] [*2*[1]]
Tho Maylin		1
Mr Wm Trantum		4
Widd Young	1 C	
Bazill Towers		2
Rich Hunt		1

	[NC]	[Ch]
Rich Lea		2
Tho Harbert		1
Jo Watts		1
Han Satchwell	1 C	
Jo Packwood		1
Tho Holmes		2
Jo Hurley	2	
Geo Baggott	1	
Essau Warring		3
Widd Crooke		3
Danll Steane		2
Edwd Heaycox	1 C	
Margt Hennock	1 C	
Jo Hodgkins	1 C	
Wm Wrighte		4
Jo Roberds		2
Jo Scrivenor		2
Alice Reade	1 C	
Bazill Warren	1 C	
Rand Langham		1
Rich Bott		1
Mr Tho Mathews		3
Sos Makepeace		1
Rich Lee		1
Clemt Hall with a forge		3
Geo Smith with a forge		2
Rich & Rob Harbert		3
Jo Baggott		2
Jo Egent	1 C	
Wm Lee		1
Tho Roberds		1
Edwd Gamball	1 C	
Jo Bird	1 C	
Rich Davenporte	1 C	
<…>Edwd Packwood	1 C	
Eliz Allen	1 C	
Jo Craftes	2 C	
Widd Capp	1 C	
Mary Holmes	1 C	
[f. 14]		
Emptie cottage	1 C	
Jos Barton	1 C	

1 TNA, E179/259/9 (1666).

	[NC]	[Ch]
Widd Woodburne	1 C	
Eliz Lythell	1 C	
A free scoole		[-] [*1*[1]]
Widd Haynes	1 C	
Tho Crook		1
Pettr Hutchins emptie		1
		59
		[60]

Brockhurst in Kerby
[in Monks Kirby par]

	[NC]	[Ch]
Rich Genoway	1 C	
Hen Grace		3
Edwd Smith with a forge	2 C	
Rich Roberts		1
Nick Baggott	1 C	
Mary Hall		2
Edwd Lea with an oven		<1>2
Widd Treavice	1 C	
Widd Paybody	1 C	
Rich Handes		1
Jo Smith		2
Nick Baggott		2
Hen Bradshaw		1
Tho Heele	1 C	
Widd Stapleton		2
Mr Wm Miller		3
Geo Baggott	1 C	
Widd Cleaney	1 C	
Mr Hen Cotton		2
Tho Andrews		1
Widd Packwood	1	
Tho Perkins		3
Tho Bridges		2
Wm Welles		1
Nick Hooke		3
		31

Strattation in
[Street Ashton
in Monks Kirby par]

	[NC]	[Ch]
Tho Clarke	1 C	
Wm Langham jun		2
Rich Clousley		1
Wm Langham sen	1 C	
Rich Goodman		1
Tho Gilbert		2
Wm Smith		3
Wm Gilbert		2
Edmd Gilbert		2
Widd Scotton	1 C	
		13

[f. 14v]
Kerby Parr
Paddock Newnham
[Newnham Paddox]

	[NC]	[Ch]
Bazill Earle of Denby		34

Little Walton
[in Monks Kirby par]

	[NC]	[Ch]
Tho Ballard		2
Mr Jo Bossworth		3
Mr Ambross Saunders		4
Wm Hookes		2
John Higgs		4
Wm Sutton		3
Widd Wright	1 C	
Fran Smith		1
		53

Cisters Over
[Cestersover in Monks Kirby par]

	[NC]	[Ch]
Mr Wm Veire		5
Mr Godff Clarke		4
Widd Boddington	1 C	
Jo Bretford	1 C	
Tho Lee [*at mill*[2]]		2
Wm Varnum	1 C	
Mr Tho Barford		2
		13

Copson
[Copston Magna
in Monks Kirby par]

	[NC]	[Ch]
Widd Perkins		1
Tho Warner		2

[1] TNA, E179/259/9 (1666).
[2] TNA, E179/259/9 (1666).

	[NC]	[Ch]
Widd Masson	1	
<...>Griff Bull	2	
Wm Perkins		2
Jos Perkins		1
Wm Steane		1
Jo Astley		2
Edwd Wale		1
Mr Rich Losbey		1
Jo Adcock		2
Jo Devonshire		2
Rich Paine	1 C	
James Bull	1 C	
Wm Clarke		2
Wm Wright	1 C	
Jo Wale emptie		2
Jo Baker	1 C	
Edwd Kenn		1
Jo Essex sen	1 C	
Jo Vincent	1 C	
Tho Baker	1 C	
Wm Moore	1 C	
Wm Wright	1 C	
Widd Watterton		1
Highcross[1]		
Tho Dafferne		3
		24

John Astly is charged with 2

[f. 15]

Stretton et
Newbold Kerby Parr

[Stretton under Fosse and Newbold Revel in Monks Kirby par]

	[NC]	[Ch]
Mr Tim St Nickolas		6
Jo Essex		3
Mr Jo Barker		4
Jo Farmer		1
Mr Charles Shuckbrugh		2
Wm Showell		2
Wm Harbert		1
Wm Palmer		3
Wm Langham	1 C	
Clemt Hurst		3
Rich Sharman		1
Wm Maw		1
Jo Newcombe		1
Edwd Hands		1
Mr Jo Binley		3
Geo Cole		2
Wm Bretford		1
Ann Scotton	1 C	
Robt Walmesley		1
Sir Fulware Skippwith bart		17
Widd Crafts	2 C	
Rich Wilcox	1 C	
Tho Thornton	1 C	
Emptie cottage	1 C	
Tho Varnum	1 C	
Jo Smith	1 C	
		53

Essenhull

[Easenhall in Monks Kirby par]

	[NC]	[Ch]
Eliz Webb		2
Widd Baseley		3
Tho Tallis		1
Wm Bosley & Tho Palmer		2
Wm Crafts		1
Alice Bates		2
Jo Sturdivant		1
Wm Woodward		1
Widd Bates		3
Anth Meadowes		2
Jo Gamage		2
Eliz Reeve		2
Tho Smith		2
Mr Hump Davis		5
Ann Eives		2
Jo Easson		1
Tho Atkins	1 C	
Wm Toone		1
Edwd Palmer		1
[f. 15v]		
Fran Currall		1

1 High Cross had a single house where the Fosse Way crossed Watling Street.

	[NC]	[Ch]
Ann Moreton	1	
Joane Bassam	1	
Rich Green	1	
Geo Smith	1	
Joyce Bromidge	1	
Tho Stockton	1	
		35

Veuied by:
Warberton Hull collector
Tho Perkins constable

Paylton
[Pailton in Monks Kirby par]

	[NC]	[Ch]
Mrs Mary Boughton		6
Mr Bazill Good		6
Jane Walker		1
Jo Kinge		2
Jos Checkland & E[l]iz Ladbrook		2
Rich Cookes		1
Fran Bayley		1
Audrey Bayley widd		1
Tho Checkland jun & [*Tho*[1]] Cleaver		3
Widd Crafts		1
Tho Checkland sen		1
Tho Ballard		1
Emptie house		3
Tho Benn		1
Mr Wm Smith		3
Wm Bodington		3
Eliz Whitmore		1
Emptie cottage		1
Wm Perkins		2
Rob Barret		1
Tho Cooke		3
Jo Steane		1
Rich Hall		3
Edwd Mobbs		1
Wm Bentley		2
Jo Cole		2
Jo Hall		2
Wm Lole with a forge		2

	[NC]	[Ch]
Rich Lole		1
Anth Lole		1
Rich Harbert		1
Jo Wright		2
Jane Bayley		3
[f. 16]		
Wm Cross		1
Wm Checkland		1
Andrew Lee		2
Wm Shuttleworth		1
Mrs Green emptie		1
Tho Smith		1
Tho Snoden		1
Jo Pearson		2
Faith Cookes		3
Mary Jordaine		1
Petter Hutchinson		1
Wm Bayley		2
Tho Knibb with an oven		3
Mary Daff		2
Mr Jo Good		4
Edwd Gilbert		2
Edwd Goulding		1
Joseph Arems		1
Tho Cooper		2
Wm Edmunds		1
Jo Checkland	1 C	<1>0
Tho Hecocks	<1>0 [<C>]	1
Rich Steane	1 C	
Fran Warde	1 C	
Rich Burbury	1 C	
Wm Lea	1 C	
Samll Lea	1 C	
Theo Fox	1 C	
Ann Lole	1 C	
Eliz Chaplin	1 C	
Wm Steane	1 C	
Wm Shuttleworth	1 C	
Mich Gilbert	1 C	
Wm Arpuds	1 C	
Tho Mathews	1 C	
Wm Cole	1 C	

[1] WCRO, QS11/29 (1673).

	[NC]		[Ch]
Wm Dawkins	1	C	
Widd Reeve	1	C	
Hen Cheaney	1	C	
Eliz Lee	1	C	
Edwd Langham emptie	1	C	
John Flowers	1	C	
Jo Watts	1	C	
Tho Neale	1	C	
Philli Checkland			1
			[100]

Veiued by:
Warberton Hull collector
Wm Smith constable

[f. 16v]

Brinkloe [Brinklow par]

	[NC]		[Ch]
Hump Lester			1
Isab Lister			1
Rob Hancock			1
Jo Showell			1
Tho Steane			1
Tho Ryley with a forge	2	C	
Tho Alder			2
Christpher Sedgley	1	C	
Edwd Clarke			1
Tho Smith			1
Allex Barloe	1	C	
Wm Varnum			1
Jo Garner			1
Robt Sedgley			3
Edwd Symonds			3
Joseph Garner			2
Tho & John Kibble			2
Geo Newcombe			1
Robt Symonds			1
Jo Bush			4
Rob Sedgley			2
Eliz Bentley			1
Mr Rich Cues			3
Wm Adler			1
Sarah How			1
Robt Varney			1
John How			2
Jo Lester			1
Jos <…>Greene			2
Wm Newcombe jun			1
Eliz Bodington			1
Wm Lea	1		
Rich Sedgley with 2 forges			3
Fran Hancock	1	C	
Wm Jyes with 1 oven			2
Wm Steane			1
Wm Lester			1
Wm Smith jun	1	C	
Edwd Lester			1
Wm Ryley	1	C	
Tho Jornes			1
Edwd Lester jun			1

[f. 17]

	[NC]		[Ch]
Robt Bray			2
Robt Randall			1
Wm Smith sen			1
Edmd Birde with a forge			2
John Astlin			5
John Astin			3
Samll Smith			4
Mr Clarke rector 2 houses			[*5,5*[1]] 10
Wm Sale			2
John Hurley			1
Tho Newcombe sen			1
Rob Newcombe empte			1
Jo Astin	1	C	
Jo Gee			1
Wm Bates			1
Margt Arnall			2
Edwd Sale			2
Wm Smith wheelwright			1
Jar Sedgley			1
Wm Stanley			1
John Sedgley			2
Tho Dawes			4
Samll Pace			4
Wm Morris			1
Jo Bush			1

1 WCRO, QS11/1 (1663).

	[NC]	[Ch]
Wm Masson		1
Wm Francis		1
David Cotton		4
Wm Lester farmer		2
Robt Varity with 1 oven		<1>2
Eliz Sedgley	1 C	
Hugh Davenporte	1 C	
Nick Sedgley	1 C	
Wm Hewett	1 C	
Bridg Cole	1 C	
[rest of page torn away[1]]		
Alice Clarke	[- *C*]	
Eliz Dawk[*ins*	- *C*]	
Eliz Thro[*ught*	- *C*]	
Jo Sedgle[*y*	- *C*]	
Hen Flint[*e*	- *C*]	
Ann Shell[*ey*	- *C*]	
Rich Be[*ntley*	- *C*]	
Edwd Sy[…	- *C*]	
Hen B[*urton*	- *C*]	
[*Mary Newcombe*	- *C*]	
[*Edw Whitman*	- *C*]	
[*Jo Soeden*	- *C*]	
[*Ann Hutt*	- *C*]	
[*Wm Boulton*	- *C*]	
[*Jo Jorne jun*	- *C*]	
[*Dorety Clarke*	- *C*]	
[*Wm Sedgley*	- *C*]	
[*Jonat Burton*	- *C*]	
[*Eliz Jorne*	- *C*]	
[*Jo Jorne sen*	- *C*]	
[*Jo Sh[a]tswell*	- *C*]	
		[117]

[f. 17v]

Branden et Bretford

[in Wolston par]

[***Brandon***[2]]

	[NC]	[Ch]
Mr Wilcox		8
Tho Mathews		3
Mrs Haddon widd		7
Rob Amner		2
Rich Hynton		1
Tho Hewet		2
Nick Wright		4
Widd Smith		4
Jo Losley		3
Alice Phillipps		1
Eliz Bosswell		1
Rich Shelley		1
Wm Walker		1
Wm Worth		3
Tho Hancock		1
Jo Spiers & Tho Sutton		5
Wm Burbury		1
Tho Carter		1
Jo Satchwell		1
Widd Francis		2
Jo Orvin		1
Nick Adkins		2
Wm Hancock		1
Eliz Smith	1 C	
Nath Smith	1 C	
Rich Knight		1
Tym Lyseman	1 C	
Edwd Clarke	1 C	
Rich Lysseman	1 C	
Widd Ashin	1 C	
Tho Lysseman		1

[***Bretford*** [3]]

[rest of page torn away[4]]

	[NC]	[Ch]
[*Will Daniell*]		4
[*Widd Button*]		2
[*Rich Drought*]		4
[*Robt Sale*]		2
[*Edwd Bennett*]		1
[*Widd Atkins*		*2*]
[*Rich Checkley*		*2*]
[*Hen Lapworth*		*1*]

1 Data inserted from TNA, E179/347: exemption certificate dated 5 August 1670.
2 WCRO, QS11/55 (1674).
3 WCRO, QS11/55 (1674).
4 Data inserted from WCRO, QS11/29 (1673).

	[NC]	[Ch]
[*Rich Bend*		*1*]
[*John Parker*	*1 C*]	
		[77]

[f. 18]

Harbury Magna

[Harborough Magna par]

	[NC]	[Ch]
Mrs Riplingham		10
Mr Benj Holloways		4
Wm Smith <& Nick Webb>		4
Mr Fran Childes		3
Tho Cleaver		2
Wm Murcott		4
Margt Satchwell		2
Tho Steane		3
Nick Webb		2
Tho Gilbert		1
Danll Checkley		1
Wm Gilbert	1 C	
Samll Gamball		1
Jo Craftes		2
Tho Steane shoomaker		1
Hen Webb		1
Rich Ward		1
Tho Scotton	<1>2 C	
Wm Cleaver sen		2
Wm Cleaver jun		1
Wm Childes		1
<Ric>Eliz Gamage		1
Rich Satchwell		2
Rich Price with a forge		2
Jo Hurst		2
Eliz Denby	1 C	
Tho Woodward	1 C	
Eliz Wright		1
Tho Staples		1
Edwd Sow	1 C	
Tho Webb	1 C	
Rich Harris	1 C	
[rest of page torn away[1]]		
Edwd Birde	[- *C*]	
Wm Price	[- *C*]	
Jane [*Mor*	- *C*]	
Hen Hook[*e*	- *C*]	
Tho Cle[*aver*	- *C*]	
[*Wm*] Child [*sen*	- *C*]	
[*Saundery Gallard*	- *C*]	
[*Ann Cleaver*	- *C*]	
[*William Smith*	- *C*]	
[*Richard Atkins*	- *C*]	
[*Michael Billinge*	- *C*]	
[*John Worth sen*	- *C*]	
		[55]

Ve[uied by:
Warberton Hull collector]

[f. 18v]

Shilton et Barnecle

[***Shilton*** par[2]]

	[NC]	[Ch]
Jo Ward		1
Edwd Hurst	1 C	
Wm Randall		1
Hen Jeffcott		1
Robt Lole		3
Mr Jo Perkins		5
Rich Jeffcott		3
Jo Johnson		2
Edwd Johnson		1
Rich Jeffcott empte		<1>2
Jos Lole		1
Rich Wakeline		4
Tho Haywood with a forge		3
Widd Butler	1 C	
Wm Ballard		1
Wm Lovett		2
Geo Million		2
Jo Smith		2
[blank] Masson made a barne	1 C	
The vikeridge emptie		2
Wm Wright	2 C	
Tho Burton	1 C	
Tho Cookes	1 C	
A cottage emptie	1 C	
Mich Elmes	1 C	

1 Data inserted from TNA, E179/347: exemption certificate dated 10 March 1670/1.

2 WCRO, QS11/55 (1674).

	[NC]	[Ch]
Widd Prockter	1 C	
Jobe Farndon	1 C	
Jo Broughton	1 C	
[page torn from here[1]]		
[*Robt?*] Ward	1 C	
[*John*] & Jane Ward	2 C	
[*Rich Tayler*]	<1>2 C	
[*Grivell Vicars*]	1 C	

[f. 19]

Barnecle

[Barnacle in Bulkington par[2]]

	[NC]	[Ch]
Mr Tym Stoughton		10
Mr Wm Hickman		4
Robt Hall		1
Rich Belcher		1
Rich Good		2
Rich Lole		1
Jo Bunce		1
Jo Johnson		2
Sarah Hunt		1
Jo Lee		3
Sarah Muston		2
Tho Smith		1
Edwd Hookes		2
Tho Overton		1
Wm Hutt		1
Widd Holliard	1 C	
Tho Dawkins	1 C	
Wm Prosser	1 C	
Tho Biggs	1 C	
Widd Overton	1 C	
		68
		[69]

Veuied by:
Warberton Hull collector

[1] Data inserted from TNA, E179/347: exemption certificate dated 28 March 1671.

[2] Part of Barnacle was in Shilton parish but it was not indicated separately in any hearth tax return (*VCH*, vi, pp. 48, 213).

Hemlingford Hundred

	[NC]	[Ch]

[WCRO, QS11/20]
[front cover]
Hemlingford Hundred
Mr Field his Division
Solihull Division
Collected per Ri Samo[n]
Anno 1670
Exchequer Roles
Theise were retorned
in att Michms 1671
[written by unknown scribe
and Richard Samon[1]]

[inside front cover]	[NC]	[Ch]
Badsley Clinton		
[Baddesley Clinton par]		
should have beene at the latter end of <Old Dich in Balshall> Packinton Parva but for want of roome is here inserted		
[see below p. 335]		
Esquire Ferrars		15
Wm Knight		3
Tho Hawkes		2
Tho Patston		1
Tho Beck		2
Tho Feild		1
John Sandleys		1
Robt Eberall		2
Richd Bird emptie		1
Robt Richeson emptie		1
Edw Beesly		1
8 poore cottages	[8] C	

Kinwalsy in the Mannor of Knoll	[NC]	[Ch]
[Kinwalsey in Hampton in Arden par]		
should have beene plac't after Longdon End in Knoll but for want of roome is here inserted		
[see below p. 332]		
Richd Ritle		3
Wm Clarke		1
Henry Newton		1
Samll Bicly		1
Tho West		4

[p. 1]
Hemlingford Hundred
Balshall in the
Parish of Hampton in Arden
[Balsall]
[***Meer End*** [2]]

	[NC]	[Ch]
John Mayoe		1
John Goodale & his son		4
Ralph Morrice		1
John Clarke		1
Wm Peaton		1
Geo Badham		1
George Gullian		1
Gregory Goodall		<1>2
Robt Lewis		1
Edward White	2	
George Beaton		1
Hen Swift		1
Hen Wooten		1
Widd Oliver	1	
Tho Turrill		1
Widd Hunt	1	
John White	1	
Rich Barnacle	1	
Widd Bowler	1	
John Hews	1	
John Eborn	1	
Widd Potter	1	
John Spires	1	

[1] The unknown scribe wrote pp. 1–28 before Richard Samon amended them, and added the entries inside the front cover, before continuing on pp. 29–32.
[2] TNA, E179/259/9 (1666).

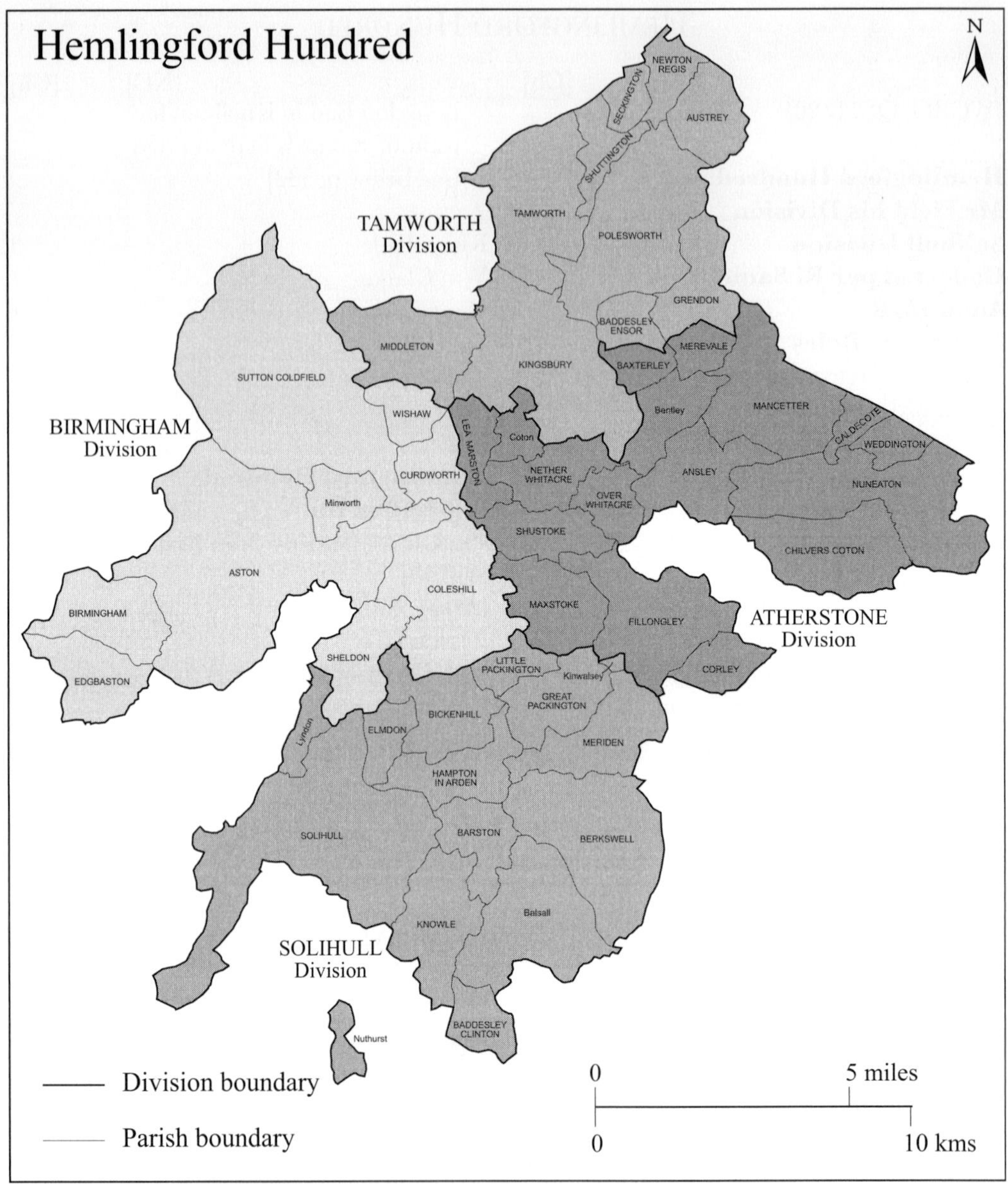

Map 17 Hemlingford Hundred with parish names. Detached parts of parishes and subsidiary parts of those in other divisions are named in lower case.

	[NC]	[Ch]
John Chesterton	1	
Widd Swift	1	
Gefery Tencher	1	
John Padiston	1	
Tho Barrackell	1	
Joseph Baddam	1	
Henery Barnacle	1	
[***Balsall Street***[1]]		
Clemt James		5
Tho Clarke sen		1
[p. 2]		
Mr Lawrence Evetts		6
Wm Edmonds		1
Mrs Evetts widd		5
Tho Butcher alias Taylor		1
Christpofer West }		2
John Richmond }		1
<…><…>		
Margrett Aylsbury		2
An emptie house Eberall landlord		1
Mr Wm Eberill		6
<Wm>Mr Francis <Browne>Evetts		3
John Winter		3
Widd Wheately		2
Widd Grooby	1	
John Linsey		1
Tho Short		2
Widd Phillips	1	
Humphry Feild		1
Widd Farr		<1>2
Widd Wrighton		2
Wm Casmore		1
Tho Arch<er>	1	
Walter Arch<er>	1	
Tho Roe		2
Robt Edwards		1
Tho Blunt		2
<… Smith>		
Robt Parsons		1
Tho Bradnock		1
Rich Smith		1
John Hammond		1
<Henry>Edw Phillipps		1

	[NC]	[Ch]
Eliz Saile		2
Tho Smith		1
Christpofer Bradnock		2
John Cattell		1
Rich Davis		1
Widd Bellet		1
Edward Farr		1
George Higgins		1
Widd Clarke		1
John Baker		1
Wm Browne		1
[p. 3]		
Anth Harrill one a funnill only		2
Widd Villers		3
Rich Higgins		1
Gilbert Darker		1
Wm Gardner		1
Tho Buttler one a funnill to an oven paid for one		2
Benj West		4
Ann Aylesbury		3
James Downes		2
<Tho Masters>		
John Clarke		1
Widd Martin house emptie and noe distress		1
<George Fry>	<1>	
John Ansty	1	
Jeoffery Martin	1	
Wm Biddle	1	
Widd Morrice	1	
John Simonds	1	
[blank space sufficient for two names]		
John Harbert	1	
Denice Boston	1	
Rich Parsons	1	
John Earle sen	1	
George Short	1	
Nich Earle jun	1	
Geo Matthews	1	
Godfery Hopkins	1	
Maur Walker	1	

[1] TNA, E179/259/9 (1666).

	[NC]	[Ch]
Widd Ball	1	
Tho Ebbrall	1	
Old Dich in Bassall		
[Oldwich in Balsall]		
Tho Fullford		1
Wm Fetherston		2
Tho Richardson		1
Widd Smith		1
Wm Paint		2
Tho Compton		4
Robt Richardson		1
[p. 4]		
John Wright		3
Law Harbon		2
Rich Bird		3
Robt Betts paid 2s		1
Will Johnson	1	
Wm Knight		1
Widd Wheeler		1
John Ell		1
John Berry		<1>2
Jonathan Yates		1
Robt Richards		1
Tho Ell		2
Dinah Fisher		1
Rich Burton		4
Robt Farr		2
Robt Collett		2
Tho <B>Prist		2
Widd Fetherstone		2
Tho Evett		1
Tho Lockyer		1
Samll Paston		1
<Widd>Samll Herbarn		3
Wm Yardly		3
Tho Carter one a funnill to an oven		4
Widd Odam		1
Eliz Dunckley		1
Widd Carley	1	

	[NC]	[Ch]
Widd Flint	1	
Rich Sole	1	
<Widd>Valent Phillips	1	
Caleb Smith	1	
Tho Nix	1	
Tho Bennett	1	
Tho Sole	1	
Chrispian Evetts	1	
[p. 5]		
[***Fen End***[1]]		
Wm Blacket		1
Mr Samll Wills		4
Mrs Evitts vidua		5
Rich Matthews		1
John Chatterlyn		1
Rich Cattell		1
Wm Ward		1
John Reves		4
Wm Tayler		1
Mrs Stanton		2
Samll Hunt		1
John Spooner		1
Clemt Fisher		6
Hen Fullford		2
John Rowe		1
Widd Row		1
Tho Shakspier		3
Widd Wattson	1	
John Tayler	1	
Widd Bellamy	1	
Christpofer Davis	1	
Widd Ward	1	
Joseph Dutchfeild	1	
John Holder	1	
John Wattson & the Widd	1	
James Rowe		1
<Francis Evetts>		

Viewed per:
Richd Samon collector
Tho Butler constable

[1] TNA, E179/259/9 (1666).

	[NC]	[Ch]
Barkeswell [Berkswell par]		
Hen Mathews esq		10
Simon Wright	2	
Wm Hurst		1
<Widd Mason>		
Tho Lea		1
Rich Mills		2
Wm Chettham		1
Wm Asten		1
Mr Humpy Harper		3
Tho Davis	1	
[p. 6]		
Daniell Harris		1
Benjamen West		1
<Tho West>		
Jer Stonell		1
Wm Margetts	1	
Tho Byfeild		1
Christpofer Wotton		1
Wm Flint emptie Kinston of Stonly landlord		3
John Rippon		2
Hen Ashby	1	
Charles French		2
Edward Higginson		5
Widd Sanders		1
John Elles		1
<Tho Ellis>		<1>
Mr Henery Buttler		6
Mr Rich Kimberly		5
Tho Ebrill	1	
Hen Scrivener	1	
Samll Savidge		2
John Baker		1
Christpfore Wooton		<1>2
John Savidge		1
Eliz Greene		1
Eliz Timsberley		1
Widd Watson		2
Wm Watson		4
John Whattcock		2
Wm Farmer		1
Rich Key		2
Tho Williams		3

	[NC]	[Ch]
Hen Wattson		1
Tho Gifford		1
Tho Gardner		1
Edw Green Jno Bennet landlord	1	<1>
Edw Stone		1
Edw Barker		2
Susanah Bishoppe		1
Tho Painter		2
Widd Povey <emptie the dore shut up & no distresse to be had>		2
<Edw>Rich Casmore		1
[p. 7]		
<...>Widd Bonney emptie the door shut up & noe distresse		2
<...>Edw Casmore		1
Mr John Whitehead		5
John Norton		3
Nich Jackson		4
Wm Gibbs		1
Robt Bennett		2
John Willson		2
Alex Casimore		1
Wm Bennet		4
John Betteridge	1	
Rich Phillips sen		1
John Gardner		2
Samll Gardner		2
Tho More		1
Phillip Fisher		1
Tho Clarke		1
John Arch		2
Joane Haywood		5
Tho Docker sen		1
John Eves<tts>		3
Tho Etherington		2
Rich Phillipps jun		1
Tho Perkins		4
George Kimberly		2
Rich Hopkins		1
Wm Flint		1
John Clarke		1
Widd Baker		1
Mr John Hartlett		5

	[NC]	[Ch]
Tho Matthews		3
Robt Boulton		1
Wm Thompson		1
Hen Flint		1
Ralph Plumpton		1
Widd Nicholes		1
Robt Cox		1
Edward Masters		2
Geo Clarke		1
Rich Baker		1
<Widd Gardner>		<1>
[p. 8]		
Tho Bassell		1
Wm Gardner		1
Tho Elletts		1
Mrs Evatts		4
John Mayo		4
Rich Witthers	1	
Geo Diall gent		4
Nich Austen		1
Mr Miles Flint		6
Tho Ward		1
Wm Wootten		1
John Casmore		1
Tho Barre		2
Wm Miller		4
John Aston		1
The free schole not endowed with £20 per annum		3
John Bannell		5
Widd Carter		3
John Fantham		1
Tho Heath		1
Rich Humphery		4
Mr Buswell		2
Gregor Chattway		1
Tho Whitehead		3
Kather Mason		1
Gilbert Docker		3
Tho Docker sen		2
Tho Docker jun		2
Ralph Byfeild		5
John Boulton		2

	[NC]	[Ch]
Widd Lowe		1
Edw Green	1	
Sir Samull Marrow		17
<Geo Feilding esq>		<17>
Samull Lugg rector		7
Christpofer Jacques		2
Widd Tayler		3
Widd Byfeild		1
Tho Gibbs		1
[p. 9]		
Rich Rowe		3
Tho Righton		1
Widd Midleton		2
Abra Austen		3
Mr Henry Hudgeford		2
Mr John Bennett		4
Wm Hickin		1
Lettice Avice	1	
Fran Chaplin	1	
John Burbridge	1	
Rich Tayler	1	
Anne Short	1	
Geo Hughes	1	
Humph Adcocks	1	
Robt Hands	1	
Widd Kimberly	1	
Anth Glover	2	
Morris Cooke	1	
Widd Clarke	1	
John Rampton	1	
Wm Hollice	1	
John Court	1	
Rich Taylor	1	
Edw Cleaver	1	
Tho Adcox	1	
Anne Readinge	1	
Widd Court	1	
Edw Stone	[-] [*1*[1]]	
Widd Hopkins	1	
Edw Court	1	
Widd Robinson	1	
Tho Robinson sen		1
Edw Wallis	1	

[1] TNA, E179/259/9 (1666).

	[NC]	[Ch]
Robt Casimore	1	
Wm Brookes	2	
Widd Hattley an empty cott[age]	1	
Wm Gould	1	
[p. 10]		
Ellinor Harris	1	
Aron Freeman	1	
John Hodgett	1	
Widd Lines	1	
Edw Marsh	1	
<Abrah Gibbs>		<1>
Tho Cooks	1	
John Davis	1	
Edw Withers	1	
Rich Davis	1	
Widd Chattway		1
Tho Willson alias Reeve	1	

Viewed per:
Richd Samon collector
R Davis thirdborough

[p. 11]

Barston and Escott[1]

[Barston par]

	[NC]	[Ch]
Samll Hunt gent [*clerk* [2]]		2
Edw Smith [*gent* [3]]		8
Tho Astly gent		8
Wm Hudgesford gent		4
Mr Geo Fisher		3
Tho Whatcock one never finisht		3
Geo Fisher		1
Tho Large		2
Rich Tayler		1
Geo Bradnock		2
Tho Hancock		1
Robt Dorman		1
John Dippell		1
Wm Farmer		1
Wm Law		1
Rand Essex	1	
Rich Wast		5
John Camell		2
Widd Hickins	2	
Hen Fisher		1
Edw Thomas alias Tomes		1
Kath Tomes	1	
Wm Fisher		2
Joseph Large		1
Widd Satchwell		1
John Fisher		1
Christopher Ailsbury		2
Tho Wrighton		1
Tho Burbridge		1
John Wrighton		2
Nich Wheeler v[ery] p[oor]		1
Clemt Docker		2
Widd Cole the house in controversie		2
<N>Michll Cox		1
Wm Law		2
Wm Owen	1	
(unpaid) Clement Gibbons		2
Nich Smith		1
Wm Whiatt		1
Nich Fisher		2
Geo Coale		2
[p. 12]		
Edw Mallener		1
Rich Mills } Sir Robt Burgin landlord		2
Stephen Downes } Sir Robt Burgin landlord		2
Tho Masters named in Bradnock Marsh		<2>
Samll Cross now empty		1
<Wheeler now Samll Cross>		<1>[4]
Widd Clarke	1	
Isack Row	1	
<Eliz Worsley the house quite down>		
John Worley	1	

1 Eastcote was in Barston parish but was not identified separately.
2 TNA, E179/259/9 (1666).
3 TNA, E179/259/9 (1666).
4 Not deleted in the manuscript although this must have been the intention.

	[NC]	[Ch]
Widd Hugginson	1	
Widd Watts	1	
John Camell emptie dore shut up & noe distress	[-] [*1*[1]]	
Hen Kimberly	1	

Viewed per:
Richd Samon collector
Wm Law constable

Bradnock Marsh
[Bradnocks Marsh in Berkswell par]

	[NC]	[Ch]
Hen Marsh gent		5
Edw Carr		1
Tho Harris		2
(unpaid) Matth Leach		<1>2
Rich Swift		1
Widd Carr		3
John Ellitt		3
[blank] Swift		1
Wm James	1	
[blank] Swift		1
Jasper Goldier	1	
John Smith	1	
Hen Cox		1
Tho Masters		2

Knoll [Knowle chap[2]]

	[NC]	[Ch]
Mr Grivill		[-] [*8*[3]]
John Burrows		2
Mr Tho Palmer		6
Robt Winn		1
Edw Ashhurst		3
John Martin		1
Rich Carter		1
[p. 13]		
Rich Fisher		1
Wm Euds		3
John Martin		2
Mr Oliver Wiggin		8
Mrs Eliz Grimshaw widd		5
Wm Vorly		2
Rich Moore		1
Mr Rich Stoaks		3
Tho Ell		1
Natth Bissell		4
John Simonds		3
Mr Joysfeild		3
Mr Andrew Palmer		6
Edward Parsons		1
Wm Smith		2
Mr Spooner		6
Mrs Porter widd	2	
Wm Perkins		3
Simon Bissell		6
Edw Driver		4
Rich Parkes		5
Archelaus Busbey		1
Rich Johnson		1
Mrs Grimshaw widd		7
Tho Carr one of them a back [oven?]		8
Eliz Carter		1
John Johnson		1
<John>Tho Masters		1
Rich Welton		1
Tho Tayler	1	
Edm Lucett	1	
Tho Chambers	2	
Tho Priest	1	
Rich Watton emptie dore shut up & noe distress	1	
Eliz Ashby	1	
John Humphery	1	
Ralph Kent	1	
Abigall Welton	1	
Jobe Doson	1	
Wm Phillips	1	
John Bradford	1	
Wm Neale	1	
Anne Shakespire	1	
Hen Ashurst	1	

1 WCRO, QS11/32 (1671).
2 Chapelry of Hampton in Arden parish.
3 TNA, E179/259/9 (1666).

	[NC]	[Ch]
[p. 14]		
Ann Cooke	1	
Widd Newton	1	
Job Eads		1
Symon Brown	1	
Widd Beaseley	1	
Widd Taylor	1	
Widd Brown	2	

Chesnett Wood end

[Chessetts Wood End in Knowle chap]

	[NC]	[Ch]
Hen Scamber		5
Paull Martine		1
Mr Tibbitts		4
Mr <A>Odams		4
Tho Shakespeire		1
Wm Cox		1
Mr James Wright		2
John Taylor		1
Mrs Anne Norton		6
Wm Ashby		1
Rich Wall		1
John Archer		5
Widd Tayler		1
John Norton		1
Tho Bett		1
Rich Grimshaw gent		7
Humph Asbury very poore & noe distress to be had		1
Tho Baldwin	1	
Geo Wheeler	1	
Widd Brigg	1	
John Allen	1	
John Johnson	1	
Rich Brage	1	
Wm Burdon	1	
Tho Hall	1	
Edw Shett	1	
Widd Tayler	1	
John Shakespire		3

[p. 15]

Knoll Wood End

[in Knowle chap]

	[NC]	[Ch]
Tho Gilbert		2
John Lanton		1
Valentine Scambler		1
Tho Bissell		2
John Willson		1
Rich Burman		2
Rich Webb		3
Andrew Edmonds		1
Mrs Sarah Herbern		8
Charl Olives		3
Rich Heath		1
Hen Tayler		1
Geofry Taylor	1	
Margrett Haywood	1	
Wm Tayler	1	
John Bratt	1	
Tho Ward	1	
Kath Haucock	1	
John Haynes	1	
John Britten	1	
Wm Audley	1	
Tho Ridle	1	
Rich Lancaster	1	

Knoll Woodney End

[Knowle Widney End in Solihull par]

	[NC]	[Ch]
Widd Truelove emptie & noe distress to be had		3
[blank] Whatcock		1
Tho Ross		1
Hen Farr		1
John Grethhead jun		1
Tho Higginson		5
Tho Simonds		1
<Widd Wilson Mr Shirly in Solihull landlord>	<2>	
John Grethhead sen		1
Giles Millard		1
Rich Talice		1
James Rice		1

	[NC]	[Ch]
Widd Holbich		3
Mr Tho Holbich		5
George Toney	1	
<Henry Palmer>		<4>
Charles Stoney	1	
Widd Colins	1	
Wm Wood		1
Henry Palmer		1
[p. 16]		
Humph Hayward	1	
John Twigger	1	
Widd Rawlins	1	
Widd Smith	1	
Widd Cotterill	1	
John Lea	1	
Tho Palmer	1	
Em Hudsford	1	
Samll Symonds	1	
John Botterell	1	
Charles Stoney jun	1	
Law Ebrall		1

Longdon End [in Solihull par]

	[NC]	[Ch]
Charles Warring gent		10
Wm Spooner gent		10
Tho Symonds		7
Wm Davis		3
John Davis		3
George Bird alias Lynold		1
Tho Burton gent		2
John Brandon		1
Edw Sandale		1
John Newbury sen		2
John Tayler		1
John Wilks		3
John Palmer		2
Edw Watton		1
Tho Brice		1
Hen Tarlton		2
Robt Fisher		3
Mary Palmer		1
Jane Rice		1
John Newbery		1
Marg Wigston		1

	[NC]	[Ch]
Tho Harper		3
Vallent Henson		1
John Haynes		1
Tho Weston		1

Viewed by:
Richd Samon collector
Tho Carr constable

	[NC]	[Ch]
[p. 17]		
Tho Cattell		1
Christpofer Greathead		1
Widd Rastell	1	
Tho Lumber	1	
Edw Hooper	1	
Widd Hobby	1	
George Newby	1	
Edw Readall	1	
Tho Wood	1	
John Large	1	
Tho Rawbone	1	

Hampton in Arden [par]

	[NC]	[Ch]
John Login gent		8
Wm Fisher		1
Wm Taylor		1
Widd Loome		1
John Burge		2
Sarah Heath		1
Mr Pretty clarke		6
Hen Richardson		2
Rich Johnson		1
Tho Davis		1
Mrs Gardner <Burmingham>		3
Tho Fentham emptie Mr Geo Fentham de Burmingham landlord		1
Isack Mason		3
Clemt Paddey		1
Geo Smith		1
Samll Barden		3
Jona Adkins one new erected at Michms 70 paid for one		2
Alice Tompson vidua		1
Simon Mason		1
Tho Heath		1

	[NC]	[Ch]
John Bidle		1
Geo Lowe		2
Eliz Thompson		1
John Fisher		5
Tho Wall		3
Josiah Vardon		1
Tho Large		1
Natth Masson		1
Tho Barber		1
Margery Smith widd		3
[p. 18]		
Ann Mortiboies	1	
Edm Smith		1
Clemt Mason		2
Wm Fentham		1
<John Haris?>		
Tho Pady		1
Mr Robt Loggin		3
Wm Harding		2
Eliz Smith widd	1	
Wm Preist	2	
Widd Loome	1	
Rich Birgg	1	
John Biddell	1	
Walt Hunt	1	
Widd Willis	1	
Joseph Birgg	1	
Hen Gardner jun	1	
Hen Mills	1	
Widd Stafford	1	
Widd Williams	1	
John Fancham sen	1	
John Fancham jun	1	
Wm Hasting	1	
Eliz Knight	1	
Widd Gey	1	
Christpofer Tatton	1	
Tho Gey		1
Eustace Fentham	1	
John Brige	1	

Viewed by:
Richd Samon collector
Wm Fisher constable

	[NC]	[Ch]
[p. 19]		
Meridon [Meriden par]		
Tho Fisher gent		12
Mart Holbech gent		12
Jarvice Wheat gent		7
Mr <S…>Snell vicar		4
Tho Feild gent		8
Widd Baggett		7
Wm Smith		10
Wm West		4
Edw Parker		5
Edw <B>Parker		5
Mr Robt Harper		4
Mrs Ann Hardinge		9
Widd Rowney		2
Tho Avery		2
Mr William Harper		3
John Smart 2 houses		6
John Kinge sen		3
John Kinge jun		4
John Holmes		3
John Hunt		2
Rich Jeofry		4
Mr Wheate in 2 houses		3
Widd Baggett		2
Edw Leather		1
John Berry		2
Hen Paine		2
Hen Bunn sen		2
Tho Barker		3
John George		2
Tho Lapworth		1
Griffin Barnett		1
Hen Hardinge		1
Geo Eborn		1
Wm Rusell		3
Edw Mothershed		2
Thomas Stoaks		<2>1
John Willkinson emptie dore shut up & noe distress		1
Edw Harris		1
Ralph Kempsey		1
Rich Clarke		1
Hen Bunn jun		1

	[NC]	[Ch]
[p. 20]		
Tho Paddey		1
John Overton		1
Edw Baker		2
Wm Daniell		1
John Featchley		1
Widd Kimberly		1
Griffin Bewfeild		4
Mrs Feild		1
Wm Hackney		1
Robt Parsons		1
Wm Gardner		5
James Adcock		1
Widd Berry	1	
Widd Worth	1	
<Wm>Edw Lapworth	1	
Job Winmyll	1	
Robt Worth dead emptie noe distress to be had		1
John Swift	1	
Wm Green	1	
Richd Sneape	1	
Tho Berry	1	
<Widd Berry twice named>		
Wm Sparks	1	
Widd Parker	1	
John Hatley	1	
Rich Wilcock	1	
Grifin Berry	1	
Wm Fetherston	1	
Wm Lucas	1	
Griffin Keelinge entered at Michms 70 paid halfe a yeare		1
Robt Bewfeild	1	
Robt Bunn	1	
Corbett Pintupp	1	
Twite Cross Elliott	1	
Tho Baker sen	1	
Widd Swift	1	
Widd Westcott	1	
Tho Hudd	1	
Tho Jefery	1	
Tho Simonds	1	

	[NC]	[Ch]
John Bosworth	1	
Rich Taylor	1	
Wm Mossely	1	
George Greene	1	
Widd Hopkins	1	
<Rich Snibb?>	<1>	

Viewed by:
Richd Samon collector
Richd Jeoffry constable

[p. 21]

Great Packington [par]

	[NC]	[Ch]
Sir Clemt Fisher baronet		32
John Knight		1
John Newy		1
Widd Adcock		1
Rich Harding 1 forge refuseth to pay for his forge		3
Widd Smith		1
Simon Lee		2
Robt Hart		1
Nath Allen		2
Wm Wilson		1
James Masters		1
Wm Parsons		2
Edm Murcutt alias Wells		1
Wm Smart		1
Rich Reeves		2
Wm Cast		1
John Cradock		1
Wm Harding		1
Tho Hasterly	<1>	1
Geo Tedd		1
Jos Mason		1
Rich Watton		1
Widd Shuttellworth		1
John Flint		1
John Daniell		3
Clemt Docker		1
Widd Daniell		2
Wm Morteboyes		1
Tho Bysacer	1	
Robt Elliott		1

	[NC]	[Ch]
John Nicholl	1	
Tho Burbridge		1
Tho Cattell		1
Fran Warrall		1
Simon Hyatt		1
Mr Geery vicar		3
Rich Taridan		1
Tho Boult	1	
Tho Brown	1	
Clemt Docker	1	
Tho Taradine	1	
John Todd	1	
Wm Heast	1	
Tho Smith		1
[p. 22]		
Clemt Willson	1	
John Allen	1	
Lawrence Mooday	1	
Widd Reeves	1	
Widd Hills		1

Viewed by:
Richd Samon collector
[blank] Parsons constable

Packington Parvay
[Little Packington par]

	[NC]	[Ch]
Mr Morrice vicar		1
Robt Smith		1
Wm Billison		<2>3
Robt Bisacre		1
Rich Buttler		2
Wm Harrison		1
<Wm Catebree>		<1>
Hen Avery		1
<Robt>Willm Kerby		1
Ralph Smith		1
John White		1
John Garner		3
Tho Mortiboies		1
Edw Willson		1
Ralph Smith jun		1
Tho Shakespire		1
Rich Adcock		2
Tho Barwicke		1
Wm Ludford		1
Clemt Milliman		2
Fran Penn		4
Widd Davis	1	
Ewstace Basacker	1	
Fran Docker	1	
Joane Smith	1	
Tho Mortiboys	1	
Wm Coxall	1	
Wm Tysall	1	
John Wyrly	1	

Viewed by:
Richd Salmon collector
C Mullyman constable

[p. 23]
Church Bicknall
[Church Bickenhill
in Bickenhill par]

	[NC]	[Ch]
Clemt Wall		4
Mr Richd Martine		5
Mr Orton vicar		2
Tho Brooke		6
Widd Wall		2
Rich Bayles		1
John Holmes		1
Luke Jarvice		1
Widd Adcocks		2
Andrew Gardner		1
Wm Foxall		2
Steph Foxall	1	
Wm Morton		1
Widd Wall		8
Rich Powell		1
Wm Rabster	1	
John Day	1	
Tho Mitchell	1	
Widd May howse emptie dore shut & noe distress	[-] [*1*[1]]	
Ann Buttler	1	

[1] TNA, E179/259/9 (1666).

	[NC]	[Ch
Wm Hill	1	
Edw Lukeman	1	
Josiah Sanders	1	

Middell Bicknell and Hill
[Middle Bickenhill and
Hill Bickenhill in Bickenhill par]

	[NC]	[Ch]
Wm Brookes		2
John Henshaw		2
Wm Henshaw		2
Tho Brooks		1
Widd Keatly		1
Edw Brooks		1
Tho Lockley		1
John Anderton		1
Abra Auton		1
John Allin		1
<John>James Wright		1
Edw Smith	1	
Wm Daniell		5

[p. 24]
Longdon End in Bricknall
[Lyndon End in Bickenhill par]

	[NC]	[Ch]
Mr Rich Lucas		5
John Shaw		2
Tho Roper Widd Chambers		2
Rich Ketley		1
Tho Evetts		2
Nath Tooksley		1
Samll Charman		1
Widd Taxley		1
John Wall		1
Rich Biddell sen		1
Wm Biddell		2
Tho Heath		1
(unpaid) Rich Biddell jun		1
Edw Withrington	<1>0	

Marston Cailey End
[Marston Green End
in Bickenhill par]

	[NC]	[Ch]
John Judge gent		3
Robt Midlemore gent		4
Mrs Anne Smith		4
Samll Jervice		3
(unpaid) Wm Archer		2
John Burr		1
Rich Hands		1
Tho Lotch		1
Wm Gobsell		2
Wm Eves		2
Rich Bucknall		1
Rich Yates sen		1
Rich Yates jun		1
Widd Smith		1
Wm Thikbrome		1
Humph Sadler		1
John Hinshaw		1
Mr Tho Chattock		4

Viewed by:
Richd Samon collector
John Shaw constable

[p. 25]
Elmdon in Hampton
[Elmdon par[1]]

	[NC]	[Ch]
John Maine gent		10
Tho Clarke		2
Ralph Maire		2
Mr John Browne		1
John Parsons jun		1
John Kendrick		2
Oliver Hancox		2
Mr Hobbey		2
Rich Poltrey		1
Tho Anderton		1
Wm Green		1
Leona Barr		1
Tho Fisher		3

[1] Elmdon was a separate parish.

	[NC]	[Ch]
Wm Blunt		1
James Parsons sen		1
Rich Lake		1
Fran Andrews	1	
Robt Doffe	1	
Widd Paidge	1	
Mr Boone vicar		3

Newthurst in the Mannor of Knoll
[Nuthurst in Hampton in Arden par]

	[NC]	[Ch]
Isack Ingram gent		6
Mrs Lovett gent widd		4
John Wooten		3
Anth Benford		2
Rich Hopkins		2
John Mortiboyes		1
Wm Hexstall		1
John Smith		1
Tho Cranmore		1
Jane Rogers		1
Edw Cranmore		1
Rich Boaster	1	
Edw Wood	1	
Tho Berwick	1	
Widd Williams	1	
Abra Cooke	1	

Viewed by:
Richd Samon collector
Ralph Maire thirdborough in Elmdon

[p. 26]
Forshaw End in Solihull [par]

	[NC]	[Ch]
Roger Baker		2
Hen Milborn		2
Wm Brooksbank		1
Hen Hyatt		1
Wm Collins		4
John Robins		1
Hen Madow		1
Tho Frost		1
John Normand	1	
Tho Parker	1	

	[NC]	[Ch]
Tho Taylor	1	
Widd Browne	1	
Tho Haywood	1	
Widd Smith	1	
Wm Brewer alias Deues one new erected at Ladyday 71		1

Woodney End in Solihull
[Widney End in Solihull par]

	[NC]	[Ch]
Rich Powell 1 forge refuseth to pay for his forge		1
Mr Grisswell rector		7
Mr Huggiford		8
Clement Fisher		1
John Madcalfe		2
Edw Flincher		1
Leno Birde		2
Widd Collyer		1
Geo Callo		1
Wm Callo		5
Widd Twist		1
John Mills		1
Edw Green		1
Geo Feilding esq		8
John Webb		3
Wm Holmes		2
Wm Moris	2	
Wm Willcox	1	
Erasmus Callo	1	
Tho Simonds	1	
John Lea very poore	1	

[p. 27]
Sherly End in Solyhull
[Shirley End in Solihull par]

	[NC]	[Ch]
Wm Wheely		1
George Barton		1
Hump Barton		1
Tho Hudgford		1
<John Lea named elcewher>		
John Burton		1
Rich Bates		2
Mr Hump Dollfin		4
Tho Hyman		2

	[NC]	[Ch]
Robt Fowler		1
John Greaves		1
Rich Brockhurst		2
Tho Camden emptie Tho Highman landlord		2
James Ashfeild	1	
Tho Highmam		4
Mr Rich Pocuck		3
Wm Palmer		1
Widd Ha<…>we		4
Tho Hall		3
Wm Meadow		3
Rich Ball	1	
Rich Newbery		1
Tho <Gibbs>Newbery or Tho Gibbs		2
Mr Wm Martin		2
Rich Hands		1
John Gap one never finisht paid but for one		<2>1
John Essex		1
Widd Arden	1	
John Jeffery misrable poore & noe distress	<1>	1
Wm Cottrell	1	
Widd Truelove	1	
Rich Ward	1	
Widd Lea	1	
Tho Kendrick	1	
<Jam Asfeild named elcewher>		
Widd Roach	1	
Rich Evans	1	
Geo Feild		2
[p. 28]		
Tho Pratt	1	
<Wm Cotterill named elcewhere>	<1>	
Fran Ward	1	
<Richard>Wm Birth	1	
Oliver Hands	1	
Rich Gardner	1	
John Cotterill		1

	[NC]	[Ch]
Wm Paine	1	
Widd Smallwood	1	
<Wm Buck non such ith parish>		
Wm Hodgett	1	
Richard Matthews	1	
Widd Sparry	1	

Oakend

[Olton End in Solihull par]

	[NC]	[Ch]
Widd Witthers, Oken End	1	
John Tandy jun		1
John Smith emptie the dore shut up & noe distress to be had		<1>
Wm Smith		1
Amos Banister		1
Hen Banister		1
John Higeston		6
Rich Mills		1
<A cottage none such>		
Tho Dyall		3
Mr Avery		4
Hen Palmer gent		6
Mr John Slough <alias Flower>		3
Robt Palmer		3
<John Anderton jun>		
John Tandy sen		<3>2
Mr Tho Daly		3
Josias Fox [&[1]] [blank] Michell		3
Mr John Griswould		3
Tho Lago		3
Rich Brandwood		3
Hen Griswould		1
Robt Harison		1
John Cotterill Edw Green landlord		2
Fran Barr		1
Edw Crooke		2
[p. 29]		
Geo Gilbert		2
Hen Veale		1
Wm Griswould		2
Geo Bott		1
Samll Avery	1	
Wm Scotton	1	

1 WCRO, QS11/45 (1673).

	[NC]	[Ch]
Widd Lake	1	
Widd Greswould	1	
Widd Smith alias Greswould	1	
Tho Chambers	1	
John Symonds	1	
Francis Brookes vid	<1>	1
Mary Swinford vidua	1	
Alice Brandon vidua	1	
Richd Ashford	1	

Whitlocks end in Solyhull [par]

	[NC]	[Ch]
Averell Paddy		2
Geo Graunt		2
Richd Taylor		1
Humphery Newy		1
John Flavell		1
Danll Hall one quite down		5
Leond Berry		1
Tho Ashby		1
Widd Astly		1
Richd Bissell		3
Widd Baldwin		1
Jno Kendrick		1
Tho Lee		2
Edw Gilkes		1
Richd Heath		2
Richd Gilson		1
Tho Palmer		4
Richd Foard		2
Wm Madue		2
Richd Avery		2
Antho Kemsey		1
[p. 30]		
Widd Cotterill		3
Edw Hawkes		4
Tho Feild	1	
Wm Tayler	1	
Edw Day	1	
Widd Crosbyes daughter	1	
John Davis	1	
Robt Breedon	1	
Mary Chatter	1	
John Pritty	1	

	[NC]	[Ch]
John Hill	1	
Widdow Lea		1
Anne Lea vidua	1	
Hen Witherington in Tamworth parish	1	
John Lea	1	
Widd Fulford	2	
Widd Waring	1	

[***Solihull borough***[1]]

	[NC]	[Ch]
(unpaid) Tho Dawes the free schoole not endowed with £30 per annum		4
Ridgly Ward		1
Widd Russen		5
Richd Sutton		1
Richd Cole		4
John Brandon		2
Widd Giles alias Sergeant		2
Widd Walker	2	
Hen Wright		2
Clem Newy		5
Hen Evans		1
Widd Blunt		1
Wm Benton		3
Mr Joss Holt		7
Tho Crooke		4
Tho Palmer		5
Widd Ensor		2
[p. 31]		
Hen Powell		5
Clemt Newy		2
Mary Sergeant	2	
John Wright		5
John Fluelling	1	<1>
John Farmer		4
Tho Barker		1
John Slacher		1
Widd Corser		1
Wm Harrison 1 forge refuseth to pay for his forge		1
Wm Powell		2
Nich Daniell		1
Tho Essex		1
Hen Bradley		1

[1] WCRO, QS11/59 (1674).

	[NC]	[Ch]
Eliz Roe vidua emptie & noe distresse	1	
Reginald Veale	1	
Geo Greswould	1	
Widd Cooper	1	
Hen Dawes sen	1	
Richd Bennion	1	
Anne Wright vidua	1	
Geo Banister sen	1	
Hen Davis jun	1	
Joss Bent	1	
Robt Clarke jun	1	
Widd Paine	1	
Widd Lea	1	
Robt Hayward	1	
Hen Smith	1	
Widd Weaver	1	
Abra Underhill	1	
Robt Herdiman	1	
James Cooper	1	
Tho Osender	1	
James Withers	1	
Hump Twist	1	
[p. 32]		
John Bissell	1	
Robt Himson	1	
Henry Graunt	1	
Richd Tandy	2	
Luke Rider newly entered	1	
[*Christopher*[1]] Green	1	
Hen Ballard	1	
Wm Pinly	1	
Widdow Newy	1	
Wid Bird	1	
Reginald Veale sen	1	
Widd Smith	1	
Robt Smith	1	
Jane Browne	1	
Francis Ridell	1	
Wm Matthews	1	
John Tomkins	2	
Geo Banister jun	1	
John Essex	1	
Jone Thorne	1	<1>
Jno Thorne 1 forge refuseth to pay for his forge	<1>	1
Tho Betterton	1	
Widd Banister	1	
Anne Bradborne	1	
Wm House	1	
[*Widow*[2]] Holt	1	
Widd Butler	1	
Hen Greswould	1	
Widd Newby entered paid halfe a yeare very poore		1
Richd Haynes	1	
Wm Bissell	1	

Viewed by:
Richd Samon collector
John Wright constable

[WCRO, QS11/22]
[f. 1: see pp. 30–2, 163]
[f. 1v]

Bermingham [Birmingham]
Division in Hemlingford Hundred
[written by Henry Hargrave]

Curdworth [par]

Jno Ridgley esq	10
Jno Hunt	1
Mrs Elizab <Brasebridge>Brinsley	2
Mr Jno Brasebridge	3
Docter Wagstaffe	8
Tho Roads	1
Ardin Lingard	1
Jno Thame	1
Humph Lingard	1

1 TNA, E179/347: undated exemption certificate for 1670/1.
2 TNA, E179/347: undated exemption certificate for 1670/1.

	[NC]	[Ch]
Tho Hart		1
Sarah Kimberly		3
Edwd Pearson		1
Jno Mahew		1
Tho Sore		1
Jno Walden		2
Jos Adcocks		2
Willm Spooner		3
Geo Hall		2
Jno Dockett emptie		1
Edwd Astley		1
Willm Marston		1
Benj Johnson		1
Jno Hancocke		1
Edwd Haswell		1
Tho Lingard		3
Jno Freeman 1 forge &		1
Jno Judd		1
Jno Heath		2
Alice Wakefeild		1
		58
Tho Courtier	1	
Edwd Haswell sen	1	
Tho Write	1	
Tho Haly	1	
Tho Horsly	1	
Humph Worstall	1	
Widd Sadler	1	
Edwd Chandler	1	
Howses upon the waste	3	

[f. 2]

Minworth [in Curdworth par]

	[NC]	[Ch]
James H<…>urde		<3>2
Tho Wilcox		3
Jno Bill		1
Geo Gilbert		1
Henr Clay		3
Edwd Eagles		1
Edwd Jackson sen		1
<Edwd>Rich Nicholls		1
Tho Somerland		3
Willm Sheffeild		1
Tho Sadler		2
Tho Guest jun		1
Mr Tho Hargrave <sen>		2
Tho Mare 1 forge &		2
Edwd Woolly		3
Robt Guest		2
Edwd Lingard		1
Willm Marston		1
Jonath Tudman		1
Rich Write		1
Edwd Waldron		1
Tho Bickley		1
Widd Hargrave		1
Henr Fisher		4
Mrs Margrtt Woolly		2
Willm Swift		1
Tho Tudman		1
		44
<Tho Write> (mistake)	<1>	
<Edwd Hustwell sen>	<1>	
<Tho Courtier>	<1>	
<Tho Haly>	<1>	
<Tho Horsley>	<1>	
Robt Burnett	2	
Edwd Jackson jun	1	
Edwd Mare	1	
Widd Hatchett	1	
James Moses	1	
Tho Morris	1	
Tho Nicholl	1	
Abrah Write	1	
Widd Thornton	1	
Tho Frewin	1	
Tho Hargrave	1	
Jno Chudd	1	
Howses upon the common	2	

[f. 2v]

Sheldon [par]

	[NC]	[Ch]
Geo Devereux esq owner (emptie)		11
Mr Willm Ball minister		5
Robt Watcocke		5
Mr Willm Bannell		5
Mr Samll Devereux (emptie)		7
Tho Donton		3

	[NC]	[Ch]
Henr Shaw		7
Tho Archer		4
Willm Ward		3
Jno Bragg		2
Jos Syer		2
James Dent		1
Tho Madue		3
Willm Bramidge		1
Low Brockhurst		2
Jno Wells		1
Widd Jarvis		2
Isaac Bragg		1
Abrah Hancocke		2
Mrs Martha Kennersly vid		6
Tho Gopsall		1
Widd Cooke		3
Jno Mantell		1
Geo Gopsall		<1>2
Jno Bolds		1
Jno Hodgetts		1
Tho Smith		1
Tho Palmer		1
Phillip Wells		3
Jos Chareman		1
Jos Callow		1
Christpofer Tatton		1
Jno Heath		1
Jno Brockhurst		1
Rich Hands		1
Widd Wells		1
Widd Allen		2
Widd Bonnell		2
Willm Rogers		1
Abrah Hancocks		3
Humph Hobday		1
Jno Allin		3
Isaac Allin		2
		108

[f. 3]

	[NC]	[Ch]
Willm Woodard	1	
Widd Brockhust	1	
Widd Somerland	1	
Rich Wells	1	
Tho Avery	1	
Tho Showell	1	
Tho Trantor	1	
Edwd Bragg	1	

Water Oarton

[Water Orton in Aston par]

	[NC]	[Ch]
(3) Mr Tho Homer		3
Jno Gee of Asly owner	(emptie)	1
Jno Hinman		3
Walter Butler		2
Humph Pearson		3
Willm Fisher		3
Digby Hancox		1
Jno Bushell		1
Edwd Groves		2
Rich Wilcox		2
Tho Barrowes		1
Jno Hancocke		4
Willm Barton		2
Jno Harris		2
Widd Voile		1
Christpofer Feare		1
Willm Smith		1
		33
Franc Grinsell	1	
Widd Dawson	1	
Widd Hancocke	1	
Widd Richards	1	
Rich Silke	1	
Rich Roads	1	

Colshill [Coleshill par]

	[NC]	[Ch]
The Lady Digby		30
Jno Mahew		1
Abigall Eaves		1
Tho Eaves		1
Edwd Elliott		1

[f. 3v]

	[NC]	[Ch]
Rich Eaves		2
Edwd Glover		2
Jno Harris		2
Willm Browne		1
Rich Eaves sen		1

	[NC]	[Ch]
Christpofer Ireland		3
Henr Past		1
Widd Crosse		2
Widd Northwood		1
Willm Butler		1
Duke Yong		1
(1) Edwd Clarke 1 payable at Mich 1671 a pauper before (not paid)		1
Widd Butler		1
Jno Sadler		1
Mr Rich Adamson		4
Tho Holbich		2
(1) Mrs Anne Waite 1 entered at Lady Day 71 a pauper before (not paid)		1
Jno Mellis		1
Jno & Geo Butler		2
Jno Pearson sen		2
Ambr Holden		5
Jonas Boles		1
Edwd Smith jun	1 forge &	1
Jno Eaves		2
Tho Gill		2
Humph Mahew		1
<Tho>Franc Bowers		6
Rich Owin		1
Rich Mahew		1
Willm Walker		4
Arth Olds		2
Rich Bolton		1
Tho Crooke		1
Widd Sadler		1
Tho Walter		2
Tho Stone		3
Geo Baley		2
Simon Grainge		2
Sarah Marston		4
Franc Bowers owner (emptie)		1
Rich Woolson		1
Tho Adams		1
Widd Sadler		2
(2) The schoole howse	[-]	[*2*[1]]

	[NC]	[Ch]
Tho Rachell		1
Tho Adcockes		2
[f. 4]		
Jno Wagstaffe		1
Rich Abell		2
Jno Cater		1
Tho Walter		1
Mrs Feild		14
Edwd Keyton		2
Tho Steppins		1
Rich Owin		1
Edwd Cox now Tho Scott		<1>0
Willm Belcher		2
Jno Castleton		4
Willm Lax		1
Tho Mahew		<3>2
Robt Sodin		1
Robt Bosworth		2
Mrs Grace Elsmore		7
<W>Jno Balis		5
Tho Kidderminster		1
Jno Clifton		<1>3
Rich Johnson		3
Samll Sanders		1
Ralph Tookey		3
Jno Hollyard	1 forge &	3
Jno Eaves jun		2
Jno Past		<2>1
Willm Tuckey		3
Widd Caster		1
Widd Paine		1
Rich Tuckey		1
Tho Overton		1
Jno Wilson		2
Widd Kidderminster		4
Mr Willm Kidderminster		8
Edwd Smith sen		1
Rich Harris		1
Char King		1
Jos Harrison		1
Jno Coles		1
Tho Smith		1

[1] TNA, E179/259/9 (1666).

	[NC]	[Ch]
Jno Ensor		1
Tho Wathall		1
Jno Stone		1
Widd Stone		1
Jno Stone sen		1
Rich Orton		1
Christpofer Kisse		1
Jno Pearson jun		2
Mr Rich Peace		4
Widd Clay		2
		[222]

[f. 4v]

Bacon End

[Bacons End in Coleshill par]

Mr Jno Bull		7
Mr Geo Cotterell		8
Mr Jno Martell		5
Mr Tho Cotterell		3
Edwd Haward		1
Mr Jno Cotterell		2
Mr Rich Sandford		4
Tho Yeats		5
Widd Rawbone		1
Simon Grainge		1
Edwd Clifton		1
Willm Harvey		1
		[39]

Hawkswell

[Hawkeswell in Coleshill par]

Widd Eads		2
Rich Rawbone		1
Widd Simonds		1
Samll Elson		<1>2
Tho Clifton		1
Jno Sanders		1
Rich Jefferies		1
Geo Barton		7
Geo Faulconbridge		1
Jno Pawlett		2
Tho Jones		1
Lawr Jones		1
Widd Bolton		1
Tho Jackson		1

	[NC]	[Ch]
Jno Simonds		1
Ralph Palmer		1
		25

Gilson [in Coleshill par]

Mr Willm Wise		7
Dorothy Jeaks		2
Widd Smith		<1>2
Willm Short		1
Isaac Nicholls		1
<…>Nicho Miller		1
[f. 5]		
Jno Smith now Willm Miller		1
(1) Rich Miller 1 new built payable at Michs 1671 (not paid)		1
Jno Minsham		1
Tho Miller		3
Mr Brookes		8
		[28]

Poore for Colshill Hawkswell Baconsend and Gilson being all one Parish

Jno Cheatly	1	
Jos Smith	1	
Tho Preston	1	
Tho Scott	1	
Widd Trimings	1	
Jno Kidderminster	1	
Rich Alpott	1	
Tho Kilpecke	1	
Widd Flavile	2	
Jno Ebton	1	
Franc Tiser	1	
Simon Grainge sen	1	
Dorothy Yeates	1	
Tho Miller	1	
Jno Mortboys	1	
Jno Hayward	2	
Widd Smith	1	
Willm Eaves	1	
Tho Cooper	1	
Franc Coslett	1	
Rich Borden	1	
Math Ablett	1	

	[NC]	[Ch]
Edwd Ball	2	
Edwd Thornton	1	
Jno Williams	1	
Jno Blackwell	1	
Franc Judd	1	
Willm Swan	1	
Geo Knight	1	
Widd Conway	1	
Cottages upon the waste	20	

[f. 5v]

Wishaw [par]

	[NC]	[Ch]
Geo Goodyer jun		2
Tho Robinson		1
Rich Horton		1
Willm Tomlinson		1
Jno Wheely		2
Willm Cooke		1
James Write		2
Doro Lovett		<1>2
Jno Lovett 1 forge &		<2>1
Tho Glover		2
Willm Smith		1
Nicho Moore		3
Widd Hall		2
Tho Hall		2
Jno Cooke		<2>1
Mr Rich Oarton		<3>2
Henr Gilbert owner (emptie)		1
Willm Wilson the last tenant owner Mr Lile of Moxall (emptie)		1
Mr Robt Lloyde		3
		31
Rich Smith	1	
Rich Harvy	1	
Tho Snape	1	
Jno Willington	1	
Anne Rockett	1	

Sutton Colefield & Maney

[Sutton Coldfield par]

Wormley quarter beyond the Wood

[Walmley and beyond the Woods]

	[NC]	[Ch]
Ambrose Cooper		2
<Mr> Henry Pudsey esq		9
Mr Tho Feild		6
Tho Sharratt		3
Mrs Alice Cradocke		4
Rich Write jun		2
Jno Balyes		2
Jno Fidler		1
Jno Cooke		3
Abrah Jorden		1
Jno Graisbrooke sen		3
Jno Glascot		1
[f. 6]		
Widd Write		4
Walter Somerland		1
Edwd Bennett		2
Abrah Pemberton		4
Phillip Best		2
Geo Gilbert		1
Tho Weaver		1
Jno White		1
Rich Somerland		3
Henr Hurst		4
James Lees		3
Henr Write		2
Jno Write		1
<Jno>Tho Cater		2
James Write		0
Robt Lea		1
Jno Thomson		2
Tho Patterton		1
Willm Dixon		2
Willm Richards		1
Jno Townsend		1
(1) Jno Hurst 1 new built payable at Michs 1671 (not paid)		1
Alice Dixon		1
Willm Wood gent of Pedemore		2
		80

	[NC]	[Ch]
[***Maney and the Wild*** [1]]		
[Maney and the Wylde in Sutton Coldfield par]		
Willm King		1
Rich Somerland		1
<Mich>Walter Farmer		1
Jno Alpott		1
Geo James		2
(2) Henr Rastell and Henr Turner entered at Midsomer (not paid)		2
Widd Rotheram		1
Willm Stephenson		1
Mr Raphiell Sedgwick		6
Mr Peter Lambert		4
<Ralph>Robt Poulton		1
Mr Benj Blacksham		6
Rich Beckley		1
Benj Cockersell		1
Edwd Fletcher		2
Widd King		2
Ralph Blakesly		3
Tho Veasy		4
Ralph Veasy		2
[f. 6v]		
Mrs Mary Martin		1
Mr Jno Adis		6
Willm Roocker		3
Jno Farmer		2
Jno Winn		0
Widd Hawksford		1
Willm Pickerill		1
Widd Stainer		4
Ralph Blaksly sen		3
Willm Peate		2
Rich Byron		1
James Heath		1
Jno Hall		1
		68

Great Sutton
[Sutton Coldfield in Sutton Coldfield par]

	[NC]	[Ch]
(7) Mr Jno Gilbert very poore & in prison 7 hearths received in p[aymen]t 14s. there being no distresse (not paid)		7
Mrs Secheverell		7
(1) Willm Warton 1 hearth entered at Lady Day 1671 (not paid)		1
Mr Samll Stephenson		3
Mr Henr Freeman		4
Robt Rogerson		5
Tho Clifton		2
Rich Rogerson		3
Danll Mosse		3
Willm Pearsall		2
Tho Reading		2
Geo Bentley		1
Mr Jno Rostell		4
Tho Mills		4
Jno Jackson		1
James Haniball		1
Willm Loynes		1
Jno Martin jun		3
Willm Spooner		2
Willm Veasy		2
Willm Norton		1
Geo James		1
Ralph Cooper		1
Willm Martin jun		2
Mrs Rebecca Wasse		5
Mr Willm Chancey		5
Tho Goodale		1
Mrs Bridgett Hanum		5
[f. 7]		
Mr Rich Best		12
Mr Jno Cooper		2
Rich Martin sen		1
James Martin		3
Jno Cartwrite		2
Jno Haniball		2
Tho Freeman		3
Mr Sturgis of London owner emptie		16

[1] TNA, E179/259/10 (1665).

	[NC]	[Ch]
Rich Foard		3
Mr Nicho Harvy		5
Tho Norris		1
(4) <Jno>Rich Foard new built & entered at Lady Day 1671	(not paid)	4
Franc James		2
Robt Write		2
Jno Cooper		2
Jno Tomlinson		1
Mrs Kath Holden		6
Mr Tho Dawny		9
		[155]

Hill Quarter & Little Sutton
[in Sutton Coldfield par]
[***Hill*** [1]]

	[NC]	[Ch]
Jno Terry		2
Widd Tailor		1
Willm Halfepenny		1
Jno Halfepenny		2
Widd Priest jun		2
Willm Balies		3
Widd Sedgwicke		3
Jno Turner		2
Rich Turner		2
Willm Gibbins		3
Jno Cooper	1 forge &	2
Jno Woodsaw	1 forge &	1
Tho Harrison		1
Geo Cooper		1
Edwd Parkes	1 forge &	1
Willm Smith		1
Ralph Dixwell		1
Widd Cartwrite		1
Tho Wilcox		1
Ralph Turner owner	(emptie)	3
<Henr>Willm Terry		1
Robt Tailor		1
Widd Elkin		1
Jno Eagles		2
Geo Cooper sen		1
[f. 7v]		
Willm Meere		1
Tho Turner		1

[***Little Sutton*** [2]]

	[NC]	[Ch]
Tho Birch		1
Abell Cooper		2
Will Cooper		2
Jno Brooks		3
Simon Cartwrite		2
Tho Aspin		1
Tho Cooper		1
Rich Burton		1
Jno Birch		1
Willm Pickwell	1 forge &	<1>3
Mrs Yardly		1
Franc Yardly		2
Willm Glover		1
Willm Taylor		2
Robt Tailor		1
Samll Asplin		1
Mr James Littleton		6
Ralph Cooper		4
<Rich>Willm Birch		1
Jno Terry		2
Jno Fox		0
Clemt Smart		2
Jno Smallwood		1
Franc North		2
Tho Waldron		1
Edwd Cooper (emptie)		1
		[87]

Moore & Ashfordlong
[Moor and Ashfurlong in Sutton Coldfield par]

	[NC]	[Ch]
Geo Sacheverell esq		17
Mr Grovener		11
Mr Tho Scott		6
Mr Jos Raynor		4
Doctor Willm Watson		10
Jno Powell		6
Widd Hall		2

1 TNA, E179/259/10 (1665).
2 WCRO, QS11/59 (1674).

	[NC]	[Ch]
Willm Hannum		7
Geo Keite gent		4
Robt Heath		1
Robt Bird		1
Willm Hunnibone		1
Edwd Hickman		1
Mary Ashford widd		1
Jno Jones		2
Rich Ashford		1
Mr Jno Davell		3
[f. 8]		
Tho Richards		2
Mr Ambr Cooper		2
Tho Bassett 1 forge &		4
Tho Eagles		1
Mich Moore		3
Willm Penn		2
		[92]
Poore of all this parish together		
Tho Creton	1	
Tho Cotterell	1	
Samll Jeffery	1	
Jno Blacher	1	
Edwd Walker	1	
Widd Duncome	1	
Sarah Duncome	1	
Hemlocke Fox	1	
Anne Tuncks	1	
Widd Tuncks	1	
Willm Parker	1	
Moses White	1	
James Martin jun	1	
Willm Farmer	<1>2	
Jno Cheatle	1	
Geo Oarton	1	
Willm Astall	2	
Jno Stephens	1	
Anne Wasse	1	
Willm Lucey	1	
Franc Ward	1	
Ralph Morris	1	
Edwd Cotton	1	
Jno Spooner	1	
Willm Bagnall	1	

	[NC]	[Ch]
Mary Woodson	1	
Edwd Luckley	1	
Jno Bird	1	
Jno Smith	1	
Geo Hampson	1	
Franc Pickerill	<1>2	
Jno Willy	1	
Edwd Cater	1	
Anne Cooper	2	
Willm Astall	<1>2	
Rich Rawthorne sen	1	
Willm Underhill	1	
Nicho Brooks	1	
Jno Smith	1	
[f. 8v]		
Tho Farley	1	
Jno Holland	1	
Jno Norris	1	
Widd Day	1	
Jos Lewis	1	
Jno Blith	1	
Ralph Blith	1	
Jno Griffin	1	
Edwd Duckman	1	
Willm Buckley	1	
Miles Johnson	1	
Widd Dale	1	
Edwd Crathorne	1	
Rich Smith	1	
Tho James	1	
Geo Nichlins	1	
Tho Binion	1	
Geo Jackson	1	
Tho Keeling	1	
Widd Silvester	1	
Widd Ashly	1	
Danll Walter	1	
Jno Horwood	1	
Edwd Cater	1	
Howses upon the common that receive collection	30	

	[NC]	[Ch]
Moxall [Moxhull in Wishaw par]		
Geo Lisle esq		14
Rich Adcock		6
Tho Jones		1
Willm Gopsall		1
Jno Plover		1
Nicho Godfrey		1
Tho Shelly		1
Edwd Write		1
Willm Naseby		1
Edwd Whitehead		1
Tho Cooke		1
Rich Nicholls		1
Ambr Cooper		1
		31
[f. 9]		
Jno Heath	1	
Widd Ellis	1	
Willm Wright	1	
Henr Write	1	
Willm Wilson	1	
Dudson [Duddeston] **in Aston Parish**		
Capt Robt Turton		8
Widd Edwards		3
Tho Warwicke		1
Martin Day		1
Franc Mills		1
Sir Robt Holt for the lodge		1
		15
Danll Winn	1	
Tho Wiggins	2	
Benj Orton	1	
Jno Hunt	1	
Vincent Legar	1	
Tho Walker	1	
Ambr Key	1	
Castle Bromwich [in Aston par]		
Jno Bridgman esq		21
Char Rotheram		3
Jno Thornton		3
Franc Weston		3

	[NC]	[Ch]
Willm Hall		2
<Franc Weston>Tho Foster		3
Willm <…>Foster		4
Mr Jno Brookes minister		3
Jos Knight		1
Widd Waldron		1
Tho Underhill		2
Symon Walden		3
Edwd Piggott		3
Widd Write		1
[f. 9v]		
Tho Elson		1
Tho Lake 1 forge &		3
Franc Vale		4
Jno Everard		1
Franc Spencer		3
Edwd Adcockes		1
Franc Sadler		2
Willm Sadler		6
Tho Day		1
Widd Eagles		2
Willm Barebone		3
Widd Oarton		1
James Compson		1
Jno Day		1
Tho Wall		2
Edwd Weston		1
Christpofer Sadler		4
Willm Sanders		2
Rich Sadler		3
Jno Sadler		3
Jno Weston sen		2
Rich Thickbroome		14
Henr Smith		3
Sir Herbert Price		12
		129
Henr Elson	1	
Tho Stanley	1	
Edwd Kendall	1	
Humph Griffin	1	
Jno Langley	1	
Jno Cater	1	
Phillip Smith	1	
Jno Hargrave	1	

	[NC]	[Ch]
Edwd Price	1	
Elizab Barbone	1	
Widd Wenn	1	
Ellianor Powell	1	
Jno Lilly	1	
Widd Bromswick	1	
Abrah Carter	1	
Willm Haycocke	1	
Humph Rogers	1	
Howses upon the common that receive collection	9	

[f. 10]

Little Bromwich [in Aston par]

	[NC]	[Ch]
Willm Wood esq		10
Edwd Branwood		4
Robt Powell		4
Robt Belcher		5
Willm Jourden		2
James Page		2
Tho Silke jun		1
Geo Portman		2
Peter Bery		1
Joseph Raynor		1
Joseph King		1
Willm Wootton		2
Robt King		1
Willm Flavell		2
Robt Silke		1
Rich Miller		1
Hugh Vincent		1
Edwd Osborne		<1>2
Edwd Hargrave		2
Jos Marsh		2
Widd Harvy		2
Jno Walker		1
Willm Russell		2
Jno Ward		4
Willm Rogers		1
Tho Lane 1 forge &		3
Willm Jourden		2
Wingfeild Bissell <owner> (emptie)		1
Jno Vaile		1
		64

	[NC]	[Ch]
Henr Smith	1	
Willm Bates	1	
Elizab Penn	1	
Willm Watton	1	
Ellianor Hopkins	1	
Jno Bates	1	
Marjery Bates	1	
Jno Hopkins	1	
Tho Smith	1	

[f. 10v]

Witton [in Aston par]

	[NC]	[Ch]
Mr Willm Booth		18
Henr Lane		4
Tho Stanley 1 forge &		1
Geo Harding		2
Edwd Willis		2
Willm Warwicke		1
Jno Jackson owner		1
Robt Jackson		1
Rich Adams		2
Widd Edwards		2
Rich Witton 1 forge &		3
Widd Holliman		1
Samll Osborne 1 forge &		1
Tho Write		1
Jno White		1
Aquilla Bancks		1
Rich Bancks		1
Jno Smith jun		1
Willm Write	1	
Tho Penn	1	
Jno Smith	1	
Tho Adcocke	<1>2	
Widd Tutle	1	
Jno Bucke	1	
Humph While	1	
Widd Holland	1	
Lucy Stanly	1	
Widd Cooper	1	
		44

Boresly [Bordesley in Aston par]

	[NC]	[Ch]
Willm Flint		1
Willm Phillips		1

	[NC]	[Ch]
Tho Worrall		1
Willm Cookes		1
Franc Harper		1
Widd Walker		1
Jos Allen		1
Willm Woodward		1
Tho Gilbert		1
Henr Foard		1
The Lady Gawdey		5
[f. 11]		
Willm Elborne		2
Willm Poultney		2
Simon Underhill		3
Willm Allin		1
Humph Poultny		1
Jno Feild		5
Jos Marsh		2
Jno Marsh		1
Geo Dolphin		3
Izab Foster		2
Isaac Tailor		2
Tho Kildale		2
Tho Owin		2
Tho Hadley		1
Widd Harper		<1>2
Steph Colemore		2
Jno Feild		1
Jno Allin		2
Mr Tho Rawton		7
Mr Rich Coomer		4
Ralph Write		1
Nicho Millard		1
Henr Hunt		3
Anne Feble & Elizabeth Cooke		2
Jone Dolphin		<1>2
Jone Sawyer		1
Mr Tho Evans		8
Edwd Dolphin		1
Edwd Walker sen		1
Tho Fowler		1
Jno Pearcy jun now Edwd Allin		1
Tho Ashbury		1
Jno Perry sen		1
Widd Flavell		1
Jone Syer		1

	[NC]	[Ch]
Geo Graves		1
Jno Russell		1
Will Middleton (empty)		1
		91
Willm Kendall	1	
Tho Brookes and Tho Ives	1	
Widd Cadducke	1	
Jno Tailor	2	
Tho Hybotome	1	
Jno Marsh	1	
Edwd Clawson	1	
Martin Jeffery	2	
Nath Rogers	1	
Jno Russell 1 forge &	1	
[f. 11v]		
Jno Taylor	1	
Willm Rogers	1	
Edwd Harrison	1	
Widd Musgrave	1	
Ellinor Harding	1	
Elizab Fitton	1	
Willm Browne	1	
Jno Cooke	1	
Widd Dolphin	1	
Henr Flabell	1	
Howses upon the common that receive collection	12	
Erdington [in Aston par]		
Harvy Baggott esq		10
Phillip Lane		5
Simon Grenold		3
Mr Jno Adis		3
Peter Cooper		1
Rich Boxidge		1
Willm Rogers jun		1
Jno Rogers		3
Vincent Eagles		1
Willm Rogers sen		3
Rich Morris		1
Willm Edgill		2
Joyce Hopkins		1
Robt Ansor		1
Tho Paine		1
Hugh Walton		1

	[NC]	[Ch]
Willm Nitingale		2
Robt Stanley 1 forge &		1
Willm Bragg		1
Jacob Whiteas		1
Tho Pincks		1
Henr Holding jun now Widd		1
Isaac Keeling		3
Henr Holding sen		1
Jno Dawson		3
Widd Eagles		1
Henr Freeman		1
[f. 12]		
Samll Harrison		2
Mr Humph Holding		6
Willm Archer		1
Edwd Goldingale		2
Jacob Bragg		1
Franc Hall		4
Lawr Edghill		2
Tho George		1
Anne Glason		1
Ralph Sedgwicke		4
Willm Hopkins		3
Samll Rodes		2
Rich Barton		1
Widd Birch very poore		3
Tho Roper		2
Tho Wells very poore		3
Humph Jennings esq		11
Mr Edwd Birch sen		4
Willm Jennings		2
Willm Heath		1
Henr Leeke		2
Jno Allen 1 forge &		1
Edwd Warwicke		3
Ambrose Fido		1
Tho Somerland		1
Alice Somerland		1
Jone Hopkins		1
Mr Edwd Birch		3
Roger Colborne		1
Willm Burton		1
Mr Jennings 2 forges		[-]
		125

	[NC]	[Ch]
Jno Underwood	1	
Willm Stokes	1	
Roger Stokes	1	
Jno Norris	1	
Zach Hews	1	
Tho Horton	1	
Tho Felton	1	
Geo Stoaks	1	
Rich Underhill	1	
James Bancks	1	
Rich Sadler	1	
Willm Hutton	1	
Jno Ashford	1	
Tho Shefeild	1	
Widd Mathews	1	
Joyce Hargrave	1	
Mary Barton	1	
[f. 12v]		
Mary Allen	1	
Rich Smart	1	
Tho Roper	1	
Jno Roper	1	
Dorothy Bidle	1	
Widd Write	1	
Cuthbd Macklin	1	
Jone Trayford	1	
Jno Hodgkins	1	
Mary Harding	1	
Izab Answer	1	
Anne Dickman	1	
Anne Crofts	1	
Geo Clifton	1	
Howses upon the common that receive collection	28	

Wishwood and Saltley

[Washwood and Saltley in Aston par]

	[NC]	[Ch]
Humph Newby		3
Willm Jourden		4
Widd Write		1
Jno Write		4
Henr Write 1 forge &		1
Jno Pearson		3
Willm Chambers		1

	[NC]	[Ch]
Robt Rotheram		9
Tho Gotch		1
Edwd Glover		1
Mary Newby		2
Samll Chaster		1
Ambrose Chesterton		<2>1
Jno Austen		1
<Jno Austen>		<1>
<Jno>George Birch		<1>2
Jno Hopkins		1
Jno Chetwin		2
Elizab Harrison		1
Widd Marman		1
		40
Rich Chatwin	1	
Jone Fellowes	1	
Lettice Griswould	1	
[f. 13]		
Jno Mayman	1	
Edwd Vincum	1	
Henr Newby	1	
Humph Warwitt	1	
Widd Rogers	1	
Tho Price	1	
Mary Hancocke	1	
Rich Overton	1	
Willm Clawson	1	
Rich Chatwin	1	
Jno Wastle	2	
Howses upon the common that receive collection	9	

Aston nere Birmingham
[Aston par]

	[NC]	[Ch]
Sir Robt Holt bart		41
Willm Pritchett 1 forge &		3
Mr Tho Yardley		7
Sarah Minard		3
Hugh Holland		1
Edwd Badley		1
Mr Rich Martin		3
Tho Whitacre		1
Amos Sparkes		1
Henr Osborne		1
Jno Gisborne		2
Tho Jenkins		1
Jno Dixon		1
		66
Jno Bridgman	1	
Jno Whitacre	1	
Rich Hargrave	1	
Geo Bicknell	<1>2	
Rich Smart	1	

[f. 13v]
Bermingham [Birmingham par]
Welch end

	[NC]	[Ch]
Nicho Samford		5
Robt Groves		6
James Gibbons		2
Willm Bolton		2
Rich Madley 1 forge &		2
Jno Wilson		6
(1) Willm Holmes 1 a pauper before entered at Lady Day 1671 (not paid)		1
Geo Worley		<1>3
Willm Weston		2
Zach Waldron		3
Willm Jones		3
Willm Homes		1
Rich Write		2
Henr Write		2
Jno Crompton		2
Jno Kendricke 1 forge &		1
Henr Bond		1
Geo Harding 1 forge &		3
Tho Harrison 1 forge &		2
Rich Unit		1
Tho Bridgens		4
(2) Jno Oxfor new built entered at Lady Day 1671 (not paid)		2
(2) Steph Newton new built entered at Michs 1670 & paid halfe a yeare (not paid)		2
(2) Nicho Bracklebancke new built entered at Midsomer 1671 (not paid)		2
(2) Tho Fleming a pauper before entered at Lady Day 1671 (not paid)		2

	[NC]	[Ch]
Henr Cooke		3
Danll Simms & Mrs Cradocke		7
Jno Parratt		2
Geo Write		3
Jos Pemerton		2
Tho Smith		4
Rich Bonner		3
Jno Bonner		2
Robt Brandwood		6
Jno Russell		4
Mr Carter		8
Tho Blith		3
Willm Whetston		2
[f. 14]		
Geo Hotham		2
(2) Samll Boys entered at Lady Day 1671 a pauper formerly (not paid)		2
Edwd Greenshill		2
Christpofer Henman		2
Mrs Mary Guest		3
Tho Pemberton		5
Peter Baker		4
Jno Neway		2
Geo Alsop		2
(2) Tho Bate 2 entered at Lady Day 1671 a pauper before (not paid)		2
Willm Jackson		3
Rich Lewis		2
(2) Jarvis Brian 2 new built entered at Lady Day 167 (not paid)		2
(2) Samll Tailor 2 new built entered at Lady Day 1671 (not paid)		2
Willm Baylie		3
Widd Bitway		4
Edwd Tailor } (formerly one house)		2
Rich Harrison } (formerly one house)		5
Willm Strain } (formerly one house)		2
Isaac Stanton		3
Antho Burrage		2
(2) Jno Willinger 2 a pauper before entered at Lady Day 1671 (not paid)		2
		[169]

	[NC]	[Ch]
High Streete on the left hand downwards		
Tho Fewtrill		5
Tho Newton		2
Samll Porter		9
Robt Seale		3
Willm Girdler		5
Jno Browne		4
Willm Price		4
Mr Franc Potter		4
Josline Pearcy		2
Widd Smith now Jno Browne		2
Humph Jennings esq		3
Mr Phillip Friers		13
Robt Bancks		8
Anne Butler		3
(3) <Edwd>Tho Birch 3 entered at Midsomer 1671 & two paupers before (unpaid)		3
(5) Samll Vaughton		5<4>
Simon Heath		15
Ann Yeates		10
		100
[f. 14v]		
Bullring		
Mr Geo Dodd		4
Mr Josiah Slater		3
Mr Turry		2
Edwd Ensor		3
		12
High Streete on the right hand downwards		
Edwd East		<3>1
Tho Rann		2
Josiah Baker		2
Jos Robinson		5
Jno Cotterell		4
Edwd Scott		2
Foulke Bray		4
(2) Henr Mayhew 2 entered at Lady day 1671 a pauper before (not paid)		2
Jno Baker		4
Jacob Austin		4

	[NC]	[Ch]
Jacob Leather		3
Mr Edwd Crancke		13
Mr Tho Mooreland		7
		53

High Streete more on the left hand downwards

	[NC]	[Ch]
Jno Wood		3
Widd Crompton		1
Edward Crompton		2
Jno Wollaxall		2
Jno Bentley		2
Samll Sely		2
Widd Baker		2
Mr Jno Birch		2
(B) Jno Wall		8
(2) Roger Auster 2 new built entered at Lady Day 1671 (not paid)		2
Willm Hall		2
Nath Pemberton		5
Jno Harding		2
Edwd Haywood		4
Widd Clement		3
Geo Fanthem		3
James Baker		3
Widd Moore		1
Mr Samll Smalbrooke		10
Jer Grigory		4
Hugh Tuncks		3
Edwd Freeman		4
Josiah Yeats		2
[f. 15]		
Mr Willm Bryersly		4
Edwd Croswell		2
Samll Groves		1
Humph Vaughton		2
Willm Nicholls		1
Mr Doley		6

Cares [Carrs] **Lane**

	[NC]	[Ch]
(2) Robt Hunt 2 new built entered at Lady Day 1671 (not paid)		2
(1) Tho Scott 1 new built entered at Lady Day 1671 (not paid)		1
		86
		[91]

Digbeth

	[NC]	[Ch]
Mr Tho Rawny		8
Rich Jencks		2
Robt Coles	2 forges &	2
Jno Stacey		2
Willm Dickins		2
Willm Bryerly		2
Rich Halfepenny		7
Rich Careles		5
Samll Lindon emptie Mr Phillips of Pancridge owner		3
Humph Buckle		2
Samll Balies		1
(1) Samll Balies more 1 hearth new built & finished at Midsomer 1671 (not paid)		1
Benj Roberts		3
Joseph Brainton		2
Rich Dolphin	1 forge &	3
(2) Edwd Horton new built 2 hearths entered at Lady Day 1671 (not paid)		2
Samll White		3
Mr James Trubshaw		5
James Piddocke		2
(2) Jno Graves 2 hearths entered at Lady Day 1671 a pauper before (not paid)		2
Jno Sharpley jun		1
Zach Gisborne		4
Jonath Toone		2
Jos Hawkes		2
Tho Dalloway		2
Jno Hunt		3
Edwd Bellamy		4
Edwd Ollives		2
Isaac Allen	1 forge &	4
Hugh Hides	1 forge &	3
[f. 15v]		
Abrah Cow		2
Willm Sanders		2
Henr Fantham		4
Antho Pointon		2
Robt Clarke		2
Mich Browne		2
Jno Capelwood		2

	[NC]	[Ch]
Robt Dalloway	1 forge &	3
Ambr Foxall		6
Samll Doley		2
Widd White		2
Jno Greene	2 forges &	3
Rich Billingsly		3
Willm Elsmore		3
Willm Medley		1
Tho Cotterell		5
Jno Brookes	1 forge &	1
Robt Bingham	1 forge &	2
James Garner		1
Danll Broughton	1 forge &	2
Jno Perry	1 forge &	2
Willm Humphry		2
Char Frite		3
Tho Timberly	1 forge &	1
Jno Brinton	1 forge &	2
Jos Lea		2
(2) Willm Silke 2 new built entered at Lady Day 1671 (not paid)		2
Jno Henn	1 forge &	2
Abrahm Foxall owner (emptie)		2
Jno Cotterell	1 forge &	2
Willm Parry	1 forge &	2
Jno Freeman		2
Jno Ashford	1 forge &	2
Rich Knight		1
Robt Smith		1
Jno Spooner		2
Jno Dalby		1
Jno Greaves sen		2
Rich Williams		2
Jno Simcox		6
Jos Hunt		1
Widd Cotterell		4
Jno Ellis		2
Jno Hopkins		6
Jno Cotterell	1 forge &	2
Samll White now Mr Jno Pemberton		2
		[194]

[f. 16]

Digbeth on the right hand downwards

	[NC]	[Ch]
Peter Farmeing		1
Willm Burton		2
Jno Allen		3
Tho Greaves		2
(1) Mr Jno Rogers 1 new built entered at Midsomer 1671 (not paid)		1
Mr Robt Smalbrooke		4
Jos Baker		2
Rich While		2
Willm Wood		2
Jno Hunt		2
Jno Walke	1 forge &	2
Tho Tailor		2
Willm Miller		1
Humph Tibbetts	1 forge &	1
Mr Willm Sprott		5
Rich Knight		1
Jno Wall		3
Rowland Cotterell		2
Edwd Crosby		1
Rich King		2
Mrs Billingsly		<2>3
Willm Borne		1
Jno Sleigh		1
Abrah Colemore		3
Mr Jno Billingsley		4
Jno Townsend		1
Jno Greenwood	<1>2 forges &	1
Jos Knight		2
Abell Bingham		3
		60

Edgbaston Streete

	[NC]	[Ch]
Widd Miller		5
Willm Suger		2
Jno Haywood		2
(3) Rich Hunt 3 very poore and blind (not paid)		3
Tho Fairfax 3 emptie and owner Rich Painton		3
Jno Gardner		2

	[NC]	[Ch]
(7) Widd Benson miserably poore 7 hearthes nothing to be found but children & raggs (not paid)		7
Tho Russell		4
[f. 16v]		
Edwd Coborne		3
Mr Jno Lander		2
Mrs Kempson		2
Willm Hawkes 1 forge &		2
Franc Darby		2
Widd Richards		4
Jno Filedust		2
Simion Harris		2
Willm Guest		4
Rich Earles		3
Robt Primer		3
(3) Dorothy Crompton 3 hearths new built entered at Lady day 71 (not paid)		3
Phillip Allin		1
Geo Gisborne		3
Tho Sanders		2
Jno Eaton		2
(1) Widd Walker 1 a pauper before entered at Midsomer 1671 (not paid)		1
Jno Weely		6
Willm Cotterell		2
Abrah Spooner		4
Jno Sanders		2
Jno Bellamy		2
Willm Cox		5
Christpofer Harris		3
Jos Tailor		2
Jno Taylor jun 1 forge &		2
Willm Southam		2
Jeremy Rotheram		2
Jos Worrall		2
Rich Mills		2
Edwd Capps		3
Mr Robt Girdler		7
Rich Hallis		4
Willm Hewkes		3
Mr Ryland archdeacon		11
Geo Hartley		2
Tho Fisher		2

	[NC]	[Ch]
Jo Faster & 3 new built		2
		139
Spicer Streete		
Edwd Carter		2
Rich Painton		2
Jno Hands		6
Mr Willm Coleman		4
Mr Rich Kempson		4
Mr Tho Whitacre		6
Jno Bradley		1
[f. 17]		
Widd Lea		2
Ambrose Lea		3
Rich Billingsly		4
Jno Belcher		4
Tho Birch		2
Antho Cooper		1
Robt Coles		5
Tho Moreland		6
(3) Jno Jesson 3 new built entered at Lady Day 1671 (not paid)		3
Jno Spooner		3
Tho Seale		3
Mrs Wilson widd		7
Mr Edwd Eades		5
Tho Rands		4
Jno Rands		2
(1) Rich Peters new built entered at Michs 1670		1
Tho George		3
		[83]
New Streete		
Henr Wood		3
Humph Ashford		7
Franc Levett		3
Robt Baylie		3
Mr Baldwin		3
Ambrose Lea		2
Samll Smith		3
Mrs Guest		4
Roger Vaughter		2
Willm Bentley		1
The schoole howse		1
Mr Nath Brooksby		8

		[NC]	[Ch]
Jos Tubbs	1 forge &		2
Tho Crompton			2
Jno Wiggen			2
Samll Wells	1 forge &		2
Danll Holloway			2
Tho Tailor			2
Phillip Knee			2
Jacob Carely			3
Tho Aston			2
Tho Hunt			2
Rich London			5
Tho Sabee			2
Rich Sabee			2
John Guest			1
[f. 17v]			
Clemt Leake			5
Isaac Careles			5
Jno Norris			2
Widd Strubshaw			2
Widd Marston			2
			87

Bull Street

		[NC]	[Ch]
Rich Tuckley	1 forge &		2
Edwd Ashford	(formerly one howse)		2
Edwd Harding			2
Henr Castleton			1
Jno Cooper			3
Jos Cooper			2
Cor Bridgens			1
Robt Whittall			4
(2) Mr Wilsby 2 hearths new built entered at Lady Day 1671 (not paid)			2
Mr Wilsby more			2
Mr Willm Miller			3
Jno Guest	1 forge &		2
Nicho Jackson			1
Widd Piggott			3
Tho Guest			4
Jno Wagstaffe			3
Rich Cotterell			4
Mr Fincher			4
Willm Marston			3
Rich Underhill	(formerly one howse)		2
Jno Michell			1
Jno Jennings			4
(4) A new howse with 4 hearths not yet finished			[-]
Jno Guest sen	1 forge &		2
			55
			[57]

Moore Streete

		[NC]	[Ch]
Jno Hunt			3
Mich Miller			4
Jno Basely			3
Willm Kettle			2
Jno Groves			2
Willm Eachell	2 forges &		3
Jno Bate			1
Edmd Forrest	1 forge &		2
Jno Banner			6
Roger Tailor			2
Jno Pemberton			2
Willm Fairfax			1
[f. 18]			
Robt Clarson			3
Geo Anderton			2
Mich Gorton			2
Jno Ashford			3
Geo Jackson			2
Elizab Balie			3
Isaac Ashford			1
Danll Ashford			2
Widd Vaughton			3
Abrahm Cash			2
Jno Hunt			1
Rich Lewis			2
Mr Foxall			4
Mr Powell			2
Widd Carter			3
Tho Ward			1
Widd Norris			1
			68

Parke Street

		[NC]	[Ch]
Humph Moore			5
Widd Hunt			4
Willm King			2
Willm Graves			6
Willm Perry			2
Franc Simonds			3

	[NC]	[Ch]
Jno Betridge and Willm Lench		
2 forges &		3
Rich Fetherstone		2
(1) Job Cowley 1 new built		
entered at Lady Day 1671 (not paid)		1
Tho Betridge 1 forge &		2
		30
Cort [Court] **Lane**		
Edwd Biggs 1 forge &		3
	Totall	1196
		[1144]
Jno Roper	1	
Widd Day	1	
Jno Roads	1	
Rich Andrews	1	
Tho Maior	1	
Widd Rooker	1	
Henr Crooke	1	
Mr Snouch	1	
Widd Cotterell	1	
Tho Cash	1	
Widd Harrison	1	
Widd Phillips	1	
Henr Cooke	1	
[f. 18v]		
Henry Chatterton	1	
Jno Tipson	1	
Rich Sheath	1	
Rich Sheath	1	
Henr Phillips	1	
Jonah Paston	1	
Tho Wakely	1	
Henr Hunt	<1>2	
Jno Weet	1	
Widd Jones	1	
Robt Phillips	1	
Willm Hanson	1	
Jno Powell	1	
Henr Onyons	1	
Jonas Wareing	1	
Willm Simms	2	
Jno Barbon	<1>2	
Jno Austin	2	

	[NC]	[Ch]
Edwd Hare	1	
Robt Raines	1	
Tho Johnson	1	
James Lewis	1	
James Raves	1	
Tho Morell	1	
Willm Worrall	1	
Tho Flavell	2	
Samll Kendicke	1	
Willm Austin	1	
Widd Grover	1	
Jno Fownes	1	
Widd Duck	1	
Widd Aston	1	
Willm Smith	1	
Elizab Vaughan	1	
Jos Hartell	1	
Jno Askall	1	
Peter Hussey	1	
Tho Cox	1	
Jno Barton	1	
Jonath Austin	1	
Jno Hutton	1	
Humph While	1	
Widd Benson	1	
Robt Smith	1	
Cor Bridgens jun	1	
Tho Mayo	1	
[f. 19]		
Nicho Milliten	1	
Widd Crofts	1	
Jno Onyon	1	
Rich Onyon	1	
Widd Adams	1	
Tho Bennett	1	
Rich Pinchett	1	
Benj Mahew	<1>2	
Henr Webster	2	
Willm Halfpeny	1	
Tho Lawrance	1	
In towne howses that receive collection	200	

		[NC]	[Ch]
Derriton [Deritend in Aston par]			
Jno Brayman	<1>2 forges &		1
Willm Palmer			1
Willm Naseby			3
Willm Pearsall	1 forge &		2
Widd Inings			3
Willm Blocksledge			2
Tho Cox			3
Edwd Brayman			1
Tho Somerland			1
Alice Pemberton			3
Isaac Pemberton			3
Jno Kempster			2
Jno Chainge			2
Rich Forrest			5
Edwd Allin sen			1
Jno Ingsly	1 forge &		3
Humph Smith			1
Tho Edwards			3
<Jno>George Greaves			1
Elizab Moore widd			2
Edwd Allin			1
Edwd Barber			4
Willm East			1
Jno Cooper			1
Anne Moore widd pearcermaker	1 forge &		2
Anne Moore widd jun sheermaker	1 forge &		2
Simon Smith			3
Joseph Bloxledge			2
Willm Hawkes	1 forge &		3
Jno Fox			4
[f. 19v]			
Rich Dolphin			1
Rich Hawkes	2 forges &		2
Rich Jenks			1
Abrah Pinley	1 forge &		1
Willm Turner			1
Willm Billinly			3
Rich Shephard	2 forges &		2
			91
			[77]
Humph Jones		1	
Ambr Pemberton		1	
Widd Hunt	<2>1 forge &	1	
Widd Hawkes		1	
Willm Cotrell	1 forge &	1	
Edwd Buck		1	
Jno Court		1	
Mordecay Sackborne		1	
Tho Hunt		1	
Rich Allen		1	
Jno Ball		1	
Willm Jencks		<1>2	
Rich Pemberton		1	
Geo Clarke		1	
Willm Hodgkins		1	
Rich Smith		1	
Tho Packinton		1	
Robt Mosse		1	
Jno White		1	
Tho Mason		1	
Widd Cox		1	
Towne howses that receive collection		17	

		[NC]	[Ch]
Edgbarston Towne [Edgbaston par]			
Sir Jno Gage for Edgbarston Hall			22
Jno Underhill			2
Robt Bowers	1 forge &		3
Rich Rootes			<2>1
Zahary Drury			1
Bartho Wheely			1
Mrs Anne Deely			1
Nicho Drury			1
Widd Orton			3
Robt Smith			3
Henr Birch			1
Isbosheth Birch	1 forge &		1
Elizab Weely	1 forge [&]		1
James Haynes (to pay)	1 forge &		1
[f. 20]			
Jno Smalwood	1 forge &		1
Jno Dale			3
Humph Hadley	1 forge &		2
Jno Scattergood	1 forge &		1

	[NC]	[Ch]
Jno Haines		1
Henr Stampe		1
Ellinor Phillips		1
Jno Cox		1
Tho Gibbins		2
Rich Williams		1
Rich Piddocke		2
Widd Freeman		8
Widd Walter		5
Willm Waldron		3
Jno Hartill		1
Jno Poole		1
Willm Bunn		1
Mr Robt Painter		3
Henr Povey		1
Tho Gaunt 1 forge &		1
Jno Loynes		1
Rich Smith <1>2 forges &		1
Jno Forrest 1 forge &		2
Leon Cowbidge		1
Jno Watton		1
Mr Peter Sadler		6
(1) Rich Clarke 1 entered at Lady day 71 a pauper before (not paid)		1
Rich Westwood		1
Geo Swingland		1
		95
		[97]
Ambr Greene	1	
Jno Kempster	1	
Nath Smalman	1	
Walter Brooks	1	
Rich Peters	1	
Nicho Robinson	1	
Widd Robinson	1	
Robt Milward	1	
Willm Clarke	1	
Edwd Smith	1	

[f. 20v]

The Forreigne of Bermingham

[The Foreign in Birmingham par]

Willm Colemore esq	13
Jno Loynes	5

	[NC]	[Ch]
Mr Parratt		2
Willm Smalwood 1 forge &		2
Tho Holyman		1
Willm Fellowes		1
Morris Piddocke		4
Willm Piddocke		4
Widd Best		2
Mr Henr Foard		7
Jno Ridle		2
Henr Ridle		1
Rich Burbidge		3
Henr Harper		1
Abrah Heath		3
(2) Jno Falford 2 entered at Lady day 1671 (not paid)		2
Willm Turner 2 forges &		2
(1) Math Mackley 1 entered at Lady Day 71 (not paid)		1
Jno Smith		6
Luke Ridle		1
		[63]
Henr Write	1	
Jno Medley	1	
Henr Sudger	<1>2	
Tho Dorman	1	
Willm Alwood	1	
Tho Watton	1	
Edwd Bucknall	1	

Viewed and collected by me Henr Hargrave collector

[WCRO, QS11/21]

[f. 1]

Atherstone Division

Part of Hemlingford Hundred

[written by Henry Hargrave]

Fillingley Green end	Hearthes
[in Fillongley par]	
Willm Shaw	2
Willm Hall	1
Tho Goodheart	1

	[NC]	[Ch]
Geo Earle		2
Jno Hide		1
Widd Dolton		1
Clemt Stone		2
Tho Beck		2
Mr Tho Holbech		7
Tho Butler		3
Edwd Parker emptie (unpaid)		4
Robt Write		2
Mr Char Shuttleworth		7
Nath Foard		1
Henrie Kimberly sen entered at Christmas (unpaid)		1
Widd Erpe		2
Rich Smith		4
Samll Rutterford		1
Christphofer Tadd		1
Mr Edwd Priest		4
Morris Hawfeild		1
Mrs Franc Holbech widd		5
Walter Beland		1
Tho Brookes		2
Mr Willm Smith		5
Mr Emillion Holbech		6
Tho Eedson		3
Edwd Holbech		1
Jno Sayle		8
Mr Tho Brooks		5
Jno Smith		2
Tho Bennett		2
Franc West new built & tenanted at Lady Day 71 (unpaid)		4
Roger Walker		6
		100

Wood end [in Fillongley par]

	[NC]	[Ch]
Adolph Owton gent		8
Mr Martin Whaitcott		5
Mr Jno Brearly		4
Jno Veare		3
Jno Tailor		2
Mr Emillion Holbech emptie		3
Tho Hinds		2
Tho Whaitcott		5
Jno Webb		1
[f. 1v]		
Henrie Flavill payable at Ladie day		1
Jno Avery		1
Widd Avery		2
Tho Brookes		2
Edwd Glover		1
Jno Newman		2
Edwd Herbert		1
Willm Kimberley		1
Roger Butler		3
Willm Foard		2
Mr Willm Brookes		2
Mr Tho Brierley		5
Giles Cave		1
Jno Walker		1
Tho Hill		3
Mr Joseph Essex		4
Mr Martin Whatcocke jun		4
Rich Hollioake		1
Rich Watkins		1
[***Metley End*** [1]]		
Mr Willm Avery		5
Willm Whare		1
Willm Crips		1
Samll Hall		2
Edwd Chamberline		2
Andrew Greene		2
Tho Brabins		4
Jno Downes		1
Mr Tho Sadler		5
Mrs Sadler widd		3
Jno Taverner		3
Henr Hollinsworth		1
Jno Cudd		2
Willm Browne		1
<W… …>		
Willm Harvy		4
Mr Jno Odill		1
Tho Cave		1

[1] WCRO, QS11/31 (1671).

	[NC]	[Ch]
Nath Greene		2
Willm Hollier		<1>2
Willm Gosse		1
Willm Hollier Mr Greene of Coventry owner (emptie)		1
Willm Write		1
Tho Hartell		2
Math Eborne		1
Widd Walker		2
Nicho Thomson		3
Willm Meeke		1
[f. 2]		
Tho Bredon		1
Widd Lovett		1
Elizab Beck		<1>2
Job Lacy		1
Widd Camell		1
Manasses Snell } entered at Ladi day		1
Rich Heath } paid ½ yeere (unpaid)		2
		135

C [Fillongley Certified]

[***Green End*** [1]]

	[NC]	[Ch]
Widd Monton	2	
Joseph Shaw	2	
Willm Watkins 1 forge &	2	
Josiah Sewell	1	
Martin Shaw	1	
Math Ebron	1	
Tho Whitman	1	
Jno Jeffery	1	
Simon Pemberton	2	
Franc Olliver	1	
Willm Arndell	1	
Bath Greene	1	
Henr Kimberly jun	1	
Giles Barton	1	
Edwd Holbech	1	
Leon Greene	1	
Widd Clarke now Willm Lynes	1	
Jno Stones	1	
Henr Marston	1	

[***Wood End*** [2]]

	[NC]	[Ch]
Jon Tolton	1	
Tho Simms	2	
Tho Boyce now Flavill payable at Ladie day	<1>0	1
Tho Barton	1	
Giles Cave	1	
Edwd Brandwood	2	
(paid) Rich Holliocke	<1>	
Danll Smith	1	
Jno White	1	
Tho Jarvis	1	
Tho Ainge	1	
Jno Todd	1	
Widd Chadman	1	
Widow Smith	1	
Roger Baker	1	
Jane Garrett	1	
Bartho Greene	1	
Rich Betridge	1	
Widd Bredon	1	
[f. 2v]		
Ellinor Weston	1	

[***Metley End*** [3]]

	[NC]	[Ch]
Jno Hollier	1	
Jno Hall	1	
Tho Gilbert	1	
		236

Corley [par]

	[NC]	[Ch]
Jno Avery		1
Mr Tho Browne clerk		3
Willm Harris		1
Ralph Bucknall		1
Rich Davis never paid beefore		1
Rich Palmer		2
Widd Smith		1
Widd Ward		1
Tho Marler		1
Tho Brickley		1
Mr Tho Watcock		6

1 WCRO, QS11/31 (1671).
2 WCRO, QS11/31 (1671).
3 WCRO, QS11/31 (1671).

	[NC]	[Ch]
Tho Butler		1
Rich Sanders 1 forge &		1
Jno Lynes		4
Jno Brothers owner (emptie)		1
Rich Rope		3
Jeffery Jefcott		2
Willm Smith		2
Jonath Adam		1
Peter Johnson		2
Widd Clarke owner (emptie)		1
Jno Hall		2
Jno Smith owner (emptie)		1
Henr Jackson		1
Tho Holbech		2
Rich Jackson		1
Jno Clarke		2
Willm Smith		3
Nath Foard		1
Mr James Hales owner		1
Willm Stonehurst		1
Jon Burbidge		1
Jon Clay never paid beefore payable at Ladie day		1
Micall Clarke		1
<Peter>Jonathan Adams		2
[f. 3]		
Willm Mathews	1	
Widd Harris	1	
Willm King	1	
		57

Maxstock [Maxstoke par]

	[NC]	[Ch]
Mrs Dilke widd		17
In the lodge		2
Jno Whatcock		3
Nath Clifton		6
Geo Webb		2
Tho Wilson		2
Rich Keeling		2
Rich Shepard		2
Rich Barrett		2
Roger Avery		1
Mr Geo Barton		2
Widd Essex		1
Rich Snell		1
Jno Mathews		1
Bartho Eaves		1
Willm White		1
Jno Smart		1
Randolph Shelly (emptie)		2
Robt Bates		1
Peter Lacy		2
Humph Smith		2
Geo Crosse		1
Tho Moorwood		3
Willm Lightborne		2
Leon Greene		1
Alice Jeffery		2
Widd Scotton		2
Tho Grainger		2
Widd Earle		2
Mrs Pollett		5
Jno Dunton		3
Willm Hawkins		1
Widd Griffin		2
Humph Maydew		1
Willm Snape		1
Tho Glascott		2
Willm Glascott		1
[f. 3v]		
Leonard Greene		1
Widd Jackson		1
Jno Sices		1
Jno Dawkins gent		10
Tho Browne		1
Widd Swift		1
Willm Perkins		1

Coaton in Maxtock [constablery] [Coton in Kingsbury par[1]]

	[NC]	[Ch]
Mr Tho Coaton sen		4
Mr Tho Coaton jun		6
Jos Croxall		2
Robt Hickcox		1
		114

[1] Walker, *Hemlingford*, pp. 68–9.

	[NC]	[Ch]
[***Maxstoke***[1]]		
Willm Newton	1	
Henr Farmer	1	
Hugh Tyso	1	
Willm Milkes	1	
Hugh Tranton	1	
Henr Wootton	1	
Walter Mold	1	
Nicho Britton	1	
Mary Greene	1	
Anne Cornwell	1	
Edmd Jacob	1	
[***Coton***[2]]		
Edwd Marler	1	
Edwd Hawksford	1	
Tho Higgins	1	
Elizab Rockett	1	
Marston [in Lea Marston par]		
Widd Bredon		3
Geo Sharrett		1
Jno Greene		2
Tho Wooward		2
Willm Perkins		1
Edwd Simons		3
Nicho Wooley		1
		13
[f. 4]		
Widd Bredon	1	
Willm Newbald	1	
Jno Bredon	1	
Tho Asman	1	
Jno Clarke	1	
Jno Miller	1	
Shustocke [Shustoke par]		
Mr Haines minister		3
Jno Wiresdell		1
Jno Moody		1
Jno Butler		1
The parsnidge howse		5
Mr Tho Croxall		8

	[NC]	[Ch]
Edwd Naylor		1
Widd White		1
Walter White		2
Tho Butler		2
Rich Proffitt		4
Mr Franc Featherston		8
Henr Corall		1
Edwd Witman		3
Anne Weaver		1
Samuell Watson		1
Tho Betridge		1
Widd Hall emptie & owner		3
Willm Alport		1
Jno Pimley		2
Willm Everard		1
Randall Croxall		5
Willm Jeakes		3
Tho Tailor		5
Rowland Erpes		3
Tho Croxall (& 3 building)		2
Nicho Wilday		3
Mr Tho Huntleech		5
Robt Veale		2
Tho Hill		1
		80
Willm Day	1	
Rich Eaves	1	
Rich White	1	
[f. 4v]		
Tho Kidderminster	1	
Rich Edwards	1	
Edwd Smith	2	
Widd Hall <…>	0	
Edwd Proffitt	1	
Tho Croxall sen	1	
Henr Chester	1	
Edmd Weston	2	
Samll Grew	1	
Willm Wilday	1	
Willm Jeakes	<1><0>	
Tho Tailor	<1><0>	
Tho Sadler	1	

[1] WCRO, QS11/31 (1671).
[2] WCRO, QS11/31 (1671).

	[NC]	[Ch
Willm Sadler	1	
Simon Hasterly	1	
Willm Ludford	1	
Jno Matchett	1	
Richard Harris	1	

Blithend in Shustocke
[Blythe End in Shustoke par]

Willm Dugdale esq		9
Mich Daniell		3
Jno Eaves		2
Willm Legg		2
Christoph Barwell		1
Robt Messinger		1
		18

Bentley in Shewstocke
[Bentley in Shustoke par]

Robt Shilton		1
Geo Yardley now Will Elton		1
H[…]enr Keene		1
Jno Belcher		1
Rich Clarke		2
Rich Hall		1
Henr Browne		1
Jno Pack		1
Rich Winspire		1
Mr Jno Glover		2
[f. 5]		
Mr Tho Butler		4
Job Power		2
Rich Brookes		1
Widd Lewis		1
Jno Harris		1
Jno Sturley		2
Benj Brearly		1
Jno Broughton		1
		25
Tho Yardley	1	
Widd Brookes	1	
Willm Smith	1	

	[NC]	[Ch]
Jno Wiseman	1	
Tho Hollier	1	
Rich Houghton	1	
Tho Tailor	1	
Jno Write	1	
Danll Write	1	
Geo Hollioake	1	
Rich Masser	1	
Widd Lewis	1	
Widd Clarke	1	

Baxterly in Shewstocke
[Baxterley par[1]]

Franc Cope		2
Steph Slaine		3
Martin Brearly		8
Jno Bickley		2
Willm Jeffery		1
Nich Waite		1
Jane Shepard		1
Tho Ward		2
Jos Carver		1
Jno Tailor		1
Robt Shorthose		1
Robt Meeke		1
Margrtt Oarton		1
Jno Slany		1
[f. 5v]		
Rich Heath		2
Jno Crowder		1
Christpofer Harrison		1
Rich Salsbury		2
Widd Walker		1
Willm Wilson		4
Geo Ball		1
Widd Walker		1
Willm Lewis		1
		40
Geo Swann	1	
Willm Alsop	1	
Widd Farmer	1	
Jno Bush	1	

1 Baxterley was a separate parish.

	[NC]	[Ch]
Sarah Bickley	1	
Tho Write	1	
Widd Write	1	
Widd Bimion	1	
Widow Carver	1	
Lea Marston [par]		
Sir Char Adderley		13
Henr Clowes		1
James Swift		1
Jno Hunt		1
Jno Montford		1
Tho Rotheram		2
Widd Eades		2
Willm Seale		3
Elizab Johnson		1
Willm Brabins		1
Mary Spooner		2
Dorothy Voile		1
Willm Eads		1
Jno Hill		1
Mr Nicho Brookes		5
<Willm>Widd Stanley		1
Susan Hill		1
Rich Browne		1
Mr Richard Briscoe		1
Edward Heartshill		1
[f. 6]		
Tho Gibson		1
Henr Gisborne		1
Rich Redding		1
Samll Clawson		2
		46
Rich Newkins	1	
Mary Wheeler	1	
Nicho Heath	1	
Henr Lemford	1	
Tho Stanley	1	
Jno Stanley	1	
Tho Keeling	1	
Nicho Perkins	2	
Elizab Heath	1	
Marie Miller	1	

	[NC]	[Ch]
Nether Whitacre [par]		
Kath Savidge		2
Tho Hitson		2
Mrs Hitson		2
Tho Lanfley		3
Tho Write		3
Willm Poole		2
Nicho Brabins		2
Jno Brookes		1
Robt Butler		1
Willm Betridge		1
Willm Eaves		1
Tho Snell		2
Jno Gilbert 1 forge &		1
Rich Snell		2
Rich Keeling		2
Jno Croxall		2
Tho Butler		1
Tho Hollier owner (emptie)		1
Willm Hollier		3
Willm Keeling		1
Ambrose Farmer		3
Tho Woodward		2
Willm Ballard		1
Willm Johnson		1
Tho Cheatly		1
Anne Winn		1
[f. 6v]		
Tho Simons		1
Geo Greenwood		1
Tho Hollier		1
Edwd Reave		1
<Willm Pooley> mistake		<1><0>
Jno Harrison		1
Simon Biddle		2
Jno Keeling		2
Jno Warwicke		<2>1
Tho Beck		4
Gabriell Olds		1
Rich Keeling		1
James Ludford		1
(1s) Abrah Allin paid ½ yeere		1
Willm Parker		1
Jno Bainton		1

	[NC]	[Ch]
Jno Walker		1
Tho Barber		1
Widd Jackson		1
Tho Draper owner (emptie)		1
Widd Michell		2
Rich Cheshire		1
Mr Collier		4
Widd Hesterly		1
James Cox		2
Jno Lindon		1
Rich Keeling		4
Tho Write		4
Rich Hall		1
Mr Franc Bickley		6
Edwd Simons now }		0
Josiah Allen }		3
The Lady Wimbleton		22
Robt Browne		1
Jno Walker		1
Rich Life		1
Willm Tompson		1
Tho Bott gent		8
(1s) Char Browne ½ yeere		1
Robt Simond		1
Willm Scarrald		1
Rich Francis		3
Jno Clarke		1
Widd Jackson		1
Mrs Kath Savidge		1
Jno Newball		1
Edwd Walton		1
(1s) Simon Daniell ½ yeere		1
Tho Write		1
(1s) Widd Walker paid ½ yeere		1
[f. 7]		
Ambrose <Walker>Bosworth		1
		146
Tho Haxford	1	
Widd Kingsbury	1	
Joane Langley	2	
Franc Smith	1	
Widd White	1	
Mary Sanders	1	

	[NC]	[Ch]
Tho Tailor	1	
Jno Bosworth	1	
Amos Barton	1	
Jno Baker	1	
Jno Lithium	1	
Tho Poole	1	
Edwd Groves	1	
Jno Croxall	1	
Sarah Aldridge	2	
Tho Poole	1	

Uper Whitacre

[Over Whitacre par]

	[NC]	[Ch]
Willm Kennam		2
Tho Halpenny		1
Tho Miller		4
Jane Miller		<1>2
Tho Cheshire		0
Tho Tailor		1
Willm Hill		3
Jno Cheshire		1
Rich Freeman (emptie)		1
Tho Browne		1
Rowland Cooper		3
Rich Sadler		6
Henr Charlton		2
Tho Randall		1
Willm Kinnill		2
Jno Lawley		1
Rich Edwards owner (emptie)		1
Mr Tho Barber		3
Jno Miller		5
Rowland Cooper		3
Nath Allen		1
Tho Sadler		2
Anne Outon		1
Jno Cade		3
[f. 7v]		
Willm Debitt		1
Widd Tailor		1
Edwd Weston		1
Jno Keene 1 forge &		1
Henr Francis		1
Tho Oughton	C	<2>

	[NC]	[Ch]
Rich Whittell		3
		58
Robt Miller	1	
Tho Cheshire	1	
Willm Harbert	1	
Widd Harbert	1	
Tho Tailor	0	
Willm Hill	0	
Widd Garrett	1	
Tho Oughton	2	
Tho Write	1	
Samll Poole	1	
Widd Jackson	1	
Willm Poole	1	

Ansley [par]

[There are eight duplicate entries, marked with an X]

	[NC]	[Ch]
Danll Scott		2
Jno Robert		4
Jno Hewett		3
Anne Scott		2
Robt Hewett		2
Jno Clarke of Paintbrok		2
Robt Power		2
Jno Power		2
Jno Darby		<2>1
Tho Higham		<1>2
Clemt Wilson		1
Willm Wooster		2
Geo Staremore		1
Mr Edwd Stratford		5
Robt Burbidge & Jno Hewett		2
Nath Smith		1
[f. 8]		
Robt Sadler		1
Robt Hill		2
Jno Haydon		3
Geo Hewitt		2
Steph Pickering		1
Willm Smith		2
Robt Everard		1
Jone Lord		1
Esquire Ludford		2
Esquire Ludford for a mill		1
Jno Oughton		2
Jno Clarke		2
Widd Clarke		3
Mr Franc Bacon		4
Mich Clarke		3
Tho Brierly		3
Humph Clarke		1
Mr Tho Sharrett		2
Samll Griffin		2
Willm Hill		2
Jno Hidson		1
Robt Guy		1
Tho Procter		1
[X] Robt Guy		1
Widd Dale		1
Widd Farmer owner (emptie)		2
Willm Mason		1
Tho Harris		2
Jno Clarke 1 forge &		1
Esquire Ludford		2
Widd Day		1
Widd Baker		1
Tho Witeman		2
Jno Barefeild		2
Tho Ison		2
Jno Lord & Jno Stephens at Bratts Hall		5
Jno Ludford esq		12
Robt Harris		1
Widd Bunny		2
[X] Willm Smith payable at Ladie day }		1
[X] Will Seawell the like }		1
[X] George Staremore		1
[X] Robert Hill		2
John Watson payable at Ladie day }		1
George Elliott the like }		1
		[122]
[f. 8v]		
Willm Clarke jun	1	
Tho George	1	
Jno Hewett	1	
Tho Brooke	1	
Robt Smart	1	

	[NC]	[Ch]
Willm Clarke	1	
James Tailor	1	
[X] Tho Ison	<1>2	
Willm Seywood	1	
Tho Hinckes	1	
Widd Jest	1	
Widd Bates	1	
Tho Robson	1	
Geo Urland jun	1	
Jno Urland	1	
Franc Holmes	1	
Mary Bunny	1	
Alice Browne	1	
Anne Harris	1	
Rich Wilson	1	
Widd Avery	1	
Widd Shaw	1	
Vallent Musson	1	
Danll Hill owner of an emptie howse but now filled with poore people & no distresse[1]	3	
Simon Lea owner (emptie no distresse)	1	
Tho Goadby sen	1	
Jno Clarke	1	
Tho Joanes	1	
Willm Goadby jun	1	
Mary Alders	1	
Tho Goadby sen	1	
[X] (paid) Geo Elliott	1	
[X] (paid) Jno Watson	1	
Rich Smith	1	
Willm Clarke	1	
Tho Shilton	1	

[f. 9]

Chilver Coaton

[Chilvers Coton par]

	[NC]	[Ch]
Tho Kind		1
<Rich>Ralph Cox		1
Abrah Keene		1
Willm Clarke		2
Jno Parker		3
Samll Johnson		1
Robt Ball		1
Rich Paul		3
Peter Holmes		1
Willm Cox		1
James Holmes		1
Alexand Rush		1
Mr Langham emptie (owner)		1
Mr Chamberline owner (emptie)		1
Rich Drakeford		1
Pawl Hinman		1
Rich Clarke		1
Rich Paul jun		1
Widd Dale		1
Tho White		1
Nicho Bull		1
Char Bale		2
Willm Bush		1
Jno Mattox		2
Willm Robinson (emptie)		3
Danll Bemish		1
Willm Hall		2
Rich Newdigate esq		32
Mr Edwd Abbott		5
Willm Hackwood		1
Samll Johnson		1
Jno Perry		2
Rich King		1
Jno Newdigate esq		4
Jno Wagstaffe		1
Willm Rawson		2
Jos Drew		2
Mr Tho Sprott		4
Robt Hill		3
Widd Jenson		1
Tho Moreton		3
Mr Edwd Stratford		7
Marmaduke Smith		1
Tho Knight		1
Franc Friswell		2
Robt Paine		2

1 This property was recorded in 1671 as 'full of poore people and given by a gent to the parish for that use' and was certified with just one hearth (WCRO, QS11/31).

	[NC]	[Ch]
Willm White		<1>2
Rich Lloyd		1
Willm Baker		1
Samll Browne 1 forge &		1
[f. 9v]		
Henr Sutton		1
Willm Greene		1
Danll Hinckley		5
Rich Hyman		1
Jno Holmes		1
Tho Kinder		2
Tho Suffolke		1
Willm Archard		1
Franc Faster		1
Tho Suffolke sen	<0>1	
(paid) <Tho Kind (emptie)>	<0>	
Rich Paul	1	
Jno Massey	1	
Willm Holmes	1	
Henr Ballard	1	
Edwd Hands	1	
Rich Knight	1	
Andrew Aron	1	
Jno Price	1	
Widd White	1	
Widd Wagstaffe	1	
Tho Cooper	1	
Jno Hancock	1	
Edwd Boswell	1	
Elizab Browne	1	
Christpofer Smith	1	
Jone Page	1	
Rich Floyd sen	1	
Jno Jeffery	1	
Tho Johnson	1	
Jno Rawson	1	
Widd Cox	1	
Jno Glascott	1	
Humph Stapley	1	
Widd Nock	1	
Christpofer Stretton	1	
Nicho Chapline	1	
Bartho White	1	
Widd Love	1	
Lewis Linton	1	
Anne Whitmore	1	
Willm Knight	1	
Mary Ireson	1	
Widd Sadler	1	
Jno Suffolke	1	
Widd Holmes	1	
Widd Goldsmith	1	
Willm Holmes	1	
Cum multis aliis [with many others] in towne howses & upon the common	35	

[f. 10]

Grief in Coaton

[Griff in Chilvers Coton par]

	[NC]	[Ch]
Danll Ball		2
Rich Bayton		4
Willm Clarke		2
Henr Brighton		4
Tho Newton		2
Jno Moore		1
Tho King		2
Rich Smith		1
Mr Coventry (emptie)		2
Tho Gibson	1	
Willm Brasely	1	
Jno Burgis	1	
Rich Shaw sen	1	
Rich Shaw jun	1	
Jno Shaw	1	
Widd Serjant	1	
Robt Hands	1	
Willm Morris	1	
Tho Basse	1	
In towne howses	4	

Woodland in Coaton

[Woodland in Chilvers Coton par]

	[NC]	[Ch]
Sarah Cotterell		1
Willm Smith		1
Edwd Fairechild		<1>2
Nicho Lloyd		3

	[NC]	[Ch]
Tho Nash		1
Tho Dugley		1
Rich Greene		1
Rich Miller		1
Tho Taylor		1
Rich Nash		1
Widd Hankinson one more building		1
Anne Dyer		1
Jno Slingsby		1
Willm Avery		1
Jno Gee		6
Edwd Browne		1
Simon Stone		1
Abrah Lucas		4
Jno Shepard		1
[f. 10v]		
Henr Smith		1
Samll Spencer		1
Willm Lucas		<1>2
Jno Atkins		1
Henr Greene		1
Willm Milhowse		1
Widd Hambrough		1
Rich Lloyd		1
		194
		[190]
Jos Smith	1	
Robt Lockley	1	
Jno Harris	1	
Widd Clarke	1	
Job Hampe	1	
Henr Turner	1	

Noneaton [Nuneaton par]

	[NC]	[Ch]
Jno Stratford esq		11
Adam Orrell		5
Mr Rich Pick		7
(not paid) The schoole		1
Widd Nutt		2
Willm Hipworth		2
Edwd White		2
Mr Womuncell		2
Willm Hall		8
Rich Oarton		5
Jno Stanton		3
Tho Watts		<1>2
Jno Beeke		1
Henr Flood		2
Edwd Bosworth		1
Jacob Pegg		1
Jos Marston		1
Jno Bosworth		3
Henr Daffron		1
Nicho Bell		2
Jno Dafforn		1
Jno Greene & [blank] Bordett		2
Rich Burdett		1
Willm Runnills		2
Henr Varnam		4
Jno Wall		1
Job Musson		3
Willm Watts		4
Widd Stone		3
Geo Harris		3
[f. 11]		
Mrs Groves widd		3
Jno Hall (b[aker][1])		3
Tho Abbotts		2
Mr Wymondsall		2
Mr Robt Shires		8
Mrs Coldecott		5
Mr Willm Trevers		4
Willm Mortimer sen		1
Willm Mortimer jun		1
Willm Smith		3
Willm Burges		1
Willm Blackwell		6
Adam Orall		5
Christpofer Knight		4
Willm Morris		4
Rich Cradducke		1
Edwd Orill		3
Willm Fausett		3

[1] Walker, *Hemlingford*, pp. 159, 179.

	[NC]	[Ch]
Willm Dudley		8
Willm Goodale		3
Jno Crosse		3
Willm Draffs		2
Geo Cox		1
Jno Judkin		6
Tho Smith		3
Edwd Jefferis		2
Tho Webb		2
Jno Ellis jun		2
Jno Ellis sen		4
Rich Wardeing		3
Edwd Healing		3
Robt Hill jun		4
Robt Smith 1 forge &		1
Jeremy Wise		<1>2
Tho Morris		4
Edwd Warden		2
Mr Robinson		5
Jno Bissell		2
Mr Jno Loaden		6
[blank] Donas		2
Geo Jeffery		3
Widd Gurne		1
Jno Alexander		1
Widd Greene		1
Jos Lakins		1
Jonath Turner		1
Alice Parker		2
Willm Robinson (emptie)		3
Roger Ellis		1
Jno Browne		1
Sarah Croxall		2
Willm Earpe		2
[f. 11v]		
Robt Wilson		2
Edwd Jeffery		2
Tho White		2
Samll Brasebridge		6
Willm Francis		2
Tho Parker		2
Edwd Blith		1
Nicho Cooke		4
Willm King		2

	[NC]	[Ch]
Rich Fassett		3
Jarvis Bussell		4
Edwd Yorke		4
Geo Rainor		3
Tho Bell		2
Mr Willm Sadler		3
Jno Hall		2
Mr Jno Parker owner (emptie)		1
Edwd Parker		3
Mary Dabbs		2
Jno Cox		5
Willm Piggott		4
Edwd Smith		3
Jno Parker		3
Widd Mulbury		1
Samll Shilton		5
Rich Farner		1
Widd Randall		3
Edwd Rimington		3
<Edw>Willm Bowman		1
Jno Binley		3
(refuseth to pay) Henr Everard (unpaid)		2
Jno Damm		1
Widd Barber		1
Widd Wright		3
Willm Hamersley		2
Christpofer Garrett owner (emptie)		2
Robt Garnett		1
Rich Jackson		2
Tho Green		1
Margt Watson		4
Nicho Hall		3
Geo Jefferis		0
Willm Corbett		2
Willm Marston		4
Jos Dalby		1
Willm Shepard		2
Jno Jefferis		1
Samll Jelleff		3
Edwd Lax		1
Hercules Fawsett		1
Robt Bradford		1
Robt Bratt		1
Geo Vincent		1

	[NC]	[Ch]
Willm Tailor (b[aker][1])		3
[f. 12]		
Widd Greene		3
Timothy Norbury (b[aker][2])		3
Willm Brent		2
(refuseth to pay) Jno Budworth		5
Jno Painter		1
[*Widd* [3]] Whiteman		3
Edwd Botnell		1
Robt Bacon		4
Mrs Grace Stratford		11
		[392]
Jno Mills	1	
Widd Moone	1	
Willm Keeling	<1>2	
Jno Harris	1	
Danll Sowtham	1	
Rich Harris	1	
Abrah Drakely	1	
Jno Burditt	1	
Jno Beake	<1>0	
Henr Flood	<1>0	
Humph Cradocke	1	
Moyses Crompton	1	
Henr Flood jun	1	
Jno Broadnicke	1	
Willm Kellett	1	
Widd Suffolke	1	
Jno Pegg	1	
Robt Watts	1	
Willm Kellett	1	
Sarah Kellett	1	
Micha Mearing	2	
Jno Greene	1	
Rich Lenton	1	
Willm Brayley	1	
(paid) Jos Marston	<1>0	
Jno Munt	1	
Doro Knight	1	
Mary Moore	1	

	[NC]	[Ch]
Jno Hall	1	
Widd Cooke	1	
(paid) Jno Bosworth	<1>0	
Rich Brodericke	1	
Geo Chatterton	1	
Robt Mortimer	1	
Edwd Birditt	1	
Susan Webb	1	
Willm Harris	1	
Anne Clay	1	
Samll Block	1	
Mrs Caldicott	1	
[f. 12v]		
Jno Pedley	1	
Moses Campion	1	
Willm Serjeant	1	
Robt Sidewell	1	
Henr Robinson	1	
Tho Smith sen	1	
Tho Smith jun	1	
Jonath Trussell	1	
In towne howses & receive collection	90	

Woodlands & Stocklingford

[Stockingford in Nuneaton par]

	[NC]	[Ch]
Rich Francey		1
Amis Simonds		1
Benj Kelsey		1
Rich Tarpe		<1>2
Robt Burbidge		1
Mary Jefcott		1
Henr Shakespeare		2
Jno Topp		2
Jno Tapp		1
Tho Tapp		1
Robt Hunter		1
Willm Browne		1
Tho Smith		1
Tho Procter sen		1
Tho Procter jun		1

1 Walker, *Hemlingford*, p. 159.
2 Walker, *Hemlingford*, p. 159.
3 WCRO, QS11/31 (1671).

	[NC]	[Ch]
Willm Ancott		3
Willm Huncocke		1
Jno Hanley		2
Jos Baylie		1
Willm Chantrell		1
Mich Arndell		1
Rich Corbett		1
Susanah Waters		2
Nicho Newman		1
Nicho Newman jun		1
Rich Gilbert		1
Tho Brookes		1
Rich Lucas (b[aker][1])		3
Robt <Wilkins>Wilkox		1
Rich Hawkins		1
Jno King		1
[f. 13]		
Jno Hocklinworth		1
Robt Roberts (refuseth to pay)		2
Edwd Parnell		1
Moses Campion		<1>3
Rich Mann		3
Joane Baley		1
(refuseth to pay) Jno Jefscott (unpaid)		1
Mary Bennett		1
Edwd Ball		1
Samll Momford		4
Jno Kelsey		2
Tho Frances		1
Tho Trapp		4
Jno Ward		1
Tho Bell		2
Tho Bennett		3
Alice Harrison		0
<Jno Neath>		0
Willm Taylor (emptie)		1
		72
Alice Harrison	1	
Jno Neath	1	
Jane Garrett	1	
Widd Asley	1	
Willm Pettie	1	
Elizab Brooker	1	

	[NC]	[Ch]
Willm Brooker	1	
Tho Rogers	1	
Widd Rowley	1	
Widd Bosnett	1	
Nicho Clay	1	
Samll Aston	1	
James Smith	1	
Willm Moore	1	
Willm Garrett	1	
Tho Hinckes	1	
Take collection & live in towne howses	6	
Jno Glover	1	

Attlebrough

[Attleborough in Nuneaton par]

	[NC]	[Ch]
Jonath White		2
Willm Musson		2
Willm Long		1
Jno Garrett		1
Jno Marston		1
[f. 13v]		
Tho Browne		2
Jno Hurst		1
Willm Smith		2
Widd Garrett		1
Samll Bramish		1
Tho Paine		2
<Tho Paine>		<2>0
Mrs Perkins		1
Samll Paine		1
Willm Wall		1
Tho Parker		2
Mich Paine		1
Widd Richards		1
Widd Perkins		3
Jos Slingsby		2
Steph Paine		2
Jno Paine		3
Willm Cooper		2
Tho Simpkin		1
Rich Cheshire		1
Morris Taylor		1

[1] Walker, *Hemlingford*, p. 195.

	[NC]	[Ch]
Tho Malborne		1
Willm Haddon		1
Tho Gunn		1
Edwd Watts		1
Atwell Chandler		2
Marmaduke Dufkin		2
Franc Goldring		2
Jno Everard		3
Willm Everett		1
		52
Danll Beamish	1	
Widd Parnell	1	
Jno Watts	1	
Tho Ballard	2	
Nicho Whitmore	1	
Geo Salsbury	1	
Robt Spencer	1	
Willm Brookes	1	
Tho Tuckey	1	
Edwd Shipman	1	
Edwd Jackson	1	
Widd Gisborne	1	
Jno Drakely	1	
In towne howses & take collection	17	
Geo Saller	1	
Willm Richards	2	

[f. 14]

Caldecott [Caldecote par]

	[NC]	[Ch]
Willm Purefoy esq		20
Jno Baylie now Jno Porter		3
Rich Shepard		4
Jno Smith		2
Martin Baylie		3
Geo Gee		2
Tho Goodacre		1
Tho Baylie		1
Edwd Shepard		1
Rich Burgis		1
Marke Ballard 1 a pauper before now 2 to be paid for at Michs 1671 (unpaid)		2

	[NC]	[Ch]
Tho Sanders		1
		[41]
Widd Melhowse	1	
Noah Bassett	1	

Weddington [par]

	[NC]	[Ch]
Wooleston Aderly esq		15
Mich Armsted clerk		7
Tho Throne		7
Jno Bancks		2
Jno Rawlinson		1
		[32]

Mancester [Mancetter par]

	[NC]	[Ch]
Mr Willm Blore clerk		3
Mr Grayman		9
Mr Grayman emptie (paid)		3
Mr Peter Thornton		5
Mr Wilson		4
Tho Wilday 1 now holds land & payable at <Ldday> Michs 71 (unpaid)		1
Henr Walford two more building		2
Jno Wilday 1 holds land & payable at Michs 1671 (unpaid)		1
Willm Baker		1
Elizab Croshaw		1
Mr Manwaring		6

[f. 14v]

	[NC]	[Ch]
Willm Cockin		7
Widd Midleton		1
Jno Goodman		1
Benj Gulston		1
Antho Midleton		1
Geo Wilday		1
Rich Bayard		1
Jos Hewett		1
<Jno Rainer> now Jer Ford		3
Mr Farmer		11
Jno Dusenip		1
(1) Edwd Abbotts 1 payble at <Lady Day> Michs 1671 now holds land (unpaide)		1

	[NC]	[Ch]
Henr Bryarlie		5
(1) Tho Ireland payable at Mich 1671 (unpaid)		1
		[72]
Rich Watkins	1	
Edwd Hagg	1	
Widd Palmer	1	
Robt Palmer	1	
Henr Parson	1	
Ralph Lilley	1	
Widd Goodman	1	
Tho Dowce	1	
Widd Clarke	1	
In towne howses & take collection	3	

Hartshill [in Mancetter par]

	[NC]	[Ch]
Tho Beck		2
Mr Edmd Parker jun		6
Nath Grascome		4
Tho Melhowse now Mich Parker		5
Tho Needham		3
Edwd Burbridge		1
<Jer>Geo Griggs		1
Abrah Miles		1
Widd Parker		1
Rich Dixon		2
Widd Grascum		5
Edwd Watts at the mill		1
<Willm>Widd Hewett		2
Geo Gee		3
Nath Newton		7
Geo Gee sen emptie		2
Geo Weaver		1
Margtt Alcott		2

[WCRO, QS11/23]
[f. 1]

Hartshill more

	[NC]	[Ch]
Robt Broughton		1
Tho Cooper		4
Tho Haywood		2
Robt Burbridge		1
Franc Cable		1
Tho Milhowse (before)		0
Mr Baylie		6
Jno Gold		2
Jonath Dixon		4
Jno Lee		1
Mich Mee		1
		72
Willm Burbidge	1	
James Dorman	1	
Henr Newsham	1	
Tho North	1	
Mich Palmer	1	
Widd Worley	1	
Widd Black	1	
In howses upon the common that take collection	8	

Atherston[e in Mancetter par]

	[NC]	[Ch]
Widd Jennings		4
Robt Mason		1
Willm Drayton		3
Jno Gee		4
Mary Habell		3
Anne Jennings		3
Nath<...> Mansfeild		3
Jno Tookeley		2
Mary Gee		2
Arth Dabbs		5
Arth Dabbs		1
Widd Petty		1
Mr Tho Mountney		2
2 more new building		[-]
Symon Drayton		1
Widd Drayton		4
Ralph Drayton		3
Ralph Pimly		1
Tho Bonds		2
Jno Power jun		1
Math Habell		4
Willm Power		2
Jno Owin		3

[f. 1v]

	[NC]	[Ch]
Lionell Crafts		6
Edwd Tomlin		2

	[NC]	[Ch]
Widd Fawx		1
Widd Smith		1
Willm Biddle		5
Mrs Mitchell now Lyonell Crafts also }		5
Rich Turley		6
Rich Preston		4
Jno Ensor		10
Henr Rowditch		3
Edwd Wilson		1
Rich Berrisford		8
Isaac Roper		2
Geo Farmer		2
Rich Bull		2
Harrington Drayton		5
Tho Baker		2
Mary Ball		4
Willm Simonds		1
Henr Wood		4
Jno Abell		2
Rich Hutchinson		4
Rich Bidle		6
Tho Wilson		3
Mich Oarton		2
Willm Everard		1
Jno Power (b[aker][1])		5
Henr <Po>Maurell		3
Jno Martin		2
Mr Tho Walker		11
Tho Barnes		3
Jos Proudman		1
Sarah Parker sen		1
Tho Shepie		3
Tho Warmsley		2
Rich Mowsley		4
Jno Radgdall	1 forge &	1
Rich Marshall		4
Willm Clare		3
Jno Draper		1
Widd Bunny		1
Widd Mold & Widd Abell		4

	[NC]	[Ch]
Jno Mason		4
Mary Higginton		2
Rich Clarke		2
Edwd Fox		2
Noah Loadsby		2
[f. 2]		
Tho Strong		2
Widd Hodgkins		3
Widd Wood		2
Edw Sadler		2
Edwd Marters		3
Benj Shepie		4
Jos Chamberline		2
Kath Grew		3
Nicho Stayford		2
Jno Warmsley		5
Henr Cheshire		2
James Bonely		4
Seabright Reppington esq		14
Samll Brasebridge		10
Tho Goodale gent		4
Mrs Shaw		4
Jos Perkins		4
Geo Baker		3
Robt Bickley		9
Tho Draper		3
Mr Jno Vincent		3
Widd Oadams & Mary Smith }		2
1 more new built &		
2 building (unpaid) }		1
Mr Willm Simonds		6
Jno Shelland	1 forge &	2
Edwd Poward		4
Mr Geo Sadler		5
Willm Roper		3
Rich Goodwin		2
Willm Goodwin		5
Robt Parker		4
Mr Lawrance		2
Jonath Biddle		5
Widd Weston		1
Alice Sabs		6

[1] Walker, *Hemlingford*, p. 250.

	[NC]	[Ch]
Roger Hunt		6
Rich Lancashire		2
Rich Shelly		2
Robt Roper 1 forge &		2
Mr Rich Simonds		7
Jno Farmer		1
Rich Shelly 1 new built (not yet payable)		1
Henry Wilson		1
Henr Farmer		1
Tho Johnson		1
Willm Fish<er>		1
Rich Jeffcott		2
Jno Simonds		1
Rich Oadams		1
Rich Baker		2
Rich Everitt		<2>1
[f. 2v]		
Willm Power		2
Widd Fox		3
Jno Croxall		1
Tho Mersh		1
Nicho Sturkey		1
Rich Oadums		1
Willm Fellowes		1
Tho Sergeant		1
Anne Whitemill		1
Geo Weaver		1
Widd Hitchinson		2
Jno Fascott		1
Franc Paine		1
Christpofer Everett		3
Jno Lego		4
Zach Parker		1
		397
		[401]
Rich Carver	1	
Chad Hesterly	1	
Doro Bull	1	
Rich Collins	1	
Ralph Gee	1	
Geo Cotton	1	
Walter Fox	1	
Jno Bray	1	

	[NC]	[Ch]
Jno Bray	2	
(paid) <Willm Power>	<1><2>	
Mary Power	<2>1	
Willm Baker	1	
Mary Everard	1	
Willm Mason	1	
Edwd Bludden	1	
Franc Veale	1	
Jno Farmer	1	
Edwd Arme	1	
Henr Garfeild	1	
Rich <Garfeild>Blander	1	
Jno Petty	1	
Rich Milday	1	
Widd Mantle	1	
Kendall William	1	
Widd Bates	1	
Tho Cheshire	1	
Anne Wheatly	1	
Simon Fisher	1	
Jno Earle	1	
Barbary Howe	1	
Robt Cowrtney	1	
Amy Simonds	1	
Tho Brookes	1	
Elizab Norbury	1	
Edwd Arme	1	
Hester Grew	2	
[f. 3]		
Tho Clay	1	
Rich Smith	1	
Rich Browne	1	
Edwd Draper	1	
Widd Gilbert	1	
Widd Smith	1	
Tho Goodman	1	
Widd Hadding	1	
Samll Light	1	
Willm Leakins	1	
Jno Miller	1	
Willm Belly	1	
Margtt Cooke	1	
Rich Mosse	1	
Henr Richardson	1	

	[NC]	[Ch]
Towne houses & receive collection	34	

Merivall [Merevale par]

	[NC]	[Ch]
Mr Jos Smith		6
Mr[s] Kath Budd		3
Jno Stratford esq		4
Mr Monsall clerk		2
Rich Biggs		2
Tho Barford		1
Mary Warner		1
Tho Spencer		1
Mr Jno Pegg		4
Tho Deeming		1
		25
David Sutton	1	
Jno Oarton	2	

Viewed & collected by me
Henr Hargrave collector

[WCRO, QS11/23]
[f. 3v]
Tamworth Division
in Hemlingford Hundred
[written by Henry Hargrave]

Tamworth [borough: part[1]]
[in Tamworth par: part[2]]
Markett Streete

	Hear[ths]
Gilbert Jourden	4
Henr Greene	2
Jno Gardner	1
Willm Eaton	1
Tho Parker	1
Jno Waters	1
Jno Hare	1

	[NC]	[Ch]
Rich Page		1
Walter Chadborne		1
Tho Heath		2
Willm Hare		2
Ralph Keeling	1 forge &	2
Mr Char Benton		5
Mr Batton emptie lives in Staffordshire		1
Edwd Beck		3
Jos Clare		1
Tho Barlow		1
Rich Hanson		2
Robt Peake		3
Steeph Jones		3
Geo Faux		1
Tho Cooper		1
Mr Geo Alsop		5
Dan Jourden		2
Jno Savidge owner and lives at Wincott (emptie)		4
Rich Johnson		1
Mr Edwd Simonds		2
Mr Edwd While		2
Robt Hartwell		3
Mr Jonath Cuningham		2
Robt Woodcocke		2
Edwd Massey to pay by the bayliffes of the towne (emptie)		1
Jno Sherman		3
Mr Tho Shilton		5
Mr Woolverston		5
Jno Allin		3
Mr Tho Egginton		4
Rich Mann		3
Jno Mason		1
Willm Wilcox		4
Jno Cox		2
Jno Osborne		2
Jno Blith now Jno Key		4
Mr Edwd Simonds		4

1 The east, centre and southern parts of the borough, including the castle, lay in Warwickshire, while the north and west, including the parish church, were predominantly in Staffordshire. In the centre of the town, the boundary between the two counties went down the middle of Church Street.

2 Altogether 377 households were recorded in Warwickshire by the hearth tax returns and 129 in Staffordshire. For more details, see the note to Table 9 on the combined data (p. 61).

	[NC]	[Ch]
[f. 4]		
Tho Denn		4
Edwd Drayton		7
Tho Vernam		2
Willm Mitchell		4
Edwd Massey		3
Ralph Gibbins		3
Mr Tho Pratt		3
Geo Write 2 hearths now but 1 formerly & a pauper payable at Lady Day 1671 (unpaide)		2
Tho Birch		2
Willm Cawne		4
Abrah Pick		2
Jno Welch		4
Jno Dawes		2
Tho Whitworth		3
Rich Gripton		1
Tho Robinson		2
Nicho Turner now Alexander 2 building		2
Tho Alcocke		4
		158

Georg[e] **Streete**

	[NC]	[Ch]
Jno Mowsley		3
Mr Ralph Adderly		9
Mr Jno Allen		5
Nicho Parker		6
Widd Lattimer		3
Jno Osborne		10
Mr Evans		3
Jno Vaughton		3
Tho Crompton		1
Franc Wilders		4
Tho Wagstaffe		3
Tho Taylor		<1>2
Tho Osborne		2
Edwd Onion		2
Geo Piggott		4
Tho Bateman		3
Nath Rice		1
Job Bateman		3
Mr Job Beardsly		7
Nath Jefferis		1
Tho Key		3
		78

Church Streete

	[NC]	[Ch]
Dorothy Williams		2
Ralp Hudson & Tho Freeman owner Ralph Freeman of Bermingham (emptie)		3
James Smith		2
Tho Keeling		1
Christpofer Haseldine		2
Tho Jones		8
James Alkins		1
Willm Morrell		1
Isaac Oarton		1
[f. 4v]		
Henr Moore		2
Jno Blith		2
Jno Watkins		2
Christpofer Osborne		2
Christpofer Hartell		1
Christpofer Glover		2
Tho Mowsley		1
Geo Piggott		4
Samll Hasden		2
Willm Wilcocke jun		2
Tho Basse		3
		44

The Castle Liberty

	[NC]	[Ch]
Jno Ferrers esq		20
Mr Geo Wagstaffe		3
Mr Edwd Oulds		6
Widd Willington		3
Gilbert Jourden		1
Mr Edwd White		2
Mr Robt Woodcocke		2
		37

Gum[Gun]**-Gate & Bowbridge Streete**

	[NC]	[Ch]
Jno Randall		1
Robt Hunt		1
Jno Drayton		1
Samll Willington formerly a pauper now payable		2
Nath Smith		1

	[NC]	[Ch]
Tho Spooner		1
Edwd Smith		1
Nicho Farmer		2
(1) Jno Allen 1 payable at Lady Day (unpaid)		1
		[11]
		325
		[328]
Widd Willington	1	
Jno Wootton	1	
Jno Fawnsworth	2	
Widd Osborne	1	
Phill Needham	<1>2	
Rich Done	2	
Tho Charles	2	
Hugh Underhill	1	
Mr Bach	<1>2	
Jno Eginton	2	
Jno Heath	2	
Widd Heath	1	
Anne Peeres	1	
Bennett Bell	1	
Widd Gorton	1	
Jno Platts	1	
Humph Dalton	1	
James Browne	1	
Willm Smith	2	
Rich Osborne	1	
Widd Miller	1	
Tho Oarton	1	
[f. 5]		
Willm Bosworth	1	
Widd Griggs	1	
Willm Pate	1	
Jno Snape	1	
Christpofer Drayton	1	
Willm Eades	1	
Steph Jones	1	
Edwd Chadborne	1	
Jno Onyon	1	
Jno Clarke	1	
Widd Smith	1	

	[NC]	[Ch]
Towne howses that receive collection	42	

Amington [in Tamworth par]

	[NC]	[Ch]
Willm Roberts		2
Widd Bate		1
Edwd Davis		1
Joseph Skellett		1
Franc Hutchinson } James How		<1>2
Samll Beardsly		3
Simon Bilson		1
Mr Geo Paine		3
Willm Leakin carpenter		2
Corn Clarke		1
Widd Traine		2
Jno Miller		4
Tho Edwards		1
Clemt Redford		1
Willm Leakin		1
Tho Boston		1
Jno Squelch		1
Tho Freeman		2
Cockin Beardsly		2
Willm Cotton		1
Willm Leakin Dog Lane		1
Cockin Gopsall 1 more at Lady Day 1671		1
Willm Stretton		1
Seabright Repington esq		15
Willm Freeman		2
Willm Brabent		1
		54
Jo Beardsly	1	
Rich Archer	1	
Widd Browne	1	
Rich Vaydalt	1	
Widd Dawman	1	
Edwd Lax	1	
Willm Wheat	1	
Howses upon the common that receive collection	6	
Widd Smith	1	

[f. 5v]

Glascott

[Glascote in Tamworth par]

	[NC]	[Ch]
Jno Collins		2
Willm Sedgwicke		2
Edwd Beck		1
Geo Starkey		2
Tho Wootton		1
Rich Harding		1
Humph Clay		1
Ralph Thorpe		1
Tho Remington		2
Steph Skellett 1 payable at Lady Day 1671 (unpaid)		1
		14
Jone Drake	1	
Tho Nailor	1	
Willm Bald	1	
Nath Taylor	1	
Geo Starkey	1	

Bolhall [Bolehall in Tamworth par]

	[NC]	[Ch]
Mr Langley minister		4
Geo Prittie		3
Rich Bloodd		3
Tho Buckland 1 new built payable at Lady Day 1671		1
Izab Moore		2
Lewis Foord		3
Tho Hoodd		2
Jno Goff 1 more building payable at Lady Day 1671		1
Geo Write		1
Franc Johnson		2
Henr Davis		2
Jermin Smith		1
		25
Robt Jeffery	1	
Mr Briggs	1	
Widd Greene	1	
Jno Greenwood	1	

Willincoate

[Wilnecote: part in Tamworth par]

	[NC]	[Ch]
Tho Smith		1
Jno Lucas		1
Jno Smith emptie Row Buckley owner		1
Willm Bird sen		1
Tho Clarke		1
Jno Wilson		1
Mich Potter		1
Willm Higgins		1
Rich Betts		1
Jarell Smith		1
Rich Hobday		2
Franc Middleton		1
Robt Martin		1
Tho Ensor jun		2
Jno Dixon		1
Tho Oarton		1
Jno Ensor sen		2
Char Stavely		2
Tho Ensor jun		3
Robt Hatton		1
Walter Ensor sen		1
Alexander Story		1
Jno Fulgham		4
Birbidge Mogg		1
Willm Elliott		2
Willm Pallett		1
Phill Buckcroft gent		3
Arthur Shipton		4
Rowland Bockley		1
Edwd Newth		3
Edwd Chiswell		2
Willm Drakeford		1
Mr Clemt Fisher		6
Tho Malin		1
Jno Betts		1
Tho Silvester		3
Rich Wicklin		2
Willm Cotton		2
Walter Ensor jun		2
Jno Ensor jun		2
Christpofer Wilcox		2

	[NC]	[Ch]
Edwd Bakewell		1
Tho Smith		1
Walter Collins		1
Willm Bird jun		1
Jno Dixon		1
[f. 6v]		
Tho Malin sen		2
Rich Archer		1
(1) Nath Smith formerly Walter Lea a pauper holds land & payable at Lady Day 71 (not paid)		1
		80
Samll Sanelts emptie owner widd Oarton	1	
Widd Ludford	1	
Jno Jenners	1	
Jno Arnold	1	
Mary Lacey emptie Mr Woolleston of Hurly owner	1	
Rowland Wilcox	1	
Dorothy Birch	1	
Willm Stinson	1	
Tho Thomson	1	
Alice Bagnall	1	
Alice Roades	1	
Jno Dixon emptie Mr Ball of Amington owner	1	
Tho Goodman	1	
Tobias Sheldon	1	
Marke Wootton	1	
Tobias Tompson	1	
Robt Cooper	1	
Sibill Bird	1	
Tho Bird	2	
Erasmus Foster	1	
Tho Marlow	1	
Jno Nicholas	1	
Willm Benford	1	
Geo Comley	1	
Rich Marlow	1	

	[NC]	[Ch]
Jno Bird	1	
Jno Buggins	1	
Geo Smith	1	
Nicho Hollier	1	
Jno Keeling	1	
Henr Roads	1	
Tho Hollier	1	
Tho Mitchell	1	
Howses upon the common that receive collection	30	

[f. 7]

Holt Slatly & Clift

[Holt, Slately & Cliff in Kingsbury par[1]]

	[NC]	[Ch]
Robt Repington		4
Jno Voyle		1
Willm Fridgen		1
Willm Hall		1
Jno Oarton		1
Jno Thomson		1
Mr Willm Crips		5
Rich Paine		1
Mr Tho Alsop		11
		26
Tho Higgin	1	
Jno Hill	1	
Elizab Brotherhood	1	
Doro Harris	1	
Geo Lee	1	
Willm Arme	1	
Tho Haywood	1	

Dosthill [in Kingsbury par[2]]

	[NC]	[Ch]
Rich Hawkins		3
Rich Drake		1
Antho Smith		2
Jno Membry		6
Jno Harris		2
Tho Oarton ei[us]d[em] owner lives at Willincoate (emptie)		2
Jno Davis		1

1 Walker, *Hemlingford*, pp. 68–9.
2 Walker, *Hemlingford*, pp. 68–9.

	[NC]	[Ch]
Tho Scott		3
Rich Mould		4
		24
Willm Taylor	1	
Nicho Voyle	1	

Middleton [par]

	[NC]	[Ch]
The Lady Willowby		26
Simon Hancox		3
Jno Browne		1
Moses Lander		1
Willm Cox		1
Margtt Jackson		1
Robt Hall jun 1 forge &		1
[f. 7v]		
Rich Fernall		1
Edwd Chapline		1
Walter Mouberly 1 forge &		<1>2
Tho Walthew		2
Jno Bond		2
Luke Darby		1
Edwd Cox sen		1
Rich Wheatly		1
Peter Layton		3
Geo Wayfeild		2
Peter Cartwrite		1
Ambr Higgumbotham sen		1
Tho Spencer		1
Math Shepard		1
Jno Moore		1
Samll Write		1
Ambr Higginbotham jun		1
Widd Rowbotham		1
Franc Bartlett		4
Widd Aldridge		2
Jno Hickman		1
Franc Pickering 1 forge &		2
Willm Cox		1
Nicho Nixon		1
Widd Cox		1
Rowland Hilton		1
Jno Potter		2
Willm Dixon		1
Robt Hall sen		2
Jno Sudbury		2
Jno Bond		2
Jno Hall		1
Willm Dixon		2
Jno Cox		1
Tho Whitehead		2
Jno Ashwood		2
Franc Yeoman 1 forge &		1
Fran Hind		2
Willm Seale		2
Franc Wharwood		2
James Gardner		2
Robt Gorton		5
Humph Meson		1
Jno Somerfeild		1
Willm Goone		1
Joseph Short		2
Geo Orme		3
Widd Darby		1
Mr Robt Grasebrooke		4
Mary Higombotham		1
[f. 8]		
Franc Worack		1
Avery Moore		1
Jno Cox		1
Willm Walker payable at Mich 1671 a pauper formerly (unpaid)		1
		120
Edwd Adcocke	<1>2	
Edwd Cox jun	1	
Elizab Cox	1	
Edwd Whitehead	1	
Widd Whitehead	1	
Widd Moore	1	
Willm Cooper	1	
Jno Cox	1	
Anne Penn	1	
Geo Willis	1	
Jno Collett	1	
Edwd Willowby	1	
Rich Hilton	1	
Alexand Layton	1	
Howses upon the common that take collection	10	

	[NC]	[Ch]
Badgly Ensor		
[Baddesley Ensor par]		
Mr Franc Leeming		5
Samll Wheatley		2
Willm Jackson		1
Henr Siddon		6
Widd Chapline		2
Danll Barefeild		7
Tho Thomson two more buildeing		3
Franc Thomson		2
Samll Oarton Samll Gold owner (emptie)		2
Jno Lane		1
Agn Collins		1
Sarah Newton		3
Widd Barefoote		3
Samll Gold		3
Widd Swinfeild		3
Mr Ralph Farmer owner (emptie)		4
Rich Mason		2
Edwd Dible		1
		51
Edwd Linckfeild	1	
Widd Tincker	1	
Willm Cotton	1	
[f. 8v]		
Geo Collins	1	
Tho Perkins	1	
Anne Goldingham	1	
Jno Keyes	1	
Jno Steele	2	
Howses upon the common that receive collection	8	

Here you must end.

	[NC]	[Ch]
Kingsbury [par]		
Robt Hopkins		1
Timothy Oarton		<1>2
Willm Congrave		1
Willm Simonlog[1]		1
Willm Browne		2
Mr Alsop		5
Nicho Bromwell		1
Timothy Owton		2
Jonath Burton		1
Mrs Mary Lewis		12
Mr Tho Fry		3
Mr Tho Brookes		2
Mr Rich Broughton new built & not finished untill Lady Day 1671 (not paid)		2
Humph Hawxford		2
Willm Litchfeild		1
Izab Carter		1
Tho Brookes at the mill		2
Jno Faulconbridge		1
<Jno>Jacob Hewett		1
Willm Rubley		1
Tho Jarvis		6
Rich Price		1
Willm Burditt		1
Tho Voile		1
Job West		2
Jno Armson		2
Robt Baker		1
Rich Woolley		2
Char Pott		1
Jno Voyle		1
Geo Repington & Widd Repington		2
Mr Willington		2
Rich Voile		1
Widd Browne payable at Lady Day 71 a pauper before (not paid)		2
		69
[f. 9]		
Anne Bowring	1	
Tho Hewett	1	
Widd Hewett	1	
Anne Chapline	1	
Kath Hartell	1	
Edwd Sleath	1	
Edwd Greene	1	
Anne Litchfeild	1	

1 Recorded as 'Wm Simonds of the lodge' in 1666 (TNA, E179/259/9).

	[NC]	[Ch]
Hurly [Hurley in Kingsbury par]		
Mr Waldine [*Willington*[1]]		7
Hugh Willington		4
Mr Willm Wilson		2
Joseph Simonds		3
Miles Padgett		3
Jno Bratt		1
Willm Carter		1
Jno Hull		<1>3
Mr Willm Cooke		4
Power Brecknock		4
Willm Nicholl		4
Willm Miller		1
Mr Franc Purefoy		3
Robt Cooper		2
Willm Savidge		1
Widd Pearce		1
Jno Ludford		2
Abrah Gilbert		1
Mr Geo Alsop of Tamworth owner (emptie)		1
Jos Mireing 1 forge &		2
Willm Mitchell		1
Tho Martin		1
Robt Ballard		1
Mr Tho Muffen		4
Mrs Muffen sen		1
Sir Jno Knightloe owner last tenant Tho Nicholl (emptie)		5
Willm Crispe		1
Antho Devitt		2
Tho Devitt		3
Geo Macham		4
Peter Chetwin		1
Edwd Brabin		1
Rich Marlow		2
Rich Warberton		1
Widd Wharr		1
Geo Goward		2
[f. 9v]		
Antho Ireland		3
Barnabie Ireland		2
Humph Hatton		2
Samll Watson		1
Willm Foard		1
Tho Chetwin		1
Edwd Harris		1
Widd Bates		1
Tho Clare		1
Willm Judd		1
Willm Oadams		1
Widd Burditt		1
Bern Simons		1
		98
Franc Brookes	1	
Jno Cratner	<1>2	
Tho Burton	1	
Jno Massey	1	
Rich Churchill	1	
Rich Harris	1	
Tho Harris	1	
Jno Harris	1	
Widd Massy	1	
Franc Massey	1	
Widd Harris	1	
Willm Greenway	1	
Olliver Hollier	1	
<Willm>Robt Blyth	1	
Henr Smith	1	
Widd Burton	1	
Elizab Carpenter	1	
Jno Tayler	1	
Jno Hewett	1	
Widd Blunt	1	
Howses upon the common & receive collection	14	
Grindon [Grendon par]		
Willm Chitwin esq now Sir Wooleston Dixey bart		20
Mr Franc Lakin		5
Mr Tho Baker		5
Widd Murrey		2
Roger Evans		1

[1] WCRO, QS11/33 (1671).

	[NC]	[Ch]
Widd Cureton		3
Geo Cooke		1
[f. 10]		
Widd Harcott		2
Tho Mellis		1
Rich Ley		1
Rich Collier		2
Jno Deane		1
Alice Skerman		1
Rich Ball		2
Widd White		2
Willm Kisse		2
Rich Wall		2
Geo Oldner		1
Jno Aldridge		2
Jno Oarton		2
Tho Hull		3
Rich Jackson		1
Jno Thomas		1
Rich Hudson		1
Jno Wootton		1
Robt Hely		2
Robt Kendall		1
Samson Bilson		1
Jno Hunter sen		1
Timothy Oarton		2
Ralph Taylor		1
Tho Barefoote		1
James Browne		1
Edwd Johnson		1
(4) Mrs Anne Gibson new built payable at Lady Day 1671 (not paid)		4
(1) Willm Rosse payable at Michs 1671 (not paid formerly cert)		1
(1) Jno Ashbury payable at Michs 1671 (not paid formerly cert)		1
(1) Robt Pickwell payable at Michs 71 (not paid formerly cert)		1
		83
Jno Walton	1	
Nicho Harper	1	

	[NC]	[Ch]
Wheatly		
[Whateley in Kingsbury par]		
<Willm>Tho Whatly		2
Jno Ensor		2
Mr Willington		8
Tho Rowlatt		3
Widd Lucas		3
Jno Cooper		2
Jno Bickly		3
		23
[f. 10v]		
Whittington [in Grendon par]		
Tho Mosely		2
Jno Thurman		2
Jno Rose		2
Edwd Johnson		1
Tho Barnes		3
Robt Merriaker		<3>1
Rich Ball		2
Jno Milner		1
Tho Chapman		2
Rich Page		1
Willm Leakin		1
Walter Newton Mr Ashley of Tamworth owner (emptie)		1
Widd Johnson		1
		20
[f. 11]		
Hall End & Holt Hall		
[in Polesworth par]		
Tho Corbin esq		16
Tho Wilmore		2
Jno Coaton		3
		21
Jno Scott	1	
Mrs Reeve	1	
Dordon [in Polesworth par]		
Tho Sropshire		3
Jno Walter		3
Willm Tovey		6
Willm Clarke		1
Jno Tovey		2

	[NC]	[Ch]
Jno Kisse		1
Jno Holmes		1
Jno Toone		1
Widd Batch owner (emptie)		3
Willm Spencer		1
Rich George		1
Willm Harris		4
Sarah Jefford emptie		1
Henr Maw		<2>1
Willm Oarton jun		1
Rich Lakin		1
Tho Harrison		1
		32
Howses upon the common	8	

Freasly
[Freasley in Polesworth par]

	[NC]	[Ch]
Jno Weston		5
Jno Orme		1
Geo Ashbeshaw		1
Tho Figleton		1
Tho Harris		2
Tho Roome		1
Rich Spitle		5
Humph Ashbury		1
Tho Cooper		1
Tho Moore emptie owner		2
		20
Widd Nicholas	1	

Willincott in Powlsworth
[Wilnecote: part in Polesworth par]

	[NC]	[Ch]
Jno Storer		2
Jno Wallis		3
Nicho Browne emptie		1
		6
Widd Walden	1	
Tho Orme	1	
Cottages upon the common	18	

[f. 11v]

Warton in Powlesworth [par]

	[NC]	[Ch]
Christpofer Broadbent		6
Rich Sheldon		<3>1
Tho Cooper 1 forge &		<2>1
Tho Bull		3
Tho Hull		2
Rich Aldridge		<1>2
Rich Decer		1
Willm Oarton sen		1
Tho Prior		1
Tho Oarton		2
Rich <Cooper>Cope sen		1
Rich Cope jun		1
Tho Lukin sen		1
Tho Oarton jun		1
Jno Taverner		2
Jonath Aldridge		2
James Harrison		1
Widd Lukin		2
Tho Lago		1
Willm Hull		2
Mary Townsend		2
		36
Aldnege Oarton	2	
Kath Cooper	1	
Susanna Norton	1	
Jno Windridge	1	
Tho Mole	2	
Jone Sadler	1	
Tho Hunter	1	
Jone Robinson	1	
Franc Lakin	1	
Widd Clarke	1	
Cottages upon the common	5	

Bramcott & Seckinton
[Seckington par[1]]

	[NC]	[Ch]
Willm Heath		2
Nath Smith		1
Mr Clarke rector		3

[1] Bramcote was not identified separately. Part of it was in Polesworth parish.

	[NC]	[Ch]
Sir Franc Burditt now Robt Burditt esq		3
Robt Burwell		2
Geo Aldridge		1
Robt Burditt Esq [*at Bramcote Hall*[1]]		11
		23
Robt Hutchinson	1	
Robt Nicholl	1	
Howses upon the common	6	

Shutington[2]

[f. 12]

The certified persons of Wheatly[3]

[Whateley in Grendon constablery]

	[NC]	[Ch]
Abrah Burton	1	
Tho Haywood	1	
Geo Lee	1	
Elizab Spittles	1	
Widd Cooke	1	
Samll Oarton	1	
Willm Procter	1	
Rich Browne	1	
Howses upon the common that receive collection	7	

Powlsworth [Polesworth par]

	[NC]	[Ch]
Rich Biddulph esq		18
Mr Ragg minister		3
Jno Tubney		3
Willm Rice		1
Mary Faulconer		1
Edwd Cart		1
Jos Heath		3
Mr Henr Hardsman		6
Isaac Ball new built 3 payable at Michs 1671 (not paid)		3
Robt Sneape		1
Tho Swindale		1
Willm Heathcote		4
Joane Heathcote		2
Jno Yong		3
Willm Mosely		3
Tho Smith		1
Jno Bilson		1
Henr Bateman sen		2
Henr Bateman jun		1
Henr Write		3
Rich Dison		1
Rich Faulks		3
Widd Hull		2
Luke Tailor		1
Tho Manning jun		1
Robt Mosely		2
Widd Lidell		3
Tho Maning sen	1 forge &	2
Henr Hull		1
Widd Clarke		1
Jno Briggs		1
Widd Holt jun		1
Widd Holt sen		2
Widd Baker		1
Edwd Browne		1
Jno Fox		2
Jacob Shilton		4
Willm Cooper		1

[f. 12v]

	[NC]	[Ch]
Willm Sadler		1
Jno Bridge jun		1
(1) Jno Wallis 1 and payable at Michs 1671 (not [paid])		1

1 Walker, *Hemlingford*, p. 17.

2 This entry implies that Shuttington parish should follow here.

3 Whateley was in Grendon constablery and Kingsbury parish, which caused considerable confusion over how it was recorded in the hearth tax, especially the exempt. Styles's attempt to disentangle them was only partly successful because he ignored the seven non-chargeable 'houses upon the common that receive collection'. In Table 28, these were allocated arbitrarily to Grendon parish, which otherwise would have had a mere two non-chargeable households, and the remaining eight to Whateley, similar to its total in the Kingsbury exemption certificate of 30 May 1671. See Walker, *Hemlingford*, pp. 68–9, 75–7, 128 & 136–7, and exemption certificates nos. 28 and 29, p. 414 below.

	[NC]	[Ch]
(6) Mrs Bidle 6 hearthes new built not yet finished		[-]
Henr Luckin		[-] [*1*[1]]
		92
		[94]
Jno Higgins	<1>2	
Tho Spare	1	
Henr Briggs	1	
Edwd Shepard	1	
Tho Adkins	1	
Antho Waite	1	
Widd Congrave	1	
Tho Twelves	1	
Widd Latimore	1	
Joseph Grontidge	1	
Jno Clay	1	
Robt Hind	1	
Tho Maundy	1	
Franc Congrave	1	
Tho Bateman	1	
Kath Lukin	1	
Bridgett Hunter	1	
Howses upon the waste that receive collection	13	
Jno Chadborne	1	

Pooly Hall [Pooley Hall in Polesworth par]

	[NC]	[Ch]
Sir Austin Cockin		19
Willm Cooper		2
Widd Hull emptie		1
		22

[**Polesworth**]

	[NC]	[Ch]
Jno Gold	1	
Widd Bredon	1	
Willm Creton	1	
Isaac Write	1	
James Blastocke	1	
Geo Sexton	1	
Henr Latimore	1	
Jno & Edwd Taunt	2	
Kaleb Clarke	1	
Willm Grontidge	1	
Robt Stretton	2	
Howses upon the common	8	

[WCRO, QS11/22]
[f. 26]

Shutington [Shuttington par]

	[NC]	[Ch]
Robt Ball of Alcott Hall		4
Samll Allin		3
Jno Pearce		2
Tho Bayliffe		2
Willm Simonds		1
Mr Drayton		2
Simon Warwicke		2
Willm Story		1
Franc Silvester		2
Henr Simonds		2
Widd Miller		1
Willm Seale		1
Henr Ensor		2
Tho Ward		1
Rich Dowler		1
		27
Willm Waxford	1	
Jno Whitehead	1	
Jeffery Hunt	1	
Tho Mowsley	1	

Newton [Newton Regis par]

	[NC]	[Ch]
Mr Tho Johnson clerk		3
Henr Woolly		3
Jno Jeffery		3
Robt Spencer		2
Tho Prinsop		1
Geo Newby		2
Olliver Walker		1
Willm Greenwood		2
Tho Bosse		1
Christpofer Smith		2
Erasmus Alpott		3
Henr Erpe		1
Tho Spencer and Ellinor Spencer		3
Tho Holding		2
Willm Hudd		2

[1] WCRO, QS11/33 (1671).

	[NC]	[Ch]
Widd Gorton 1 forge &		1
Jno Hill		2
Christoph Spencer		1
Willm Prinsop		3
Robt Prinsop		1
Tho Page		1
<Tho>Jno Spencer 1 forge &	1	
[f. 26v]		
Tho Taylor jun		1
Rich Spencer sen		1
Henr Beck		1
Simon Prinsop		2
Widd Prinsop		1
Rich Cooper		1
Tho Watson		1
Jno Prinsop		1
Tho Asbury		1
Tho Bosse		1
		52
Willm Taylor	1	
Willm Wilson	1	
Henr Broadhurst	1	
Rich Corbett	1	
Jno Page	1	

Austry [Austrey par]

	[NC]	[Ch]
Willm Beck		2
Ralph Browne		1
Jno Barwell		1
Samll Foster		1
Tho Barwell sen		1
Jno Robinson		1
Willm King		2
Jno Spencer		1
Willm Crips		2
Willm Leming		2
Willm Smith 1 forge &		1
Robt Arnoll		1
Tho Miller		1
Willm Page		1
Tho Hanson		1
Widd Tailor		<1>2
Rich Read		1
Tho Page		1

	[NC]	[Ch]
Widd Joane Dabor		1
Jos Oarton		2
Jno Beck		1
Jno Buntingdale		1
Robt Warner		1
Willm Page		1
Jno Kendall		1
Jno Sutton		1
Willm Smart jun		1
Robt Erpe sen		1
Tho Robinson sen		1
Mr Shakespeare clerk		3
[WCRO, QS11/22]		
[f. 1]		
Robt Lilly		4
Robt Crosse		1
Rich Tailor		1
Kath Dester		1
Tho Taverner		2
Widd Crispe emptie		2
Mr Cooke		1
Willm Branson		1
Widd Heyes		1
Tho Write		1
Tho Varnum		2
Mr Willm Lewin		5
Mr Jno Monke		4
Mr Jno Smith		4
Rich Spencer		1
Robt Spencer		1
Jno Cooper		1
Robt Clarke		1
Henr Spencer		1
Rich Farrin		1
Simon Wiggin		1
Willm Varnum		1
Rich Hincks		2
Willm Smart sen		1
Jno Poltney		1
Edwd Wilkes		1
Willm Taylor		1
Hugh Smart		1
Willm Boston		1
Tho Palmer		1

	[NC]	[Ch]
Henr Merry		3
Robt Erpe jun		1
Henr Kendall gent		4
Mr Amy		3
(1) Math Petcher 1 payable at Lady day 1671 a pauper before (not paid)		1
Robt Taverner		1
Tho Beck		1
Jno Spencer jun		1
Tho Arnoll		1
Samll Foster		1
Rich Read		1
Tho Mould		1
		138
		[104]
Jno Smith	1	
Ralph Gadsby	1	
Alice Smith	1	
Rich Tallis	1	
Rich Page	1	
Tho Hatchett	1	
Nicho Poltney	1	
Howses upon the common that receive collection	8	

Viewed and collected by me
Henry Hargrave collector

Warwickshire: Selected Exemption Certificates 1670–74

These certificates have been selected for those parishes and places where significant numbers of exempt householders were not named in, or omitted from, their hearth tax return. All but three were entered onto printed forms, headed as in the first example below, and indicated thereafter by '[printed]'. The wording was based upon the second exemption clause in the 1662 Hearth Tax Act that required annual certification, plus the two-hearth limit. It ignored the first clause that gave automatic exemption to most householders who were already excused from paying the local levies to church and poor. During the 1670s the attempt by the government to jettison this clause was opposed as unjust if not illegal in many parishes. This is revealed by the three manuscript certificates (Nos 20, 24, 25) and some additions to several others. After the first certificate, the names of the signatories have been omitted.

[ch] indicates that the householder was recorded as chargeable in the 1670 return.

Barlichway Hundred

Alcester division

1. **Tardebigg par:**
Tutnall and Cobley[1] 14 December 1670 [printed] 15 names

Wee the Minister of the Parish of *Tutnell et Cobley in the County of Warwick with the Churchwardens & Overseeres* of the said Parish doe hereby Certifie unto his Majesties Justices of the Peace for the said *County* That we do believe That the respective Houses wherein the Persons hereunder named doe Inhabit are not of greater vallue then twenty shillings per annum upon the full Improved rent, And that neither the Person so inhabiting, nor any other using the same Messuages hath, useth, or Occupieth any Lands or Tenements of their own or others of the yearly vallue of Twenty shillings per annum, Nor hath any Lands, Tenements, Goods or Chattels of the vallue of Ten pounds in their own Possession, or in the Possession of any other in trust for them. And that the said houses have not above two Chimneys, Fire-hearthes and Stoves in them respectively.

Witness our hands this *14*th day of *December 1670*
Edward Cookes Churchwarden Rich Mence Overseer of the poore

1 TNA, E179/347. Tutnall and Cobley was a detached part of Tardebigg parish. No minister signed this particular certificate, just two officials, but it was still endorsed by two local justices. Although the 15 names were counted correctly, only the last five can be added to the nine non-chargeable in the 1670 hearth tax return because William Davenporte was already assessed there as chargeable.

Rich Button
Wm Davenporte [ch]
Hen Palmer
Widd Loxley
Fran Chapman
Tho Lewis
Mich Jordane
John Kendrick
John Baker
Wm Dunn
Wm Manning
Jane Manning
John Chaundler
Wm Bibbins
John Woodes

We Allow of this Certificate containing *15* names
John Clopton Tho Rawlins

Bidford division

2. **Bidford on Avon**[1] 23 June 1671 [printed] 95 [91] names

Bidford poore
Widd Handy
Geo Tayler
Rich Baylis
John Grimitt
Jobe Bushell
Widd Mills
Fran Leighton
Kempe Abell[?]
Arther Ingram
Simon Hill
Rich Williams
Robert Tovy
Margret Jones
Tho Mince
John Tayler
Margret Bayles now Kath Baker
John Beamone now payable Bayles
Eliz Jones
Tho Sharp
Barnaby Trimnell
William Greete
John Tovy
Alce Baylis widd
Jeffrey Grimet
John Baker now Atho Heming
Rich Ingraham
Tho Chapman
Tho Baylis
Tho Butler
Tho Blundell now with Sheepard
Tho Freeman
John Harris
John Woodward now Bridgett Reason
Tho Alcock
Robert Baldwin
Eliz Heming
Darothy Harward
Darothy Dowler
Tho Harward sen
Tho Haynes
John Buggin
Henry Tredwell
Ales Shakspeare
William Pearce
Widd Welles
Arthare Richardson
William Baylis
John Clark
George Sale
William Holmes sen
Widd Hiam
George Perkins
Marcleeve [Marlcliff]
John Godsoe
John Broome
Ed Harbidg
John Harbidg
Eliz Sharlett
John Dance
John Leighton
Richard Salter
Ann Roberts now Tho Handy
Richard Mumford
Barton
John Peet[e]rs
Tho Tayler
Peeter Standly
John Caning
Widd Bennet
Ursula Jones now Jone Bennet
Tho Harris now Ed Simons
Fran Handy
Richard Handy
Tho Godwin now Tho Heming
John Bennet
Widd Rascall
John Hiron
Richard Mascall
William Willmore
Burnells Broome

[1] TNA, E179/347. This total of 95 certified exempt was boosted by including the four place names.

[Bidford on Avon contd.]
Richard Bennet
Richard Satchwell
Margret Blundell widd
Widd Penn
Widd Berry
Richard Blundell
John Quiney now
  Tho Quiney
Hugh Jones now
  Jone Jones
James Wise now
  William Harris
Tho Goringe
Widd Bee
William Harris
Ed Oackly [ch]
Richard Garet

3. **Bidford on Avon par:**
Kings Broom[1] 15 November 1670 [printed] 38 names

Tho Harris
Jo Robinson
Wm Bartlam
Tho Warmington
John Lye
Rich Garret
Jo Bent
Jo Layton
Wm George
Hen Lett
Widd Houltam
Roger Bayley
Wm Bayley
Tho Layton
Jo Layton jun
Widd Chapman
Tho Morris
Roger Kinson
Wm Shutter sen
Robt Williams
Widd Roberts
Jo Edkins
Robt Shutter
Wm Layton
Widd Robins
Hen Harwood
John Leaffeild
Hen Layton
Math Layton
Hump Wrighte
Edwd Grimett
Rich Elton
Jo Gray
Edwd Saunders
Wm Shutter jun
Wm Kinson
John Stanley
Tho Hipkins

Hemlingford Hundred

Atherstone division

4. **Chilvers Coton**[2] 15 November 1671 [printed] 107 names

Christopher Paine	1	Edward Hands	1	Wid Hews	1
Christopher Stretton	1	Richard Knight	1	Tho Cooper	1
Michael Chaplin	1	William Whitmore	1	Margery Wagster	1
Ralph Randall	1	Mary Ireson	1	Nicolas Lacy	1
Bartholomew White	1	Willm Browne	1	Wid Smart	1
Michael Paine	1	Wid Stretton	1	Edward Boswell	1
John Morton	1	Joseph Smiths school	1	Sam Suffolk	1
Elias Lentall	1	William Wright	1	Wid Goldsmith	1
Thomas Suffolk sen	1	Wid Perry	1	Willm Shaw	1

[1] TNA, E179/347. Because Kings Broom lay in Temple Grafton constablery, it had a separate certificate from the rest of Bidford parish. In 1669 a dispute over the assessment of its constables' levies was settled in Bidford's favour (*Quarter Sessions*, v, p. 116).

[2] TNA, E179/194/334/42–3. Several of these names were duplicates or else inhabited Nuneaton parish, but all of them cannot be identified with certainty. This certificate is one of the few that recorded hearth numbers as well as names.

Wid Holmes 1
John Massy 1
An uninhabited tenement 1
Christopher Smith 1
Wid Baker 1
Charles Lentall 1
Wid Millis 1
Will Knight 1
Anne Cooper 1
John Wagster 1
Wid Love 1
Wid Cooper 1
Roger Herbert 1
William Holmes 1
Wid Robinson 1
Richard Floyd jun 1
Robert Green 1
Ellen Burges 1
Willm Wilson 1
<Edward Goldby> <1>
Richard Johnson 1
John Walker 1
Willm Sergent 1
Barthol Sergent 1
Willm Brookes 1
Edward Randall 1
Willm Randall 1
Willm Mortimore 1
Gilbert Mortimore 1
Robert Sergent 1
Wid Swaine 1
John Stonell 1
Wid Checkly 1
Francis Sergent 1
Wid White 1
Willm Wagster 1
Wid Orchard 1
John Britaine 1
Alex Knight 1
Ri Robinson 1

Woodl[and]

Hen Ballard 1
John Hancox 1
Willm Sergent 1
Willm Hill 1
Willm Suffolk 1
Job Hamp 1
Joseph Smith 1
Henry Turner 1
Wid Hankison 1
Elizabeth Browne
John Hall 1
John Harris 1
Willm Lucas 1
Robert Lockley 1

Wash lane

Humph Staples 1
Nicolas Staples 1
Wid Glascott 1
Wid Cox 1
Wid Knock 1
Wid Freestone 1
John Rason sen 1
John Rason jun 1
Richard Parnell 1
Wid Tilecott or Cornelius Carver } 1
An house lately Daniel Beamish his } 1
John Jeffery 1
Wid Page 1

Griffe

Wid Gibson 1
[blank] Beesly 1
John Burges 1
Ri Shaw 1
Ri Holmes 1
Willm Morris 1
Wid Bass 1
Wid Newton 1
Michael Sergent 1
John Shaw 1
Willm Morton 1
Ro Hands 1
Wm Sergent 1

5. **Corley**[1] 1 December 1671 [printed] 12 names

Widdow Harris
Widdow Walton
Widdow Lee
Robert Hudson
John Kinge
William Davye
Robert Norman
Thomas Stone
Edward Walter
John Burbage [ch]
John Smart
William Kinge

6. **Mancetter par: Atherstone**[2] 3 November 1671 [printed] 121 names

Richard Carver
Thomas Pettey
George Pettey
Thomas Ball
Richard Collins
Ralph Jee
Widd Armson
Widd Hartell
Joseph Deay
Mathew Arme
Widd Power jun
Widd Ludford

[1] TNA, E179/194/334/52.
[2] TNA, E179/194/334/36–7.

[Atherstone contd.]
John Bray
John Barlow
Francis Veale
William Musson
Widd Everitts jun
Edward Bladon
Cadwalliter Preist
John Farmer jun
John Moore
Edward Arme jun
Thomas Renney
Widd Guoyte
Richard Bladon
Phillop Dan
Widd Walplate
William Hall jun
Thomas Wilday
Richard Wilday
John Pettey
John Flemings
Widd Mantle
Widd Wheatley
Thomas Chesshire
Symon Fisher
John Earle
Richard Barson
William Hall sen
Thomas Bladon
John Smyth glover
Widd Clemons
John Smart
William Kendall
Randall Holding
Francis Orton
Samuell Dilkes
Thomas Bilson
Thomas Hardyman
Widd Chapman
Widd Faulks
Richard Proudman
Andrew Bull
William Follows sen
Thomas Symmonds
Widd Vincent
William Flood
Henery Garfeild
Widd Kemster
Widd Pickering
Katherine Fisher
William Mathews
Nicolas Meering
Thomas Rowell
Widd Lakin
Widd Hatfeild
Widd Higham
Francis Paine
Widd Smyth
Humphry Swane
Rodger Grew
John Peete
Mary Grew widd
Elizabeth Heath
William Ballinton
William Hollyock
Maxamillion Ballerd
Widd Drayton
John Loveday
Widd Mosse
Widd Pettey
William Lakin
Goodier Lattymore
Widd Elkinton
Henery Richardson
Margarett Cooke
John Milner
William Bayley
Widd Haddon
Samuell Leete
Thomas Goodman
Chad Hesterley
John Smyth mason
Esther Grew widd
William Miller
Edward Arme sen
Widd Narborow
Thomas Brookes
Joseph Drayton
Amias Symons
Widd How
Robert Coatley
Widd Farmer
Jeffery Ward
Samuell Fox
John Bayley
<William>Widd Everitt
Widd Bonney
William Baker
Widd Power sen
Zac Parker sen
Thomas Gilbert
Johnathan Abell
Edward Gilbert
John Draper
Soloman Smyth
John Mason ith horse faire
George Cotton
Widd Gilbert
Edward Draper
Richard Smyth

7. **Mancetter par: Hartshill**[1] 30 October 1671 [printed] 14 names

<C…y B…>
Sarah Black
Thomas Poultney
Thomas Garrett
Edward Bonne[?]
Israell Astley
Thomas Sandes
Joane Rawley
James Dorman

[1] TNA, E179/194/334/38.

Henry Newcomb
Thomas North
William Burbidg
Micah Palmer
Simon Miles
William Alrigh

8. **Mancetter par: Mancetter**[1] 1 May 1672 [printed] 17 names

John Miles
Richard Barson
Thomas Downes
Willm Burman
Symon Everett
George Smith
Widdow Clarke
Widdow White
Robert Palmer
Ralph Lilly
Widdow Goodman
Edward Hegge
Izabel Sea
John Jusnip [ch]
Lewis Key
John Dowell
Widdow Palmer

9. **Merevale**[2] 2 November 1671 [printed] 18 names

John Orton
Tho Cope
Jo Spode
Wm Clifford
Sam Foxe
Rich Smith
Robt Smith
Francis Keen vid
Walter Keen
Tho Sherman
Walter Bailie
Eliz Baylie widd
Hen Fairefeild
John Gerson
Rich Tomson
Jo Cley
Lewis Camps
Maurice Smeton

10. **Nether Whitacre**[3] 1 May 1671 [printed] 24 names

Joane Langley
<… …>
John Bosworth
Thomas Tayler
Thomas Poole sen
Thomas Poole jun
John Hartlew
Mary White widdow
Anne Walker widow [ch]
Johane Hawkesford widdow
Sara Alderidge widdow
John Croxall sen [ch]
John Croxall jun
Edward Groves
Amos Barton sen
Amos Barton jun
Thomas Hawksford
Richard Kinge
Francis Smith
John Litham
John Baker
Elizabeth Saunders
Joseph Spiers
[seven illegible names deleted]
Thomas Loft[?]
Mary Warwick

11. **Nuneaton**[4] 7 November 1671 [printed] 219 [214] names

Thomas Turnor
Humphery Cooper
Mary Greene wid
Elizabeth Browne
Edward Wilkinson
Cristopher Fawcett
William Forrin
William Paine
Ann Harris wid
Edward Mobes c[onstable?]
Frances Wilkinson
Will Sidwell sen & jun
Herculos Turnor
John Greene
Thomas Alexander
Richard Greene
John Garnett
Tho Garnett jun

1 TNA, E179/194/334/39.
2 TNA, E179/194/334/35.
3 TNA, E179/194/334/46.
4 TNA, E179/194/334/41.

[Nuneaton contd.]
Patience Parker
Nathaniell Varneham
Henery Greene
Tho Randle
Nic Halloday
Tho Wotson
Will Greene
Edward Fawcett
Tho Greene
John Man
Wid Wilkinson
John Chipman
William Poultny
Jane Pignutt
Sam Allin
Eliz Waters wid
Richard Greene
Edward Newland
Henery Scetchly
Ann Chapman wid
Eliz Jeffry
John Wilkinson
John Marson
Michaell Starkey
Jane Haddon
Mary Orton wid
Tho Orton
Antony Robbinson
Tho Adkines
James Francis
Will Francis
Tho Hill
Hugh Adderston
Robbert Sidwell
John Pegg
John Biswell
Ed Orrill sen
<Will Halsey>
Widdow Logings
Henery Worley
John Allin
Anna Wagster wid
Sam Jacom
Widd Bratt
Will Sidwell
Edward Ireson
Luke Roggers
Will Barber sen
Roger Newland
John Standly
Tho Barber
Sam Wheatly
Robbert Walker
Wid Musston
Will Veanes
Widd Mathew
Will Glascock
Will Ballard
Ann Jeffrye wid
John Woodcock
Tho Garnett
Wid Sharpe
Will Barber jun
Mary Fox
<… Goldby>
John Webb
<Edward Blythe>
Alice Scattergood
Ralfe Jeffrey
William Addams
Robbert Teb
Will Strickland
Humphery Vincent
Robbert Gascock
Susanna Gee
Wid Burbury
Luce Winterton
Ann Turnor
Will Medcalfe
Edward Parke
Robert Hill sen
Alice Taylor wid
<Wid Smith>
Tho Web
Edward Jeffrey
Jonarthan Truswell
Tho Griffin
Tho Smith
Henery Flood
<Joseph Copsall?>
Ann & Mary Cooke
Nicholas Broadnock
John Broadnock
John Hall
John Moore
Edward Knight c[onstable?]
John Mount
George Chatterton
Will Brearly
Will Buckler
Will Kellett
Wid Suffolke
Aron Champion
Widdow Lenton
John Pegg
John Greene
Jacob Pegg
Michaell Meering
Sarah Kellett
Rob Wots
Rich Knock
Rich Wagstaf
John Lenton
Will Harris
Ann Clay wid
Sam Block
Widdow Boswell
Nathaniall Varneham
John Peddle
Tho Mould
Isaack Gumbly
Luke Mortimer
Humphery Craddock
Widdow Kellett
Will Loader
Abram Drakely
Richard Harris
Will Varneham
Daniell Sowtherne
John Harris
Luce Harvey
Will Keeling
Widdow Moore
John Miller

Mary Densheire wid
Will Farneham
Tho Willemett
Robbert Bratt sen
Will Sargent
Edward Burdett
Robbert Mortimer
John Burdett
Job Vears
Mary Orton
John Greene

Attelborrow hamblet
[Attleborough]
Sam Palmer
Edward Chipman
Ed Harris
James Lestor
Tho Paine
Will Brookes
Robbert Willimson
Jarvis Loomehouse
Sarah Browne
Tho Tookey
Richard Chessheire
Will Earpe
Will Bushell
Widdow Mount
Robbert Spensor
Widdow Greene
George Salesbury
Will Rickard
Katherine Paine
Sam Paine
Nic Whitmore
Richard Hunt
John Parnell
John Pinchback sen
John Pinchback jun
Will Lawkines
Widow Gisborne
John Drakely
Robbert Burgis
Katherine Parnill
Danniell Be…s
Rich Jacson
Ann Paine wid
Water Flawne

Stockingfford hamblet
John Glover
John Neath
Tho Balife
Widdow Glover
Simon Bosworth
Widdow Garratt
William Moore
James Smith
William Petty
Widdow Bosstock
Henery Greene
Nic Clay
John Astly
Widdow Rowly
Robbert Huntor
Widdow Waters
Henery Houlmes
John Jefcoat
Roger Warin
Will Twiswell
<John Arndell>
Michaell Arndell
Will Brookes

Birmingham division

12. **Aston par: Deritend**[1] 20 October 1671 [printed] 55 names

Joseph Gillbird
George Rilley
Joseph Harde
Widdoe Monford
William Penton
John Gossedy
Thomas Arther
Thomas Latham
Richard Jenckes sen
William Pallmer
James Hearst
Thomas Joans
Hennery Fisher
Humphery Sabill
<Nathaniell …beard?>
Widdoe Warde
Widow Wood
Richard Hancox
Robert Hancox
Arther Griffits
Phillip Phindley
Richard Higginson
Edward Trowle
Widdoe Packington
Thomas Masson
Robert Kendall
Richard Bedworth
William Moss
Thomas Ashbury
Robert Moss
Wid Joans
William Hodgkins
George Clarke
Thomas Packington
Richard Pemberton
Thomas Smith
Widdoe Shackspeare
Widoe Jemkes
<Richard Smith>
<John Baulle?>
William Tap
Thomas Hunt
Richard Allin
Edward Walker
William Williss

[1] TNA, E179/194/334/58. Deritend was a separate constablery from the rest of Aston parish.

[Deritend contd.]
John Cavert
John …ratt
Edward Buck
William Cotterill
Robert Bedford
Widdoe Hunt
Humphery Joans
William Pinchback
Amoss Pemberton
Richard White
Robber Wodall
Robb Dalaway
Mary Fantham widoe
Robert Hancox

13. **Aston**[1] 2 May 1672 [printed] 166 [168] names

The Libbertie of Aston towne
Henry Willis
Tho Whittaker deceased
Edward Hill
Widdoe Jones
Ellen Barton deceased
John Bridgman
John Bradshaw
Rich Hargreve
George Bicknell
The Libbertie of Witton
John Smith
Widdoe Holland
Thomas Penn
William Wright
John Buck
John Adcocks
Joseph Jackson
Widdoe Tuttell
Widdoe Stanly
Humfry White
Tho Kesterton
Widdoe Cooper
John Kemson
The Lordshipp or Libbertie of Eardington
Thomas Warwick
Richard Smarte
John Rooper
Widdoe Mathews
Widdoe Boseworth
John Sheffeild
William Ashford
Edward Shepard
Thomas Ashford
Widdoe Brockhurst
Thomas Pearsall
Cuthberd Mackline
Thomas Rooper
Widdoe Hartley
John Rooper
John Allon
William Stoakes
Widdoe Write
John Malpus
Thomas Holden
Joseph Hodgskins
Widdoe Moore
Widdoe Ensor
Thomas Bloxich
Widdoe Hutton
George Clifton
George Stoakes
Richard Sadlett
William Dickman
Ann Crofts
Robert Jue
Richard Underhill
Thomas Hulkes
Widdoe Hargreve
William Freeman
Humfry Holden
Widdoe Taylor
John Higgenbottom
Widdoe Hues
Thomas Horton
Edward Hill
Thomas Underhill
Edward Eagles
Francis Baylis
Henry Charles
Thomas George
Henery Hulkes
Richard Weston
John Dawson
The Lordshipp of Castell Bromwitch
Walter Smith alias Kenley
Edward Smith alias Kenley
John Grinder
Thomas Handes
Widdoe Sadler
Widdoe Smith
William Stanley
John Cater
Widdoe Thornton
Henry Morrish
William Acock
Widdoe Brounsett
John Lillie
Abraham Cater
Humfry Rogers
John Langley
Thomas Locke
John Hargreve
Widdoe Barebone
Thomas Stanley
Widdoe Naïve
William Horton
Edward Prise
Henry Elssonn
Martine Holden
Thomas Massey

[1] TNA, E179/194/334/62–4.

Humfry Griffen
Ann Haycocke
Phylipp Smith alias Stanley
William Lambert
Gregorie Lambert
William Cater

The Lordshipp or Libbertie of Water Orton

Richard Loades
Francis Greencill
Thomas Burges
William Eagles
Widdoe Dawson
Sarah Bather
Widdoe Wright
Widdoe Richardson
Widdoe Hancoxx

The Lordshipp or Libbertey of Bordesley

Henry Flavell
John Boyer sen
John Boyer jun
Nathan Roogers
Richard Pratt
William Syer
Raphiell Higgenbottom
Ann Ensor
Martine Jefferies
Zachary Pratt
Dorathy Hodgskins
William Middelton
Alce Right
John Taylor
Humfry Crofts
Widdoe Dalphine
Widdoe Caddock
Abraham Coock
Widdoe Polton
Widdoe Hardinge
Edward Harrisson
John Baxford
William Roogers
John Marsh
Thomas Higgenbotton

The Lordshipp or Libbertie of Littell Bromwitch

Widdoe Penn
William Batch
John Batch
Ellinor Hopkins
John Hopkins
Widdoe Batch
John Allen
Edward Smith

The Lordshipp or Libbertie of Saltley

Thomas Roogers
Thomas Osburne
Thomas Price
Daniell Blackham
Richard Overton
Christopher Tibbins
John Dunn
William Oliver
Richard Chetwin sen
Robt Oliver
Richard Chetwin jun
Widdoe Wastell
William Handes
Widdoe Benson
Widdoe Roogers
Widdoe Phillipts
Edward Wells
Widdoe Mills
Edward Vincent jun
John Weaver
and William Chambers

The Lordshipp of Dudston and Neachels [Nechells]

Benjamine Overton
David Winn

14. **Birmingham**[1] 5 February 1671/2 [printed] 359 [365] names

The Forran [Foreign] **and Welch end**

John Medey
Danell Smith
Hendry Shuger
Will Huitt
Will Smith
Hendry Wright
Humfry Townesend
Edward Burbrig
Will Alwood
John Burbidg
Widdow Watton
Edward Bucknall
Roger Walldron
Hendry Crooke
John Snoth
Richard Andrus
Thomas More
John Rowcher
Tho Mayer
Wido Daye
Tho Bennett
John Roper
Tho Harison
John Pick
John Mathewes
Joseph Swift
Nickolas Arther
Wido Cottrell
Tho Cash
Will Harisson
Hendry Band
John Tibson
Richard Sheath
Ambrose While

1 TNA, E179/194/334/65.

[Birmingham, Foreign contd.]
Tho Wackland
John Wheeler
Wido Jones
Humphfry Tayler
Robart Smith
John Powell
Henery Ouianes
Will Andrus
Wido Willinger
John Driver
Will Simes
Tho Cash sen
Tho Cash jun
Joseph Awestin
John Awstine
John Weele
Will Hill
Edward Tayler
Tho Fleeminge
John Michall
Hendry Chadelton
John Wright
Robart Phillpes
Samuell Phillpes
Henery Phillipes
Henery Watten
John Robery
Nickolas Millington
Tho Mayoe
John Heelis
John Hare
Edward Hare
Samuell Vaighan
Edward Harding
Audryan Fitter
Wido Benson
Cornelias Brigenes jun
Wido Treene
Henery Hunte
Joane Adkines
John Rodes
Johnathan Paston
Will Stonton
Wido Rowcher
Mary Emorton
Elener Horton
Richard Pritchett
Tho Harrison
Will Clarcke
Richard Ounianes

New Streete

Edward Tounkes
Robart Gest
John Fownes
Wido Juckes
Will Smith
Anne Stockwell
John Aschall
Wido Farmor
Wido Hill
Tho Cox
Johnatham Awstin
John Hutton
Wido Groves
Humprey Whille
Danell Farmer
Abraham Walldron
John Barton
Wido Hammon
Will Smith
Will Harison
John Haman
Wido Aston

Digbeth

Dorithye Davis
Abraham Haddock
Richard Wattkines
Richard Carlis
John Smith
John Blackmore
Wido Penn
Wido Day
Will Rodes
Wido Townesend
Wido Bellemy
Will Right
Thomas Woosly
Richard Howes
Jacob Townesend
George Vaughan
Aron Dallby
Aron Mockly
John Hunt
Joseph Woode
Bengamin Woode
Anthony Penn
John Moris
Humfry Tibbettes
Tho Batch
Wido Holmes
Wido Bayes
Wido Hunt
Will Wall
Robart Tune
Richard Price
Rice Edwardes
John Lewes
Edward Cromton
Wido Penn
John Bycker
Dorithye Barber
Henery Smith
Richard Wallis
Wido Bricklestafe
John Fox
Wido Groves
Goodman Wall

Couert Lane

Henery Forist
James Barnesly
Gillbeart Patchett
Henery Allputt
Will Boyce
Wido Evanes
Wid Walldan
Wido Welles
John Hogkines
Raphell Martine
Roger Cromton

Spicell [Spicer] **Streete**

Wido Brickellstafe
Richard Eedes
Wido Man
Hendry Webester

Bengamen Mayoe
Will Hapeney
Tho Handes
John Gosshidge
Richard Eavenes
Richard Lawrance

Edgbaston Streette

Wido Harisse
Raphell Stich
Richard Powell
Humphry Heely
Will Browne
Micheall Orton
Samuell Welles
Josuah Hunt
Tho Girdler
Wido Spouner
Josuah Grifen
Tho Golde
John Grifin
Abrose Freeman
Richard Ensor
Tho Clarcke
John Nayler
Will Keeling
Will Danckes
Tho Cade
Richard Daye
Will Heles
Francis Saford
John Filde
Wido Leather
John Browne
Will Francis
Richard Coleburne
Will Worre
Tho Betteredg
John Woodall
John Bellomie
Edward Newcombe
Robart Priner
Roger Cartricke
Wido Weete
Josiah Bande
John Groves
David Owen
Wido Gorton
Abraham Bellomy
Samuell Tayler
John Eedes
Mathewe Davis
Tho Yeates
John Greaves
Tho Jackson
Sanders Heartly
Richard Hunt
Henery Davis
John Tayler sen
Raphell Kesterton
Caleb Hunt
John Filde
Will Townesend
Samuell Townesend
Richard Whille
Wido Cox
Mary Colye
Richard Fox
Raphell Worly

Pinfold Streete

John Goold
Wido Colye
Wido Quilliames
Wido Turner
Will Newcombe
Raphell Deane
Benjamen Baner
John Tombson
Will Owen
Edward Jackson
Richard Davis
John Field
Tho Barnes
Will Hille
Robart Jackson
Mary Pratt
Mary Swift
Richard Day
Richard Hedges
Joseph Newcomb
Thomas Newcomb
John Waring
Will Sassill
Francis Barton
Wido Balldin
Tho Rider
Will Strayne

Park Streete

John Simmones sen
Wido Dayer
Tho Trapher
Nickolas Newcombe
Wido Smith
Wido Treene
Robart Handes
Mary Thornely
Wido Hawckes
Wido Whyle
Henerey Tayler
Edward Woode
Will Lench
Edward Wackman
Richard Pinly

More Streete

John Bently
Wido Backer
Tho Cowper
Wido Fearforx
John Brigenes
Joane Chambers
Mary Ball
Wido Norris
Josyah Blackam
Tho Lane
John Dimock
Robart Wright
John Suger
Humphfry Edmands
Tho Cooke
Wido Slye
Elener Day
Wido Croly
Elizabeth Hunt
Tho Day
Wido Charety
Will Dalloway

[Birmingham, Moor St contd.]
Richard Heyles
Wido Wise
John Tomson
Jane Cash
Tho Bennet jun
David Beary
Ambrose Cash
Richard Partridg
Wido Yeates
John Greatrix
John Tomson
John Groves
Will Heawood
John Weete
Edward Welles
Humphry Byrum
John Pearsall
Wido Fearefax
Francis Harper
Edward Fox
Edward Harpar
Henery Walcker
Mary Grisell
John Tounckes
John Harison
Edward Moles
Tho Bently
Will Fearfox
Tho Cr[o]wly
Jone Tomson
John Greene
Humphrey Richards
Tho Marlowe
Wido Norton

Hight Streete

Robart Raines
James Ramese[?]
<Abraham Guest>
Jarvis Donne
Tho Johnson
Will Whorall
Richard Weele
Will Lawe
Jobe Cowlye
Will Austine
Samuell Suger
John Oniones
Wido Holtam
Tho Hunte
James Tayler
Will Hanson
Will Hanson jun
Nickolas Brickelbenck
Will Wonly
Jeremia Cade
Richard Day
John Turner
Samuell Tayler
John Barebone
John Webester
Ambrose Browne
Francis Eddes
Will Bettredg
John Spowner
Abraham Est
Joseph Tayler
Wido Croftes
Wido Hart
Henery Baund
Wid Charety
Wido Ward
Henery Carlis

15. **Coleshill**[1] 24 June 1671 [printed] 55 [58] names

John Martyboyes
Radle Croxall
Joane Triming
Isabell Mills widdow
John Heward
Oliver Perkins
Richard Hewse
Humfrey Greene
Will Tarran
Widdow Perrey
Tho Jackson
Richard Right
Elizabeth King
Widdow Smiths dauters
Francis Tysall
Rich Tysall
Widdow Martin
Widdow Jerland
Widdow Northwood
John Chettland
Widdow Jackson
Thomas Preston
Edward Thornton
John Chetly
Tho Dyall
Tho Everitt
Widow [?]Stonett
Widow Corslett
Ric Wakefield
Joane Mayou
Ambrose Smith
Mary Worman
Widdow Stanley
Widdow Craten
Will Harris
Widdow Erpe
Widdow Martin jun
Widdow Cowper
Widdow Milner
Will Stretch
Georg Knight
Widdow Conway
Will Swan
Henry Jordan
Francis Judd

[1] TNA, E179/194/334/54. Neither the certificate nor the returns for Coleshill show to which of the four different areas within the parish its exempt householders belonged.

John Williams
John Walton
Widdow Steephenton
Edmund Lovitt
Henry Cowper
Widdow Trimins
John Kittermaster
John Empton
Will Eaves
Rich Smith
John Tysall
Ed Sterdman
Gilson
Widdow Smith

16. **Curdworth and Minworth**[1] 11 December 1671 [printed] 26 names

[**Curdworth**]
Widdow Hauxford
Widow Ashford
Thomas Hawley
Humfrey Wastell
Richard Freeman
Thomas Horseley
Widdow Biddle
Thomas Wright
Edward Veysey
[**Minworth**]
Thomas Hargrave
Thomas Fruin
Widdow Thornton
Abraham Wright
John Tudman
Widdow Hargrave
Widdow Mosse
Thomas Nichalls
Edward Meare
Widdow Lewis
Widdow Adsit
Edward Jackson jun
Henry Cley
Widdow Soar
John Hauxford
Thomas Morris
Widdow Mekins

17. **Edgbaston**[2] 24 July 1671 [printed] 17 names

John Prabee
Widow Rabbison
Ruchard Rabbison
Robbart Millard
John Cemster
Ambros Greene
Ann Harte
Nathanuell Tayler
Frances Millard
Samuell Cemster
Rogger Parceall
Gilbart [?]Hall
Thomas Parcevall
Widdow …arme
Edward Smyth
Walter Brookes[?]
John Smalewood

18. **Sheldon**[3] 10 May 1671 [printed] 20 names

William Smeyth
Thomas Hamton
Widdowe Hanes
Widdowe Paddey
Seymon Donton
William Owen
William Radford
Widdow Rooedes
Abraham Hanes
Widdow Sumarland
William Wodwards
William Showell
Edward Brag
Will Tranter
Thomas Radford
Goodman Hasler
Goodey Withington
Judeth Howe
Widdow Silck
Deuoris Sumarland

1 TNA, E179/194/334/55.
2 TNA, E179/194/334/61.
3 TNA, E179/194/334/57.

19. **Sutton Coldfield**[1] 10 August 1671 [printed] 116 [117] names

Greatt Sutton
William Askall
Mathew Howes
Widdow Hewer
Robert Eavins
Joseph Lewes
Valentine Martin
Widdow Ensor
George Dawes
Widdow Brookes
Widd Eavins
Widd Smith
Widd Walker
Rich Martin jun
Tho Gretton
Willm Gretton
Widd Martin
Nicholas Madew
Ann Wass spinster
Francis Roleson
John Elkine
Ciseley Wright spinster
Robert Dogged
Widdow Wright
Robert Griffin
John Steevens
John Griffin
Willm Martin
Willm Farmer
John …uall[?]
James Martin jun
In Hill & Little Sutton
Robert Asburie
Joseph Wooderson
Tho Lewsey
Edward Dickman
Michaell Jonson
Ralph Millner
Willm Rigge
Widd Dale
John Thorley
Widd Buttler
James Smallwood
Willm Undrill
James Lewes
John Lewes
Widd Blyth
John Blyth
Edw Selvester
Willm Bickley jun
Rich Smallwood
Nicholas Brookes
John Norris
Hugh Lees
Tho Cotterill
Edw Ensor
John Holland
Tho Asplin
John Tayler
Joseph Ashford
Widd Rabone
William Harrison
George Nicklin
Widdow Asaby
John Paine
John Smith
Edward Crathorne
George Syer
Thomas Kinge
Widd Wright
Widd Glover
John Suger
Sameuel Grevin
[?]Meda Day
Moore & Ashforlong
Georg Jackson
John Wootton
Isaack Whorwood
John Whorwood
Thomas Keeling
Widdow Lambard
Thomas Benian
Edward Walker
Robert Huniborne
Henry Smyth
Willm Smith
James Huniborne
Isaack Vale
Widd Goodwin
Ann Cotterill spinster
Thomas Whatley sen
Tho Whatley jun
Widd Bromley
Beyond the Wood
Widd Lane
Walter Valiante
Francis Warde
Hen Mathews
Richard Thomas
Robert Adcox
Warmley [Walmley]
John Greeway
William Whatley
Ann Spooner spinster
Raphaell Lashford
Joane & Eliza Walker
John Hurste
Many & Wilde
[Maney and the Wylde]
Margery Cotterill spinster
John Blackham
John Duncombe
Benjamin Harris
<Margarett Duncombe>
John Owers
Ann Tunkes wid
William Parker
Peter Lambert
Wenlocke Fox
Henry Vale

1 TNA, E179/194/334/59–60. This certificate not only contains 24 more names than the 1670 return but also distributes them between Sutton Coldfield's five quarters.

Briggitt Wynne
Ann Fullslanes
Widdow Spencer
Widdow White
Margret Duncum

Solihull division

20. **Baddesley Clinton**[1] 1674 [manuscript] 11 names

This is a true certificate to certifie you to whome it doth concern that those inhabitants that are underwritten live in cottages upon the waste and they doe not pay to neither Church nor poore and they are not chargeable accordinge to the Actt.

Edward Sides
Edward Joanes
William Johnsons
Thomas Bollten
Trustrum Bollten
Thomas Hawkins
William Bollten
Widdow Hawkins
Robert Beatts
George Wallker
Widdow Rawlins

21. **Berkswell**[2] 13 May 1671 [printed] 81 names

Simon Right
Thomas Davyes
Willid Margetts
John Betridge
Henery Ashby
Tho Ebrall
Hen Scrivener
Edward Greene
Lettice Avis
Francis Chaplyn
John Burbage
Richard Taylor
Anne Short
George Hughs
Humphry Adcox
Robert Hands
Widdow Kimberly
Anthony Glover
Widdow Chataway
Widdow Wolfe
Maurice Cooke
Julyan Clerke
John Rampton
William Hollis
John Court
Richard Taylor
Edward Clever
Thomas Adcox
Ann Readinge
Widdow Court
Wid Hopkins
Edward Court
Widdow Robinson
Edward Wallis
Robert Casemore
William Brookes
Widdow Garner
William Goulbee
Ellinor Harris
Richard Westley
Aron Freeman
Rich Withers
Jo Hodgetts
Wid Lynes
Edward March
Thomas Cooke
John Davyes
Thomas Willson alias Reeve
Edward Withers
Richard Davyes
Joseph Goulbee
William Jones
John Davyle
Hen Gambal
Francis Times
Robert Bissaker
Richard White sen
John Marle
Alice Willson
Wid Woodard
Nic Baker
Hen Wood
William Hyman
Richard Taylor, **Burton Green**
Thomas Radford
Gregory Radford
John Adds

1 TNA, E179/347. No exempt were named for Baddesley Clinton in the 1670s earlier than 1674. The wording of this manuscript certificate derives from the first exemption clause and ignores the one that the government wanted to be applied.
2 TNA, E179/347.

[Berkswell contd.]
Widdow Kimberly
Philip Weblyn
Thomas Bonny
Isabell Bonny
Rich White jun
John Preist
John Collyns
Wid Ellyot
Wid Smith
John Kimby
Bradnock Marsh in Berkswell
John Swift [ch]
William James
Jasper Gouldeir
Widdow Higgenson

22. **Bickenhill**[1] 14 April 1671 [printed] 33 [32] names

Dorothy Withington
Elizabeth Marteboyes
William Rabster
John Day
Thomas Michell
Henry Bales
Matthewe Morris
Dorothy Foxe
Nicolas Smith
Robert Fisher
Edward Collins
Henry Pindley
John Becke
Alice Prime
Henry Smith
John Butler
Anne Butler
Anne Bayleis
William Pindley
John Smallbrooke
Elizabeth Wall
Barnaby Pinkes
John Smith
Josias Saunders
Widdow Chambers
Henry Cartricke
Robert Taylour
Stephen Foxall
Mary Hitson
Edward Smith
Edwin Luckman
William Hill

23. **Knowle [Constablery]**[2] 12 April 1671 [printed] 88 names

[Knowle Chapelry]
Knoll towne
Widd Porter
Tho Taylor
Edmd Lucett
Tho Preist
Eliz Ashly
Jno Humphery
Ralph Kent
Abigail Welton
Job Doson
Wm Phillips
Jno Bradford
Wm Neale
Anne Shakespeire
Hen Ashhurrst
Anne Cooke
Widdow Newton
Simon Browne
Widd Beasley
Widdow Taylor
Widdow Brown
Tho Norten
Margery Hyat
Baldwin Palmer
Hewin Astley
Tho Chambers
Jno Baylies
Mary Eady
Rich Edson
Hen Hancox
Rich Hancox
Hen Price
Robt Reading
Knoll Woodend
Jeofrey Taylor
Margett Haywood
Wm Taylor
Jno Pratt
Tho Ward
Katherine Hanconck
John Haynes
John Britten
Wm Audely
Tho Riddell
Rich Lancaster
Widdow Taylor
Widdow Taylor [X]
Widdow Britten
Tho Hancox
Widdow Parsons
Jno Dent
Jno Carter
Ow Maudley
Chestnet [Chessetts]
Woodend
Tho Baldwin

1 TNA, E179/347. This certificate contains 20 more non-chargeable householders in Bickenhill than in the seven other lists from the 1670s (see Table 29).

2 TNA, E179/347. Most unusually, the part of Solihull parish that was in Knowle constablery was included here. The entries for Nuthurst (6) and Elmdon (3) have been omitted.

Geo Wheeler
Widdow Bragg
John Allen
John Johnson
Rich Brage
Wm Pawden
Tho Hales
Edw Shett
Widd Tayler
Margett Hayward vidua [X]

[Solihull Parish]

Woodney end
[Knowle Widney End]
Geo Stoney
Charles Stoney
Widdow Collins
Wm Wood [ch]
Hump Haywood
Jno Twigger
Widdow Rawlins
Widdow Smith
Widdow Cotterill
Wm Lea
Tho Palmer
Wm Huddesford
Sam Symonds
John Botterill
Charles Stoney jun
Longdon end
Widdow Rasted
Tho Lumber
Widdow Hooper
Widdow Hobby
Geo Newby
Edward Readell
Tho Wood
John Lardge
Tho Rawbone
Geo Kendrick
John Hilton
<John ?Botterill>

24. **Meriden**[1] 27 March 1671 [manuscript] 38 names

Wee the minister and churchwardens of Mereden in the County of Warwick do hereby certifie our belief that the persons hereafter named by reason of their poverty are exempted from our usuall taxes payments contribucons towards our church and poor and that the house wherein any one of them doth inhabit is not of greater value than of twentie shillings per annum upon the full improved rent and that neither the person so inhabiting nor any other using the same mess[u]age hath useth or occupieth any lands or tenements of their owne or others of the yearly value of 20s per annum; nor hath any lands tenements goods or chattels of the value of ten pounds in their own possession, or in the possession of any other in trust for them neither hath any one of them more than two chimneys, in witness whereof we have hereunto put our hands this 27th of March Anno Domino 1671

Wid Berry
Wid Worth
Job Windmill
John Swift
William Green
R. Sneape
Tho Berry
William Sparks
Wid Parker
John Heatly
Ri Wilcox
Griffin Berry
William Fetherston
W. Lucas
<Gr Keeling>
R. Bewfeild
R. Bunn
Corbet Printopp
T. Elliot
T. Parker sen
Wid Swift
Wid Wescot
T. Wood
T. Jeffry
T. Simons
John Boswth
R. Taylour

[1] TNA, E179/347. This certificate is reproduced in Figure 24. Its manuscript preamble inserts the first exemption clause from 1662 before the second. Its inclusion was an act of defiance by the parochial officers of Meriden against the government's push to deprive those who were excused from paying the local levies to church and poor of automatic exemption.

[Meriden contd.]
W. Mousley
G. Green
Wid Hopkins
W. Taylour
Wid Lathum
Wid Boswth
W. Belston
William Alderidg
William Printopp
John Harrison
John Grant
E. Lapworth

25. **Solihull**[1] no date [1670/1] [manuscript] 118 names

These are to certify by us whose names are subscribed, that none of the inhabitants of this Parish of Solyhull in the County of Warwick underwritten, have chimnys, fire-hearthes, or stoves in their respective houses to the number of three nor doe they pay to Church or Poore, but are themselves so poore, that they receive yearely pay or Almes of the said parish, so therefore are, as we conceive, so qualifyd as to be exempted by the statutes in that behalf made, from paying Hearth-mony.

Borough
Widow Walker
Widow Gyles alias Serjeant [ch]
Geo Callow
John Lluellyn
Elizabeth Rowe widow
Reynold Veale jun
Geo Greswold
Widow Cooper
Hen Dawes sen
Richd Benion
Anne Wright widow
Geo Banister sen
Hen Dawes jun
Joseph Bent
Robert Clarke
Widow Payne
Widow Lea
Robt Heyward
Hen Smith
Widow Weaver v [or] Ellenor Cheshire
Abraham Underhill
Robt Hardyman
James Cooper
Tho Ossender
John Withyes
Humphry Twist
John Bissell
Robert Hinson
Hen Grant
Richd Tandy
Luke Ryder pro preterito[2]
Christopher Greene
Henry Bollard
William Pinly
Widow Newy
Widow Bird
Reynold Veale sen
Widow Smith
Robert Smith
Jane Browne
Francis Ridle
William Mathews
John Tompkins
John Essex
Joane Thorne
Tho Betterton
Widow Banister
Anne Bradborne
Willm Howes
Widow Holt
Widow Butler
Richd Heynes
Willm Byssell
Geo Banister jun
Richd Brick
Widow Morrice
Foshaw [Forshaw] **End**
Tho Tayler
<Edward>Widow Browne
Tho Haywood
Widow Smith
Widow Hunt
Widow Parker
John Norman
Edward Browne
Widny End
William Morrice
Willm Willcoxe
Erasmus Callow
Thomas Simons
John Lea

1 TNA, E179/347. This manuscript certificate, which was written by the rector of Solihull, Henry Greswold, was even more defiant than No. 20 from Baddesley Clinton. For his next certificate in 1672 Greswold used the standard printed form, but inserted an additional section with 19 names of those who he claimed were receiving yearly alms and so were qualified for exemption only under the first clause and not the second. See certificate No. 23 for the remainder of this parish.

2 Luke Ryder had recently occupied his house.

The rest of Widny End are
in Knoll certificate
as likewise all Longdon End

Sherly End
Richard Ball
Widow Arden
William Cottrell
Rich Ward
Widow Ley
Tho Kendrick
James Ashfield
Widow Roch
Richard Evans
Tho Pratt
Frances Ward
Willm Birch
Oliver Hanns
Richd Gardner
John Cottrell [ch]
John Cottrell
Richd Cottrell
Willm Payne
Widow Smallwood
Willm Hodgetts
Richd Mathews
Widow Sparry
Thomas Field
Widow Watton

Olton End
Samuell Averell
Willm Scotton
Widow Lake
Widow Greswold
Widow Smith alias Greswold
Tho Chambers
John Simons
Widow Swinford
Alice Brandon
Richd Ashford

Whitlox End
Tho Field
William Tayler
Edward Day
Widow Crosby's daughters
John Davyes
Robt Breedon
Mary Chater widow
John Pretty
John Hill
Widow Lea
John Lea
Widow Fullford
Widow Wareing
Widow Veale
John Veale

Tamworth division

26. **Austrey**[1] 30 May 1671 [printed] 11 names

Ralfe Gadsbye
Alice Smith spinster
Richard Tallis
Thomas Daniell
Anne Page widd
John Hatchett
Nicholas Poultney
Thomas Kendall
John Simkin
John Smith laborer
Richard Farren

27. **Baddesley Ensor**[2] 17 June 1671 [printed] 13 names

Perse Barfoote widdow
William Wills
Richard Browne
Nathaniell Sneape
Richard Browne sen
William Vernon
John Colman
Katherine Hutchinson wid
Thomas Barwell
Margerie Bilson
Hellen Twisle wid
Widdow Coton
Thomas Perkens

[1] TNA, E179/194/334/10.
[2] TNA, E179/194/334/18.

28. **Grendon**[1] 29 May 1671 [printed] 15 names

John Tomson
Richard Ball
William Edes
Alies Cooke
Francis Richards
Elizabeth Spittell
John Hunter jun
John Albrighton
John Walton
Alies Asbrey
Thomas Skermon
Jone Standley
John Grotwidg
Samuell Orton
Nicklas Harper

29. **Kingsbury**[2] 30 May 1671 [printed] 61 names

Hurley
Widowe Burton
John Capenhurst
Henery Greenway
John Taylour
Richard Churchill
Robert Harris
Widow Bracebridge
Widow Harris
Thomas Harris
John Massey
Widow Massey
John Harris
Gabriel Hollier
Widow Chetwyn
William Greenway
Widowe Hawxford
Robert Blythe
Henery Smith
Widow Blount
Widow Mills
Thomas Goyle
Thomas Banks
Widow Rubley
Joane Collins
Widow Howe
Joyce Watson
Thomas Orton
John Hewit
Richard Wright
Alice Ashmore
William Sleigh
Robert Tims
William Judde
Whateley in the constablery of Grindon[3]
Abraham Barton
William Orme
Thomas Heywood
John Hill
Widow Brotherhood
George Lees
William Harris
Thomas Wright
Dosthill in the constablery of Manceter
Thomas Tomlinson
William Taylour
Nicholas Voyle
Widow Hawkins
Halloughton in the constablery of Whitacre
Joseph Spires
Elizabeth Saunders
John Baker
Heathhouses in Kingsbury
Widowe Hartill
Coton in the constablery of Mackstock
John Lytherham
Edward Hawxford
Edward Marlour
Elizabeth Rocket
The hamlet of Kingsbury
Edward Greene
Anne Bowring
Winefred Voyle
Edward Sleigh
Anne Chaplyn
Thomas Hewit
<Francis Brookes>
<Humphrey Heatley>
John Cratnor
Thomas Burton

1 TNA, E179/194/334/17. The certificates from 1671 are almost certainly more reliable for Grendon parish and Whateley in Kingsbury parish than their 1670 returns, but they still do not distinguish the exempt in Whittington from those in Grendon village. One of the former was probably Alice Asbrey (Walker, *Hemlingford*, p. 136).

2 TNA, E179/194/334/16.

3 This certificate from 1671 is almost certainly more reliable for Whateley in Kingsbury parish than the 1670 return.

30. **Middleton**[1] 5 May 1672 [printed] 22 names

Joane Cope widow
Elizebeath Cope wid
Thomas Nixson
Edward Cope jun
Widdow Whitehead
Widdow Moore
William Cooper
John Croocke
Anne Penne
George Willis
Alexander Lighton
William Symes
John Seargant
Thomas Standley
Widdow Shorte
Edward Roberts
Edward Standley
Anne Goonne widdow
James Faussitt
John Seale
Joane Blewe
William Jackeson

31. **Polesworth**[2] 16 June 1671 [printed] 94 [100] names

Polesworth
Edward Shepherd
John Chadburne
Thomas Atkins
Anthony Wright
Widow Congrave
Thomas Twelves
Thomas Banks
Robert Stretton
John Clay
Robert Hinds
Francis Congrave
Widow Lakin
Widow Hunter
Joseph Blastock
Henry Briggs
John Boles
<John>Edward Tant
Joseph Groutage
Henry Lattimer
Will Ballard
James Blastock
Caleb Clarke
Edward Groutage
Will Groutage
Alice Getley
Thomas Bilson
John Atkins
Robert Briggs
Widow Rabye
John Nicols
Humphrey Massye
Widow Gretton
Widow Rogers
Widow Bott
Thomas Colman
Widow Breedon
Thomas Taverner
Daniel Ward
Thomas Mandue
Henry Massye
David Corbison
Cockaine Martin
Abigaile Wright
Thomas Batman
George <…>S…eston
Henry Batman jun

Warton in the parish of Polesworth
William Poultnye
Widow Browne
Widow Kinge
Aldridge Orton
Robert <Orton>Smith
Robert Higginson
Widow Aldridge
Katharine Cooper
Richard Lakin
Richard Clarke
Joane Robinson
Frances Lakin
Richard Cope
Thomas Hunter
Thomas Mole
Sarah Sadler
Susanna Norton

Dordon in the parish of Polesworth
Samuel Briggs
Widow Yeld
Widow Mellis
Widow Lithal
Will Harris
Edward Atkins
Widow Hinds
John Baxter
John Gartage
Widow Hull
Widow Tomson
Henry Snow

Street-way [Watling Street] **and Hall-end in the parish of Polesworth**

[1] TNA, E179/194/334/19.
[2] TNA, E179/194/334/15. This certificate is reproduced in Figure 23. In it the vicar of Polesworth appears to have made the best case possible in support of the four householders who did not qualify for exemption as defined by its preamble.

[Polesworth contd.]
Thomas Mills
Thomas Moore
Will Baxter
<William>Widow Reeves
Widow Greaves
Widow Hill
Fraaslye [Freasley] **in the parish of Polesworth**
Josiah Moore
Henry Moore
Dorothy Greenwood
Widow Musson
Widow Arme
Widow Nicolls
George Bird
Robert Slater
John Breedon
Thomas Arme
Wilncoate and Streetway [Wilnecote and Watling Street] **in the parish of Polesworth**
Mary Burnes
George Smith
Margaret Litheram
Thomas <Tayler>Arme
Widow Waldrom
John Congrave
Richard Wise
Richard Hunter
Lenhard <…>White

These are also humbly to certifye that although Henry Wright, Thomas Spare & John Higgins of Polesworth as also John Wendridge of Warton are liable to pay in respect of what they rent yet they are miserably poore & worth little or nothing.

32. **Seckington and Bramcote**[1] 27 October 1671 [printed] 9 names

Dorothy Gardner
Emaniel Thomson
Widdow Cooper
John Martyn
Dorothy Hutchinson
Widdow Cope
John Johnson
Robert Nicholls
Henry Riley

All which have received contribution

33. **Tamworth par: Corporation** [borough][2] 29 May 1671 [printed] 53 names

Thomas Clark
Henry Keene
Ralph …eves
Andrew Ballard
John Howes
William Dickison
William Wright
Henry Smith labourer
John …atts
Elizabeth Smith widow
Mary Allin widow
Ann Peeres
John Sneape
Eedy …ennings widow
Nicholas Keeling
Humphry Dolton
Christopher Drayton
John Onyon
John Briggs
William Farmer
William Peat mason
Anthony Alsop glover
George Godwin
John Milner
Thomas Orton
Henry Sketchley
Henry Read
John Clark
Margery Brittain widow
[blank] Willington widow
Ann Batham
John Egginton
<… …>
John Swinston
Richard Dones
Thomas Charles alias Bedworth

[1] TNA, E179/194/334/13. The information in the final comment was not relevant to the wording of this certificate and was almost certainly false, so it may have been conceived as a smokescreen to conceal the dubious qualifications of some of these householders.

[2] TNA, E179/194/334/21. The preamble to the last 18 names in this transcript bases their claim to exemption on their reduced circumstances and on the first exemption clause and not on the wording of the printed certificate, which applies to the rest.

These persons undernamed in this collume, we do believe, are very poor & indigent, who by reason of their poverty pay none of the usuall taxes payments & contributions towards the church & poore but doe receive almes.

Robert Silk
Thomas Vernon
John Tornsworth
Hugh Underhill
Isabel Osburn widow
An Gorton widow
Benedict Bell
Dorothy Harding widow
Thomas Ashmore
Jeffery Bathe
Nathaniel Rice
William Smith of Church Street
Philip Needham
William Boldsworth
John Smart
James Smith alias Brown
Widow Hely
Randle Thornsworth

34. **Tamworth par: Amington and Bolehall**[1] 3 June 1671 [printed] 38[37] names

Poore of Amington
Henry Curson
Isaac Gun
Richard Lees
Widow Maud
Edward James
Joane Parker widow
Cornelius Clark
[blank] Blew
William Browns wife
Robert Taylor
Joseph Taylor
Amie Skellet
Edward Orton
Widow Clark

Poore in Stonidelph within the constablery of Amington
Widow Da[w]man
Thomas [?]Kellet
Edward Lax
William Waite
Richard Voydall
Gregory Horne
William …unter
William <…>Baker
Widow Smart
John Aston
Henry Orgall

Poore in Bolehall and Glascot
Widow Grin
Widow Greene
Ann Jackson
Widow Sneape
Thomas Sylvester
James Bird
Thomas Briggs
John Greenwood
Robt Jefferis

Poore in Glascott
Thomas Naylor
Georg Starkey
Widow Ball

35. **Tamworth par: Wilnecote**[2] 30 May 1671 [printed] 49 names

William Stintson
Robert Thompson
George Birch
Palmer Buggins
Henry Collins
George Smyth
John Jennings
Thomas Michell
Thomas Hollyer
Thomas Wright
Thomas Marlor
Robert Arnold
Widdow Cotten
Henry Roades
John Whateley
Thomas Lillie
John Thompson jun
Widdow Keeleing
Thomas Goodman
Richard Smyth
Walter Lea
John Bird
Robert Coupper
John Marlor
Widdow Bagnall
John Tompson
Widdow Nicholes

1 TNA, E179/194/334/20. Amington was a separate constablery within Tamworth parish and Bolehall and Glascote another.
2 TNA, E179/194/334/14. Wilnecote was another constablery, mainly in Tamworth parish.

[Wilnecote contd.]
Anthony Marlor
George Cumley
Alce Roades
Widdow Cope
John Greeneway
William Boumford
Widdow Martin
Elizebeth Hollyer
Henry Cotten
Richard Marlor
Tobias Sheldon
Widdow Morton
Rowland Wilcoxe
John Birbidge
William Squelch
Thomas Bird
William Cumley
Marmaduke Wotton
John Wilcoxe
John Armeshaw
Widdow Hollyer
Erasmus Foster

Kineton Hundred

Brailes division

36. **Brailes**[1] July 1670 [printed] 79 names

Gregory Luke
Thomas Wadley
James Momford
Thomas Cross
Richard Blackman
William Bradley
John Momford
Widow Perkinson [ch]
William George
Nicholas Perkinson
John Bumpas
Widow Spicer
Widow Wrench
[Ma]rgret Walker [*wid*]
[*John*] Gardner
[*Geo?*] Pitway [ch]
… et Miles [*widd*]
[Wid]ow Rendall
[*John?*] [?]Hood
[Rich?]d Godson
[Wi]dow Napton
... ll Godson
William Hunt
William Herbert
Thomas Humfris [ch]
John Wood
Widow West
William Gardner
Thomas James
John Robinson
Laurence Walker
Elizabeth Stiler
Widow Collins
Robert Durram
John White
William Hemminge
John Prestidge
William Albury
John Upton
Ralph Prestidge [ch]
Edward Humfris
James Phipps
James Gardner
John Eddon
Widow Hancoke
George Becket
Nathaniell Smith [ch]
Robert Hone [ch]
James Hone
Joane Moore
James Chadburne
John Brian
William Whiting [ch]
Widow Thornit
John Cockbill sen [ch]
John Cockbill jun
Walter Gregory
Thomas Genings
Ralph Harrison
John Bishop [ch]
<William Aston>
Richard Bishop [ch]
William Saule
Gerard Whitinge
Thomas Freeman
William Wrench
Anthony Hambidge
Thomas Bishop
William Carter
Francis Moore
<John Marshull>
Robert Eddon
Catherine Tayler
John Wilkes [ch]
Richard Hone

[1] TNA, E179/347. Eleven of these names were returned as chargeable in the 1670 return for Brailes. This may be explained by the parish officers being more generous than the chimney men in their interpretation of exemption. Where this certificate has been damaged, parts of a few names have been inserted from the return for 1670, which is transcribed above.

<Thomas Phillips>
John Teale
Esay Walker
William Kilby
John Kinge
John Beards
William Brewer

37. **Long Compton**[1] 29 October 1670 [printed] 37 names

John Chisnolde
John Davis
Margaret Weston
Jane Harris widdow
Will Smith
Bridget Collet vid
James Cousens
Richard Haile
Will Milloway sen
John Becke
Anne Taylor widdow
Anne Joyner widdow
Robert Welch
Richard Willcoxe
Richard Tomes
Kinnye[Kimberry] Hunt
Will Savage
John Oliver
John Alder
Thomas Tyler
Edward Hewes
Will Bivins
John Laurence
Michael Poole
Tho Leadbeater
Mary Haile
Margaret Fisher
Anthonye Lane
Margaret Leadbeater
Saunders Herbert
Margaret Goldicot wid
John Crosse
Winnye[Winifride] Hunt
Robert Sherlye
Anne Savage
Will Staple
Mathew Harbard

Priors Marston division

38. **Avon Dassett**[2] 13 October 1670 [printed] 13 names reduced to 8

[This certificate was duly signed by the rector, a churchwarden and an overseer of the poor, but was rejected by the receiver, John Newsham, who deleted five names and then wrote out a second list, which the rector and parish officers then refused to sign.]

Thomas Gibes
William Round
Joh Smith
Elisha Smith
<John Rawlings jun>
<Richard Glover>
Widdow Walker
Wid Phips
Richard Hancox
Thomas Petipher
<John Tinsell>
<John Bachehler>
<William Sharpe>

The persons duly to be certified for are vizt

Tho Gibes
Will Round
Jon Smith
Elizabeth Smith
Widow Walker
Widow Phipps
Richard Handcox
Tho Petipher

I would intreate the minister Mr Staunton to make a new certificate
John Newsham

[1] TNA, E179/347.
[2] TNA, E179/347. Deadlock ensued after Warwickshire's receiver, John Newsham, refused to accept five of the names certified by Avon Dassett's minister and officers. When Newsham demanded a revised certificate, they stood firm even though he then recorded the five as chargeable in the relevant return.

Knightlow Hundred

Rugby division

39. **Rugby**[1] 31 August 1674 [printed] 69 names

Francis Trusse
Willm Satchwel
John Ladbrook
John Wright
Wm Lathbury
Abraham Kidney
John Bourne
Wm Bromwich
John Hobley
Henry Hobley
Thomas Bunting
John Foster
Tho Mabs
Wid Pen
Wid Willis
George Biddle
Nicholas Baldwin
Tho Trusse
Edward Robins
Wid Francis
Tho Currall
Wm Currall
Walter Ilet
Rich Trusse

Greg Billing
John Highrous
Wid Sharp
Wid Trusse
Tho Satchwel
Highgate Berry
Roger Groome
Rich Bret
Wm Prince
Wid Joyner
Ralph Horsley
Tho Bishell
Wid Blizzard
Wid Satchwel
Wid Sefton
Wid Shell
John Satchwel
Tho Wright
Edw Bucknal
Wid Harrold
Susan Greene
Tho Jackson
Francis Palmer
James Wilson

Anthony Joyner
Ward Kauton
Benj Hall
Wid Preston
Tho Tant
Wid Ilet
Tho Prince
Jo Jarvis
Jo Smith
<Jas Seal jun>
Jo Harrold
Edw Wright
Jo Bradshaw
Wm Bayly
<Wid Cooper>
Jane Bourn
<Wm Lee>
Mich Loome
Greenaway's wife
Rands his wife
Cotons wife
Wid Hawks
Rich Gent
James Seal

Southam division

40. **Napton on the Hill**[2] 20 February 1670/1 [printed] 47 names

Math Biddle
Rich Loe
Wm Evans
Jo Kiteley

Tho Eales
Jo Mallin
Jo Barnecle
Wm Houltam

John Powell
Jo Taft
Jo Sheesby sen
Tho Pratt

1 TNA, E179/347. Most unusually, the March 1671 certificate for Rugby exempted '40 cotts miserable poore and not at all liable to pay the duty of hearth money' without giving their householders' names. The next two certificates referred similarly to the same group. Thus this certificate from August 1674 is the only one that names the occupants of these cottages, although of course they were not all the same people who lived in them at Michaelmas 1670.

2 TNA, E179/347.

Edwd Whithead sen
Hen Pickstocke
Fran Barnett
Wm Barrett
James Marriott
Wm Griffin
Jo Nasbey
Tho Mallin
Peetter Beaver
Rich Hyerne
Wm Malline
Sus Powell
Robt Hust
James Tidman
Jo Biddle jun
Tho Budd
Hen Budd
Widd Horley
Widd Hixson
Wm Harwood
Widd Naseby
Wm Mortibus
Robt Trepas
Wm Makepeace labourer
Robt Talbutt
Jo Parker
Widd Jeffes
Jo Clarke
John Garrett
Rich Beane
Wm Watt
Jo Jefes
Rob Gee
Wm Orton
Wm Gente

41. **Southam**[1] 7 February 1670/1 [printed] 60 names

Mary Turner widd
Widd Spicer
Tho Jadkin
Wm Gilbert
Widd Banbury
Rich Maunton
<Marg Cox>
Rich Wootton
Wm Beasley
Mary Cox
Edwd Horne
John Goode
Widd Higham
Wm Chester
Rich Pettifer
Widd Jackson
Eph Benson
Rob Browne
Widd Goode
Wm Wright
John Freeman
Rich Freeman
Rob Hill
Wm Jeffes
Tho Freeman
Tho Basley
Widd Ladd
Wm Goode
Wm Kinge
Widd Perry
Widd Webb
Wm Hayward
Widd Cox
John Edmunds
Rich Worrall
Wm Sharman
Joseph Julian
Hen Biddle
Fran Cox
Widd Castle
Tho Clarke
Tho Stollard
Geo Worrall
Hen Pitcher
Edwd Horne [X]
Joseph Tomes
Abrah Clarke
Widd Wright
Tho Gibbs
Danll Lea
Sym Julians
John Turner
Tho Queeney
Wm Collins
Rich Queeney [ch]
Margt Freeman
Sarah Sheepard widd [ch]
Widd Mallin
Tim Mordicke [ch]
Luke Winkley
John Williams

[1] TNA, E179/347.

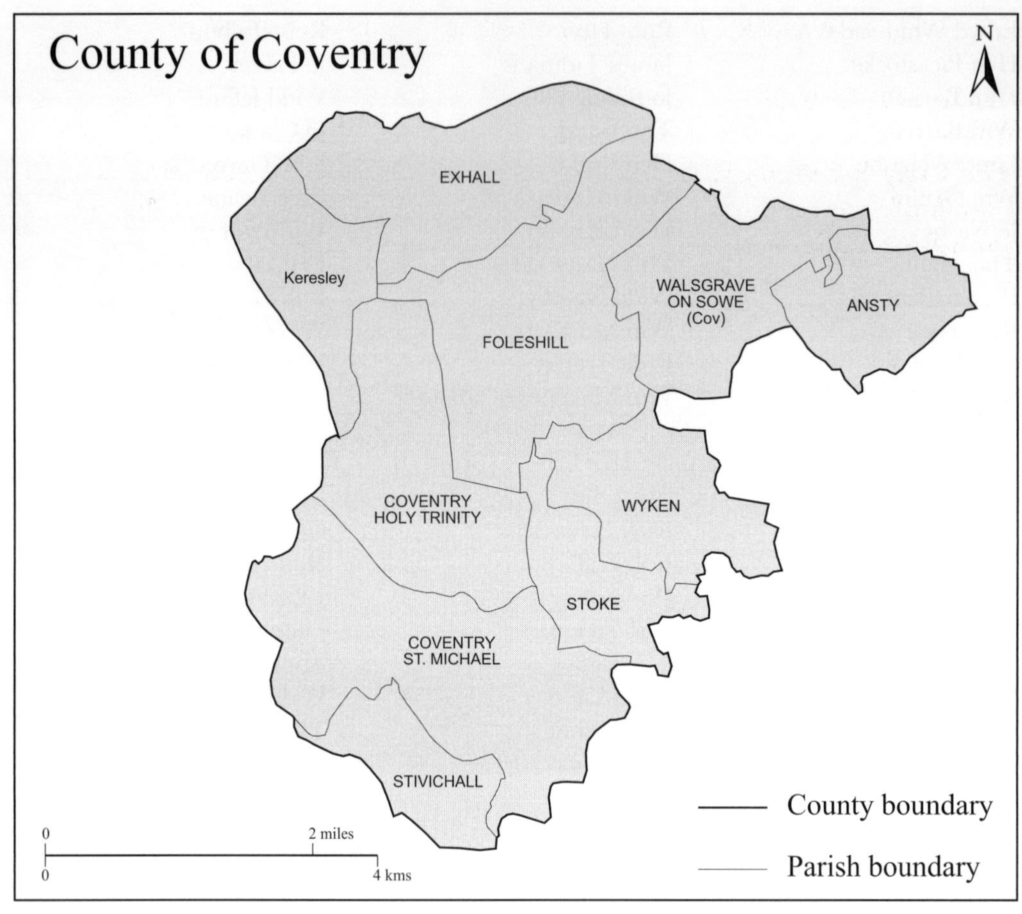

Map 18 County of Coventry with parish names. Detached parts of parishes are named in lower case.

Coventry Hearth Tax Return Lady Day 1666

[TNA, E179/259/9]
[p. 1]
The Citty & Countye of the City of Coventry with the liberties thereof
One halfe yeares duty of Hearth money ended March 25th 1666
John Best Collector

	[Paid]	[Unpaid]	
[City of Coventry]			
Gosford Streete Ward [in Holy Trinity & St Michael pars[1]]			
Mr Thomas Blakes	6		
Zephaniah Louke	2		
Mr William Vale	3		
Mr Humphry Rogers	6		
Robert Bedford owner		3	empty
John Harrison	3		
Mr Cotton		3	empty
Mrs Pywell	6		
Henry Packwood	1		
Jonathan Mason	6		
John Smyth	4		
John Smyth fuller	3		
John Collins	5		
Paul Wood		2	cert
Samuell Collins	3		
Edward Harper		1	in building
John Scare		1	pauper
John Bott	4		
and one publiq oven		1	
Richard Newcomb		2	cert
Goodwyfe West		2	cert
Samuell Bedford	6		
Mrs Wedgwood		2	cert
[blank]		3	empty
James Ward sen	2		
Samuell Utting		2	cert
Wm Wightman	3		

	[Paid]	[Unpaid]	
James Ward jun		2	cert
Edward Taylor		2	cert
Samuell Smyth	6		
Mrs Stretton	6		
George Delworth	1		
Joane Bristow		1	cert
James Mades		1	dead
John Fosson		1	cert
Emanuell Small		3	empty
Widd Bryan		2	cert
Alderman Vale owner		3	empty
Joseph Ceely	4		
Tho Blackslye		3	puld up 1 & refuseth
Widd Sandrey		1	cert
George Wilkinson		1	cert
Rich Hall		1	cert
Jonathan Fullflowe	3		
Richard Visand	4		
Thomas Hewett	3		
[p. 2]			
John Ambrose jun	3		
Henry Lapworth		1	cert
Wm Bosworth	3		
George Copson	1		
Math Taylor owner over the gate		[-]	
William Smyth sen		2	
Widd Lowe		2	cert
Wm Partridge	5		
Edward Lapworth	4		

1 The surviving exemption certificates that included Gosford St Ward recorded 30 exempt in Holy Trinity parish and 27 in St Michael in 1672, compared with 35 and 28 respectively in 1674 (Table 29, pp. 471–2). Unfortunately no document indicates how the payable households were subdivided.

[Gosford Street Ward contd.]	[Paid]	[Unpaid]	
[blank] Eades		1	cert
Henry Ward		3	dead & no distresse
Rich Armstrong	2		
Daniell Grimston	<3>2	& 1	decayed
Wm Smyth jun		2	cert
Henry Langley		1	cert
William Petman		3	very poore
John Kinnington		2	
John Ward	2	& 1	decayed
Roger Fisher		1	cert
William Abell		1	cert
Wm W<e>oster		2	puld downe 1 & refuseth
Wm Smyth		1	cert
Thomas Ward	5		
Mr Hopkins owner		[-][*10*[1]]	empty
John Baker		3	no distresse takes alms
Richard Barne		2	gone
Tho Humfry	5		
John Ambrose sen		2	
Sarah Haw		3	no distresse
Wm Pinder		2	cert
Widd Pinder		1	cert
Widd Gardner		1	cert
Wm Parker		1	cert
Wm Sceares		2	cert
Edward Rogers	5		
Mrs Duckett		1	cert
Mrs Hicks	7		
Mr Stretton owner		[-]	empty
Thomas Gardner		1	dead
John Hobson		1	cert
John Rawbone		1	cert
Symon Challinghowse		1	cert
John Carelesse		1	cert
William Smyth sen		1	cert
Widd Chapling		1	cert

	[Paid]	[Unpaid]	
Job Mathewes		1	cert
Joseph Clideny		1	cert
Samuell S<...>eares		1	cert
Wm Hilton		1	cert
Joane Kelby		1	cert
Widd Hassekine		1	cert
Widd Harvile		1	cert
Joseph Lelseys		2	
Mrs Sarah Rusworth	4		
Wm Gardner		2	cert
Edward Sturton		2	cert
Thomas Barker	3		
Thomas Past	5		
[p. 3]			
Hugh Lawlesse	3		
Mr Wright of Stoake owner		[-]	empty
Widd Perkins		1	cert
Thomas Hands		2	cert
Thomas Clowdes		3	no distresse almes
John Burton		1	cert
Widd Andrewes		1	cert
Tho Mambrasse		1	cert
Hump Crew		1	cert
Wm Rowland		1	cert
Rich Showell		1	cert
Widd Wilkins		1	cert
Randall Gardner		1	cert
Rich Orchard		1	cert
Widd Merry		1	cert
Widd Burton		1	cert
John Fosson		1	cert
Wm Brockett		1	cert
John Scotton		1	cert
Wm Townsend		1	cert
Tho Adington		1	cert
Abrah Woster		1	cert
Henry Bristow		1	cert
John Arch		1	cert
Dan Messenger		1	cert

[1] TNA, E179/259/10 (1665).

	[Paid]	[Unpaid]	
Wm Woster		1	cert
Thomas Clowes		1	cert
William Hoult	2		
Will Allibone		2	cert
Edward Astell	3		
Anne Edson		1	
Thomas Butler	2		
	156	136	

Smythfordstreete Ward
[in St Michael par]

	[Paid]	[Unpaid]	
Wm Greeneway	5		
Thomas Abee	5	& 1	decayed
George Pickering	6		
Edward Owen	4		
Wm Smyth owner		3	empty
Samuell Flavell	3		
Abrah Walding	8		
Mr Naylor owner		[-]	empty
Tho Lawrence	2		
John Morgan	5		
James Taytom	3		
John Carver	1		
Wm Cooke		1	cert
Henry Pinder		2	cert
Mary Young		1	cert
Francis Tedd	6	& 1	decayed
Edward Good		2	cert
Wm Sowtherne		1	cert
Thomas Chissell	4		
Edward Biddle		2	empty
Edward Childes	21		
[p. 4]			
John Clearke	5		
Richard Cavett	4	& 1	oven
Anne Johnson		1	cert
Widd Carpenter		1	cert
Anne Wills		1	cert
Anne Copson		1	cert
Mary Fletcher		1	cert
Samuell West	7		
Thomas Smyth		1	cert
Tymo Cooke	1		
Thomas Godfrey		2	cert

	[Paid]	[Unpaid]	
Edward Sheldon		1	cert
John Higginson	4	& 1	taken downe
Rich Edson		4	no distresse
Wm Mathewes		2	empty
Edward Looe	4	& 1	stopt up
William King		5	poore & lives by almes
Richard Jeffcott		3	
Thomas Stookes	2		
Richard Hunt	2		
Thomas Cavett	4	& 1	tooke of by oath
Alexander Edwards	4		
John Hullee	2	& 1	decayd
Wm Pollard		2	cert
Thomas Johnson		1	cert
William Lucas	1		
Nicolas Dornell	3		
Wm Browne		1	cert
Sarah Billingsley		2	empty
Gregory Achell	1		
Joseph Woster	4		
John Hopkins		1	cert
Mary Alsop		1	cert
Susanna Bull		2	cert
Alderman Chambers owner	2		
William Willcox	5<5>0		
Judith Upsion	3		
Thomas Butterlesse	4		
Mr Rich Terry		8	paid 4 shillings
Wm Smyth		3	with a forge
George Wright	2		
Thomas Symonds	3		
Edward Snell	4		
Robt Lee	2		
John Logues	3		
Sampson Clearke	5		
William Swift	1		
Mr Anstie owner		[-]	empty

[Smithford Street Ward contd.]	[Paid]	[Unpaid]	
Samuell Ward	3		
John Jones	2		
Sam Wattson	3		
Anne Record	3		
George Alliett	5		
Sam Watson		1	
	171	64	

[p. 5]

Sponstreete Ward

[in St Michael par]

	[Paid]	[Unpaid]	
Edward Forster		2	in building
Richard Launder	7		
Wm Waring	1		
John Houlding	1		
John Barr		1	cert
Richard Cave	1		
Wm Webster	5		
Rich Benion		2	cert
Tho Benion		1	cert
Wm Forster		3	no distresse, takes almes
Anne Draper	1		
Wm Ryley	3		
Wm Pickering		2	cert
Mary Jackson		1	cert
Eliza Shewell		1	cert
Tho Pickering		1	cert
Wm Gardner		1	cert
Richard Murrill		1	cert
Thomas Rudiard	1		
Widd Pickering		1	cert
Edward Murcott		1	cert
Widd Atkins		2	cert
Symon Pickering	<4>3	& 1	blowne downe
Edward Smyth		2	cert
Wm Buswell		1	
John Whitehead sen	2		
James Roach		1	cert
Thomas Browne		1	empty
Will Hall		1	cert
George Henbury		1	cert
Wm Ebron		1	cert
Will Price		1	cert
Widd Higgins		1	cert
Henry Clearke		1	cert
Wm Hall jun		1	cert
John Smyth		1	cert
John Mussage owner	2		
John Croxall		1	cert
Wm Burbridge		1	cert
John Whiteheade jun		1	cert
John Houlding		1	cert
Wm Bates		1	cert
Robert Lee		1	cert
Richard Mathewes		1	cert
Alderman Smyth	11		
Widd W[illia]mson		1	cert
Hannah Swallow		1	cert
Richard Ireson		1	cert
Richard Walker		1	cert
Thomas Showell	4		
Rob Mallett		1	cert
Wm Lyndsey		1	cert
Richard Miller	3		
Wm Dickson		1	cert
Widd Taff		1	cert
Rich Mathewes		1	cert
John Gilbert		1	cert
Christpofer Checkley		1	cert
Thomas Dudley		1	cert
Symon Burt		1	cert

[p. 6]

	[Paid]	[Unpaid]	
Widd Bosworth		1	cert
Wm Cosford		1	cert
Henry Deacon		1	cert
Widd Moore		1	cert
John Lloyd	2		
Robert Cunigrave	2		
John Ebron		1	cert
Robert Knight	2		
John Tilson	3		
Thomas Gilbert	1		
Mr Beale owner		2	empty
George Kerby	3		

	[Paid]	[Unpaid]	
Richard Bates	2		
Rich Parman	5		
Richard Parlin		1	cert
Wm Southerne	2		
and 1 forge		1	
Richard Gardner	1		
Wm Robison	2		
Henry Babbs	1		
Wm Monke	2		
John Bennett		1	cert
Richard King	5		
Anne Backhowse		1	cert
Mathew Wood	4		
An almes house[1]		10	under endowed
Widd Poole		1	cert
Wm Skinner		1	cert
Henry Muddock	2		
Rebecca Painton		1	cert
Widd Wood		1	cert
Mathew Aston		1	cert
Wm Howard		1	cert
Edward Dutchman		1	cert
Edmond Fox	4		
Edwd Hurst	3<2>0		
William Ward		2	
Fran Clearke sen	4		
Katherine Wright	3		
John Holmes		1	cert
Tho Walker		1	
and a forge		1	
John Hawkesford	3		
Wm Villers	<1>2		
Thomas Ashborne		1	cert
Eliza Estwick		1	cert
John Boughs	3		no distresse
John Clement	1		
Rich Stanton		1	cert
Marg Turne		1	cert
Hum Naylor		1	cert
John Johnson		1	cert

	[Paid]	[Unpaid]	
Jeremiah Walter	2		
Wm Charles	8		
John Patrick		2	cert
Mr Gibbons owner		1	empty
Richard Gibbons	5		
John Murdock	5		
and a publiq oven		1	
Mr Yeardley owner	<5>3		
John Wright	4		
[p. 7]			
John Charles	3		
John Wildee	1		
and a forge		1	
Anthony England		1	cert
John Browne		2	
John Gunn		2	
Edward Stoakes		2	cert
Fra Chambers		1	cert
Roger Bellamy		1	cert
William Feild		2	cert
Eliza Denham		2	cert
Lattin Richards	6		
Joane Holding	4		
Tho Arnell		1	cert
Henry Marler		1	cert
Wm Arnell		1	cert
Anne Smyth		3	poore & no distresse
Anne Nicolls		2	cert
Widd Bissacar		1	cert
Wm Griffin		1	
John Jackson		1	cert
and a forge		1	
Francis Keale	7		
Peter Pettipher		2	empty
Tho Hilliard		1	cert
Thomas Villidge		1	cert
Wm Knibbs		1	cert
Mr Edward Looe owner		[-]	empty
John Bayly		3	no distresse
Wm Mason		2	cert

[1] It has been assumed that this entry represents five separate dwellings with two hearths each, as in the four almshouses with eight hearths in Cross Cheaping Ward below.

[Spon Street Ward contd.]	[Paid]	[Unpaid]	
Rich Brockhowse	4		
George Vernon	4		
Sarah Kinnington		1	cert
Tho Wilcox		2	cert
Eliza Porter		1	cert
George Porter	3		
Edward Craddock	6		
John Walker	3		
Samuell Bale	2		
Thomas Porter	2		
Edward Blacksley	<3>0	3	puld downe 1 & refuseth
Edw Harford		2	cert
Anne Butler		1	empty
Thomas Smyth	1		
Wm Wood	1		
Marg Brookes		1	cert
Francis Clearke jun	3		
George Greene	1		
Henry Gibbons	3		
Tho Hollyer	4		
Benja Miller	2		
George Rushton	1		
Major Slaughter owner		[-]	in 2 empty howses
John Lawrence	2		
Tho Borne jun	3		
John Snell	3		
Jane Mason		2	
[p. 8]			
Mr Thomas Gayrie	3		
and 1 in building		1	
Thomas Moore		2	cert
Edward Deacon	4		
Luke Oliver & Jno Aston		4	no distresse
Rob Backhowse	2		
Wm Clearke	3		
Robt Chandler	5		
John Charnley	7		

	[Paid]	[Unpaid]	
Joseph Ebron	4		
John Smyth in 2 tenements	5		
Idem John [Smyth] an empty howse	3		
Thomas Mustion	4		
and a publiq oven		1	
Wm Tackey	3		
Eliza Adcox	4		
Tho Borne sen	6		
Symon Borne	[-]	[*3*[1]]	
	[256]	[154]	

Litle Parke Streete Ward[2]

[in St Michael par]			
Henry Cooke	3		
Henry Diston	2		
Wm Bent	2		
John Spell	1		
Joane Butler	2		
Anthony Blakesbye	2		
Mrs Susan Westley		6	empty
Anne Gullifer	2		
<…> Twa Maydes		1	gone
John Price		2	cert
John Herbert	3		
Samu Alsop	6		
Alice Ridlee	1<1>0		
Wm Sutton		2	empty
Luke Milborne	2		
Samuell Wheate		1	in building
Thomas French	2		
Tho Dawson	3		
Tymo Bird	1		
Henry Jeffcott	5		
Nathaniell Stephens	2		
John Cranwell	3		
Sam Chadbourne		1	cert
John Haw sen	1		
John Haw jun	1		
Clem Gullifer	1<1>0		

1 TNA, E179/259/10 (1665).
2 Also known as Earl Street Ward.

	[Paid]	[Unpaid]	
Eliza Payne	<3>2	<2>0	
Eliza Wilson		1	cert
Alderman Love	8		
Rich Hunt & Wm Pollard	4		
Wm Clifton	4		
and a publiq oven		1	
Abraham Carter	2		
John Lilly	1		
[p. 9]			
Mary Moore	1	& 1	in building
Avis Lilly		1	
John Whiteheade	<3>2	& 1	decayed
John Timbrill	3		
Tho Pickering	1		
Mr John Lax	15		
Thomas Fox	2		
John Cleyton	3		
William Philipps	6		
John Gorton	2		
Richard Garrett	3		
Fran Bayly	6		
Widd Woodley	2		
James Swinerton	2		
Wm Wright	<2>0	2	empty
Fran Clearke	1		
Samuell Withers	4		
John Falkener	2		
Sir Richard Hopkins	<17>16	& 1	in his hall which hee will not pay for
John Bird	2		
Francis Davenport	6		
Mrs Frances Brookes	2		
John Tunnill	1		
Joseph Chambers	12		
Joyce Ford	4		
Mr Hayles owner		[-]	empty
Henry Hople	3		
Fran Cater	4		
Wm Benford	2		
Widd Parker	2		
Judeth Ouldham		1	cert

	[Paid]	[Unpaid]	
Rich Bush		1	cert
Richard Sadler		1	cert
Eliza Morris		1	cert
John Holloway		1	cert
Henry Lawrence	1		
John Porter	2		
Rich Robinson	2		
Wm Heycock	3		
Judith Astlee	4		
Mr Abrah Gibbons owner		10	empty
Thomas Bennett	3		
Dr Rich Higgs	15		
Jesse Poole	<5>3	& 2	puld downe
Eliza Rice	3		
Moses Higham		1	cert
Daniell Gilbert	4		
Marke Gulston	5		
James Morgan	5	& 1	puld downe
Widd Randall		1	cert
Widd Love	4		
Dorothy Bishop	3		
Richard Greene		3	empty
John Ragdell	2		
Edward Hill	9		
Tho Bowater	3		
Wm Pickering	2		
Wm Wetherley		1	cert
[blank] Wright		1	cert
Ursula Wetherley		1	cert
Mary Crofts		1	cert
Widd Jenkins		1	cert
[p. 10]			
Mary Shakespeare	5		
John Barton		1	cert
Widd Walker		1	cert
Robert Turner	2		
John Davies		1	cert
John Pickering		1	cert
Mich Fisher		1	cert
Widd Andrewes		1	cert
Rich Waring		1	cert
Goodwyfe Gardner		1	cert
Edward Walker		2	cert

[Little Park Street Ward contd.]	[Paid]	[Unpaid]	
The Wheate Sheafe		[-]	empty not viewed
Thomas Woolson		1	cert
Widd Leakins		1	cert
Edward Sanders		1	cert
Widd Parker		2	cert
Thomas Feanne		1	cert
Anne Browne		1	cert
John Tymme	1		
Richard Lee	3		
Michaell Parker	5		
John Bradshaw	4		
Gilbert Adderley		3	
Mr Cartwright		1	
John Fairefax	6		
John Ichenor	4		
George King	3		
Abrah Allen		1	cert
Joseph Ellis	1		
Mr Jesson owner of 2 empty houses	18	& 1	decayed
Mr Butler	7		
Sam Higham	3		
John Kennington	3		
William Jesson owner		[-]	empty
Rich Cranwell	3		
Mrs Stoughton	2		
Katherine Holdbridge	3		
Sir Thomas Norton	12		
Mrs Warner		<…>1	cert
Edward Palmer	11		
Mr Capper	8		
John Berry	3		
Widd Dye		1	cert
Widd Blackslye		1	cert
John Borne	12		
Mrs Eliza Ball	10		
John Woolston	4		
William Hill	8		

	[Paid]	[Unpaid]	
William Quinborough 2 howses	4		
Widd Taylor		1	cert
[blank]		1	empty
	393	78 [77]	

Jordayne Well Ward

[in Holy Trinity & St Michael pars[1]]

	[Paid]	[Unpaid]	
Jonah Abell	3		
William Neale		3	in building
Wm Kenning	3		
Richard Hayes	6		
Foulke Waldron	4		
and a forge		1	
John Edmonds	2		
Price Devereux	3		
Humphry Knipe	3		
Richard Ferreman	4		
Edward Cooke		[-]	in building
John Bishop		4	
Thomas Cart	4		
Edward Lowke	4		
Richard Newcombe		2	empty
John Wright	2		
Robert Parker	2		
Richard Wall	2		
Widd Burnham		1	cert
Thomas Jeffery		1	cert
Mathew Eades		1	cert
Abrah Copson	2		
Abrah Avery		2	cert
Widd Sanders		2	cert
Mich Poole		2	cert
Widd Starkey		2	cert
John Cooper		1	cert
Manasses King		2	cert
Charles Winterton	3		
and a publiq oven		1	
Thomas Bradshaw		1	cert

[1] According to the exemption certificates for 1672 and 1674, the certified exempt in Jordan Well Ward rose from 39 in Holy Trinity parish and 17 in St Michael to 42 and 18 respectively in 1674 (Table 29, pp. 471–2).

	[Paid]	[Unpaid]	
Edward Vaus		1	cert
Widd Hicks		1	cert
John Lindon		1	cert
Simon Osshewan	5		
Widd Candle		1	cert
George King		1	cert
John Carle<y>s	3		
Abrah Carles	1		
Henry Wooten		1	cert
Humph King		1	cert
John Thompson		2	cert
Robt Thompson		1	cert
Tho Collins		1	cert
George Keene		1	cert
Wm Harbert		1	cert
John Massey	3		
Wm Busbye	2		
John Mackland		1	cert
Robt Rotton		2	cert
Widd Moorecroft		1	cert
John Booth		1	cert
Christpofer Woodburne		1	cert
John Fisher		1	cert
Jesse Poole		1	cert
[p. 12]			
John Raynor		1	cert
Samuell Phipps		1	cert
John Huffey		1	cert
Wm Bryent		1	cert
Daniell Wilson		1	cert
Widd Eachell		1	cert
Walter Moore	1		
Jane Moore		1	
William Holmes	4		
George Wadgley		1	cert
Wm Rylie		1	cert
Thomas Wooten		1	cert
Richard Chaplin	2		
Wm Chapman		1	cert
Rich Bratton		2	cert
Robt Johnson		1	cert
Richard Westley		1	cert
Widd Cooper		1	cert
John Bradney		1	cert

	[Paid]	[Unpaid]	
Mr Jesson owner		1	empty
Symon Lucas	2		
Abrah Parsons	1		
Widd Atherley		1	cert
Peter Barnes		1	cert
John Chaplin		2	cert
Hellen Whittley	6		
Abraham Bird		1	cert
John Yardley	3		
Joseph Ash	3		
Wm Sollomon		1	cert
Michaell Cranor	2		
Thomas Hansell	2		
Joseph Ash sen		3	
Widd Packwood		1	cert
John Poole	2		
Widd Hill		4	no distresse
George Mobbs		2	cert
Joseph Hewett		3	no distresse
John Thompson	2		
Joseph Chaplin		1	cert
John Edwin		2	cert
Edwd Fairebrother	4		
Robert Chering		1	cert
Richard Archer	1		
Widd Newcombe		1	cert
Samu Eades	1		
Widd Glasse		1	cert
John Love		1	cert
Tho Bowman		1	cert
Nathaniell Gilbert	4	& 2	decayed
Widd Newby		1	cert
Mr James Jesson	7		
Thomas Miller		1	cert
Tho Graunt		1	cert
Sarah Rushworth	4		
Widd Barr		1	cert
[p. 13]			
Edwd Smyth	3		
Anne Geary	2		
Mr Kerton	7		
Robert Bedford	6		
Henry Merry		1	
Robert Remington	4		

[Jordan Well Ward contd.]	[Paid]	[Unpaid]	
John Quinborough	2		
Mary Shotton	3		
William Kyeler		1	cert
William Adderley		1	empty
Anne Moore		1	empty
	139	102	

Much Parkestreete Ward

[in St Michael par]			
Hum Lee esq	11		
John Ford	1		
Thomas Webb	3		
John Yorke	2		
Henry Musson		6	puld downe 1 & refused to pay for all
John Joynes	3		
Fran Jarvis		2	prisoner in his howse
Edwd Grovener		6	
John Bassnett	5		
Thomas Jesson	11		
Luke Witherley	2		
Sarah Thompson		1	cert
Thomas Smyth	<3>0	3	no distresse
Joseph Hasseldon		2	empty
George Tyler		2	cert
Isaack Losson		2	cert
George Baker	7		
Wm Ashmore		1	cert
Wm Blackwell	6	& 3	taken downe
and a publiq oven		1	
Susan Carelesse		1	cert
Isaack Price		2	
Nathan Alsop	6		
Elinor Hite		1	cert
John Hite	1		
Joan Higham		1	empty
Rich Gregory		1	
and a forge		1	

	[Paid]	[Unpaid]	
Mr Owen owner		1	empty
Richard Crump		2	
John Stretton	2		
Wm Stretton	1		
The corner howse		[-]	empty
John Wright		2	no distresse
Wm Irons		2	cert
Edwrd Cooke		1	cert
Ralph Atherley		1	cert
John King		3	no distresse
Wm Blackwell	1		
Edwrd Hill	13		
Gilb Atherley		4	not finished
and a forge		1	
[p. 14]			
Wm Fisher		1	cert
John Cave	1		
Francis Birch	3		
Henry Gram	2		
John Quiney	2		
At the gate		2	two poor people
Mrs Jane Hales	19	& 4	decayed
Widd Smyth		1	take almes
Widd Smyth sen		1	take almes
Nathan Lisson		1	take almes
Roger Ludford	3		
Rich Hamblett		1	cert
Wm Pigbridge		1	cert
Widd Holly		1	cert
Widd Foxly		1	cert
Mary Bunbury		1	cert
Randall Hamblett		1	cert
John Clifton	3		
and a publiq oven		1	
Wm Preston	8		
Lewis Hands		1	cert
Edward Large	3		
John Lawrence		3	no distresse
Sander Cradock	3		
Edwrd Smyth		1	cert
Nicol Barton		1	cert
John Hanson	2		
Wm Hobson		2	cert

	[Paid]	[Unpaid]	
John Goddard		1	
Richard King		1	cert
Widd Lowson		2	cert
Tho Robinson		1	dead
Marg Hope	2		
Goodwyfe Bayly		1	cert
John Newcombe		1	cert
Rich Webb	2		
James Marshall		2	cert
Mathew Cleaver		2	cert
Wm Cooper		1	cert
Thomas Bott	3		
Richard Cleaver		1	cert
Wm Johnson		1	cert
A cottage		1	empty
Abrah Cesterson		2	gone & empty
Marg Underhill		1	cert
George Buswell	<2>0	2	empty
Edwrd Smyth		2	cert
[blank] Burnham		1	empty
Nico Davies		1	cert
Wm Long		1	cert
John Holloway		1	cert
Bryan Adgertom		1	cert
Wm Cleavor		1	cert
Widd Pickard		1	cert
Rich Ward		1	cert
John Whale		1	cert
Henry Colly		1	cert
John Bristow		1	cert
[p. 15]			
Widd Johnson		2	cert
John Bennett		1	cert
Mr Moore owner		[-]	empty
Thomas Pigbrig		1	cert
Humphry Musson	4		
Richard Moore	7		
Widd Sherewood	2		
Mr Painton owner		2	empty
Mathew Brandon	<4>2	& 2	puld downe
Mr Bedford owner	4		
Robt Conygrave	3		

	[Paid]	[Unpaid]	
Geo Buswell		2	cert
Mr Atherley owner		1	empty
Mr Boroughbie	7		
Mr Palmer owner		[-]	empty
Thomas Robinson	1		
Thomas French	2		
Jane Thompson		<3>2	
John Binion	4		
Wm Copson	2		
Tho Lapworth	3		
Thomas Warren	2		
John Deacon	4		
Thomas Hobson	8		
Tho Lee		1	cert
Henry Whale	7		
Widd Dawkins		1	cert
Widd Rawbone		1	cert
Daniell Shaw	4		
Thomas Shaw		3	empty
Hannah Webster		2	cert
Michaell Man	4		
Robt Johnson	2		
Thomas Lee		3	empty
Edward Gravener	2		
Anthony Edwards		1	cert
John Edwards		1	cert
Jonah Nicolls		1	cert
George Rugg	2		
Eliza Sanders		2	cert
Tho Wotton		3	no distresse
Mary Blunt	1		
John Merry	1		
Rich Grovener		2	cert
Widd Gower		1	cert
Widd Wedgett		1	cert
Henry Gamb	1		
Gilbert Power		2	cert
Anthony Fisher		2	cert
Tho Dikes	1		
Edwrd Jackson		1	cert
Roger Steares		1	cert
Daniell Austin	3		
	214	153	

[p. 16]	[Paid]	[Unpaid]	
Crosse Cheaping Ward			
[in Holy Trinity par]			
Samuell Pitts	3		
Elizabeth Whaler	4		
Francis Wright		6	gone away
Samuell Peaseley	9		
Humphry Burton	11		
Nathan Whanley	5		
Benj Carleton	6		
Rich Bradnock		2	cert
Robt Dowell	2		
Henry Hunt		1	cert
Joane Lester		2	cert
John Ashton		2	cert
Rich Johnson		2	cert
John Browne		1	cert
Sarah Higginson	2		
Robt Bryan		2	cert
John Sherewood		4	puld downe 1 & refuseth
Rosamand Smallwood		1	cert
Thomas Hughes		1	cert
Thomas Lyndsey	5		
Wm Crispe		2	cert
Widd Howell		2	cert
Wm Neale	2		
Samuell Gravener	2		
Sam Gravener sen		1	cert
Mr Perkins of Noble hall		[-]	
John Higginson	2		
Abrah Grascome	2		
Sam Eales		2	cert
Sarah Binkes		3	no distresse
Samuell Bryan	6	& 1	in building
Richard Walding	11		
Christpofer Goddard		1	cert
Goodman Pitts		3	no distresse
Mrs Bayly		4	no distresse
Jno Falkner		1	cert
George Feake		1	cert
Widd Gravener		1	cert
Tho Shakespeare		2	

	[Paid]	[Unpaid]	
Benja Mayo		2	cert
Tho Shakespeare sen	2		
John Bennett	2		
Alice Slater		1	cert
John Sherman	2		
Tho Greatbach	2		
Nath Hobson	5		
Tho Hudson	4		
Wm Gilbert	3		
Rich Webster	1		
John Moore	3		
Tho Greatbach sen	3		
Edwrd Greatebach		1	
[p. 17]			
Wm Gravener	2		
Wm Warding	2		
John Lester	2		
Ralph Ashborne	2		
Fran Webster	2		
Thomas Rotton	2		
Wm Wright		2	empty
Tho Johnson		2	cert
Widd Kelbye	3		
George Towers		1	cert
A howse		[-]	empty
Thomas Grascome	4		
Goodman Greene		1	cert
Goodman Prest		1	cert
Thomas Smyth		1	cert
Wm Pilkington		2	
Edward Crusoe	4		
Widd Hamond		1	cert
John Coleman		1	cert
Joane Berry		1	cert
Mary Haydon		1	cert
Wm Smyth		1	cert
Jos Lord		2	cert
Henry Thompson		1	cert
Sarah & Mary Hamond		2	cert
Jos Spencer		1	cert
Tho Greason		1	cert
Math Smyth jun	4		
Oliver Katherines	4		
John Bates	1		

	[Paid]	[Unpaid]	
John Moyes		[-]	
Alice Owen		1	cert
Thomas Marson	4		
Christpofer Hurt	3		
Wm Hurt	2		
Edwrd Browne	3		
Ralfe Houghton		1	cert
John May	2		
Robt Bryerlye	7		
Wm Essex	1		
Tho Hardeway	5		
Wm Essex	3		
Mrs Susan Barnard	3		
Daniell Kelbye		[-]	
Rich Phillipps	2		
Mary Lindsey	1		
Robt Hill	2		
Wm Houghton	2		
Tho Francis	4		
John Mayo		1	
Abell Brooksbye	4		
Wm Rowney	7		
Ralph Hoope	3		
John Dowell	2		
Francis Harryman	3		
Sam Heywood		1	empty
John Brownewell	11		
[p. 18]			
Richard Palmer	3		
Fran Collins owner		[-]	empty
Mr Wm Austen	[-]	[*11*[1]]	empty
Joan Meare	3		
Christpofer Owen	5		
Thomas Sargison	7		
Katherine Scotten	4		
Mrs Joane Pigeon	10		
Wm Pickhorne	4		
James Bushell	11		
John Ratten		1	cert
Tho Throgmorton	6		
Mr John Dicker	13		
The Mayors parlour		2	
Mr Jno Burbridge	10		

	[Paid]	[Unpaid]	
Stephen Beale	7		
Rich Hunt	1		
Thomas Flent	2		
Hugh Carter	3		
John Dinnes	6		
Sam Martin	3		
Mary Mayo	4		
John Mayo	2		
Mr Birton owner		1	empty
Wm Hayward	3		
Rich Taylor	2		
Robt Ireland		1	cert
John Johnson		1	cert
Fran Bird		1	cert
Sam Martin		2	cert
Tho Mayo		1	cert
Anne Brunt		1	cert
George Allen		1	cert
Wm Wells		1	cert
Tho Rogers	3		
Abrah Philipps	2		
John Fox		1	in building
Francis Gibson	2		
Robert Hayward	2		
Eliza Overton		2	
Thomas Towers		1	cert
Mrs Judith Murdock	5		
Humph Wellton	7		
John Hayward	3		
Widd Bragdale		1	cert
Wm Dawes		1	cert
Mathew King		2	cert
Hannah Oulds	3		
Rich Howcutt		1	cert
Ralph Ireland		2	cert
Robt Allen		1	cert
Sam Poole		1	cert
Andrew Warner		3	cert
Thomas Fox	2		
[p. 19]			
Edward Carter	3		
Idem Edward [Carter]		[-]	a new house

[1] TNA, E179/259/10 (1665).

[Cross Cheaping Ward contd.]	[Paid]	[Unpaid]	
John Kemp	1		
Sam Tissell	4		
Anne Gravener		1	cert
John Bennett sen	3		
Hamlett Harwell	1		
Uslin Wood		1	cert
Eliza Smyth		1	cert
Richard Wildye		1	cert
John Everett		1	cert
Edwrd Tarsoe		1	cert
Fower almes howses		8	
Math Harryman	6		
Mary Baker	1		
Mathew Smyth alderman	5		
Sam Heywood	6		
Rich Pinder	2		
Rich Waterfeild	3		
Wm Smyth	4		
John Webb	3		
Henry Heycock	1		
John Man	6		
and a forge		1	
Abrah Owen	3		
Mr King owner	6		
Wm Smyth	4		
John Winterton	2		
Anne Rewe	2		
Wm Benion	6		
Mr Hugh Caple	8		
Livewell Coates	2<2>0		
Marga Downes	2		
Alderman Billers	9		
Wm Johnson	1		
Richard Webster	2		
Thomas Lyndsey	2		
Ursula Archer		1	cert
Joseph Mayo		[-]	
Mrs Billingsley	5		
	446	123	

Bishopsgate Ward

[Bishop Street Ward in Holy Trinity par]	[Paid]	[Unpaid]	
John Voyall	2		
Joane Cooke	4		
George Barrow	4		
Sam Gilbert	1		
Benj Palmer	2		
Samu Ellett	2		
and 1 publiq oven		1	
Robert Whittle	4		
Tho Portman		2	cert
Widd Hollyer & tenements		3	no distresse
Richard Bates	2		
[p. 20]			
Job Marson		1	cert
Henry Croxall		1	cert
Widd Worley		1	cert
Henry Wotten	3		
Joseph Powers	4		
Sam Sherewood	6	& 1	decayed
Oliver Childerson		2	empty
Jonas Grymes	5		
Robt Farmer	2		
Thomas Webb	5		
James Bird		2	cert
Nicolas Wilcox	5		
Thomas Murdock	3		
Robt Stone		2	cert
Thomas Johnson		2	empty
Mr Jeremy Wheate owner	6		
Edward Liddall		1	cert
Mathew Unyon owner		1	cert
Dor & Eliza Randall		1	cert
Widd Woodward		1	cert
Rebecca Smyth		4	puld downe 1 & refuseth
Mathew Smyth		1	cert
Anne Hayberd		1	cert
Jeremy Towers		1	cert
Richard Aston	2		
Samu Lawton	3		

	[Paid]	[Unpaid]	
William Ward		1	cert
Wm Waring	1		
Tho Waring	1		
Sam Pickering	2		
Vadiman Ayre	3		
Francis Bates	2		
Sam Shaw		1	cert
Widd Smyth		1	cert
Widd Loynes		1	cert
Widd Randall		1	cert
Rich Elliott		1	cert
John Smyth		1	cert
Widd Blackwell		1	cert
Widd Hands		1	cert
John Kendall		1	cert
John Richardson		1	cert
Henry Smyth		1	cert
Mr Hooper	4		
Mr Sargison owner		2	empty
John Murdock	7		
Richard Haycock		1	cert
Jane Robinson		1	cert
Wm Townsend	4		
and 1 publiq oven	1		
Mary Raboe		2	
John Essex	4		
Robert Peirce		1	cert
Obediah Poole		1	cert
John Elliott		1	cert
Wm Leader		1	cert
Sarah Smyth		1	cert
Sam Smyth	1		
Widd Marle		2	empty
[p. 21]			
William Choyce	3		
Joan Sanders	2		
Hugh Peter	1		
Samuell Meigh		3	
Symon Craver		1	cert
Anne Carpenter		1	cert
Samuell Shaw		1	cert
Hannah Ash		2	cert
John Graysley	2		
Dorothy Harris		1	cert

	[Paid]	[Unpaid]	
Mrs Sarah Burbury	9		
Nicolas Smyth	4		
John Holmes		<3>2	
William Gest a forge		1	
John Hasledon	9		
Mich Packwood owner		[-]	empty
Widd Parke		2	cert
Robt Gilbert	2		
Humfrey Webb	2		
Thomas Satchwell	7		
Dorothy Philipps	5		
Sam Holmes		2	
Thomas King	11		
Ralph Philipps	7		
Tho Luddington		2	cert
Wm Strong	6		
John Wallis	3		
and a forge		1	
Randall Pywell	1		
Robert Michell		1	
Humph Newburgh	6		
Mich Packwood	5		
John Haycocks	1		
John Ashley		1	
John Bootes	3		
Eliza Smyth	1	& 1	in building
Thomas Bootes		1	cert
Millicent Smyth	5		
And Ridgley		2	dead
Moses Robinson		2	empty
Widd Noble		1	cert
John Rew		1	cert
Widd Ebion		1	empty
William Keely		1	cert
Widd Grascome		1	cert
Widd Shelley		1	cert
Mary Yeoman		1	cert
Wm Spitle	2		
John Ward	2		
Wm Langton	2		
Benj Sanders		1	cert
Wm Whale	4		
Samuell Francklyn	3		
Sam Craver	3		

[Bishop Street Ward contd.]	[Paid]	[Unpaid]	
Thom Clift	2		
John Burbridge		1	cert
Wm Haycock		1	cert
Phill Glasse		1	empty
Peter Pitts		1	cert
Robert Paul	2		
Antho Ashmore		2	cert
Eliza Cooper		1	cert
Math Shaw		2	cert
[p. 22]			
Eliza Shaw		2	cert
Obediah Poole		1	cert
Robt Trewman		1	cert
Joane Allett		1	cert
Widd Gilbert		1	cert
Ursula Tayler		1	cert
Francis Griffton		1	cert
Thomas Bough		1	cert
John Creake		1	cert
Widd Knight		1	cert
Rich Lovitt		1	cert
Richard Bennett		1	empty
Tho Hobson		1	cert
John Newell		1	cert
John Arshley		1	cert
Widd Gross		1	cert
Widd Johnson		1	cert
William Shelley		1	cert
Robert Cooper		1	cert
John Botterill		1	cert
Edwrd Dyke		1	cert
Wm Shelley sen		2	
Tho Bruce	2		
Daniell Butler		1	cert
Thomas Shugar	1		
Rich Bascubbe		1	pauper
Richard Clearke	1		
John Potton		3	no distresse
Richard Piper		2	cert
Widd Million	1		
Thomas Turner		1	cert
Widd Swift		1	cert

	[Paid]	[Unpaid]	
John Smyth		1	cert
Widd Dash		1	cert
Widd Player		1	empty
Wm Bascuboe	1		
Mrs Williams owner		1	empty
Thomas Shugar owner		1	empty
Thomas Bewley	5		
Sam Falkener	2		
Rich Lovitt		1	cert
Wm Bradshaw	4		
Antho Cave		1	cert
John Buttwell		1	
Thomas Barton		1	
John Broomesgrave		1	cert
Mrs Million owner	3		
John Fearne	4		
Vincent Crispe		2	cert
Richard Margaretts		2	in building
Natha Showell	3		
and a publiq oven		1	cert
Alice Robberts		1	cert
Widd Griffen		1	cert
John Yates		1	cert
Edward Litchfeild		1	cert
Rich Butler		1	cert
Bridgett Johnson		1	cert
John Sapcott		<3>2	
Samuell Fenton	1		
Sam Ambrose		1	empty
Humph Slow	5		
Mrs Angers owner		[-]	empty
Edwrd Lynes	6	& 1	decayed
Jeremiah Bratt	6		
[p. 23]			
Abrah Pitts		2	cert
Robt Horton	2		
Mr Alderman Snell	[-]	[*5*[1]]	
Alice Fletcher		1	cert
Alderman Joliffe	8		
Mr Cleark of Granborough owner		9	empty
	257	176	

[1] TNA, E179/259/10 (1665).

	[Paid]	[Unpaid]	
Baylie Lane Ward			
[in St Michael & Holy Trinity pars[1]]			
Daniell Wright	3		
Henry Nettleton	4		
Thomas Smyth		2	cert
Widd Cooke		1	cert
Richard Barker		2	cert
Widd Cooper		1	cert
Edwrd Urne		2	cert
Rob Bedson		2	cert
Thomas Catterns		1	cert
Richard Randall		1	cert
Thomas Savadge	2		
Widd Hurt & Ra Barker		2	cert
Widd Gibson		1	cert
Joseph Kathernes		2	cert
Thomas Dudley	3		
George Newcombe		1	cert
Nicolas Brookes	2		
Henry Cooke	3		
Christpofer Low		2	cert
and 1 forge		1	
Thomas Porter	4		
Samuell Feake	6		
John West	2		
Thomas Browne		1	cert
Tho Benion		1	cert
Wm Tomlinson		1	cert
John Berry		2	cert
Kath Prest		1	cert
Widd Murvill		1	cert
John Sherman		1	cert
Richard Clowes		1	cert
Richard Voyall		1	cert
Thomas Friswell		1	cert
Joseph Symcox	2	& 1	taken up
Sam Webster		2	
Christpofer Pitts	3		
Rich Thompson		2	empty
Kath Caniball		2	cert

	[Paid]	[Unpaid]	
Widd Angell		1	cert
Christpofer Biddle		1	cert
Fran Ashborne		1	cert
Alderman Naylor owner		1	empty
Sarah Bootes		1	cert
Henry Ashborne	2		
John Catternes	2		
Francis Beardsley		1	cert
and a publiq oven		1	
Anne Hill		1	empty
Wm Comebridge		1	cert
Alderman James Naylor	8		
Robert Burton	3		
[p. 24]			
Wm Bedson		<3>2	& 1 decayed
Constant Turloe	2		
Wm Herbert	3		
Ben Lowson	3		
William Ellis	2		
John Bearsley	2		
Christpofer Shrowley		1	cert
William Hill		1	cert
Gilbert Adderley	9		
Benj Baies	2		
John Mustion	5		
Thomas Dadley	9		
Joyce Darker	2		
George Rotton	2		
Tho Godfrey		1	cert
Francis Wright	6		
Anne Dolbye		1	cert
Mr Villers owner		[-]	empty
Joane Falkener		1	empty
Abrah Watts	3		
Fran Colling	3		
John Daniell	5		
Joseph Herrett with 2 forges	6		

1 All 31 certified exempt for Bayley Lane Ward in 1672 appeared in the certificate for St Michael parish, but they were divided in 1674 between St Michael with 20 and Holy Trinity with 7 (Table 29, pp. 471–2).

[Bailey Lane Ward contd.]	[Paid]	[Unpaid]	
Abig Biddle	2		
George Owen	1		
Wm Ward		1	empty
Joseph Nicolls	5		
Hugh Bucknell		2	cert
Gilbert Wood		2	no distresse
Bridgett Unick		1	no distresse
Thomas Hurt	4		
Rich Mitchell	1		
Rich Wild	1		
Wm Baggett	2		
John Love	2		
Thomas Hawkes		1	cert
Tho Martin		1	cert
Henry Allens <…> owner	4		
Jane Gilbert	5		
Tho Grascome	1	& 1	in building
Walter Gilbert owner		[-]	empty
John Harbert	2		
Fowlke Waldron	1		
Eliza Portman	3		
Widd Edwards		1	cert
George Bearsley		1	cert
Martin Noble	4	& 1	broken
The vestry of St Michaell	2		
	153	67	

Broadgate Ward

[in St Michael par]

	[Paid]	[Unpaid]	
James Griffen	2		
John Ted	4		
John Craner	3		
Richard Downes	11		
John Marler		1	cert
Tho Webster		1	cert
Robt Buntes		1	cert
[p. 25]			
Thomas Bates		1	cert
Widd Man		1	cert
Moyses Merrye	2		
John Downes owner	3		
William Marlow		1	cert
John Carelesse		1	cert
Thomas Walker		2	cert
Wm Benford		2	new built
John Mussage	2		
John Thurston	1		
Thomas Wilson	1		
Tho Montgomery		2	cert
Tho Craner		1	cert
John Gee	2		
Widd Newland		1	cert
Widd Taylor		1	cert
Samuell Swift		1	cert
Rich Ash		1	cert
Widd Ellis & her sonne		2	cert
Ann Smyth		1	cert
Katherine Coleman		1	cert
William Abbitt		1	cert
<…>A cottage empty		1	cert
Richard Muddiman		1	cert
Richard Coles	4		
Samuell Low	2		
Rebecka Fitter	2		
Edward Wheatly		1	cert
George Dawes		1	cert
Nicolas Bissaker	<4>3	& 1	taken downe
Widd Brisco	3		
An empty howse		1	
Daniell Drayton		1	cert
Joyce Cheyny		1	cert
Thomas Benford		2	cert
Ralph Johnson		1	empty
Thomas Mills		1	cert
Robert Rawson	6		
An empty cottage		1	empty
Sir Robt Townsends howse	9		
Rich Ratten sen	1		
Wm Meacock	5		
Widd Wood		1	cert
Richard Morris		1	cert
Joseph Philipps		1	
Widd Cowley		1	cert

	[Paid]	[Unpaid]	
Richard Brookes		2	
Thomas West	2		
Wm Bowter		1	
Edward Browne	3		
Richard Brunt	4		
William Moore		1	cert
Richard Welch		1	cert
Edwrd Unyon	2		
John Skripes	1		
Sam Marlow		1	no distresse
Widd Marson		1	cert
Gilb Witherley		1	cert
Richard Walter	1		
John Fearne		1	cert
Robt Lovett		2	gone
[p. 26]			
Richard Ratton jun		1	cert
Thomas Hall		1	cert
Newsham Smyth		1	cert
Mrs Darker		[-]	no tennant
An almes howse		[-]	
Rowland Tomkins	2		
Humfrey Allen		1	cert
Widd Brookesby		[-]	empty
William Forster	1		
Widd Pindall		1	cert
Richard Dobson		1	cert
Sam Raydall & Sam Wells	3		
Thomas Crafts		1	cert
William Tedds		1	cert
Mrs Susan Bassett	9		
Isaack Waldron	5		
Henry Taylor	2		
Samuell Lee	3		
Wm Rogers	6		
John Wooldridge	8		
Mr Wm Mosse	15		
Samuell Ashley	5		
Richard Hayward	4		
Mr Clearke owner		[-]	empty
William Snell	3		
Robert Pashley	7		
Richard Lyndsey	2		

	[Paid]	[Unpaid]	
Samuell Moody	<5>0	5	very poore & no distresse
Margarett Crow	3		
Susana Hall		2	cert
John Bowyer	2		
Thomas Prestwood		2	empty
Anne Baldwin	3		
John North	1		
Mich Earle	4		
John Cretchlow	4		
Mathew Parker	2		
William Rowney	5		
Mrs Eliza Cooke	12		
Richard Low	6		
John Harbert		1	
	196	69	

[Outlying parts]

Exall in Coventry Lybertye [Exhall par]

John Harding	1		
Wm Harding		1	cert
Thomas Butler	2		
Widd Smyth	1		
John Smart	1		
Henry Cleyton	4	& 2	in building
Widd Hurst		1	no distresse
Widd Bradwell	2		
James Gulliner	1		
Jos Boyle	2		
Sir Arthur Calye	15		
John Heathcock	2		
Oliver Woolfe	2		
John Wright	4		
Math Neale	3		
Widd Woolfe	1		
[p. 27]			
Thomas Fearne	1		
William Drake	1		
Thomas Whestley		2	no distresse
Edwrd Catterns	2		
John Betteridge		1	
Widd Ware	1		

[Exhall par contd.]	[Paid]	[Unpaid]	
[blank] Cox owner		[-]	empty
Widd Drake		1	cert
Nicolas Lockley		1	cert
John Randall		5	empty
<John Wright>		<5>	entered before
George Nevill	1		
Widd Good		1	cert
Henry Good		1	empty
John Cox	1		
Idem [John] Cox	1		
Widd Hobbington		1	cert
Thomas Lee		1	
Widd Jennings	1		
Rich Waster		1	cert
William Young	1		
Elizabeth Fletch		1	cert
Mr Francis Turner	9		
Gabriell Stafford	1		
John Clare	4	& 1	stopt up
Edwrd Hoxtall	2		
John Robberts	4		
Henry Arnies		1	cert
Widd Hunt		1	cert
Thomas Smyth	1		
Widd Woodton	1		
Richard Pickard	1		
George Browne	3		
Tho Batchnitt		1	cert
John Baldwin		1	cert
Tho Dickinson		1	cert
Roger Weatherby		1	cert
Dorothy Lester		1	cert
Stephen Lacy		1	cert
Widd Carpenter		1	cert
Widd Deeping		1	cert
Wm Godfrey		1	cert
William Palmer		1	cert
Will Drake		1	cert
Joshua Lager	2		
Edwrd Philipps		1	cert
Thomas Clearke	1		
Richard Cayle	4		
and 1 publiq oven		1	
Thomas Philipps	9		

	[Paid]	[Unpaid]	
Bridgett Kathrine		1	cert
Thomas Lee	1		
Wm Drake 2 howses		4	empty
Sam Wymack		1	
Widd Horne		2	
Eliza Frost		1	cert
Eliza Farington		1	cert
Joane Hounds		1	cert
Isabell Gould		1	cert
Rich Wagstaffe		1	cert
Joane Shepheard		1	cert
William Walker	1		
	95	50	

[p. 28]

Stivechall

[Stivichall par]

	[Paid]	[Unpaid]	
John Marsh		1	cert
John Kimberley	1		
Henry Newett	1		
Will Campen		1	cert
Widd Shereman		1	cert
John Walker		1	cert
Wm Walker	1		
William Smyth	1		
Robert Burton	1		
Benja Lynes	1		
Mr Hales	2		
Robt Burbury	2		
Rich Franckland	2		
Susan Ansell	1		
Richard Stone	1		
Thomas Arnell	1		
Hugh Coomeby		1	cert
Robt Jeas		1	cert
Stephen Crosse		1	cert
Susan Marton		2	cert
Humphy Hales	5	& 2	stopt up
Thomas Bull		1	
Anne Tedd		2	cert
Benja Hall		1	cert
Widd Coles		1	cert
Widd Worley		1	cert
Edward Hall	2		
and 1 forge		1	
Benja Walton	6		

	[Paid]	[Unpaid]	
William Cox	1		
Benja Godfrey		2	empty
Mary Keeling	2		
Widd Lee		1	cert
Widd Sharpe		1	cert
Thomas Lea		1	cert
Thomas Arnell	10		
Wm Nall	1		
John Kimberley	1		
	43	23	

Focell [Foleshill par]

	[Paid]	[Unpaid]	
William Atkins		2	cert
and 1 forge		1	
An empty cottage		1	
William Tame	2		
Richard Judge sen	1		
Widd Hill		1	cert
Widd Cheyney		1	cert
William Reade		1	cert
John Done		1	cert
Wm Bartholmew		1	cert
Jno Bingham		1	cert
Widd Bartholmew		1	cert
John Chesse		1	cert
Joseph Thompson	5		
Rich Michell	1		
Widd Benam		1	downe
Thomas Cottage	1		
Henry Longdon	1		
Samu Frissell	2		
[p. 29]			
Christpofer Judge	3		
Robt Mussell sen	1		
An empty howse		1	
Mr Tame a workehowse		1	
Thomas Little		1	cert
Fran Blackwell		1	cert
Thomas Jackson		1	no distresse
Alice Burbridge		1	cert
Mrs Eliza Bayle	5		
George Taylor		1	cert
Thomas Lenton		1	cert
Francis Pickett	2		

	[Paid]	[Unpaid]	
Henry Pickerd		1	cert
Richard Lenton		1	cert
William Taylor		1	cert
Thomas Taylor		1	cert
Ralph Drake		1	cert
Susan Avery		1	cert
John Lenton	1		
John Davis		1	cert
Widd Smyth		1	cert
Jos Moseley		1	cert
Arthur Drake		1	cert
John Carpenter		1	cert
John Davy		1	cert
Rich Drake		1	cert
Wm Clement		1	cert
Thomas Wishyre		1	cert
Widd Parsons		1	cert
Richard Lucas		1	cert
Rich Lenton sen		1	cert
John Lenton		1	cert
Widd Freeman		1	cert
Widd Jackson		1	cert
Barth Hall		1	cert
John Jackson jun	1		
Thomas Land	1		
Richard Trussell	1		
Thomas Bosworth	1		
George Hopkins		1	cert
Widd Cruse		1	cert
Thomas Dencher		1	cert
Wm Linall	2		
Rich Gowin		1	cert
Thomas Messenger		2	cert
and a forge		1	
William Smyth	2		
Edwrd Smyth	3		
John Goodson	4		
John Jackson	2		
Wm Jackson	1		<cert>
Widd Baker		1	cert
Livewell Smyth	2		
Widd Chessen		1	cert
John Haddon		1	cert
Thomas Ashmore	1		

[Foleshill contd.]	[Paid]	[Unpaid]	
John Smyth		1	cert
Wm Cooke	1		
Rich Madesley		1	
Tho Westleheade		1	

Bell Greene
[in Foleshill par]

	[Paid]	[Unpaid]	
Henry Pinkman	2		
Thomas Greene	1		
Wi<lliam>ddow Greene	1		
[p. 30]			
John Smyth	<2>1		no distresse
and 1 forge		1	
Jude Hethersteech	1		
Wm Spence	<1>0	1	cert
William Harris		1	cert
Wm Goodby	2		
Widd Webb		1	cert
William Bayly	2		
Thomas Jude	1		
Samuell Hart	2		
Joseph Langworth	1		
Widd Hetherstich		1	cert
Samuell Johnson		1	cert
Robert Garrett	2		
Widd Smyth		1	cert

Coltwest Greene
[Court Waste Green[1] in Foleshill par]

	[Paid]	[Unpaid]	
James Smyth	2		
Rich Jude	1		
Richard Melling	1		
John Merry		1	cert
William Joyce		1	cert
Anne Joyce		1	cert
Mary Johnson		1	cert
John Humfry		1	cert
Thomas Jude	1		
and 1 publiq oven		1	
An empty howse		1	

	[Paid]	[Unpaid]	
Fran Perkins	1		
	69	70	

Church End
[in Foleshill par]

	[Paid]	[Unpaid]	
Thomas Welton	1		
John Smyth	3		
An empty howse		1	
Fran Pickerd		2	
Wm Pickerd		1	cert
Richard Newcombe		1	cert
	4	5	

Focell Heath
[in Foleshill par]

	[Paid]	[Unpaid]	
William Deane	1		
Clement Smyth	1		
John Burbury		1	cert
Richard Lloyd		1	cert
John Roe		1	cert
John Clare	1		
Rich Welling sen		1	cert
Mr Cooke	2		
William Royley		2	
Widd Catherns		1	cert
Abrah Hatt owner		1	empty
John Stafford	1		
Mr James Hales	7		
Thomas Smyth	2		
Tho Warner		1	cert
John Collett	1		
Wm Langdon	1		
Eliza Fisher		1	cert
Widd Deacon		1	cert
Henry Good	1		
Christpofer Hollyoake	1		
Eliza Cristling		2	cert
Widd White		2	cert
Moses Godfrey		1	cert
John Miller	4		
Thomas Rowley	2		
Thomas Westley		1	cert

1 *VCH*, viii, p. 58.

	[Paid]	[Unpaid]	
[p. 31]			
Eliza Bedington		1	cert
Edwrd Boyle		1	cert
Thomas Rowley		1	cert
Widd Yates	1		

Pinley & Whitley
[in St Michael par]

	[Paid]	[Unpaid]	
Mr Bowatar	5	& 7	in building
Mr Thomas Hales	8		
Indiah Washington	5		
Edward Rose	1		
Thomas Hooton at mill		5	puld down one & refuseth to pay
Clement Smyth	1		
	46	32	

Sow [Walsgrave on Sowe par: part]

	[Paid]	[Unpaid]	
Thomas Jordan		1	cert
Marg White		1	cert
Rich Darby		1	cert
Tho Newcombe		1	cert
Henry Haward		1	cert
William George alias Tanner		1	cert
Hum Lenton sen } Hum Lenton jun }		2	cert
Anthony Goulding		1	cert
Empty cottage		1	cert
Widd Fairefox		1	cert
Alice Allen		1	cert
Wm Parker		1	cert
Mary Hampton		1	cert
Thomas Moe	1		
George March	1		
Jane Hoer		1	
Wm Cock		1	
Eliza Higginson	4		
Thomas Hane		1	cert
Joane Walker		1	cert
Wm Deeping		1	cert

	[Paid]	[Unpaid]	
Widd Hewes		1	cert
William Browne		1	cert
Rich Westley		2	cert
Sam Higginson	3	& 1	decayed
Sam Scotton	1		
John Lee		1	cert
Hanah Westley		1	cert
Edwrd Bush		1	cert
Eliza Wilkinson		1	cert
Kather Deane		1	cert
John Coleman		2	cert
Thomas Essex	1		
Tho Iliff		2	
Thomas Eales		1	no distresse
Tho Bushell		1	cert
Thomas Dulkett		1	cert
Henry Clearke		1	cert
<Tho Bushell>		<1>	<cert>
George Owen		1	cert
Major Slawter owner		4	empty
Mr Estwick owner		2	empty
William Steane		1	
William Wale	2		
Eliza Horsley		1	cert
Robt Legley		1	cert
[p. 32]			
Wm Jackson		1	no distresse
Robt Symonds	3		
John Pettifer	3		
William Hewett	1		
Thomas Lucas		1	cert
Wm Coleborne	2		
Mich Cowdale	3		
Wm Maline	3	& 1	stopt up
Widd Webb		1	cert
Wm Hewett		1	cert
Mr Philipps & Ma Porter		1	cert
William Abbotts	1		
John Arndoll		1	cert
Wm Jordan		1	empty
Thomas Skellett		1	cert
Mary Jackson		1	cert
Arthur Round		1	cert
Martin Killingsley		1	cert

	[Paid]	[Unpaid]	
[Walsgrave on Sow contd.]			
Richard Hayward	6	& 3	decayed
Tymothy Gibberts	6	& 5	decayed
	29	67	
	[41]		
Stoake [Stoke par]			
Mary Ange		1	cert
Henry Payne		1	burnt down
John Ange		1	cert
John Powell		1	cert
Edwrd Jennings		1	cert
Thomas Haxtex		3	no distresse
Tho Vinars howse		[-]	empty
Thomas Billings		1	cert
George Bryan		2	gone
Thomas Ware		1	cert
John Rowe		1	cert
Randall English		1	cert
Abrah English	2		
Theoph Shereman		1	dead
Widd Baxter		1	cert
Widd Jordane		1	cert
John Blockley		2	puld downe 1 & refuseth
John Abbott		2	cert
Thomas Loggett		1	cert
Rich Smyth		1	cert
Thomas Adnett		1	
Elinor Pratt		1	cert
Mr Estwick	10		
John Midleton	1		
Thomas Wighett	1		
Henry Horne	9		
Thomas Holbatch	8		
Randall Sherman		1	cert
Widd Crump		1	cert
Thomas Hebb		1	cert
Samuell Harwar	9	& 2	decayed
Samuell Ashton	7		
Christofer Randall	5		
Tho Everett		2	cert
and 1 forge		1	

	[Paid]	[Unpaid]	
John Thompson		1	cert
Woolfrey Remington	3		
Robt Bryan		1	cert
Will Patridge		9	
Mr Partridge owner		1	empty
Samuell Hayes	1		
Paul Boswell	1		no distresse
[p. 33]			
Tobias Newcombe	1		
Thomas Corner		2	cert
Mary Cheyney		1	cert
Mary Hopkins	9		
Thomas Wagstaffe	7		
Mrs Hopkins owner		1	empty
Thomas Corner owner		1	empty
Adrian Slim	1		
Widd Whale		1	cert
John Taylor		1	cert
Richard Webb		1	cert
Cassandir Crowder		1	cert
Wm Ward	2		
Thomas Hall	2		
and 1 forge		1	
Robert Bates		2	cert
Andrew Davies		1	cert
Robt Jenkins		1	cert
Isaack Snowden		1	cert
James Holt	6	& 1	stopt up
Valentine Chrisworth		1	
<John Tayler>		<1>	entered before
<Thomas Lockett>		<1>	entered before[1]
	85	62	
Kersley [Keresley] [in St Michael par]			
Nicolas Ashborne	3		
Ursula Brothers	1		
Hump Newes	1		
George Dale		1	cert
Robt Smyth		2	in building
Sarah Golding	4		

1 Recorded above as Thomas Loggett.

	[Paid]	[Unpaid]	
John Burges	1		
William Baldwin	1		
Christofer Smyth	4		
Thomas Whyam		5	
William Hounes	1		
William Keele	1		
Richard Jeakeman		3	gone
Thomas Norr		1	cert
Alexander Price		1	cert
John Burgis		1	cert
John Hall	2		
Robert King		6	would pay but 5
Thomas Treene	5		
Richard Newis	1		
Mrs Walding	8		
Wm Chipman		1	cert
Antho Golding		1	cert
Sam Clearke		22	howse in building
	33	44	

Radford [in Holy Trinity par]

	[Paid]	[Unpaid]	
John Brothers		1	no distresse
Wm Newis	1		
Tho Ingram	2		
Gabriell Kathrones	3	& 2	in building
Mr Hales owner		1	no distresse
John Wale	2		
John Keyte	1		
Henry Cooke		1	no distresse
Widd Smyth	1	& 1	forge, refuseth
John Payne		1	gone
Widd Brockurst		2	no distresse
Phillip Cooke	3	& 1	decayd
and 1 forge		1	refuseth
Thomas Harvy		1	pauper
Mr Hicks owner		[-]	empty
Ralph Phillips	2	& 2	in building
	16	13	

[p. 34]

Anstye [Ansty par]

	[Paid]	[Unpaid]	
Richard Taylor	9		
Hannah Horne	3		
Thomas Russell	2		
Rich Amstone	1		
John Wilkinson	5		
William Hicks	1<1>0		
John Nibbs		3	no distresse
Widd Rylye		1	no distresse
Richard Barlee		1	no distresse
Rich Coles		1	no distresse
Thomas Farndon	2<2>0		
Wm Jefcott	2		
Henry Jefcott	4	& 2	stopt up
Jonah Ballard	4		
Edward Farndon	<4>2	& 2	stopt up
George Morris	2		
Jona Clearke	2		
Wm Narmanton	1		
John Ball owner	1		
Rich Flower	1<1>0		
Richard Pettifer	3		
Wm Stratford	2		
Widd Warden		1	no distresse
Thomas Aume		1	no distresse
Nicolas Atkins	1		
Abig Mason		1	no distresse
Richard Hutt	1		
Grissell Viccars		1	no distresse
	49	14	

Wicken [Wyken par]

	[Paid]	[Unpaid]	
Wm Carter	2		
Thomas Barford	2		
Mr Greene owner		1	no distresse
Richard Hollier		1	no distresse
John Harding	1		
Eliza Tant		1	no distresse
Major Tymo Slater		4	
Wm Skynner	2		
Henry Greene	10		

[Wyken contd.]	[Paid]	[Unpaid]	
Mary Symonds		1	almes
Tho Oliver alias Mayer	2		
Wm Nibbs	1		
Eliza Clouse		1	no distresse
Tho Chambers	1		
Henry Greene		[-]	
Mathew Washbroock	1		
Widd Clearke		1	no distresse
Edwrd Lawson		1	no distresse
Nicolas Skynner	2		

	[Paid]	[Unpaid]	
John Biddle	1	& 2	in building
John Binch	1		
Thomas Muslon	1		
William Compton		1	no distresse
Samuell Biddle	3		
Edward Rasen		1	no distresse
	30	15	

Finis Citty & County of Coventry & libertyes

4182 [at bottom of page]

Appendix

Table 28 **Detailed digest of the transcribed hearth tax returns**

Table 29 **Exempt household totals in the hearth tax returns and exemption certificates**

Table 28 Detailed digest of the transcribed hearth tax returns

Key and Notes

Ch = chargeable
NC = not chargeable
(inc. cert) indicates the numbers of not chargeable households that were omitted from the 1670 returns but have been identified in a contemporary exemption certificates. They have been included in the totals of the not chargeable and are summarised in Table 29 below.

[1] indicates an exemption certificate from 1670–1 in TNA, E179/347.
[2] indicates an exemption certificate from 1671–2 in TNA, E179/194/334.

The column headed [1] indicates the number of not chargeable entries that record groups of householders' names without giving any hearth numbers. All are assumed to have had only one hearth each and are additional to the totals in the one-hearth household column. They are derived from either the 1670 return or the omitted entries identified in contemporary exemption certificates.

The figures in [square brackets] after the 10+ column show the hearth numbers for each of these households.

The figures in (brackets) in the columns for the two- and three-hearth entries indicate the number that were not chargeable. These are included in, and are not additional to, the relevant totals.

* indicates an estimated total.

Where two or more places have been enumerated separately within a parish or its equivalent, their overall totals are provided additionally in italics within <*angle brackets*>.

When part of a parish was enumerated in another division, that division is indicated as follows:
Ath = Atherstone   Ken = Kenilworth   PM = Priors Marston
Bid = Bidford   MK = Monks Kirby   Sou = Southam

con = constablery; det = detached portion; e.p. = extra parochial

Those non-house hearths that were recorded as forges or ovens have been omitted from this analysis, as has the one vine house.

Wherever possible, entries that covered two or more households have been separated for these calculations.

The minimum number of exempt households per parish that have been added to these totals from contemporary exemption certificates is five. Similarly, duplicate entries of five or more in a parish have been excluded; this applies only to Ansley which had eight duplicates.

(a) Warwickshire 1670

Places enumerated	*Total h'holds* *All*	*Ch*	*NC(inc.cert)*	*[1]*	*Household totals by number of hearths* *1*	*2*	*3*	*4*	*5*	*6*	*7*	*8*	*9*	*10+*		*Total hearths*
Barlichway Hundred																
Alcester Division																
Alcester	270	145	125		172	(9)54	20	15	5	1	-	2	1			456
Arrow parish	*<60*	*33*	*27*		*42*	*9*	*2*	*2*	*4*	-	-	-	-	*1*		*114>*
Arrow	30	19	11		21	5	2	-	1	-	-	-	-	1	[20]	62
Oversley	30	14	16		21	(1)4	-	2	3							52
Coughton parish	*<94*	*68*	*26*		*61*	*13*	*9*	*5*	*1*	*2*	*1*	-	-	*2*		*205>*
Coughton	41	24	17		29	5	3	1	-	-	1	-	-	2	[10,37]	106
Sambourne	53	44	9		32	8	6	4	1	2						99
Great Alne	53	37	16		39	5	4	2	2	-	-	1				87
Ipsley	55	32	23		36	9	5	2	1	-	-	-	-	2	[12,20]	114
Kinwarton	14	8	6		9	1	2	-	-	2						29
Morton Bagot	40	19	21		26	(1)5	3	3	1	1	1					75
Spernall	16	14	2		7	2	3	2	1	1						39
Studley	121	64	57		93	10	8	4	2	1	-	-	2	1	[26]	213
Tardebigg (part)																
Tutnall & Cobley	56	42	14 (5)[1]	5	27	13	2	6	2	-	-	-	-	1	[10]	108
Weethley chapelry	15	7	8		11	(1)3	-	-	1							22
Bidford Division																
Aston Cantlow parish	*<105*	*69*	*36*		*73*	*19*	*10*	*1*	-	*1*	-	-	-	*1*		*161>*
Aston Cantlow	42	22	20		35	5	2									51
Little Alne	13	10	3		8	2	2	-	-	1						24
Newnham	16	13	3		10	3	3									25
Shelfield	22	14	8		16	3	2	-	-	-	-	-	-	1	[10]	38
Wilmcote	12	10	2		4	6	1	1								23
Bidford on Avon parish	*<190*	*62*	*128 (20)*[1]	*20*	*141*	*18*	*7*	*1*	-	-	*1*	-	*1*	*1*		*253>*
Barton	27	11	16		23	2	2									33
Bidford	76	26	50 (15)	15	51	7	2	-	-	-	1					93
Bidford Grange	2	2	0		1	-	-	-	-	-	-	-	1			10
Burnells Broom	18	5	13 (3)	3	12	(1)2	-	-	-	-	-	-	-	1	[15]	34
Kings Broom	50	12	38 (2)	2	39	7	2									61
Marlcliff	17	6	11		15	-	1	1								22
Binton	25	19	6		17	2	1	3	2							46
Exhall	15	10	5		9	4	-	-	-	1	-	1				31
Haselor	58	37	21		40	16	1	1								79
Salford Priors parish	*<133*	*69*	*64*		*94*	*28*	*6*	*1*	*2*	-	-	*1*	-	*1*		*206>*
Abbots Salford	30	12	18		20	7	1	1	-	-	-	-	-	1	[16]	57
Salford Priors	103	57	46		74	(2)21	5	-	2	-	-	1				149
Temple Grafton	45	26	19		34	1	3	2	1	-	3	1				87
det: Billesley	1	1	0		-	-	-	-	-	-	-	-	-	1	[25]	25
Welford (part)																
Lt Dorsington & Bickmarsh	5	4	1		3	1	-	-	1							10
Weston on Avon (part)																
Milcote	5	5	0		4	-	-	-	1							9
Wixford	23	12	11		16	4	1	-	-	1	-	-	-	1	[18]	51
Henley Division																
Beaudesert	26	12	14		20	(1)4	1	1								35
Claverdon parish	*<87*	*61*	*26*		*58*	*16*	*5*	*5*	*3*							*140>*
Claverdon	61	46	15		39	11	5	3	3							103

	Total h'holds			*Household totals by number of hearths*												*Total*
Places enumerated	*All*	*Ch*	*NC(inc.cert)*	*[1]*	*1*	*2*	*3*	*4*	*5*	*6*	*7*	*8*	*9*	*10+*		*hearths*
Langley	26	15	11		19	(1)5	-	2								37
Henley in Arden chapelry	137	60	77		99	(8)25	4	4	3	2						204
Preston Bagot	15	9	6		9	2	2	2								27
Rowington	131	79	52		68	(4)25	16	12	6	1	2	-	1			273
Ullenhall chapelry	*<60*	*33*	*27*		*39*	*12*	*4*	*2*	*1*	*1*	*1*					*101>*
Aspley & Forde Hall	10	7	3		5	2	1	1	-	-	1					23
Ullenhall	50	26	24		34	(2)10	3	1	1	1						78
Wootton Wawen parish	*<69*	*47*	*22*		*52*	*8*	*6*	*1*	-	-	-	-	-	*2*		*125>*
Edstone	4	4	0		3	-	-	-	-	-	-	-	-	1	[13]	16
Whitley	8	5	3		6	-	1	1								13
Wootton Provost	14	10	4		9	2	3									22
Wootton Wawen	43	28	15		34	6	2	-	-	-	-	-	-	1	[22]	74
Stratford Division																
Alveston parish	*<72*	*42*	*30*		*48*	*13*	*7*	*2*	-	-	-	*1*	*1*			*120>*
Alveston	22	20	2		11	6	4	-	-	-	-	1				43
Tiddington	50	22	28		37	7	3	2	-	-	-	-	1			77
Bearley	17	11	6		12	2	2	1								26
Budbrooke parish	*<61*	*39*	*22*		*45*	*9*	*4*	*1*	-	*1*	-	-	-	*1*		*101>*
Budbrooke	10	9	1		6	2	2									16
Hampton on the Hill	30	19	11		24	3	1	-	-	1	-	-	-	1	[16]	55
Lower Norton	21	11	10		15	4	1	1								30
Hampton Lucy	54	38	16		35	9	5	2	2	-	1					93
Haseley	40	21	19		31	6	-	2	-	-	-	-	-	1	[16]	67
Hatton parish	*<107*	*63*	*44*		*76*	*20*	*7*	*3*	-	-	*1*					*156>*
Beausale	42	22	20		32	(2)8	1	1								55
Hatton	30	20	10		21	(1)6	1	1	-	-	1					47
Shrewley	35	21	14		23	6	5	1								54
Honiley	18	13	5		12	(1)2	2	1	-	-	-	-	-	1	[14]	40
Loxley	25	15	10		16	6	1	-	1	-	-	-	-	1	[10]	46
Norton Lindsey	27	17	10		23	2	-	1	1							36
Sherbourne	44	26	18		34	(1)6	2	-	-	2						64
Snitterfield parish	*<69*	*44*	*25*		*42*	*12*	*7*	*6*	-	*1*	-	-	-	*1*		*145>*
Fulbrook e.p.	4	4	0		2	1	-	1								8
Snitterfield	65	40	25		40	11	7	5	-	1	-	-	-	1	[28]	137
Stratford upon Avon parish (all)	*<562*	*298*	*264*		*335*	*83*	*64*	*34*	*18*	*13*	*4*	*2*	*2*	*7*		*1140>*
Bishopton	14	9	5		6	4	4									26
Bridge Town	8	6	2		3	3	1	1								16
Clopton	3	2	1		1	-	-	1	-	-	-	-	-	1	[14]	19
Old Stratford	37	10	27		27	3	1	2	-	1	-	-	1	2	[11,15]	85
Ruin Clifford	2	2	0		-	1	-	-	-	1						8
Shottery	41	19	22		26	8	4	-	2	-	1					71
Welcombe	3	2	1		2	-	-	-	-	1						8
Drayton (Bid)	5	5	0		1	2	1	1								12
Luddington (Bid)	22	13	9		17	2	2	1								31
Stratford upon Avon borough	*<427*	*230*	*197*		*252*	*60*	*51*	*28*	*16*	*10*	*3*	*2*	*1*	*4*		*864>*
Bridge St	37	34	3		8	(2)11	5	8	1	2	1	-	-	1	[10]	111
Church & Chapel St	107	42	65		77	8	10	3	2	1	1	2	1	2	[10,10]	203
Henley St	69	31	38		49	(1)8	7	2	-	2	-	-	-	1	[11]	117
High St	31	31	0		1	4	7	6	9	3	1					124
Sheep St	97	33	64		70	(3)15	7	2	2	1						145

Places enumerated	*Total h'holds*					*Household totals by number of hearths*											*Total*
	All	*Ch*	*NC(inc.cert)*		*[1]*	*1*	*2*	*3*	*4*	*5*	*6*	*7*	*8*	*9*	*10+*		*hearths*
Wood St	86	59	27			47	(3)14	15	7	2	1						164
det: Bushwood	18	5	13			14	(1)2	1	1								25
Wolverton	16	15	1			11	1	1	2	-	-	1					31
Wroxall	31	23	8			14	13	1	1	-	1	-	-	-	1	[22]	75
Hemlingford Hundred																	
Atherstone Division																	
Ansley	89	56	33			53	25	(1)6	2	2	-	-	-	-	1	[12]	151
Baxterley	32	23	9			24	5	1	1	-	-	-	1				49
Caldecote	14	12	2			7	3	2	1	-	-	-	-	-	1	[20]	43
Chilvers Coton parish	*<188*	*95*	*93*		*39*	*115*	*18*	*6*	*5*	*2*	*1*	*1*	-	-	*1*		*283>*
Chilvers Coton	132	59	73		35	75	11	5	2	2	-	1	-	-	1	[32]	204
Griff	23	9	14		4	12	5	-	2								34
Woodland	33	27	6			28	2	1	1	-	1						45
Corley	46	35	11	(8)[2]	8	25	8	3	1	-	1						68
Fillongley	*<136*	*96*	*40*			*72*	*32*	*9*	*9*	*8*	*2*	*2*	*2*				*281>*
Green End	53	34	19			26	(4)13	2	4	3	2	2	1				123
Metley End	37	34	3			20	10	3	2	2							67
Wood End	46	28	18			26	(2)9	4	3	3	-	-	1				91
Lea Marston parish	*<47*	*31*	*16*			*35*	*7*	*3*	-	*1*	-	-	-	-	*1*		*76>*
Lea Marston	34	24	10			26	(1)5	1	-	1	-	-	-	-	1	[13]	57
Marston	13	7	6			9	2	2									19
Mancetter parish	*<341*	*189*	*152*	*(41)*[2]	*86*	*127*	*45*	*26*	*24*	*13*	*9*	*3*	*1*	*2*	*5*		*699>*
Atherstone	257	136	121	(37)	71	86	(2)37	21	20	9	6	1	1	1	4	[10,10, 11,14]	524
Hartshill	43	28	15		8	18	7	2	3	2	2	1					87
Mancetter	41	25	16	(4)	7	23	1	3	1	2	1	1	-	1	1	[11]	88
Maxstoke	55	44	11			31	17	3	-	1	1	-	-	-	2	[10,17]	112
Merevale (most)	28	10	18	(16)[2]	16	5	(1)3	1	2	-	1						44
Nether Whitacre	97	75	22	(6)[2]	6	62	(2)16	6	4	-	1	-	1	-	1	[22]	170
Nuneaton parish	*<439*	*226*	*213*	*(24)*[2]	*137*	*164*	*62*	*41*	*17*	*8*	*4*	*1*	*3*	-	*2*		*733>*
Attleborough	66	34	32		17	32	(2)14	3									86
Nuneaton	302	144	158	(24)	114	82	(2)40	33	15	8	4	1	3	-	2	[11,11]	552
Stockingford	71	48	23		6	50	8	5	2								95
Over Whitacre	39	29	10			24	(1)6	6	1	1	1						69
Shustoke parish	*<54*	*36*	*18*			*30*	*9*	*7*	*1*	*4*	-	-	*2*	*1*			*118>*
Blythe End	6	6	0			2	2	1	-	-	-	-	-	1			18
Shustoke	48	30	18			28	(2)7	6	1	4	-	-	2				100
det: Bentley	31	18	13			26	4	-	1								38
Weddington	5	5	0			1	1	-	-	-	-	2	-	-	1	[15]	32
Birmingham Division																	
Aston parish	*<521*	*283*	*238*	*(23)*[2]	*98*	*269*	*69*	*49*	*16*	*5*	*2*	*2*	*2*	*1*	*8*		*929>*
Aston	18	13	5			11	(1)2	3	-	-	-	1	-	-	1	[41]	72
Bordesley	81	49	32		12	47	(2)14	3	1	2	-	1	1				125
Castle Bromwich	70	38	32	(6)	15	28	7	13	3	-	1	-	-	-	3	[12,14, 21]	161
Deritend	92	37	55	(17)	34	34	(1)11	10	2	1							133
Duddeston	13	6	7			10	(1)1	1	-	-	-	-	1				23
Erdington	116	57	59		28	61	9	11	3	1	1	-	-	-	2	[10,11]	184
Little Bromwich	38	29	9			21	11	1	3	1	-	-	-	-	1	[10]	73
Washwood & Saltley	42	19	23		9	24	(1)4	2	2	-	-	-	-	1			64
Water Orton	23	17	6			13	5	4	1								39

Places enumerated	Total h'holds All	Ch	NC(inc.cert)		[1]	Household totals by number of hearths 1	2	3	4	5	6	7	8	9	10+		Total hearths
Witton	28	18	10			20	(1)5	1	1	-	-	-	-	-	1	[18]	55
Birmingham	780	415	365	(88)[2]	288	126	(8)186	79	45	21	14	8	5	1	7	[10,10, 11,13,13, 13,15]	1582
Coleshill	197	139	58	(8)[2]	28	104	(3)35	9	7	4	1	4	3	-	2	[14,30]	379
Curdworth parish																	
Curdworth	40	29	11		3	26	5	4	-	-	-	-	1	-	1	[10]	69
det: Minworth	41	27	14		2	27	7	4	1								59
Edgbaston	60	43	17	(7)[2]	7	38	5	6	-	1	1	-	1	-	1	[22]	114
Sheldon	63	43	20	(12)[2]	12	27	9	7	1	3	1	2	-	-	1	[11]	128
Sutton Coldfield parish	*<304*	*187*	*117*	*(24)*[2]	*54*	*135*	*54*	*23*	*15*	*5*	*8*	*3*	-	*2*	*5*		*604>*
Hill & Little Sutton	94	52	42		*22	*49	15	6	1	-	1						129
Maney & the Wylde	46	31	15		*3	*27	7	3	3	-	3						83
Moor & Ashfurlong	41	23	18		*10	*15	5	2	3	-	2	1	-	-	3	[10,11, 17]	110
Sutton Coldfield	76	46	30		*11	*26	(5)17	7	4	5	1	2	-	1	2	[12,16]	190
Walmley & beyond the Woods	47	35	12		*8	*18	10	5	4	-	1	-	-	1			92
Wishaw parish	*<42*	*32*	*10*			*30*	*8*	*2*	-	-	*1*	-	-	-	*1*		*72>*
Moxhull	18	13	5			16	-	-	-	-	1	-	-	-	1	[14]	36
Wishaw	24	19	5			14	8	2									36
Solihull Division																	
Baddesley Clinton	19	11	8		8	6	3	1	-	-	-	-	-	-	1	[15]	38
Barston	52	41	11			30	(1)16	2	1	1	-	-	2				93
Berkswell parish	*<216*	*136*	*80*	*(28)*[1]	*28*	*116*	*34*	*15*	*10*	*8*	*2*	*1*	-	-	*2*		*383>*
Berkswell	202	125	77	(28)	28	108	(3)31	13	10	7	2	1	-	-	2	[10,17]	358
Bradnocks Marsh	14	11	3			8	3	2	-	1							25
Bickenhill parish				*(22)*[1]													
Bickenhill	*69	44	*25	(*15)	15	34	10	2	4	2	1	-	1				115
det: Lyndon End	*20	13	*7	(*7)	7	8	4	-	-	1							28
Elmdon	20	17	3			12	5	2	-	-	-	-	-	-	1	[10]	38
Great Packington	49	37	12			40	6	2	-	-	-	-	-	-	1	[32]	91
Hampton in Arden	58	37	21			42	(1)7	6	-	1	1	-	1				93
det: Balsall	*<168*	*113*	*55*			*122*	*24*	*10*	*6*	*3*	*3*						*257>*
Balsall	100	63	37			77	(1)13	4	2	2	2						145
Oldwich	68	50	18			45	11	6	4	1	1						112
det: Kinwalsey	5	5	0			3	-	1	1								10
det: Nuthurst	16	11	5			11	2	1	1	-	1						28
Knowle chapelry	*<126*	*66*	*60*	*(17)*[1]	*17*	*70*	*11*	*9*	*4*	*4*	*5*	*3*	*3*				*247>*
Chessetts Wood End	28	18	10			20	1	1	2	2	1	1					56
Knowle	68	36	32	(10)	10	33	(3)7	6	2	2	4	2	2				147
Knowle Wood End	30	12	18	(7)	7	17	3	2	-	-	-	-	1				44
Little Packington	28	20	8			22	3	2	1								38
Meriden	95	57	38	(8)[1]	8	53	12	5	7	3	-	2	1	1	3	[10,12, 12]	208
Solihull parish	*<319*	*176*	*143*	*(10)*[1]	*10*	*218*	*40*	*22*	*11*	*9*	*2*	*3*	*2*	-	*2*		*532>*
Forshaw End	17	9	8	(2)	2	12	2	-	1								22
Knowle Widney End	30	16	14			26	-	2	-	2							42
Longdon End	38	27	11	(2)	2	24	4	5	-	-	-	1	-	-	2	[10,10]	76
Olton End	38	27	11			22	5	8	1	-	2						72
Shirley End	50	27	23	(3)	3	34	7	3	3								72
Solihull Borough	86	30	56	(2)	2	63	(4)10	1	4	5	-	1					136

Places enumerated	*All*	*Total h'holds* *Ch*	*NC(inc.cert)*	*[1]*	*1*	*Household totals by number of hearths* *2*	*3*	*4*	*5*	*6*	*7*	*8*	*9*	*10+*		*Total hearths*
Whitlocks End	39	24	15 (1)	1	25	(1)8	2	2	1							61
Widney End	21	16	5		12	(1)4	1	-	1	-	1	2				51
Tamworth Division																
Austrey	87	72	15	8	61	10	3	4	1							119
Baddesley Ensor	34	18	16	8	11	(1)6	5	1	1	1	1					68
Grendon	66	51	15 (6)[2]	13	30	16	3	1	2	-	-	-	-	1	[20]	118
Kingsbury parish (all)	*<175*	*112*	*63*	*14*	*100*	*30*	*12*	*9*	*3*	*3*	*1*	*1*	-	*2*		*317>*
Dosthill	11	9	2		4	3	2	1	-	1						26
Holt, Slately & Cliff	16	9	7		13	-	-	1	1	-	-	-	-	1	[11]	33
Hurley	83	49	34	14	45	(1)10	6	6	1	-	1					133
Kingsbury	42	34	8		25	13	1	-	1	1	-	-	-	1	[12]	77
Whateley	15	7	8		8	3	3	-	-	-	-	1				31
Coton (Ath)	8	4	4		5	1	-	1	-	1						17
Middleton	85	61	24	10	49	(1)19	3	2	1	-	-	-	-	1	[26]	145
Newton Regis	37	32	5		23	8	6									57
Polesworth parish	*<195*	*99*	*96*	*52*	*91*	*26*	*15*	*3*	*2*	*3*	-	-	-	*3*		*333>*
Dordon	25	17	8	8	11	1	3	1	-	1						40
Freasley	11	10	1		7	2	-	-	2							21
Hallend	5	3	2		2	1	1	-	-	-	-	-	-	1	[16]	23
Polesworth	92	42	50	21	48	10	9	2	-	1	-	-	-	1	[18]	148
Pooley Hall	3	3	0		1	1	-	-	-	-	-	-	-	1	[19]	22
Warton	36	21	15	5	19	10	1	-	-	1						53
Wilnecote (part)	23	3	20	18	3	1	1									26
Seckington	15	7	8	6	4	2	2	-	-	-	-	-	-	1	[11]	31
Shuttington	19	15	4		10	7	1	1								31
Tamworth parish (part)	*<377*	*216*	*161*	*78*	*162*	*72*	*32*	*18*	*5*	*3*	*2*	*1*	*1*	*3*		*671>*
Amington	40	26	14	6	23	7	2	1	-	-	-	-	-	1	[15]	68
Bolehall	16	12	4		8	4	3	1								29
Glascote	15	10	5		11	4										19
Tamworth borough (part)	194	119	75	42	58	44	23	14	5	2	2	1	1	2	[10,20]	411
Wilnecote (most)	112	49	63	30	62	13	4	2	-	1						144
Kineton Hundred																
Brailes Division																
Barcheston parish	*<25*	*16*	*9*		*15*	*2*	*2*	*2*	*1*	*3*						*56>*
Barcheston	4	4	0		2	-	-	-	1	1						13
Willington	21	12	9		13	2	2	2	-	2						43
Barton on the Heath	30	17	13		13	(1)7	3	2	1	1	1	-	-	2	[12,18]	92
Brailes parish	*<188*	*118*	*70*		*130*	*30*	*18*	*5*	*4*	-	-	-	-	*1*		*294>*
Chelmscote	2	1	1		1	1										3
Lower Brailes	111	61	50		81	(2)13	10	3	3	-	-	-	-	1	[10]	174
Upper Brailes	51	39	12		29	13	7	2								84
Winderton	24	17	7		19	3	1	-	1							33
Burmington	28	17	11		21	4	1	1	-	-	1					43
Cherington	41	28	13		25	9	6	-	1							66
Great Wolford parish	*<84*	*54*	*30*		*60*	*12*	*5*	*3*	-	-	*1*	*2*	-	*1*		*145>*
Great Wolford	42	27	15		26	(1)10	2	2	-	-	1	1				75
Little Wolford	42	27	15		34	2	3	1	-	-	-	1	-	1	[11]	70
Honington	52	31	21		32	(5)13	4	-	-	1	-	1	-	1	[17]	101
Idlicote	22	14	8		12	4	1	3	-	-	1	-	-	1	[15]	57
Long Compton	103	70	33	30	34	(1)14	17	4	1	1	-	1	-	1	[38]	216
Pillerton Hersey	29	22	7		20	2	4	2	1							49

	Total h'holds				Household totals by number of hearths											Total
Places enumerated	*All*	*Ch*	*NC(inc.cert)*	*[1]*	*1*	*2*	*3*	*4*	*5*	*6*	*7*	*8*	*9*	*10+*		*hearths*
Pillerton Priors	28	22	6		20	4	2	1	-	1						44
Stretton on Fosse	46	31	15		29	7	5	2	1	1	-	-	-	1	[10]	87
Whatcote	28	24	4		20	6	2									38
Whichford parish	*<101*	*72*	*29*		*51*	*23*	*16*	*7*	*1*	*-*	*1*	*1*	*1*			*202>*
Ascott	27	20	7		12	5	7	2	-	-	1					58
Stourton	32	24	8		20	5	2	4	1							57
Whichford	42	28	14		19	(2)13	7	1	-	-	-	1	1			87
Kineton Division																
Atherstone on Stour parish	*<18*	*13*	*5*		*9*	*3*	*3*	*2*	*-*	*-*	*1*					*39>*
Ailstone	10	7	3		5	3	-	2								19
Atherstone on Stour	8	6	2		4	-	3	-	-	-	1					20
Butlers Marston	35	30	5		21	5	4	2	1	-	1	-	-	1	[10]	73
Chadshunt	24	21	3		19	4	-	-	-	-	-	-	-	1	[13]	40
Combrook chapelry	*<31*	*24*	*7*		*23*	*4*	*3*	*-*	*1*							*45>*
Brookhampton	2	2	0		1	-	-	-	1							6
Combrook	29	22	7		22	4	3									39
Compton Wynyates	4	3	1		3	-	-	-	-	-	-	-	-	1	[26]	29
Ettington parish	*<67*	*51*	*16*		*49*	*6*	*5*	*4*	*1*	*-*	*-*	*-*	*1*	*1*		*119>*
Ettington	55	43	12		39	6	5	3	1	-	-	-	1			92
Fulready	8	5	3		7	-	-	1								11
Lower Ettington	4	3	1		3	-	-	-	-	-	-	-	-	1	[13]	16
Gaydon	37	33	4		21	6	7	2	1							67
Halford	37	25	12		24	(2)3	7	1	1	1						66
Ilmington parish	*<95*	*62*	*33*		*61*	*17*	*8*	*5*	*2*	*-*	*-*	*-*	*-*	*2*		*170>*
Compton Scorpion	3	3	0		1	-	-	1	-	-	-	-	-	1	[11]	16
Foxcote	5	3	2		4	-	-	-	-	-	-	-	-	1	[10]	14
Ilmington	87	56	31		56	(1)17	8	4	2							140
Kineton parish	*<124*	*95*	*29*		*90*	*18*	*11*	*3*	*1*	*-*	*-*	*-*	*-*	*1*		*191>*
Kineton	88	65	23		63	13	8	3	1							130
Little Kineton	36	30	6		27	5	3	-	-	-	-	-	-	1	[15]	61
Lighthorne parish	*<33*	*27*	*6*		*17*	*10*	*-*	*3*	*1*	*-*	*1*	*-*	*-*	*1*		*82>*
Compton Verney e.p.	3	3	0		2	-	-	-	-	-	-	-	-	1	[21]	23
Lighthorne	30	24	6		15	10	-	3	1	-	1					59
Oxhill	41	33	8		24	9	2	2	2	1	1					79
Radway parish (all)	*<53*	*43*	*10*		*32*	*12*	*7*	*1*	*-*	*-*	*-*	*1*				*89>*
Radway	45	35	10		29	9	5	1	-	-	-	1				74
Radway in Burton con (PM)	8	8	0		3	3	2									15
Tysoe parish	*<150*	*121*	*29*		*100*	*15*	*19*	*11*	*5*							*256>*
Lower Tysoe	45	36	9		25	4	8	4	4							93
Middle Tysoe	64	45	19		49	(3)6	6	3								91
Upper Tysoe	41	40	1		26	5	5	4	1							72
Whitchurch parish	*<29*	*20*	*9*		*20*	*4*	*2*	*1*	*-*	*-*	*1*	*1*				*53>*
Crimscote & Bruton	10	8	2		6	2	1	1								17
Whitchurch	4	4	0		2	-	-	-	-	-	1	1				17
Wimpstone	15	8	7		12	2	1									19
Priors Marston Division																
Avon Dassett	34	26	8		19	6	4	1	2	-	-	2				73
Burton Dassett parish	*<76*	*52*	*24*		*44*	*13*	*9*	*3*	*1*	*3*	*1*	*1*	*-*	*1*		*158>*
Burton Dassett	6	4	2		3	-	-	1	-	-	-	1	-	1	[11]	26
Knightcote	33	24	9		20	5	6	1	1							57

Places enumerated	*Total h'holds* *All*	*Ch*	*NC(inc.cert)*	*[1]*	*Household totals by number of hearths* *1*	*2*	*3*	*4*	*5*	*6*	*7*	*8*	*9*	*10+*		*Total hearths*
Little Dassett	9	6	3		4	(1)3	1	-	-	-	1					20
Northend	28	18	10		17	5	2	1	-	3						55
Cropredy (part)																
Mollington	19	14	5		9	4	4	-	-	1	-	-	-	1	[10]	45
Farnborough	43	25	18		27	(3)8	1	5	-	-	-	1	-	1	[11]	85
Fenny Compton parish	*<94*	*61*	*33*		*74*	*11*	*2*	*2*	*1*	*1*	*2*	*1*				*143>*
Fenny Compton	91	58	33		74	10	1	2	1	1	1	1				131
Hodnell/Watergall e.p (Sou:Kn)	3	3	0		-	1	1	-	-	-	1					12
Lower Shuckburgh chapelry	34	23	11		23	(1)8	1	1	1							51
Priors Hardwick	36	29	7		16	9	8	2	1							71
Priors Marston chapelry	102	68	34		70	14	9	5	3	1						166
Ratley parish	*<36*	*25*	*11*		*18*	*7*	*5*	*1*	*2*	*1*	-	-	-	*2*		*89>*
Ratley	34	23	11		18	(1)6	5	1	2	1	-	-	-	1	[11]	76
Upton	2	2	0		-	1	-	-	-	-	-	-	-	1	[11]	13
Shotteswell	55	38	17		39	8	7	-	-	-	-	1				84
Warmington parish	*<63*	*50*	*13*		*43*	*5*	*7*	*2*	*2*	*2*	*2*					*118>*
Arlescote	5	4	1		1	-	1	1	1	-	1					20
Warmington	58	46	12		42	5	6	1	1	2	1					98
Wormleighton	16	11	5		11	2	2	-	-	-	-	-	-	1	[15]	36
Tanworth Division																
Avon																
Barford	75	46	29		59	7	4	1	2	1	-	-	1			114
Bishops Tachbrook parish (all)	*<64*	*46*	*18*		*47*	*6*	*7*	*2*	-	-	*1*	-	-	*1*		*109>*
Bishops Tachbrook	58	40	18		45	4	6	2	-	-	1					86
Tachbrook Mallory (Ken:Kn)	6	6	0		2	2	1	-	-	-	-	-	-	1	[14]	23
Charlecote	19	12	7		10	5	2	1	-	-	-	-	-	1	[42]	72
Chesterton parish	*<22*	*16*	*6*		*14*	*3*	*1*	*1*	*1*	*1*	-	-	-	*1*		*54>*
Chesterton	19	13	6		14	3	1	-	1							28
Kingston	3	3	0		-	-	-	1	-	1	-	-	-	1	[16]	26
Moreton Morrell parish	*<30*	*21*	*9*		*16*	*9*	*4*	-	-	-	-	-	-	*1*		*58>*
Moreton	22	16	6		13	(1)6	2	-	-	-	-	-	-	1	[12]	43
Moreton Morrell	8	5	3		3	(1)3	2									15
Newbold Pacey parish	*<36*	*20*	*16*		*27*	*4*	*1*	-	-	*2*	*1*	-	*1*			*66>*
Ashorne	18	13	5		12	4	1	-	-	1						29
Newbold in Wellesbourne con	8	1	7		8											8
Newbold Pacey	10	6	4		7	-	-	-	-	1	1	-	1			29
Wasperton	20	14	6		13	(1)4	2	-	-	1						33
Wellesbourne parish	*<80*	*48*	*32*		*50*	*12*	*8*	*3*	*3*	*1*	-	*2*	-	*1*		*157>*
Walton Deyville	14	6	8		11	1	-	-	1	-	-	-	-	1	[10]	28
Wellesbourne Hastings	27	20	7		14	(1)5	5	2	1							52
Wellesbourne Mountford	39	22	17		25	(2)6	3	1	1	1	-	2				77
Arden																
Lapworth parish	*<89*	*57*	*32*		*55*	*17*	*6*	*8*	*2*	*1*						*155>*
Kingswood Brook	16	10	6		10	3	1	1	1							28
Lapworth	73	47	26		45	(2)14	5	7	1	1						127
Packwood	63	36	27		47	9	5	-	-	1	-	-	-	1	[10]	96
Tanworth in Arden parish	*<293*	*177*	*116*		*218*	*41*	*20*	*7*	*2*	*2*	*2*	-	-	*1*		*438>*
Clayside	126	85	41		91	(1)17	11	3	1	1	1	-	-	1	[14]	202

Places enumerated	*Total h'holds* *All*	*Ch*	*NC(inc.cert)*	*[1]*	*Household totals by number of hearths* *1*	*2*	*3*	*4*	*5*	*6*	*7*	*8*	*9*	*10+*		*Total hearths*
Heathside	143	85	58		110	(1)19	8	3	1	1	1					202
Tanworth	24	7	17		17	(1)5	1	1								34
Warwick Borough	*<617*	*372*	*245*		*301*	*100*	*67*	*58*	*31*	*17*	*10*	*5*	*6*	*22*		*1689>*
Warwick: St Mary	*<471*	*276*	*195*		*225*	*76*	*48*	*43*	*27*	*12*	*9*	*4*	*6*	*21*		*1370>*
Castle St	49	33	16		20	(1)8	8	3	5	2	-	-	-	3	[10,10, 47]	176 1
High St	58	48	10		12	14	6	10	4	2	2	-	2	6	[10,13, 14,17, 18,20]	254
Jury St	30	25	5		4	(1)4	(1)6	4	2	3	1	-	2	4	[11,12, 13,14]	149
Market Place	112	92	20		29	(7)24	17	12	12	3	5	4	2	4	[10,11, 11,14]	385
Saltisford	114	36	78		85	(8)13	5	4	2	1	1	-	-	3	[10,10, 36]	221
West St	108	42	66		75	(3)13	(1)6	10	2	1	-	-	-	1	[10]	185
Warwick: St Nicholas	*<146*	*96*	*50*		*76*	*24*	*19*	*15*	*4*	*5*	*1*	*1*	*-*	*1*		*319>*
Bridge End	46	31	15		30	(2)8	2	3	1	1	1					82
Smith St	100	65	35		46	(5)16	17	12	3	4	-	1	-	1	[13]	237
Knightlow Hundred																
Kenilworth Division																
Ashow	23	18	5		15	5	3									34
Baginton	35	26	9		20	7	3	2	-	1	-	1	-	1	[13]	78
Bubbenhall	35	23	12		19	9	3	2	2							64
Cubbington	67	37	30		50	4	7	2	3	-	-	1				110
Harbury	118	90	28		94	(1)14	5	3	1	-	-	1				162
Kenilworth	*<244*	*144*	*100*		*172*	*30*	*13*	*14*	*5*	*8*	*-*	*2*				*416>*
Augmentation	140	76	64		103	(5)18	5	5	4	4	-	1				226
Duchy	104	68	36		69	(5)12	8	9	1	4	-	1				190
Leamington Priors	56	31	25		43	(1)5	4	2	2							83
Leek Wootton parish	*<58*	*44*	*14*		*46*	*7*	*1*	*1*	*1*	*1*	*-*	*-*	*-*	*1*		*89>*
Hill Wootton	11	11	0		10	1										12
Leek Wootton	40	27	13		33	4	1	-	1	1						55
Woodcote & Woodloes	7	6	1		3	2	-	1	-	-	-	-	-	1	[11]	22
Lillington	40	22	18		29	11										51
Milverton	28	22	6		20	3	2	1	-	1	-	-	-	1	[10]	52
Offchurch	40	19	21		34	4	1	-	-	-	-	-	-	1	[14]	59
Radford Semele	54	42	12		37	11	4	-	1	-	-	-	-	1	[12]	88
Stoneleigh parish	*<145*	*105*	*40*	*10*	*86*	*22*	*12*	*4*	*2*	*2*	*3*	*1*	*1*	*2*		*332>*
Canley	14	12	2		9	2	1	-	-	1	1					29
Cryfield	4	3	1		1	-	1	2								12
Finham	12	8	4		8	2	-	-	-	1	-	1				26
Fletchamstead	31	21	10		20	(1)4	2	-	2	-	2	-	-	1	[10]	68
Hill	9	8	1		6	2	-	1								14
Hurst	12	12	0		7	2	3									20
Stareton	12	12	0		6	5	1									19
Stoneleigh	51	29	22	10	29	5	4	1	-	-	-	-	1	1	[70]	144
Ufton	32	22	10		19	(1)10	2	1								49
Whitnash	28	23	5		17	6	2	-	3							50

Places enumerated	*Total h'holds*				*Household totals by number of hearths*											*Total*
	All	*Ch*	*NC(inc.cert)*	*[1]*	*1*	*2*	*3*	*4*	*5*	*6*	*7*	*8*	*9*	*10+*		*hearths*
Monks Kirby Division																
Allesley	110	94	16		59	(2)21	8	10	6	-	1	2	2	1	[12]	248
Arley	33	29	4		13	13	3	3	-	-	-	-	-	1	[12]	72
Astley	49	42	7		26	(1)14	4	3	-	-	1	-	-	1	[18]	103
Bedworth	281	58	223		261	(9)17	-	2	-	1						309
Binley parish	*<42*	*31*	*11*		*25*	*8*	*3*	*3*	*1*	*-*	*1*	*-*	*-*	*1*		*125>*
Binley	28	17	11		17	(1)4	3	3	1							51
Combe Fields e.p.	14	14	0		8	4	-	-	-	-	1	-	-	1	[51]	74
Brinklow	99	65	34	21	54	12	4	5	3							146
Bulkington parish	*<145*	*118*	*27*		*91*	*37*	*10*	*3*	*-*	*-*	*1*	*1*	*-*	*2*		*243>*
Barnacle	20	15	5		13	4	1	1	-	-	-	-	-	1	[10]	38
Bramcote	19	16	3		13	5	1									26
Bulkington	41	37	4		28	8	3	1	-	-	-	-	-	1	[11]	68
Marston Jabbett	21	12	9		12	4	3	1	-	-	1					40
Ryton	22	18	4		14	(1)6	2									32
Weston in Arden	22	20	2		11	10	-	-	-	-	-	1				39
Burton Hastings parish	*<28*	*23*	*5*		*14*	*8*	*4*	*-*	*2*							*52>*
Burton Hastings	22	18	4		8	(2)8	4	-	2							46
Stretton Baskerville etc	6	5	1		6											6
Coventry: Holy Trinity (part)																
det: Coundon	24	20	4		17	4	-	2	-	-	1					40
det: Willenhall	15	12	3		6	5	2	-	1	-	-	-	1			36
Harborough Magna	44	25	19	12	18	(1)8	2	3	-	-	-	-	-	1	[10]	74
Monks Kirby parish	*<263*	*175*	*88*		*161*	*60*	*26*	*9*	*2*	*3*	*-*	*-*	*-*	*2*		*474>*
Brockhurst	26	17	9		15	6	4	-	-	-	-	-	-	1	[34]	73
Cestersover	7	4	3		3	2	-	1	1							16
Copston Magna	27	16	11		17	(1)9	1									38
Easenhall	26	19	7		15	8	2	-	1							42
Little Walton	8	7	1		2	2	2	2								20
Monks Kirby	55	32	23		36	(2)11	4	4								86
Pailton	78	55	23		53	14	8	1	-	2						121
Street Ashton	10	7	3		5	4	1									16
Stretton under Fosse	26	18	8		15	(1)4	4	1	-	1	-	-	-	1	[17]	62
Shilton	32	17	15		18	(3)10	2	1	1							53
Walsgrave on Sowe (part)	38	26	12		20	(2)12	2	1	-	3						72
Wibtoft chapelry	18	13	5		9	3	1	4	1							39
Willey	28	17	11		19	5	2	1	-	1						45
Withybrook	49	36	13		27	(1)16	2	1	2	1						85
Wolvey parish	*<84*	*53*	*31*		*63*	*13*	*3*	*2*	*-*	*-*	*-*	*2*	*-*	*1*		*133>*
Smockington	37	13	24		33	2	1	-	-	-	-	1				48
Wolvey	47	40	7		30	(2)11	2	2	-	-	-	1	-	1	[11]	85
Rugby Division																
Bilton	65	29	36		55	6	1	1	1	-	-	-	-	1	[12]	91
Bourton on Dunsmore parish	*<53*	*32*	*21*		*33*	*14*	*2*	*-*	*1*	*2*	*1*					*91>*
Bourton	27	15	12		17	7	-	-	-	2	1					50
Draycote	26	17	9		16	(1)7	2	-	1							41
Brownsover chapelry	14	14	0		5	6	2	1								27
Church Lawford	35	23	12		30	1	1	1	2							49
Churchover	52	37	15		39	5	3	2	-	1	1	-	-	1	[10]	89
Clifton upon Dunsmore parish	*<81*	*54*	*27*		*53*	*13*	*7*	*5*	*1*	*-*	*1*	*1*				*140>*

Places enumerated	*Total h'holds* *All*	*Ch*	*NC(inc.cert)*	*[1]*	*Household totals by number of hearths* *1*	*2*	*3*	*4*	*5*	*6*	*7*	*8*	*9*	*10+*		*Total hearths*
Clifton upon Dunsmore	48	32	16		31	7	4	4	-	-	1	1				88
Newton & Biggin	33	22	11		22	6	3	1	1							52
Dunchurch parish	*<133*	*68*	*65*		*88*	*22*	*11*	*4*	*3*	*2*	*-*	*1*	*-*	*2*		*242>*
Cawston	3	2	1		2	-	-	-	-	-	-	-	-	1	[16]	18
Dunchurch	53	26	27		33	(1)7	5	3	1	2	-	1	-	1	[10]	109
Thurlaston	66	32	34		48	(1)13	3	-	2							93
Toft	11	8	3		5	2	3	1								22
Frankton	34	22	12		18	(2)11	2	1	-	1	-	-	1			65
Hillmorton	107	68	39		75	23	3	2	3	1						159
Kings Newnham	11	8	3		5	4	1	-	-	-	-	-	-	1	[17]	33
Newbold on Avon parish	*<111*	*65*	*46*		*75*	*18*	*10*	*5*	*1*	*1*	*-*	*-*	*-*	*1*		*194>*
Cosford	19	11	8		11	(2)4	1	2	1							35
Harborough Parva	4	4	0		1	2	1									8
Long & Little Lawford	57	35	22		44	9	2	1	-	-	-	-	-	1	[22]	94
Newbold on Avon	31	15	16		19	3	6	2	-	1						57
Rugby	177	104	73	40	80	16	21	9	3	5	-	1	-	2	[12,12]	333
Ryton on Dunsmore	47	32	15		34	(2)8	2	1	1	-	-	1				73
Stretton on Dunsmore chapelry	*<68*	*39*	*29*		*52*	*10*	*1*	*1*	*-*	*1*	*1*	*2*				*108>*
Princethorpe	18	15	3		13	3	-	-	-	1	-	1				33
Stretton on Dunsmore	50	24	26		39	(3)7	1	1	-	-	1	1				75
Willoughby	52	34	18		35	(1)9	3	3	-	-	1	-	-	1	[12]	93
Wolston parish (all)	*<103*	*77*	*26*		*68*	*20*	*3*	*6*	*1*	*1*	*1*	*1*	*-*	*2*		*191>*
Wolston & Marston	62	43	19		45	12	-	2	-	1	-	-	-	2	[11,13]	107
Brandon (MK)	31	25	6		19	4	3	2	1	-	1	1				64
Bretford (MK)	10	9	1		4	4	-	2								20
Southam Division																
Birdingbury	27	21	6		17	6	1	1	1	-	-	-	-	1	[19]	60
Bishops Itchington	56	37	19		38	(1)10	4	-	1	2	-	-	-	1	[15]	102
Grandborough parish	*<67*	*49*	*18*		*36*	*(1)21*	*4*	*3*	*-*	*2*	*-*	*1*				*122>*
Grandborough	53	36	17		34	(1)15	2	1	-	-	-	1				82
Woolscott	14	13	1		2	6	2	2	-	2						40
Hunningham	29	17	12		19	(1)6	3	-	-	-	-	-	-	1	[10]	50
Ladbroke	54	34	20		36	8	7	-	2	1						89
Leamington Hastings parish	*<94*	*49*	*45*		*63*	*22*	*2*	*5*	*1*	*-*	*-*	*-*	*-*	*1*		*149>*
Broadwell	42	22	20		30	(2)10	-	2								58
Hill	16	10	6		10	4	1	1								25
Kites Hardwick	13	7	6		8	3	1	1								21
Leamington Hastings	23	10	13		15	(1)5	-	1	1	-	-	-	-	1	[11]	45
Long Itchington parish	*<105*	*56*	*49*		*78*	*17*	*4*	*3*	*1*	*-*	*-*	*1*	*-*	*1*		*159>*
Bascote	26	16	10		19	5	1	-	-	-	-	1				40
Long Itchington	77	38	39		58	12	3	3	1							108
Stoney Thorpe	2	2	0		1	-	-	-	-	-	-	-	-	1	[10]	11
Marton parish	*<50*	*23*	*27*		*36*	*7*	*4*	*-*	*3*							*77>*
Birdingbury in Marton	8	0	8		8											8
Marton	42	23	19		28	7	4	-	3							69
Napton on the Hill parish	*<158*	*110*	*48 (8)*[1]	*8*	*117*	*25*	*3*	*3*	*1*	*1*						*207>*
Napton on the Hill	155	108	47 (8)	8	116	24	2	3	1	1						201
Radbournes e.p.	3	2	1		1	1	1									6
det: Chapel Ascote e.p.	1	1	0		-	1										2
Southam	140	83	57 (5)[1]	5	80	(3)29	11	5	5	3	-	1	1			256
Stockton	42	20	22		30	(1)9	-	2	-	-	-	-	1			65

Places enumerated	*Total h'holds* *All*	*Ch*	*NC(inc.cert)*	*[1]*	*Household totals by number of hearths* *1*	*2*	*3*	*4*	*5*	*6*	*7*	*8*	*9*	*10+*		*Total hearths*
Upper Shuckburgh parish	*<19*	*11*	*8*		*18*	-	-	-	-	-	-	-	-	*1*		*40>*
'Lower' Shuckburgh	15	7	8		15											15
Upper Shuckburgh	4	4	0		3	-	-	-	-	-	-	-	-	1	[22]	25
Wappenbury parish	*<42*	*23*	*19*		*28*	*9*	-	*1*	*1*	*1*	*1*	-	*1*			*77>*
Eathorpe	23	12	11		18	2	-	1	-	-	1	-	1			42
Wappenbury	19	11	8		10	7	-	-	1	1						35
Weston under Wetherley	23	16	7		11	7	3	1	-	-	-	-	-	1	[20]	58
Wolfhampcote parish	*<85*	*68*	*17*		*52*	*20*	*6*	*5*	*1*	*1*						*141>*
Flecknoe	56	40	16		38	13	4	1								80
Nethercote	6	6	0		1	2	1	1	-	1						18
Sawbridge	20	19	1		12	5	1	1	1							34
Wolfhampcote	3	3	0		1	-	-	2								9
Warwickshire totals	17,243		6,574	1,217		2,869		701		201		84		175		31,226
		10,669	(386)		10,209		1,309		342		101		35			
						(234)	(3)									

(b) County of Coventry 1666

Places enumerated	*Total h'holds* *All*	*Pay*	*Cert(e.c.)*		*[–]*	*Household totals by number of hearths* *1*	*2*	*3*	*4*	*5*	*6*	*7*	*8*	*9*	*10+*		*Total hearths*
Coventry city	*<29+1399*	*825*	*574*		*29*	*611*	*(113)342*	*(1)174*	*100*	*53*	*46*	*21*	*13*	*10*	*29*		*3456>*
Bayley Lane	2+ 95	56	39		2	39	(10)31	10	6	4	2	-	1	2			213
Bishop St	2+198	107	91		2	107	(12)43	13	12	9	6	3	1	3	1	[11]	428
Broadgate	4+105	62	43		4	52	(5)22	10	6	5	3	1	1	2	3	[11,12, 15]	264
Cross Cheaping	7+197	132	65		7	59	(19)60	(1)27	17	8	10	5	1	2	8	[10,10, 11,11,11, 11,11,13]	577
Gosford St	3+131	64	67		3	58	(16)29	23	6	6	7	1	-	-	1	[10]	298
Jordan Well	118	55	63		-	62	(11)26	13	11	1	3	2					234
Little Park St	3+144	109	35		3	51	(2)32	23	11	5	6	1	4	1	10	[10,10, 10,11,12, 12,12,15, 15,17]	461
Much Park St	3+146	86	60		3	68	(15)40	17	6	1	4	4	2	-	4	[11,11, 13,19]	350
Smithford St	2+ 73	54	19		2	20	(5)17	11	11	8	2	1	2	-	1	[21]	227
Spon St	3+192	100	92		3	95	(18)42	27	14	6	3	3	1	-	1	[11]	404
Outlying parts																	
Ansty	28	20	8	(4)		14	7	(1)3	2	1	-	-	-	1			59
Exhall	1+76	48	28		1	53	12	2	5	1	-	-	-	2	1	[15]	141
Foleshill parish	*<140*	*67*	*73*			*110*	*(4)22*	*3*	*2*	*2*	-	*1*					*188>*
Bell Green	17	11	6			12	5										22
Church End	6	4	2			4	1	1									9
Court Waste Green	11	6	5			10	1										12
Foleshill	75	30	45			61	(2)9	2	1	2							99
Foleshill Heath	31	16	15			23	(2)6	-	1	-	-	1					46
Holy Trinity: Radford	1+14	13	1	(1)	1	8	4	2									22

Places enumerated	Total h'holds *All*	*Pay*	*Cert(e.c.)*	*[–]*	Household totals by number of hearths *1*	*2*	*3*	*4*	*5*	*6*	*7*	*8*	*9*	*10+*	*Total hearths*
St Michael: Keresley (det)	22	16	6		13	1	2	2	2	1	-	1			53
St Michael: Pinley & Whitley	6	6	0		2	-	-	-	3	-	-	1			25
Stivichall	37	22	15		26	(2)8	-	-	1	1	-	-	-	1 [10]	63
Stoke	1+60	30	30	1	39	(4)9	2	-	1	1	2	1	4	1 [10]	142
Walsgrave on Sowe (part)	65	25	40		49	(3)7	5	2	-	2					98
Wyken	24	17	7 (7)		16	5	1	1	-	-	-	-	-	1 [10]	43
County totals	*<3+472*	*264*	*208 (12)*	*3*	*330*	*(13)75*	*(1)20*	*14*	*11*	*5*	*3*	*3*	*7*	*4*	*834>*
Coventry totals	32+1871	1089	782 (12)	32	941	(126)417	(2)194	114	64	51	24	16	17	33	4290

Additional key and Notes for Coventry

Pay = payable. In addition to those who had paid, this column includes those householders who had not paid, but were not certified as exempt.

Cert = certified exempt.

(e.c.) indicates the number of certified exempt households that have been added to the 1666 Cert totals from the exemption certificates for 1672 and have therefore been deducted from the relevant payable totals.

[-] This column contains the number of entries without any hearth numbers. These are also indicated separately in the totals for all households (e.g. *29* in *29+1399* in the first line of the table).

Hearths that were described as having been destroyed or were in the process of being built have been omitted from these calculations but refusals to pay have been included.

Table 29 Exempt household totals in the hearth tax returns and exemption certificates

For key, see p. 472

(a) Warwickshire 1670–4

Parish etc	*HT70*	*EC70–1*	*HT71*	*EC71–2*	*HT73*	*EC72–3*	*HT74*	*EC73–4*
Barlichway Hundred								
Alcester Division								
Alcester	125	-	-	124	133	133	121(113)	121
Arrow par	27	23*	-	25	27	27	29(28)	26
Arrow	*11*	*10*		*11*		*11*	*26(26)*	*11*
Oversley	*16*	*13*		*14*		*16*	*3(2)*	*15*
Coughton par	26	24	-	26	30	30	21(19)	-
Coughton	*17*			*17*		*19*	*19(19)*	
Sambourne	*9*			*9*		*11*	*2*	
Great Alne	16	15*	-	7	15	15	2	19
Ipsley	23	23	-	21	25	24*	2	24*
Kinwarton	6	6	7	6	5	5	4(4)	7
Morton Bagot	21	20*	-	20	20	20	18(18)	18
Spernall	2	2	2	-	1	1	1	-
Studley	57	59*	-	60	59	59	58(58)	58
Tardebigg (pt) +	9	15	-	11	12	12	0	-
Weethley chap	8	6	6	6	6	6	2	6
Bidford Division								
Aston Cantlow par	36	35*	-	34*	36	37*	39(39)	39
Aston Cantlow	*20*	*19*			*19*	*20*		
Little Alne	*3*	*4*			*5*	*5*		
Newnham	*3*	*2*			*3*	*3*		
Shelfield	*8*	*8*			*7*	*7*		
Wilmcote	*2*	*2*			*2*	*2*		
Bidford on Avon par +	106	129*	-	64*	106(21)	106(21)	82(54)	54
Barton	*16*	*15*			*16(5)*	*16(5)*		*9*
Bidford	*35*	*52**		*31*	*34*	*34*		*19*
Burnells Broom	*10*	*14*			*12(5)*	*12(5)*		
Kings Broom	*34*	*38*		*33**	*33*	*33*	*28*	*18*
Marlcliff	*11*	*10*			*11(11)*	*11(11)*		*8*
Binton	6	4	-	5	6	6	2	-
Exhall	5	6	-	5	5	5	4	4
Haselor	21	-	-	21	20	20	0	-
Salford Priors par	64	63*	-	58	65	63*	16(14)	14
Abbots Salford	*18*				*18*	*18*		*14*
Salford Priors	*46*				*47*	*45**		-
Temple Grafton	19	18	-	17	16	16	15	15
Welford (pt)	1	-	-	-	1	-	1	-
Weston on Avon (pt)	0	-	-	-	1	-	0	-
Wixford	11	10	-	9	9	9	8	8
Henley Division								
Beaudesert	14	13	-	14	14	14	12	12
Claverdon par	26	24	-	23	25	25	25	-
Claverdon	*15*	*15*		*15*	*15*	*14*	*14*	
Langley	*11*	*9*		*8*	*10*	*11*	*11*	
Henley in Arden chap	77	65	-	44	47	47*	67	69*
Preston Bagot	6	-	-	6	6	8	10	10

Parish etc	*HT70*	*EC70–1*	*HT71*	*EC71–2*	*HT73*	*EC72–3*	*HT74*	*EC73–4*
Rowington	52	52	-	51	38	39	34	34
Ullenhall chap	27	22*	-	24	26	25*	21	18
Aspley	*3*			*3*	*3*	*3*	*3*	
Ullenhall	*24*			*21*	*23*	*22**	*18*	*18*
Wootton Wawen par	22	17*	-	21	23	23	23	-
Whitley	*3*			*3*	*3*	*3*	*3*	
Wootton Wawen	*19*			*18*	*20*	*20*	*20*	
Stratford Division								
Alveston par	30	28*	-	27	38	41*	30	37
Alveston	*2*				*7*		*7*	
Tiddington	*28*				*31*		*23*	
Bearley	6	-	-	7	7	7	8	7
Budbrooke par	22	20	-	15	12	13	11	14
Budbrooke	*1*	*1*		*2*	*1*	*2*	*1*	
Hampton on the Hill	*11*	*10*		*10*	*10*	*10*	*9*	
Lower Norton	*10*	*9*		*3*	*1*	*1*	*1*	
Hampton Lucy	16	18	-	16	16	16	15	13
Haseley	19	20* ^	-	18	20	20	18	18
Hatton par	44	43	-	40	42	42*	36	27
Beausale	*20*	*20*		*20*	*17*	*18**	*15*	*21*
Hatton	*10*	*9*		*5*	*9*	*9*	*8*	*6*
Shrewley	*14*	*14*		*15*	*16*	*15*	*13*	
Honiley	5	5	6	-	12	11*	12	11
Loxley	10	10	-	10	10	10	9	11
Norton Lindsey	10	10	10	11	11	11	10	7
Sherbourne	18	17	-	18	19	18	18	19
Snitterfield	25	23	-	21	24	24(6)	18	16
Stratford upon Avon par								
Old Stratford	58	-	-	50*	57	55(10)	53(19)	85*
Bishopton	*5*			*5*	*5*	*4*	*5*	*5*
Bridge Town	*2*			*2*	*2*	*2*	*2*	*2*
Clopton & Welcombe	*2*			*1*	*2*	*2*	*1*	*1*
Old Stratford	*27*			*24*	*26*	*27(10)*	*26(19)*	*60*
Shottery	*22*			*18*	*22*	*20*	*19*	*17*
Stratford borough	197(12)	153*	-	173*	174(12)	194	156	-
Bridge St	*3*			*4*	*3*		*3*	
Church & Chapel St	*65(12)*			*48*	*66(12)*		*51*	
Henley St	*38*			*40*	*32*		*33*	
High St	-			-	-		-	
Sheep St	*64*			*51*	*50*		*48*	
Wood St	*27*			*30*	*23*		*21*	
Bid: Luddington	9	-	-	11	-	-	-	-
Bushwood (det)	13	-	-	11	13	12	12(8)	12
Wolverton	1	2	-	-	2	2	1	2
Wroxall	8	-	-	-	10	10*	8	8
Hemlingford Hundred								
Atherstone Division								
Ansley	33	-	28	32*	31(6)	26	29	29
Baxterley	9	-	8	12	8(6)	12	0	-
Caldecote	2	-	3	4	3	4	4	4
Chilvers Coton par +	93(39)	-	88	106*	90(55)	95* ^	96	99
Chilvers Coton	*73(35)*		*69*	*79*	*70(43)*	*77**	*75*	*78*

Parish etc	*HT70*	*EC70–1*	*HT71*	*EC71–2*	*HT73*	*EC72–3*	*HT74*	*EC73–4*
Griff	*14(4)*		*12*	*13*	*12(12)*	*18*	*12*	*12*
Woodland	*6*		*7*	*14*	*8*		*9*	*9*
Corley +	3	-	2	12	2	12	12	12
Fillongley	40	-	37	42	34	43	38	38
Lea Marston par	16	-	16	16	9	9	9	9
Lea Marston	*10*		*10*		*3*		*6*	
Marston	*6*		*6*		*6*		*3*	
Mancetter par +	111(45)	-	95(76)	152	112(69)	98*	116	115
Atherstone	*84(34)*	-	*71(60)*	*121*	*88(50)*	*89**	*92*	*91*
Hartshill	*15(8)*		*15(11)*	*14*	*13(11)*	-	*14*	*14*
Mancetter	*12(3)*		*9(5)*	*17*	*11(8)*	*9*	*10*	*10*
Maxstoke	11	-	12	14	10(10)	13	13	13
Merevale (most) +	2	-	18(16)	18	2	17	17	18
Nether Whitacre +	16	-	14	24	17	28	21	21*
Nuneaton par +	189(113)	-	171(112)	214*	196(41)	209	188	196
Attleborough	*32(17)*		*28(22)*	*34*	*31(12)*	*36*	*29*	*33 ^*
Nuneaton	*134(90)*		*126(73)*	*158**	*143(22)*	*151*	*142*	*146*
Stockingford	*23(6)*		*17(17)*	*22*	*22(7)*	*11*	*17*	*17*
Over Whitacre	10	-	7	12	8	9	12	12
Shustoke	18	-	16	15	15	16	12	12*
Bentley (det)	13	-	14	14	14(13)	13	12	12
Birmingham Division								
Aston par +	215(75)	-	-	223*	212(154)	229*	239	231*
Aston	*5*			*9*	*6*	*9*	*9*	*9*
Bordesley	*32(12)*			*25*	*30(27)*	*33*	*31*	*30*
Castle Bromwich	*26(9)*			*32*	*32(28)*	*31*	*31*	*31*
Little Bromwich	*9*			*8*	*8(6)*	*8**	*9*	*8*
Deritend	*38(17)*			*55*	*42(23)*	*54*	*59*	*56*
Duddeston & Nechells	*7*			*2*	*7*	-	*3 ?*	-
Erdington	*59(28)*			*49*	*53(45)*	*53 ^*	*58*	*58**
Saltley & Washwood	*23(9)*			*21*	*16(11)*	*18**	*20*	*20*
Water Orton	*6*			*9*	*6(6)*	*8*	*5*	*5*
Witton	*10*			*13*	*12(8)*	*15*	*14*	*14*
Birmingham +	277(200)	-	-	365*	256(160)	369	368	368
Bull St				-	*11*	-	*1*	-
Court Lane				*11*	-	*11*	-	*11*
Digbeth				*43*	*19*	*45*	*55*	*44*
Edgbaston St				*61*	*13*	*56*	*88*	*60*
High St				*36*	*5*	*35*	*33*	*35*
Moor St				*56*	*11*	*57*	*57*	*58*
New St				*22*	*2*	*21*	*22*	*21*
Park St				*15*	*3*	*20*	*16*	*16*
Pinfold St				*27*	-	*27*	-	*28*
Spicer St				*10*	*12*	*11*	*11*	*11*
The Foreign				*84*	*20*	*86*	*85*	*84*
Coleshill +	50(20)	-	-	58*	24	42	45	45
Curdworth +	11(3)	-	-	9	11(8)	13	13	13
Minworth (det)	14(2)	-	-	17	16(11)	17*	16	16
Edgbaston +	10	-	-	17	18	19	18	18
Sheldon +	8	-	-	20	7	18	18	22
Sutton Coldfield par +	93(30)	-	-	117*	115(86)	129	126	127
Hill & Little Sutton				*42*	*9*	*45*	*48*	*48*
Maney & the Wylde				*15*	*8*	*15*	*13*	*13*

Parish etc	*HT70*	*EC70–1*	*HT71*	*EC71–2*	*HT73*	*EC72–3*	*HT74*	*EC73–4*
Moor & Ashfurlong				*18*	*2*	*23*	*19*	*19*
Sutton Coldfield				*30*	*6*	*34*	*33*	*34*
Walmley & the Woods				*12*	*4*	*12*	*13*	*13*
Wishaw par	10	-	-	9	7	8	8	8
Moxhull	*5*				*2*	*3*	*2*	*2*
Wishaw	*5*				*5*	*5*	*6*	*6*
Solihull Division								
Baddesley Clinton +	8(8)	-	8(8)	-	8(8)	-	11	11
Barston	11	10	10	14	12(8)	12	10	10
Berkswell par +	51	81	50	81	50(39)	46(20)	43	43
Berkswell	*48*	*77*	*47*		*48(39)*			
Bradnocks Marsh	*3*	*4*	*3*		*2*			
Bickenhill +	9	32*	12	11*	11(8)	10	10	11
Elmdon	3	3	2	2	2	-	0	-
Great Packington	12	12	12	12	13(10)	12 ^	13	13
Hampton in Arden	21	21	19	20*	19	-	20	20
Balsall (det)	55	56*	58	57	58(48)	55	57	58
Balsall	*37*	*37*	*39*		*8*			
Oldwich	*18*	*19*	*19*		*2*			
Nuthurst (det)	5	6	5	5	5(5)	-	5	5
Knowle chap +	43	62*	45	69*	46(40?)	61	39	39
Chessetts Wood End	*10*	*11*	*11*	*14*	*2*		*8*	
Knowle	*22*	*32*	*22*	*31*	*2*		*20*	
Knowle Wood End	*11*	*19*	*12*	*24*	*2*		*11*	
Little Packington	8	8	8	8	0	8 ^	8	8
Meriden +	30	38	31	40	31(31)	29	29	38*
Solihull par +	133	144	126	130	26(23?)	128 ^	127	128
Forshaw End	*6*	*8*	*6*	*8*		*8*	*8*	*8*
Knowle Widney End	*14*	*15*	*13*	*23*	*23(23?)*	*12*	*11*	*19*
Longdon End	*9*	*11*	*9*			*8*	*8*	
Olton End	*11*	*10*	*10*	*10*		*10*	*9*	*10*
Shirley End	*20*	*24*	*21*	*24*	*3*	*24*	*20*	*24*
Solihull borough	*54*	*56*	*50*	*48*		*49*	*40*	*50*
Whitlocks End	*14*	*15*	*12*	*12*		*12*	*8*	*12*
Widney End	*5*	*5*	*5*	*5*		*5*	*23*	*5*
Tamworth Division								
Austrey +	15(8)	-	13(12)	11	15(9)	15 ^	20	20
Baddesley Ensor +	16(8)	-	11(11)	13	10	11	13	13
Grendon +	9(7?)	-	9(7)	15	9(6)	14	7	7
Kingsbury par +	63(14?)	-	56(47)	61*	56(43)	55	52	55*
Dosthill	*2*		*5(5)*	*4*	*4*	*3*	*3*	*3*
Holt etc	*7*		*3(3)*	*4*		*7*		*7*
Hurley	*34(14?)*		*31(26)*	*33*	*34(30)*	*31*	*32*	*32*
Kingsbury	*8*		*7(7)*	*8*	*7(7)*	*7*	*8*	*7*
Whateley	*8*		*6(6)*	*8*	*7(6)*	*7*	*6*	*6*
Ath: *Coton*	*4*		*4*	*4*	*4*	-	*3*	-
Middleton +	24(10)	-	16(16)	22	16	16	18	18
Newton Regis	5	-	5(5)	4	4	4	4	4
Polesworth par +	96(52)	-	77(32)	100*	76(68)	102	92	92
Dordon	*8(8)*		-	*12*	-	*12*	*13*	*13*
Freasley	*1*		*1*	*10*	*1*	*8*	*8*	*8*
Hallend	*2*		*1*	*6*	*1*	*6*	*6*	*6*

Parish etc	*HT70*	*EC70–1*	*HT71*	*EC71–2*	*HT73*	*EC72–3*	*HT74*	*EC73–4*
Polesworth	*50(21)*		*43*	*46*	*44(41)*	*51*	*45*	*45*
Warton	*15(5)*		*24(24)*	*17*	*22(19)*	*18*	*12*	*12*
Wilnecote	*20(18)*		*8(8)*	*9*	*8(8)*	*7*	*8*	*8*
Seckington +	8(6)	-	9(9)	9	8(8)	7	8	8
Shuttington	4	-	6(6)	8	6	6	8	8
Tamworth (pt) +	161(78)	-	93(74)	139*	132(108)	142	148	146(28)
Amington etc	*14(6)*		*9(9)*	*14*	*10(8)*	*13*	*26*	*16*
Bolehall	*4*		*5(5)*	*9**	*5(5)*	*9*	*10*	*10*
Glascote	*5*		*5(5)*	*3*	*3*	*4*	*4*	*4*
Stonydelph				*11*		*10*		*10*
Tamworth borough (pt)	*75(42)*		*39(26)*	*53*	*58(45)*	*56*	*53*	*50(28)*
Wilnecote	*63(30)*		*35(29)*	*49*	*56(50)*	*50*	*55*	*56*
Kineton Hundred								
Brailes Division								
Barcheston	9	9	9	9	9	9	9	9
Barton on the Heath	13	15	20	20	20	20	17	17
Brailes par +	70	79	82	86	82	81*	86(85)	85
Chelmscote	*1*		*1*		*1*	*1*		
Lower Brailes	*50*		*60*		*59*	*58*		
Upper Brailes	*12*		*13*		*12*	*12*	*1*	
Winderton	*7*		*8*		*10*	*10*		
Burmington	11	11	10	9	9	9	9	9
Cherington	13	13	12	12	12	12	13	13
Great Wolford par	30	32	34	34	34	37	29	29
Great Wolford	*15*	*17*	*18*	*18*	*18*	*19*	*14*	*14*
Little Wolford	*15*	*15*	*16*	*16*	*16*	*18*	*15*	*15*
Honington	21	20	17	18	19	19	17	16
Idlicote	8	8	9	9	9	9	9	9
Long Compton +	33(30)	37	43(39)	43	35	36	37	36*
Pillerton Hersey	7	7	9	9	8	9	6	6*
Pillerton Priors	6	8	6	6	6	6	6	6
Stretton on Fosse	15	16	18	18	18	18	18	18
Whatcote	4	5	5	5	4	4	3	3
Whichford par	29	30	33	33	32	31	29	29
Ascott	*7*		*8*	*8*	*8*	*8*		
Stourton	*8*		*9*	*9*	*8*	*8*	*11*	*11*
Whichford	*14*		*16*	*16*	*16*	*15*	*18*	*18*
Kineton Division								
Atherstone on Stour par	5	5	5	5	5	5	5	5
Ailstone	*3*		*3*	*3*	*3*	*3*	*1*	
Atherstone on Stour	*2*		*2*	*2*	*2*	*2*	*4*	
Butlers Marston	5	5	5	5	5	5	6	6
Chadshunt	3	3	3	3	3	3	2	-
Combrook chap	7	-	7	7	7	7	5	5
Compton Wynyates	1	-	1	-	0	-	0	2
Ettington par	16	16 ^	15	15	14	14	14	13
Ettington	*12*		*11*	*11*	*10*	*10*	*10*	
Fulready	*3*		*3*	*3*	*3*	*3*	*3*	
Lower Ettington	*1*		*1*	*1*	*1*	*1*	*1*	
Gaydon	4	4	4	4	4	4	4	-
Halford	12	12/11	12	12	12	12	10	10
Ilmington par	33	40/33 ^	41	44*	36	41	35	35*

Parish etc	*HT70*	*EC70–1*	*HT71*	*EC71–2*	*HT73*	*EC72–3*	*HT74*	*EC73–4*
Foxcote	*2*		*2*	*2*	*2*	*2*	*2*	*2*
Ilmington	*31*		*39*	*42**	*34*	*39*	*33*	*33*
Kineton par	29	29	20	22	19	22	17	17
Great Kineton	*23*	*23*	*15*	*17*	*15*	*18*	*14*	*14*
Little Kineton	*6*	*6*	*5*	*5*	*4*	*4*	*3*	*3*
Lighthorne	6	6	7	9	6	10/6*	7	6
Oxhill	8	16/8	10	10	6	6	6	6
Radway	10	11	14	14	13	13	5	5
Tysoe par	29	32/30	38	32	33	38*	42	42
Lower Tysoe	*9*	*9*	*10*	*10*	*10*	*11*	*12*	*12*
Middle Tysoe	*19*	*20*	*25*	*19*	*22*	*23*	*26*	*26*
Upper Tysoe	*1*	*1*	*3*	*3*	*1*	*4*	*4*	*4*
Whitchurch	9	9	9	9	9	9	11	11
Crimscote	*2*		*2*	*2*	*2*	*2*	*3*	
Wimpstone	*7*		*7*	*7*	*7*	*7*	*8*	
Priors Marston Division								
Avon Dassett +	8	13/8	13	13	10	11	10	10
Burton Dassett par	24	24*	26	23	21	21*	17	17
Burton Dassett	*2*		*2*	*5*	*1*	*1*		
Knightcote	*9*		*9*	*8*	*7*	*7*		
Little Dassett	*3*		*3*		*2*	*3*		
Northend	*10*		*12*	*10*	*11*	*10*		
Cropredy (pt)	5	5	5	10	10	9	9	9
Farnborough	18	19*/14	17	17*	17	18	18	18*
Fenny Compton	33	33	34	33	34	33	34	34
Lower Shuckburgh chap	11	11	11	11	11	12	9	10
Priors Hardwick	7	7	8	8	7	7	13	13
Priors Marston chap	34	34	38	37	34	33	34	34
Ratley	11	14/10	12	12	10	11	10	9
Shotteswell	17	17	16	17	16	16	17	17
Warmington	13(3)	10	12	12	11	12	11	11
Wormleighton	5	5	5	5	4	5	4	4
Tanworth Division								
Avon								
Barford	29	29	28	28	31	30	0	-
Bishops Tachbrook par	18	14	15	14	15	15	19	19
Bishops Tachbrook	*18*		*15*		*15*		*18*	*18*
Ken: *Tachbrook Mallory*	-		-		-		*1*	*1*
Charlecote	7	7	8	8	7	7	7	7
Chesterton	6	6	6	6	6	6	6	6
Moreton Morrell par	9	9	9	9	9	9	11	11
Moreton	*6*		*6*	*6*	*6*	*6*		
Moreton Morrell	*3*		*3*	*3*	*3*	*3*		
Newbold Pacey par	16	17	18	18*	18	18	12	12
Ashorne	*5*	*5*	*5*	*5*	*5*	*5*	*4*	*4*
Newbold in Wellesbourne	*7*	*8*	*7*	*7*	*6*	*6*	-	-
Newbold Pacey	*4*	*4*	*6*	*6*	*7*	*7*	*8*	*8*
Wasperton	6	7	6	9 ^	7	9	10	10
Wellesbourne par	32	33	33	34	39	35	29	31* ^
Walton Deyville	*8*	*6*	*9*	*9*	*10*	*7*	*6*	*6*
Wellesbourne Hastings	*7*	*8*	*8*	*9*	*11*	*10*	*8*	*8*
Wellesbourne Mountford	*17*	*19*	*16*	*16*	*18*	*18*	*15*	*17*

Parish etc	*HT70*	*EC70–1*	*HT71*	*EC71–2*	*HT73*	*EC72–3*	*HT74*	*EC73–4*
Arden								
Lapworth par	32	34	35	29	33	33	31	31
Kingswood Brook	*6*		*6*	*5*	*6*	*6*		*5*
Lapworth	*26*		*29*	*24*	*27*	*27*		*26*
Packwood	27	31*	30	30	28	30*	26	26
Tanworth in Arden par	116	114	108	107	100	106*	109	109
Clayside	*41*		*35*			*51*		
Heathside	*58*		*59*			*55*		
Tanworth	*17*		*14*					
Warwick Borough	245	229*	236	229*	201	207	223	222
St Mary	195	180*	189	187*	160	160	161	160
Castle St	*16*	*15*	*17*	*17*	*16*	*16*	*15*	*15*
High St	*10*	*10*	*8*	*10*	*6*	*6*	*2*	
Jury St	*5*	*4*	*4*	*4*	*5*	*5*	*5*	*6*
Market Place	*20*	*18*	*19*	*19*	*14*	*18*	*30*	*30*
Saltisford	*78*	*70*	*76*	*71*	*62*	*57*	*67*	*67*
West St	*66*	*63*	*65*	*66*	*57*	*58*	*42*	*42*
St Nicholas	50	49	47	42	47	47	62	62
Bridge End	*15*	*15*	*13*	*16*	*17*	*17*		
Smith St	*35*	*34*	*34*	*26*	*30*	*30*		
Knightlow Hundred								
Kenilworth Division								
Ashow	5	-	5	6	5	5	6	6
Baginton	9	12	-	15	16	16	15	15
Bubbenhall	12	13	-	12	10	10	14	14
Cubbington	30	29	-	28	27	27	30	30
Harbury	28	30	-	29	23	22	28	-
Kenilworth	100	102*	-	88*	97(6)	95*	76	78
Augmentation	*64*	*62*		*52*	*61(6)*	*60(6)*	*45*	
Duchy	*36*	*40*		*36*	*36*	*35*	*31*	
Leamington Priors	25	25	-	24	21	21	25	25
Leek Wootton	14	15	-	17	13	13	14	14
Lillington	18	19	-	19	19	19	19	-
Milverton	6	6	-	6	6	6	6(4)	-
Offchurch	21	13	-	16	12	12	11	11
Radford Semele	12	12	-	12	11	11	13	13
Stoneleigh par	40(10)	27	-	24*	42(10)	38*(10)	30	40*(10)
Canley	*2*	*3*		*2*				
Cryfield	*1*	*1*		*-*				
Finham	*4*	*4*		*5*				
Fletchamstead	*10*	*6*		*6*				
Hill	*1*	*1*		*-*				
Hurst	*-*	*1*		*1*				
Stoneleigh	*22(10)*	*11*		*10*				
Ufton	10	12	-	12	12	11	11(8)	1
Whitnash	5	5	-	5	6	6	5	5
Monks Kirby Division								
Allesley	16	17	-	15	27	27	19	19
Arley	4	5	-	5	5	5	6	6
Astley	7	5	-	-	7	7(3)	5	5

Parish etc	*HT70*	*EC70–1*	*HT71*	*EC71–2*	*HT73*	*EC72–3*	*HT74*	*EC73–4*
Bedworth	223	206	-	202*	221	224	204(204)	205*
Binley	11	-	-	12	11	11	9	9
Brinklow	34?	31	-	29	31	31	32	32
Bulkington par	27	27	-	24	21	25	32	32
Barnacle	*5*	*5*				*5*		*5*
Bramcote	*3*	*3*		*3*			*7*	*2*
Bulkington	*4*	*4*		*7*		*20*	*8*	*8*
Marston Jabbett	*9*	*9*		*6*			*8*	*8*
Ryton	*4*	*4*		*4*			*5*	*5*
Weston in Arden	*2*	*2*		*4*			*4*	*4*
Burton Hastings	4	6	-	6	3	4	3	4
Stretton Baskerville e.p.	1	-	-	-	1	-	1	-
Coventry Holy Trinity (pt)								
Coundon (det)	4	-	-	-	3	-	6(3)	6
Willenhall (det)	3	-	3	-	3	-	0	-
Harborough Magna	19	19	-	9	-	17	18(11)	18
Monks Kirby par	88	86	-	79	86	85	71	71
Brockhurst	*9*	*8*		*6*	*7*		*9*	*9*
Cestersover	*3*	*3*		*3*	*3*			
Copston Magna	*11*	*10*		*11*	*10*		*6*	*6*
Easenhall	*7*	*6*		*7*	*7*		*7*	*7*
Little Walton	*1*	*2*		*1*	*2*		*1*	*1*
Monks Kirby	*23*	*23*		*19*	*24*		*23*	*23*
Pailton	*23*	*24*		*23*	*24*		*12*	*12*
Street Ashton	*3*	*3*		*3*	*3*		*2*	*2*
Stretton under Fosse	*8*	*7*		*6*	*6*		*11*	*11*
Shilton	15?	14	-	15	9	12*	21	21
Walsgrave on Sowe (pt)	12	8	-	12	12	12(4)	10	10
Wibtoft chap	5	-	-	5	5	5	5	5
Willey	11	4	-	2	3	3	8	8
Withybrook	13	-	-	15	15	15	14	14
Wolvey par	31	31	-	31	30	29	36(19)	36*
Smockington	*24*							
Wolvey	*7*							
Rugby Division								
Bilton	36	-	-	34	29	34	29	32*
Bourton on Dunsmore	21	12	-	15	15	13	12	12
Bourton	*12*	*8*			*12*		*12*	
Draycote	*9*	*4*			*3*			
Church Lawford	12	-	-	12	12	12	11	7
Churchover	15	13	-	13	13	13*	12	13
Clifton upon Dunsmore par	27	29	-	29	29	29	29	29
Clifton upon Dunsmore	*16*	*16*		*16*	*16*	*16*	*17*	*17*
Newton and Biggin	*11*	*13*		*13*	*13*	*13*	*12*	*12*
Dunchurch par	65	65	-	61	63	61	26	55
Dunchurch	*28*	*30*		*27*	*27*		*26*	*26*
Thurlaston	*34*	*35*		*34*	*36*			*29*
Toft	*3*							
Frankton	12	11	-	12	12	12	8	8
Hillmorton	39	37	-	36	37	37*	36	38
Kings Newnham	3	-	3	4	3	3	0	4
Newbold on Avon par	46	-	-	43	44(16)	44*(16)	36	36
Cosford	*8*				*8(3)*	*8(3)*	*6*	*6*

Parish etc	*HT70*	*EC70–1*	*HT71*	*EC71–2*	*HT73*	*EC72–3*	*HT74*	*EC73–4*
Long Lawford	*22*			*20*	*20(13)*	*36(13)*	*15*	*15*
Newbold on Avon	*16*			*23*	*16*		*15*	*15*
Rugby +	73(40)	70*(40)	-	70(40)	71(40)	69(40)	68	69
Ryton on Dunsmore	15	12	-	12	15	14*	14	14
Stretton on Dunsmore chap	29	25	-	19	23(10)	21(10)	24	24
Princethorpe	*3*	*3*		*3*			*4*	*4*
Stretton on Dunsmore	*26*	*22*		*16*			*20*	*20*
Willoughby	18(2)	17(2)	-	14	15	14	18	15
Wolston par	26	17	-	28	25(9)	24	26	26
Wolston & Marston	*19*	*17*		*21*	*18(9)*	*18(9)*	*18*	*18*
MK: *Brandon & Bretford*	*7*	*-*		*7*	*7*	*6*	*8*	*8*
Southam Division								
Birdingbury	6	8*	-	17	10	18	8	8
Bishops Itchington	19	20	-	13*	22	22	17	19*
Grandborough	18	-	-	16	20	33(3)	14	21
Hunningham	12	9	10	9	8	7*	7	8
Ladbroke	20	19	-	20	21	21*	17	17
Leamington Hastings par	45(6)	31	-	30	33	33*	29	29
Broadwell	*20*				*17*			
Hill	*6*				*6*			
Kites Hardwick	*6*				*5*			
Leamington Hastings	*13(6)*				*5*			
Long Itchington par	49	49	-	45	63	62	38	39
Bascote	*10*			*9*				
Long Itchington	*39*			*36*				
Marton par	27	27	-	17	26	19	14	14
Birdingbury in Marton	*8*				*8*			
Marton	*19*				*18*			*14*
Napton on the Hill +	39	47	-	37*	38	37	33	33
Radbournes e.p.	1	-	1	-	1	-	0	-
Southam +	52	60	-	56	60	59	47	47
Stockton	22	24	-	15	21	25	18	18
Upper Shuckburgh par	8	-	-	6	7	7	6	-
Wappenbury par	19	-	-	17	21	20*	17	17
Eathorpe	*11*						*10*	
Wappenbury	*8*						*7*	
Weston under Wetherley	7	-	-	7	9	-	11	11
Wolfhampcote	17	-	-	16	21	21	15	15

(b) Coventry 1666–74

Parish etc	*HT66*	*EC72*	*EC73*	*EC74*
Coventry city	574	510	-	567*
Holy Trinity (most)		208	-	246*
Bayley Lane (pt)				*7*
Bishop St	*91*	*88*		*107*
Cross Cheaping	*65*	*51*		*55*
Gosford St (all/pt)	*67*	*30*		*35*
Jordan Well (all/pt)	*63*	*39*		*42*

Parish etc	*HT66*	*EC72*	*EC73*	*EC74*
St Michael (most)		302		321*
Bayley Lane (all/pt)	*39*	*31*		*20*
Broadgate	*43*	*42*		*48*
Gosford St (pt)		*27*		*28*
Jordan Well (pt)		*17*		*18*
Little Park St	*35*	*34*		*34*
Much Park St	*60*	*50*		*73*
Smithford St	*19*	*15*		*16*
Spon St	*92*	*86*		*84*
Outlying parts				
Ansty	4	8	7	-
Exhall	28	31	29	-
Foleshill	73	73*	59*	-
Holy Trinity (pt)				
Radford	-	1		
St Michael (pt)				
Keresley	6	5	-	5
Stivichall	15	17	16	-
Stoke	30	37	30	-
Walsgrave on Sowe (pt)	40	40*	31*	-
Wyken	-	7	6	-

Key

EC = exemption certificate
HT = hearth tax return
chap = chapelry
det = detached
e.p. = extra parochial
par = parish
pt = part
Ath = Atherstone division
Bid = Bidford division
Ken = Kenilworth division
MK = Monks Kirby division

(brackets) indicate groups of exempt who were not named, but are included within the given total.
? indicates uncertainty over the data or area covered.
/ dividing two figures indicates an exemption certificate that was challenged and altered by the receiver etc.
* indicates that this total is different from the total that is recorded in an exemption. certificate or, where no total is given, the exclusion of some names because of duplication etc.
^ indicates the survival of another exemption certificate for the same collection.
+ indicates that there is a transcript of one or more exemption certificates for this parish on pp. 394–421 above.

The very time-consuming vetting for duplicate entries in the exemption certificates that relate to the 1670 returns has not been applied to most of the other certificates.

Sources: WCRO, QS11/7–59; TNA, E179/259/9, E179/347, E179/194/334.

Bibliography and Short References

Alcock, 'Broadgate' — N.W. Alcock, 'Documentary records' in M. Rylatt & M.A. Stokes, *The excavations at Broadgate East, Coventry 1974–5* (Coventry, 1996), pp. 1–24.

Alcock, *Grazier* — N.W. Alcock, *Warwickshire grazier and London skinner 1532–1555* (British Academy, 1981).

Alcock, *People at home* — N.W. Alcock, *People at home* (Chichester, 1993).

Alcock, 'Innovation' — N.W. Alcock, 'Innovation and conservatism: the development of Warwickshire houses in the late 17th and 18th centuries', *Transactions of the Birmingham & Warwickshire Archaeological Society*, 100 (1996), pp. 133–54.

Alcock, 'Rich man' — N.W. Alcock, 'The rich man in his castle …' in Dyer & Richardson, pp. 143–63.

Alcock, 'Smoke bay' — N.W. Alcock, 'Smoke bay or open hall? Cuttle Pool Farm, Knowle, Warwickshire', *Vernacular Architecture*, 29 (1998), pp. 82–84.

Alcock, 'Warwickshire' — N.W. Alcock, 'The hearth tax in Warwickshire' in Barnwell & Airs, pp. 106–19.

Alcock, Faulkner & Jones, 'Maxstoke Castle' — N.W. Alcock, P.A. Faulkner & S.R. Jones, 'Maxstoke Castle, Warwickshire', *Archaeological Journal*, 135 (1978), pp. 195–235.

Alcock & Meeson, 'Baddesley Clinton' — N.W. Alcock & R.A. Meeson, 'Baddesley Clinton: architectural responses to social circumstances', *Antiquaries Journal*, 87 (2007), pp. 295–345.

Alcock & Moir, 'Alcester' — N.W. Alcock & A.K. Moir, 'A medieval urban house with two heated open rooms: 3, 5 Butter Street, Alcester', *Vernacular Architecture*, 35 (2004), pp. 63–5.

Arkell, 'Exemption' — T. Arkell, 'Understanding exemption from the hearth tax' in Barnwell & Airs, pp. 18–21.

Arkell, 'Instructions' — T. Arkell, 'Printed instructions for administering the hearth tax' in Schurer & Arkell, pp. 38–64.

Arkell, 'Inventories' — T. Arkell, 'Interpreting probate inventories', in T. Arkell, N. Evans & N. Goose, eds, *When death do us part* (Oxford, 2000), pp. 72–102.

Arkell, 'King' — T. Arkell, 'Illuminations and distortions: Gregory King's Scheme calculated for the year 1688 and the social structure of later Stuart England', *The Economic History Review*, 59 (2006), pp. 32–69.

Arkell, 'Multiplying factors' — T. Arkell, 'Multiplying factors for estimating population totals from the hearth tax', *Local Population Studies*, 28 (1982), pp. 51–7.

Arkell, 'Poll taxes' — T. Arkell, 'An examination of the poll taxes of the later seventeenth century, the Marriage Duty Act and Gregory King' in Schurer & Arkell, pp. 142–80.

Arkell, 'Poverty' — T. Arkell, 'The incidence of poverty in England in the later seventeenth century', *Social History*, 12 (1987), pp. 23–47.

Arkell, 'Regional' — T. Arkell, 'Identifying regional variations from the hearth tax', *The Local Historian*, 33 (2003), pp. 148–74.

Arkell, 'Warwickshire' — T. Arkell, 'Assessing the reliability of the Warwickshire hearth tax returns of 1662–74', *Warwickshire History*, 6 (1986–7), pp. 183–97.

Barnwell, 'Houses' — P.S. Barnwell, 'Houses, hearths and historical enquiry' in Barnwell & Airs, pp. 177–83.

Barnwell & Airs — P.S. Barnwell & M. Airs, eds, *Houses and the hearth tax: the later Stuart house and society* (Research Report 150, Council for British Archaeology, 2006).

Barratt, 'Wasperton' — D.M. Barratt, 'The inclosure of the manor of Wasperton in 1664', *University of Birmingham Historical Journal*, 3 (1952), pp. 138–152.

Beier, 'Poverty' — A.L. Beier, 'Poverty and progress in early modern England' in A.L. Beier, D. Cannadine & J.M. Rosenheim, eds, *The first modern society* (Cambridge, 1989), pp. 201–39.

Borsay, 'Towns' — P. Borsay, 'Warwickshire towns in the age of Dugdale' in Dyer & Richardson, pp. 187–208.

Braddick, *Taxation* — J.M. Braddick, *Parliamentary taxation in seventeenth-century England* (Woodbridge, 1994).

Chandaman, *Revenue* — C.D. Chandaman, *The English public revenue 1660–1688* (Oxford, 1975).

Cooper, *Houses* — N. Cooper, *Houses of the gentry* (New Haven & London, 1999).

CSPD — *Calendar of State Papers Domestic 1666–1667* (London, 1860).

CTB — *Calendar of Treasury Books*, vii (London, 1916).

Dictionary of surnames — P. Hanks & F. Hodges, *A dictionary of surnames* (Oxford, 1988).

Downing, *Knowle* — T.W. Downing, ed., *The records of Knowle* (Coventry, 1914).

Dugdale, *Antiquities* — William Dugdale, *The Antiquities of Warwickshire*, 2nd edn, revised by William Thomas (London, 1730).

Dyer, 'Towns' — A. Dyer, 'Warwickshire towns under the Tudors and Stuarts', *Warwickshire History*, 3 (1976–7), pp. 122–35.

Dyer, 'Introduction' — C. Dyer, 'Introduction' in Dyer, *Self-contained*, pp. 1–5.

Dyer, *Self-contained* — C. Dyer, ed., *The self-contained village?* (University of Hertfordshire, 2007).

Dyer, 'Village' C. Dyer, 'Were late medieval villages "self-contained"?' in Dyer, *Self-contained*, pp. 6–27.

Dyer & Richardson C. Dyer & C. Richardson, eds, *William Dugdale historian 1605–86: his life, his writings and his county* (Woodbridge, 2009).

Edwards, 'Horse trade' P.R. Edwards, 'The horse trade of the midlands in the seventeenth century', *Agricultural History Review*, 27 (1979), pp. 90–100.

Eveleigh, *Firegrates* D.J. Eveleigh, *Firegrates and kitchen ranges* (Princes Risborough, 2004).

Everitt, 'Market' A. Everitt, 'The market town' in J. Thirsk, *The agrarian history of England and Wales*, 4 (Cambridge, 1967), pp. 467–90.

Farr, *Great fire* M.W. Farr, ed., *The great fire of Warwick 1694: the records of the commissioners appointed under an Act of Parliament for rebuilding the town of Warwick* (Dugdale Society, 36, 1992).

French, *Middle sort* H.R. French, *The middle sort of people in provincial England 1600–1750* (Oxford, 2007).

Gerhold, *Putney* D. Gerhold, *Putney and Roehampton in 1665* (Roehampton University London & Wandsworth Historical Society, 2007).

Gooder, *Arbury* E. Gooder, *The squire of Arbury* (Coventry Branch of the Historical Association, 1990).

Goose, 'Wealth' N. Goose, 'How accurately do the hearth tax returns reflect wealth? A discussion of some urban evidence', *Local Population Studies*, 67 (2001), pp. 44–63.

Grant, 'Coalfield' E.G. Grant, 'Changing perspectives in the Warwickshire coalfield' in Slater & Jarvis, pp. 323– 45.

Green, 'Durham' A. Green, 'Introduction' in E. Parkinson, *Durham*, pp. xv–xci.

Gribbin, *Science* J. Gribbin, *Science: a history 1543–2001* (London, 2002).

Guillery, 'London' P. Guillery, 'London's suburbs, house size and the hearth tax' in Barnwell & Airs, pp. 35–45.

Hey, 'West Riding' D. Hey, 'The West Riding in the late seventeenth century' in D. Hey, C. Giles, M. Spufford & A. Wareham, eds, *Yorkshire West Riding hearth tax assessment Lady Day 1672* (British Record Society, 2007), pp. 11–60.

Hindle, 'Great survey' S. Hindle, 'Sir Richard Newdigate and the "great survey" of Chilvers Coton: fiscal seigneurialism in late-seventeenth-century Warwickshire' in Dyer & Richardson, pp. 164–86.

Hindle, *Parish* S. Hindle, *On the parish? The micro-politics of poor relief in rural England c1550–1750* (Oxford, 2004).

Hindle, *State* S. Hindle, *The state and social change in early modern England, 1550–1640* (Basingstoke, 2000).

Hindle, *Welfare* S. Hindle, '*The birthpangs of welfare: poor relief and parish governance in seventeenth-century Warwickshire* (Dugdale Society Occasional Papers, 40, 2000).

Hoskins, *Exeter* — W.G. Hoskins, *Industry, trade and people in Exeter, 1688–1800* (Manchester, 1935).

Hughes, *Warwickshire* — A. Hughes, *Politics, society and civil war in Warwickshire, 1620–1660* (Cambridge, 1987).

Husbands, 'Hearths' — C. Husbands, 'Hearths, wealth and occupations: an exploration of the hearth tax in the later seventeenth century' in Schurer & Arkell, pp. 65–77.

Kain & Oliver, *Parishes* — R.J.P. Kain & R.R. Oliver, *Historic parishes of England & Wales* (Colchester, 2001).

Kerby, *Inequality* — G. Kerby, 'Inequality in a pre-industrial society: a study of wealth, status, office and taxation in Tudor and Stuart England with particular reference to Cheshire', unpublished PhD Thesis, University of Cambridge (1983).

Larminie, *Wealth* — V. Larminie, *Wealth, kinship and culture: the seventeenth-century Newdigates of Arbury and their world* (Royal Historical Society, Studies in History 72, 1995).

Laslett, *World* — P. Laslett, *The world we have lost* (London, 1st edn, 1965, 3rd edn, 1983).

Levine & Wrightson, *Whickham* — D. Levine & K. Wrightson, *The making of an industrial society: Whickham 1560–1765* (Oxford, 1991).

Marshall, 'Levying' — L.M. Marshall, 'The levying of the hearth tax 1662–1688', *English Historical Review,* 51 (1936), pp. 628–46.

Meekings, *Accounts* — C.A.F. Meekings, *Analysis of hearth tax accounts 1666–1699* (List & Index Society, 163, 1980).

Meekings, *Dorset* — C.A.F. Meekings, *Dorset hearth tax assessments 1662–1664* (Dorchester, 1951).

Meekings, 'Loans' — C.A.F. Meekings, 'The City loans on the hearth tax 1664–1668' in A.E.J. Hollander & W. Kellaway, eds, *Studies in London history* (London, 1969), pp. 335–70.

Meekings, Porter & Roy, *Worcester* — C.A.F. Meekings, S. Porter & I. Roy, eds, *The hearth tax collectors' book for Worcester 1678–1680* (Worcestershire Historical Society, NS, 11, 1983).

Orlin, 'Fictions' — L.C. Orlin, 'Fictions of the early modern English probate inventory' in H.S. Turner, ed., *The culture of capital: property, cities and knowledge in early modern England* (London, 2002), pp. 57–63.

Overton et al., *Households* — M. Overton, J. Whittle, D. Dean & A. Hann, *Production and consumption in English households, 1600–1750* (London, 2004).

Parkinson, *Durham* — E. Parkinson, ed., *Durham hearth tax Lady Day 1666* (British Record Society, 2006).

Parkinson, *Establishment* — E. Parkinson, *The establishment of the hearth tax 1662–1666* (List & Index Society, special series, 43, 2008).

Parkinson, 'Understanding' — E. Parkinson, 'Understanding the hearth tax returns: historical and interpretative problems' in Barnwell & Airs, pp. 7–17.

Pearson, 'Kent' — S. Pearson, 'Introduction' in D. Harrington, ed., *Kent hearth tax assessment Lady Day 1664* (British Record Society, 2000), pp. xxiii-cii.

Phillimore Atlas — C.R. Humphery-Smith, ed., *The Phillimore atlas and index of parish registers* (Chichester, 1984).

Poole, *Coventry* — B. Poole, *Coventry: its history and antiquities* (Coventry, 1870).

Power, 'London' — M.J. Power, 'The social topography of Restoration London' in A.L. Beier & R. Finlay, eds, *London 1500–1700* (Harlow, 1986), pp. 199–223.

Quarter Sessions — S.C. Ratcliff & H.C. Johnson, eds, *Warwick county records: Quarter Sessions records*, i-vii (Warwick, 1935–46).

Ramsden, *Westmorland* — N. Ramsden, ed., *The Westmorland hearth tax for the year 1674* (Cumbria Family History Society, 1998).

Richardson, *Architectural remains* — C.J. Richardson, *Architectural remains of the reigns of Elizabeth and James I* (London, 1840).

Roberts, 'Village' — B.K. Roberts, 'Village forms in Warwickshire; a preliminary discussion' in Slater & Jarvis, pp. 125–46.

Rowlands, 'Society' — M. Rowlands, 'Society and industry in the West Midlands at the end of the seventeenth century', *Midland History*, 4 (1977), pp. 48–60.

Schurer & Arkell — K. Schurer & T. Arkell, eds, *Surveying the people* (Oxford, 1992).

Seaward, *Cavalier* — P. Seaward, *The Cavalier Parliament and the reconstruction of the old regime 1661–1667* (Cambridge, 1988).

Skipp, *Crisis* — V. Skipp, *Crisis and development: an ecological study of the Forest of Arden 1570–1674* (Cambridge, 1978).

Slater & Jarvis — T.R. Slater & P.J. Jarvis, eds, *Field and Forest: an historical geography of Warwickshire and Worcestershire* (Norwich, 1982).

Spufford, 'Chimneys' — M. Spufford, 'Chimneys, wood and coal' in Barnwell & Airs, pp. 22–32.

Spufford, 'Limitations' — M. Spufford, 'The limitations of the probate inventory' in J. Chartres & D. Hey, eds, *English rural society 1500–1800* (Cambridge, 1990), pp. 139–74.

Spufford, 'Potential' — M. Spufford, 'The scope of local history, and the potential of the hearth tax returns', *The Local Historian*, 30 (2000), pp. 202–21.

Spufford, *Poverty* — M. Spufford, *Poverty portrayed: Gregory King and the parish of Eccleshall* (Staffordshire Studies 7, Keele, 1995).

Styles, 'Census' — P. Styles, 'A census of a Warwickshire village in 1698' in Styles, *Studies*, 90–107 (first published in 1951).

Styles, 'Hearth tax'	P. Styles, 'Introduction to the Warwickshire hearth tax records' in Walker, *Hemlingford*, pp. xi–xcvii.
Styles, 'Heralds'	P. Styles, 'The heralds' visitation of Warwickshire 1682–3' in Styles, *Studies*, pp. 108–49 (first published in 1955).
Styles, 'Kineton'	P. Styles, 'The social structure of Kineton hundred in the reign of Charles II' in Styles, *Studies*, pp. 150–74 (first published in 1962).
Styles, 'Settlement'	P. Styles, 'The evolution of the law of settlement' in Styles, *Studies*, pp. 175–204 (first published in 1963).
Styles, *Studies*	P. Styles, *Studies in seventeenth century West Midlands history* (Kineton, 1978).
Thirsk, 'Midlands'	J. Thirsk, 'The South-West Midlands' in J. Thirsk, ed., *The agrarian history of England and Wales*, 5, part 1 (Cambridge, 1984), pp. 159–93.
Trinder & Cox, *Telford*	B. Trinder & J. Cox, eds, *Yeomen and colliers in Telford* (Chichester, 1980).
Trinder & Cox, *Severn Gorge*	B. Trinder & N. Cox, eds, *Miners and mariners of the Severn Gorge* (Chichester, 2000).
Tyack, *Country houses*	Geoffrey Tyack, *Warwickshire country houses* (Chichester, 1994).
VCH	*Victoria history of the county of Warwick*, ii-viii (Oxford, 1908–69).
Walker, *Hemlingford*	M. Walker, ed., *Warwick county records: hearth tax returns, 1: Hemlingford hundred: Tamworth and Atherstone divisions* (Warwick, 1957).
Ward, 'Taxes'	W.R. Ward, 'The office for taxes, 1665–1798', *Bulletin of the Institute of Historical Research*, 25 (1952), pp. 204–12.
Weatherill, *Consumer*	L. Weatherill, *Consumer behaviour and material culture in Britain 1660–1760* (London, 1988).
Whiteman, *Compton*	A. Whiteman, ed., *The Compton census of 1676: a critical edition* (British Academy, 1986).
Wilson, *Apprenticeship*	C. Wilson, *England's apprenticeship 1603–1763* (London, 1965).
Wood, *Medieval house*	M. Wood, *The English medieval house* (London, 1983).
Wood-Jones, *Banbury*	R.B. Wood-Jones, *Traditional domestic architecture of the Banbury region* (Manchester, 1963).
Woodall, *Hroca*	J. Woodall, *From Hroca to Anne* (Solihull, 1974).
Wrightson, 'Order'	K. Wrightson, 'The social order of early modern England: three approaches' in L. Bonfield, R.M. Smith & K. Wrightson, eds, *The world we have gained* (Oxford, 1986), pp. 177–202.
Wrightson, 'Sorts'	K. Wrightson, ' "Sorts of people" in Tudor and Stuart England' in J. Barry & C. Brooks, eds, *The middling sort of people* (London, 1994), pp. 28–51.
Youngs, *Guide*	F.A. Youngs, *Guide to the local administrative units of England*, ii (Royal Historical Society, 1991).

Index of Persons

For easier searching and to reduce the size of the index, spelling variants and closely similar surnames have been grouped together though this is not intended to suggest that the grouped names necessarily relate to the same family. Cross-references to the indexed name forms are only given when the indexed form is located more that about 10 places away from the original name. Forenames have been expanded and standardised when this could be done unambiguously. However, users should be aware of the need to look both for alternative surname spellings and for alternative forenames: e.g. Edmund as well as Edward; Michael (generally expanded from Mich') as well as Nicholas (Nich'). Numbers in brackets identify multiple occurrences on the same page. For names of historians, see the Subject Index.

Index of Places

Places are in Warwickshire unless otherwise stated.

Index of Subjects

Introduction

Transcripts

Key for Hearth Tax Mapping Units
(Back end-paper map)

The key is given in two versions. The first is a key from map numbers to places, the second a key from places to numbers.

Number key

The map is numbered within hundreds, broadly from north to south, with the County of Coventry placed after Knightlow hundred; subdivisions of parishes are given consecutive numbers wherever possible (with obvious anomalies for parishes in more than one hundred). The five sections are grouped as follows:

Hemlingford	1–73	County of Coventry 164–174	Barlichway	175–226
Knightlow	74–163		Kineton	227–290

Number key

Hemlingford hundred (1–73)

No	*Place*
1	Newton Regis
2	Seckington
3	Austrey
4	Shuttington
5	Polesworth
6	Tamworth, Amington and Stonydelph
7	Tamworth, Bolehall and Glascote
8	Tamworth, Borough (part)
9	Tamworth, Castle Liberty
10	Tamworth, Wilnecote
11	Grendon, Grendon
12	Grendon, Whittington
13	Baddesley Ensor
14	Merevale
15	Mancetter, Atherstone
16	Mancetter, Mancetter
17	Mancetter, Hartshill
18	Caldecote
19	Weddington
20	Kingsbury, Dosthill
21	Kingsbury, Whateley
22	Kingsbury, Holt, Slately & Cliff
23	Kingsbury, Hurley
24	Kingsbury, Kingsbury
25	Kingsbury, Coton
26	Sutton Coldfield
27	Middleton
28	Baxterley
29	Shustoke, Bentley
30	Ansley
31	Nuneaton, Stockingford
32	Nuneaton, Nuneaton
33	Nuneaton, Attleborough
34	Chilvers Coton
35	Wishaw
36	Lea Marston
37	Curdworth, Curdworth
38	Curdworth, Minworth
39	Nether Whitacre
40	Over Whitacre
41	Aston, Witton
42	Aston, Erdington
43	Aston, Castle Bromwich
44	Aston, Water Orton
45	Aston, Aston
46	Aston, Duddeston
47	Aston, Washwood and Saltley
48	Aston, Little Bromwich
49	Aston, Deritend
50	Aston, Bordsley
51	Birmingham
52	Edgbaston
53	Coleshill
54	Shustoke, Shustoke
55	Maxstoke
56	Fillongley
57	Corley
58	Sheldon
59	Little Packington
60	Great Packington
61	Hampton in Arden, Kinwalsey
62	Bickenhill
63	Bickenhill, Lyndon
64	Elmdon
65	Solihull
66	Hampton in Arden
67	Meriden

Hemlingford hundred (contd)

No	*Place*
68	Barston
69	Berkswell
70	Knowle
71	Hampton in Arden, Balsall
72	Baddesley Clinton
73	Hampton in Arden, Nuthurst

Knightlow hundred (74–163)

No	*Place*
74	Hydes Pasture
75	Stretton Baskerville
76	Burton Hastings
77	Wolvey
78	Bulkington
79	Bedworth
80	Astley
81	Arley
82	Shilton
83	Withybrook
84	Monks Kirby, Copston Magna
85	Wibtoft
86	Willey
87	Monks Kirby, Monks Kirby
88	Monks Kirby, Cestersover
89	Monks Kirby, Pailton
90	Monks Kirby, Stretton under Fosse
91	Binley, Combe Fields
92	Walsgrave on Sowe (War)
93	Binley, Binley
94	Brinklow
95	Monks Kirby, Easenhall
96	Harborough Magna
97	Churchover
98	Kings Newnham
99	Newbold on Avon, Harborough Parva
100	Newbold on Avon, Cosford
101	Newbold on Avon, Newbold on Avon
102	Newbold on Avon, Long and Little Lawford
103	Brownsover
104	Clifton on Dunsmore, Newton and Biggin
105	Clifton on Dunsmore, Clifton on Dunsmore
106	Rugby
107	Bilton
108	Hillmorton
109	Church Lawford
110	Wolston, Wolston
111	Wolston, Brandon and Bretford
112	Willenhall
113	Baginton
114	Ryton on Dunsmore
115	Stoneleigh
116	Kenilworth
117	Allesley
118	Coundon
119	Bubbenhall
120	Stretton on Dunsmore, Stretton
121	Stretton on Dunsmore, Princethorpe
122	Frankton
123	Bourton on Dunsmore
124	Dunchurch, Cawston
125	Dunchurch, Dunchurch
126	Dunchurch, Thurlaston
127	Ashow
128	Leek Wootton
129	Milverton
130	Lillington
131	Cubbington
132	Weston under Wetherley
133	Wappenbury, Wappenbury
134	Wappenbury, Eathorpe
135	Hunningham
136	Marton
137	Birdingbury
138	Leamington Hastings
139	Grandborough, Woolscott
140	Grandborough, Grandborough
141	Willoughby
142	Wolfhampcote, Wolfhampcote & Sawbridge
143	Wolfhampcote, Flecknoe
144	Upper Shuckburgh
145	Offchurch
146	Long Itchington
147	Stockton
148	Southam
149	Napton on the Hill
150	Leamington Priors
151	Radford Semele
152	Whitnash
153	Bishops Tachbrook, Tachbrook Mallory
154	Ufton
155	Harbury
156	Ladbrooke
157	Bishops Itchington
158	Napton on the Hill, Chapel Ascote
159	Napton on the Hill, Upper Radbourne
160	Napton on the Hill, Lower Radbourne
161	Fenny Compton, Hodnell
162	Napton on the Hill, Wills Pastures

163 Fenny Compton, Watergall

County of Coventry (164–174)

No *Place*
164 Exhall (Coventry)
165 Keresley
166 Foleshill
167 Walsgrave on Sowe (Coventry)
168 Ansty
169 Coventry Holy Trinity (incl. Radford)
170 Wyken
171 Stoke
172 Coventry St Michael
173 Pinley & Whitley
174 Stivichall

Barlichway hundred (175–226)

No *Place*
175 Wroxall
176 Honiley
177 Rowington
178 Stratford upon Avon, Bushwood
179 Haseley
180 Hatton, Beausale
181 Hatton, Hatton
182 Hatton, Shrewley
183 Tardebigg, Tutnall and Cobley
184 Ullenhall
185 Beaudesert
186 Henley in Arden
187 Preston Bagot
188 Claverdon, Claverdon
189 Claverdon, Langley
190 Budbrooke
191 Wolverton
192 Norton Lindsey
193 Sherbourne
194 Ipsley
195 Studley
196 Morton Bagot
197 Wootton Wawen
198 Bearley
199 Snitterfield
200 Snitterfield, Fulbrook
201 Hampton Lucy
202 Coughton, Sambourn
203 Spernall
204 Aston Cantlow
205 Coughton, Coughton
206 Great Alne
207 Alcester
208 Kinwarton
209 Weethley
210 Arrow, Arrow
211 Arrow, Oversley
212 Haselor
213 Temple Grafton, Billesley
214 Stratford upon Avon, Old Stratford
215 Stratford upon Avon, Drayton and Luddington
216 Stratford upon Avon, Stratford Borough
217 Alveston
218 Loxley
219 Weston on Avon, Milcote
220 Salford Priors
221 Wixford
222 Exhall (War)
223 Temple Grafton, Temple Grafton
224 Binton
225 Bidford
226 Welford on Avon, Bickmarsh

Kineton hundred (227–290)

No *Place*
227 Tanworth in Arden
228 Packwood
229 Lapworth
230 Warwick St Mary
231 Warwick St Nicholas
232 Barford
233 Bishops Tachbrook, Bishops Tachbrook
234 Wasperton
235 Newbold Pacey
236 Charlecote
237 Moreton Morrell
238 Wellesbourne, Wellesbourne Hastings
239 Wellesbourne, Wellesbourne Mountford
240 Wellesbourne, Walton Deyville
241 Chesterton
242 Lighthorne, Lighthorne
243 Lighthorne, Compton Verney
244 Chadshunt
245 Gaydon
246 Burton Dassett, Burton and Little Dassett
247 Burton Dassett, Knightcote & Northend
248 Fenny Compton, Fenny Compton
249 Wormleighton
250 Priors Hardwick
251 Priors Marston
252 Lower Shuckburgh
253 Atherstone on Stour
254 Ettington
255 Combrook
256 Kineton
257 Butlers Marston
258 Pillerton Hersey
259 Pillerton Priors
260 Radway
261 Avon Dassett

Kineton hundred (contd)

No	*Place*
262	Farnborough
263	Warmington
264	Cropredy, Mollington
265	Shotteswell
266	Ratley, Ratley
267	Ratley, Upton
268	Tysoe
269	Oxhill
270	Whitchurch
271	Ilmington
272	Stretton on Fosse
273	Halford
274	Idlicote
275	Whatcote
276	Compton Wynyates
277	Honington
278	Barcheston, Barcheston
279	Barcheston, Willington
280	Brailes, Upper Brailes & Chelmscote
281	Brailes, Winderton
282	Brailes, Lower Brailes
283	Burmington
284	Cherington
285	Whichford, Stourton
286	Whichford, Ascott & Whichford
287	Long Compton
288	Great Wolford, Little Wolford
289	Great Wolford, Great Wolford
290	Barton on the Heath

Place key

Place	*No*
Alcester	207
Allesley	117
Alveston	217
Ansley	30
Ansty	168
Arley	81
Arrow, Arrow	210
Arrow, Oversley	211
Ashow	127
Astley	80
Aston Cantlow	204
Aston, Aston	45
Aston, Bordsley	50
Aston, Castle Bromwich	43
Aston, Deritend	49
Aston, Duddeston	46
Aston, Erdington	42
Aston, Little Bromwich	48
Aston, Washwood and Saltley	47
Aston, Water Orton	44
Aston, Witton	41
Atherstone on Stour	253
Austrey	3
Avon Dassett	261
Baddesley Clinton	72
Baddesley Ensor	13
Baginton	113
Barcheston, Barcheston	278
Barcheston, Willington	279
Barford	232
Barston	68
Barton on the Heath	290
Baxterley	28
Bearley	198
Beaudesert	185
Bedworth	79
Berkswell	69
Bickenhill	62
Bickenhill, Lyndon	63
Bidford	225
Bilton	107
Binley, Binley	93
Binley, Combe Fields	91
Binton	224
Birdingbury	137
Birmingham	51
Bishops Itchington	157
Bishops Tachbrook, Bishops Tachbrook	233
Bishops Tachbrook, Tachbrook Mallory	153
Bourton on Dunsmore	123
Brailes, Lower Brailes	282
Brailes, Upper Brailes & Chelmscote	280
Brailes, Winderton	281
Brinklow	94
Brownsover	103
Bubbenhall	119
Budbrooke	190
Bulkington	78
Burmington	283
Burton Dassett, Burton and Little Dassett	246
Burton Dassett, Knightcote & Northend	247
Burton Hastings	76
Butlers Marston	257
Caldecote	18
Chadshunt	244
Charlecote	236
Cherington	284
Chesterton	241
Chilvers Coton	34
Church Lawford	109
Churchover	97
Claverdon, Claverdon	188
Claverdon, Langley	189
Clifton on Dunsmore, Clifton on Dunsmore	105
Clifton on Dunsmore, Newton and Biggin	104
Coleshill	53

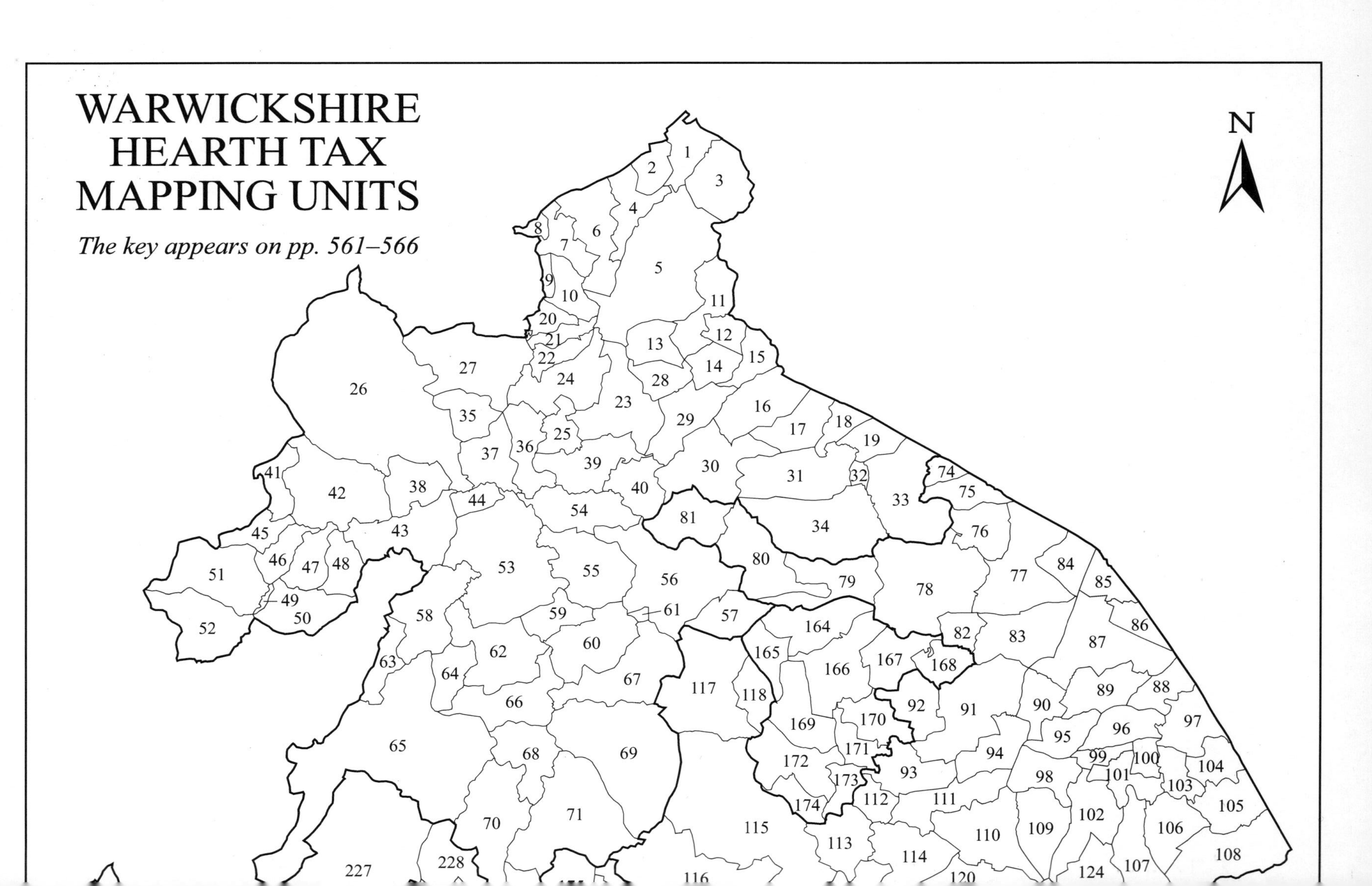
WARWICKSHIRE
HEARTH TAX
MAPPING UNITS
The key appears on pp. 561–566
N